THIRD EDITION

programming the **world wide web**

THIRD EDITION

programming the **world wide web**

ROBERT W. SEBESTA

University of Colorado at Colorado Springs

PEARSON

Addison
Wesley

Boston San Francisco New York
London Toronto Sydney Tokyo Singapore Madrid
Mexico City Munich Paris Cape Town Hong Kong Montreal

Publisher	Greg Tobin
Acquisitions Editor	Matt Goldstein
Project Editor	Katherine Harutunian
Marketing Manager	Michelle Brown
Production Assistant	Sarah Bartlett
Production Services	Argosy Publishing, Inc.
Cover Design	Joyce Cosentino Wells
Text Design	Sandra Rigney
Prepress and Manufacturing	Caroline Fell
Media Producer	Bethany Tidd

Cover image © 2005 PictureQuest

Access the latest information about Addison-Wesley titles from our World Wide Web site:
http://www.aw-bc.com/computing

Many of the designations used by manufacturers and sellers to distinguish their products are claimed as trademarks. Where those designations appear in this book, and Addison-Wesley was aware of a trademark claim, the designations have been printed in initial caps or all caps.

The programs and applications presented in this book have been included for their instructional value. They have been tested with care, but are not guaranteed for any particular purpose. The publisher does not offer any warranties or representations, not does it accept any liabilities with respect to the programs or applications.

Library of Congress Cataloging-in-Publication Data
Sebesta, Robert W.
 Programming the World Wide Web / Robert W. Sebesta. — 3rd ed.
    p. cm.
 Includes bibliographical references and index.
 ISBN 0-321-30332-6
 1. Internet programming. 2. World Wide Web. I. Title.
 QA76.625.S42 2005
 006.7'6—dc22

                                        2005004051

ISBN 0-321-30332-6

12345678910-CRS-08070605

To Aidan

Contents

2   Introduction to XHTML   29

3 Cascading Style Sheets   93

4   The Basics of JavaScript   129

5   JavaScript and HTML Documents   189

8   Introduction to XML   297

9 The Basics of Perl   345

10   Using Perl for CGI Programming   389

11   Servlets and Java Server Pages   429

14 Database Access through the Web 565

Preface

OVERVIEW

It is difficult to overestimate the effect the World Wide Web has had on the day-to-day lives of people, at least those in the developed countries. In just a few years, we have learned to use the Web for a myriad of disparate tasks, ranging from the mundane task of shopping for airline tickets to the crucial early-morning gathering of business news for a high-stakes day trader.

The speed at which millions of Web sites have appeared would seem to indicate that the technologies used to build them were sitting on the shelf, fully developed and ready to use, even before the Web was developed. Also, one might guess that the tens of thousands of people who built those sites were sitting around unemployed, waiting for an opportunity and already possessing the knowledge and abilities required to carry out this mammoth construction task when it appeared. Neither of these was true. The need for new technologies was quickly filled by a large number of entrepreneurs, some at existing companies and some who started new companies. A large part of the programmer need was filled, at least to the extent to which it has been filled, by new programmers, some straight from high school. Many, however, were previously employed by other sectors of the software development industry. All of them had to learn to use new languages and new software systems.

Until recently, programmers learned Web software technologies through company in-house training, a scattering of courses focused on one specific Web technology at colleges and universities, or on their own. A visit to a local bookstore will turn up a large supply of books on those technologies aimed at the practicing professional. In the last few years college courses have begun to appear that attempt to cover a broad spectrum of Web programming technologies. One difficulty encountered by those teaching these courses is the lack of a textbook that is targeted to their needs. Most of the books that discuss Web programming were written for professionals, rather than college students. Such books are typically written to fulfill the needs of professionals, which are quite different from those of college students. One major difference between an academic book and a professional book lies in the assumptions made by the author about the prior knowledge and experience of the audience. The backgrounds of professionals vary widely, making it difficult to assume much of anything. On the other hand, a book written for junior computer science majors can make some definite assumptions about the background of the reader. This book is written for those students.

The goal of this book is to provide the reader with a comprehensive introduction to the programming tools and skills required to build and maintain server sites on the Web. A wide variety of technologies are used in the construction of a Web site. There are now many books available, for professionals that focus on these technologies. For example, there are dozens of books that specifically address only XHTML. The same is true for a half-dozen other technologies. This book provides an overview of how the Web works, as well as descriptions of many of the most widely used Web technologies.

The first and second editions of this book were used to teach a junior-level Web programming course at the University of Colorado at Colorado Springs. The challenge for students in the course is to learn to use several different programming languages and technologies in one semester. A heavy load of programming exercises is essential to the success of the course. Students build a basic, static Web site using only XHTML as the first assignment. Throughout the remainder of the semester they add features to their site as the new technologies are discussed in the course. Our students' prior course work in Java, data structures, and assembly language are helpful, as is the fact that many of them know some XHTML before taking the course.

The most important prerequisite to the material of this book is a solid background in programming in some language that supports object-oriented programming. It is helpful to have some knowledge of a second programming language and a bit of UNIX, which helps with the Perl part of the course. Also, UNIX is still a popular platform choice for Web servers. Familiarity with a second language makes learning the new languages easier.

TABLE OF CONTENTS

The book is organized into three sections, introduction (Chapter 1), client-side technologies (Chapters 2–8), and server-side technologies (Chapters 9–14).

Chapter 1 lays the groundwork for the rest of the book. A few fundamentals are introduced, including the history and nature of the Internet, the World Wide Web, browsers, servers, URLs, MIME types, and HTTP. Also included in Chapter 1 are brief overviews of the most important topics of the rest of the book.

Chapter 2 provides an introduction to XHTML, including images, links, lists, tables, frames, and forms. Small examples are used to illustrate the many XHTML elements that are discussed in this chapter.

The topic of Chapter 3 is Cascading Style Sheets, which have quickly become the standard way of imposing style on the content specified in XHTML tags. Because of the size and complexity of the topic, the chapter does not cover all of the aspects of style sheets. The topics discussed are levels of style sheets, style specification formats, selector formats, property values, and color. Among the properties covered are those for fonts, lists, and margins. Small examples are used to illustrate the subjects being discussed.

Chapter 4 introduces the core of JavaScript, a powerful language that could be used for a variety of different applications. Our interest, of course, is its use in Web programming. Although JavaScript has become a large and complex language, we use the student's knowledge of programming in some other language to leverage our discussion, thereby providing a useful introduction to the language in a manageably small number of pages. Topics covered are the object model of JavaScript, its control statements, objects, arrays, functions, constructors, and pattern matching.

In Chapter 5 we discuss some of the features of JavaScript that are related to XHTML documents. Included is the use of the basic and DOM 2 event and event-handling model, which can be used in conjunction with some of the elements of XHTML documents.

Perhaps the most exciting and interesting application of JavaScript is for building dynamic XHTML documents using the Document Object Model (DOM). Chapter 6 provides descriptions of a collection of some of the document changes that can be made using JavaScript and the DOM. Included are element positioning, moving elements, changing the visibility of elements, changing the color, style, and size of text, changing the content of tags, changing the stacking order of overlapped elements, slow movement of elements, and dragging and dropping elements.

Java applets are described in Chapter 7. First, the fundamentals of applet activities and the `paintComponent` method are introduced. Then, the `<object>` tag and applet parameters are discussed. Next, the chapter introduces the graphics that can be created by applets. Applets that can interact with the user through Swing widgets are then covered.

Java is now being used in the introductory programming sequence at many colleges and universities. This allows us to discuss Java applets without first introducing Java. For those institutions that do not use Java as the language vehicle for their introductory programming courses, we provide a quick introduction to Java in an appendix.

Chapter 8 presents an introduction to XML, which provides the means to design topic-specific markup languages that can be shared among users with common interests. Included are the syntax and document structure used by

XML, data type definitions, namespaces, schemas, and the display of XML documents with both Cascading Style Sheets and XML Transformations. Also included is an introduction to Web services and XML processors.

Chapter 9 introduces the characteristics and capabilities of Perl as a general-purpose programming language. Both before and since the arrival of the Web, the power and flexibility of Perl have been used on a variety of non-Web applications, including UNIX system administration and as the language for many of the small to medium size programming tasks formally done in C. For the most part, we limit our focus on Perl to those parts of the language that are needed for CGI programming. Control statements, arrays, hashes, references, functions, pattern matching, and file input and output are discussed.

Chapter 10 introduces the use of Perl for Common Gateway Interface (CGI) programming. Although there are now alternatives to CGI, it is still widely used, and when it is, it is most often done in Perl. CGI and CGI linkage are introduced first. Then the form of query strings for form data is described. Finally, the CGI.pm module is introduced, which greatly simplifies CGI programming in Perl. Several examples are used to show how common CGI tasks are designed and programmed in Perl using CGI.pm.

Java servlets and JSP are discussed in Chapter 11. The chapter introduces the mechanisms for building Java servlets and presents several examples of how servlets can be used to present interactive Web documents. Then, two approaches to storing information on clients using servlets, cookies and session tracking, are introduced and illustrated with examples. Finally, JSP is introduced through a series of examples.

Chapter 12 introduces PHP, a server-side scripting language that is currently gaining popularity, especially as a database access language. The basics of the language are discussed, as well as the use of cookies and session tracking. The use of PHP as a Web database access language is covered in Chapter 14.

Chapter 13 is an introduction to ASP.NET, though it begins with a brief introduction to C#. ASP.NET controls are among the topics discussed in this chapter. Constructing Web services with ASP.NET is also introduced.

Chapter 14 provides an introduction to database access through the Web. This chapter includes an introduction to the nature of relational databases, architectures for database access, the structured query language, SQL, and the free database system, MySQL. Then, three approaches to Web access to databases are discussed: using Perl, using PHP, and using Java JDBC. The JDBC section is lengthy, including a complete Java database application program, as well as metadata and the use of JDBC in servlets. All of the program examples in the chapter use MySQL.

This book includes an appendix that introduces Java to those who have experience with C++ and object-oriented programming. Students who do not know Java can learn enough of the language from this appendix to allow them to understand the Java applets, servlets, JSP, and JDBC that appear in this book.

SUPPORT MATERIALS

The supplements for the book are available at Addison-Wesley's Web site www.aw.com/cssupport. Support materials available to all readers of this book include

- A set of lecture notes in the form of PowerPoint files. The notes were developed to be the basis for class lectures on the book material.
- Code for example programs
- PowerPoint slides of all the figures

Additional support material including solutions to selected exercises are available only to instructors adopting this textbook for classroom use. Please contact your school's Addison-Wesley representative for information on obtaining access to this material.

SOFTWARE AVAILABILITY

Most of the software systems described in this book are available free to students. These include browsers, which provide an interpreter for JavaScript and the Java Virtual Machine. Also, Perl, PHP, and Java language processors, as well as Java class libraries to support servlets and Java JDBC, are available and free. ASP.NET is supported by the .NET software available from Microsoft.

DIFFERENCES BETWEEN THE SECOND EDITION AND THE THIRD EDITION

The third edition differs significantly from the second. Chapter 13, on ASP.NET, is entirely new. Chapter 11 was dramatically changed: the material on Web servers was moved to Chapter 1 and a lengthy section on JSP was added. Chapter 3 was reorganized to a more rational order. Also, sections were added on borders and selector formats. Chapter 5 was also reorganized. A section on Web services was added to Chapter 8. (The new Chapter 13 also includes a section on Web services.) Finally, the section on running applets in Java threads in Chapter 7 was eliminated.

Throughout the book, the XHTML was updated to conform to the XHTML 1.1 recommendation, and all documents were validated under the 1.1 standard. Also, numerous small changes were made to improve the correctness and clarity of the material.

ACKNOWLEDGEMENTS

The quality of this book was significantly improved as a result of the extensive suggestions, corrections, and comments provided by its reviewers. It was reviewed by:

Dunren Che
Southern Illinois University

Richard C. Deter
Middle Tennessee State University

George Holmes
University of Arkansas

Kadathur Lakshmanan
State University of New York at Brockport

Tim Margush
University of Akron

Robert Noonan
College of William and Mary

Jeff Offutt
George Mason University

Marius C. Silaghi
Florida Institute of Technology

Chen-chi Shing
Radford University

Donald S. Szarkowicz
Indiana University Northwest

Michael Weiss
Carleton University

Jonwook Woo
California State University, Los Angeles

Tom Wulf
University of Cincinnati

Mir Farook Ali

Elizabeth Leboffee

Matt Goldstein, Editor, Katherine Harutunian, Project Editor, Patty Mahtani, Managing Editor, and Sarah Bartlett, Production Assistant, all deserve my gratitude for their encouragement and help in completing the manuscript. Also, thanks to Tarida Anantachai at Argosy Publishing for quickly converting the collection of files I provided into a bound book.

Finally, I thank my children, Jake and Darcie, for their patience in enduring my absence from them throughout the many hours I invested in writing this book.

1

Fundamentals

The lives of most inhabitants of industrialized countries, as well as some in unindustrialized countries, have been changed forever by the advent of the World Wide Web. Although this has had some downsides—for example, easier access to pornography and the ease with which those with destructive ideas can propagate those ideas to others—on balance, the changes have been enormously positive. Many of us use the Internet and the World Wide Web on a daily basis, communicating with friends, relatives, and business associates through e-mail, shopping for virtually anything that can be purchased anywhere, and digging up a limitless variety and amount of information, from movie theater schedules to hotel room prices in cities halfway around the world to the history and characteristics of the culture of some small and obscure society of humans. Constructing the software and data that provide all of this information requires knowledge of several different technologies, such as markup languages and meta-markup languages, as well as programming skills in a myriad of different programming languages, some specific to the World Wide Web and some designed for general-purpose computing. This book is meant to provide the required background and a basis for acquiring the knowledge and skills necessary to build the World Wide Web sites that provide both the information users want and the advertising that helps pay for its presentation.

This chapter lays the groundwork for the remainder of the book. It begins with introductions to and some history of the Internet and the World Wide Web. It then discusses the purposes and some of the characteristics of Web browsers and servers. Next, it describes uniform resource locators (URLs), which specify addresses for resources available on the Web. Following this, it introduces Multipurpose Internet Mail Extensions, which provide ways in which file types can be specified—and which are required because of the many different formats in which information can be represented in files. Next, it discusses the Hypertext Transfer Protocol (HTTP), which provides the communication interface for connections between browsers and Web servers. Finally, the chapter provides brief overviews of some of the tools commonly used by Web programmers, including XHTML, XML, JavaScript, Java, Perl, and PHP. All of these are discussed in far more detail in the remainder of the book (XHTML in Chapters 2 and 3; JavaScript in Chapters 4, 5, and 6; XML in Chapter 8; Perl in Chapters 9 and 10; PHP in Chapter 12; and Java in Chapters 7, 11, and Appendix A).

1.1

A BRIEF INTRODUCTION TO THE INTERNET

Virtually every topic discussed in this book is related to the Internet. Therefore, we begin with a quick introduction to the Internet itself.

1.1.1 Origins

The U.S. Department of Defense (DoD) became interested in developing a new large-scale computer network in the 1960s. The purposes of this network were communications, program sharing, and remote computer access for researchers working on defense-related contracts. One fundamental requirement was that the network be sufficiently robust so that even if some network nodes were lost due to sabotage, war, or some more benign reason, the network could continue to function. The DoD's Advanced Research Projects Agency (ARPA)[1] funded the construction of the first such network, which connected about a dozen ARPA-funded research laboratories and universities. The first node of this network was established at UCLA in 1969.

Because it was funded by the ARPA, the network was named ARPAnet. Despite the initial intentions, the primary early use of ARPAnet was simple text-based communications through e-mail. Because ARPAnet was available only to laboratories and universities that conducted ARPA-funded research, the great

---

1. ARPA was renamed Defense Advanced Research Projects Agency (DARPA) in 1972.

majority of educational institutions were not connected. As a result, a number of other networks were developed during the late 1970s and early 1980s, with BITNET and CSNET among them. BITNET, which is an acronym for Because It's Time Network, began at the City University of New York. It was built initially to provide electronic mail and file transfers. CSNET, which is an acronym for Computer Science Network, connected the University of Delaware, Purdue University, the University of Wisconsin, RAND Corporation, and Bolt, Beranek, and Newman. Its initial purpose was to provide electronic mail. For a variety of reasons, neither of these became a dominant national network.

A new national network was created in 1986, NSFnet, sponsored, of course, by the National Science Foundation (NSF). NSFnet initially connected the NSF-funded supercomputer centers at five universities. Soon after being established, it became available to other academic institutions and research laboratories. By 1990, NSFnet had replaced ARPAnet for most nonmilitary uses, and a wide variety of organizations had established nodes on this network—by 1992, NFSnet connected more than 1 million computers around the world. In 1995, a small part of NSFnet returned to being a research network. The rest became known as the Internet, although this term was used much earlier for both ARPAnet and NSFnet.

1.1.2 What the Internet Is

The Internet is a huge collection of computers connected in a communications network. These computers are of every imaginable size, configuration, and manufacturer. In fact, some of the devices connected to the Internet—such as plotters and printers—are not computers at all. The innovation that allows all of these diverse devices to communicate with each other is a single, low-level protocol, the Transmission Control Protocol/Internet Protocol (TCP/IP). TCP/IP became the standard for computer network connections in 1982, and it can be used directly to allow a program on one computer to communicate with a program on another computer via the Internet. In most cases, however, a higher-level protocol runs on top of TCP/IP. Nevertheless, it's important to know that TCP/IP provides the low-level interface that allows all computers (and other devices) connected to the Internet to appear exactly the same.

Rather than connecting every computer on the Internet directly to every other computer on the Internet, the individual computers in an organization normally are connected to each other in a local network. One node on this local network is physically connected to the Internet. So, the Internet is actually a network of networks rather than a network of computers.

Obviously, all devices connected to the Internet must be uniquely identifiable.

1.1.3 Internet Protocol Addresses

For people, Internet nodes are identified by names; for computers, they are identified by numeric addresses. This exactly parallels the relationship between a variable name in a program, which is for people, and the variable's numeric memory address, which is for the machine.

The Internet Protocol (IP) address of a machine connected to the Internet is a unique 32-bit number. IP addresses usually are written (and thought of) as four 8-bit numbers, separated by periods. The four parts are separately used by Internet-routing computers to decide where a message must go next to get to its destination.

Organizations are assigned blocks of IPs, which they in turn assign to their machines that need Internet access—this now includes most computers. For example, a small organization may be assigned 256 IP addresses, such as `191.57.126.0` to `191.57.126.255`. Very large organizations, such as the Department of Defense, may be assigned 16 million IP addresses, which include all IP addresses with one particular first 8-bit number, such as `12.0.0.0` to `12.255.255.255`.

In late 1998, a new IP standard, IPv6, was approved, although it has not yet been widely implemented. The most significant change was to expand the address size from 32 bits to 128 bits. This is a change that is soon to be essential because the number of remaining unused IP addresses is diminishing rapidly. This new standard can be found at `ftp://ftp.isi.edu/in-notes/rfc2460.txt`.

1.1.4 Domain Names

Because people have difficulty dealing with and remembering numbers, machines on the Internet also have textual names. These names begin with the name of the host machine, followed by progressively larger enclosing collections of machines, called *domains*. There may be two, three, or more domain names. The first domain name, which appears immediately to the right of the hostname, is the domain of which the host is a part. The second domain name gives the domain of which the first domain is a part. The last domain name identifies the type of organization in which the host resides, which is the largest domain in the site's name. For organizations in the United States, `edu` is the extension for educational institutions, `com` specifies a company, `gov` is used for the U.S. government, and `org` is used for many other kinds of organizations. In other countries, the largest domain is often an abbreviation for the country—for example, `se` is used for Sweden, and `kz` is used for Kazakhstan.

Consider this sample address:

```
movies.comedy.marxbros.com
```

Here, `movies` is the hostname and `comedy` is `movies`'s local domain, which is a part of `marxbros`'s domain, which is a part of the `com` domain. The hostname and all of the domain names are together called a *fully qualified domain name*.

Because IP addresses are the addresses used internally by the Internet, the fully qualified domain name of the destination for a message, which is what is given by a browser user, must be converted to an IP address before the message can be transmitted on the Internet to the destination. These conversions are done by software systems called *name servers*, which implement the Domain Name System (DNS). Name servers serve a collection of machines on the Internet and are operated by organizations that are responsible for the part of the Internet to which those machines are connected. All document requests from browsers are routed to the nearest name server. If the name server can convert the fully qualified domain name to an IP address, it does so. If it cannot, the name server sends the fully qualified domain name to another name server for conversion. Like IP addresses, fully qualified domain names must be unique. Figure 1.1 shows how fully qualified domain names requested by a browser are translated into IPs before they are routed to the appropriate Web server.

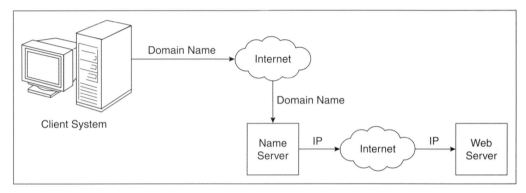

FIGURE 1.1 Domain name conversion

One way to determine the IP address of a Web site is by using `telnet` on the fully qualified domain name. This is illustrated in Section 1.7.1.

By the mid-1980s, a collection of different protocols that run on top of TCP/IP had been developed to support a variety of uses of the Internet. Among these, the most common were `telnet`, which was developed to allow a user on one computer on the Internet to log on to and use another computer on the Internet; File Transfer Protocol (`ftp`), which was developed to transfer files among computers on the Internet; Usenet, which was developed to serve as an electronic bulletin board; and `mailto`, which was developed to allow messages to be sent from the user of one computer on the Internet to other users on other computers on the Internet.

This variety of protocols, each with its own user interface and useful for only the purpose for which it was designed, restricted the growth of the Internet. Users were required to learn all the different interfaces to gain all the advantages of the Internet. Before long, however, a better approach appeared: the World Wide Web.

1.2

THE WORLD WIDE WEB

Programming for the World Wide Web is the topic of this book, so a brief overview of the Web is certainly in order here.

1.2.1 Origins

In 1989, a small group of people led by Tim Berners-Lee at CERN (Conseil European pour la Recherce Nucleaire, or the European Laboratory for Particle Physics) proposed a new protocol for the Internet as well as a system of document access to use it.[2] The intent of this new system, which the group named the World Wide Web, was to allow scientists around the world to use the Internet to exchange documents describing their work.

The proposed new system was designed to allow a user anywhere on the Internet to search for and retrieve documents from databases on any number of different document-serving computers. By late 1990, the basic ideas for the new system had been fully developed and implemented on a NeXT computer at CERN. In 1991, the system was ported to other computer platforms and released to the rest of the world.

For the form of its documents, the system used *hypertext*, which is text with embedded links to text in other documents to allow nonsequential browsing of textual material. The idea of hypertext had been developed earlier and had appeared in Xerox's NoteCards and Apple's HyperCard in the mid-1980s.

From here on, we will refer to the World Wide Web simply as "the Web." The units of information on the Web have been referred to by several different names; among them, the most common are *pages*, *documents*, and *resources*. Perhaps the best of these is *documents*, although that seems to imply only text. *Pages* is widely used but is misleading in that Web units of information often have more than one of the kind of pages that make up printed media. There is some merit to calling these units *resources* because that covers the possibility of nontextual information. This book will use *documents* and *pages* more or less interchangeably, but we prefer *documents* in most situations.

Documents are sometimes just text, usually with embedded links to other documents, but they often also include images, sound recordings, or other kinds of media. When a document contains nontextual information, it is called *hypermedia*.

In an abstract sense, the Web is merely a vast collection of documents, some of which are connected by links. These documents are accessed by Web browsers, introduced in Section 1.3, and are provided by Web servers, introduced in Section 1.4.

---

2. Although Berners-Lee's college degree was in physics (from Oxford), his first stint at CERN was as a consulting software engineer. Berners-Lee was born and raised in London.

1.2.2   Web or Internet?

It is important to understand that the Internet and the Web are not the same thing. The *Internet* is a collection of computers and other devices connected by equipment that allows them to communicate with each other. The *Web* is a collection of software and protocols that has been installed on most, if not all, of the computers on the Internet. The Internet was quite useful before the Web was developed, and it is still useful without it. However, it is now the case that most users of the Internet use it through the Web.

1.3

WEB BROWSERS

When two computers communicate over some network, in many cases one acts as a client and the other as a server. The client initiates the communication, which is often a request for information stored on the server, which sends that information back to the client. The Web, as well as many other systems, operates in this client/server configuration.

Documents provided by servers on the Web are requested by *browsers*, which are programs running on client machines. They are called browsers because they allow the user to browse the resources available on servers. The first browsers were text based—they were not capable of displaying any sort of graphic information, nor did they have a graphical user interface. This effectively constrained growth of use of the Web. In early 1993, this changed with the release of Mosaic, the first browser with a graphical user interface. Mosaic was developed at the National Center for Supercomputer Applications (NCSA) at the University of Illinois. This interface provided convenient access to the Web for users who were neither scientists nor software developers. The first release of Mosaic ran on UNIX systems using the X Window system. By late 1993, versions of Mosaic for Apple Macintosh and Microsoft Windows systems had been released. Finally, users of the computers connected to the Internet around the world had a powerful way to access anything on the Web anywhere in the world. The result of this power and convenience was explosive growth in usage of the Web.

A browser is a client on the Web because it initiates the communication with a server, which waits for a request from a client before doing anything. In the simplest case, a browser requests a static document from a server. The server locates the document and sends it to the browser, which displays it for the user. However, more complicated situations are common. For example, the server may provide a document that requests input from the user through the browser. After the user supplies the requested input, it is transmitted from the browser to the server, which may perform some computation using it and then return a new document to the browser to inform the user of the results of the computation. Sometimes a browser directly requests the execution of a program stored on the server. The output of the program is then returned to the browser.

Although the Web supports a variety of protocols, the most common one is the Hypertext Transfer Protocol (HTTP). HTTP provides a standard form of communications between browsers and Web servers. Section 1.7 provides an introduction to HTTP.

The most commonly used browsers are Microsoft Internet Explorer (IE), which runs only on PCs that use one of the Microsoft Windows operating systems,[3] and Netscape's browser, which comes in versions for many different computing platforms. There are several other browsers available, such as the Opera and Mozilla browsers. However, the great majority of browsers in use are from Microsoft, and most of the others are from Netscape, so we focus on those two in this book.

1.4

WEB SERVERS

Web servers are programs that provide documents to requesting browsers. Servers are slave programs: They act only when requests are made to them by browsers running on other computers on the Internet.

The most commonly used Web servers are Apache, which has been implemented for a variety of computer platforms, and Microsoft's Internet Information Server (IIS), which runs under Windows operating systems. As of November 2004, there were over 50 million Web sites in operation, 68% of which were Apache, about 21% of which were IIS, and the remainder were spread thinly over a large number of others. (The third-place server was SunONE, with just over 3%.)[4]

1.4.1 Web Server Operation

Although having clients and servers is a natural consequence of information distribution, this configuration offers some additional benefits for the Web. Serving information does not take a great deal of time. On the other hand, displaying information on client screens is time consuming. Because Web servers need not be involved in this display process, they can handle many clients. So, it is both a natural and an efficient division of labor to have a small number of servers provide documents to a large number of clients.

Web browsers initiate network communications with servers by sending them URLs (discussed in Section 1.5). A URL can specify one of two different things: the address of a data file stored on the server that is to be sent to the cli-

---

3. Actually, versions 4 and 5 of IE (IE4 and IE5) were also available for Macintosh computers, and IE4 was available for UNIX systems. However, IE6 is currently available only for Windows platforms.

4. These statistics are from http://www.netcraft.com.

ent, or a program stored on the server that the client wants executed, with the output of the program returned to the client.

All the communications between a Web client and a Web server use the standard Web protocol, Hypertext Transfer Protocol (HTTP), which is discussed in Section 1.7.[5]

When a Web server begins execution, it informs the operating system under which it is running that it is now ready to accept incoming network connections through a specific port on the machine. While in this running state, the server runs as a background process in the operating system environment. A Web client, or browser, opens a network connection to a Web server, sends information requests and possibly data to the server, receives information from the server, and closes the connection. Of course, other machines exist between browsers and servers on the network—specifically, network routers and domain-name servers. This section, however, focuses on just one part of Web communication: the server.

Simply put, the primary task of a Web server is to monitor a communications port on its host machine, accept HTTP commands through that port, and perform the operations specified by the commands. All HTTP commands include a URL, which includes the specification of a host machine. When the URL is received, it is translated into either a filename (in which case the file is returned to the requesting client) or a program name (in which case the program is run and its output is sent to the requesting client). This sounds pretty simple, but as is the case in many other simple-sounding processes, a large number of complicating details are involved.

All current Web servers have a common ancestry: the first two servers, developed at CERN in Europe and NCSA at the University of Illinois. Currently, the most common server configuration is Apache running on some version of UNIX.

1.4.2 General Server Characteristics

Most available servers share common characteristics, regardless of their origin or the platform on which they run. This section provides brief descriptions of some of these characteristics.

The file structure of a Web server has two separate directories. The root of one of these is called the *document root*. The file hierarchy that grows from the document root stores the Web documents to which the server has direct access and normally serves to clients. The root of the other directory is called the *server root*. This directory, along with its descendent directories, stores the server and its support software.

The files stored directly in the document root are those available to clients through top-level URLs. Typically, clients do not access the document root directly in URLs; rather, the server maps request URLs to the document root,

---

5. Actually, some of these communications use the secure version of HTTP, HTTPS.

whose location is not known to clients. For example, suppose that the site name is `www.bloomers.com`, which happens to be a UNIX-based system. Further suppose that the document root is named `topdocs` and is stored in the `/admin/web` directory, making its address `/admin/web/topdocs`. A request for a file from a client with the URL `http://www.bloomers.com/petunias.html` will cause the server to search for the file with the file path `/admin/web/topdocs/petunias.html`. Likewise, the URL `http://www.bloomers.com/bulbs/tulips.html` will cause the server to search for the file with the address `/admin/web/topdocs/bulbs/tulips.html`.

Many servers allow part of the servable document collection to be stored outside the directory at the document root. The secondary areas from which documents can be served are called *virtual document trees*. For example, the original configuration of a server might store all its servable documents from the primary system disk on the server machine. Later, the collection of servable documents might outgrow that disk, in which case part of the collection could be stored on a secondary disk. This secondary disk might reside on the server machine or on some other machine on a local area network. To support this arrangement, the server is configured to direct request URLs with a particular file path to a storage area separate from the document-root directory. Sometimes files of different content, such as images, are stored outside the document root.

Early servers provided few services other than the basic process of returning requested files or the output of programs whose execution had been requested. The list of additional services has grown steadily in the past few years. Contemporary servers are large and complex systems that provide a wide variety of client services. Many servers can support more than one site on a computer, potentially reducing the cost of each site and making their maintenance more convenient. Such secondary hosts are called *virtual hosts*.

Some servers can serve documents that are in the document root of other machines on the Web; in this case, they are called *proxy servers*.

Although Web servers were originally designed to support only the HTTP protocol, many now support `ftp`, Gopher, News, and mail. Nearly all Web servers can interact with database systems through Common Gateway Interface (CGI) programs and server-side scripts.

1.4.3 Apache

Apache began as the NCSA server, `httpd`, with some added features. The name Apache has nothing to do with the Native American tribe of the same name. Rather, it came from the nature of its first version, which was *a patch*y version of the `httpd` server. As seen in the usage statistics given at the beginning of this section, Apache is by far the most widely used Web server. The primary reasons for this are as follows: It is an excellent server, both fast and reliable. Furthermore, it is open-source software, which means it is free and is managed by a large team of volunteers, a process that efficiently and effectively maintains the system. Finally, it is one of the best available servers for Unix-based systems, which are the most popular for Web servers.

Apache is capable of providing a long list of services beyond the basic process of serving documents to clients. It takes an entire book to describe all these services. It also takes a long list of words to explain how an Apache server can be configured to the tastes of the site manager. Only a tiny glimpse of how the actions of Apache can be customized is given here.

When Apache begins execution, it reads its configuration information from a file and sets its parameters to operate accordingly. A new copy of Apache includes default configuration information for "typical" operation. The site manager modifies this configuration information to fit his or her particular needs and tastes.

For historical reasons, there are three configuration files in an Apache server: `httpd.conf`, `srm.conf`, and `access.conf`. Only one of these, `httpd.conf`, actually stores the directives that control an Apache server's behavior. The other two point to `httpd.conf`. This file contains the list of directives that specify the server's operation.

Table 1.1 lists some of the most commonly changed Apache directives.

TABLE 1.1 The Most Commonly Used Apache Directives

Directive Name	Purpose
ServerName	Names the server system
ServerRoot	Path to the server root
ServerAdmin	The site administrator's address
DocumentRoot	Path to the document root
Alias	The document root's virtual and physical paths
Redirect	A pointer to a document or document directory on a different server
DirectoryIndex	Names of the welcome pages
UserDir	Specifies whether local users can add and/or delete documents

After changes have been made to `httpd.conf`, Apache must be stopped and restarted before they will take effect.

1.4.4 IIS

Although Apache has been ported to the Windows platforms, it is not the most popular server on those systems. Because the Microsoft IIS server is supplied as part of Windows—and because it is a reasonably good server—most Windows-based Web servers use IIS. Apache and IIS provide similar varieties of services.

From the point of view of the site manager, the most important difference between Apache and IIS is that Apache is controlled by a configuration file that is edited by the manager to change Apache's behavior. With IIS, server behavior is modified by changes made through a window-based management program, named the IIS snap-in, which controls both IIS and `ftp`. This program allows the site manager to set parameters for the server.

Under Windows XP, the IIS snap-in is accessed by going to Control Panel, Administrative Tools, and IIS Admin. Clicking on this last selection takes you to a window that allows starting, stopping, or pausing IIS. This same window allows IIS parameters to be changed when the server has been stopped.

1.5

UNIFORM RESOURCE LOCATORS

Uniform (or universal)[6] resource locators (URLs) are used to identify documents (resources) on the Internet. There are many different kinds of resources, identified by different forms of URLs.

1.5.1 URL Formats

All URLs have the same general format:

scheme:object-address

The scheme is often a communications protocol. Common schemes include `http`, `ftp`, `gopher`, `telnet`, `file`, `mailto`, and `news`. Different schemes use object addresses that have differing forms. Our main interest is in the HTTP protocol, which supports the Web. It is used to request and send eXtensible Hypertext Markup Language (XHTML) documents. In the case of HTTP, the form of the object address of a URL is as follows:

//fully-qualified-domain-name/path-to-document

Another scheme of interest to us is `file`. The `file` protocol means that the document resides on the machine running the browser. This is useful for testing documents to be made available on the Web, without actually making them visible to any other browser. When `file` is the protocol, the fully qualified domain name is always omitted, making the form of such URLs as follows:

file://path-to-document

---

6. Fortunately, resource addresses are usually referred to as URLs, so whether it is *uniform* or *universal* is usually irrelevant.

Because we focus on XHTML documents in this book, we limit the remainder of our discussion of URLs to the HTTP protocol.

The hostname is the name of the server computer that stores the document (or provides access to it on some other computer). Messages to a host machine must be directed to the appropriate process running on the host for handling. Such processes are identified by their associated port numbers. The default port number of Web server processes is 80. If a server has been configured to use some other port number, it is necessary to attach that port number to the hostname in the URL. For example, if the Web server is configured to use port 800, the hostname must have `:800` attached.

URLs can never have embedded spaces.[7] Also, there is a collection of special characters that cannot appear in a URL, including semicolons, colons, and ampersands (`&`). To include a space or one of the disallowed special characters in a URL, the character must be coded as a percent sign (`%`) followed by the two-digit hexadecimal ASCII code for the character. For example, if `San Jose` is a domain name, it must be typed as `San%20Jose` (20 being the hexadecimal ASCII code for a space). All of the details of URLs can be found at `http://www.w3.org/Addressing/URL/URI_Overview.html`.

1.5.2 URL Paths

The path to the document for the HTTP protocol is similar to a path to a file or directory in the file system of an operating system: a sequence of directory names and a filename, all separated by whatever separator character the operating system uses. For UNIX servers, the path is specified with forward slashes; for Windows servers, it is specified using backward slashes. Most browsers allow the user to specify the separators incorrectly—for example, using forward slashes in a path to a document file on a Windows server. For example, for UNIX, you might have this:

```
http://www.gumboco.com/files/f99/storefront.html
```

The path in a URL can differ from a path to a file because a URL need not include all directories on the path. A path that includes all directories along the way is called a *complete path*. In most cases, the path to the document is relative to some base path that is specified in the configuration files of the server. Such paths are called *partial paths*. For example, if the server's configuration specifies that the root directory for files it can serve is `files/f99`, the previous URL is specified as follows:

```
http://www.gumboco.com/storefront.html
```

---

7. Actually, some browsers incorrectly accept spaces in URLs, although this is nonstandard behavior.

If the specified document is a directory rather than a single document, the directory's name is followed immediately by a slash, as in the following:

```
http://www.gumboco.com/departments/
```

Sometimes a directory is specified (with the trailing slash) but its name is not given, as in this example:

```
http://www.gumboco.com/
```

The server then searches at the top level of the directory in which servable documents are normally stored for something it recognizes as a home page. By convention, this is often a file named `index.html`. The home page usually includes links that allow the user to find the other related servable files on the server.

If the directory does not have a file that the server recognizes as being a home page, a directory listing is constructed and returned to the browser.

1.6

MULTIPURPOSE INTERNET MAIL EXTENSIONS

A browser needs some way of determining the formats of the documents it receives from Web servers. Without knowing the form of a document, the browser would be unable to render it. The forms of these documents are specified with the Multipurpose Internet Mail Extensions (MIME).

1.6.1   Type Specifications

MIME was developed to allow different kinds of documents to be sent using Internet mail. These could be various kinds of text, video data, or sound data. Because the Web has similar needs, MIME was adopted as the way to specify document types transmitted over the Web. A Web server attaches a MIME format specification to the beginning of the document that it is about to provide to a browser. When the browser receives the document from a Web server, it uses the included MIME format specification to determine what to do with the document. If the content is text, for example, the MIME code tells the browser that it is text and also indicates the particular kind of text it is. If the content is sound, the MIME code tells the browser that it is sound and then gives the particular representation of sound so that the browser can choose a program to which it has access to produce the transmitted sound.

MIME specifications have the following form:

```
type/subtype
```

The most common MIME types are text, image, and video. The most common text subtypes are plain and html. The most common image subtypes are gif and jpeg. The most common video subtypes are mpeg and quicktime. A list of MIME specifications is stored in the configuration files of every Web server. In the remainder of this book, when we say *document type*, we mean both the document's type and its subtype.

Servers determine the type of a document by using the filename's extension as the key into a table of types. For example, the extension .html tells the server that it should attach text/html to the document before sending it to the requesting browser.[8]

Browsers also maintain a conversion table for looking up the type of a document by its filename extension. However, this is used only when the server does not specify a MIME type, which may be the case for some older servers. In all other cases, the browser gets the document type from the MIME header provided by the server.

1.6.2 Experimental Document Types

Some experimental subtypes are being used. The name of an experimental subtype begins with x-, as in video/x-msvideo. Any Web provider can add an experimental subtype by having its name added to the list of MIME specifications stored in the Web provider's server. For example, a Web provider might have a handcrafted database whose contents he or she wants to make available to others through the Web. Of course, this raises the issue of how the browser can display the database. As you might expect, the Web provider must supply a program that the browser can call when it needs to display the contents of the database. These programs either are external to the browser, in which case they are called *helper applications*, or are code modules that are inserted into the browser, in which case they are called *plug-ins*.

Every browser has a set of MIME specifications it can handle. All can deal with text/plain (unformatted text) and text/html (HTML files), among others. Often a particular browser cannot handle some document type, even though the type is widely used. These cases are handled in the same way as the experimental types described previously. The browser determines the helper application or plug-in it needs by examining the browser configuration file, which provides an association between file types and their required helpers or plug-ins.

A browser can indicate to the server the document types it prefers to receive, as discussed in Section 1.7.

---

8. This is not necessarily correct. XHTML documents also use the .html file extension, but strictly speaking should use a different MIME type.

1.7

THE HYPERTEXT TRANSFER PROTOCOL

All Web communications transactions use the same protocol, the Hypertext Transfer Protocol (HTTP). The current version of HTTP is 1.1. It is formally defined as RFC 2616, which was approved in June 1999. RFC 2616 is available at the Web site for the World Wide Web Consortium (W3C), `http://www.w3.org`. This section provides a brief introduction to HTTP.

HTTP consists of two phases, the request and the response. Each HTTP communication (request or response) between a browser and a Web server consists of two parts, a header and a body. The header contains information about the communication; the body contains the data of the communication, if there is any.

1.7.1 The Request Phase

The general form of an HTTP request is as follows:

1. HTTP method   Domain part of the URL   HTTP version
2. Header fields
3. Blank line
4. Message body

The following is an example of the first line of an HTTP request:

```
GET  /storefront.html  HTTP/1.1
```

Only a few request methods are defined by HTTP, and even a smaller number of these are typically used. Table 1.2 lists the most commonly used methods.

TABLE 1.2 HTTP Request Methods

Method	Description
GET	Returns the contents of the specified document
HEAD	Returns the header information for the specified document
POST	Executes the specified document, using the enclosed data
PUT	Replaces the specified document with the enclosed data
DELETE	Deletes the specified document

GET and POST are the most commonly used methods. POST was originally designed for tasks such as posting a news article to a newsgroup. Its most common use now is to send form data to the server, along with a request to execute a program on the server that will process the form data.

Following the first line of an HTTP communication is any number of header fields, most of which are optional. The format of a header field is the field name followed by a colon and the value of the field. There are four categories of header fields:

1. *General:* For general information, such as the date
2. *Request:* Included in request headers
3. *Response:* For response headers
4. *Entity:* Used in both request and response headers

One common request field is the Accept field, which specifies a preference of the browser for the MIME type of the requested document. More than one Accept field can be specified if the browser is willing to accept documents in more than one format. For example:

```
Accept: text/plain
Accept: text/html
Accept: image/gif
```

A wildcard character, the asterisk (*), can be used to specify that part of a MIME type can be anything. For example, if any kind of text is acceptable, the Accept field could be as follows:

```
Accept: text/*
```

The Host: *host* request field gives the name of the host. The Host field is required for HTTP 1.1. The If-Modified-Since: *date* request field specifies that the requested file should be sent only if it has been modified since the given date.

If the request has a body, the length of that body must be given with a Content-length field, which gives the length of the response body in bytes. POST method requests require this field because they send data to the server.

The header of a request must be followed by a blank line, which is used to separate the header from the body of the request. Requests that use the GET, HEAD, and DELETE methods do not have bodies. In these cases, the blank line is used to signal the end of the request.

A browser is not necessary to communicate with a Web server; telnet also can be used. Consider the following command, given at a UNIX command line:

```
> telnet blanca.uccs.edu http
```

This command creates a connection to the `http` port on the `blanca.uccs.edu` server. The server responds with the following:[9]

```
Trying 128.198.162.60 ...
Connected to blanca
Escape character is '^]'.
```

The connection to the server is now complete, and HTTP commands can be given. For example:

```
GET /respond.html HTTP/1.1
Host: blanca.uccs.edu
```

The header of the response to this request is given in Section 1.7.2.

1.7.2   The Response Phase

The general form of an HTTP response is as follows:

1. Status line
2. Response header fields
3. Blank line
4. Response body

The status line includes the HTTP version used, a three-digit status code for the response, and a short textual explanation of the status code. For example, most responses begin with this:

```
HTTP/1.1  200  OK
```

The status codes begin with 1, 2, 3, 4, or 5. The general meanings of the five categories specified by these first digits are shown in Table 1.3.

TABLE 1.3 First Digits of HTTP Status Codes

First Digit	Category
1	Informational
2	Success
3	Redirection
4	Client error
5	Server error

---

9. Notice that this `telnet` request returns the IP of the server.

One of the more common status codes is one users never want to see: 404 Not Found, which means the requested file could not be found.

After the status line, the server sends a response header, which can contain several lines of information about the response, each in the form of a field. The only essential field of the header is Content-type.

The following is the response header for the request given near the end of Section 1.7.1:

```
HTTP/1.1  200  OK
Date: Tues, 18 May 2004 16:45:13 GMT
Server: Apache (Red-Hat/Linux)
Last-modified: Tues, 18 May 2004 16:38:38 GMT
ETag: "1f1223-16c-92dc9f80"
Accept-ranges: bytes
Content-length: 364
Connection: close
Content-type: text/html, charset=ISO-8859-1
```

The response header must be followed by a blank line, as is the case for request headers. The response data follows the blank line. In the preceding example, the response body would be the html file, respond.html.

In HTTP versions prior to 1.1, when a server finished sending a response to the client, the communications connection was closed. However, the default operation of HTTP 1.1 is that the connection is kept open for a time so that a client can make several requests over a short period of time without needing to reestablish the communications connection with the server. This change led to significant increases in the efficiency of the Web.

1.8

THE WEB PROGRAMMER'S TOOLBOX

This section provides an overview of the most common tools used in Web programming—some are programming languages, but some are not. The tools discussed are XHTML, a markup language; XML, which is a meta-markup language; JavaScript, Java, Perl, and PHP, which are programming languages; and a few high-level editing systems, which are neither. Web programs and scripts are divided into two categories, client side and server side, according to where they are interpreted or executed. XHTML and XML are client-side languages; Perl and PHP are server-side languages; JavaScript is most often a client-side language, although it can be used for both; and Java is commonly used for both.

We begin with the most basic tool, XHTML.

1.8.1   Overview of XHTML

At the onset, it is important to realize that XHTML is not a programming language. It cannot be used to describe computations. Its purpose is to describe the general form and layout of documents to be displayed by a browser.

The word *markup* comes from the publishing world, where it is used to describe what production people do with a manuscript to specify to a printer how the text, graphics, and other elements in the book should appear in printed form. XHTML is not the first markup language used with computers. TeX and LaTeX are older markup languages for use with digital text; they are now used primarily to specify how mathematical expressions and formulas should appear in print.

An XHTML document is a mixture of content and controls. The controls are specified by the tags of XHTML. Most XHTML tags consist of a pair of syntactic markers that are used to delimit particular kinds of content. The pair of tags and their content are together called an *element*. For example, a paragraph element specifies that its content, which appears between its opening tag, `<p>`, and its closing tag, `</p>`, is a paragraph. A browser has a default style (font, font style, font size, and so forth) for paragraphs, which is used to display the content of a paragraph element.

Some tags include attribute specifications that provide some additional information for the browser. In the following example, the attribute specifies the location of its nontextual content:

```
<img src = "redhead.jpg">
```

In this case, the image document stored in `redhead.jpg` is to be displayed as an image at the position in the document in which this tag appears.

XHTML 1.0 was introduced in early 2000 by the W3C as an alternative to HTML 4.01, which was at that time (and still is) the latest version of HTML. XHTML 1.0 is nothing more than HTML 4.01 with stronger syntactic rules. These stronger rules are those of XML (see Section 1.8.4). The current version, XHTML 1.1, was released in May 2001 as a replacement for XHTML 1.0. Chapter 2, "Introduction to XHTML," provides a description of a large subset of XHTML.

1.8.2   Tools for Creating XHTML Documents

XHTML documents can be created with a general-purpose text editor. There are two kinds of tools that can simplify this task: XHTML editors and what-you-see-is-what-you-get (WYSIWYG, pronounced *wizzy-wig*) XHTML editors.

XHTML editors provide shortcuts to producing repetitious tags such as those used to create the rows of a table. They also may provide a spell-checker and a syntax-checker, and they may color-code the XHTML in the display to make it easier to read and edit.

A more powerful tool for creating XHTML documents is a WYSIWYG XHTML editor. Using a WYSIWYG XHTML editor, the writer can see the document that the XHTML describes while writing the XHTML. WYSIWYG XHTML editors are very useful for beginners who want to create simple documents without learning XHTML and for users who want to prototype the appearance of a document. On the other hand, these editors sometimes produce poor-quality XHTML. In some cases, they create proprietary tags that some browsers will not recognize.

Three examples of WYSIWYG XHTML editors are Microsoft FrontPage, Macromedia Dreamweaver, and Adobe PageMill. All three allow the user to create XHTML-described documents without requiring the user to know XHTML. They cannot handle all of the tags of XHTML, but they are very useful for creating many of the common features of documents. Among these three, FrontPage is by far the most widely used. Information on PageMill is available at `http://www.adobe.com/`, information on Dreamweaver is available at `http://www.macromedia.com/`, and information on FrontPage is available at `http://www.microsoft.com/frontpage/`.

1.8.3   Plug-ins and Filters

Two different kinds of converters can be used to create XHTML documents. First are *plug-ins*, which are programs that can be integrated with a word processor. Plug-ins add new capabilities to the word processor, such as toolbar buttons and menu elements that provide convenient ways to insert XHTML into the document being created or edited. After such insertions, the document is displayed using the XHTML. So, the plug-in makes the word processor appear to be an XHTML editor that provides WYSIWYG XHTML document development. The end result of this process is an XHTML document. The plug-in also makes available all the tools that are inherent to the word processor during XHTML document creation, such as a spell-checker and a thesaurus.

A second kind of converter is a *filter*, which converts an existing document in some form, such as LaTeX or Microsoft Word, to XHTML. Filters are never part of the editor or word processor that created the document. This is an advantage because they can be platform-independent. For example, a Word-Perfect user working on a Macintosh computer can provide documents that can be later converted to XHTML using a filter running on a UNIX platform. The disadvantage of filters is that creating XHTML documents with a filter is a two-step process: You first create the document and then use a filter to convert it to XHTML.

Neither plugs-ins nor filters produce XHTML documents that, when displayed by browsers, have the identical appearance of that produced by the word processor.

The two advantages of both plug-ins and filters, however, are that existing documents produced with word processors can be easily converted to XHTML and that users can produce XHTML documents using a word processor with which they are familiar. This obviates the need to learn to format text using

XHTML directly. For example, once you learn to create tables with your word processor, it is easier to use that process than to learn to define a table directly in XHTML.

The XHTML output produced by both filters and plug-ins often must be modified, usually using a simple text editor, to perfect the appearance of the displayed document on the browser. Because this new XHTML file cannot be converted back to its original form (regardless of how it was created), you will have two different source files for a document. This inevitably leads to version problems during maintenance of the document. This is clearly a disadvantage of using converters.

1.8.4   Overview of XML

HTML is defined using the Standard Generalized Markup Language (SGML), which is a language for defining markup languages (such languages are called meta-markup languages). XML (eXtensible Markup Language) is a simplified version of SGML, designed to allow users to easily create markup languages that fit their own needs. XHTML is defined using XML. Whereas XHTML users must use the predefined set of tags and attributes, when a user creates his or her own markup language using XML, the set of tags and attributes are designed for the application at hand. For example, if a group of users wants a markup language to describe data about weather phenomena, that language could have tags for cloud forms, thunderstorms, and low-pressure centers. The content of these tags would be restricted to relevant data. If such data is described using XHTML, cloud forms could be put in paragraphs, but then they could not be distinguished from thunderstorm elements, which would also be paragraphs.

Whereas XHTML describes the overall layout and some presentation hints for general information, XML-based markup languages describe data and its meaning through their individualized tags and attributes. XML does not specify any presentation details.

The great advantage of XML is that application programs can be written to use the meanings of the tags in the given markup language to find specific kinds of data and process it accordingly. The syntax rules of XML, along with the syntax rules for a specific XML-based markup language, allow documents to be validated before any application attempts to process their data. This means that all documents that use a specific markup language can be checked to determine whether they are in the standard form for such documents. This greatly simplifies the development of application programs that process the data in XML documents.

1.8.5   Overview of JavaScript

JavaScript is a client-side scripting language whose primary uses in Web programming are to validate form data and to create dynamic XHTML documents.

The name JavaScript is misleading because the relationship between Java and JavaScript is tenuous, except for some of the syntax. One of the most important differences between JavaScript and most common programming languages is that JavaScript is dynamically typed. This is virtually the opposite of the strongly typed languages such as C++ and Java.

JavaScript "programs" are usually embedded in XHTML documents.[10] These XHTML documents are downloaded when they are requested by browsers. The JavaScript code in an XHTML document is interpreted by the browser on the client.

One of the most important applications of JavaScript is to dynamically create and modify documents. JavaScript defines an object hierarchy that matches a hierarchical model of an XHTML document. Elements of an XHTML document are accessed through these objects, providing the basis for dynamic documents.

Chapter 4, "The Basics of JavaScript," provides a more detailed look at Java-Script. Chapter 5, "JavaScript and XHTML Documents," and Chapter 6, "Dynamic Documents with JavaScript," discuss the use of JavaScript to provide access to and dynamic modification of XHTML documents.

1.8.6 Overview of Java

Java is based on C++ but differs from that language in several important ways. First, Java is much smaller than C++ and is considerably safer, particularly in the areas of pointers and array index range errors. Although simpler than C++, Java is not a simple language by any measure. Appendix A provides a quick introduction to Java, focusing on the parts of the language most often used for writing applets and servlets.

Java was designed by Sun Microsystems, which controls its continuing development. It was originally developed to program household appliances. As always, timing is exquisitely important: Java was still in development when Web usage began to explode. Java's designers realized that Java would be a powerful way to provide a computational capability for XHTML documents. Rather than running programs on the Web server to provide a computational capability, a special kind of Java program called an *applet* can be resident on the server, but a compiled version of the applet can be downloaded to the browser when requested by the XHTML document being displayed by the browser.

Compiled Java is represented in an idealized machine language called *bytecodes*. When the browser receives a bytecode applet, it "executes" it using a Java virtual machine, which is an interpreter for bytecodes. Java applets are discussed in Chapter 7, "Java Applets." The use of applets moves these computations from servers, which are often very busy, to the browser, which often has little to do. This is similar to how JavaScript works. The primary differences are that Java-Script code is physically part of an XHTML document, whereas applets are stored separately from the XHTML. Moreover, JavaScript is less powerful than Java.

---

10. We quote the word *programs* to indicate that these are not programs in the general sense of the self-contained collections of C++ or C code we normally call programs.

There are many computational tasks in a Web interaction that must occur on the server, such as processing order forms and accessing server-resident databases. A form of Java class called a *servlet* can be used for these applications.

Java can also be used as a server-side scripting language. An XHTML document with embedded Java scriptlets is one form of Java Server Pages. Both servlets and Java Server Pages are discussed in Chapter 11, "Servlets and Java Server Pages."

Microsoft also provides a system for embedding programming code in an XHTML document, this time in any of a variety of programming languages. This system is named Active Server Pages (ASP.NET). ASP.NET is discussed in Chapter 14, "Introduction to ASP.NET."

1.8.7 Overview of Perl

Before applets and embedded scripts were developed, a computational capability was provided for XHTML documents by allowing the document to request the execution of virtually any program on the server. This is done using the Common Gateway Interface (CGI). Briefly, CGI is a standard way in which a browser and a server communicate to run a program on the server and return the output of that program to the browser.

CGI programs can be written in any programming language that is supported by the server machine. The most commonly used language for CGI programs is Perl. Perl dominates the CGI programming business because it is highly portable and because it has several capabilities that are needed for this kind of programming. No other programming language fits the application as well.

The features of Perl that make it ideal for CGI programming are its direct access to operating system functions, its powerful character string pattern-matching operations, and its ability to include database operations. Perl is a very expressive and powerful language whose use is not limited to CGI programming. In recent years, it has replaced C for many small to medium applications. Although Perl began as a UNIX language, it has been ported to all common computer systems, including PCs running Windows and Apple Macintosh systems.

Perl's syntax is similar to that of C. However, Perl code is not compiled into machine language and executed, as is C. Instead, it is compiled to an intermediate language and interpreted.

The subset of Perl that is most useful for CGI programming is introduced in Chapter 9, "The Basics of Perl." Its use in CGI programming is discussed in Chapter 10, "Using Perl for CGI Programming."

1.8.8 Overview of PHP

PHP is a server-side scripting language specifically designed for Web applications (unlike Perl, which is a general-purpose language that happens to be good for server-side software). PHP code is embedded in XHTML documents, as is the case with JavaScript. With PHP, however, the code is interpreted on the server before the XHTML document is returned to the requesting client. A requested document that includes PHP code is preprocessed to interpret the PHP code and insert its output into the XHTML document. The browser never sees PHP code and is not aware that a requested document originally included PHP code.

PHP is similar to JavaScript, both in terms of its syntactic appearance and in terms of the dynamic nature of its strings and arrays. Both JavaScript and PHP use dynamic data typing, meaning that the type of a variable is controlled by the last assignment to it. PHP's arrays are a combination of Perl's arrays and Perl's hashes (associative arrays). The language includes a large number of predefined functions for manipulating arrays.

PHP allows simple access to XHTML form data, so form processing is easy with PHP. PHP provides support for many different database management systems. This makes it an excellent language for building programs that need Web access to databases.

1.9
SUMMARY

The Internet began in the late 1960s as the ARPAnet, which was eventually replaced by NSFnet for nonmilitary users. NSFnet later became known as the Internet. There are now millions of computers around the world connected to the Internet. Although much of the network control equipment is different and many kinds of computers are connected, all of these connections are made through the TCP/IP protocol, making them all appear, at least at the lowest level, the same to the network.

Two kinds of addresses are used on the Internet: IP addresses for computers, which are four-part numbers; and fully qualified domain names for people, which are words separated by periods. Fully qualified domain names are translated to IP addresses by name servers running DNS. A number of different information interchange protocols have been created, including `telnet`, `ftp`, and `mailto`.

The Web began in the late 1980s at CERN as a means for physicists to efficiently share the results of their work with colleagues at other locations. The fundamental idea of the Web is to transfer hypertext documents among computers using the HTTP protocol on the Internet.

Browsers request XHTML documents from Web servers and display them for users. Web servers find and send requested documents to browsers. All documents are addressed on the Internet using URLs; the specific protocol to be used is the first field of the URL. URLs also include the fully qualified domain name and a file path to the specific document on the server. The type of a document that is delivered by a Web server appears in the first line of the document as a MIME specification. Web sites can create their own experimental MIME types, provided that they also furnish a program that allows the browser to present the document's contents to the user.

HTTP is the standard protocol for Web communications. HTTP requests are sent on the Internet from browsers to Web servers; HTTP responses are sent from Web servers to browsers to fulfill those requests. The most commonly used HTTP requests are GET and POST, both of which require URLs.

Web programmers use several languages to create the documents that servers can provide to browsers. The most basic of these is XHTML, the standard markup language for describing how Web documents should be presented by browsers. Tools that can be used without specific knowledge of XHTML are available to create XHTML documents. A plug-in is a program that can be integrated with a word processor to make it possible to use the word processor to create XHTML. A filter converts a document written in some other format to XHTML. XML is a meta-markup language that provides a standard way to define new markup languages.

JavaScript is a client-side scripting language that can be embedded in XHTML to describe simple computations. JavaScript code is interpreted by the browser on the client machine; it provides access to the elements of an XHTML document, as well as the ability to dynamically change those elements.

Java is a modern, widely used, general-purpose programming language. The two most interesting constructs provided by Java for Web programmers are applets and servlets. Applets reside on the Web server but can be requested by browsers, at which time a compiled version of the applet is transferred to the browser, which interprets the applet. This provides another means of specifying computations for Web documents that take place on the browser. Servlets are server-side Java programs that can be used for form processing and database access.

Perl is a programming language that is often used as a server-side vehicle to describe computations upon request from browsers. Interactions between browsers and Perl programs on the server are done through CGI. PHP is a server-side, XHTML-embedded scripting language. Its uses are similar to those of CGI programs.

1.10 Review Questions

1. What was one of the fundamental requirements for the new national computer network proposed by the DoD in the 1960s?

2. What protocol is used by all computer connections to the Internet?

3. What is the form of an IP address?

4. Describe a fully qualified domain name.

5. What is the task of a DNS name server?

6. What is the purpose of `telnet`?

7. In the first proposal for the Web, what form of information was to be interchanged?

8. What is hypertext?

9. What category of browser, introduced in 1993, led to a huge expansion in use of the Web?

10. In what common situation is the document returned by a Web server created after the request is received?

11. What is the document root of a Web server?

12. What is a virtual document tree?

13. What is the server root of a Web server?

14. What is a virtual host?

15. What is a proxy server?

16. What does the `file` protocol specify?

17. How do partial paths to documents work in Web servers?

18. When a browser requests a directory without giving its name, what is the name of the file that is normally returned by the Web server?

19. What is the purpose of a MIME type specification in a request/response transaction between a browser and a server?

20. What must a Web server furnish the browser when it returns a document with an experimental MIME type?

21. Describe the purposes of the five most commonly used HTTP methods.

22. What is the purpose of the `Accept` field in an HTTP request?

23. What response header field is most often required?

24. Prior to HTTP 1.1, how long were connections between browsers and servers normally maintained?

25. What important capability is lacking in a markup language?

26. What is a plug-in?

27. What is a filter XHTML converter?

28. Why must code generated by a filter often be modified by hand before use?

29. What is the great advantage of XML over XHTML for describing data?

30. How many different tags are predefined in an XML-based markup language?

31. What is the relationship between Java and JavaScript?

32. Where is JavaScript code interpreted?

33. Where are Java applets interpreted?

34. Where are Java servlets interpreted?

35. What is the purpose of the Common Gateway Interface?

36. What features of Perl make it ideal for CGI programming?

37. Where are CGI programs executed (or interpreted)?

38. Where is PHP code interpreted?

39. In what ways is PHP similar to JavaScript?

1.11 Exercises

1. For the following products, what brand do you have access to, what is its version number, and what is the latest available version?

   a. Browser

   b. Web server

   c. Perl

   d. Java

   e. PHP

2. Search the Web for information on the history of the following technologies and write a brief overview of those histories.

   a. TCP/IP

   b. SGML

   c. XHTML

   d. ARPAnet

   e. BITNET

   f. XML

Introduction to XHTML

This chapter introduces the most commonly used subset of the eXtensible Hypertext Markup Language (XHTML). Because of the simplicity of XHTML, the discussion moves quickly. The chapter begins with a brief history of the evolution of HTML and XHTML, followed by a description of the form of tags and the structure of an XHTML document. Then tags used to specify the presentation of text are discussed, including those for line breaks, paragraph breaks, headings, and block quotations, as well as tags for specifying the style and relative size of fonts. This is followed by a description of the formats and uses of images in Web documents. Next, hypertext links are introduced. Three kinds of lists—ordered, unordered, and definition—are then covered. After that, the XHTML tags and attributes used to specify tables are discussed. The next section of the chapter introduces forms, which provide the means to collect information from Web clients. The following section discusses frames, which provide a way to divide the browser window into smaller rectangles, each of which can display a different document. Finally, the last section describes the syntactic differences between HTML and XHTML.

2.1

ORIGINS AND EVOLUTION OF HTML AND XHTML

HTML is derived from the Standard Generalized Markup Language (SGML), which is an International Standards Organization (ISO) standard for describing text-formatting languages.[1] The original intent of HTML was different from those of other text-formatting languages, which dictate all of the presentation details of text, such as font style, size, and color. Rather, HTML was designed to specify document structure at a higher and more abstract level, necessary because HTML-specified documents had to be displayable on a variety of computer systems, often using different browsers.

The addition of style sheets to HTML in the late 1990s advanced its capabilities closer to those of other text-formatting languages by providing a way to include the specification of presentation details. These are introduced in Chapter 3, "Cascading Style Sheets."

2.1.1 Versions of HTML and XHTML

HTML has gone through a sequence of versions, ending with 4.01, which was approved in late 1999. The XHTML 1.0 standard was approved in early 2000. XHTML 1.0 is a reformulation of HTML 4.01 as an XML markup language.[2] The XHTML 1.1 standard was recommended by W3C in May 2001. This standard, primarily a modularization of XHTML 1.0, drops some of the features of its predecessor, most notably frames. The development and evolution of HTML and XHTML is controlled by the World Wide Web Consortium (W3C).[3]

In the early days of the Web, there was no standard for HTML, which was acceptable as long as the number of users was small. Dramatic growth in the use of the Web and HTML changed this, and a standard version became a necessity. One problem with HTML standards, a problem that also occurs with some other standards, is that the people who should follow the standard—in this case, those who design and distribute browsers—often do not. At one time, Netscape's browser implemented a number of HTML features that were not part of the standard, such as layers, which allowed Web-document elements to be absolutely positioned anywhere on the browser display. Microsoft is also guilty of adding extensions to HTML for its browser, such as filters, which provide a number of different visual effects for text and images. These extensions

---

1. Not all text-formatting languages are based on SGML; for example, PostScript and LaTeX are not.
2. XML (eXtensible Markup Language) is the topic of Chapter 8, "Introduction to XML."
3. The W3C Web site is http://www.w3.org.

were in part due to the slowness of the W3C's release of new HTML standards. With HTML 4.0, released in 1997, the standard moved ahead of the browser makers, at least in some of its features. Neither layers nor filters were included in HTML 4.0. The latest versions of the most popular browsers, Microsoft Internet Explorer 6 (IE6) and Netscape 7 (NS7), come close to supporting the latest standard, XHTML 1.1.

The addition of presentation details through style sheets in HTML 4.0 made some features of earlier versions obsolete. These features, as well as some others, have been *deprecated*, meaning that they will be dropped from HTML at some time in the future. Deprecating a feature is a warning to users to stop using the feature because it will not be supported forever. Although even the latest releases of browsers still support the deprecated parts of HTML, we do not include descriptions of most of them in this book. The only exception is frames, which are discussed in Section 2.10.

XHTML 1.0 was defined in three levels, one of which, named Transitional, allowed the inclusion of HTML 4.0's deprecated tags and attributes. XHTML 1.1 eliminated these deprecated features. All of the XHTML documents in this book, except those illustrating frames, conform to the XHTML 1.1 standard.

2.1.2 HTML versus XHTML

There are some commonly heard arguments for using HTML rather than XHTML, especially XHTML 1.1. First, because of its lax syntax rules, HTML is much easier to write, whereas XHTML requires a level of discipline many of us naturally resist. Second, because of the huge number of HTML documents available on the Web, browsers will continue to support it as far as one can see into the future. However, some older browsers have problems with some parts of XHTML.

There are, however, strong reasons why one should use XHTML. One of the most compelling is that quality and consistency in any endeavor, be it electrical wiring, software development, or Web-document development, rely on standards. HTML has few syntactic rules, and HTML processors (for example, browsers) do not enforce the rules it does have. Therefore, HTML authors have a high degree of freedom to create documents using their own syntactic preferences. Because of this, HTML documents lack consistency, both in low-level syntax and overall structure. Conversely, XHTML has strict syntactic rules that impose a consistent structure on all XHTML documents. Also, the fact that there are a large number of poorly structured HTML documents on the Web is a poor excuse for generating more.

Another significant reason for using XHTML is that when you create an XHTML document, its syntactic correctness can be checked, either by an XML browser or by a validation tool (see Section 2.4). This checking process may find errors that could otherwise go undetected until after the document is posted on a site and requested by a client, possibly with only a specific browser.

The argument that XHTML is difficult to write correctly is obviated by the availability of XTHML editors, which provide a simple and effective approach to creating syntactically correct XHTML documents.[4]

It is also possible to convert legacy HTML documents to XHTML documents using software tools. Tidy, which is available at `http://tidy.sourceforge.net`, is one such tool.

The remainder of this chapter provides an introduction to the most commonly used tags and attributes of XHTML 1.1.

2.2

BASIC SYNTAX

The fundamental syntactic units of HTML are called *tags*. In general, tags are used to specify categories of content. For each category, a browser has default presentation specifications for the specified content. The syntax of a tag is the tag's name surrounded by pointed brackets (<>). Tag names must be written in all lowercase letters. Most tags appear in pairs: an opening tag and a closing tag. The name of a closing tag is the name of its corresponding opening tag with a slash attached to the beginning. For example, if the tag's name is p, the corresponding closing tag is named /p. Whatever appears between a tag and its closing tag is the *content* of the tag. A browser display of an XHTML document shows the content of all of the document's tags; it is the information the document is meant to portray. Not all tags can have content.

The opening tag and its closing tag together specify a container for the content they enclose. The container and its content together are called an *element*. For example, consider the following:

```
<p> This is extremely simple. </p>
```

The paragraph tag, <p>, marks the beginning of the content, and the </p> tag marks the end of the content of the paragraph element.

Attributes, which are used to specify alternative meanings of a tag, can appear between an opening tag's name and its right-pointed bracket. They are specified in keyword form, which means that the attribute's name appears, followed by an equals sign and the attribute's value. Attribute names, like tag names, are written in lowercase letters. Attribute values must be delimited by double quotes.

---

4. One such editor system is available at `http://www.xstandard.com`.

Comments in programs increase the readability of those programs. Comments in XHTML have the same purpose. They can appear in XHTML in the following form:

```
<!-- whatever you want to say -->
```

Browsers ignore XHTML comments—they are for people only. Comments can be spread over as many lines as are needed. For example, you could have the following comment:

```
<!-- PetesHome.html
This document describes the home page of Pete's Pickles
-->
```

Besides comments, several other kinds of text may appear in an XHTML document but be ignored by browsers. Browsers ignore all unrecognized tags. They also ignore line breaks. Line breaks that show up in the displayed content can be specified but only with tags designed for that purpose. The same is true for multiple spaces and tabs.

Programmers find XHTML a bit frustrating. In a program, the statements specify exactly what the computer must do. XHTML tags are treated more like suggestions to the browser. If a reserved word is misspelled in a program, the error is usually detected by the language implementation system, and the program is not executed. However, a misspelled tag name results in the tag being ignored by the browser, with no indication to the browser user that anything is out of the ordinary. Browsers are even allowed to ignore tags that they recognize. Furthermore, the browser user can configure his or her browser to react to specific tags in different ways.

2.3

STANDARD XHTML DOCUMENT STRUCTURE

Every XHTML document must begin with an `xml` declaration element that simply identifies the document as being one based on XML. This element includes the version number, which is still 1.0, as an attribute. It also specifies the Unicode encoding format, `utf-8`, as the value of the `encoding` attribute code. The following is the `xml` declaration element, which must be the first line of every XHTML document:

```
<?xml version = "1.0" encoding = "utf-8"?>
```

Immediately following the `xml` declaration element is an SGML `DOCTYPE` command, which specifies the particular SGML document-type definition (DTD) with which the document complies, among other things.[5] The following command states that the document in which it is included complies with the XHTML 1.1 standard:

```
<!DOCTYPE html PUBLIC "-//w3c//DTD XHTML 1.1//EN"
  "http://www.w3.org/TR/xhtml11/DTD/xhtml11.dtd">
```

A complete explanation of the `DOCTYPE` command requires more effort, both to write and to read, than is justified at this stage of our introduction to XHTML.

XHTML documents must include the four tags `<html>`, `<head>`, `<title>`, and `<body>`. The `<html>` tag identifies the root element of the document. So, XHTML documents always have an `<html>` tag immediately following the `DOCTYPE` command, and they always end with `</html>`. The `html` element includes an attribute, `xmlns`, that specifies the XHTML namespace, as shown in the following:

```
<html xmlns = "http://www.w3.org/1999/xhtml">
```

Although the `xmlns` attribute's value looks like a URL, it does not specify a document. It is just a name that happens to have the form of a URL. Namespaces are discussed in Chapter 8, "Introduction to XML."

An XHTML document consists of two parts, the *head* and the *body*. The `<head>` element contains the head part of the document, which provides information about the document rather than its content. The body of a document provides the content of the document, which itself typically includes tags and attributes.

The content of the title element is displayed by the browser at the top of its display window, usually in the browser's window title bar.

Standards prior to XHTML 1.1 allowed a document to have either a body element or a frameset element. The Frameset alternative of the XHTML 1.0 DTD standards applies when the document has a frameset element. The Transitional alternative of the XHTML 1.0 standard allows deprecated HTML features to be used. Both of these will be used in Section 2.10.

---

5. A document-type definition specifies the syntax rules for a particular category of XHTML documents.

2.4

BASIC TEXT MARKUP

This section describes how the text content of an XHTML document can be formatted with XHTML tags. By *formatting*, we mean layout and some presentation details. For now, we will ignore the other kinds of content that can appear in an XHTML document.

2.4.1 Paragraphs

Text is normally organized into paragraphs in the body of a document. In fact, the XHTML standard does not allow text to be placed directly in a document body. Paragraphs appear as the content of a paragraph element, specified with the tag <p>. In displaying the content of a paragraph, the browser puts as many words as will fit on the lines in the browser window. The browser supplies a line break at the end of each line. As stated in Section 2.2, line breaks embedded in text are ignored by the browser. For example, the following paragraph might[6] be displayed by a browser, as shown in Figure 2.1.

```
<p>
   Mary had
a
   little lamb, its fleece was white as snow. And
 everywhere that
  Mary went, the lamb
 was sure to go.
</p>
```

> Mary had a little lamb, its fleece was white as snow. And everywhere that Mary went, the lamb was sure to go.

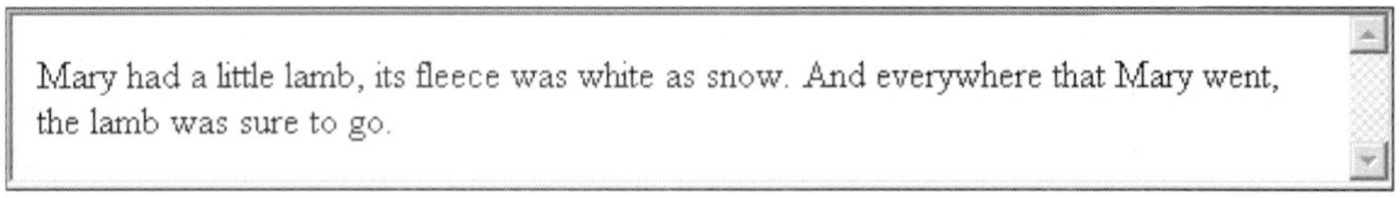

FIGURE 2.1 Filling lines

Notice that multiple spaces in the source paragraph element are replaced by single spaces in the display of Figure 2.1.

---

6. We say "might" because the width of the display that the browser uses determines how many words will fit on a line.

The following is our first example of a complete XHTML document:

```
<?xml version = "1.0" encoding = "utf-8"?>
<!DOCTYPE html PUBLIC "-//w3c//DTD XHTML 1.1//EN"
  "http://www.w3.org/TR/xhtml11/DTD/xhtml11.dtd">

<!-- greet.html
     A trivial document
     -->
<html xmlns = "http://www.w3.org/1999/xhtml">
  <head> <title> Our first document </title>
  </head>
  <body>
    <p>
      Greetings from your Webmaster!
    </p>
  </body>
</html>
```

Figure 2.2 shows a browser display of greet.html.

Greetings from your Webmaster!

FIGURE 2.2 Display of greet.html

If the paragraph tag is preceded by other text, it breaks the current line and inserts a blank line. For example, the following line would be displayed, as shown in Figure 2.3.

```
<p> Mary had a little lamb, </p> <p> its fleece was
white as snow. </p>
```

Mary had a little lamb,

its fleece was white as snow.

FIGURE 2.3 The paragraph element

2.4.2   XHTML Document Validation

The W3C provides a convenient way to validate XHTML documents against its standards. The URL of the service is `http://validator.w3.org/file-upload.html`. Figure 2.4 shows a browser display of `file-upload.html`.

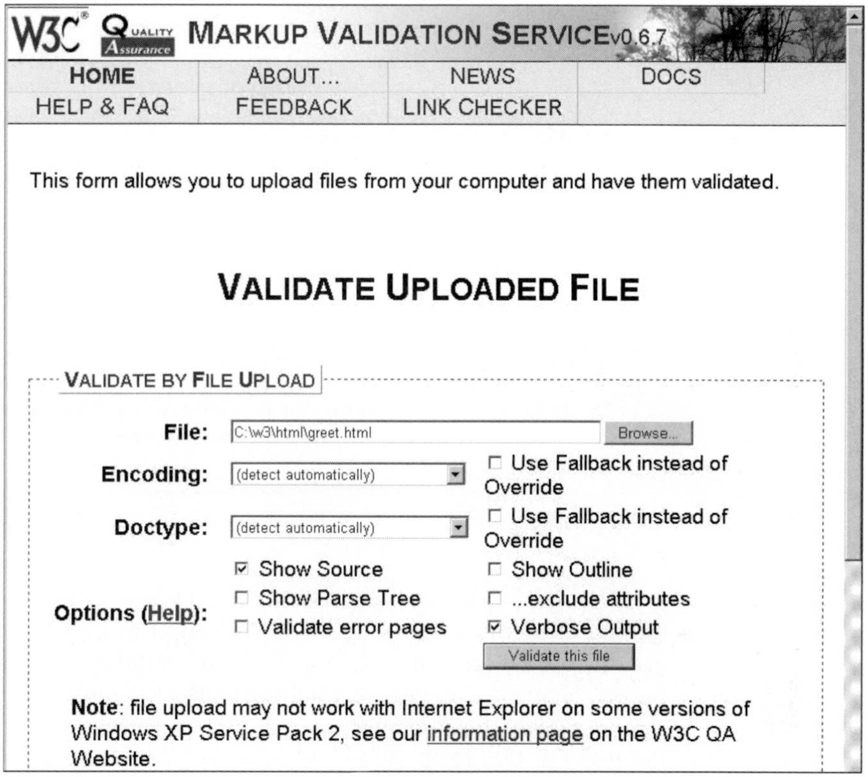

FIGURE 2.4 Display of `file-upload.html`, the W3C HTML validation document

The filename of the document to be validated is entered (including the pathname) or found by browsing. When the `Validate this file` button is pressed, the specified file is uploaded to the `validator` server, where the validation system is run on it. We recommend that the `Show Source` checkbox be checked because that causes the validation system to furnish a listing of the document in which the lines are numbered. These numbers are referenced in the report provided by the validation system.

Figure 2.5 shows a browser display of the document returned by the validation system for our sample document `greet.html`. Notice that we cut the source listing off in the figure, simply to prevent the figure from spanning more than one page.

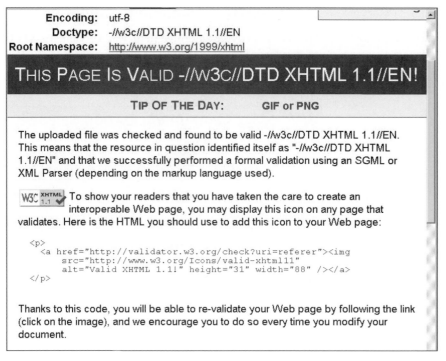

FIGURE 2.5 HTML validation output for `greet.html`

One of the most common errors made in crafting XHTML documents is putting elements where they do not belong. For example, putting text directly in a body element is illegal. The XHTML validation system is a valuable tool for producing documents that adhere to W3C standards. The specific standard against which the document is checked is given in the DOCTYPE command. Because the DOCTYPE command in `greet.html` specifies the `xhtml11.dtd` DTD, this document is checked against the XHTML 1.1 standard.

2.4.3   Line Breaks

Sometimes text requires a line break without the preceding blank line. This is exactly what the break tag does. The break tag differs from the paragraph tag in that it can have no content and therefore has no closing tag (because it would serve no purpose). The break tag is specified as `<br />`. The slash indicates that the tag is both an opening and closing tag. The space before the slash represents the absent content.[7]

---

7. Some older browsers have trouble with the tag `<br/>` but not with `<br />`.

Consider the following:

```
<p>
Mary had a little lamb, <br />
  its fleece was white as snow.
</p>
```

This would be displayed as shown in Figure 2.6.

Mary had a little lamb,
its fleece was white as snow.

FIGURE 2.6 Line breaks

2.4.4 Headings

Text is often separated into sections in documents by beginning each section with a heading. Larger sections sometimes have headings that appear in larger fonts than headings for sections nested inside them. In XHTML, there are six levels of headings, specified by the tags <h1>, <h2>, <h3>, <h4>, <h5>, and <h6>, where <h1> specifies the largest heading. Headings are displayed in a boldface font whose default size depends on the number in the heading tag. On most browsers, <h1>, <h2>, and <h3> use font sizes that are larger than that of the default size of text, <h4> uses the default size, and <h5> and <h6> use smaller sizes. The heading tags always break the current line, so their content always appears on a new line. Browsers usually insert some vertical space before and after all headings.

The following example illustrates the use of headings:

```
<?xml version = "1.0" encoding = "utf-8"?>
<!DOCTYPE html PUBLIC "-//w3c//DTD XHTML 1.1//EN"
   "http://www.w3.org/TR/xhtml11/DTD/xhtml11.dtd">

<!-- headings.html
     An example to illustrate headings
     -->
<html xmlns = "http://www.w3.org/1999/xhtml">
  <head> <title> Headings </title>
  </head>
```

continued

```
<body>
  <h1> Aidan's Airplanes (h1) </h1>
  <h2> The best in used airplanes (h2) </h2>
  <h3> "We've got them by the hangarful" (h3) </h3>
  <h4> We're the guys to see for a good used airplane (h4) </h4>
  <h5> We offer great prices on great planes (h5) </h5>
  <h6> No returns, no guarantees, no refunds,
      all sales are final! (h6) </h6>
</body>
</html>
```

Figure 2.7 shows a browser display of `headings.html`.

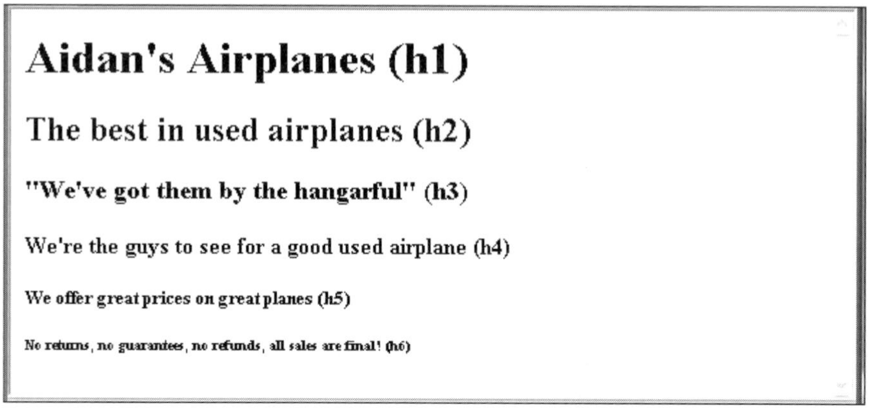

FIGURE 2.7 Display of `headings.html`

2.4.5   Block Quotations

Sometimes we want a block of text to be set off from the normal flow of text in a document. In many cases, such a block is a long quotation. The `<blockquote>` tag is designed for this situation. Browser designers determine how the content of `<blockquote>` can be made to look different from the surrounding text. In many cases, the block of text is indented, either on the left or right side or both. Another possibility is that the block is set in italic. Consider the following sample document:

```
<?xml version = "1.0" encoding = "utf-8"?>
<!DOCTYPE html PUBLIC "-//w3c//DTD XHTML 1.1//EN"
   "http://www.w3.org/TR/xhtml11/DTD/xhtml11.dtd">


<!-- blockquote.html
     An example to illustrate a blockquote
     -->
<html xmlns = "http://www.w3.org/1999/xhtml">
  <head> <title> Blockquotes </title>
  </head>
  <body>
    <p>
       Abraham Lincoln is generally regarded as one of the greatest
       presidents of the U.S. His most famous speech was delivered
       in Gettysburg, Pennsylvania, during the Civil War. This
       speech began with
    </p>
    <blockquote>
      <p>
        "Fourscore and seven years ago our fathers brought forth on
         this continent, a new nation, conceived in Liberty, and
         dedicated to the proposition that all men are created equal.
      </p>
      <p>
         Now we are engaged in a great civil war, testing whether
         that nation or any nation so conceived and so dedicated,
         can long endure."
      </p>
    </blockquote>
    <p>
       Whatever one's opinion of Lincoln, no one can deny the
       enormous and lasting effect he had on the U.S.
    </p>
  </body>
</html>
```

Figure 2.8 shows a browser display of blockquote.html.

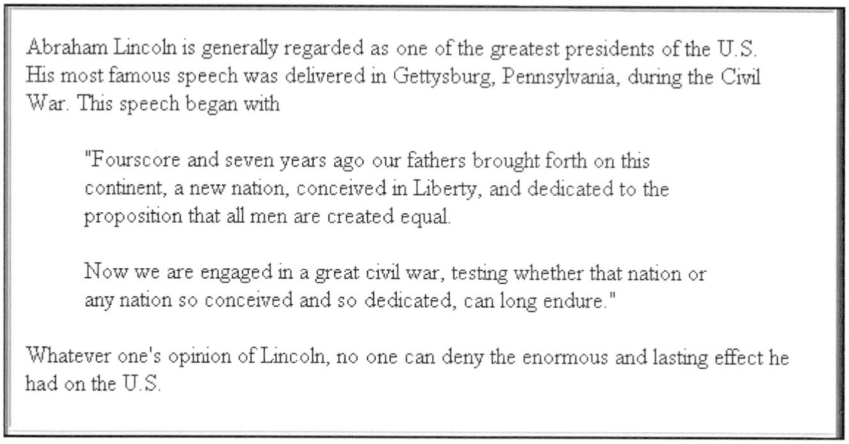

Abraham Lincoln is generally regarded as one of the greatest presidents of the U.S.
His most famous speech was delivered in Gettysburg, Pennsylvania, during the Civil
War. This speech began with

"Fourscore and seven years ago our fathers brought forth on this
continent, a new nation, conceived in Liberty, and dedicated to the
proposition that all men are created equal.

Now we are engaged in a great civil war, testing whether that nation or
any nation so conceived and so dedicated, can long endure."

Whatever one's opinion of Lincoln, no one can deny the enormous and lasting effect he
had on the U.S.

FIGURE 2.8 Display of `blockquote.html`

2.4.6   Font Styles and Sizes

Frequently, one needs to set off or emphasize words or phrases in text. This is
usually done by using different font styles or different font sizes for the text that
is to be emphasized. XHTML includes a few tags for doing this. The simplest
of these are `<b>` and `<i>`, which change the font style of the text in their content to boldface and italic, respectively. If the font of text in its content is already
italic, the `<i>` tag has no effect; similarly, if the font is already boldface, the `<b>`
tag has no effect.

XHTML tags are categorized as being either block or inline. The content
of an *inline* tag appears on the current line. A *block* tag breaks the current line so
that its content appears on a new line. The heading and blockquote tags are
block tags, where `<b>` and `<i>` are inline tags. In XHTML, block tags cannot
appear in the content of inline tags. Therefore, a block tag can never be nested
directly in an inline tag. Also, inline tags and text cannot be directly nested in
body or form elements. That is why the example, `greet.html`, has the text
content of its body nested in a paragraph element.

The `<big>` and `<small>` tags provide the means to specify relative sizes of
characters. Characters that appear between the `<big>` and `</big>` tags are set
in a font size that is larger than the preceding and following text. How much
larger is decided by the browser. If it happens that the font is already at its maximum size, `<big>` has no effect. `<big>` tags can be nested, still having the
expected effect. For example, consider the following:

```
Mary <big> had <big> a <big> little <big> lamb
</big></big></big></big>
```

This text would be displayed as shown in Figure 2.9.

FIGURE 2.9 The `<big>` element

The `<small>` tag does the opposite of `<big>`. For example,

```
Mary <small> had <small> a </small></small>
```

would be displayed as shown in Figure 2.10.

FIGURE 2.10 The `<small>` element

Subscript and superscript characters can be specified by the `<sub>` and `<sup>` tags, respectively. For example,

```
X<sub>2</sub><sup>3</sup> + y<sub>1</sub><sup>2</sup>
```

would be displayed as shown in Figure 2.11.

FIGURE 2.11 The `<sub>` and `<sup>` elements

The `<tt>` tag is used to specify a monospace font. For example,

```
<tt> Mary <big> had <big> a </big> little </big> lamb
</tt>
```

would be displayed as shown in Figure 2.12.

```
Mary had a little lamb
```

FIGURE 2.12 The `<tt>` element

Character-modifying tags are not affected by `<blockquote>` except when there is a conflict. For example, if the text content of `<blockquote>` is set in italic and a part of that text is made the content of an `<i>` tag, the `<i>` tag would have no effect.

Although the tags described in this subsection are not deprecated, the preferred way to specify font styles and font sizes is with style sheets, which are discussed in Chapter 3. Style sheets offer a much more precise and consistent way to control font size and style, as well as other presentation details.

2.4.7   Character Entities

XHTML provides a collection of special characters that are sometimes needed in a document but cannot be typed as themselves. In some cases, these characters are used in XHTML in some special way, for example >, <, and &. In other cases, the characters do not appear on a keyboard, such as the small raised circle that represents "degrees" in a reference to temperature. Finally, there is the nonbreaking space, which browsers regard as a hard space—they do not squeeze them out like they do other multiple spaces. These special characters are defined as *entities*, which are names for the characters by the browser. An entity in a document is replaced by its associated character by the browser. Table 2.1 lists some of the most commonly used entities.

TABLE 2.1 Some Commonly Used Entities

Character	Entity	Meaning
&	`&amp;`	Ampersand
<	`&lt;`	Less than
>	`&gt;`	Greater than
"	`&quot;`	Double quote
'	`&apos;`	Single quote (apostrophe)
$\frac{1}{4}$	`&frac14;`	One quarter
$\frac{1}{2}$	`&frac12;`	One half
$\frac{3}{4}$	`&frac34;`	Three quarters
°	`&deg;`	Degree
(space)	` `	Nonbreaking space

2.4.8   Horizontal Rules

The parts of a document can be delineated for each other, making the document easier to read, by placing horizontal lines between them. Such lines are called *horizontal rules*, and the block tag that creates them is `<hr />`. The `<hr />` tag causes a line break (ending the current line) and draws a line across the screen. The browser chooses the thickness, length, and horizontal placement of the line. Typically, browsers display lines that are 3 pixels thick.

Note again the slash in the `<hr />` tag, indicating that this tag has no content and no closing tag.

2.4.9   The `meta` Element

The meta element is used to provide additional information about a document. It has no content; rather, all of the provided information is specified through attributes. The two attributes that are used to provide information are `name` and `content`. The user makes up a name as the value of the `name` attribute and specifies information through the `content` attribute. One commonly chosen name is `keywords`; the value of the `content` attribute associated with the keywords are those that a document author believes characterizes his or her document. For example:

```
<meta name = "keywords"  content = "binary trees,
linked lists, stacks" />
```

Web search engines use the information provided with the meta element to categorize Web documents in their indices. So, if the author of a document seeks widespread exposure for the document, one or more meta elements are included to ensure that it will be found by at least some Web searches.

2.5
IMAGES

The inclusion of images in a document can dramatically enhance its appearance (although images slow the document-download process considerably for clients that do not have high-speed Internet access). The image is stored in a file, which is specified by an XHTML request. The image in the file is inserted into the display of the document by the browser.

2.5.1   Image Formats

The two most common methods of representing images are Graphic Interchange Format (GIF, pronounced like the first syllable of *jif-fy*) and Joint Photographic Experts Group (JPEG, pronounced *jay-peg*) format. Most contemporary browsers can render images in either of these two formats. Files in both of these formats are compressed to reduce storage needs and provide faster transfer over the Internet.

The GIF format was developed by the CompuServe network service provider for the specific purpose of moving images. It uses 8-bit color representations for pixels, allowing a pixel to have 256 different colors. If you are not familiar with color representations, this may seem to be entirely adequate. However, with the color displays on most contemporary computers, this leaves a huge number of colors that can be displayed but that cannot be represented in a GIF image. Files containing GIF images use the `.gif` (or `.GIF`) extension on their names. GIF images can be made to appear transparent.

The JPEG format uses 24-bit color representations for pixels, which allows JPEG images to include more than 16 million different colors. Files that store JPEG images use the `.jpg` (or `.JPG` or `.jpeg`) extension on their names. The compression algorithm used by JPEG is better at shrinking an image than the one used by GIF. This compression process actually loses some of the color accuracy of the image, but because there is so much to begin with, the loss is rarely discernable by the user. Because of this powerful compression process, even though a JPEG image has much more color information than a GIF image of the same subject, the JPEG image can still be smaller than the GIF image. Because of this, JPEG images are often preferred to GIF images. The disadvantage of JPEG is that it does not support transparency.

A third image format is now gaining popularity, Portable Network Graphics (PNG, pronounced *ping*). PNG was designed in 1996 as a free replacement for GIF after the patent owner for GIF, Unisys, suggested it may begin charging royalties for documents that included GIF images.[8] Actually, PNG provides a good replacement for both GIF and JPEG because it has the best characteritics of both (the possibility of transparency, as provided by GIF, and a much larger number of colors than GIF, as with JPEG). One drawback of PNG is that because its compression algorithm does not sacrifice picture clarity, its images require more space than comparable JPEG images.[9] Information on PNG can be found at `www.w3.org/Graphics/PNG`.

2.5.2 The `<img />` Tag

The image tag, `<img />`, which is an inline tag, specifies an image that is to appear in a document. In its simplest form, the image tag includes two attributes: `src`, which specifies the file containing the image; and `alt`, which specifies text to be displayed when it is not possible to display the image. If the file is in the same directory as the XHTML file of the document, the value of

---

8. The patent expired in the United States in 2003.

9. Space is not the direct issue; download time, which depends on file size, is the real issue.

src is just the image's filename. In many cases, image files are stored in a subdirectory of the directory where the XHTML files are stored. For example, the image files might be stored in a subdirectory named images. If the image file's name is stars.jpg and it is stored in the images subdirectory, the value of src would be as follows:

```
"images/stars.jpg"
```

Some seriously aged browsers are not capable of displaying images. When such a browser finds an <img /> tag, it simply ignores its content, possibly leaving the user confused by the text in the neighborhood of where the image was supposed to be. Also, graphical browsers, which *are* capable of displaying images, may have image downloading disabled. This is done when the Internet connection is slow and the user chooses not to wait for images to be downloaded. It is also done by visually impaired users. In any case, it is helpful to have some text displayed in place of the ignored image. For these reasons, the alt attribute is required by XHTML.

Two optional attributes of img, width and height, can be included to specify (in pixels) the size of the rectangle for the image. These can be used to scale the size of the image (that is, to make it larger or smaller). Care must be taken to ensure that the image is not distorted in the resizing. For example, if the image is square, the width and height attribute values must be equal.

The following is an example of an image element:

```
<img src = "c210.jpg"  alt = "(Picture of a Cessna 210)" />
```

The following example extends the airplane ad document to include information about a specific airplane and an image of it.

```
<?xml version = "1.0" encoding = "utf-8"?>
<!DOCTYPE html PUBLIC "-//w3c//DTD XHTML 1.1//EN"
  "http://www.w3.org/TR/xhtml11/DTD/xhtml11.dtd">

<!-- image.html
     An example to illustrate an image
     -->
<html xmlns = "http://www.w3.org/1999/xhtml">
  <head> <title> Images </title>
  </head>
  <body>
    <h1> Aidan's Airplanes </h1>
    <h2> The best in used airplanes </h2>
    <h3> "We've got them by the hangarful" </h3>
```

continued

```
<h2> Special of the month </h2>
<p>
   1960 Cessna 210 <br />
   577 hours since major engine overhaul<br />
   1022 hours since prop overhaul <br /><br />
   <img src = "c210new.jpg"  alt = "Picture of a Cessna 210" />
   <br />
   Buy this fine airplane today at a remarkably low price
   <br />
   Call 999-555-1111 today!
</p>
</body>
</html>
```

Figure 2.13 shows a browser display of image.html.

FIGURE 2.13 Display of image.html

There is much more to the `<img />` tag than we have led you to believe. In fact, the `<img />` tag can include up to 30 different attributes. For descriptions of the rest, visit `http://www.w3.org/TR/html401/index/attributes.html`.

2.6
HYPERTEXT LINKS

A hypertext link in an XHTML document, which we simply call a *link* here, acts as a pointer to some resource. That resource can be an XHTML document anywhere on the Web, or it may just be another place in the document currently being displayed. It could also be a specific place (rather than the top) in some other document. Without links, Web documents would be boring and tedius to read. There would be no convenient way for the browser user to get from one document to any logically related document. Most Web sites consist of many different documents, all linked together in some sensible way. Therefore, links are essential to building any interesting Web site.

2.6.1 Links

A link that points to a different document specifies the address of that document. Such an address might be a filename, a directory path and a filename, or a complete URL. If a link points to a specific place in any document other than the beginning, that place somehow must be marked.

All links are specified in an attribute of an anchor tag (`<a>`), which is an inline tag. A document that includes an anchor tag that specifies a link is called the *source* of that link. The document whose address is specified in a link is called the *target* of that link. When the target is in the same document as the link to it, the document is both the source and the target of the link.

As is the case with many tags, the anchor tag can include many different attributes. However, for creating links only one is required, `href` (an acronym for hypertext `reference`). The value assigned to `href` specifies the target of the link. If the target is in another document in the same directory, the target is just the document's filename. If the target document is in some other directory, the UNIX pathname conventions are used. So, an XHTML file named `c210data.html` in a subdirectory of the directory in which the source XHTML file—say, named `airplanes`—is stored has the address `airplanes/c210data.html`. This is the relative method of document addressing. Absolute file addresses could be used in which the entire pathname for the file is given. However, relative links are easier to maintain, especially if a hierarchy of XHTML files must be moved. If the document is on some other machine (not on the server providing the document that includes the link), the complete URL obviously must be used.

The content of an anchor tag, which becomes the clickable link the user sees, is restricted to text, line breaks, images, and headings. Although some browsers allow other nested tags, that is not standard XHTML and should not be used if you want your code to work on all browsers. Links are usually implicitly rendered in a different color than the surrounding text. Sometimes they are also underlined. When the mouse cursor is placed over the anchor-tag content and the left mouse button is pressed, the link is taken by the browser. If the target is a different document, that document is loaded and displayed, replacing the currently displayed document. If the target is in the current document, the document is scrolled by the browser to display the target of the link. As an example, consider the following document, which adds a link to the document displayed in Figure 2.6:

```
<?xml version = "1.0" encoding = "utf-8"?>
<!DOCTYPE html PUBLIC "-//w3c//DTD XHTML 1.1//EN"
  "http://www.w3.org/TR/xhtml11/DTD/xhtml11.dtd">

<!-- link.html
     An example to illustrate a link
     -->
<html xmlns = "http://www.w3.org/1999/xhtml">
  <head> <title> A link </title>
  </head>
  <body>
    <h1> Aidan's Airplanes </h1>
    <h2> The best in used airplanes </h2>
    <h3> "We've got them by the hangarful" </h3>
    <h2> Special of the month </h2>
    <p>
      1960 Cessna 210 <br />
      <a href = "C210data.html"> Information on the Cessna 210 </a>
    </p>
  </body>
</html>
```

In this case, the target is a complete document that is stored in the same directory as the XHTML document. Figure 2.14 shows a browser display of link.html. When the link shown in Figure 2.14 is clicked, the browser displays the screen shown in Figure 2.15.

Aidan's Airplanes

The best in used airplanes

"We've got them by the hangarful"

Special of the month

1960 Cessna 210
Information on the Cessna 210

FIGURE 2.14 Display of `link.html`

1960 Cessna 210 Information

577 hours since major engine overhaul
622 hours since prop overhaul

Buy this fine airplane today at a remarkably low price
Call 999-555-1111 today!

FIGURE 2.15 Following the link from `link.html`

Links can include images in their content, in which case the browser displays the image with the link:

```
<a href = "c210data.html"
  <img src = "small-airplane.jpg"
      alt = "An image of a small airplane">
    Information on the Cessna 210
</a>
```

An image itself can be an effective link (the content of the anchor element). For example, an image of a small house can be used for the link back to the home document of a site. The content of an anchor element for such a link is just the image element.

2.6.2   Targets within Documents

If the target of a link is not at the beginning of a document, it must be some element within a document, in which case there must be some means of specifying it. The target element can include an `id` attribute, which can then be used to identify it in an `href` attribute. Consider the following example:

```
<h2 id = "avionics"> Avionics </h2>
```

Nearly all elements can include an `id` attribute. The value of an `id` attribute must be unique within the document because it is used to reference a specific element.

If the target is in the same document as the link, the target is specified in the `href` attribute value by preceding the `id` value with a pound sign (#), as in this example:

```
<a href = "#avionics"> What about avionics? <a/>
```

When the `What about avionics?` link is taken, the browser moves the display so that the `h2` element whose `id` is `avionics` is at the top.

When the target is a part or fragment of another document, the name of the part is specified at the end of the URL, separated by a pound sign (#), as in this example:

```
<a href = "AIDAN1.html#avionics"> Avionics </a>
```

2.6.3   Using Links

The most common use of links to parts of the same document is to provide a table of contents in which each entry has a link. This provides a convenient way for the user to get to the various parts of the document simply and quickly. Such a table of contents is implemented as a stylized list of links, using the list specification capabilities of XHTML, which are discussed in Section 2.7.

Links exemplify the true spirit of hypertext. The reader can click on links to learn more about a particular subtopic of interest and then return to the location of the link. Designing links requires some care because they can be annoying if the designer tries too hard to convince the user to take them. For example, making them stand out too much from the surrounding text can be distracting. A link should blend into the surrounding text as much as possible so that reading the document without taking any of the links should be easy and natural.

2.7

LISTS

We frequently make and use lists in daily life—for example, to-do lists and grocery lists. Likewise, both printed and displayed information is permeated with lists. XHTML provides simple and effective ways to specify lists in documents. The primary supported list types are those with which most people are already familiar: unordered lists such as grocery lists and ordered lists such as the assembly instructions for a new bicycle. Definition lists can also be defined. The tags to specify unordered, ordered, and definition lists are described in this section.

2.7.1 Unordered Lists

The <ul> tag, which is a block tag, creates an unordered list. Each item in a list is specified with an <li> tag. Any tags can appear in a list item, including nested lists. Each list item is implicitly preceded with a bullet. For example, consider the following:

```
<?xml version = "1.0" encoding = "utf-8"?>
<!DOCTYPE html PUBLIC "-//w3c//DTD XHTML 1.1//EN"
  "http://www.w3.org/TR/xhtml11/DTD/xhtml11.dtd">

<!-- unordered.html
     An example to illustrate an unordered list
     -->
<html xmlns = "http://www.w3.org/1999/xhtml">
  <head> <title> Unordered list </title>
  </head>
  <body>
    <h3> Some Common Single-Engine Aircraft </h3>
    <ul>
      <li> Cessna Skyhawk </li>
      <li> Beechcraft Bonanza </li>
      <li> Piper Cherokee </li>
    </ul>
  </body>
</html>
```

Figure 2.16 shows a browser display of unordered.html.

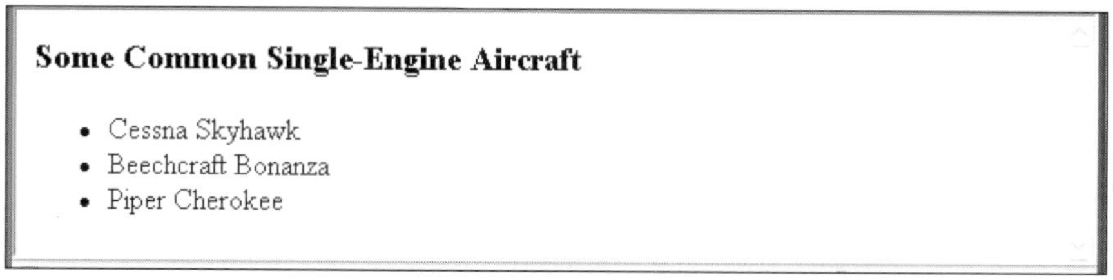

Some Common Single-Engine Aircraft

- Cessna Skyhawk
- Beechcraft Bonanza
- Piper Cherokee

FIGURE 2.16 Display of `unordered.html`

2.7.2 Ordered Lists

Ordered lists are those in which the order of items is important. This ordered-ness of a list is shown in the display of the list by the implicit attachment of a sequential value to the beginning of each item. The default sequential values are Arabic numerals, beginning with 1.

An ordered list is created within the block tag `<ol>`. The items are specified and displayed just like those for unordered lists, except that the items in an ordered list are preceded by sequential values instead of bullets. Consider the following example of an ordered list:

```
<?xml version = "1.0" encoding = "utf-8"?>
<!DOCTYPE html PUBLIC "-//w3c//DTD XHTML 1.1//EN"
  "http://www.w3.org/TR/xhtml11/DTD/xhtml11.dtd">


<!-- ordered.html
     An example to illustrate an ordered list
     -->
<html xmlns = "http://www.w3.org/1999/xhtml">
  <head> <title> Ordered list </title>
  </head>
  <body>
    <h3> Cessna 210 Engine Starting Instructions </h3>
    <ol>
      <li> Set mixture to rich </li>
      <li> Set propeller to high RPM </li>
      <li> Set ignition switch to "BOTH" </li>
      <li> Set auxiliary fuel pump switch to "LOW PRIME" </li>
      <li> When fuel pressure reaches 2 to 2.5 PSI, push
           starter button
      </li>
    </ol>
  </body>
</html>
```

Figure 2.17 shows a browser display of `ordered.html`.

Cessna 210 Engine Starting Instructions

1. Set mixture to rich
2. Set propeller to high RPM
3. Set ignition switch to "BOTH"
4. Set auxiliary fuel pump switch to "LOW PRIME"
5. When fuel pressure reaches 2 to 2.5 PSI, push starter button

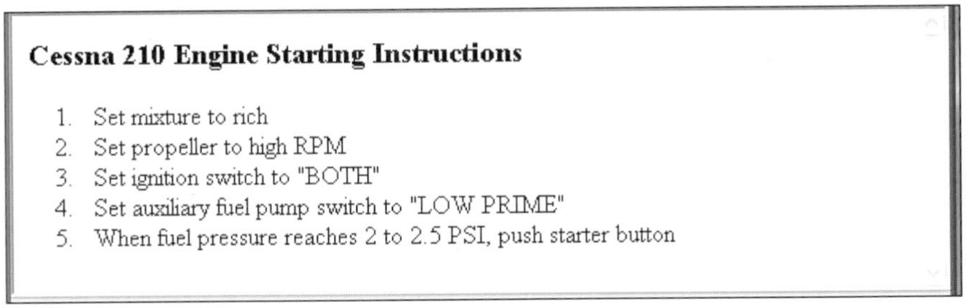

FIGURE 2.17 Display of `ordered.html`

As noted earlier, lists can be nested. However, a list cannot be directly nested; that is, an `<ol>` tag cannot immediately follow an `<ol>` tag. Rather, the nested list must be the content of an `<li>` tag. The following example illustrates nested ordered lists:

```
<?xml version = "1.0" encoding = "utf-8"?>
<!DOCTYPE html PUBLIC "-//w3c//DTD XHTML 1.1//EN"
  "http://www.w3.org/TR/xhtml11/DTD/xhtml11.dtd">

<!-- nested_lists.html
     An example to illustrate nested lists
     -->
<html xmlns = "http://www.w3.org/1999/xhtml">
  <head> <title> Nested lists </title>
  </head>
  <body>
    <h3> Aircraft Types </h3>
    <ol>
      <li> General Aviation (piston-driven engines)
        <ol>
          <li> Single-Engine Aircraft
            <ol>
              <li> Tail wheel </li>
              <li> Tricycle </li>
            </ol> <br />
          </li>
          <li> Dual-Engine Aircraft
            <ol>
              <li> Wing-mounted engines </li>
              <li> Push-pull fuselage-mounted engines </li>
            </ol>
```

continued

```
        </li>
      </ol> <br />
    </li>
    <li> Commercial Aviation (jet engines)
      <ol>
        <li> Dual-Engine
          <ol>
            <li> Wing-mounted engines </li>
            <li> Fuselage-mounted engines </li>
          </ol> <br />
        </li>
        <li> Tri-Engine
          <ol>
            <li> Third engine in vertical stabilizer </li>
            <li> Third engine in fuselage </li>
          </ol>
        </li>
      </ol>
    </li>
  </ol>
  </body>
</html>
```

Figure 2.18 shows a browser display of nested_lists.html.

Aircraft Types

1. General Aviation (piston-driven engines)
    1. Single-Engine Aircraft
        1. Tail wheel
        2. Tricycle

    2. Dual-Engine Aircraft
        1. Wing-mounted engines
        2. Push-pull fuselage-mounted engines

2. Commercial Aviation (jet engines)
    1. Dual-Engine
        1. Wing-mounted engines
        2. Fuselage-mounted engines

    2. Tri-Engine
        1. Third engine in vertical stabilizer
        2. Third engine in fuselage

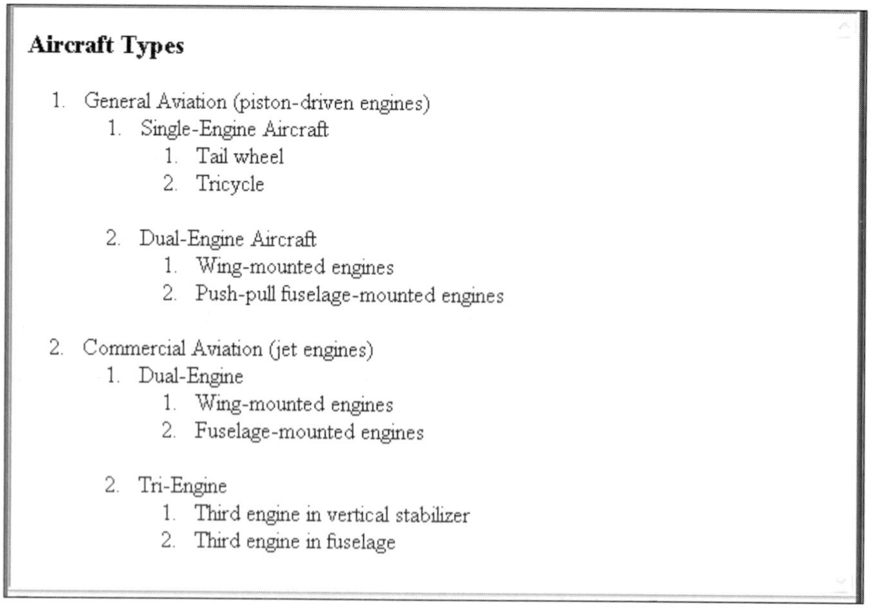

FIGURE 2.18 Display of nested_lists.html

One problem with the nested lists in Figure 2.11 is that all three levels use the same sequence values. Chapter 3 describes how style sheets can be used to specify different sequence systems for different lists.

The `nested_lists.html` example uses nested ordered lists. There are no restrictions on list nesting, provided the nesting is not direct. For example, ordered lists can be nested in unordered lists and vice versa.

2.7.3   Definition Lists

As the name implies, definition lists are used to specify lists of terms and their definitions, such as in glossaries. A definition list is given as the content of a `<dl>` tag, which is a block tag. Each term to be defined in the definition list is given as the content of a `<dt>` tag. The definitions themselves are specified as the content of `<dd>` tags. The defined terms of a definition list are usually displayed on the left margin; the definitions are usually shown on the line or lines following the term, which are indented. Consider the following example:

```
<?xml version = "1.0" encoding = "utf-8"?>
<!DOCTYPE html PUBLIC "-//w3c//DTD XHTML 1.1//EN"
  "http://www.w3.org/TR/xhtml11/DTD/xhtml11.dtd">


<!-- definition.html
     An example to illustrate definition lists
     -->
<html xmlns = "http://www.w3.org/1999/xhtml">
  <head> <title> Definition lists </title>
  </head>
  <body>
    <h3> Single-Engine Cessna Airplanes </h3>
    <dl>
      <dt> 152 </dt>
      <dd> Two-place trainer </dd>
      <dt> 172 </dt>
      <dd> Smaller four-place airplane </dd>
      <dt> 182 </dt>
      <dd> Larger four-place airplane </dd>
      <dt> 210 </dt>
      <dd> Six-place airplane - high performance </dd>
    </dl>
  </body>
</html>
```

Figure 2.19 shows a browser display of `definition.html`.

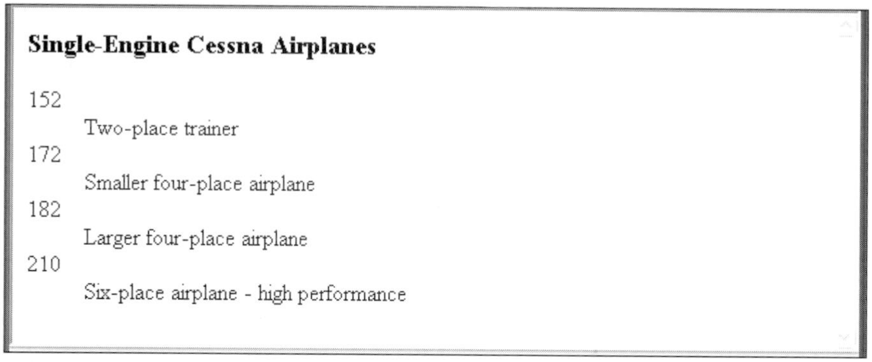

Single-Engine Cessna Airplanes

152

Two-place trainer

172

Smaller four-place airplane

182

Larger four-place airplane

210

Six-place airplane - high performance

FIGURE 2.19 Display of `definition.html`

2.8

TABLES

Tables are common fixtures in printed documents, books, and of course, Web documents. Tables provide a highly readable way of presenting many kinds of information.

A table is a matrix of rows and columns, in which each intersection of a row and a column is called a *cell*. Some of the cells contain column or row labels; most of the rest contain the information, or data, of the table. The information in a cell can be almost any document element, including text, headings, horizontal rules, images, and nested tables.

2.8.1 Basic Table Tags

A table is specified as the content of the block tag `<table>`. The most common attribute for the `<table>` tag is `border`. A table that does not include the `border` attribute will be a matrix of cells with neither horizontal nor vertical lines separating the cells. The browser has a default width for table borders, which is used if the `border` attribute is assigned the value `"border."` Otherwise, a number can be given as `border`'s value, which specifies the border width in pixels. For example, `border = "3"` specifies a border 3 pixels wide. All table borders are beveled to give a three-dimensional appearance, although this is ineffective with narrow border widths.

In most cases, a displayed table is preceded by a title, which is given as the content of a `<caption>` tag, which can immediately follow the `<table>` tag. The cells of a table are specified one row at a time. Tables usually have column labels and row labels. Each row of a table is specified with a row tag, `<tr>`. Within each row, the row label is specified by the table heading tag, `<th>`. Although the `<th>` tag has *heading* in its name, we call these things *labels* to avoid confusion with headings created with the `<hx>` tags. Each data cell of a row is specified with the table data tag, `<td>`. The first row of a table usually has the table's column labels. For example, if a table has three data columns and their column labels are `Apple`, `Orange`, and `Screwdriver`, the first row can be specified by the following:

```
<tr>
   <th> Apple </th>
   <th> Orange </th>
   <th> Screwdriver </th>
</tr>
```

Each data row of a table is specified with a heading tag and one data tag for each data column. For example, the first data row for our work-in-progress table might be as follows:

```
<tr>
   <th> Breakfast </th>
   <td> 0 </td>
   <td> 1 </td>
   <td> 0 </td>
</tr>
```

In tables that have both row and column labels, the upper-left corner cell is often empty. This empty cell is specified with a table header tag that includes no content (either `<th></th>` or just `<th />`).

The following document describes the whole table:

```
<?xml version = "1.0" encoding = "utf-8"?>
<!DOCTYPE html PUBLIC "-//w3c//DTD XHTML 1.1//EN"
   "http://www.w3.org/TR/xhtml11/DTD/xhtml11.dtd">


<!-- table.html
     An example of a simple table
     -->
<html xmlns = "http://www.w3.org/1999/xhtml">
   <head> <title> A simple table </title>
   </head>
   <body>
      <table border = "border">
         <caption> Fruit Juice Drinks </caption>
         <tr>
            <th> </th>
            <th> Apple </th>
```

continued

```
      <th> Orange </th>
      <th> Screwdriver </th>
    </tr>
    <tr>
      <th> Breakfast </th>
      <td> 0 </td>
      <td> 1 </td>
      <td> 0 </td>
    </tr>
    <tr>
      <th> Lunch </th>
      <td> 1 </td>
      <td> 0 </td>
      <td> 0 </td>
    </tr>
    <tr>
      <th> Dinner </th>
      <td> 0 </td>
      <td> 0 </td>
      <td> 1 </td>
    </tr>
  </table>
</body>
</html>
```

Figure 2.20 shows a browser display of this table.

Fruit Juice Drinks

	Apple	Orange	Screwdriver
Breakfast	0	1	0
Lunch	1	0	0
Dinner	0	0	1

FIGURE 2.20 Display of `table.html`

2.8.2 The `rowspan` and `colspan` Attributes

In many cases, tables have multiple levels of row or column labels in which one label covers two or more secondary labels. For example, consider the display of a partial table shown in Figure 2.21. In this table, the label "Fruit Juice Drinks" spans the three lower-level label cells. Multiple-level labels can be specified with the rowspan and colspan attributes.

FIGURE 2.21 Two levels of column labels

The colspan attribute specification in a table header or table data tag tells the browser to make the cell as wide as the specified number of rows in the table. For the previous example, the following code could be used:

```
<tr>
  <th colspan = "3"> Fruit Juice Drinks </th>
</tr>
<tr>
  <th> Orange </th>
  <th> Apple </th>
  <th> Screwdriver </th>
</tr>
```

If there are fewer cells in the rows above or below the spanning cell than the colspan attribute specifies, the browser stretches the spanning cell over the number of cells that populate the column in the table.[10] The rowspan attribute of the table heading and table data tags does for rows what colspan does for columns.

A table that has two levels of column labels and also has row labels must have an empty upper-left corner cell that spans both the multiple rows of column labels and the multiple columns. Such a cell is specified by including both rowspan and colspan attributes. Consider the following table specification, which is a minor modification of the previous table:

```
<?xml version = "1.0" encoding = "utf-8"?>
<!DOCTYPE html PUBLIC "-//w3c//DTD XHTML 1.1//EN"
  "http://www.w3.org/TR/xhtml11/DTD/xhtml11.dtd">
```

continued

---

10. Some browsers add empty row cells to allow the specified span to occur.

```
<!-- cell_span.html
     An example to illustrate rowspan and colspan
     -->
<html xmlns = "http://www.w3.org/1999/xhtml">
  <head> <title> Rowspan and colspan </title>
  </head>
  <body>
    <table border = "border">
      <caption> Fruit Juice Drinks and Meals </caption>
      <tr>
        <td rowspan = "2"> </td>
        <th colspan = "3"> Fruit Juice Drinks </th>
      </tr>
      <tr>
        <th> Apple </th>
        <th> Orange </th>
        <th> Screwdriver </th>
      </tr>
      <tr>
        <th> Breakfast </th>
        <td> 0 </td>
        <td> 1 </td>
        <td> 0 </td>
      </tr>
      <tr>
        <th> Lunch </th>
        <td> 1 </td>
        <td> 0 </td>
        <td> 0 </td>
      </tr>
      <tr>
        <th> Dinner </th>
        <td> 0 </td>
        <td> 0 </td>
        <td> 1 </td>
      </tr>
    </table>
  </body>
</html>
```

Figure 2.22 shows a browser display of cell_span.html.

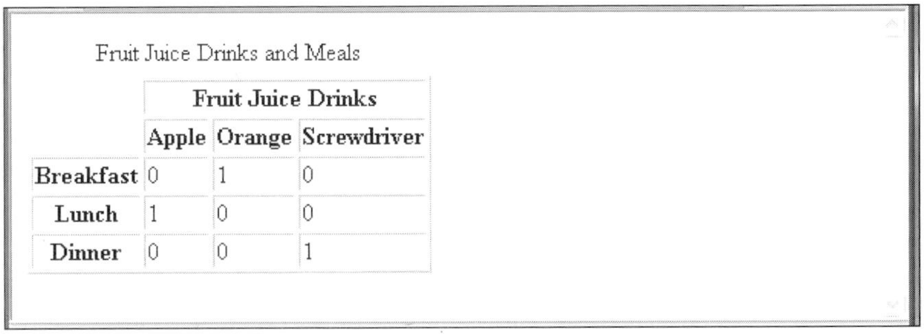

Fruit Juice Drinks and Meals			
	Fruit Juice Drinks		
	Apple	Orange	Screwdriver
Breakfast	0	1	0
Lunch	1	0	0
Dinner	0	0	1

FIGURE 2.22 Display of `cell_span.html`: multiple-labeled columns and labeled rows

2.8.3   The `align` and `valign` Attributes

The placement of the content within a table cell can be specified with the `align` and `valign` attributes in the `<tr>`, `<th>`, and `<td>` tags. The `align` attribute has the possible values `left`, `right`, and `center`, with the obvious meanings for horizontal placement of the content within a cell. The default alignment for headers is `center`; for data, it is `left`. If `align` is specified in a `<tr>` tag, it applies to all of the cells in the row. If it is included in a `<th>` or `<td>` tag, it only applies to that cell.

The `valign` attribute of the `<th>` and `<td>` tags has the possible values `top` and `bottom`. The default vertical alignment for both headings and data is `center`. Because `valign` applies only to a single cell, there is never any point in specifying `center`.

The following example illustrates the `align` and `valign` attributes:

```
<?xml version = "1.0" encoding = "utf-8"?>
<!DOCTYPE html PUBLIC "-//w3c//DTD XHTML 1.1//EN"
  "http://www.w3.org/TR/xhtml11/DTD/xhtml11.dtd">

<!-- cell_align.html
     An example to illustrate align and valign
     -->
<html xmlns = "http://www.w3.org/1999/xhtml">
  <head> <title> Alignment in cells </title>
  </head>
  <body>
    <table border = "border">
      <caption> The align and valign attributes </caption>
```

continued

```
    <tr align = "center">
      <th> </th>
      <th> Column Label </th>
      <th> Another One </th>
      <th> Still Another One </th>
    </tr>
    <tr>
      <th> align </th>
      <td align = "left"> Left </td>
      <td align = "center"> Center </td>
      <td align = "right"> Right </td>
    </tr>
    <tr>
      <th> <br /> valign <br /> <br /> </th>
      <td> Default </td>
      <td valign = "top"> Top </td>
      <td valign = "bottom"> Bottom </td>
    </tr>
  </table>
 </body>
</html>
```

Figure 2.23 shows a browser display of `cell_align.html`.

The align and valign attributes

	Column Label	Another One	Still Another One
align	Left	Center	Right
valign	Default	Top	Bottom

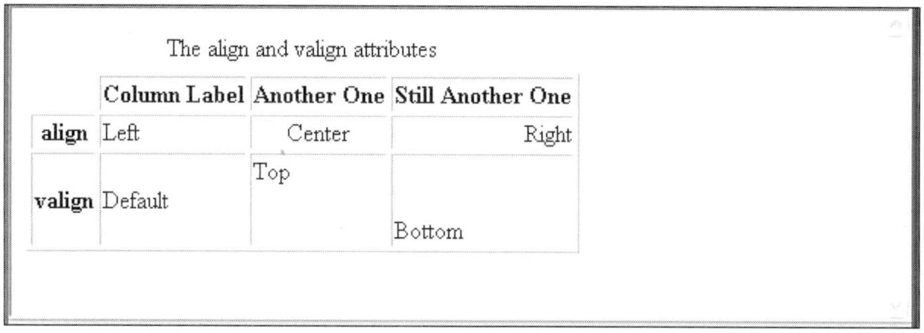

FIGURE 2.23 Display of `cell_align.html`: the `align` and `valign` attributes

2.8.4 The `cellpadding` and `cellspacing` Attributes

The table tag has two attributes that can be used to specify the spacing between the content of a table cell and the cell's edge and the spacing between adjacent cells. The `cellpadding` attribute is used to specify the spacing between the content of a cell and the inner walls of the cell. This is often used to prevent text in a cell from being too close to the edge of the cell. The `cellspacing` attribute is used to specify the distance between cells in a table.

The following document, `space_pad.html`, illustrates the `cellpadding` and `cellspacing` attributes:

```
<?xml version = "1.0" encoding = "utf-8"?>
<!DOCTYPE html PUBLIC "-//w3c//DTD XHTML 1.1//EN"
  "http://www.w3.org/TR/xhtml11/DTD/xhtml11.dtd">


<!-- space_pad.html
     An example that illustrates the cellspacing and
     cellpadding table attributes
     -->
<html xmlns = "http://www.w3.org/1999/xhtml">
  <head> <title> Cell spacing and cell padding </title>
  </head>
  <body>
    <b>Table 1 (space = 10, pad = 30) </b><br /><br />
    <table border = "5"  cellspacing = "10"  cellpadding = "30">
      <tr>
        <td> Small spacing, </td>
        <td> large padding </td>
      </tr>
    </table>
    <br /><br /><br /><br />
    <b>Table 2 (space = 30, pad = 10) </b><br /><br />
    <table border = "5"  cellspacing = "30"  cellpadding = "10">
      <tr>
        <td> Large spacing, </td>
        <td> small padding </td>
      </tr>
    </table>
  </body>
</html>
```

Figure 2.24 shows a browser display of `space_pad.html`.

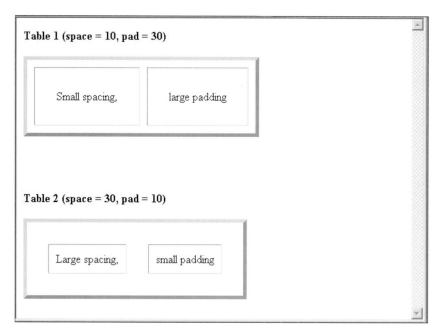

FIGURE 2.24 Display of `space_pad.html`

2.8.5   Table Sections

Tables naturally occur in two and sometimes three parts: header, body, and footer (not all tables have a natural footer). These three parts can be denoted in XHTML with the `thead`, `tbody`, and `tfoot` elements. The header includes the column labels, regardless of number of levels in those labels. The body includes the data of the table, including the row labels. The footer, when it appears, sometimes has the column labels repeated after the body. In some tables, the footer contains totals for the columns of data above. A table can have multiple body sections, in which case the browser may delimit them with horizontal lines that are thicker than those that delimit the rows within a body section.

2.9

FORMS

The most common way for a user to communicate information from a Web browser to the server is through a form. Forms, which are modeled on the paper forms that people continually are required to fill out, can be described in XHTML and displayed by the browser. XHTML provides tags to generate the commonly used objects on a screen form. These objects are called *controls* or *widgets*. There are controls for single-line and multiple-line text collection, checkboxes, radio buttons, and menus, among others. All control tags are inline tags. Most controls are used to gather information from the user in the form of either text or button selections. Each control can have a value, usually given through user input. Together, the values of all of the controls (that have values) in a form are called the *form data*. Every form requires a Submit button (see Section 2.9.5). When the user clicks the Submit button, the form data is encoded and sent to the Web server for processing.

2.9.1 The `<form>` Tag

All of the components of a form appear in the content of a `<form>` tag. `<form>`, which is a block tag, can have several different attributes, only one of which, `action`, is required. The `action` attribute specifies the URL of the application on the Web server that is to be called when the user clicks the Submit button.

In this chapter, our examples of form elements will not have corresponding application programs, so the value of their `action` attributes will be the empty string (`""`). Chapters 10 through 13 discuss several approaches to building form-processing programs and scripts.

The `method` attribute of `<form>` specifies one of the two techniques, `get` or `post`, used to pass the form data to the server. `get` is the default, so if no `method` attribute is given in the `<form>` tag, `get` will be used. The alternative technique is `post`. In both techniques, the form data is coded into a text string when the user clicks the Submit button.

The `get` and `post` techniques are further discussed in Chapter 10, "Using Perl for CGI Programming."

2.9.2 The `<input>` Tag

Many of the commonly used controls are specified with the inline tag `<input>`, which is used for text, passwords, checkboxes, radio buttons, and the special buttons Submit and Reset. The one attribute of `<input>` that is required for all of the controls discussed in this section is `type`, which specifies the particular kind of control. The control's kind is its type name, such as `checkbox`. All of the previously listed controls except Reset and Submit also require a `name` attribute, which becomes the name of the value of the control within the form data. The controls for checkboxes and radio buttons require `value` attributes, which initializes the value of the control.

A text control, which we usually refer to as a text box, creates a horizontal box into which the user can type a line of text. Text boxes are often used to gather information from the user, such as the user's name or address. The default size of a text box is often 20 characters. Because the default size can vary among browsers, it is a good idea to include a size on each text box. This is done with the `size` attribute of `<input>`. If the user types more characters than will fit in the box, the box is scrolled. If you do not want the box to be scrolled, you can include the `maxlength` attribute to specify the maximum number of characters that the browser will accept in the box. Any additional characters are ignored. For example, consider the following text box:

```
<form action = "">
  <p>
    <input type = "text"  name = "Name"  size = "25" />
  </p>
</form>
```

Suppose the user typed the following line:

```
Alfred Paul von Frickenburger
```

The text box would collect the whole string, but the string would be scrolled to the right, leaving the following shown in the box:

```
ed Paul von Frickenburger
```

The left end of the line would be part of the value of `Name`, even though it does not appear in the box. The ends of the line can be viewed in the box by moving the cursor off the ends of the box.

Notice that controls cannot appear directly in the form content—they must be placed in some block container, usually a paragraph.

Now consider a similar text box that includes a `maxlength` attribute.

```
<form action = "">
  <p>
    <input type = "text"  name = "Name"  size = "25"
           maxlength = "25" />
  </p>
</form>
```

If the user typed the same name as in the previous example, the resulting value of the `Name` text box would be this:

```
Alfred Paul von Frickenbu
```

No matter what was typed after the u in that person's last name, the value of `Name` would be as shown.

If the contents of a text box should not be displayed when it is entered by the user, a password control can be used. For example:

```
<input type = "password"  name = "myPassword"
       size = "10" maxlength = "10" />
```

Regardless of what characters are typed into a password control, only bullets or asterisks are displayed by the browser.

There are no restrictions on the characters that can be typed into a text box. So, the string `"?!34,:"` could be entered into the text box meant for names. Therefore, the entered contents of text boxes nearly always must be validated, either on the browser or on the server to which the form data is passed for processing.

Checkbox and radio controls are used to collect multiple-choice input from the user. A checkbox control is a single button that is either on or off (checked or not). If a checkbox button is on, the value associated with the name of the button is the string assigned to its `value` attribute. A checkbox button does not contribute to the form data if it is off. Every checkbox button requires a `name` attribute and a `value` attribute in its `<input>` tag. For form processing on the server, the name identifies the button and the value is its value (if it is checked). The attribute `checked`, which is assigned the value `checked`, specifies that the checkbox button is initially on. In many cases, checkboxes appear in lists, with every one having the same name. The content of the `<input>` tag is displayed next to the checkbox button, providing a label. Consider the following example:

```
<?xml version = "1.0" encoding = "utf-8"?>
<!DOCTYPE html PUBLIC "-//w3c//DTD XHTML 1.1//EN"
  "http://www.w3.org/TR/xhtml11/DTD/xhtml11.dtd">

<!-- checkbox.html
     An example to illustrate a checkbox
     -->
<html xmlns = "http://www.w3.org/1999/xhtml">
  <head> <title> Checkboxes </title>
  </head>
  <body>
    <p>
      Grocery Checklist
    </p>
    <form action = "">
      <p>
        <input type = "checkbox"  name = "groceries"
               value = "milk"  checked = "checked" /> Milk
        <input type = "checkbox"  name = "groceries"
               value = "bread" /> Bread
        <input type = "checkbox"  name = "groceries"
               value= "eggs" /> Eggs
      </p>
    </form>
  </body>
</html>
```

Figure 2.25 shows a browser display of `checkbox.html`.

Grocery Checklist

☑ Milk ☐ Bread ☐ Eggs

FIGURE 2.25 Display of `checkbox.html`

If the user does not turn on any of these checkbox buttons, `milk` will be the value for `groceries` in the form data. If the `milk` checkbox is left on and the `eggs` checkbox is also turned on by the user, the values of `groceries` in the form data would be `milk` and `eggs`.

Radio buttons are closely related to checkbox buttons. The difference between a group of radio buttons and a group of checkboxes is that only one radio button can be on or pressed at any time. Every time a radio button is pressed, the button in the group that was previously on is turned off. Radio buttons are named after the mechanical push buttons on the radios of cars of the 1950s—when you pushed one button on such a radio, the previously pushed button was mechanically forced out. The `type` value for radio buttons is `radio`. All radio buttons in a group must have the `name` attribute set in the `<input>` tag, and all radio buttons in a group have the same name. A radio button definition may specify which button is to be initially in the pressed, or on, state. This is indicated by including the `checked` attribute, set to the value `checked`, in the `<input>` tag of the button's definition. If no radio button in a group is specified as being checked, the browser usually checks the first button in the group. Consider the following radio button example:

```
<?xml version = "1.0" encoding = "utf-8"?>
<!DOCTYPE html PUBLIC "-//w3c//DTD XHTML 1.1//EN"
  "http://www.w3.org/TR/xhtml11/DTD/xhtml11.dtd">

<!-- radio.html
     An example to illustrate radio buttons
     -->
<html xmlns = "http://www.w3.org/1999/xhtml">
  <head> <title> Radio </title>
  </head>
  <body>
    <p>
      Age Category
    </p>
```

```
    <form action = "handler">
      <p>
        <input type = "radio"  name = "age"  value = "under20"
               checked = "checked" /> 0-19
        <input type = "radio"  name = "age"  value = "20-35" />
          20-35
        <input type = "radio"  name = "age"  value = "36-50" />
          36-50
        <input type = "radio"  name = "age"  value = "over50" />
          Over 50
      </p>
    </form>
  </body>
</html>
```

Figure 2.26 shows a browser display of `radio.html`.

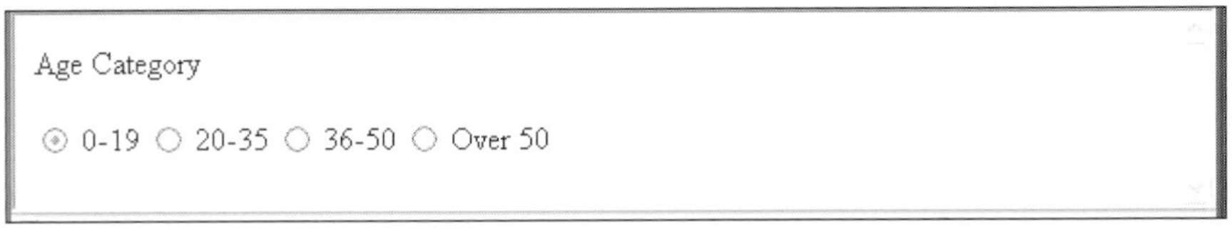

FIGURE 2.26 Display of `radio.html`

2.9.3   The `<select>` Tag

Checkboxes and radio buttons are effective methods for collecting multiple-choice data from a user. However, if the number of possible choices is large, the displayed form becomes too long to display. In these cases, a menu should be used. A menu is specified with a `<select>` tag (rather than the `<input>` tag). There are two kinds of menus: those in which only one menu item can be selected at a time (which are related to radio buttons) and those in which multiple menu items can be selected at any given time (which are related to checkboxes). The default option is the one related to radio buttons. The other option can be specified by adding the `multiple` attribute, which takes the value "multiple," to the `<select>` tag. When only one menu item is selected, the value sent in the form data is the value of the `name` attribute of the `<select>` tag and the chosen menu item. When multiple menu items have been selected, the value for the menu in the form data includes all selected menu items. If no menu item is selected, no value for the menu is included in the form data. The `name` attribute, of course, is required in the `<select>` tag.

The `size` attribute can be included in the `<select>` tag. `size` specifies the number of menu items that are to be displayed for the user. If no `size` attribute is specified, the value 1 is used. If the value for the size attribute is 1 and multiple is not specified, just one menu item is displayed with a downward scroll arrow. If the scroll arrow is clicked, the menu is displayed as a pop-up menu. If either multiple is specified or the size attribute is set to a number larger than 1, the menu is usually displayed as a scrolled list.

Each of the items in a menu is specified with an <option> tag, nested in the select element. The content of an <option> tag is the value of the menu item, which is just text (no tags may be included). The <option> tag can include the selected attribute, which specifies that the item is preselected. The value assigned to selected is "selected." This preselection can be overridden by the user. The following document describes a menu with the default value (1) for size:

```
<?xml version = "1.0" encoding = "utf-8"?>
<!DOCTYPE html PUBLIC "-//w3c//DTD XHTML 1.1//EN"
  "http://www.w3.org/TR/xhtml11/DTD/xhtml11.dtd">

<!-- menu.html
     An example to illustrate menus
     -->
<html xmlns = "http://www.w3.org/1999/xhtml">
  <head> <title> Menu </title>
  </head>
  <body>
    <p>
      Grocery Menu - milk, bread, eggs, cheese
    </p>
    <form action = "">
      <p>
        With size = 1 (the default)
        <select name = "groceries">
          <option> milk </option>
          <option> bread </option>
          <option> eggs </option>
          <option> cheese </option>
        </select>
      </p>
    </form>
  </body>
</html>
```

Figure 2.27 shows a browser display of menu.html. Figure 2.28 shows a browser display of menu.html after clicking the scroll arrow. Figure 2.29 shows a browser display of menu.html with size = "2."

FIGURE 2.27 Display of `menu.html` (default `size` of 1)

FIGURE 2.28 Display of `menu.html` after the scroll arrow is clicked

FIGURE 2.29 Display of `menu.html` with `size` set to 2

When the `multiple` attribute of the `<select>` tag is set, adjacent options can be chosen by dragging the mouse cursor over them while the left mouse button is held down. Nonadjacent options can be selected by clicking on each while holding down the keyboard Ctrl key.

2.9.4 The `<textarea>` Tag

In some situations, a multiline text area is needed. The `<textarea>` tag is used to create such controls. The text typed into the area created by `<textarea>` is not limited in length, and there is implicit scrolling both vertically and horizontally. The default size of the visible part of the text in a text area is often quite small, so the `rows` and `cols` attributes should usually be included and set to reasonable sizes. If some default text is to be included in the text area, it can be included as the content of the text area element. The following document describes a text area whose window is 40 columns wide and 3 lines tall:

```
<?xml version = "1.0" encoding = "utf-8"?>
<!DOCTYPE html PUBLIC "-//w3c//DTD XHTML 1.1//EN"
  "http://www.w3.org/TR/xhtml11/DTD/xhtml11.dtd">

<!-- textarea.html
     An example to illustrate a textarea
     -->
<html xmlns = "http://www.w3.org/1999/xhtml">
  <head> <title> Textarea </title>
  </head>
  <body>
    <p>
      Please provide your employment aspirations
    </p>
    <form action = "handler">
      <p>
        <textarea name = "aspirations"  rows = "3"  cols = "40">
          (Be brief and concise)
        </textarea>
      </p>
    </form>
  </body>
</html>
```

Figure 2.30 shows a browser display of `textarea.html` after some text has been typed into the area.

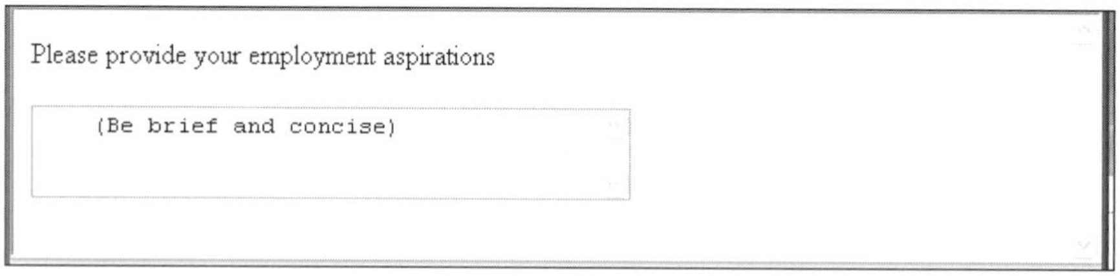

FIGURE 2.30 Display of `textarea.html` after some text entry

2.9.5 The Submit and Reset Buttons

The Reset button clears all of the controls in the form to their initial states. The Submit button has two actions: First, the form data is encoded and sent to the server. Second, the server is requested to execute the server-resident program specified in the `action` attribute of the `<form>` tag. The purpose of such a server-resident program is to process the form data and return some response to the user. Every form requires a Submit button. The Submit and Reset buttons are created with the `<input>` tag, as is illustrated in the following example:

```
<form action = "">
  <p>
    <input type = "submit"  value = "Submit Form" />
    <input type = "reset"  value = "Reset Form" />
  </p>
</form>
```

Figure 2.31 shows a browser display of Submit and Reset buttons.

FIGURE 2.31 Submit and Reset buttons

2.9.6   A Complete Form Example

The following document describes a form for taking sales orders for popcorn. Three text boxes are used at the top of the form to collect the buyer's name and address. These are placed in a borderless table to force the text boxes to align vertically. A second table is used to collect the actual order. Each row of this table names a product with the content of a `<td>` tag, displays the price with another `<td>` tag, and uses a text box with `size` set to 2 to collect the quantity ordered. The payment method is input by the user through one of four radio buttons.

```
<?xml version = "1.0" encoding = "utf-8"?>
<!DOCTYPE html PUBLIC "-//w3c//DTD XHTML 1.1//EN"
  "http://www.w3.org/TR/xhtml11/DTD/xhtml11.dtd">


<!-- popcorn.html
     This describes popcorn sales form page
     -->
<html xmlns = "http://www.w3.org/1999/xhtml">
  <head> <title> Popcorn Sales Form </title>
  </head>
```

continued

```
<body>
  <form action = "http://cs.ucp.edu/cgi-bin/sebesta/popcorn.pl"
        method = "post">
    <h2> Welcome to Millennium Gymnastics Booster Club Popcorn
         Sales
    </h2>

<!-- A borderless table of text widgets for name and address -->

    <table>
      <tr>
        <td> Buyer's Name: </td>
        <td> <input type = "text"  name = "name"
                    size = "30" /> </td>
      </tr>
      <tr>
        <td> Street Address: </td>
        <td> <input type = "text"  name = "street"
                    size = "30" /> </td>
      </tr>
      <tr>
        <td> City, State, Zip: </td>
        <td> <input type = "text"  name = "city"
                    size = "30" /> </td>
      </tr>
    </table>
    <p />

<!-- A bordered table for item orders -->

    <table border = "border">

<!-- First, the column headings -->

      <tr>
        <th> Product Name </th>
        <th> Price </th>
        <th> Quantity </th>
      </tr>

<!-- Now, the table data entries -->
```

```
        <tr>
          <th> Unpopped Popcorn (1 lb.) </th>
          <td> $3.00 </td>
          <td> <input type = "text"  name = "unpop"
                       size ="2" /> </td>
        </tr>
        <tr>
          <th> Caramel Popcorn (2 lb. canister) </th>
          <td> $3.50 </td>
          <td> <input type = "text"  name = "caramel"
                 size = "2" /> </td>
        </tr>
        <tr>
          <th> Caramel Nut Popcorn (2 lb. canister) </th>
          <td> $4.50 </td>
          <td> <input type = "text"  name = "caramelnut"
                 size = "2" /></td>
        </tr>
        <tr>
          <th> Toffey Nut Popcorn (2 lb. canister) </th>
          <td> $5.00 </td>
          <td> <input type = "text"  name = "toffeynut"

        </tr>

      </table>

<!-- The radio buttons for the payment method -->

      <h3> Payment Method: </h3>
      <p>
        <input type = "radio"  name = "payment"  value = "visa"
               checked = "checked" /> Visa
        <input type = "radio"  name = "payment"  value = "mc" />
          Master Card
        <input type = "radio"  name = "payment"
               value = "discover" /> Discover

        <input type = "radio"  name = "payment"
               value = "check" /> Check <br/>
      </p>

<!-- The submit and reset buttons -->
```

continued

```
        <p>
          <input type = "submit"  value = "Submit Order" />
          <input type = "reset"  value = "Clear Order Form" />
        </p>
      </form>
    </body>
  </html>
```

Figure 2.32 shows a browser display of `popcorn.html`.

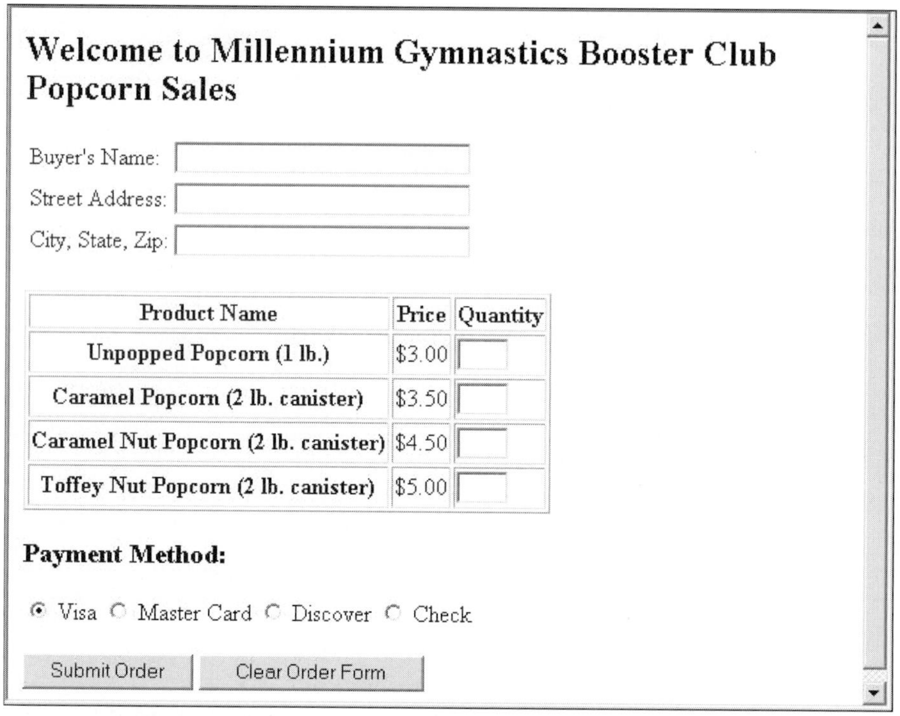

FIGURE 2.32 Display of `popcorn.html`

In Chapter 10, a Perl program is developed to process the form data from the popcorn form example. Chapter 12, "Introduction to PHP," has a PHP script for processing the data from the same form.

2.10

FRAMES

The browser display window can be used to display more than one document at a time. The window can be divided into rectangular areas, each of which is a *frame*. Each frame is capable of displaying its own document. Frames can be used for a number of different display situations. Among the most common of these is having a table of contents displayed in one frame and parts of the main document displayed in another. The table of contents can include links that, when followed, lead to the targeted parts of the main document being displayed in the other frame. Using frames, the table of contents can be displayed while the various documents are being displayed.

There are some problems with frames, which led W3C to begin discouraging their use as early as 1999 (with the release of HTML 4.0). They are entirely left out of XHTML 1.1. This means documents that include frames cannot be validated using the XHTML 1.1 standard. However, frames are commonly found in legacy HTML documents. Furthermore, they are still being included in new documents and are still supported by the latest versions of the popular browsers. Therefore, we retain our discussion of them.

2.10.1 Framesets

The number of frames and their layout in the browser window are specified with the `<frameset>` tag. A frameset element takes the place of the body element in a document. A document has either a body or a frameset but cannot have both.

The `<frameset>` tag must have either a `rows` or a `cols` attribute, and they often have both. The `rows` attribute specifies the number of rows of frames that will occupy the window. There are three kinds of values for rows: numbers, percentages, and asterisks. Normally, two or more values, separated by commas, are given in a quoted string. When a number is used as a value, it specifies the height of one row in pixels. A percentage is given as a number followed immediately by a percent sign. When used, a percent value specifies the percentage of the total browser window height that a row should occupy. When an asterisk is used as the value of `rows`, it means the remainder of the window height.

Consider the following example:

```
<frameset rows = "200, 300, 400">
```

This frameset will have three rows of frames. Because no `cols` attribute was included, the frames extend over the entire width of the browser window. If the window height happens to be 900 pixels, the three rows will have the heights 200, 300, and 400 pixels. If the window height is not exactly 900, the actual height will be divided so that the first frame will have $\frac{2}{9}$ of the height, the second $\frac{1}{3}$ of the height, and the last one $\frac{4}{9}$ of the height. It is more practical to specify rows with percentages, as in this example:

```
<frameset rows = "22%, 33%, 45%">
```

The frameset specified with the following has the same dimensions as the previous one:

```
<frameset rows = "22%, 33%, *">
```

If two asterisks are given in the `rows` attribute value, they each get half of what remains of the height of the window.

The `cols` attribute is very much like the `rows` attribute, except that it specifies the number of columns of frames. For example, the following tag specifies that the window is to have six frames in three equal-height rows and two columns:

```
<frameset rows = 33%, 33%, 33%"  cols = "25%, *">
```

Figure 2.33 shows a browser display of the window described by this frameset. The documents that appear in the frames in Figure 2.33 contain nothing more than frame labels.

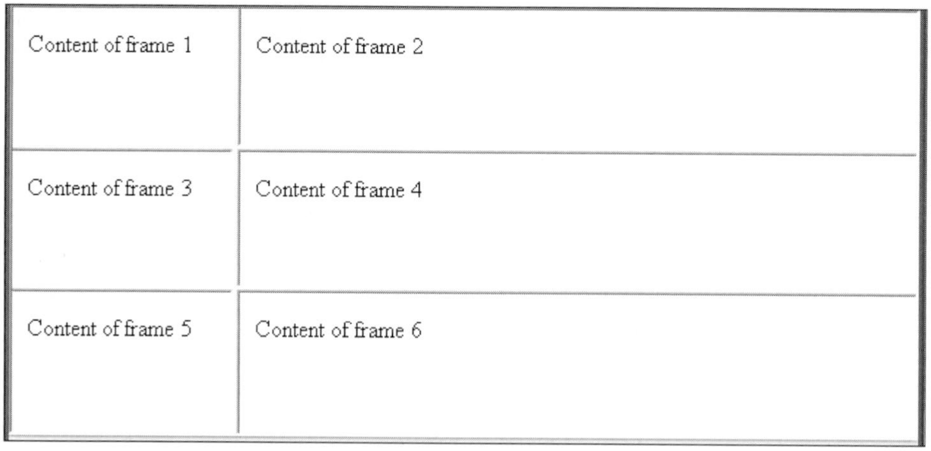

Content of frame 1	Content of frame 2
Content of frame 3	Content of frame 4
Content of frame 5	Content of frame 6

FIGURE 2.33 A simple frameset of six frames

2.10.2   Frames

The content of a frame is specified with the `<frame>` tag, which can appear only in the content of a frameset element. Each frame defined in a frameset has an associated <frame> tag that gives the filename of a document that describes its content. The sequence of <frame> tags in a frameset is important because the order dictates which frame gets which content. The frames in the frameset appear by rows. For example, if the frameset has two rows and two columns, the first two frames fill the two columns of the first row of frames. The content of a frame is specified as the value of the src attribute in the <frame> tag. For example:

```
<frame src = "apples.html">
```

If a <frame> tag has no src attribute, the browser displays an empty frame. If the frameset specifies more frames than <frame> tags, the unspecified frames are displayed as empty frames. Empty frames are rarely useful because they cannot be filled later.

If the content of a frame does not fit into the given frame, scroll bars are implicitly included. If you want a frame to have scroll bars, regardless of the size of its content, the <frame> attribute scrolling can be set to yes.

If a <frame> tag includes a name attribute, the content of its associated frame can be changed by the selection of a link in some other frame that specifies that name. For example, consider the following simple document:

```
<?xml version = "1.0" encoding = "utf-8"?>
<!DOCTYPE html PUBLIC "-//w3c//DTD XHTML 1.0 Frameset//EN"
  "http://www.w3.org/TR/xhtml1/DTD/xhtml1-frameset.dtd">

<!-- frames.html
     An example to illustrate frames
     -->
<html xmlns = "http://www.w3.org/1999/xhtml">
  <head> <title> Frames </title>
  </head>
  <frameset cols = "20%, *">
    <frame src = "contents.html" />
    <frame src = "fruits.html"  name = "descriptions" />
  </frameset>
</html>
```

This document has two frames. The left frame displays contents.html; the right frame displays fruits.html. Because the second frame has a name, it can be the target of a link from another frame (in this case, contents.html, shown below).

Notice that the frames.html document uses a different DOCTYPE than previous examples. This is because frames are not included in XHTML 1.1. Also, in XHTML 1.0, frames were specified with the Frameset alternative DTD of XHTML 1.0.

The `contents.html` document is a list of links to the fruit description documents. Each link must give both an `href` attribute for the document filename and a `target` attribute to specify the name of the frame in which the document is to be displayed. For example, consider the following document:

```
<?xml version = "1.0" encoding = "utf-8"?>
<!DOCTYPE html PUBLIC "-//w3c//DTD XHTML 1.0 Transitional//EN"
  "http://www.w3.org/TR/xhtml1/DTD/xhtml1-transitional.dtd">

<!-- contents.html
     The contents of the first frame of frames.html,
     which is the table of contents for the second frame
     -->
<html>
<head> <title> Table of Contents Frame </title>
</head>
<body>
<h4> Fruits </h4>
<ul>
    <li> <a href = "apples.html"  target = "descriptions">
            apples </a>
    </li>
    <li> <a href = "bananas.html"  target = "descriptions">
            bananas </a>
    </li>
    <li> <a href = "oranges.html"  target = "descriptions">
            oranges </a>
    </li>
</ul>
</body>
</html>
```

Yet another DOCTYPE is used in `contents.html`. This is because its particular use of frames was deprecated in HTML 4.0.[11] The standard used here, XHTML 1.0 Transitional, allows deprecated features of HTML. Recall that frames were completely removed from XHTML 1.1.

---

11. Specifically, the `target` attribute of the anchor tag, as used in `contents.html`, was deprecated.

Next, consider the `fruits.html` document, which is the initial document displayed in the second frame:

```
<?xml version = "1.0" encoding = "utf-8"?>
<!DOCTYPE html PUBLIC "-//w3c//DTD XHTML 1.1//EN"
  "http://www.w3.org/TR/xhtml11/DTD/xhtml11.dtd">

<!-- fruits.html
     The initial contents of the second frame
     of frames.html - a general description of fruit
     -->
<html xmlns = "http://www.w3.org/1999/xhtml">
  <head> <title> General Information on Fruits </title>
  </head>
  <body>
    <p>
      A fruit is the mature ovary in a flowering plant.
      Fruit is clasified by several characteristics, the
      most important being the number of ovaries included.
      If only a single ovary is included, it is called a
      simple fruit.
    </p>
  </body>
</html>
```

Figure 2.34 shows a browser display of `frames.html`.

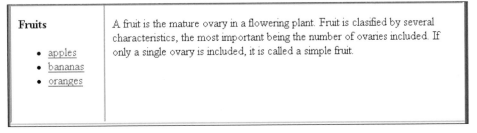

FIGURE 2.34 Display of `frames.html`

Assuming that `bananas.html` has been defined, after choosing the bananas link from the document `contents.html`, the resulting browser display may appear as shown in Figure 2.35.

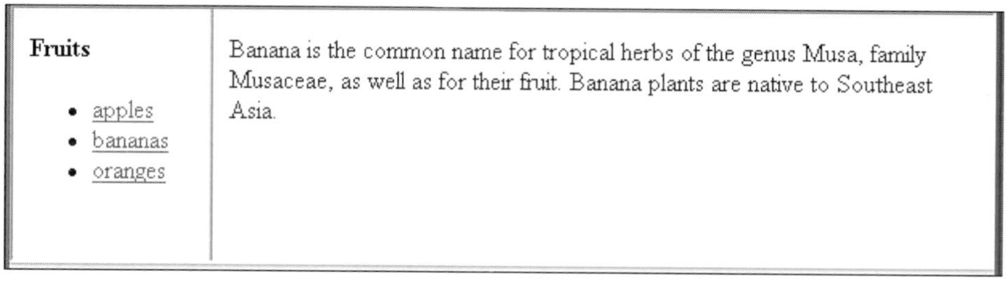

Fruits	Banana is the common name for tropical herbs of the genus Musa, family Musaceae, as well as for their fruit. Banana plants are native to Southeast Asia.
• apples • bananas • oranges	

FIGURE 2.35 Display of `frames.html` after taking the `bananas` link

Frames, as we have described them so far, are actually relatively boring. Although they allow multiple documents to be displayed in different parts of the browser display at the same time, their layout is tediously regular. Fortunately, frames can be arranged in more interesting ways. The mechanism to support this is simple—framesets can be nested. For example, the outermost frameset can define some number of columns. Each of these columns then can be divided with a nested frameset into whatever collection of frames is useful. The following example, `nested_frames.html`, illustrates this approach to dividing the display into irregular frames.

```
<?xml version = "1.0" encoding = "utf-8"?>
<!DOCTYPE html PUBLIC "-//w3c//DTD XHTML 1.0 Frameset//EN"
  "http://www.w3.org/TR/xhtml1/DTD/xhtml1-frameset.dtd">

<!-- nested_frames.html
     An example to illustrate nested frames
     -->
<html xmlns = "http://www.w3.org/1999/xhtml">
  <head> <title> Nested frames </title>
  </head>
  <frameset cols = "40%, *">
    <frameset rows = "50%, *">
      <frame src = "frame1.html" />
      <frame src = "frame2.html" />
    </frameset>
    <frameset rows = "20%, 35%, *">
      <frame src = "frame3.html" />
      <frame src = "frame4.html" />
      <frame src = "frame5.html" />
    </frameset>
  </frameset>
</html>
```

Figure 2.36 shows a browser display of `nested_frames.html`. As was the case with the frames in Figure 2.33, the frames here contain only labels that identify them.

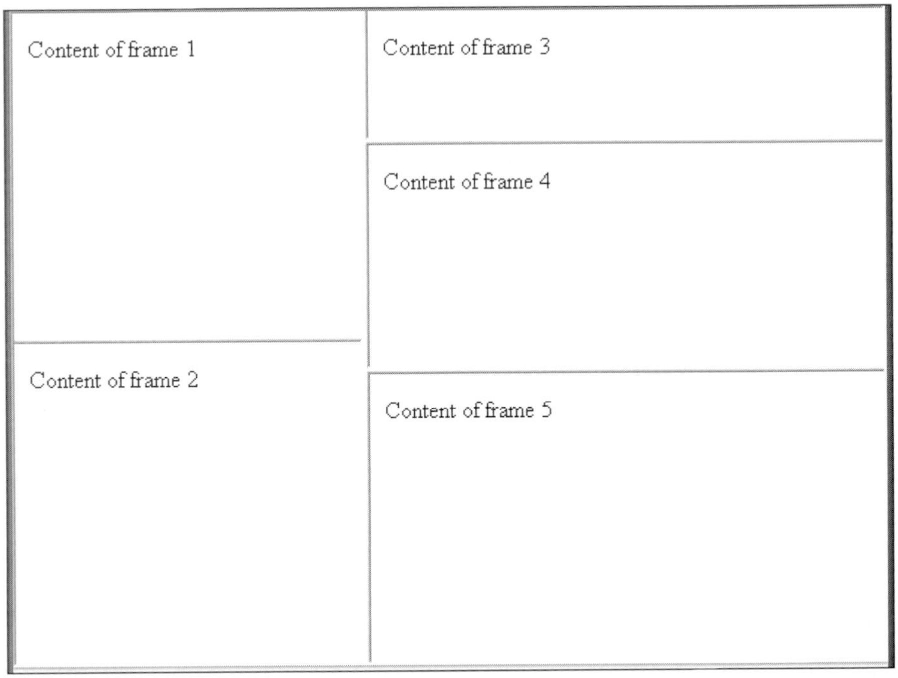

Content of frame 1

Content of frame 3

Content of frame 4

Content of frame 2

Content of frame 5

FIGURE 2.36 Display of `nested_frames.html`

2.11

SYNTACTIC DIFFERENCES BETWEEN HTML AND XHTML

There are some significant differences between the syntactic rules of HTML (or lack thereof) and those of XHTML. This section describes these differences.

Case sensitivity. In HTML, tag and attribute names are case insensitive, meaning that `<FORM>`, `<form>`, and `<Form>` are equivalent. In XHTML, all tag and attribute names must be in lowercase.

Closing tags. In HTML, closing tags may be omitted if the processing agent (usually a browser) can infer their presence. For example, in HTML, paragraph elements often do not have closing tags. The appearance of another opening paragraph tag is used to infer the closing tag on the previous paragraph. For example:

```
<p>
During Spring, flowers are born. ...
<p>
During Fall, flowers die. ...
```

In XHTML, all elements must have closing tags. For elements that do not include content, in which the closing tag appears to serve no purpose, a slash can be included at the end of the opening tag as an abbreviation of the closing tag. For example, the following two lines are equivalent:

```
<input type = "text"  name = "address" > </input>
```

and

```
<input type = "text"  name = "address" />
```

Recall that some browsers can be confused if the slash at the end is not preceded by a space.

Quoted attribute values. In HTML, attribute values must be quoted only if there are embedded special characters or whitespace characters. Numeric attribute values are rarely quoted in HTML. In XHTML, all attribute values must be double quoted, regardless of what characters are included in the value.

Explicit attribute values. In HTML, some attribute values are implicit; that is, they need not be explicitly stated. For example, if the border attribute appears in a <table> tag without a value, it specifies a default width border on the table. For example:

```
<table border>
```

This is illegal in XHTML, in which such an attribute is assigned a string of the name of the attribute. For example:

```
<table border = "border">
```

Other such attributes are checked, multiple, and selected.

id *and* name *attributes.* HTML markup often uses the name attribute for elements. This attribute was deprecated for some elements in HTML 4.0. The id attribute was added to nearly all elements with this same version of HTML. In XHTML, the use of id is encouraged, and the use of name is discouraged. In fact, the name attribute was removed for the anchor and map elements in XHTML 1.1. However, form elements must still use the name attribute because it is used in the form data.

Element nesting. Although HTML has rules against improper nesting of elements, they are not enforced. Examples of nesting rules are: 1) an anchor element cannot contain another anchor element, and a form element cannot contain another form element; 2) if an element appears inside another element, the closing tag of the inner element must appear before the closing tag of the outer element; 3) block elements cannot be nested in inline elements; 4) text cannot be directly nested in body or form elements; and 5) list elements cannot be directly nested in list elements. In XHTML, these nesting rules are strictly enforced.

All of the XHTML syntactic rules are checked by the W3C validation software.

2.12

SUMMARY

XHTML was derived from SGML, unlike some other popular text-formatting languages such as LaTeX and PostScript. Without the style sheets described in Chapter 3, XHTML is capable of specifying only the general layout of documents, with few presentation details. The current version of XHTML is XHTML 1.1; it was released in 2001.

The tags of XHTML specify how content is to be arranged in a display by a browser. Most tags consist of opening and closing tags to encapsulate the content that is to be affected by the tag. XHTML documents have two parts, the head and the body. The head describes some things about the document but does not include any content. The body includes the content and the tags and attributes to describe the layout of that content.

Line breaks in text are ignored by browsers. The browser fills lines in its display window and provides line breaks when needed. Line breaks can be specified with the `<br />` tag. Paragraph breaks can be specified with `<p>`. Headings can be created with the `<hx>` tags, where *x* can be any number from 1 to 6. The `<blockquote>` tag is used to set off a section of text. The `<big>` and `<small>` tags are used to request larger and smaller fonts, respectively. The `<sub>` and `<sup>` tags are used to create subscripts and superscripts, respectively. Horizontal lines can be specified with the `<hr />` tag.

Images in either GIF or JPEG format can be inserted into documents from files where they are stored with the `<img />` tag. The `alt` attribute of `<img />` is used to present a message to the user when his or her browser is unable (or unwilling) to present the associated image.

Links support hypertext by allowing a document to "point to" other documents, enabling the user to move easily from one document to another. The target of a link can be a different part of the current document or the top or some other part of a different document.

XHTML supports both unordered lists, using the `<ul>` tag, and ordered lists, using the `<ol>` tag. Both of these kinds of lists use the `<li>` tag to define list elements. The `<dl>` tag is used to describe definition lists. The `<dt>` and `<dd>` tags are used to specify the terms and their definitions, respectively.

Tables are easy to create with XHTML, using a collection of tags designed for that purpose. `<table>` is used to create a table, `<tr>` is used to create table rows, `<th>` is used to create column label cells, and `<td>` is used to create data cells in the table. The `colspan` and `rowspan` attributes, which can appear in both `<th>` and `<td>` tags, provide the means of creating multiple levels of column and row labels, respectively. The `align` and `valign` attributes of the `<tr>`, `<th>`, and `<td>` tags are used to tell the browser exactly where to put data or label values within their respective table cells. The `cellpadding` and `cellspacing` attributes are used to specify the distance between the content of a cell and its boundary and the distance between cells in a table, respectively.

XHTML forms are sections of documents that contain controls used to collect input from the user. The data specified in a form can be sent to a server-resident program in either of two methods, `get` or `post`. The most commonly used controls (text boxes, checkboxes, passwords, radio buttons, and the special buttons Submit and Reset) are specified with the `<input>` tag. The Submit button is used by the user to indicate that the form data is to be sent to the server for processing. The Reset button is used to clear all of the controls in a form. The text control is used to collect one line of input from the user. Checkboxes are one or more buttons used by the user to select one or more elements of a list. Radio buttons are like checkboxes, except that within a collection, only one button can be on at a time. A password is a text box whose content is never displayed by the browser.

Menus are used to allow the user to select items from a list when the list is too long to use checkboxes or radio buttons. Menu controls are created with the `<select>` tag. A text-area control, which is created with the `<textarea>` tag, creates a multiple-line text-gathering box, with implicit scrolling in both directions.

In HTML and XHTML 1.0, the browser window can be divided into rectangles called *frames*, each of which can display a different document. The screen layout of frames is specified in a `<frameset>` tag, using the `rows` and `cols` attributes. The values of these attributes can be numbers, for which the implied units are pixels; percentages of the window; or asterisks, which specify whatever is left of the browser window. One `<frame>` tag is given in the frameset content for each frame. The `src` attribute of `<frame>` gives the address of the document to be displayed in the frame. If a `<frame>` tag includes a `name` attribute, there can be a link in a different frame that refers to that name. When the link is selected, a different document can be displayed in the named frame. The anchor tag that defines the link includes a `target` attribute to specify the name of the frame where the document is to be displayed.

2.13 Review Questions

1. What does it mean for a tag or attribute of XHTML to be deprecated?

2. What is the form of an XHTML comment?

3. How does a browser treat line breaks in text to be displayed?

4. What is the difference in the effect of a paragraph tag and a break tag?

5. Which heading tags use fonts that are smaller than the normal text font size?

6. How do browsers usually set block quotations differently from normal text?

7. What does the `<tt>` tag do to its content?

8. What are the differences between the JPEG and GIF image formats?

9. What are the two required attributes of an `<img />` tag?

10. What is the purpose of the `alt` attribute of `<img />`?

11. What tag is used to define a link?

12. What attribute is required in all anchor tags?

13. Does XHTML allow nested links?

14. How is the target of a link usually identified in a case where the target is in the currently displayed document but not at its beginning?

15. What is the form of the value of the `href` attribute in an anchor tag when the target is a fragment of a document other than the one in which the link appears?

16. What is the default bullet form for the items in an unordered list?

17. What are the default sequence values for the items in an ordered list?

18. What tags are used to define the terms and their definitions in a definition list?

19. What is specified when the `border` attribute of a `<table>` tag is set to `"border"`?

20. What is the purpose of the `colspan` attribute of the `<th>` tag?

21. What is the purpose of the `rowspan` attribute of the `<td>` tag?

22. What are the `align` and `valign` attributes of the `<tr>`, `<th>`, and `<td>` tags used for?

23. What is the difference between the `cellspacing` and `cellpadding` attributes?

24. Describe the possible values of the `rows` attribute of `<frameset>`.

25. What does the `src` attribute of `<frame>` specify?

26. Of what use is a frame that does not initially have a document?

27. How is a frame specified in a link from a different frame?

28. What are controls?

29. Which controls discussed in this chapter are created with the `<input>` tag?

30. What is the default size of a text control's text box?

31. What is the difference between the `size` and `maxlength` attributes of `<input>` for text controls?

32. What is the difference in behavior between a group of checkbox buttons and a group of radio buttons?

33. Under what circumstances is a menu used instead of a radio button group?

34. What is the drawback of specifying the `multiple` attribute with a menu?

35. How are scroll bars specified for text-area controls?

2.14 Exercises

1. Create, test, and validate an XHTML document for yourself, including your name, address, and e-mail address. If you are a student, you must include your major and your grade level. If you work, you must include your employer, your employer's address, and your job title. This document must use several headings and `<big>`, `<small>`, `<hr />`, `<p>`, and `<br />` tags.

2. Add pictures of yourself and at least one other image (your friend, spouse, or pet) to the document created for Exercise 1.

3. Add a second document to the document created for Exercise 1 that describes part of your background, using `background` as the link content. This document should have a few paragraphs of your personal or professional history.

4. Create, test, and validate an XHTML document to describe an unordered list of a typical grocery shopping list you write. (If you've never made up such a list, use your imagination.)

5. Create, test, and validate an XHTML document to describe an unordered list of at least four states. Each element of the list must have a nested list of at least three cities in the state.

6. Create, test, and validate an XHTML document to describe an ordered list of your five favorite movies.

7. Modify the list of Exercise 6 to add nested, unordered lists of at least two actors and/or actresses in your favorite movies.

8. Create, test, and validate an XHTML document to describe an ordered list with the following contents: The highest level should be the names of your two parents, with your mother first. Under each parent, you must have a

3.2

LEVELS OF STYLE SHEETS

The three levels of style sheets, in order from lowest level to highest level, are *inline*, *document* level, and *external*. Inline style sheets apply to the content of a single tag, document-level style sheets apply to the whole body of a document, and external style sheets can apply to the bodies of any number of documents. Inline style sheets have precedence over document style sheets, which have precedence over external style sheets. For example, if an external style sheet specifies a value for a particular property of a particular tag, that value is used until a different value is specified in either a document style sheet or an inline style sheet. Likewise, document style sheet property values can be overridden by different property values in an inline style sheet. In effect, the properties of a specific tag are those that result from a merge of all applicable style sheets, with lower-level style sheets having precedence in cases of conflicting specifications.

If no style-sheet information is specified, the browser default property values are used.

As is the case with tags and tag attributes, a particular browser may not be capable of using the property values specified in a style sheet. For example, if the value of the `font-size` property of a paragraph is set to 48 points, but the browser can only display the particular font being used in sizes up to 44 points, the browser obviously cannot fulfill the property specification. In this case, the browser either would substitute an alternative value or would simply ignore the given property value.

Inline style specifications appear within the opening tag and apply only to the content of that tag. This fine-grain application of style defeats one of the primary advantages of style sheets—that of imposing a uniform style on the tags of at least one whole document. Another disadvantage of inline style sheets is that they result in style information, which is expressed in a language distinct from XHTML markup, being embedded in various places in documents. It is much better to keep style specifications separate from XHTML markup. For this reason, among others, W3C deprecated inline style sheets in XHTML 1.1. Therefore, inline style specifications should be used sparingly. This chapter discusses inline style sheets, but we follow our own advice and make little use of them in our examples.

Document-level style specifications appear in the document head section and apply to the entire body of the document. This is obviously the way to impose a uniform style on the presentation of all of the content of a document.

In many cases, it is desirable to have a style sheet apply to more than one document. This is the purpose of external style sheets. External style sheets are not part of any of the documents to which they apply. They are stored separately and are specified in all documents that are meant to use them. External style sheets are written as text files with the MIME type `text/css`. They can be stored on any computer on the Web. The browser fetches external style sheets just as it fetches documents. The `<link>` tag is used to specify external style sheets. Within `<link>`, the `rel` attribute is used to specify the relationship of the linked-to document to the document in which the link appears. The `href` attribute of `<link>` is used to specify the URL of the style sheet document, as in this example:

```
<link rel = "stylesheet"  type = "text/css"
     href = "http://www.cs.usc.edu/styles/wbook.css" />
```

The link to an external style sheet must appear in the head of the document. If the external style sheet resides on the Web server computer, only its path address must be given as the value of `href`. An example of an external style sheet appears in Section 3.6.

External style sheets can be validated with the service provided at `http://jigsaw.w3.org/css-validator/validator-upload.html`.

3.3

STYLE SPECIFICATION FORMATS

The format of a style specification depends on the level of style sheet. Inline style specifications appear as values of the `style` attribute of a tag[1], the general form of which is as follows:

$$style = \text{"}property\_1\text{: }value\_1\text{; }property\_2\text{:}value\_2\text{; ...;}$$
$$property\_n\text{: }value\_n\text{;"}$$

Although it is not required, it is recommended that the last property/value pair be followed by a semicolon.

The scope of an inline style specification is restricted to the content of the element in which it appears.

Document style specifications appear as the content of a style element within the header of a document, although the format of the specification is quite different from that of inline style sheets. The general form of the content of a style element is as follows[2]:

```
<style type = "text/css">
     rule_list
</style>
```

---

1. The style attribute is deprecated in the XHTML 1.1 recommendation.

2. Browsers so old that they do not recognize the `<style>` tag may display the content of the style element at the top of the document. There are now so few such browsers in use that we ignore the issue here. Those who are concerned put the rule list in an XTHML comment.

The `type` attribute of the `<style>` tag tells the browser the type of style specification, which is always `text/css`. The type of style specification is necessary because there are other kinds of style sheets. For example, JavaScript also provides style sheets that can appear in style elements.

The content of a style element is CSS code, which uses a different form of comments. Such comments are introduced with `/*` and terminated with `*/`.[3] For example:

```
<style type = "text/css">
    /* Styles for initial paragraph */
    ...
    /* Styles for other paragraphs */
    ...
</style>
```

Each style rule in a rule list has two parts: a selector, which indicates the tag or tags affected by the rule, and a list of property/value pairs. The list has the same form as the quoted list for inline style sheets, except the list is delimited by braces rather than double quotes. So, the form of a style rule is as follows:

```
selector {property_1: value_1; property_2: value_2; . . .;
          property_n: value_n;}
```

If a property is given more than one value, those values usually are separated by spaces. For some properties, however, they are separated with commas.

External style sheets have a form similar to that of document style sheets. The external file consists of a list of style rules. An example of an external style sheet appears in Section 3.6.

3.4
SELECTOR FORMS

The selector can have a variety of forms, which are described in this section.

3.4.1 Simple Selector Forms

The simplest selector form is a single element name, such as `h1`. In this case, the property values in the rule apply to all occurrences of the named element. The selector could be a list of element names, separated by commas, in which case the property values apply to all occurrences of all of the named elements. If the

---

3. This form of comment is adopted from the C programming language and some of its descendants.

selector is an asterisk (*), the property values apply to every element in the document. Consider the following examples, in which the property is `font-size` and the property value is a number of points:

```
h1 {font-size: 24pt;}
h2, h3 {font-size: 20pt;}
```

The first of these specifies that the text content of all `h1` elements must be set in 24-point font size. The second specifies that the text content of all `h2` and `h3` elements must be set in 20-point font size.

Selectors can also specify that the style should only apply to elements in certain positions in the document. This is done by listing the element hierarchy in the selector, with only white space separating the element names. For example, the rule

```
body b i {font-size: 30pt;}
```

only applies its style to the content of italic elements that are descendants of bold elements in the body of the document. This is a *contextual* selector. It would not apply to the content of an italic element that did not have a boldface element as an ancestor. Note that descendant selectors are recognized by IE6 browsers but not by NS7 browsers.

3.4.2 Class Selectors

Style-class selectors are used to allow different occurrences of the same tag to use different style specifications. A style class is defined in a style element by giving it a name, which is attached to the tag's name with a period. For example, if you want two paragraph styles in a document—say, `normal` and `narrow`—you could define these two classes in the comment of a `<style>` tag as follows:

```
p.normal {property-value list}
p.narrow {property-value list}
```

Within the document body, the particular style class that you want is specified with the `class` attribute of the affected tag—in the preceding example, the paragraph tag. For example, you might have the following:

```
<p class = "normal">
A paragraph of text that we want to be presented in
'normal' presentation style
</p>
<p class = "narrow">
A paragraph of text that we want to be presented in
'narrow' presentation style
</p>
```

3.4.3   Generic Selectors

Sometimes it is convenient to have a class of style specifications that applies to the content of more than one kind of tag. This is done by using a generic class, which is defined without a tag name in its name. In place of the tag name, you use the name of the generic class, which must begin with a period. For example:

```
.special {property-value list}
```

Now, in the body of a document, you could have the following:

```
<h3 class = "special"> Chapter 3 </h3>
...
<p class = "special">
...
</p>
```

3.4.4   `id` Selectors

An `id` selector allows the application of a style to one specific element. The general form of an `id` selector is as follows[4]:

```
#specific-id {property-value list}
```

As you can probably guess, the style specified in the `id` selector applies to the element with the specific `id`. For example,

```
#section14 {font-size: 20}
```

specifies a font size of 20 points to the element

```
<h2 id = "section14">1.4 Calico Cats </h2>
```

CSS2 added still more selector forms. However, because of the lack of browser support for them, they are not discussed here.

3.4.5   Pseudo Classes

Pseudo classes are styles that apply when something happens rather than because the target element simply exists. CSS1 included some pseudo classes, and CSS2 added more. Unfortunately, support for the pseudo classes is sorely lacking, at least among the most popular browsers. However, two pseudo classes, `hover` and `focus`, are supported by NS7 (but not IE6), so we introduce them here.

---

4. For the oddly curious reader, the Bell Labs name for the # symbol is *octothorpe*. It was named that when it was first put on the dial of telephones.

While the names of style classes and generic classes begin with a period, the names of pseudo classes begin with colons. The style of the hover pseudo class applies when its associated element has the mouse cursor over it. The style of the focus pseudo class applies when its associated element has focus. For example, consider the following document:

```
<?xml version = "1.0" encoding = "utf-8"?>
<!DOCTYPE html PUBLIC "-//w3c//DTD XHTML 1.1//EN"
  "http://www.w3.org/TR/xhtml11/DTD/xhtml11.dtd">

<!-- pseudo.html
     Illustrates the :hover and :focus pseudo classes
     -->
<html xmlns = "http://www.w3.org/1999/xhtml">
  <head> <title> Checkboxes </title>
    <style type = "text/css">
      input:hover {color: red;}
      input:focus {color: green;}
    </style>
  </head>
  <body>
    <form action = "">
      <p>
        Your name:
        <input type = "text"  />
      </p>
    </form>
  </body>
</html>
```

In pseudo.html, the content of an input element (a text box) is colored red when the mouse cursor is placed over its content. This happens only when the text box does not have focus. If no text has been typed into the text box, the hover pseudo class has no affect. When the text box acquires focus (typically by clicking the left mouse button while the cursor is in the box), the text turns green and stays that color until the left mouse button is clicked outside the box.

3.5

PROPERTY VALUE FORMS

CSS1 includes 60 different properties in seven categories: fonts, lists, alignment of text, margins, colors, backgrounds, and borders. As you probably would guess, we will not discuss all of these properties. The complete details of all properties and property values can be found at the W3C Web site.

Property values can appear in a variety of forms. Keyword property values are used when there are only a few possible values and they are predefined—for example, `large`, `medium`, and `small`. Keyword values are not case sensitive, so `Small`, `SmAlL`, and `SMALL` are all the same as `small`.

Number values are used when no meaningful units can be attached to a numeric property value. A number value either can be an integer or a string of digits with a decimal point and can be preceded by a sign (+ or -).

Length values are specified as number values that are followed immediately by a two-character abbreviation of a unit name. There can be no space between the number and the unit name. The possible unit names are `px` for pixels, `in` for inches, `cm` for centimeters, `mm` for millimeters, `pt` for points, and `pc` for picas, which are 12 points. There are also two relative length values: `em`, which is the height of the letter *m*, and `ex`, which is the height of the letter *x*.

Percentage values are used to provide a measure that is relative to the previously used measure. Percentage values are numbers that are followed immediately by percent signs. For example, if the font size were set to `75%`, it would make the new current size for the font 75% of whatever it was. Font size would stay at the new value until it was changed again. Percentage values can be signed. If preceded by a plus sign, the percentage is added to the previous value; if negative, the percentage is subtracted.

URL property values use a form that is slightly different from references to URLs in links. The actual URL, which can be either absolute or relative, is placed in parentheses and preceded by `url`, as in the following:

```
url(tetons.jpg)
```

There can be no space between `url` and the left parenthesis.

Color property values can be specified as color names, as six-digit hexadecimal numbers, or in RGB form. RGB form is just the word `rgb` followed by a parenthesized list of three numbers that specify the levels of the three colors red, green, and blue. The RGB values can be given as either decimal numbers between 0 and 255 or as percentages. Hexadecimal numbers must be preceded with pound signs (#), as in `#43AF00`. For example, white could be specified with

```
white
```

or

```
rgb(255, 255, 255)
```

or

```
#FFFFFF
```

CSS2 specifies that some property values are inherited by elements nested in the element for which the values are specified. For example, the property `background-color` is not inherited but `font-size` is. Using a style sheet to set a value for an inheriting property for the `<body>` tag effectively sets it as a default property value for the whole document. For example:

```
body {font-size: 20pt}
```

Unless overridden by a style sheet that applies to paragraph elements, every paragraph element in the body of this document would inherit the font size of 20 points. Unfortunately, at the time of the writing of this chapter, neither IE6 nor NS7 implements inheritance completely or correctly.

3.6

FONT PROPERTIES

The font properties are among the most commonly used of the style-sheet properties. Virtually all XHTML documents include text, which is often used in a variety of different situations. This creates a need for text in many different fonts, font styles, and sizes. The font properties allow us to specify these different forms.

3.6.1 Font Families

The `font-family` property is used to specify a list of font names. The browser will use the first font in the list that it supports. For example, the following could be specified:

```
font-family: Arial, Helvetica, Courier
```

In this case, the browser will use Arial if it supports that font. If not, it will use Helvetica if it supports it. If the browser supports neither Arial nor Helvetica, it will use Courier if it can. If the browser does not support any of the specified fonts, it will use an alternative of its choosing.

A generic font can be specified as a `font-family` value. The possible generic fonts and examples of each are shown in Table 3.1. Each browser has a font defined for each of these generic names.

If a font name has more than one word, the whole name should be delimited by single quotes,[5] as in the following example:

```
font-family: 'Times New Roman'
```

---

5. We use single quotes here because, in the case of inline style sheets, the whole property list is delimited by double quotes.

TABLE 3.1 Generic Fonts

Generic Name	Examples
serif	Times New Roman, Garamond
sans-serif	MS Ariel, Helvetica
cursive	Caflisch Script, Zapf-Chancery
fantasy	Critter, Cottonwood
monospace	Courier, Prestige

In practice, the quotes may not be mandatory, but their use is recommended because they may be required in the future.

3.6.2 Font Sizes

The `font-size` property does what its name implies. For example, the following property specification sets the font size for text to 10 points:

```
font-size: 10pt
```

Many relative `font-size` values are defined, namely `xx-small`, `x-small`, `small`, `medium`, `large`, `x-large`, and `xx-large`. In addition, `smaller` or `larger` could be specified. Furthermore, the value can be a percentage, which would be relative to the current font size.

The disadvantage of the relative font sizes is the lack of strict font size control. Different browsers can use different values for them. For example, `small` might mean 10 points on one browser and 8 points on another. On the other hand, using a specific font size has the risk that some browsers may not support the particular size, making the document display appear different on different browsers.

3.6.3 Font Styles

The `font-style` property is most commonly used to specify italic, as in the following:

```
font-style: italic
```

An alternative to `italic` is `oblique`, but when displayed, the two are nearly identical, so `oblique` is not a terribly useful font style. In fact, some browsers do not support oblique, so they display all oblique fonts in italic.

3.6.4 Font Weights

The `font-weight` property is used to specify the degree of boldness. For example:

```
font-weight: bold
```

Besides `bold`, the values `normal` (the default), `bolder`, and `lighter` can be specified. The `bolder` and `lighter` values are taken as relative to the current level of boldness. Specific numbers also can be given in multiples of 100 from 100 to 900, where `400` is the same as `normal` and `700` is the same as `bold`.

3.6.5 Font Shorthands

If more than one font property must be specified, the values can be stated in a list as the value of the `font` property—the browser has the responsibility for determining from the forms of the values which properties to assign. For example, consider the following specification:

```
font: bold 14pt 'Times New Roman' Palatino
```

This specifies that the font weight should be `bold`, the font size should be 14 points, and either Times New Roman or Palatino font should be used, with precedence given to Times New Roman.

The order in which the property values are given in a `font` value list is important. The order must be: font style, font weight, font size, and finally the list of font names. Only the font size and the font family are required in the `font` value list.

The following sample XHTML document illustrates some aspects of style-sheet specification of the font properties in headings and paragraphs using a document style sheet:

```
<?xml version = "1.0" encoding = "utf-8"?>
<!DOCTYPE html PUBLIC "-//w3c//DTD XHTML 1.1//EN"
  "http://www.w3.org/TR/xhtml11/DTD/xhtml11.dtd">

<!-- fonts.html
     An example to illustrate font properties
     -->
<html xmlns = "http://www.w3.org/1999/xhtml">
  <head> <title> Font properties </title>
    <style type = "text/css">
```

```
        p.big {font-size: 14pt;
               font-style: italic;
               font-family: 'Times New Roman';
              }
        p.small {font: 10pt bold 'Courier New';}
        h2 {font-family: 'Times New Roman';
            font-size: 24pt; font-weight: bold}
        h3 {font-family: 'Courier New'; font-size: 18pt}
    </style>
  </head>
  <body>
    <p class = "big">
      If a job is worth doing, it's worth doing right.
    </p>
    <p class = "small">
      Two wrongs don't make a right, but they certainly
      can get you in a lot of trouble.
    </p>
    <h2> Chapter 1 Introduction </h2>
    <h3> 1.1 The Basics of Computer Networks </h3>
  </body>
</html>
```

Figure 3.1 shows a browser display of fonts.html.

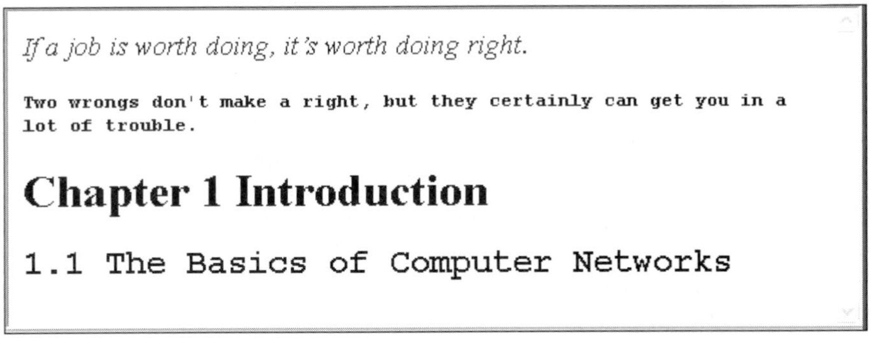

FIGURE 3.1 Display of fonts.html

The following is a revision of fonts.html, fonts2.html, which uses an external style sheet in place of the document style sheet used in fonts.html. The external style sheet, styles.css, follows the revised document.

```
<?xml version = "1.0" encoding = "utf-8"?>
<!DOCTYPE html PUBLIC "-//w3c//DTD XHTML 1.1//EN"
  "http://www.w3.org/TR/xhtml11/DTD/xhtml11.dtd">

<!-- fonts2.html
     An example to test external style sheets
     -->
<html xmlns = "http://www.w3.org/1999/xhtml">
  <head> <title> External style sheets </title>
    <link rel = "stylesheet"  type = "text/css"
          href = "styles.css" />
  </head>
  <body>
    <p class = "big">
      If a job is worth doing, it's worth doing right.
    </p>
    <p class = "small">
      Two wrongs don't make a right, but they certainly
      can get you in a lot of trouble.
    </p>
    <h2> Chapter 1 Introduction </h2>
    <h3> 1.1 The Basics of Computer Networks </h3>
  </body>
</html>
```

```
/* styles.css - an external style sheet
     for use with fonts2.html
   */
  p.big {font-size: 14pt;
         font-style: italic;
         font-family: 'Times New Roman';
        }
  p.small {font: 10pt bold 'Courier New';}
  h2 {font-family: 'Times New Roman';
      font-size: 24pt; font-weight: bold}
  h3 {font-family: 'Courier New';
      font-size: 18pt}
```

3.6.6 Text Decoration

The text-decoration property is used to specify some special features of text. The available values are line-through, overline, underline, and none, which is the default. Many browsers underline links. The none value can be used to avoid this. The following example illustrates the line-through, overline, and underline values.

```
<?xml version = "1.0" encoding = "utf-8"?>
<!DOCTYPE html PUBLIC "-//w3c//DTD XHTML 1.1//EN"
  "http://www.w3.org/TR/xhtml11/DTD/xhtml11.dtd">


<!-- decoration.html
     An example that illustrates several of the
     possible text decoration values
     -->
<html xmlns = "http://www.w3.org/1999/xhtml">
  <head> <title> Text decoration </title>
    <style type = "text/css">
      p.through {text-decoration: line-through}
      p.over {text-decoration: overline}
      p.under {text-decoration: underline}
    </style>
  </head>
  <body>
    <p class = "through">
      This illustrates line-through
    </p>
    <p class= "over">
      This illustrates overline
    </p>
    <p class = "under">
      This illustrates underline
    </p>
  </body>
</html>
```

Figure 3.2 shows a browser display of decoration.html.

FIGURE 3.2 Display of decoration.html

The `letter-spacing` property controls the amount of space between characters in text. The possible values of `letter-spacing` are any length property values, for example 3px. Sometimes the width of the letter 'm' is used, which is specified with em.

3.7

LIST PROPERTIES

Two presentation details of lists often are specified in XHTML documents: the shape of the bullets that precede the items in an unordered list and the sequencing values that precede the items in ordered lists. The `list-style-type` property is used to specify both of these.

The `list-style-type` property of an unordered list can be set to `disc`, `circle`, `square`, or `none`. The default property value for bullets is `disc`. For example, the following illustrates a document style sheet to set the bullet type in all items in unordered lists to `square`:

```
<!-- bullets1 -->
<style type = "text/css">
  ul {list-style-type: square}
</style>
...
<h3> Some Common Single-Engine Aircraft </h3>
  <ul>
    <li> Cessna Skyhawk </li>
    <li> Beechcraft Bonanza </li>
    <li> Piper Cherokee </li>
            </ul>
```

Style classes can be defined to allow different list items to have different bullet types:

```
<!-- bullets2 -->
<style type = "text/css">
  li.disc {list-style-type: disc}
  li.square {list-style-type: square}
  li.circle {list-style-type: circle}
</style>
...
<h3> Some Common Single-Engine Aircraft </h3>
  <ul>
    <li class = "disc"> Cessna Skyhawk </li>
    <li class = "square"> Beechcraft Bonanza </li>
    <li class = "circle"> Piper Cherokee </li>
  </ul>
```

Figure 3.3 shows a browser display of these two lists.

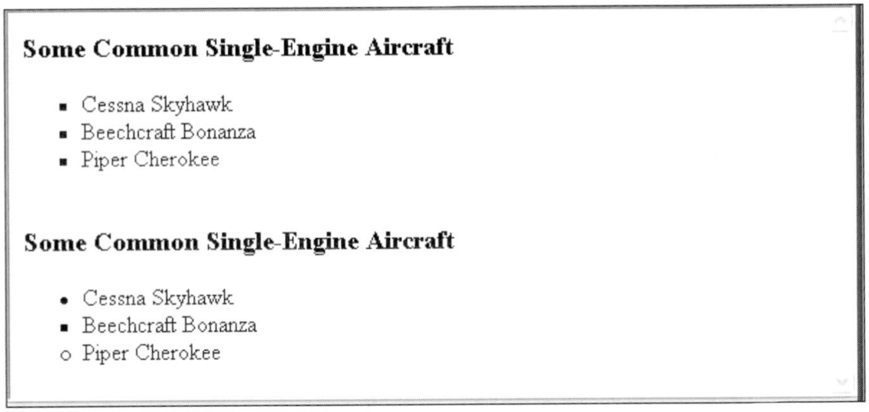

Some Common Single-Engine Aircraft

- Cessna Skyhawk
- Beechcraft Bonanza
- Piper Cherokee

Some Common Single-Engine Aircraft

- Cessna Skyhawk
- Beechcraft Bonanza
- Piper Cherokee

FIGURE 3.3 Examples of unordered lists

We are not limited to discs, squares, and circles for bullets in unordered lists. Any image can be used in a list item bullet. Such a bullet is specified with the `list-style-image` property, whose value is specified with the `url` form. For example, if `small_plane.gif` is a small image of an airplane that is stored in the same directory as the XHTML document, it could be used as follows:

```
<style type = "text/css">
  li.image {list-style-image: url(small_airplane.gif)}
</style>
    ...
  <li class = "image"> Beechcraft Bonanza </li>
```

When ordered lists are nested, it is best to use different kinds of sequence values for the different levels of nesting. The `list-style-type` property can be used to specify the types of sequencing values. Table 3.2 lists the different possibilities.

TABLE 3.2 Possible Sequencing Values for Ordered Lists

Property Values	Sequence Type	First Four Values
decimal	Arabic numerals	1, 2, 3, 4
upper-alpha	Uppercase letters	A, B, C, D
lower-alpha	Lowercase letters	a, b, c, d
upper-roman	Uppercase Roman numerals	I, II, III, IV
lower-roman	Lowercase Roman numerals	i, ii, iii, iv

The following example illustrates the use of different sequence value types in nested lists:

```
<?xml version = "1.0" encoding = "utf-8"?>
<!DOCTYPE html PUBLIC "-//w3c//DTD XHTML 1.1//EN"
  "http://www.w3.org/TR/xhtml11/DTD/xhtml11.dtd">

<!-- sequence_types.html
     An example to illustrate sequence type styles
     -->
<html xmlns = "http://www.w3.org/1999/xhtml">
  <head> <title> Sequence types </title>
    <style type = "text/css">
      ol {list-style-type: upper-roman;}
      ol ol {list-style-type: upper-alpha;}
      ol ol ol {list-style-type: decimal;}
    </style>
  </head>
  <body>
    <h3> Aircraft Types </h3>
    <ol>
      <li> General Aviation (piston-driven engines)
        <ol>
          <li> Single-Engine Aircraft
            <ol>
              <li> Tail wheel </li>
              <li> Tricycle </li>
            </ol>
          </li>
          <li> Dual-Engine Aircraft
            <ol>
              <li> Wing-mounted engines </li>
              <li> Push-pull fuselage-mounted engines </li>
            </ol>
          </li>
        </ol>
      </li>
      <li> Commercial Aviation (jet engines)
        <ol>
          <li> Dual-Engine
            <ol>
              <li> Wing-mounted engines </li>
              <li> Fuselage-mounted engines </li>
            </ol>
          </li>
```

```
        <li> Tri-Engine
          <ol>
            <li> Third engine in vertical stabilizer </li>
            <li> Third engine in fuselage </li>
          </ol>
        </li>
      </ol>
    </li>
  </ol>
  </body>
</html>
```

Figure 3.4 shows a browser display of `sequence_types.html`.

Aircraft Types

I. General Aviation (piston-driven engines)
    A. Single-Engine Aircraft
        1. Tail wheel
        2. Tricycle
    B. Dual-Engine Aircraft
        1. Wing-mounted engines
        2. Push-pull fuselage-mounted engines
II. Commercial Aviation (jet engines)
    A. Dual-Engine
        1. Wing-mounted engines
        2. Fuselage-mounted engines
    B. Tri-Engine
        1. Third engine in vertical stabilizer
        2. Third engine in fuselage

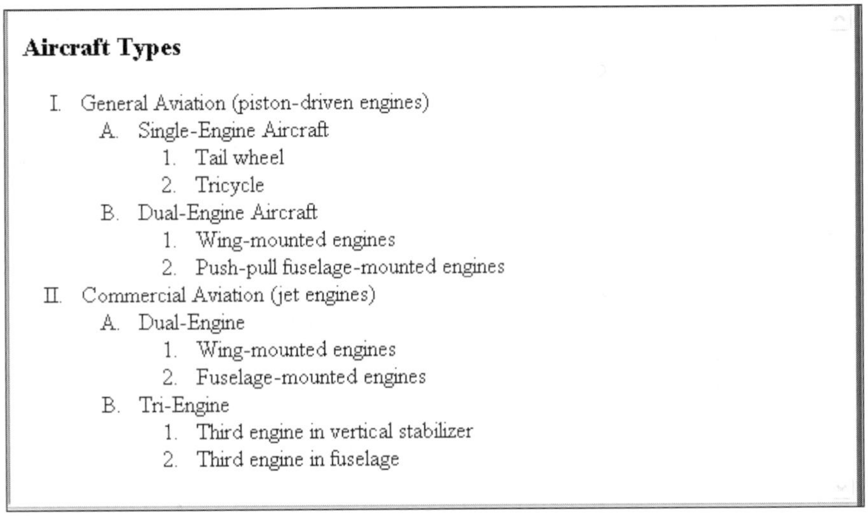

FIGURE 3.4 Display of `sequence_types.html`

CSS2 added more sequence types such as `hebrew` and `lower-greek`, but they are not yet supported by the popular browsers.

3.8
COLOR

If older browsers and older client machines are taken into account, color is not a simple issue. For one thing, the document may be displayed on monitors of widely varying capabilities. Also, the document may be rendered by browsers that have different abilities to deal with colors. This section provides an introduction to how Web sites can deal with these difficulties.

3.8.1 Color Groups

Three levels of collections of colors might be used by an XHTML document. The smallest useful set of colors includes only those that have standard names and are guaranteed to be correctly displayable by all browsers on all color monitors. This collection of colors is called the *named colors*. The names and hexadecimal codes for the named colors are shown in Table 3.3.

TABLE 3.3 Named colors

Name	Hexadecimal code	Name	Hexadecimal code
black	000000	green	008000
silver	C0C0C0	lime	00FF00
gray	808080	olive	808000
white	FFFFFF	yellow	FFFF00
maroon	800000	navy	000080
red	FF0000	blue	0000FF
purple	800080	teal	008080
fuchsia	FF00FF	aqua	00FFFF

Most Web browsers now recognize 140 named colors, although these names are not part of a W3C standard. This collection of colors is given in Appendix B.

A larger set of colors, called the *Web palette*, includes 216 colors. These colors, which are often called Web-safe colors, are displayable by Windows- and Macintosh-based browsers but may not be correctly displayed with some older terminals used on UNIX systems. Elements of this set of colors have hexadecimal values for red, green, and blue that are restricted to 00, 33, 66, 99, CC, and FF. These numbers are all combinations of all increments of 20% of each of the three basic colors, red, green, and blue. The colors of the Web palette are shown on the back inside cover of this book.

When the limitations of older browsers and monitors are not a consideration, 24-bit (or six-hexadecimal-digit) numbers can be used to specify any one of 16 million colors. When a color is specified that the browser or monitor cannot display, a (hopefully) similar color will be used.

3.8.2 Color Properties

The color property is used to specify the foreground color of XHTML elements. For example, consider the following small table:

```
<style type = "text/css">
  th.red {color: red}
```

```
      th.orange {color: orange}
</style>
  ...
<table border = "5px">
  <tr>
    <th class = "red"> Apple </th>
    <th class = "orange"> Orange </th>
    <th class = "orange"> Screwdriver </th>
  </tr>
</table>
```

The `background-color` property is used to set the background color of an element, where the element could be the whole body of the document. For example, consider the following paragraph element:

```
<style type = "text/css">
  p.redback {font-size: 24pt; color: blue;
           background-color: red">
</style>
...
<p class = "redback">
  To really make it stand out, use a red background!
</p>
```

When displayed by a browser, this might appear as in Figure 3.5.

FIGURE 3.5 The `background-color` property

3.9

ALIGNMENT OF TEXT

The first line of a paragraph can be indented using the `text-indent` property. This property takes either a length or a percentage value. For example:

```
<style type = "text/css">
  p.indent {text-indent: 0.5in}
</style>
```

```
...
<p class = "ident">
  Now is the time for all good Web programmers to begin
    using cascading style sheets for all presentation
    details in their documents. No more deprecated tags
    and attributes, just nice, precise style sheets.
</p>
```

This paragraph would be displayed as follows:

```
Now is the time for all good Web programmers to begin using
cascading Style sheets for all presentation details in
their documents. No more deprecated tags and attributes,
just nice, precise style sheets.
```

The `text-align` property, for which the possible keyword values are `left`, `center`, `right`, and `justify`, is used to arrange text horizontally. For example, the following document-level style sheet entry causes the content of paragraphs to be aligned on the right margin:

```
p {text-align: right}
```

The default value for `text-align` is `left`.

The `float` property, which is often set for images and tables, is used to specify that text should flow around some element. The possible values for `float` are `left`, `right`, and `none`, which is the default. For example, suppose we want an image to be on the right side of the display and have text flow around its left side. To specify this, the `float` property of the image is set to `right`. Because the default value for `text-align` is `left`, `text-align` need not be set for the text. In the following example, the text of a paragraph is specified to flow to the left of an image until the bottom of the image is reached, at which point the paragraph text flows across the whole window.

```
<?xml version = "1.0" encoding = "utf-8"?>
<!DOCTYPE html PUBLIC "-//w3c//DTD XHTML 1.1//EN"
  "http://www.w3.org/TR/xhtml11/DTD/xhtml11.dtd">

<!-- float.html
     An example to illustrate the float property
     -->
<html xmlns = "http://www.w3.org/1999/xhtml">
  <head> <title> The float property </title>
    <style type = "text/css">
      img {float: right}
    </style>
  </head>
```

```
<body>
  <p>
    <img src = "c210new.jpg"  alt = "Picture of a Cessna 210" />
  </p>
  <p>
    This is a picture of a Cessna 210. The 210 is the flagship
    single-engine Cessna aircraft. Although the 210 began as a
    four-place aircraft, it soon acquired a third row of seats,
    stretching it to a six-place plane. The 210 is classified
    as a high-performance airplane, which means its landing
    gear is retractable and its engine has more than 200
    horsepower. In its first model year, which was 1960,
    the 210 was powered by a 260-horsepower fuel-injected
    six-cylinder engine that displaced 471 cubic inches.
    The 210 is the fastest single-engine airplane ever
    built by Cessna.
  </p>
</body>
</html>
```

When rendered by a browser, `float.html` might appear as shown in Figure 3.6, depending on the width of the browser display window.

FIGURE 3.6 Display of `float.html`

3.10

THE BOX MODEL

Virtually all document elements can have borders. These borders have various styles such as color and width. Furthermore, the amount of space between the content of an element and its border, known as *padding*, can be specified, as well as the space between the border and an adjacent element, known as the *margin*. This model is illustrated in Figure 3.7.

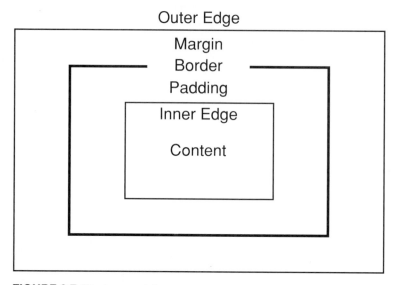

FIGURE 3.7 The box model

3.10.1 Borders

Every element has a property, `border-style`, that controls whether the element's content has a border, as well as the style of the border. CSS1 requires that borders be available for any element, but the only required style is `solid` (the default style when the border attribute of a table element is set to `border` or a pixel width). CSS2 provides several different border styles, among them `dotted`, `dashed`, and `double`, all three of which are supported by IE6 and NS7. The default value for `border-style` is none, which is why the contents of elements do not normally have borders.

The `border-width` property is used to specify the thickness of a border. Its possible values are `thin`, `medium` (the default), `thick`, or a length value in pixels. The width of the four borders of an element can be different. These are specified with `border-top-width`, `border-bottom-width`, `border-left-width`, and `border-right-width`. All of the border width properties are part of CSS1.

The color of a border is controlled by the `border-color` property, which is part of CSS1. Once again, the individual borders of an element can be colored differently through the CSS2 properties, `border-top-color`, `border-bottom-color`, `border-left-color`, and `border-right-color`. All of the border color properties are supported by IE6 and NS7.

The following document, `borders.html`, illustrates borders, using a table and a short paragraph as examples.

```
<?xml version = "1.0" encoding = "utf-8"?>
<!DOCTYPE html PUBLIC "-//w3c//DTD XHTML 1.1//EN"
  "http://www.w3.org/TR/xhtml11/DTD/xhtml11.dtd">

<!-- borders.html
     An example of a simple table with various borders
     -->
<html xmlns = "http://www.w3.org/1999/xhtml">
  <head> <title> Table borders </title>
    <style type = "text/css">
      table {border-top-width: medium;
             border-bottom-width: thick;
             border-top-color: red;
             border-bottom-color: blue;
             border-top-style: dotted;
             border-bottom-style: dashed;
            }
        p {border-style: dashed; border-width: thin;
           border-color: green
          }
    </style>
  </head>
  <body>
    <table border = "5">
      <caption> Fruit Juice Drinks </caption>
      <tr>
        <th> </th>
        <th> Apple </th>
        <th> Orange </th>
        <th> Screwdriver </th>
      </tr>
```

continued

```
      <tr>
        <th> Breakfast </th>
        <td> 0 </td>
        <td> 1 </td>
        <td> 0 </td>
      </tr>
      <tr>
        <th> Lunch </th>
        <td> 1 </td>
        <td> 0 </td>
        <td> 0 </td>
      </tr>
      <tr>
        <th> Dinner </th>
        <td> 0 </td>
        <td> 0 </td>
        <td> 1 </td>
      </tr>
    </table>
    <p>
      Now is the time for all good Web programmers to
      learn to use style sheets.
    </p>
  </body>
</html>
```

The display of `borders.html` is shown in Figure 3.8.

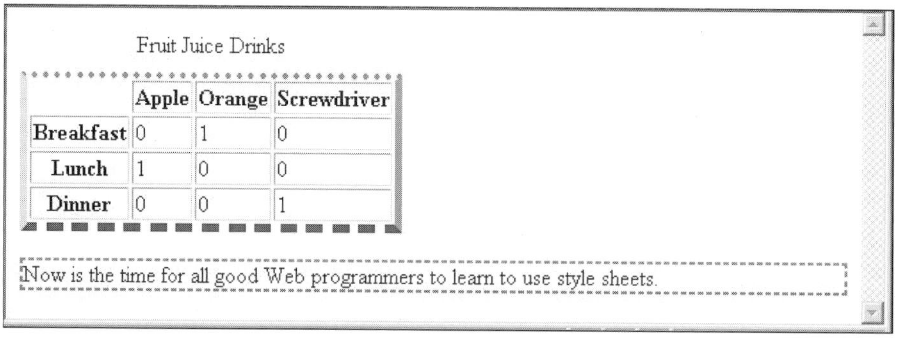

FIGURE 3.8 Borders

If the border attribute had been left out of the table element in `borders.html`, the table would have a top border and a bottom border only. It would not have left and right borders, nor would it have borders around the cells.

3.10.2   Margins and Padding

Recall from the box model that *padding* is the space between the content of an element and its border. The *margin* is the space between the border of an element and the element's neighbor. When there is no border, the margin plus the padding is the space between the content of an element and its neighbor. In this scenario, it may appear there is no difference between padding and margins. However, there is a difference when the element has a background. In this case, the background extends into the padding but not into the margin.

The margin properties are named margin, which applies to all four sides of an element, margin-left, margin-right, margin-top, and margin-bottom. The padding properties are named padding, which applies to all four sides, padding-left, padding-right, padding-top, and padding-bottom.

The following example, marpads.html, illustrates several combinations of margins and padding, both with and without borders.

```
<?xml version = "1.0" encoding = "utf-8"?>
<!DOCTYPE html PUBLIC "-//w3c//DTD XHTML 1.1//EN"
  "http://www.w3.org/TR/xhtml11/DTD/xhtml11.dtd">


<!-- marpads.html
     An example to illustrate margins and padding
     -->
<html xmlns = "http://www.w3.org/1999/xhtml">
  <head> <title> Table borders </title>
    <style type = "text/css">
      p.one   {margin: 0.2in;
               padding: 0.2in;
               background-color: #C0C0C0;
               border-style: solid;
              }
      p.two   {margin: 0.1in;
               padding: 0.3in;
               background-color: #C0C0C0;
               border-style: solid;
              }
      p.three {margin: 0.3in;
               padding: 0.1in;
               background-color: #C0C0C0;
               border-style: solid;
              }
```

continued

```
        p.four   {margin:0.4in;
                  background-color: #C0C0C0;}
        p.five   {padding: 0.4in;
                  background-color: #C0C0C0;
                  }
      </style>
    </head>
    <body>
      <p>
        Here is the first line.
      </p>
      <p class = "one">
        Now is the time for all good Web programmers to
        learn to use style sheets. <br /> [margin = 0.2in,
        padding = 0.2in]
      </p>
      <p class = "two">
        Now is the time for all good Web programmers to
        learn to use style sheets. <br /> [margin = 0.1in,
        padding = 0.3in]
      </p>
      <p class = "three">
        Now is the time for all good Web programmers to
        learn to use style sheets. <br /> [margin = 0.3in,
        padding = 0.1in]
      </p>
      <p class = "four">
        Now is the time for all good Web programmers to
        learn to use style sheets. <br /> [margin = 0.4in,
        no padding, no border]
      </p>
      <p class = "five">
        Now is the time for all good Web programmers to
        learn to use style sheets. <br /> [padding = 0.4in,
        no margin, no border]
      </p>
      <p>
        Here is the last line.
      </p>
    </body>
  </html>
```

Figure 3.9 shows a browser display of `marpads.html`.

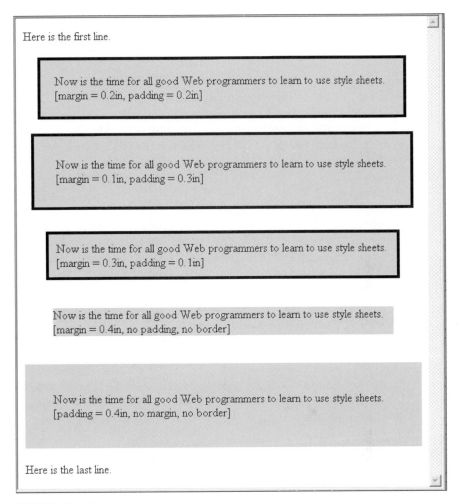

FIGURE 3.9 Display of `marpads.html`

3.11

BACKGROUND IMAGES

The `background-image` property is used to place an image in the background of an element. For example, an image of an airplane might be an effective background for text about the airplane. Consider the following example:

```
<?xml version = "1.0" encoding = "utf-8"?>
<!DOCTYPE html PUBLIC "-//w3c//DTD XHTML 1.1//EN"
  "http://www.w3.org/TR/xhtml11/DTD/xhtml11.dtd">
```

continued

```
<!-- back_image.html
     An example to illustrate background images
     -->
<html xmlns = "http://www.w3.org/1999/xhtml">
  <head> <title> Background images </title>
    <style type = "text/css">
      body {background-image: url(c172.gif);}
      p {margin-left: 30px; margin-right: 30px;
         margin-top: 50px; font-size: 14pt;}
    </style>
  </head>
  <body>
    <p >
      The Cessna 172 is the most common general aviation airplane
      in the world. It is an all-metal, single-engine piston,
      high-wing four-place monoplane. It has fixed-gear and is
      categorized as a non-high-performance aircraft. The current
      model is the 172R.
      The wingspan of the 172R is 36'1". Its fuel capacity is 56
      gallons in two tanks, one in each wing. The takeoff weight
      is 2,450 pounds. Its maximum useful load is 837 pounds.
      The maximum speed of the 172R at sea level is 142 mph.
      The plane is powered by a 360 cubic inch gasoline engine
      that develops 160 horsepower. The climb rate of the 172R
      at sea level is 720 feet per minute.
    </p>
  </body>
</html>
```

Figure 3.10 shows a browser display of back_image.html.

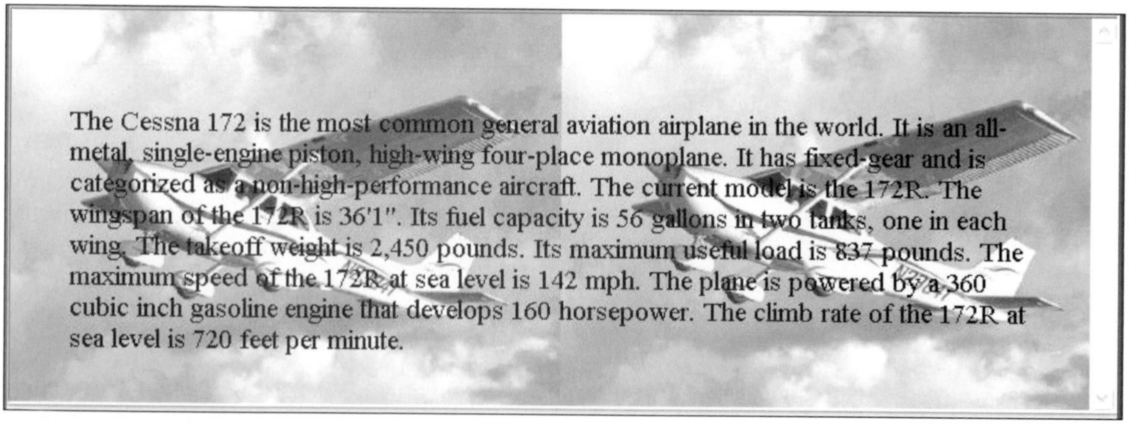

FIGURE 3.10 Display of back_image.html

Text over a background image can be difficult to read if the image has areas that are nearly the same color as the text. Therefore, care must be taken in selecting background images. In many cases, images of various kinds of textures in light gray colors are best.

Notice that, in the example, the background image is replicated as necessary to fill the area of the element. This repetition can be controlled with the `background-repeat` property, which can take the value `repeat` (the default), `no-repeat`, `repeat-x`, or `repeat-y`. The `no-repeat` value specifies that just one copy of the image is to be displayed. The `repeat-x` value means the image is to be repeated horizontally; `repeat-y` means repeat vertically. Additionally, the position of a nonrepeated background image can be specified with the `background-position` property, which can take a large number of different values. The keyword values are `top`, `center`, `bottom`, `left`, and `right`. These can be used in many different combinations. The simplest uses of these are to use one keyword to specify the horizontal placement and one for the vertical placement, such as `top left`, `bottom right`, and `top center`. If only one keyword is given, the other is assumed to be `center`. So, `top` is equilivent to `top center` (or `center top`), and `left` is the same as `center left` (or `left center`).

3.12

THE `<span>` AND `<div>` TAGS

In many situations, we want to apply special font properties to less than a whole paragraph of text. For example, it is often useful to have a word or phrase in a line appear in a different font size or color. The `<span>` tag is designed for just this purpose. Unlike most other tags, there is no default layout for the content of `<span>`. So, in the following example, the word `total` is not displayed differently from the rest of the paragraph:

```
<p>
  It sure is fun to be in <span> total </span>
    control of text
</p>
```

The purpose of `<span>` is to change property values with an inline style sheet:

```
<style type = "text/css" >
  p.spanred {font-size: 24pt;
            font-family: Ariel; color: red}
</style>
...
```

```
<p>
  It sure is fun to be in
  <span class = "spanred"> total </span>
  control of text
</p>
```

The display of this paragraph is shown in Figure 3.11

It sure is fun to be in total control of text

FIGURE 3.11 The `<span>` tag

It is common for documents to have sections, each consisting of some number of paragraphs, that have their own presentation styles. Using style classes on paragraphs, you can do this with what we have already discussed. It is more convenient, however, to be able to apply a style to a section of a document rather than each paragraph. This can be done with the `<div>` tag. As with `<span>`, there is no implied layout for the content of the `<div>` tag, so its primary use is to specify presentation details for a section or division of a document.

Consider the following example, in which a section, or division, of a document is to use a specific paragraph style:

```
<div class = "indented">
  <p>
  ...
  </p>
  <p>
  ...
  </p>
  <p>
  ...
  </p>
</div>
```

The span and div elements are further illustrated in examples in Chapter 6.

3.13

SUMMARY

Cascading style sheets were introduced to provide a uniform and consistent way to specify presentation details in XHTML documents. Many of the style tags and attributes designed for specifying style that had crept into HTML were deprecated in HTML 4.0 in favor of style sheets. Style sheets can appear at three levels: inline, which apply only to the content of one specific tag; document, which apply to all appearances of specific tags in the body of a document; and external, which are stored in files by themselves and can apply to any number of documents. The property values in inline style sheets are specified in the string value of the `style` attribute. Document style sheets are specified in a comment that is the content of a `<style>` tag in the head of the document. External style sheets appear in separate files. Both document-level and external style specifications have the form of a list of style rules. Each style rule has a list of the names of tags and a list of property/value pairs. The property/value pairs apply to all occurrences of the named tags.

A style class, which is defined in the content of a `<style>` tag, allows different occurrences of the same tag to have different property values. A generic style-class specification allows tags with different names to use the same presentation style. A pseudo class takes effect when a particular event occurs. There are many different property value forms, including lengths, percentage values, URLs, and colors. Several different properties are related to fonts. The `font-family` property specifies one or more font names. Because different browsers support different sets of fonts, there are five generic font names. Each browser supports at least one font in each generic category. The `font-size` property can specify a length value or one of a number of different named size categories. The `font-style` property can be set to `italic` or `normal`. The `font-weight` property is used to specify the degree of boldness of text. The `font` property provides an abbreviated form for font-related properties. The `text-decoration` property is used to specify underlining, overlining, and line-through text.

The `list-style-type` property is used to specify the bullet form for items in unordered lists. It is also used to specify the sequence type for the items in ordered lists.

A Web content designer must be concerned with the color capabilities of clients' browsers and monitors. The safest set of colors includes just 16 basic colors. A much larger set of relatively safe Web colors is the Web palette, which includes 216 colors. The foreground and background colors of the content of a document are specified by the `color` and `background-color` properties, respectively.

The first line of a paragraph can be indented with `text-indent`. Text can be aligned with the `text-align` property, whose values are `left`, `right`, and `justify`, which means both left and right alignment. When the `float` property is set to `left` or `right`, text can be made to flow around it on the right or left, respectively, in the display window.

Borders can be specified to appear around any element. These borders can appear in any color and any of the forms, dotted, solid, dashed, or double. The margin, which is the space between the border (or the content of the element if it has no border) and the element's neighbor, can be set with the margin properties. The padding, which is the space between the content of an element and its border (or neighbor if it has no border) can be set with the padding properties.

The `background-image` property is used to place an image in the background of an element.

The `<span>` tag provides a way to include an inline style sheet that applies to a range of text that is smaller than a line or a paragraph. The `<div>` tag provides a way to define a section of a document that has its own style properties.

3.14 Review Questions

1. What is the advantage of document-level style sheets over inline style sheets?

2. What is the purpose of external style sheets?

3. What attributes are required in a link to an external style sheet?

4. What is the format of an inline style sheet?

5. What is the format of a document-level style sheet, and where does it appear?

6. What is the format of an external style sheet?

7. What is the form of comments within the rule list of a document-level style sheet?

8. What is the purpose of a style class selector?

9. What is the purpose of a generic class?

10. Are keyword property values case sensitive or case insensitive?

11. Why is a list of font names given as the value of a `font-family` property?

12. What are the five generic fonts?

13. In what order must property values appear in the list of a `font` property?

14. In what ways can text be modified with `text-decoration`?

15. How is the `list-style-type` property used with unordered lists?

16. What are the possible values of the `list-style-type` property when it is used with ordered lists?

17. If you want text to flow around the right side of an image, which value, `right` or `left`, must be assigned to the `float` property of the image?

18. Why must background images be chosen with care?

19. What are the possible values for the `text-align` property?

20. What purpose does the `text-indent` property serve?

21. What properties are used to set margins around elements?

22. What are the three ways color property values can be specified?

23. If you want a background image to be repeated vertically but not horizontally, what value must be set to what property?

24. What properties and what values must be used to put a dotted border around a text box, where the border is red and thin on the left and blue and thick on the right?

25. What layout information does a `<span>` tag by itself indicate to the browser?

26. What is the purpose of the `<div>` tag?

3.15 Exercises

1. Create an external style sheet for the chapters of this book.

2. Create and test an XHTML document that displays a table of football scores from some collegiate football conference in which the team names have one of the primary colors of their respective schools. The winning scores must appear larger and in a different font than the losing scores. The team names must be in a script font.

3. Create and test an XHTML document that includes at least two images and enough text to precede the images, flow around them (one on the left and one on the right), and continue after the last image.

4. Create and test an XHTML document that has at least a half page of text and that has a small box of text embedded on the left margin, with the main text flowing around the small box. The embedded text must appear in a smaller font and also must be set in italic.

5. Create and test an XHTML document that has six short paragraphs of text that describe various aspects of the state in which you live. You must define three different paragraph styles, p1, p2, and p3. The p1 style must use left and right margins of 20 pixels, a background color of pink, and foreground color of blue. The p2 style must use left and right margins of 30 pixels, a background color of black, and a foreground color of yellow. The p3 style must use a text indent of 1 centimeter, a background color of green, and a foreground color of white. The first and fourth paragraph must use p1, the second and fifth must use p2, and the third and sixth must use p3.

6. Create and test an XHTML document that describes nested ordered lists of cars. The outer list must have three entries: compact, midsize, and sports. Inside each of these three lists there must be two sublists of body styles. The compact and midsize car sublists are two door and four door; the sports car sublists are coupe and convertible. Each body-style sublist must have at least three entries, each of which is the make and model of a particular car that fits the category. The outer list must use uppercase Roman numerals, the middle lists must use uppercase letters, and the inner lists must use Arabic numerals. The background color for the compact car

list must be pink; for the midsize car list, it must be blue; for the sports car list, it must be red. All of the styles must be in a document style sheet.

7. Rewrite the document of Exercise 6 to put all style-sheet information in an external style sheet. Validate your external style sheet with the W3C CSS validation service.

8. Rewrite the document of Exercise 6 to use only inline style sheets.

9. Create and test an XHTML document that contains at least five lines of text from a newspaper story. Every verb in the text must be green, every noun must be blue, and every preposition must be yellow.

10. Create and test an XHTML document that describes an unordered list of at least five popular books. The bullet for each book must be a small image of the book's cover. Find the images on the Web.

4

The Basics
of JavaScript

This chapter takes you on a quick tour of the basics of JavaScript, introducing its most important concepts and constructs but leaving out many of the details of the language. Topics discussed include the following: primitive data types and their operators and expressions, screen output and keyboard input, control statements, objects and constructors, arrays, functions, and pattern matching. In spite of this chapter's brevity, if you are an experienced programmer, you should be able to learn how to be an effective JavaScript programmer by studying this chapter, along with Chapter 5, "JavaScript and XHTML Documents," and Chapter 6, "Dynamic Documents with JavaScript." More comprehensive descriptions of JavaScript can be found in the numerous books devoted solely to JavaScript.

4.1

OVERVIEW OF JAVASCRIPT

This section discusses the origins of JavaScript, a few of its characteristics, and some of its uses. Included are a comparison of JavaScript and Java and a brief introduction to event-driven programming.

4.1.1   Origins

JavaScript, which was originally named LiveScript, was developed by Netscape. In late 1995, LiveScript became a joint venture of Netscape and Sun Microsystems and its name was changed to JavaScript. Netscape's JavaScript has gone through extensive evolution, moving from version 1.0 to version 1.5, primarily by adding many new features. A language standard for JavaScript was developed in the late 1990s by the European Computer Manufacturers Association (ECMA) as ECMA-262. This standard has also been approved by the International Standards Organization (ISO) as ISO-16262. The ECMA-262 standard is now in version 3, which corresponds to Netscape's version 1.5 of JavaScript. Microsoft's JavaScript is named JScript. The Netscape 7 (NS7) and Internet Explorer 6 (IE6) browsers both implement languages that conform to ECMA-262 v3. The current standard specification can be found at `http://www.ecma.ch`. The official name of the standard language is ECMAScript. Because it is nearly always called JavaScript elsewhere, we will use that term exclusively in this book.

JavaScript can be divided into three parts: the core, client side, and server side. The *core* is the heart of the language, including its operators, expressions, statements, and subprograms. *Client-side* JavaScript is a collection of objects that support control of a browser and interactions with users. For example, with JavaScript, an XHTML document can be made to be responsive to user inputs such as mouse clicks and keyboard use. *Server-side* JavaScript is a collection of objects that make the language useful on a Web server, for example, to support communication with a database management system.

Server-side JavaScript is used far less frequently than client-side JavaScript. Because of this, this book does not cover server-side JavaScript.

Client-side JavaScript is an XHTML-embedded scripting language. We refer to every collection of JavaScript code as a *script*. An XHTML document can include any number of embedded scripts.

4.1.2   JavaScript and Java

Although JavaScript's name appears to connote a close relationship with Java, JavaScript and Java are actually very different. One important difference is support for object-oriented programming. Although JavaScript is sometimes said to be an object-oriented language, its object model is quite different from that of Java and C++, as you will see in Section 4.2. In fact, JavaScript does not support the object-oriented software development paradigm.

Java is a strongly typed language. Types are all known at compile time, and operand types are checked for compatibility. Variables in JavaScript need not be declared and are dynamically typed, making compile-time type checking impossible. One more important difference between Java and JavaScript is that objects in Java are static in the sense that their collection of data members and methods is fixed at compile time. JavaScript objects are dynamic—the number of data members and methods of an object can change during execution.

The main similarity between Java and JavaScript is the syntax of their expressions, assignment statements, and control statements.

4.1.3   Uses of JavaScript

The original goal of JavaScript was to provide programming capability at both the server and the client ends of a Web connection. Since then, JavaScript has grown into a full-fledged programming language that can be used for a variety of application areas. This book focuses on client-side JavaScript.

Client-side JavaScript can serve as an alternative for some of what is done with server-side programming, in which computational capability resides on the server and is requested by the client. Client-side JavaScript, on the other hand, is embedded in XHTML documents (either physically or logically) and is interpreted by the browser. This transfer of load from the often-overloaded server to the normally underloaded client can obviously benefit all other clients. Client-side JavaScript cannot replace all of server-side computing. In particular, while server-side software supports file operations, database access, and networking, client-side JavaScript supports none of these.

JavaScript can be used as an alternative to Java applets. JavaScript has the advantage of being easier to learn and use than Java. Also, Java applets are downloaded separately from the XHTML documents that call them; many JavaScript scripts, however, are an integral part of the XHTML document, so no secondary downloading is necessary. On the other hand, Java applets are far more capable of producing graphics in documents than are JavaScript scripts.

Interactions with users through form elements, such as buttons and menus, can be conveniently described in JavaScript. Because events, such as button clicks and mouse movements, are easily detected with JavaScript, they can be used to trigger computations and provide feedback to the user. For example, when a user moves the mouse curser from a text box, JavaScript can detect that movement and check the appropriateness of the textbox's value (which presumedly was just filled by the user). Even without forms, user interactions are both possible and simple to program. These interactions, which take place in dialog windows, include getting input from the user and allowing the user to make choices through buttons. It is also easy to dynamically generate new content in the browser display.

Another interesting capability of JavaScript has been made possible by the development of the Document Object Model (DOM), which allows JavaScript scripts to access and modify the CSS properties and content of any element of a displayed XHTML document, making formally static documents highly dynamic. Making XHTML documents dynamic with JavaScript is discussed in Chapter 6.

4.1.4 Event-Driven Computation

Much of what JavaScript scripts typically do is event driven, meaning that the actions often are executed in response to actions of the users of documents, among them mouse clicks and form submissions. This form of computation supports user interactions through the elements of the client display. One of the common uses of JavaScript is to check the values provided in forms by users to determine whether the values are sensible. Without client-side checks of such values, form values must be transmitted to the server for processing without any prior reality checks. The program or script on the server that processes the form data must find input errors and transmit that information back to the browser, which then must ask the user to resubmit alternative input. It is obviously more efficient to perform input data checks and carry on this user dialog entirely on the client. It saves both server time and Internet time. Note, however, that validity checking on form data is often also performed on the server, in part because client-side validity checking can be subverted by an unscrupulous user. For certain form data, validity is very important. One example is if the data is to be put in a database where invalid data could possibly corrupt the database.

The actual mechanics of event-driven computation in JavaScript are discussed in detail in Chapter 5.

4.1.5 Browsers and XHTML/JavaScript Documents

If an XHTML document does not include any embedded scripts, the browser reads the lines of the document and renders its window according to the tags, attributes, and content it finds. When a JavaScript script is encountered in the document, the browser uses its JavaScript interpreter to "execute" the script. When the end of the script is reached, the browser goes back to reading the XHTML document and displaying its content.

The two parts of an XHTML document, the head and the body, have distinct purposes. JavaScript scripts can appear in either part of a document, depending on their purpose. Scripts that produce content only when requested or that react to user interactions are placed in the head of the document. Generally, this means function definitions and code associated with form elements such as buttons. On the other hand, scripts that are to be interpreted just once, when the interpreter finds them, are placed in the document body. Accordingly, the interpreter notes the existence of scripts that appear in the head of a document, but it does not interpret them while going through the head. Scripts that are found in the body of a document are interpreted as they are found.

4.2
OBJECT ORIENTATION AND JAVASCRIPT

As stated previously, JavaScript is not an object-oriented programming language. Rather, it is an object-based language. JavaScript does not have classes. Its objects serve both as objects and as models of objects. Without classes, JavaScript cannot have class-based inheritance, as is supported in object-oriented languages such as C++ and Java. It does support a technique that can be used to simulate some of the aspects of inheritance. This is done with the prototype object; thus, this form of inheritance is called *prototype-based inheritance*. Prototype-based inheritance is not discussed in this book.

Without class-based inheritance, JavaScript cannot support polymorphism. A polymorphic variable can reference related objects of different classes within the same class hierarchy. A method call through such a polymorphic variable can be dynamically bound to the method in the object's class.[1]

Despite the fact that JavaScript is not an object-oriented language, much of its design is rooted in the concepts and approaches used in object-oriented programming. Specifically, client-side JavaScript deals in large part with documents and document elements, which are modeled with objects.

4.2.1 JavaScript Objects

In JavaScript, objects are collections of properties, which correspond to the members of classes in Java and C++. Each property is either a data property or a method property. Data properties appear in two categories: primitive values and references to other objects. (In JavaScript, variables that refer to objects are often called *objects* rather than *references*.) Sometimes we will refer to the data properties simply as *properties;* we often refer to the method properties simply as *methods*.

The more general category of object properties is other objects. JavaScript uses nonobject types for some of its simplest data types; these types are called *primitives*. Primitives are used because they often can be implemented directly in hardware, resulting in faster operations on their values (faster than if they were treated as objects). Primitives are like the simple scalar variables of non-object-oriented languages such as C. C++, Java, and JavaScript all have both primitives and objects; JavaScript's primitives are described in Section 4.4.

All objects in a JavaScript program are indirectly accessed through variables. Such a variable is like a reference in Java. All primitive values in JavaScript are accessed directly—these are like the scalar types in Java and C++. These are often called *value types*. The properties of an object are referenced by attaching the name of the property to the variable that references the object. For example,

---

1. This is often called *dynamic binding*. It is a significant part of full support for object-oriented programming in a language.

if `myCar` is a variable that is referencing an object that has the property `engine`, the `engine` property can be referenced with `myCar.engine`.

The root object in JavaScript is `Object`. It is the ancestor, through prototype inheritance, of all objects. `Object` is the most generic of all objects, having some methods but no properties. All other objects are specializations of `Object`, and all inherit its methods (although they are often overriden).

A JavaScript object appears, both internally and externally, as a list of property/value pairs. The properties are names; the values are data values or functions. All functions are objects and are referenced through variables. The collection of properties of a JavaScript object is dynamic—properties can be added or deleted at any time.

Every object is characterized by its collection of properties, although objects do not have types in any formal sense. Recall that `Object` is characterized by having no properties. Futher discussion of objects appears in Sections 4.7 and 4.11.

4.3

GENERAL SYNTACTIC CHARACTERISTICS

In this book, all JavaScript scripts are embedded, either directly or indirectly, in XHTML documents. Scripts can appear directly as the content of a `<script>` tag. The `type` attribute of `<script>` must be set to `"text/javascript"`. The JavaScript script can be indirectly embedded in an XHTML document using the `src` attribute of a `<script>` tag, whose value is the name of a file that contains the script. For example:

```
<script type = "text/javascript" src = "tst_number.js"/>
```

The indirect method of embedding JavaScript in XHTML documents has the advantage of hiding the script from the browser user. It also avoids the problem of hiding scripts from older browsers, which is discussed later in this section.

Identifiers, or names, in JavaScript are similar to those of other common programming languages. They must begin with a letter, an underscore (_), or a dollar sign ($).[2] Subsequent characters may be letters, underscores, dollar signs, or digits. There is no length limitation for identifiers. The letters in a variable name are case sensitive, meaning that `FRIZZY`, `Frizzy`, `FrIzZy`, `frizzy`, and `frizzy` are all distinct names. However, by convention, programmer-defined variable names do not include uppercase letters.

JavaScript has 25 reserved words, which are listed in Table 4.1.

---

2. Dollar signs are not intended to be used by user-written scripts, although it is legal.

TABLE 4.1 The Reserved Words of JavaScript

break	delete	function	return	typeof
case	do	if	switch	var
catch	else	in	this	void
continue	finally	instanceof	throw	while
default	for	new	try	with

Besides its reserved words, another collection of words is reserved for future use in JavaScript—these can be found at `http://www.ecma.ch`. In addition, JavaScript has a large collection of predefined words, including `alert`, `open`, `java`, and `self`.

JavaScript has two forms of comments, both of which are used in other languages. First, whenever two adjacent slashes (`//`) appear on a line, the rest of the line is considered a comment. Second, both single- and multiple-line comments can be written using `/*` to introduce the comment and `*/` to terminate it.

There are two issues regarding embedding JavaScript in XHTML documents. First, there are some browsers still in use that recognize the `<script>` tag but do not have JavaScript interpreters. These browsers simply ignore the contents of the script element and cause no problems. Second, there are still a few browsers in use that are so old they do not recognize the `<script>` tag. Such a browser would display the contents of the script element as if it were just text. It has been customary to enclose the contents of all script elements in XHTML comments to avoid this problem. Because there are so few browsers that do not recognize the `<script>` tag, we believe this is no longer a problem. However, the XHTML validator also has a problem with embedded JavaScript. When the embedded JavaScript happens to include recognizable tags—for example `<br />` tags in the output of the JavaScript—they often cause validation errors. Therefore, we still enclose embedded JavaScript in XHTML comments.

The XHTML comment introduction (`<!--`) works as a hiding prelude to JavaScript code. However, the syntax for closing a comment that encloses JavaScript code is special. It is the usual XHTML comment closer, but it must be on its own line and must be preceded by two slashes (which makes it a JavaScript comment). The following XHTML comment form hides the enclosed script from browsers that do not have JavaScript interpreters, but makes it visible to browsers that do support JavaScript:

```
<!--
-- JavaScript script --
// -->
```

There are other problems with putting embedded JavaScript in comments in XHTML documents. These are discussed in Chapter 6. The best solution to all of these problems is to put all JavaScript scripts in separate files.

The use of semicolons in JavaScript is unusual. The JavaScript interpreter tries to make semicolons unnecessary, but it does not always work. When the end of a line coincides with what could be the end of a statement, the interpreter effectively inserts a semicolon there. But this can lead to problems. For example, consider the following:

```
return
x;
```

The interpreter puts a semicolon after `return`, making `x` an illegal orphan. The safest way to organize JavaScript statements is to put each on its own line whenever possible and terminate each statement with a semicolon. If a statement does not fit on a line, be careful to break the statement at a place that will ensure that the first line does not have the form of a complete statement.

4.4

PRIMITIVES, OPERATIONS, AND EXPRESSIONS

The primitive data types, operations, and expressions of JavaScript are similar to those of other common programming languages. Therefore, our discussion of them is brief.

4.4.1 Primitive Types

JavaScript has five primitive types: Number, String, Boolean, Undefined, and Null.[3] All primitive values have one of these types. JavaScript includes predefined objects that are closely related to the Number, String, and Boolean types, named `Number`, `String`, and `Boolean`.[4] These three objects are called *wrapper objects*. Each contains a property that stores a value of the corresponding primitive type. Their purpose is to provide properties and methods that are convenient for use with values of the primitive types. In the case of `Number`, the properties are more useful; in the case of `String`, the methods are more useful. Because JavaScript coerces values between the Number type and `Number` objects and between the String type and `String` objects, the methods of `Number` and `String` can be used on variables of the corresponding primitive

---

3. Undefined and Null are often called *trivial* types, for reasons that will be obvious when these types are discussed in Section 4.4.3.

4. Is this confusing yet?

types. In fact, in most cases, you can simply treat Number and String type values as if they were objects.

The difference between primitives and objects is illustrated in the following example. Suppose that `prim` is a primitive variable with the value `17` and `obj` is a `Number` object whose property value is `17`. Figure 4.1 shows how `prim` and `obj` are stored.

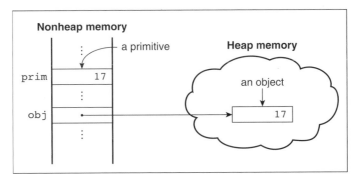

FIGURE 4.1 Primitives and objects

4.4.2 Numeric and String Literals

All numeric literals are values of type Number. The numeric values of Java-Script are represented internally in double-precision floating-point form. Because of this single numeric data type, numeric values in JavaScript are often called *numbers*. Literal numbers in a script can have the forms of either integer or floating-point values. Integer literals are strings of digits. Floating-point literals can have decimal points or exponents or both. Exponents are specified with an uppercase or lowercase `e` and a possibly signed integer literal. The following are legal numeric literals:

```
72    7.2    .72    72.    7E2    7e2    .7e2    7.e2    7.2E-2
```

Integer literals can be written in hexadecimal form by preceding their first digit with either `0x` or `0X` (the first character is zero, not o).

A string literal is a sequence of zero or more characters delimited by either single quotes (`'`) or double quotes (`"`). String literals can include characters specified with escape sequences, such as `\n` and `\t`. If you want an actual single-quote character in a string literal that is delimited by single quotes, the embedded single quote must be preceded by a backslash:

```
'You\'re the most freckly person I\'ve ever met'
```

A double quote can be embedded in a double-quoted string literal by preceding it with a backslash. An actual backslash character in any string literal must be itself backslashed, as in this example:

```
"D:\\bookfiles"
```

There is no difference between single-quoted and double-quoted literal strings. The null string (one with no characters) can be denoted with either `' '` or `""`. All string literals are primitive values.

4.4.3 Other Primitive Types

The only values of type Boolean are `true` and `false`. These values are usually computed as the result of evaluating a relational or Boolean expression (see Section 4.6.1). The existence of both the Boolean primitive type and the `Boolean` object can lead to some confusion (also discussed in Section 4.6.1).

The only value of type Null is the reserved word `null`, which indicates no value. An object reference variable has the `null` value when it does not refer to any object. When interpreted as a primitive Boolean value, `null` is `false`; as a number, it is interpreted as 0. Unlike C and C++, however, `null` is not the same as 0.

The only value of type Undefined is `undefined`. Unlike `null`, there is no reserved word `undefined`. Although `null` and `undefined` are not actually the same, in many cases they can be thought of as being the same. If a variable does not exist or has been declared but not assigned a value, it has the value `undefined`. If used as a Boolean, `undefined` is interpreted as `false`; when used as a number, it is interpreted as `NaN` (see Section 4.4.7).

4.4.4 Declaring Variables

One of the characteristics of JavaScript that sets it apart from most other common programming languages is that it is dynamically typed. This means that a variable can be used for anything. It can have the value of any primitive type, or it can be a reference to any object. The type of a particular appearance of a variable in a program is determined by the interpreter. In many cases, the interpreter converts the type of a variable to whatever is needed for the context in which it appears.

A variable can be declared either by assigning it a value, in which case the interpreter implicitly declares it to be a variable, or by listing it in a declaration statement that begins with the reserved word `var`. Initial values can be included in a `var` declaration, as with some of the variables in the following declaration:

```
var counter,
    index,
    pi = 3.14159265,
    quarterback = "Elway",
    stop_flag = true;
```

We recommend that all variables be explicitly declared.

As stated previously, a variable that has been declared but not assigned a value has the value `undefined`.

4.4.5 Numeric Operators

JavaScript has the typical collection of numeric operators. These are the binary operators + for addition, – for subtraction, * for multiplication, / for division, and % for modulus. The unary operators are negate (–), decrement (– –), and increment (++). The increment and decrement operators can be either prefix or postfix.[5] As with other languages that have the increment and decrement unary operators, the prefix and postfix uses are not always equivalent. Consider an expression consisting of a single variable and one of these operators. If the operator precedes the variable, the value of the variable is changed and the expression evaluates to the new value. If the operator follows the variable, the expression evaluates to the current value of the variable, and then the value of the variable is changed. For example, if the variable a has the value 7, the value of the following expression is 24:

```
(++a) * 3
```

But the value of the following expression is 21:

```
(a++) * 3
```

In both cases, a is set to 8.

All numeric operations are done in double-precision floating point.

The *precedence rules* of a language specify which operator is evaluated first when two operators with different precedence are adjacent in an expression. Adjacent operators are separated by a single operand. For example, * and + are adjacent here:

```
a * b + 1
```

The *associativity rules* of a language specify which operator is evaluated first when two operators with the same precedence are adjacent in an expression. The precedence and associativity of the numeric operators of JavaScript are given in Table 4.2.

---

5. *Prefix* means that the operator precedes its operand; *postfix* means that the operator follows its operand.

TABLE 4.2 Precedence and Associativity of the Numeric Operators

Operator	Associativity
++, --, unary -	Right (though it is irrelevant)
*, /, %	Left
Binary +, binary -	Left

The first operators listed have the highest precedence.

As examples of operator precedence and associativity, consider the following code:

```
var a = 2,
    b = 4,
    c,
    d;
    c = 3 + a * b;
// * is first, so c is now 11 (not 24)
    d = b / a / 2;
// / associates left, so d is now 1 (not 4)
```

Parentheses can be used to force any desired precedence. For example, the addition will be done before the multiplication in the following expression:

```
(a + b) * c
```

4.4.6 The Math Object

The Math object provides a collection of properties of Number objects and methods that operate on Number objects. The Math object has methods for the trigonometric functions, such as sin (for sine) and cos (for cosine), as well as for other commonly used mathematical operations. Among these are floor, to truncate a number; round, to round a number; and max, to return the largest of two given numbers. The floor and round methods are used in the example script in Section 4.10. All of the Math methods are referenced through the Math object, as in Math.sin(x).

4.4.7 The Number Object

The Number object includes a collection of useful properties that have constant values. Table 4.3 lists the properties of Number. These properties are referenced through Number. For example:

```
Number.MIN_VALUE
```

TABLE 4.3 Properties of Number

Property	Meaning
MAX_VALUE	Largest representable number
MIN_VALUE	Smallest representable number
NaN	Not a number
POSITIVE_INFINITY	Special value to represent infinity
NEGATIVE_INFINITY	Special value to represent negative infinity
PI	The value of π

Any arithmetic operation that results in an error (for example, division by zero) or that produces a value that cannot be represented as a double-precision floating-point number, such as one that is too large (overflow), returns the value "not a number," which is displayed as NaN. If NaN is compared for equality against any number, the comparison fails. Remarkably, in a comparison, NaN is not equal to itself. To determine whether a variable has the NaN value, the predefined predicate function isNaN() must be used. For example, if the variable a has the NaN value, isNaN(a) returns true.

The Number object has a method, toString, which it inherits from Object but overrides, that converts the number through which it is called to a string. Because numeric primitives and Number objects are always coerced to the other when necessary, toString can be called through a numeric primitive. For example:

```
var price = 427,
  str_price;
...
str_price = price.toString();
```

4.4.8   The String Catenation Operator

JavaScript strings are not stored or treated as arrays of characters; rather, they are unit scalar values. String catenation is specified with the operator denoted by a plus sign (+). For example, if the value of first is "Freddie", the value of the following expression is "Freddie Freeloader":

```
first + " Freeloader"
```

4.4.9   Implicit Type Conversions

The JavaScript interpreter performs several different implicit type conversions. Such conversions are called *coercions*. In general, when a value of one type is used in a situation that requires a value of a different type, JavaScript attempts to convert the value to the type that is required. The most common examples of these conversions involve primitive string and number values.

If either operand of a + operator is a string, the operator is interpreted as a string catenation operator. If the other operand is not a string, it is coerced to a string. For example, consider the following expression:

```
"August " + 1977
```

In this expression, because the left operand is a string, the operator is considered to be a catenation operator. This forces string context on the right operand, so the right operand is implicitly converted to a string. Therefore, this expression evaluates to the following:

```
"August 1997"
```

The number 1977 in the following expression is also coerced to a string:

```
1977 + "August"
```

Now consider this expression:

```
7 * "3"
```

In this expression, the operator is one that is only used with numbers. This forces numeric context on the right operand. JavaScript therefore attempts to convert it to a number. In this example, the conversion succeeds, and the value of this expression is 21. If the second operand were a string that could not be converted to a number, such as "August", the conversion would produce NaN, which would be the value of the expression.

As we shall see in Section 4.6.1, the relational operators also cause implicit type conversions.

4.4.10 Explicit Type Conversions

There are several different ways to force type conversions, primarily between strings and numbers. Strings that contain numbers can be converted to numbers with the String constructor, as in the following:

```
var str_value = String(value);
```

This conversion could also be done with the toString method, which has the advantage that it can be given a parameter to specify the base of the resulting number (although the base of the number to be converted is taken to be decimal). For example:

```
var num = 6;
var str_value = num.toString();
var str_value_binary = num.toString(2);
```

In the first conversion, the result is `"6"`; in the second, it is `"110"`.

A number also can be converted to a string by catenating it with the empty string. Strings can be explicitly converted to numbers in a variety of ways. The `Number` constructor can be used, as in the following:

```
var number = Number(aString);
```

The same conversion could be specified by subtracting zero from the string, as in the following:

```
var number = aString - 0;
```

Both of these conversions have the following restriction: The number in the string cannot be followed by any character except a space. For example, if the number happens to be followed by a comma, the conversion will not work.

JavaScript has two predefined string functions that do not have that problem. These two, `parseInt` and `parseFloat`, are not `String` methods, so they are not called through `String` objects. However, they operate on the strings given as parameters. The `parseInt` function searches the string for an integer literal. If one is found at the beginning of the string, it is converted to a number and returned. If the string does not begin with a valid integer literal, `NaN` is returned. The `parseFloat` function is similar to `parseInt`, but it searches for a floating-point literal, which could have a decimal point or an exponent. In both `parseInt` and `parseFloat`, the numeric literal could be followed by any nondigit character without causing any problems.

Because of the coercions JavaScript normally does, as discussed in Section 4.4.9, `parseInt` and `parseFloat` are not often needed.

4.4.11 `String` Properties and Methods

Because JavaScript coerces primitive string values to and from `String` objects when necessary, the differences between the `String` object and the String type have little effect on scripts. `String` methods can always be used through String primitive values, as if the values were objects. The `String` object includes one property, `length`, and a large collection of methods.

The number of characters in a string is stored in the `length` property:

```
var str = "George";
var len = str.length;
```

In this code, `len` is set to the number of characters in `str`, 6. In the expression `str.length`, `str` is a primitive variable, but we treated it as if it were an object (referencing one of its properties). In fact, when `str` is used with the `length` property, JavaScript implicitly builds a temporary `String` object with a property whose value is that of the primitive variable. After the second statement is executed, the temporary `String` object is discarded.

A few of the most commonly used `String` methods are shown in Table 4.4.

TABLE 4.4 `String` Methods

Method	Parameters	Result
charAt	A number	The character in the `String` object that is at the specified position
indexOf	One-character string	The position in the `String` object of the parameter
substring	Two numbers	The substring of the `String` object from the first parameter position to the second
toLowerCase	None	Converts any uppercase letters in the string to lowercase
toUpperCase	None	Converts any lowercase letters in the string to uppercase

For example, suppose `str` has been defined as follows:

```
var str = "George";
```

The following expressions have the shown values:

```
str.charAt(2)    is 'o'
str.indexOf('r') is 3
str.substring(2, 4) is 'org'
str.toLowerCase() is 'george'
```

Several `String` methods associated with pattern matching are described in Section 4.12.

4.4.12   The `typeof` Operator

The `typeof` operator returns the type of its single operand. This is quite useful in some circumstances in a script. `typeof` evaluates to `"number"`, `"string"`, or `"boolean"` if the operand is of primitive type Number, String, or Boolean, respectively. If the operand is an object or `null`, `typeof` evaluates to `"object"`. This illustrates a fundamental characteristic of JavaScript—objects do not have types. If the operand is `undefined`, `typeof` evaluates to the string `"undefined"`. Notice that the `typeof` operator always returns a string. The operand for `typeof` can be placed in parentheses, making it appear to be a function. Therefore, `typeof x` and `typeof(x)` are equivalent.

4.4.13 Assignment Statements

The assignment statement in JavaScript is exactly like the assignment statement in other common C-based programming languages. There is a simple assignment operator, denoted by =, and a host of compound assignment operators, such as += and /=. For example, the statement

```
a += 7;
```

means the same as this one:

```
a = a + 7;
```

4.4.14 The Date Object

There are occasions when information about the current date and time is useful in a program. Likewise, sometimes it is convenient to be able to create objects that represent a specific date and time and manipulate them. These capabilities are available in JavaScript through the Date object and its rich collection of methods. In the following, we describe this object and some of its methods.

A Date object is created, naturally, with the new operator and the Date constructor, which has several forms. Because we focus on uses of the current date and time, we use only the simplest Date constructor, which takes no parameters and builds an object with the current date and time for its properties. For example:

```
var today = new Date();
```

The date and time properties of a Date object are in two forms, local and Coordinated Universal Time (UTC, which was formally named Greenwich Mean Time). We only deal with local time in this section.

Table 4.5 shows the methods, along with the descriptions, that retrieve information from a Date object.

TABLE 4.5 Methods for the Date Object

Method	Returns
toLocaleString	A string of the Date information
getDate	The day of the month
getMonth	The month of the year, as a number in the range of 1 to 31
getDay	The day of the week, as a number in the range of 0 to 6

continued

TABLE 4.5 Methods for the `Date` Object (Continued)

Method	Returns
getFullYear	The year
getTime	The number of milliseconds since January 1, 1970
getHours	The number of the hour, as a number in the range of 0 to 23
getMinutes	The number of the minute, as a number in the range of 0 to 59
getSeconds	The number of the second, as a number in the range of 0 to 59
getMilliseconds	The number of the millisecond, as a number in the range of 0 to 999

The use of the `Date` object is illustrated in Section 4.6.

4.5

SCREEN OUTPUT AND KEYBOARD INPUT

A JavaScript script is interpreted when the browser finds the script in the body of the XHTML document. Thus, the normal output screen for JavaScript is the same as the screen in which the content of the host XHTML is displayed. Java-Script models the XHTML document with the `Document` object. The window in which the browser displays an XHTML document is modeled with the `Window` object. The `Window` object includes two properties, `document` and `window`. The `document` property refers to the `Document` object. The `window` property is self referential; it refers to the object, `Window`.

The `Document` object has several properties and methods. The most interesting and useful of its methods, at least for now, is `write`, which is used to create script output, which is dynamically created XHTML document content.[6] This content is specified in the parameter to `write`. For example, the following produces the screen shown in Figure 4.2:

```
document.write("The result is: ", result, "<br />");
```

The result is: 42

FIGURE 4.2 An example of the output of `document.write`

---

6. The XML Document Object Model does not require XML agents (processors) to implement `write`, although that was likely the intention. Therefore, if an XHTML document is served as XML, some browsers may reject any embedded calls to `write`. However, most XHTML documents are now served as HTML and we believe most browsers will implement `write` for their XML parsers, so we will use `write` in many of our examples.

Because `write` is used to create XHTML code, the only useful punctuation in its parameter is in the form of XHTML tags. Therefore, the parameter to `write` often includes `<br />`. The `writeln` method implicitly adds `"\n"` to its parameter, but since browsers ignore line breaks when displaying XHTML, is has no effect on the output.[7]

The parameter to `write` can include any XHTML tags and content. The parameter is simply given to the browser, which treats it exactly like any other part of the XHTML document. The `write` method actually can take any number of parameters. Multiple parameters are concatenated and placed in the output.

As stated previously, the `Window` object is the JavaScript model for the browser window. `Window` includes three methods that create dialog boxes for specific kinds of user interactions. The default object for JavaScript is the `Window` object currently being displayed, so calls to these methods need not include an object reference.

The `alert` method opens a dialog window and displays its parameter in that window. It also displays a button labeled OK. The parameter string to `alert` is not XHTML code; it is plain text. Therefore, the string parameter to `alert` may include \n but never `<br />`. As an example of an `alert`, consider the following code, which produces the dialog window shown in Figure 4.3:

```
alert("The sum is:" + sum + "\n");
```

FIGURE 4.3 An example of the output of `alert`

The `confirm` method opens a dialog window in which it displays its string parameter, along with two buttons, OK and Cancel. `confirm` returns a Boolean value that indicates the user's button input: `true` for OK and `false` for Cancel. This method is often used to offer the user the choice of continuing some process. For example, the following statement produces the screen shown in Figure 4.4:

```
var question =
      confirm("Do you want to continue this download?");
```

---

7. The `writeln` method is useful only if the browser is used to view a non-XHTML document, which is rarely done.

After the user presses one of the buttons in the confirm dialog window, the script can test the variable, question, and react accordingly.

FIGURE 4.4 An example of the output of confirm

The prompt method creates a dialog window that contains a text box. The text box is used to collect a string of input from the user, which prompt returns as its value. The window also includes two buttons, OK and Cancel. prompt takes two parameters: the string that prompts the user for input and a default string in case the user does not type a string before pressing one of the two buttons. In many cases, an empty string is used for the default input. Consider the following example:

```
name = prompt("What is your name?, "");
```

Figure 4.5 shows the screen created by this call to prompt.

Explorer User Prompt

Script Prompt:

What is your name?

OK

Cancel

FIGURE 4.5 An example of the output of prompt

alert, prompt, and confirm cause the browser to wait for a user response. In the cases of alert and prompt, the OK button must be pressed for the JavaScript interpreter to continue. The confirm method waits for either OK or Cancel to be pressed.

The following example, roots.html, illustrates some of the JavaScript features described so far. It gets the coefficients of a quadratic equation from the user with prompt and computes and displays the real roots of the given equation. If the roots of the equation are not real, the value NaN is displayed. This value comes from the sqrt function, which returns NaN when given a negative parameter. This corresponds mathematically to the equation not having real roots.

```
<?xml version = "1.0" encoding = "utf-8"?>
<!DOCTYPE html PUBLIC "-//w3c//DTD XHTML 1.1//EN"
  "http://www.w3.org/TR/xhtml11/DTD/xhtml11.dtd">


<!-- roots.html
     Compute the real roots of a given quadratic
     equation. If the roots are imaginary, this script
     displays NaN, because that is what results from
     taking the square root of a negative number
     -->
<html xmlns = "http://www.w3.org/1999/xhtml">
  <head>
    <title> Real roots of a quadratic equation </title>
  </head>
  <body>
    <script type = "text/javascript">
      <!--

// Get the coefficients of the equation from the user

        var a = prompt("What is the value of 'a'? \n", "");
        var b = prompt("What is the value of 'b'? \n", "");
        var c = prompt("What is the value of 'c'? \n", "");

// Compute the square root and denominator of the result

        var root_part = Math.sqrt(b * b - 4.0 * a * c);
        var denom = 2.0 * a;

// Compute and display the two roots

        var root1 = (-b + root_part) / denom;
        var root2 = (-b - root_part) / denom;
        document.write("The first root is: ", root1, "<br />");
        document.write("The second root is: ", root2, "<br />");
        // -->
    </script>
  </body>
</html>
```

4.6

CONTROL STATEMENTS

This section introduces the flow-control statements of JavaScript. Before discussing the control statements, we must describe the control expressions, which provide the basis for controlling the order of execution of statements. Once again, the similarity of these JavaScript constructs to their counterparts in Java and C++ makes them easy to learn for those who are familiar with one of those languages.

Control statements often require some syntactic container for sequences of statements whose execution they are meant to control. In JavaScript, that container is the compound statement. A *compound statement* in JavaScript is a sequence of statements delimited by braces. A *control construct* is a control statement and the statement or compound statement whose execution it controls.

Unlike several related languages, JavaScript does not allow compound statements to create local variables. If a variable is declared in a compound statement, access to it is not confined to that compound statement. Such a variable is visible in the whole XHTML document.[8] Local variables are discussed in Section 4.9.2.

4.6.1 Control Expressions

The expressions upon which statement flow control can be based include primitive values, relational expressions, and compound expressions. The result of evaluating a control expression is one of the Boolean values `true` or `false`. If the value of a control expression is a string, it is interpreted as `true` unless it is either the empty string (`""`) or a zero string (`"0"`). If the value is a number, it is `true` unless it is zero (`0`).

A relational expression has two operands and one relational operator. Table 4.5 lists the relational operators.

If the two operands are not of the same type and the operator is neither `===` nor `!==`, JavaScript will attempt to convert the operands to a single type. In the case in which one operand is a string and the other is a number, JavaScript attempts to convert the string to a number. If one operand is Boolean and the other is not, the Boolean value is converted to a number (`1` for `true`, `0` for `false`).

The last two operators in Table 4.6 disallow type conversion of either operand. Thus, the expression `"3" === 3` evaluates to `false`, while `"3" == 3` evaluates to `true`.

---

8. The exception to this rule is if the variable is declared in a function.

TABLE 4.6 Relational Operators

Operation	Operator
Is equal to	==
Is not equal to	!=
Is less than	<
Is greater than	>
Is less than or equal to	<=
Is greater than or equal to	>=
Is strictly equal to	===
Is strictly not equal to	!==

Comparisons of variables that reference objects are rarely useful. If a and b reference different objects, a == b is never true, even if the objects have identical properties. a == b is true only if a and b reference the same object.

JavaScript has operators for the AND, OR, and NOT Boolean operations. These are && (AND), || (OR), and ! (NOT). Both && and || are short-circuit operators, as they are in Java and C++. This means that if the value of the first operand of either || or && determines the value of the expression, the second operand is not evaluated, and the Boolean operator does nothing. JavaScript also has bitwise operators, but they are not discussed in this book.

The properties of the object Boolean must not be confused with the primitive values true and false. If a Boolean object is used as a conditional expression, it evaluates to true if it has any value other than null or undefined. The Boolean object has a method, toString, which it inherits from Object, that converts the value of the object through which it is called to one of the strings "true" or "false".

The precedence and associativity of all operators discussed so far in this chapter are shown in Table 4.7.

4.6.2 Selection Statements

The selection statements (if-then and if-then-else) of JavaScript are similar to those of the common programming languages. Either single statements or compound statements can be selected. For example:

```
if (a > b)
    document.write("a is greater than b <br />");
else {
    a = b;
    document.write("a was not greater than b <br />",
                "Now they are equal <br />");
}
```

TABLE 4.7 Operator Precedence and Associativity

Operators	Associativity
++, --, unary -	Right
*, /, %	Left
+, -	Left
>, <, >= ,<=	Left
==, !＝	Left
===,!==	Left
&&	Left
||	Left
=, +=, -=, *=, /=, &&=, ||=, %=	Right

Highest-precedence operators are listed first.

4.6.3   The `switch` Statement

JavaScript has a `switch` statement that is similar to that of C. The form of this construct is shown here:

```
switch (expression) {
    case value_1:
        // statement(s)
    case value_2:
        // statement(s)
    ...
    [default:
        // statement(s)]
}
```

In any case, the statement(s) can be either a statement sequence or a compound statement.

The semantics of a `switch` construct are as follows: The expression is evaluated when the `switch` statement is reached in execution. The value is compared to the values in the cases in the construct (those values that immediately follow the `case` reserved words). If one matches, control is transferred to the statements immediately following that case value. Execution then continues through the remainder of the construct. In the great majority of situations, it is intended that only the statements in one case be executed in each execution of the construct. To implement this, a `break` statement appears as the last statement in each sequence of statements following a case. The break statement is exactly like the break statement in Java and C++. It transfers control out of the compound statement in which it appears.

The control expression of a switch statement could evaluate to a number, a string, or a Boolean value. Case labels also can be numbers, strings, or Booleans, and different case values can be of different types. Consider the following document, which includes a script with a switch construct:

```
<?xml version = "1.0" encoding = "utf-8"?>
<!DOCTYPE html PUBLIC "-//w3c//DTD XHTML 1.1//EN"
  "http://www.w3.org/TR/xhtml11/DTD/xhtml11.dtd">


<!-- borders2.html
     An example of a switch statement for table border
     size selection
     -->
<html xmlns = "http://www.w3.org/1999/xhtml">
  <head> <title> A switch statement </title>
  </head>
  <body>
    <script type = "text/javascript">
      <!--
      var bordersize;
      bordersize = prompt("Select a table border size \n" +
                     "0 (no border) \n" +
                     "1 (1 pixel border) \n" +
                     "4 (4 pixel border) \n" +
                     "8 (8 pixel border) \n");

      switch (bordersize) {
        case "0": document.write("<table>");
              break;
        case "1": document.write("<table border = '1'>");
              break;
        case "4": document.write("<table border = '4'>");
              break;
        case "8": document.write("<table border = '8'>");
              break;
        default:  document.write("Error - invalid choice: ",
                        bordersize, "<br />");
      }
```

continued

```
        document.write("<caption> 2003 NFL Divisional",
                        " Winners </caption>");
        document.write("<tr>",
                        "<th />",
                        "<th> American Conference </th>",
                        "<th> National Conference </th>",
                        "</tr>",
                        "<tr>",
                        "<th> East </th>",
                        "<td> New England Patriots </td>",
                        "<td> Philadelphia Eagles </td>",
                        "</tr>",
                        "<tr>",
                        "<th> North </th>",
                        "<td> Baltimore Ravens </td>",
                        "<td> Green Bay Packers </td>",
                        "</tr>",
                        "<tr>",
                        "<th> West </th>",
                        "<td> Kansas City Chiefs </td>",
                        "<td> St. Louis Rams </td>",
                        "</tr>",
                        "<tr>",
                        "<th> South </th>",
                        "<td> Indianapolis Colts </td>",
                        "<td> Carolina Panthers </td>",
                        "</tr>",
                        "</table>");
        // -->
      </script>
    </body>
</html>
```

The entire table element is produced with write. Alternatively, we could have given all of the elements for the table, except the <table> and </table> tags, directly as XHTML. Because <table> is in the content of the script element, the validator would not see it. Therefore, the </table> tag would also need to be hidden.

Browser displays of the prompt dialog box and the output of borders2.html are shown in Figures 4.6 and 4.7, respectively.

FIGURE 4.6 Dialog box from `borders2.html`

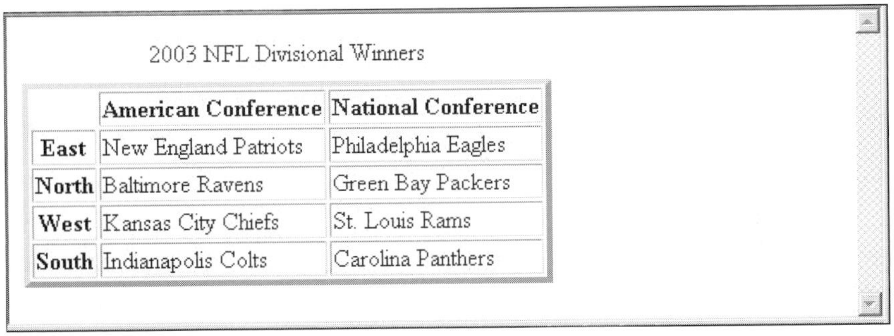

FIGURE 4.7 Display of `borders2.html`

4.6.4 Loop Statements

The JavaScript `while` and `for` statements are similar to those of Java and C++. The general form of the `while` statement is as follows:

`while` *(control expression)* *statement or compound statement*

The following is an example that illustrates the `Date` object and a simple `while` loop.

```
<?xml version = "1.0" encoding = "utf-8"?>
<!DOCTYPE html PUBLIC "-//w3c//DTD XHTML 1.1//EN"
  "http://www.w3.org/TR/xhtml11/DTD/xhtml11.dtd">

<!-- date.html
     Illustrates the use of the Date object by
     displaying the parts of a current date and
     using two Date objects to time a calculation
     -->
```

continued

```
<html xmlns = "http://www.w3.org/1999/xhtml">
  <head>
    <title> Illustrates Date </title>
  </head>
  <body>
    <script type = "text/javascript">
      <!--

// Get the current date

      var today = new Date();

// Fetch the various parts of the date

      var dateString = today.toLocaleString();
      var day = today.getDay();
      var month = today.getMonth();
      var year = today.getFullYear();
      var timeMilliseconds = today.getTime();
      var hour = today.getHours();
      var minute = today.getMinutes();
      var second = today.getSeconds();
      var millisecond = today.getMilliseconds();

// Display the parts

      document.write(
        "Date: " + dateString + "<br />",
        "Day: " + day + "<br />",
        "Month: " + month + "<br />",
        "Year: " + year + "<br />",
        "Time in milliseconds: " + timeMilliseconds + "<br />",
        "Hour: " + hour + "<br />",
        "Minute: " + minute + "<br />",
        "Second: " + second + "<br />",
        "Millisecond: " + millisecond + "<br />");

// Time a loop

      var dum1 = 1.00149265, product = 1;
      var start = new Date();

      for (var count = 0; count < 10000; count++)
        product = product + 1.000002 * dum1 / 1.00001;
```

```
      var end = new Date();
      var diff = end.getTime() - start.getTime();
      document.write("<br />The loop took " + diff +
                  " milliseconds <br />");
      // -->
    </script>
  </body>
</html>
```

A display of `date.html` is shown in Figure 4.8.

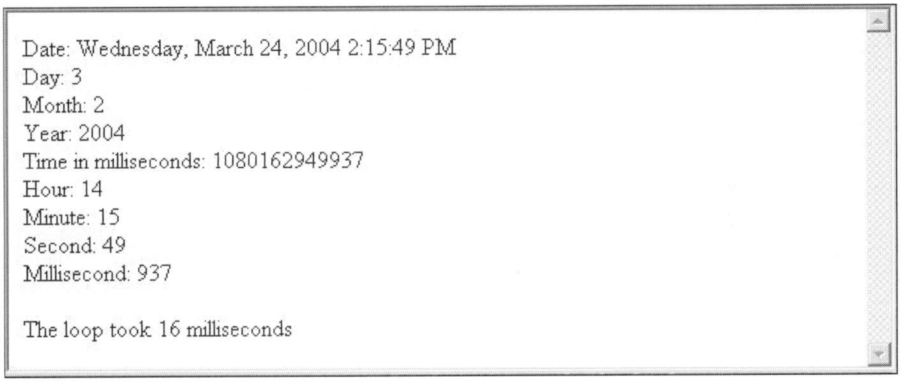

```
Date: Wednesday, March 24, 2004 2:15:49 PM
Day: 3
Month: 2
Year: 2004
Time in milliseconds: 1080162949937
Hour: 14
Minute: 15
Second: 49
Millisecond: 937

The loop took 16 milliseconds
```

FIGURE 4.8 Display of `date.html`

The general form of the `for` statement is as follows:

`for` (*initial expression; control expression; increment expression*)
     statement or compound statement

Both the initial expression and the increment expression can be multiple expressions, separated by commas. The initial expression of a `for` statement can include variable declarations. Such variables are visible in the entire script unless the `for` statement is in a function definition, in which case the variable is visible in the whole function. The following illustrates a simple `for` construct:

```
var sum = 0,
    count;
for (count = 0; count <= 10; count++)
    sum += count;
```

In addition to the `while` and `for` loop statements, JavaScript also has a `do-while` statement, whose form is as follows:

`do` *statement or compound statement* `while` (*control expression*)

The `do-while` statement is related to the `while` statement, but the test for completion is logically at the end rather than the beginning of the loop construct. The body of a `do-while` construct is always executed at least once. The following is an example of a `do-while` construct:

```
do {
    count++;
    sum = sum + (sum * count);
} while count <= 50;
```

JavaScript includes one more loop statement, the `for-in` statement, which is most often used with objects. The `for-in` statement is discussed in Section 4.7.

4.7

OBJECT CREATION AND MODIFICATION

Objects are often created with a `new` expression, which must include a call to a constructor method. The constructor that is called in the `new` expression creates the properties that characterize the new object. In an object-oriented language such as Java, the `new` operator creates a particular object, meaning an object with a type and a specific collection of members. Thus, in Java, the constructor initializes members but does not create them. In JavaScript, however, the `new` operator creates a blank object, or one with no properties. Furthermore, JavaScript objects do not have types. The constructor both creates and initializes the properties.

The following statement creates an object that initially has no properties:

```
var my_object = new Object();
```

In this case, the called constructor is that of `Object`, which endows the new object with no properties, although it does have some methods. The variable `my_object` references the new object. Calls to constructors must include parentheses, even if there are no parameters. Constructors are discussed in detail in Section 4.11.

The properties of an object are accessed using dot notation, in which the first word is the object name and the second is the property name. Properties are not actually variables—they are just the names of values. They are used with object variables to access property values. Because properties are not variables, they are never declared.

The number of members of a class in a typical object-oriented language is fixed at compile time. The number of properties in a JavaScript object is dynamic. At any time during interpretation, properties can be added to or deleted from an object. A property for an object is created by assigning a value to that property. Consider the following example:

```
// Create an Object object
var my_car = new Object();
// Create and initialize the make property
my_car.make = "Ford";
// Create and initialize model
my_car.model = "Contour SVT";
```

This code creates a new object, `my_car`, with two properties, `make` and `model`. Because objects can be nested, you can create a new object that is a property of `my_car` with properties of its own:

```
my_car.engine = new Object();
my_car.engine.config = "V6";
my_car.engine.hp = 200;
```

Properties can be accessed in two ways. First, any property can be accessed in the same way it is assigned a value, using the object-dot-property notation. Second, the property names of an object can be accessed as if they were elements of an array, using the property name (as a string literal) as a subscript. For example, consider the following statements:

```
var prop1 = my_car.make;
var prop2 = my_car["make"];
```

After executing these two statements, the variables `prop1` and `prop2` both have the value `"Ford"`.

If an attempt is made to access a property of an object that does not exist, the value `undefined` is used. A property can be deleted with `delete`, as in the following example:

```
delete my_car.model;
```

JavaScript has a loop statement, `for-in`, that is perfect for listing the properties of an object. The form of `for-in` is as follows:

```
for (identifier in object) statement or compound statement
```

Consider the following example:

```
for (var prop in my_car)
document.write("Name: ", prop, "; Value: ",
               my_car[prop], "<br />");
```

The variable, `prop`, takes on the values of the properties of the `my_car` object, one for each iteration. So, this code lists all of the values of the properties of `my_car`.

4.8

ARRAYS

Arrays in JavaScript are objects that have some special functionality. Array elements can be primitive values or references to other objects, including other arrays. JavaScript arrays have dynamic length.

4.8.1 Array Object Creation

`Array` objects, unlike most other JavaScript objects, can be created in two distinct ways. The usual way to create any object is with the `new` operator and a call to a constructor. In the case of arrays, the constructor is named `Array`:

```
var my_list = new Array(1, 2, "three", "four");
var your_list = new Array(100);
```

In the first declaration, an `Array` object of length 4 is created and initialized. Notice that the elements of an array need not have the same type. In the second declaration, a new `Array` object of length 100 is created, without actually creating any elements. Whenever a call to the `Array` constructor has a single parameter, that parameter is taken to be the number of elements, not the initial value of a one-element array.

The second way to create an `Array` object is with a literal array value, which is a list of values enclosed in brackets:

```
var my_list_2 = [1, 2, "three", "four"];
```

The array `my_list_2` has the same values as the `Array` object `my_list` created previously with `new`.

4.8.2 Characteristics of Array Objects

The lowest index of every JavaScript array is zero. Array element access is specified with numeric subscript expressions placed in brackets. The length of an array is the highest subscript to which a value has been assigned, plus 1. So, if the assignment to `my_list` that has the highest subscript is the following, then the length of `my_list` is 48:

```
my_list[47] = 2222;
```

The length of an array is both read- and write-accessible through the `length` property, which is added to every array object by the `Array` constructor. Consequently, the length of an array can be set to whatever you like by assigning the `length` property:

```
my_list.length = 1002;
```

Now, the length of `my_list` is 1002, regardless of what it was previously. Assigning a value to the `length` property can lengthen, shorten, or not affect the array's length (if the value assigned happens to be the same as the previous length of the array).

Only the assigned elements of an array actually occupy space. For example, if it is convenient to use the subscript range of 100 to 150 but not 0 to 99, an array of length 151 can be created. But if only the elements indexed 100 to 150 are assigned values, the array will require the space of 51 elements, not 151. Remember that the `length` property of an array is not necessarily the number of defined or even allocated elements. For example, the following statement sets the `length` property of `my_list` to 1002, but `my_list` may have no elements that have values or occupy space:

```
my_list.length = 1002;
```

To support JavaScript's dynamic arrays, all array elements are allocated dynamically from the heap.

The following example, `insert_names.html`, illustrates JavaScript arrays. This script has an array of names, which are in alphabetical order. It uses `prompt` to get new names, one at a time, and inserts them into the existing array. Our approach is to move elements down one at a time, starting at the end of the array, until the correct position for the new name is found. Then the new name is inserted, and the new array is displayed. Notice that each new name causes the array to grow by one element.

```
<?xml version = "1.0" encoding = "utf-8"?>
<!DOCTYPE html PUBLIC "-//w3c//DTD XHTML 1.1//EN"
  "http://www.w3.org/TR/xhtml11/DTD/xhtml11.dtd">

<!-- insert_names.html
    The script in this document has an array of
    names, name_list, whose values are in
    alphabetic order. New names are input through
    prompt. Each new name is inserted into the
    name array, after which the new list is
    displayed.
    -->
```

continued

```
<html xmlns = "http://www.w3.org/1999/xhtml">
  <head> <title> Name list </title>
  </head>
  <body>
    <script type = "text/javascript">
      <!--
// The original list of names

      var name_list = new Array("Al", "Betty", "Kasper",
                      "Michael", "Roberto", "Zimbo");
      var new_name, index, last;

// Loop to get a new name and insert it

      while (new_name =
              prompt("Please type a new name", "")) {

// Loop to find the place for the new name

        last = name_list.length - 1;

        while (last >= 0 && name_list[last] > new_name) {
          name_list[last + 1] = name_list[last];
          last--;
        }

// Insert the new name into its spot in the array

        name_list[last + 1] = new_name;

// Display the new array

        document.write("<p><b>The new name list is:</b> ",
                  "<br />");
        for (index = 0; index < name_list.length; index++)
          document.write(name_list[index], "<br />");
        document.write("</p>");
      } //** end of the outer while loop
      // -->
    </script>
  </body>
</html>
```

4.8.3 Array Methods

Array objects have a collection of useful methods, most of which are described here. The join method converts all of the elements of an array to strings and catenates them into a single string. If no parameter is provided to join, the values in the new string are separated by commas. If a string parameter is provided, it is used as the element separator:

```
var names = new Array["Mary", "Murray",
                       "Murphy", "Max"];
...
var name_string = names.join(" : ");
```

The value of name_string is now "Mary : Murray : Murphy : Max".

The reverse method does what you would expect: It reverses the order of the elements of the Array object through which it is called.

The sort method coerces the elements of the array to strings, if they are not already strings, and sorts them into alphabetical order:

```
names.sort();
```

The value of names is now ["Mary", "Max", "Murphy", "Murray"]. Section 4.9.4 discusses the use of sort for different orders and for nonstring elements.

The concat method catenates its actual parameters to the end of the Array object on which it is called. For example, consider this code:

```
var names = new Array["Mary", "Murray",
                       "Murphy", "Max"];
...
var new_names = names.concat("Moo", "Meow");
```

The new_names array now has length 6, with the elements of name, along with "Moo" and "Meow" as its fifth and sixth elements.

The slice method does for arrays what the substring method does for strings. It returns the part of the Array object specified by its parameters, which are used as subscripts. The returned array has the elements of the array object through which it is called from the first parameter up to but not including the second parameter. For example:

```
var list = [2, 4, 6, 8, 10];
...
var list2 = list.slice(1, 3);
```

The value of `list2` is now `[4, 6]`. If `slice` is given just one parameter, the returned array has all of the elements of the object, starting with the specified index:

```
var list = ["Bill", "Will", "Jill", "dill"];
...
var listette = list.slice(2);
```

The value of `listette` is `["Jill", "dill"]`.

When the `toString` method is called through an `Array` object, each of the elements of the object is converted (if necessary) to a string. These strings are concatenated, separated by commas. So, for `Array` objects, the `toString` method behaves much like `join`.

The `push`, `pop`, `unshift`, and `shift` methods of `Array` allow the easy implementation of stacks and queues in arrays. The `pop` and `push` methods remove and add an element to the high end of an array, respectively. For example, consider the following code:

```
var list = ["Dasher", "Dancer", "Donner", "Blitzen"];
var deer = list.pop();     // deer is "Blitzen"
list.push("Blitzen");
  // This puts "Blitzen" back on list
```

The `shift` and `unshift` methods remove and add an element to the beginning of an array, respectively. For example, assume that `list` is created as previously and consider the following code:

```
var deer = list.shift();   // deer is now "Dasher"
list.unshift("Dasher");
  // This puts "Dasher" back on list
```

A two-dimensional array is implemented in JavaScript as an array of arrays. This can be done with the new operator or with nested array literals, as illustrated in the following example:

```
<?xml version = "1.0" encoding = "utf-8"?>
<!DOCTYPE html PUBLIC "-//w3c//DTD XHTML 1.1//EN"
  "http://www.w3.org/TR/xhtml11/DTD/xhtml11.dtd">

<!-- nested_arrays.html
     An example illustrate an array of arrays
     -->
<html xmlns = "http://www.w3.org/1999/xhtml">
  <head> <title> Array of arrays </title>
  </head>
```

```
    <body>
      <script type = "text/javascript">
        <!--
// Create an array object with three arrays as its elements

        var nested_array = [[2, 4, 6],
                            [1, 3, 5],
                            [10, 20, 30]
                           ];

// Display the elements of nested_list

        for (var row = 0; row <= 2; row++) {
          document.write("Row ", row, ":  ");

          for (var col = 0; col <=2; col++)
            document.write(nested_array[row][col], " ");

          document.write("<br />");
        }
        // -->
      </script>
    </body>
</html>
```

Figure 4.9 shows a browser display of `nested_arrays.html`.

```
Row 0: 2 4 6
Row 1: 1 3 5
Row 2: 10 20 30
```

FIGURE 4.9 Display of `nested_arrays.html`

4.9

FUNCTIONS

JavaScript functions are similar to those of other C-based languages such as C, C++, and PHP. This section describes these functions.

4.9.1 Fundamentals

A *function definition* consists of the function's header and a compound statement that describes its actions. This compound statement is called the *body* of the function. A function *header* consists of the reserved word `function`, the function's name, and a parenthesized list of parameters, if there are any.

A `return` statement returns control from the function in which it appears to the function's caller. It optionally includes an expression, whose value is returned by the function. A function body may include one or more `return` statements. If there are no `return` statements in a function, or if the specific `return` that is executed does not include an expression, the returned value is `undefined`. This is also the case if execution reaches the end of the function body without executing a `return` statement.

Syntactically, a call to a function with no parameters is the function's name followed by an empty pair of parentheses. A call to a function that returns `undefined` is a standalone statement. A call to a function that returns a useful value appears as the operand in an expression (often the whole right side of an assignment statement). For example, if `fun1` is a parameterless function that returns `undefined`, and if `fun2`, which also has no parameters, returns a useful value, they can be called with this code:

```
fun1();
result = fun2();
```

JavaScript functions are objects, so variables that reference them can be treated as other object references. They can be passed as parameters, assigned to other variables, and can be the elements of an array. Consider the following example:

```
function fun() { document.write(
                    "This surely is fun! <br/>");}
ref_fun = fun;
  // Now, ref_fun refers to the fun object
fun();          // A call to fun
ref_fun();      // Also a call to fun
```

Because JavaScript functions are objects, their addresses can be properties in other objects, in which case they act as methods.

To ensure that the interpreter sees the definition of a function before it sees a call to the function, which is required in JavaScript, function definitions are placed in the head of an XHTML document. Calls to functions normally, but not always, appear in the document body.

4.9.2 Local Variables

The *scope* of a variable is the range of statements over which it is visible. When JavaScript is embedded in an XHTML document, the scope of a variable is the range of lines of the document over which the variable is visible.

A variable that is not declared with a `var` statement is implicitly declared by the JavaScript interpreter at the time it is first encountered in the script. Variables that are implicitly declared, even if the implicit declaration occurs within a function definition, have *global scope*—that is, they are visible in the entire XHTML document. Variables that are explicitly declared outside function definitions also have global scope. As stated earlier, we recommend that all variables be explicitly declared.

It is usually best for variables that are used only within a function to have *local scope*, meaning that they are visible and can be used only within the body of the function. Any variable explicitly declared with `var` in the body of a function has local scope.

If a variable that is defined both as a local variable and as a global variable appears in a function, the local variable has precedence, effectively hiding the global variable with the same name. This is the advantage of local variables: When you make up their names, you need not be concerned that a global variable with the same name may exist somewhere in the collection of scripts in the XHTML document.

Although JavaScript function definitions can be nested, the need for nested functions in client-side JavaScript is minimal. Furthermore, they can greatly complicate scripts. Therefore, we do not recommend the use of nested functions and do not discuss them.

4.9.3 Parameters

The parameter values that appear in a call to a function are called *actual parameters*. The parameter names that appear in the header of a function definition, which correspond to the actual parameters in calls to the function, are called *formal parameters*. JavaScript uses the pass-by-value parameter-passing method. When a function is called, the values of the actual parameters specified in the call are, in effect, copied into their corresponding formal parameters, which behave exactly like local variables. Because references are passed as the actual parameters for objects, the function has access to the objects and can change them, thereby providing the semantics of pass-by-reference parameters.

Because of JavaScript's dynamic typing, there is no type checking of parameters. The called function can itself check the types of parameters with the `typeof` operator. However, recall that `typeof` cannot distinguish between different objects. The number of parameters in a function call is not checked against the number of formal parameters in the called function. In the function, excess actual parameters that are passed are ignored; excess formal parameters are set to `undefined`.

All parameters are communicated through a property array, `arguments`, which, like other array objects, has a property named `length`. By accessing `arguments.length`, a function can determine the number of actual parameters that were passed. Because the `arguments` array is accessible directly, all actual parameters specified in the call are available, including actual parameters that do not correspond to any formal parameters (because there were more actual parameters than formal parameters). Consider the following example:

```
<?xml version = "1.0" encoding = "utf-8"?>
<!DOCTYPE html PUBLIC "-//w3c//DTD XHTML 1.1//EN"
  "http://www.w3.org/TR/xhtml11/DTD/xhtml11.dtd">


<!-- parameters.html
     The params function and a test driver for it.
     This example illustrates function parameters
     -->
<html xmlns = "http://www.w3.org/1999/xhtml">
  <head> <title> Parameters </title>
    <script type = "text/javascript">
      <!--
// Function params
// Parameters: two named parameters and one unnamed
//             parameter, all numbers
// Returns: nothing

      function params(a, b) {
        document.write("Function params was passed ",
            arguments.length, " parameter(s) <br />");
        document.write("Parameter values are: <br />");

        for (var arg = 0; arg < arguments.length; arg++)
          document.write(arguments[arg], "<br />");

        document.write("<br />");
        }
      // -->
    </script>
  </head>
  <body>
    <script type = "text/javascript">

// A text driver for params
```

```
        params("Mozart");
        params("Mozart", "Beethoven");
        params("Mozart", "Beethoven", "Tchaikowsky");
      </script>
    </body>
</html>
```

Figure 4.10 shows a browser display of `parameters.html`.

```
Function params was passed 1 parameter(s)
Parameter values are:
Mozart

Function params was passed 2 parameter(s)
Parameter values are:
Mozart
Beethoven

Function params was passed 3 parameter(s)
Parameter values are:
Mozart
Beethoven
Tchaikowsky
```

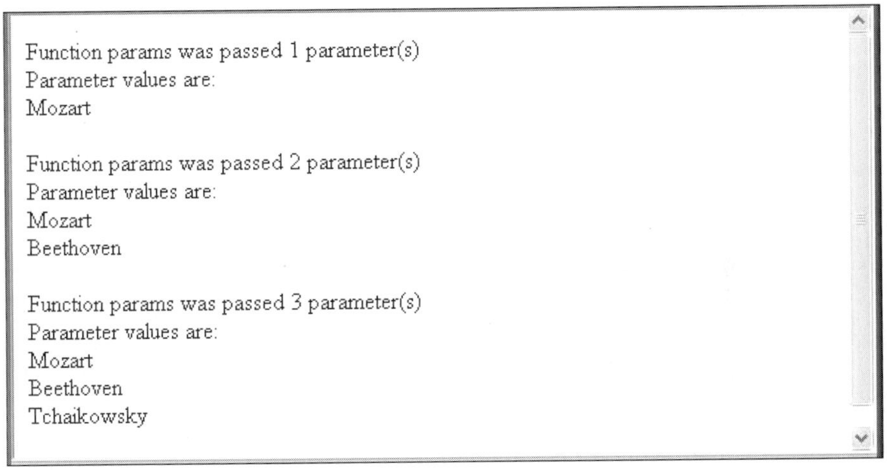

FIGURE 4.10 Display of `parameters.html`

There is no elegant way in JavaScript to pass a primitive value by reference. One inelegant way is to put the value in an array and pass the array. This works because arrays are objects. For example, consider the following script:

```
// Function by10
//    Parameter: a number, passed as the first element
//                of an array
// Returns: nothing
// Effect: multiplies the parameter by 10

function by10(a) {
    a[0] *= 10;
}
...
var x;
var listx = new Array(1);
...
```

```
listx[0] = x;
by10(listx);
x = listx[0];
```

Another way to have a function change the value of a primitive type actual parameter is to have the function return the new value:

```
function by10_2(a) {
    return 10 * a;
}
...
var x;
...
x = by10_2(x);
```

4.9.4 The sort Method, Revisited

Recall that the sort method for array objects converts the array's elements to strings, if necessary, and then sorts them into alphabetical order. If you need to sort something other than strings, or if you want an array to be sorted in some order other than alphabetic for strings, the comparison operation must be supplied to the sort method by the caller. Such a comparison operation is passed as a parameter to sort. The comparison function must return a negative number if the two elements being compared are in the desired order, zero if they are equal, and a number greater than zero if they must be interchanged. For numbers, simply subtracting the second from the first produces the required result. For example, if you want to sort the array of numbers num_list into ascending order using the sort method, the following could be used:

```
// Function num_order
// Parameter: Two numbers
// Returns: If the first parameter belongs before the
//           second, a negative number
//        If the two parameters are equal, 0
//        If the two parameters must be
//           interchanged, a positive number

function num_order(a, b) {return a - b;}

// Sort the array of numbers, list, into
// ascending order
  num_list.sort(num_order);
```

Rather than defining a comparison function elsewhere and passing its name, the function definition can appear as the actual parameter in the call to sort. This is illustrated in the script in Section 4.10.

4.10

AN EXAMPLE

The following is an example of an XHTML document containing a JavaScript function to compute the median of an array of numbers. The function first sorts the array using the sort method. If the given array has an odd length, the median is the middle element. The middle element is determined by dividing the length by 2 and truncating the result using floor. If the length is even, the median is the average of the two middle elements. The result of the average computation is rounded to an integer using round.

```
<?xml version = "1.0" encoding = "utf-8"?>
<!DOCTYPE html PUBLIC "-//w3c//DTD XHTML 1.1//EN"
  "http://www.w3.org/TR/xhtml11/DTD/xhtml11.dtd">

<!-- medians.html
     A function and a function tester
     Illustrates array operations
     -->
<html xmlns = "http://www.w3.org/1999/xhtml">
  <head> <title> Median Computation </title>
    <script type = "text/javascript">
      <!--
/* Function median
        Parameter: An array of numbers
        Result: The median of the array
        Return value: none
        */

     function median(list) {
       list.sort(function (a, b) {return a - b;});
       var list_len = list.length;

// Use the modulus operator to determine whether
//  the array's length is odd or even
// Use Math.floor to truncate numbers
// Use Math.round to round numbers

       if ((list_len % 2) == 1)
         return list[Math.floor(list_len / 2)];
       else
         return Math.round((list[list_len / 2 - 1] +
                    list[list_len / 2]) / 2);
```

continued

```
      }  // end of function median
      // -->
   </script>
</head>
<body>
   <script type = "text/javascript">
     <!--
     var my_list_1 = [8, 3, 9, 1, 4, 7];
     var my_list_2 = [10, -2, 0, 5, 3, 1, 7];
     var med = median(my_list_1);
     document.write("Median of [", my_list_1, "] is: ",
                 med, "<br />");
     med = median(my_list_2);
     document.write("Median of [", my_list_2, "] is: ",
                 med, "<br />");
     // -->
   </script>
</body>
</html>
```

Figure 4.11 shows a browser display of medians.html.

```
Median of [1,3,4,7,8,9] is: 6
Median of [-2,0,1,3,5,7,10] is: 3
```

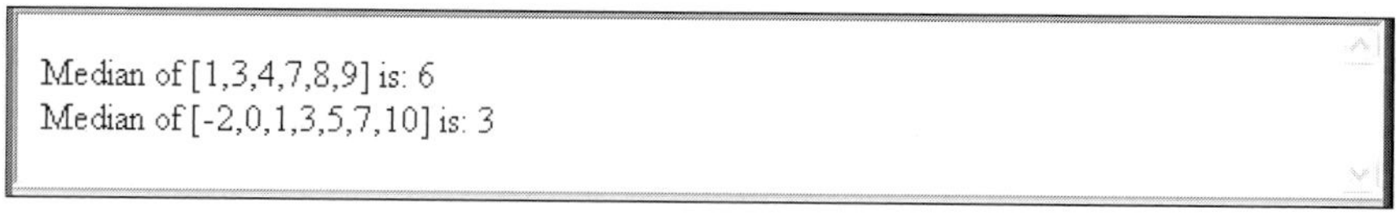

FIGURE 4.11 Display of medians.html

One significant side effect of the median function is that it leaves the given array in ascending order. This may not always be acceptable. If not, the array could be moved to a local array in median before the sorting operation.

Notice that this script uses Math.floor to determine the median of an odd-length list. If the list subscripts began at 1, this would be wrong; because they begin at 0, it is correct.

4.11

CONSTRUCTORS

JavaScript constructors are special methods that create and initialize the properties for newly created objects. Every new expression must include a call to a constructor, whose name is the same as the object being created. As you saw in

Section 4.8, for example, the constructor for arrays is named `Array`. Constructors are actually called by the `new` operator, which immediately precedes them in the new expression.

A constructor obviously must be able to reference the object on which it is to operate. JavaScript has a predefined reference variable for this purpose, named `this`. When the constructor is called, `this` is a reference to the newly created object. The `this` variable is used to construct and initialize the properties of the object. For example, consider the following constructor:

```
function car(new_make, new_model, new_year) {
    this.make = new_make;
    this.model = new_model;
    this.year = new_year;
}
```

This constructor could be used as in the following:

```
my_car = new car("Ford", "Contour SVT", "2000");
```

So far we have considered only data properties. If a method is to be included in the object, it is initialized the same way as if it were a data property. For example, suppose you wanted a method for `car` objects that listed the property values. A function that could serve as such a method could be written as follows:

```
function display_car() {
    document.write("Car make: ", this.make, "<br/>");
    document.write("Car model: ", this.model, "<br/>");
    document.write("Car year: ", this.year, "<br/>");
}
```

The following line must be added to the `car` constructor:

```
this.display = display_car;
```

Now, the code `my_car.display();` would produce the following:

```
Car make: Ford
Car model: Contour SVT
Car year: 2000
```

The collection of objects created using the same constructor is related to the concept of class in an object-oriented programming language. All such objects have the same set of properties and methods, at least initially. However, there is no convenient way to determine in the script whether two objects have the same set of properties and methods.

4.12

PATTERN MATCHING USING REGULAR EXPRESSIONS

JavaScript has powerful pattern-matching capabilities based on regular expressions. There are two approaches to pattern matching in JavaScript: one that is based on the `RegExp` object and one that is based on methods of the `String` object. The regular expressions used by these two approaches are the same. They are based on the regular expressions of the Perl programing language. This book covers only the `String` methods for pattern matching.

As stated previously, patterns are specified in a form that is based on regular expressions, which were developed to define members of a simple class of formal languages. Elaborate and complex patterns can be used to describe specific strings or categories of strings. Patterns, which are sent as parameters to the pattern-matching methods, are delimited with slashes.

4.12.1 Character and Character-Class Patterns

Within a pattern, "normal" characters match themselves. *Normal* means that they are not metacharacters, which are characters that have special meanings in some contexts in patterns. The metacharacters are these:

```
\ | ( ) [ ] { } ^ $ * + ? .
```

Metacharacters can themselves be matched by being immediately preceded by a backslash. Before discussing the use of metacharacters in patterns, we show how normal characters are used. Because they match themselves, this is simple.

The simplest pattern-matching method is `search`, which takes a pattern as a parameter. The `search` method returns the position in the `String` object (through which it is called) where the pattern matched. If there is no match, `search` returns –1. For example, consider the following:

```
var str = "Rabbits are furry";
var position = str.search(/bits/);
if (position > 0)
    document.write("'bits' appears in position", position,
                   "<br />");
else
    document.write("'bits' does not appear in str <br />");
```

The output of this code is as follows:

```
'bits' appears in position 3
```

A period matches any character except newline. So, the following pattern matches "snowy", "snowe", and "snowd", among others:

/snow./

To match a period in a string, the pattern must backslash the period. For example, the pattern /3\.4/ matches 3.4. The pattern /3.4/ would match 3.4 but also 374.

It is often convenient to be able to specify classes of characters rather than individual characters. Such classes are defined by placing the desired characters in brackets. Dashes can appear in class definitions, making it easy to specify sequences of characters. For example, you could have the following character class, which matches 'a', 'b', or 'c':

[abc]

Also, you could have the following character class, which matches any lowercase letter from 'a' to 'h':

[a-h]

If a circumflex character (^) is the first character in a class, it inverts the specified set. For example, the following character class matches any character except the letters 'a', 'e', 'i', 'o', and 'u':

[^aeiou]

Because they are frequently used, some character classes are predefined and can be specified by their names. These are shown in Table 4.8, which gives the names of the classes, their literal definitions as character classes, and descriptions of what they match.

TABLE 4.8 Predefined Character Classes

Name	Equivalent Pattern	Matches
\d	[0-9]	A digit
\D	[^0-9]	Not a digit
\w	[A-Za-z_0-9]	A word character (alphanumeric)
\W	[^A-Za-z_0-9]	Not a word character
\s	[\r\t\n\f]	A whitespace character
\S	[^ \r\t\n\f]	Not a whitespace character

Consider the following examples of patterns that use predefined character classes:

```
/\d\.\d\d/     // Matches a digit, followed by a period,
               // followed by two digits
/\D\d\D/       // Matches a single digit
/\w\w\w/       // Matches three adjacent word characters
```

In many cases, it is convenient to be able to repeat a part of a pattern, often a character or character class. To repeat a pattern, a numeric quantifier, delimited by braces, is attached. For example, the following pattern matches xyyyyz:

```
/xy{4}z/
```

There are also three symbolic quantifiers: asterisk (*), plus (+), and question mark (?). An asterisk means zero or more repetitions, a plus sign means one or more repetitions, and a question mark means one or none. For example, the following pattern matches strings that begin with any number of x's (including zero), followed by one or more y's, possibly followed by z:

```
/x*y+z?/
```

These quantifiers are often used with the predefined character class names, as in the following pattern, which matches a string of one or more digits followed by a decimal point and possibly more digits:

```
/\d+\.\d*/
```

As another example, consider the following pattern:

```
/[A-Za-z]\w*/
```

This pattern matches the identifiers in some programming languages (a letter, followed by zero or more letters, digits, or underscrores).

There is one additional named pattern that is often useful. This is\b (boundary), which matches the boundary position between a word character (\w) and a nonword character (\W), in either order. For example, the following pattern matches "A tulip is a flower" but not "A frog isn't":

```
/\bis\b/
```

It does not match the second string because the 'is' is followed by another word character ('n').

The boundary pattern is different from the named character classes in that it does not match a character; it matches a position between two characters.

4.12.2   Anchors

It is frequently useful to be able to specify that a pattern must match at a particular position in the string. The most common example of this is requiring a pattern to match at one specific end of the string. A pattern is tied to a string position with an anchor. A pattern can be specified to match only at the beginning of the string by preceding it with a circumflex (^) anchor. For example, the following pattern matches `"pearls are pretty"` but does not match `"My pearls are pretty"`:

```
/^pearl/
```

A pattern can be specified to match only at the end of a string by following it with a dollar-sign anchor. For example, the following pattern matches `"I like gold"` but does not match `"golden"`:

```
/gold$/
```

Anchor characters are like boundary-named patterns. They do not match specific characters in the string; rather, they match positions before, between, or after characters. When a circumflex appears in a pattern at a position other than the beginning of the pattern or at the beginning of a character class, it has no special meaning. (It matches itself.) Likewise, if a dollar sign appears in a pattern at a position other than the end of the pattern, it has no special meaning.

4.12.3   Pattern Modifiers

Modifiers can be attached to patterns to change how they are used, thereby increasing their flexibility. The modifiers are specified as letters just after the right delimiter of the pattern. The i modifier makes the letters in the pattern match either uppercase or lowercase letters in the string. For example, the pattern `/Apple/i` matches 'APPLE', 'apple', 'APPle', and any other combination of uppercase and lowercase spellings of the word "apple."

The x modifier allows whitespace to appear in the pattern. Because comments are considered whitespace, this provides a way to include explanatory comments in the pattern. For example:

```
/\d+          # The street number
\s            # The space before the street name
[A-Z][a-z]+   # The street name
/x
```

This pattern is equivalent to the following:

```
/\d+\s[A-Z][a-z]+/
```

4.12.4 Other Pattern-Matching Methods of `String`

The `replace` method is used to replace substrings of the `String` object that match the given pattern. The `replace` method takes two parameters: the pattern and the replacement string. The `g` modifier can be attached to the pattern if the replacement is to be global in the string, in which case the replacement is done for every match in the string. The matched substrings of the string are made available through the predefined variables `$1`, `$2`, and so on. For example, consider these statements:

```
var str = "Fred, Freddie, and Frederica were siblings";
str.replace(/Fre/g, "Boy");
```

In this example, `str` is set to `"Boyd, Boyddie, and Boyderica were siblings"`, and `$1`, `$2`, and `$3` are all set to `"Fre"`.

The `match` method is the most general of the `String` pattern-matching methods. The `match` method takes a single parameter, a pattern. It returns an array of the results of the pattern-matching operation. If the pattern has the `g` modifier, the returned array has all of the substrings of the string that matched. If the pattern does not include the `g` modifier, the returned array has the match as its first element, and the remainder of the array has the matches of parenthesized parts of the pattern, if there are any.

```
var str =
  "Having 4 apples is better than having 3 oranges";
var matches = str.match(/\d/g);
```

In this example, `matches` is set to `[4, 3]`.

Now consider a pattern that has parenthesized subexpressions:

```
var str = "I have 428 dollars, but I need 500";
var matches = str.match(/(\d+)([^\d]+)(\d+)/);
document.write(matches, "<br />");
```

The following is the value of the `matches` array after this code is interpreted:

```
["428 dollars, but I need 500", "428",
"dollars, but I need ", "500"]
```

In this result array, the first element is the match; the second, third, and fourth elements are the parts of the string that matched the parenthesized parts of the pattern.

The `split` method of `String` splits its object string into substrings, based on a given string or pattern. The substrings are returned in an array. For example, consider the following code:

```
var str = "grapes:apples:oranges";
var fruit = str.split(":");
```

In this example, `fruit` is set to `[grapes, apples, oranges]`.

As mentioned at the beginning of this section, there is a second way to do pattern matching in JavaScript. A pattern can be a `RegExp` object, in which case the methods of that object are used and the string on which the pattern is to be matched is sent as the parameter to the method. We do not discuss the use of `RegExp` objects for pattern matching.

4.13

ANOTHER EXAMPLE

One of the common uses for JavaScript is to check the format of input from XHTML forms, which is discussed in detail in Chapter 5. The example in this section illustrates the use of a simple function to check a given string that is supposed to contain a phone number to determine whether its format is correct. The function uses a simple pattern match to check the phone number.

```
<?xml version = "1.0" encoding = "utf-8"?>
<!DOCTYPE html PUBLIC "-//w3c//DTD XHTML 1.1//EN"
  "http://www.w3.org/TR/xhtml11/DTD/xhtml11.dtd">

<!-- forms_check.html
     A function tst_phone_num is defined and tested.
     This function checks the validity of phone
     number input from a form
     -->
<html xmlns = "http://www.w3.org/1999/xhtml">
  <head> <title> Phone number tester </title>
    <script type = "text/javascript">
      <!--
/* Function tst_phone_num
   Parameter: A string
   Result: Returns true if the parameter has the form of a legal
           seven-digit phone number (3 digits, a dash, 4 digits)
   */
```

continued

```
        function tst_phone_num(num) {

// Use a simple pattern to check the number of digits and the dash

            var ok = num.search(/\d{3}-\d{4}/);

            if (ok == 0)
              return true;
            else
              return false;

        }   // end of function tst_phone_num
        // -->
      </script>
    </head>
    <body>
      <script type = "text/javascript">
        <!--

// A script to test tst_phone_num

            var tst = tst_phone_num("444-5432");
            if (tst)
              document.write("444-5432 is a legal phone number <br />");
            else
              document.write("Error in tst_phone_num <br />");

            tst = tst_phone_num("444-r432");
            if (tst)
              document.write("Error in tst_phone_num <br />");
            else
              document.write(
                        "444-r432 is not a legal phone number <br />");

            tst = tst_phone_num("44-1234");
            if (tst)
              document.write("Error in tst_phone_num <br />");
            else
              document.write("44-1234 is not a legal phone number <br /");
            // -->
      </script>
    </body>
</html>
```

Figure 4.12 shows a browser display of `forms_check.html`.

444-5432 is a legal phone number
444-r432 is not a legal phone number
44-1234 is not a legal phone number

FIGURE 4.12 Display of `forms_check.html`

4.14

ERRORS IN SCRIPTS

The JavaScript interpreter is capable of detecting various problems with scripts. These are primarily syntax errors, although uses of undefined variables are also detected. Debugging a script is a bit different from debugging a program in a more typical programming language, mostly because errors that are detected by the JavaScript interpreter are found while the browser is attempting to display a document. In most cases, script errors cause the browser to not display the document, without producing any error message. Without a diagnostic message, you must simply examine the code to find the problem. This is, of course, unacceptable for all but the smallest and simplest scripts. Fortunately, there are ways to get some assistance.

The default settings for IE6 provide no debugging help for JavaScript. However, this can be changed as follows. Select Internet Options from the Tools menu and choose the Advanced tab there. This opens a window with a long list of checkboxes. Uncheck the box labeled "Disable script debugging" and check the box labeled "Display a notification about every script error." Then press the Apply button in this window. From then on, JavaScript errors will cause the browser to open and display a small window with an explanation of the problem. For example, consider the following sample XHTML document:

```
<?xml version = "1.0" encoding = "utf-8"?>
<!DOCTYPE html PUBLIC "-//w3c//DTD XHTML 1.1//EN"
  "http://www.w3.org/TR/xhtml11/DTD/xhtml11.dtd">


<!-- debugdemo.html
     An example to illustrate debugging help
     -->
```

continued

```
<html xmlns = "http://www.w3.org/1999/xhtml">
  <head> <title> Debugging help </title>
  </head>
  <body>
    <script type = "text/javascript">
      <!--
      var row;
      row = 0;

      while(row != 4 {
        document.write("row is ", row, "<br />");
        row++;
      }
      // -->
    </script>
  </body>
</html>
```

Notice the syntax error in the `while` statement. Figure 4.13 shows the browser display of what happens when an attempt is made to display `debugdemo.html`.

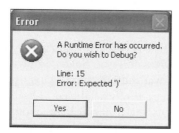

FIGURE 4.13 Display of `debugdemo.html` with Internet Explorer 6

The NS7 browser has a special console window that displays script errors. Select Tools, Web Development, and JavaScript Console to open this window. When using this browser to display documents that include JavaScript, this window should be kept open. After an error message has appeared and has been used to fix a script, press the Clear button on the console. Otherwise, the old error message will remain there and possibly cause confusion about subsequent problems. An example of the NS7 JavaScript Console window is shown in Figure 4.14.

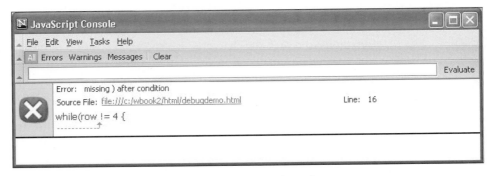

FIGURE 4.14 Display of the Netscape 7 JavaScript Console

The more interesting and challenging programming problems are only detectable during execution or interpretation. For these problems, a debugger is used. Both IE6 and NS7 have debuggers for JavaScript.

The IE6 JavaScript debugger is part of the browser. Documentation on it can be found at `http://www.microsoft.com/scripting/debugger/default.htm`.

The JavaScript debugger for NS7, which was produced by Mozilla and is named Venkman, is available at `http://developer.netscape.com/software/tools/index.html`.

4.15

SUMMARY

Client-side JavaScript scripts are embedded in XHTML files as the content of `<script>` tags. The `type` attribute of `<script>` must be set to `"text/javascript"`. A file containing a script can be included by specifying its name as the value of the `<script>` attribute `src`. The script itself must appear in a special XHTML comment.

Values in JavaScript are either primitives or objects. The primitive types are Number, String, Boolean, Undefined, and Null. Numbers are represented in double-precision floating-point format. The Number, String, and Boolean types have corresponding objects named `Number`, `String`, and `Boolean`, which act as wrapper objects. String literals can use either single or double quotes as delimiters.

JavaScript is dynamically typed, which is not the same as being a typeless language. A variable has a type, but that type can change every time a new value is assigned to the variable. It is best to explicitly declare all variables.

The `Number` object includes a collection of useful properties such as `MIN_VALUE` and `PI`. The `Math` object has many methods for commonly used operations on numbers, such as `round` and `cos`. The catenation operator, +, creates a new string by putting the two operand strings together. The `String` property `length` stores the number of characters in a string. There are `String` methods to return the character at a specified position in the string, the position of a specified character in the string, and a specified substring of the string. There are a large number of other `String` methods.

The `typeof` operator returns the type name of its operand if the operand is a primitive type; otherwise, it returns `"object"`.

The `Date` object provides the current time and date. It includes a large number of methods to produce various parts of time and date, such as the day of the week and the hour of the day.

The `alert` method of `Window` produces output in a dialog box. The `confirm` method of `Window` asks the user to select either an OK button or a Cancel button. The `prompt` method of `Window` asks the user for textual input. The `document.write` method dynamically produces XHTML content. The control statements of JavaScript are closely related to those of other common programming languages. Included is a `switch` statement.

Arrays in JavaScript are objects, as they are in Java. They have dynamic length. An `Array` object can be created in a `new` expression, which includes a call to the `Array` constructor, or by simply assigning an `Array` literal to a variable. `Array` literals are lists of values enclosed in brackets. Every `Array` object has a `length` property, which is both readable and writable, that stores the number of elements in the array. `Array` objects have a collection of useful methods, among which are `join`, for joining the elements of an array together in a string; `reverse`, which reverses the order of elements in an array; `sort`, which converts the elements of the array to strings and sorts them into alphabetical order; and `slice`, which returns a specified part of the array. The array methods `pop`, `push`, `shift`, and `unshift` were designed to implement stacks and queues in arrays.

Function definitions name their formal parameters but do not include type names. All functions return values, but the type of the value is not specified in the function's definition. Variables declared in a function with `var` are local to that function. Parameters are passed by value, resulting in pass-by-value semantics for primitives and pass-by-reference semantics for objects. The `arguments` property stores the values of the passed parameters. Neither the types of the parameters nor the number of parameters are checked by the JavaScript interpreter.

The regular expressions used in the pattern-matching facilities of JavaScript are modeled on the regular expressions of Perl. Pattern matches are specified by one of the three methods—`search`, `replace`, or `match`—of the `String` object. The regular expressions, or patterns, are made up of special characters, normal characters, character classes, and operators. Patterns are delimited by slashes. Character classes are delimited with brackets. If a circumflex appears at the left end of a character class, it inverts the meaning of the characters in the class. Several of the most common character classes are predefined. Subpatterns can be followed by numeric or symbolic quantifiers. Patterns can be anchored at the left or right end of the string against which the pattern is being matched.

The `search` method searches its object string for the pattern given as its parameter. The `replace` method replaces matches in its object string with its second parameter. The `match` method searches its object string for the given pattern and returns an array of all matches.

4.16 Review Questions

1. Describe briefly three major differences between Java and JavaScript.

2. Describe briefly three major uses of JavaScript on the client side.

3. Describe briefly the basic process of event-driven computation.

4. What are the two categories of properties in JavaScript?

5. Why does JavaScript have two categories of data variables, primitives and objects?

6. Describe the two ways to embed a JavaScript script in an XHTML document.

7. What are the two forms of JavaScript comments?

8. Why are JavaScript scripts sometimes hidden in XHTML documents by putting them in XHTML comments?

9. What are the five primitive data types in JavaScript?

10. Do single-quoted string literals have any different characteristics than double-quoted string literals?

11. In what circumstances would a variable have the value `undefined`?

12. If the value `undefined` is used as a Boolean expression, is it interpreted as `true` or `false`?

13. What purpose do rules of operator precedence serve in a programming language?

14. What purpose do rules of operator associativity serve in a programming language?

15. Describe the purpose and characteristics of `NaN`.

16. Why is `parseInt` not used more often?

17. What value does `typeof` return for an object operand?

18. What is the usual end-of-line punctuation for the string operand to `document.write`?

19. What is the usual end-of-line punctuation for the string operand to `alert`?

20. Describe the operation of the `prompt` method.

21. What is a control construct?

22. Must the `then` clause of an `if` statement in JavaScript always be a compound statement?

23. What are the three possible forms of control expressions in JavaScript?

24. What is the difference between == and ===?

25. Explain what short-circuit evaluation of an expression means.

26. What are the semantics of a `break` statement?

27. What is the difference between a `while` statement and a `do-while` statement?

28. When is a JavaScript constructor called?

29. What is the difference between a constructor in Java and one in JavaScript?

30. What properties does an object created with a `new` operator and the `Object` constructor have?

31. Describe the two ways the properties of an object can be referenced.

32. How is a new property of an object created?

33. Describe the semantics of the `for-in` statement.

34. Describe the two ways an `Array` object can be created.

35. What relationship is there between the value of the `length` property of an `Array` object and the actual number of existing elements in the object?

36. Describe the semantics of the `join` method of `Array`.

37. Describe the semantics of the `slice` method when it is given just one parameter.

38. What is the form of a nested array literal?

39. What value is returned by a function that contains no `return` statement?

40. Define the scope of a variable in a JavaScript script embedded in an XHTML document when the variable is not declared in a function.

41. Is it possible to reference global variables in a JavaScript function?

42. What is the advantage of using local variables in functions?

43. What parameter-passing method does JavaScript use?

44. Does JavaScript check the types of actual parameters against the types of their corresponding formal parameters?

45. How can a function access actual parameter values for those actual parameters that do not correspond to any formal parameter?

46. What is one way in which primitive variables can be passed by reference to a function?

47. What exactly does a constructor do in JavaScript?

48. What is a character class in a pattern?

49. What are the predefined character classes, and what do they mean?

50. What are the symbolic quantifiers, and what do they mean?

51. Describe the two end-of-line anchors.

52. What does the i pattern modifier do?

53. What exactly does the String method replace do?

54. What exactly does the String method match do?

4.17 Exercises

Write, test, and debug (if necessary) XHTML files that include JavaScript scripts for the following problems. When required to write functions, you must include a script to test the function with at least two different data sets.

1. *Output:* A table of the numbers from 5 to 15 and their squares and cubes, using alert.

2. *Output:* The first 20 Fibonacci numbers, which are defined as in the following sequence

$$1, 1, 2, 3, \ldots$$

   where each number in the sequence after the second is the sum of the two previous numbers. You must use document.write to produce the output.

3. *Input:* Three numbers, using prompt to get each.

   Output: The largest of the three input numbers.

   Hint: Use the predefined function Math.max.

4. Modify the script of Exercise 2 to input a number, n, using prompt, which is the number of the Fibonacci number required as output.

5. *Input:* A text string, using prompt.

   Output: Either "Legal name" or "Illegal name", depending on whether the input names fit the required format, which is

   Last name, first name, middle initial

   where neither of the names can have more than 15 characters.

6. *Input:* A line of text, using prompt.

   Output: The words of the input text, in alphabetical order.

7. Modify the script for Exercise 6 to get a second input from the user, which is either `"ascending"` or `"descending"`. Use this input to determine how to sort the input words.

8. *Function:* `no_zeros`

   Parameter: An array of numbers.

   Result: The given array must be modified to remove all zero values.

   Returns: `true` if the given array included zero values; `false` otherwise.

9. *Function:* `e_names`

   Parameter: An array of names, represented as strings.

   Returns: The number of names in the given array that end in either `"ie"` or `"y"`.

10. *Function:* `first_vowel`

    Parameter: A string.

    Returns: The position in the string of the leftmost vowel.

11. *Function:* `counter`

    Parameter: An array of numbers.

    Returns: The numbers of negative elements, zeros, and values greater than zero in the given array.

    Note: You must use a `switch` statement in the function.

12. *Function:* `tst_name`

    Parameter: A string.

    Returns: `true` if the given string has the form

    ```
    string1, string2 letter
    ```

    where both strings must be all lowercase letters except the first letter, and `letter` must be uppercase; `false` otherwise.

13. *Function:* `row_averages`

    Parameter: An array of arrays of numbers.

    Returns: An array of the averages of each of the rows of the given matrix.

14. *Function:* `reverser`

    Parameter: A number.

    Returns: The number with its digits in reverse order.

5

JavaScript and HTML Documents

Client-side JavaScript does not include language constructs that are not in core JavaScript. Instead, it defines the collection of objects, methods, and properties that allow scripts to interact with XHTML documents on the client. This chapter describes some of these features and illustrates their use with examples.

The chapter begins with a description of the execution environment of client-side JavaScript, which means the object hierarchy that corresponds to the structure of documents. It then gives a brief overview of the Document Object Model (DOM), noting that you need not know the details of this model to be able to use client-side JavaScript. Next, the techniques for accessing XHTML document elements in JavaScript are discussed. The fundamental concepts of events and event handling are then introduced, using the basic event model. Although the event-driven model of computation is not a new idea in programming, it has become more important to programmers with the advent of Web programming. Next, the chapter describes the relationships between event objects, XHTML tag attributes, and tags, primarily by means of two tables.

Applications of basic event handling are introduced through a sequence of complete document/JavaScript examples. The first of these illustrates handling the `load` event from a body element. The next two examples demonstrate the use of the `click` event created when radio buttons are pressed. This is followed by an example that uses the `blur` event to compare multiply-input passwords. The next example demonstrates the use of the `change` event to validate the format of input to a text box. The last example shows the use of the `blur` event to prevent user changes to the values of text-box elements.

Next, the current standard event model, DOM 2, is introduced, using a revision of an earlier example to illustrate the new features of this model. Finally, the chapter discusses the use of the `navigator` object to determine which browser is being used.

5.1

THE JAVASCRIPT EXECUTION ENVIRONMENT

A browser displays an XHTML document in a window on the screen of the client. The JavaScript `Window` object represents the window that displays the document.

All JavaScript variables are properties of some object. The properties of the `Window` object are visible to all JavaScript scripts that appear in the window's XHTML document, so they include all of the global variables. When a global variable is implicitly created in a client-side script, it is created as a new property of the `Window` object. The `Window` object provides the largest enclosing referencing environment for JavaScript scripts.

There can be more than one `Window` object. Each such object creates a global scope and is the parent object of all objects in the window. A variable declared in one `Window` object is not a global variable in another `Window` object, although it is possible to reference it in the other object.

The JavaScript `Document` object represents the displayed XHTML document. Every `Window` object has a property named `document`, which is a reference to the `Document` object that the window displays. Because a `Window` object can include multiple frames, it has a property array, `frames`, whose elements are references to the frames.

Every `Document` object has a `forms` array, each element of which represents a form in the document. Each `Forms` array element has an `elements` array as a property, which contains the objects that represent the XHTML form elements such as buttons and menus. The JavaScript objects associated with the elements in a document can be addressed in a script in several ways. These are discussed in Section 5.3.

`Document` objects also have property arrays for anchors, links, images, and applets. There are many other objects in the object hierarchy below a `Window` object, but in this chapter we are primarily interested in documents, forms, and form elements.

5.2

THE DOCUMENT OBJECT MODEL

The Document Object Model (DOM) has been under development since the mid-1990s by the W3C. At the time of this writing, DOM Level 2 (usually referred to as DOM 2) was the latest approved version, and DOM 3 was under development. The original motivation for the DOM was to provide a specification that would make Java programs and JavaScript scripts that deal with XHTML documents portable among various browsers.

Although the W3C never produced such a specification, DOM 0 is the name often used to describe the document model used by the early browsers that supported JavaScript. The DOM 0 model was partially documented in the HTML 4 specification.

DOM 1, the first W3C DOM specification, issued in October 1998, focused on the XHTML and XML (see Chapter 8, "Introduction to XML") document model. DOM 2, issued in November 2000, specifies a style sheet object model and defines how style information attached to a document can be manipulated. It also includes document traversals and provides a complete and comprehensive event model. DOM 3 will deal with content models for XML (DTDs and schemas), document validation, and document views and formatting, as well as key events and event groups. As stated previously, DOM 0 is supported by all JavaScript-enabled browsers. DOM 2 is nearly completely supported by Netscape 7 (NS7), but Internet Explorer 6 (IE6) leaves significant parts unimplemented.

The DOM is an application programming interface (API) that defines an interface between XHTML documents and application programs. It is an abstract model because it must apply to a variety of application programming languages. Each language that interfaces with the DOM must define a binding to that interface. The actual DOM specification consists of a collection of interfaces, including one for each document tree node type. These interfaces are similar to Java interfaces and C++ abstract classes. They define the objects, methods, and properties that are associated with their respective node types. With the DOM, users can write code in programming languages to create documents, move around in their structures, and change, add, or delete elements and their content.

Documents in the DOM have a treelike structure, but there can be more than one tree in a document (though that is unusual). Because the DOM is an abstract interface, it does not dictate that documents must be implemented as trees or collections of trees. Therefore, in an implementation, the relationships among the elements of a document can be represented in any number of different ways. In the JavaScript binding to the DOM, the elements of a document are objects, with both data and operations. The data are called *properties*, and the operations are, naturally, called *methods*.

The following XHTML document and its corresponding DOM tree illustrate the relationship between them.

```
<html xmlns = "http://www.w3.org/1999/xhtml">
  <head> <title> A simple document </title>
  </head>
  <body>
    <table>
      <tr>
        <th> Breakfast </th>
        <td> 0 </td>
        <td> 1 </td>
      </tr>
      <tr>
        <th> Lunch </th>
        <td> 1 </td>
        <td> 0 </td>
      </tr>
    </table>
  </body>
</html>
```

Figure 5.1 shows the DOM structure for this table.

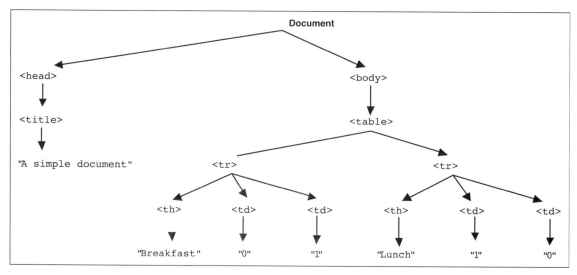

FIGURE 5.1 The DOM structure for a simple document

A language that is designed to support the DOM must have a binding to the DOM constructs. This binding amounts to a correspondence between constructs in the language and elements in the DOM. In the JavaScript binding to the DOM, XHTML elements are represented as objects, and element attributes are represented as properties. For example, the following element would be represented as an object with two properties, `type` and `name`, with the values `"text"` and `"address"`, respectively:

```
<input type = "text"  name = "address">
```

In most cases, the property names in JavaScript are the same as their corresponding attribute names in XHTML.

Anything resembling a complete explanation of the DOM is far beyond the scope of this book. Therefore, our introduction to the DOM here is intended only to provide the basis for our discussion of how JavaScript can be used to respond to document-related events and dynamically modify element attributes and content.[1] Specifically, we do not cover document tree traversal, adding and deleting nodes, or reordering nodes. A detailed description of the DOM can be found at the W3C Web site.

5.3

ELEMENT ACCESS IN JAVASCRIPT

The elements of an XHTML document have corresponding objects in an embedded JavaScript script. The addresses of these objects are required, both by the event handling discussed in this chapter and by the code to make dynamic changes to documents, which is discussed in Chapter 6, "Dynamic Documents with JavaScript."

There are several ways the object associated with an XHTML form element can be addressed in JavaScript. The original (DOM 0) way is to use the `forms` and `elements` arrays of the `Document` object, which is referenced through the `document` property of the `Window` object. As an example, consider the following XHTML document:

```
<html xmlns = "http://www.w3.org/1999/xhtml">
  <head> <title> Access to form elements </title>
  </head>
  <body>
    <form action = "">
      <input type = "button"  name = "turnItOn" />
    </form>
  </body>
</html>
```

---

1. We will discuss modifications of style properties in Chapter 6.

We refer to the address of the JavaScript object that is associated with an XHTML element as its *DOM address*. The DOM address of the button in this example, using the `forms` and `elements` arrays, is as follows:

```
document.forms[0].elements[0]
```

The problem with this approach to element addressing is that the DOM address is defined by address elements that could change, namely, the `forms` and `elements` arrays. For example, if a new button were added before the `turnItOn` button, the DOM address shown would be wrong.

Another approach to DOM addressing is to use element names. For this, the element and its enclosing elements, up to but not including the body element, must include `name` attributes. For example, consider the following document:

```
<html xmlns = "http://www.w3.org/1999/xhtml">
  <head> <title> Access to form elements </title>
  </head>
  <body>
    <form name = "myForm"  action = "">
      <input type = "button"  name = "turnItOn" />
    </form>
  </body>
</html>
```

Using the `name` attributes, the button's DOM address is as follows:

```
document.myForm.turnItOn
```

One drawback of this approach is that the XHTML 1.1 standard does not allow the `name` attribute in the form element, even though the attribute is now legal for form elements. This is a validation problem, but it causes no difficulty for browsers.

Even though a `name` attribute may not be the best way to address form elements in client-side JavaScript, names are nevertheless essential. `name` attributes are required on all form elements by the server-side programs and scripts that process form data, in which the form data value for a widget is identified by the widget's name attribute value.

Yet another approach to element addressing is to use the JavaScript method `getElementById`, which is defined in DOM 1. Because an element's identifier (`id`) is unique in the document, this approach works, regardless of how deeply the element is nested in other elements in the document. For example, if the `id` attribute of our button is set to `"turnItOn"`, the following could be used to get the DOM address of that button element:

```
document.getElementById("turnItOn")
```

The parameter of `getElementById` can be any expression that evaluates to a string. In many cases, it is a variable.

Because `ids` are most useful for DOM addressing and `names` are required for form-processing code, form elements often have both `ids` and `names`, both set to the same value.

Buttons in a group of checkboxes often share the same name. The buttons in a radio button group *always* have the same name. In these cases, the names of the individual buttons obviously cannot be used in their DOM addresses. Of course, each radio button and checkbox can have an `id`, which would make it easy to address using `getElementById`. However, using this approach does not provide a convenient way to search a group of radio buttons or checkboxes to determine which is checked.

An alternative to both `names` and `ids` is provided by the implicit arrays associated with each checkbox and radio button group. Every such group has an array, which has the same name as the group name, that stores the DOM addresses of the individual buttons in the group. These arrays are properties of the form in which the buttons appear. To access the arrays, the DOM address of the form object first must be obtained. For example:

```
<form id = "vehicleGroup">
  <input type = "checkbox"  name = "vehicles"
         value = "car" />  Car
  <input type = "checkbox"  name = "vehicles"
         value = "truck" />  Truck
  <input type = "checkbox"  name = "vehicles"
         value = "bike" />  Bike
</form>
```

The implicit array, `vehicles`, has three elements, which reference the three objects associated with the three checkbox elements in the group. This array provides a convenient way to search the list of checkboxes in a group. The `checked` property of a checkbox object is set to `true` if the button is checked. For the preceding sample checkbox group, the following code would count the number of checkboxes that were checked:

```
var numChecked = 0;
var dom = document.getElementById("vehicleGroup");
for (index = 0; index < dom.vehicles.length; index++)
  if (dom.vehicles[index].checked)
    numChecked++;
```

Radio buttons can be addressed and handled exactly as we have addressed and handled checkboxes in the above code.

5.4

EVENTS AND EVENT HANDLING

The HTML 4.0 standard provided the first specification of an event model for documents. This is sometimes referred to as the DOM 0 event model. Although the DOM 0 event model is limited in scope, it is the only one that is supported by all browsers that support JavaScript. A complete and comprehensive event model was specified by DOM 2. The DOM 2 model is supported by NS7 and the Mozilla browser. However, inexplicably, IE6 does not support it. Our discussion of events and event handling is divided into two parts, one for the DOM 0 model and one for the DOM 2 model. We describe the DOM 2 standard, even though IE6 does not support it. It is our hope that Microsoft will soon recognize the error of its ways and implement the DOM 2 event model in its browsers.

5.4.1 Basic Concepts of Event Handling

One important category of use of JavaScript for Web programming is to detect certain activities of the browser and the browser user and provide computation when these activities occur. These computations are specified using a special form of programming called *event-driven programming*. In conventional (non-event-driven) programming, the code itself specifies the order in which that code is executed, although the order is usually affected by the program's input data. In event-driven programming, parts of the program are executed at completely unpredictable times, often triggered by user interactions with the executing program.

An *event* is a notification that something specific has occurred, either with the browser, such as the completion of the loading of a document, or because of a browser user action, such as a mouse click on a form button. Strictly speaking, an event is an object that is implicitly created by the browser and the JavaScript system in response to something happening.

An *event handler* is a script that is implicitly executed in response to the appearance of an event. Event handlers enable a Web document to be responsive to browser and user activities. One of the most common uses of event handlers is to check for simple errors and omissions in the elements of a form, either when they are changed or when the form is submitted. This saves the time of sending the form data to the server, where its correctness then must be checked by a server-resident program or script before it can be processed.

If you are familiar with the exceptions and exception-handling capabilities of a programming language such as C++ or Java, you should see the close relationship between events and exceptions. Both events and exceptions occur at unpredictable times, and both often require some specific program actions.

Because events are JavaScript objects, their names are case sensitive. The names of all event objects have only lowercase letters. For example, `click` is an event, but `Click` is not.

Events are created by activities associated with specific XHTML elements. For example, the `click` event can be caused by the browser user clicking on a radio button or the link of an anchor tag, among other things. Thus, an event's name is only part of the information pertinent to handling the event. In most cases, the specific XHTML element that caused the event is also needed.

The process of connecting an event handler to an event is called *registration*. There are two distinct approaches to event handler registration, one that assigns tag attributes and one that assigns handler addresses to object properties. These are further discussed and illustrated in Sections 5.5 and 5.6.

The `write` method of `document` should never be used in an event handler. Remember that a document is displayed as its XHTML code is parsed. Events usually occur after the whole document is displayed. If `write` appears in an event handler, the content generated by it might be placed over the top of the existing document.

The remainder of this section and Sections 5.5 to 5.7 describe the DOM 0 event model and some of its uses.

5.4.2 Events, Attributes, and Tags

HTML 4 defined a collection of events, which browsers implement and with which JavaScript can deal. These events are associated with XHTML tag attributes, which can be used to connect the events to handlers. The attributes have names that are closely related to their associated events. Table 5.1 lists the most commonly used events and their associated tag attributes.

TABLE 5.1 Events and Their Tag Attributes

Event	Tag Attribute
blur	onblur
change	onchange
click	onclick
focus	onfocus
load	onload
mousedown	onmousedown
mousemove	onmousemove
mouseout	onmouseout

continued

TABLE 5.1 Events and Their Tag Attributes (Continued)

Event	Tag Attribute
mouseover	onmouseover
mouseup	onmouseup
select	onselect
submit	onsubmit
unload	onunload

In many cases, the same attribute can appear in several different tags. The circumstances under which an event is created are related to a tag and an attribute, and they can be different for the same attribute when it appears in different tags.

An XHTML text element is said to *get focus* when the user puts the mouse cursor over it and clicks the left mouse button. An element can also get focus when the user tabs to the element. Focus on an element can be forced with the focus method, which is described in Section 5.4.5. When a text element has focus, any keyboard input goes to that element. Obviously, only one text element can have focus at one time. An element becomes blurred when the user moves the cursor away from the element and clicks the left mouse button, or tabs away from the element. An element obviously becomes blurred when another element gets focus. Several nontext elements can also have focus, but the condition is less useful in those cases.

Table 5.2 shows the most commonly used attributes related to events, tags that can include the attributes, and the circumstances under which the associated events are created. Only a few of the situations shown in Table 5.2 are discussed in this chapter.

TABLE 5.2 Event Attributes and Their Tags

Attribute	Tag	Description
onblur	<a>	The link loses the input focus.
	<button>	The button loses the input focus.
	<input>	The input element loses the input focus.
	<textarea>	The text area loses the input focus.
	<select>	The selection element loses the input focus.
onchange	<input>	The input element is changed and loses the input focus.

TABLE 5.2 Event Attributes and Their Tags (Continued)

Attribute	Tag	Description
	`<textarea>`	The text area is changed and loses the input focus.
	`<select>`	The selection element is changed and loses the input focus.
`onclick`	`<a>`	The user clicks on the link.
	`<input>`	The input element is clicked.
`onfocus`	`<a>`	The link acquires the input focus.
	`<input>`	The input element receives the input focus.
	`<textarea>`	A text area receives the input focus.
	`<select>`	A selection element receives the input focus.
`onload`	`<body>`	The document is finished loading.
onmousedown	Most elements	The user clicks the left mouse button.
onmousemove	Most elements	The user moves the mouse cursor within the element.
`onmouseout`	Most elements	The mouse cursor is moved away from being over the element.
`onmouseover`	Most elements	The mouse cursor is moved over the element.
onmouseup	Most elements	The left mouse button is unclicked.
`onselect`	`<input>`	The mouse cursor is moved over the element.
	`<textarea>`	The text area is selected within the text area.
`onsubmit`	`<form>`	The Submit button is pressed.
`onunload`	`<body>`	The user exits the document.

As mentioned previously, there are two ways to register an event handler in the DOM 0 event model. One of these is by assigning the event handler script to an event tag attribute, as in the following example:

```
<input type = "button" name = "myButton"
       onclick = "alert('You clicked my button!');" />
```

In many cases, the handler consists of more than a single statement. For these, a function often is used, and the literal string value of the attribute is the call to the function:

```
<input type = "button" name = "myButton"
       onclick = "myHandler();" />
```

5.5

HANDLING EVENTS FROM BODY ELEMENTS

The events most often created by body elements are `load` and `unload`. As our first example of event handling, we consider the simple case of producing an alert message when the body of the document has been loaded. In this case, we use the `onload` attribute of `<body>` to specify the event handler.

```
<?xml version = "1.0" encoding = "utf-8"?>
<!DOCTYPE html PUBLIC "-//w3c//DTD XHTML 1.1//EN"
  "http://www.w3.org/TR/xhtml11/DTD/xhtml11.dtd">

<!-- load.html
     An example to illustrate the load event
     -->
<html xmlns = "http://www.w3.org/1999/xhtml">
  <head>
    <title> onLoad event handler </title>
    <script type = "text/javascript">
      <!--
// The onload event handler

      function load_greeting () {
        alert("You are visiting the home page of \n" +
            "Pete's Pickled Peppers \n" +
            "WELCOME!!!");
      }
      // -->

    </script>
  </head>
  <body onload="load_greeting();">
    <p />
  </body>
</html>
```

Figure 5.2 shows a browser display of `load.html`.

FIGURE 5.2 Display of `load.html`

The `unload` event is probably more useful than the `load` event. It is used to do some cleanup before a document is unloaded, such as when the browser user goes on to some new document. For example, if the document opened a second browser window, that window should be closed by an `unload` event handler.

5.6

HANDLING EVENTS FROM BUTTON ELEMENTS

Buttons in a Web document provide a simple and effective way to collect simple input from the browser user. The most commonly used event created by button actions is `click`.

5.6.1 Plain Buttons

A plain button presents a simple situation. Consider the following button element:

```
<input type = "button"  name = "freeOffer"
       id = "freeButton" />
```

A handler function can be registered for this button with the input attribute `onclick`, as in the following:

```
<input type = "button"  name = "freeButton"
       id = "freeButton"
       onclick = "freeButtonHandler();" />
```

It could also be registered by the assignment to the associated event property on the button object:

```
document.getElementById("freeButton").onclick =
                                    freeButtonHandler;
```

This statement must follow both the handler function and the form element so that JavaScript has seen both before assigning the property.

5.6.2 Checkboxes and Radio Buttons

Consider the following example of a set of radio buttons that enables the user to choose information about a specific airplane. The `click` event is used in this example to trigger a call to `alert`, which presents a brief description of the selected airplane. In this example, the calls to the event handlers send the value of the pressed radio button to the handler. This is another way the handler can determine which of a group of radio buttons is pressed.

```
<?xml version = "1.0" encoding = "utf-8"?>
<!DOCTYPE html PUBLIC "-//w3c//DTD XHTML 1.1//EN"
  "http://www.w3.org/TR/xhtml11/DTD/xhtml11.dtd">


<!-- radio_click.hmtl
     An example of the use of the click event with radio buttons,
     registering the event handler by assignment to the button
     attributes
     -->
<html xmlns = "http://www.w3.org/1999/xhtml">
  <head>
    <title> Illustrate messages for radio buttons </title>
  <script type = "text/javascript">
    <!--

// The event handler for a radio button collection

     function planeChoice (plane) {

// Produce an alert message about the chosen airplane

        switch (plane) {
          case 152:
            alert("A small two-place airplane for flight training");
            break;
```

```
                    case 172:
                      alert("The smaller of two four-place airplanes");
                      break;
                     case 182:
                      alert("The larger of two four-place airplanes");
                      break;
                    case 210:
                      alert("A six-place high-performance airplane");
                      break;
                    default:
                      alert("Error in JavaScript function planeChoice");
                      break;
                }
            }
            // -->
        </script>
    </head>
    <body>
        <h4> Cessna single-engine airplane descriptions </h4>
        <form id = "myForm"  action = "handler">
            <p>
                <input type = "radio"  name = "planeButton"  value = "152"
                       onclick = "planeChoice(152)" />
                Model 152
                <br />
                <input type = "radio"  name = "planeButton"  value = "172"
                       onclick = "planeChoice(172)" />
                Model 172 (Skyhawk)
                <br />
                <input type = "radio"  name = "planeButton"  value = "182"
                       onclick = "planeChoice(182)" />
                Model 182 (Skylane)
                <br />
                <input type = "radio"  name = "planeButton"  value = "210"
                       onclick = "planeChoice(210)" />
                Model 210 (Centurian)
            </p>
        </form>
    </body>
</html>
```

Figure 5.3 shows a browser display of `radio_click.html`. Figure 5.4 shows the `alert` window that results from choosing the Model 182 radio button in `radio_click.html`.

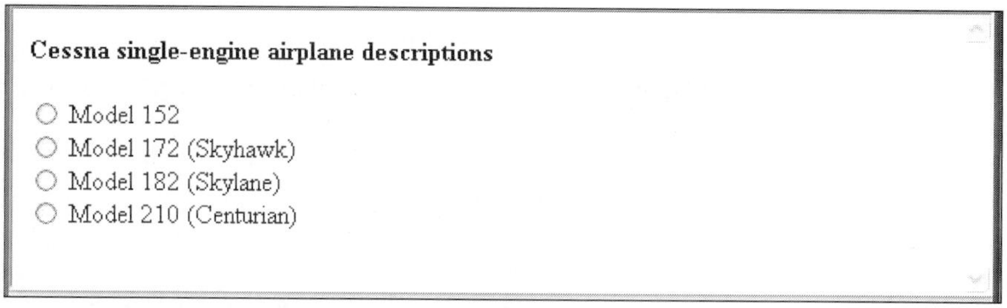

FIGURE 5.3 Display of `radio_click.html`

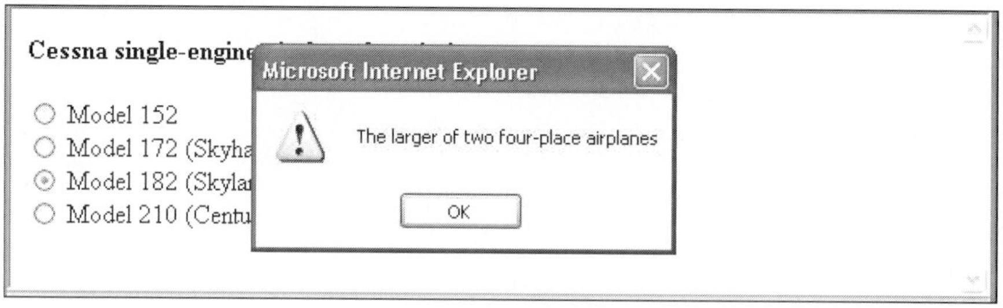

FIGURE 5.4 The result of pressing the Model 182 button in `radio_click`

In `radio_click.html`, the event handler is registered by assigning its call to the `onclick` attribute of the radio buttons. The specific button that was clicked is identified by the parameter sent in the handler call in the button element. An alternative to using the parameter would be to include code in the handler to determine which radio button was pressed.

The next example, `radio_click2.html`, whose purpose is the same as that of `radio_click.html`, registers the event handler by assigning the name of the handler to the event properties of the radio button objects. For example, the following registers the handler on the first radio button:

```
document.getElementById("myForm").elements[0].onclick = planeChoice;
```

Recall that this statement must follow both the handler function and the XHTML form specification so that JavaScript has seen both before assigning to the property.

```
<?xml version = "1.0" encoding = "utf-8"?>
<!DOCTYPE html PUBLIC "-//w3c//DTD XHTML 1.1//EN"
  "http://www.w3.org/TR/xhtml11/DTD/xhtml11.dtd">
```

```
<!-- radio_click2.hmtl
     An example of the use of the click event with radio buttons,
     registering the event handler by assigning an event
     property
     -->
<html xmlns = "http://www.w3.org/1999/xhtml">
  <head>
    <title> Illustrate messages for radio buttons </title>
  <script type = "text/javascript">
    <!--
// The event handler for a radio button collection

     function planeChoice (plane) {

// Put the DOM address of the elements array in a local variable

       var dom = document.getElementById("myForm");

// Determine which button was pressed

       for (var index = 0; index < dom.planeButton.length;
            index++) {
         if (dom.planeButton[index].checked) {
           plane = dom.planeButton[index].value;
           break;
         }
       }

// Produce an alert message about the chosen airplane

       switch (plane) {
         case "152":
          alert("A small two-place airplane for flight training");
          break;
         case "172":
           alert("The smaller of two four-place airplanes");
           break;
         case "182":
           alert("The larger of two four-place airplanes");
           break;
```

continued

```
              case "210":
                alert("A six-place high-performance airplane");
                break;
              default:
                alert("Error in JavaScript function planeChoice");
                break;
          }
        }
        // -->
      </script>
   </head>
   <body>
     <h4> Cessna single-engine airplane descriptions </h4>
     <form id = "myForm"  action = "handler">
       <p>
        <input type = "radio"  name = "planeButton"  value = "152" />
         Model 152
         <br />
        <input type = "radio"  name = "planeButton"  value = "172" />
         Model 172 (Skyhawk)
         <br />
        <input type = "radio"  name = "planeButton"  value = "182" />
         Model 182 (Skylane)
         <br />
        <input type = "radio"  name = "planeButton"  value = "210" />
         Model 210 (Centurian)
       </p>
     </form>

     <script type = "text/javascript">
       <!--
       var dom = document.getElementById("myForm");
       dom.elements[0].onclick = planeChoice;
       dom.elements[1].onclick = planeChoice;
       dom.elements[2].onclick = planeChoice;
       dom.elements[3].onclick = planeChoice;
       // -->
     </script>
   </body>
</html>
```

There is no way to specify parameters on the handler function when it is registered by assigning its name to the event property. Therefore, event handlers that are registered this way cannot use parameters—clearly a disadvantage of this approach. In `radio_click2.html`, the handler includes a loop to determine which radio button created the `click` event.

There are two advantages to registering handlers as properties over registering them in XHTML attributes. First, it is good to keep XHTML and JavaScript separated in the document. This allows a kind of modularization of XHTML documents, resulting in a cleaner design that will be easier to maintain. Second, having the handler function registered as the value of a property allows for the possibility of changing it during use. This could be done by registering a different handler for the event when some other event occurred. This would be impossible if the handler were registered using XHTML.

5.7

HANDLING EVENTS FROM TEXT BOX AND PASSWORD ELEMENTS

Text boxes can create four different events: `blur`, `focus`, `change`, and `select`.

5.7.1 The Focus Event

Suppose JavaScript is used to precompute the total cost of an order and display it to the customer before the order is submitted to the server for processing. An unscrupulous user may be tempted to change the total cost before submission, thinking that somehow an altered (and lower) price would not be noticed at the server end. Such a change to a text box can be prevented by an event handler that blurs the text box every time the user attempts to put it in focus. Blur can be forced on an element with the `blur` method. The following example illustrates this process:

```
<?xml version = "1.0" encoding = "utf-8"?>
<!DOCTYPE html PUBLIC "-//w3c//DTD XHTML 1.1//EN"
  "http://www.w3.org/TR/xhtml11/DTD/xhtml11.dtd">

<!-- nochange.html
     This document illustrates using the focus event
     to prevent the user from changing a text field
     -->
<html xmlns = "http://www.w3.org/1999/xhtml">
  <head> <title> The focus event </title>

    <script type = "text/javascript">
      <!--
```

continued

```
// The event handler function to compute the cost

   function computeCost() {
     var french = document.getElementById("french").value;
     var hazlenut = document.getElementById("hazlenut").value;
     var columbian = document.getElementById("columbian").value;

// Compute the cost

     document.getElementById("cost").value =
     totalCost = french * 3.49 + hazlenut * 3.95 +
                 columbian * 4.59;
   } //* end of computeCost
   -->
  </script>
 </head>
 <body>
  <form action = "">
   <h3> Coffee Order Form </h3>

<!-- A bordered table for item orders -->

   <table border = "border">

<!-- First, the column headings -->

     <tr>
       <th> Product Name </th>
       <th> Price </th>
       <th> Quantity </th>
     </tr>

<!-- Now, the table data entries -->

     <tr>
       <th> French Vanilla (1 lb.) </th>
       <td> $3.49 </td>
       <td> <input type = "text"  id = "french"
                 size ="2" /> </td>
     </tr>
```

```
                <tr>
                  <th> Hazlenut Cream (1 lb.) </th>
                  <td> $3.95 </td>
                  <td> <input type = "text"  id = "hazlenut"
                        size = "2" /> </td>
                </tr>
                <tr>
                  <th> Columbian (1 lb.) </th>
                  <td> $4.59 </td>
                  <td> <input type = "text"  id = "columbian"
                        size = "2" /></td>
                </tr>
            </table>

<!-- Button for precomputation of the total cost -->

            <p>
              <input type = "button"  value = "Total Cost"
                    onclick = "computeCost();" />
              <input type = "text"  size = "5"  id = "cost"
                    onfocus = "this.blur();" />
            </p>

<!-- The submit and reset buttons -->

            <p>
              <input type = "submit"  value = "Submit Order" />
              <input type = "reset"  value = "Clear Order Form" />
            </p>
          </form>
        </body>
    </html>
```

5.7.2 Validating Form Input

As stated earlier, checking the format and completeness of form input is a common application of JavaScript. This approach shifts this task from the usually busy server to the client, which in most cases is only lightly used. It also results in less network traffic and allows quicker responses to users.

When a user fills in a form input element incorrectly and a JavaScript event-handler function detects the error, the function should do several things. First, it should produce an alert message indicating the error to the user and specifying the correct format of the input. Next, it should cause the input element to be put in focus, which positions the cursor in the element. This is done with the `focus` method, which must be called through the DOM address of the element. For example, if the element's `id` is `phone`, the element can be put in focus with this statement:

```
document.getElementById("phone").focus();
```

This puts the cursor in the `phone` text box. Finally, the function should select the element, which highlights the text in the element. This is done with the `select` method, as in this example:

```
document.getElementById("phone").select();
```

The implementations of the `focus` and `select` methods in the IE6 and NS7 browsers are neither consistent nor correct. With IE6, both `focus` and `select` operate correctly, but only if the handler is registered by assigning an event property. With NS7, `select` works properly, but `focus` is apparently not implemented.

If an event handler returns `false`, that tells the browser not to perform any default actions of the event. For example, if the event is a click on the Submit button, the default action is to submit the form data to the server for processing. If user input is being validated in an event handler that is called when the `submit` event occurs and some of the input is incorrect, the handler should return `false` to avoid sending the bad data to the server. We use the convention that event handlers that check form data always return `false` if they detect an error, and `true` otherwise.

When a form requests a password from the user and that password will be used in future sessions, the user is often asked to enter the password a second time for verification. A JavaScript function can be used to check that the two entered passwords are the same.

The form in the following example includes the two password input elements, along with Reset and Submit buttons. The JavaScript function that checks the passwords is called either when the Submit button is pressed, using the `onsubmit` event to trigger the call, or when the second text box loses focus, using the `blur` event. The function performs two different tests. First, it determines whether the user typed the initial password (in the first input box) by testing the value of the element against the empty string. If no password has been typed into the first field, the function calls `alert` to produce an error message, calls `focus` on the field, and returns `false`. The second test is to determine whether the two typed passwords are the same. If they are different, the function calls `alert` to generate an error message, calls both `focus` and `select` on the first password field, and returns `false`. If they are the same, it returns `true`. The following is the document that implements the password input and checking processes.

Figure 5.5 shows a browser display of `pswd_chk.html` after the two password elements have been input but before Submit has been clicked.

```
<?xml version = "1.0" encoding = "utf-8"?>
<!DOCTYPE html PUBLIC "-//w3c//DTD XHTML 1.1//EN"
  "http://www.w3.org/TR/xhtml11/DTD/xhtml11.dtd">


<!-- pswd_chk.html
     An example of input password checking, using the submit
     event
     -->
<html xmlns = "http://www.w3.org/1999/xhtml">
  <head>
    <title> Illustrate password checking> </title>
    <script type = "text/javascript">
      <!--
// The event handler function for password checking

      function chkPasswords() {
        var init = document.getElementById("initial");
        var sec = document.getElementById("second");
        if (init.value == "") {
          alert("You did not enter a password \n" +
                "Please enter one now");
          init.focus();
          return false;
        }

        if (init.value != sec.value) {
          alert("The two passwords you entered are not the same \n"
              + "Please re-enter both now");
          init.focus();
          init.select();
          return false;
        } else
          return true;
      }
      // -->
    </script>
  </head>
  <body>
    <h3> Password Input </h3>
    <form id = "myForm"  action = "">
      <p>
      Your password
```

continued

```
              <input type = "password"  id = "initial"   size = "10" />
              <br /><br />

              Verify password
              <input type = "password"  id = "second"   size = "10" />
              <br /><br />

              <input type = "reset"  name = "reset" />
              <input type = "submit"  name = "submit" />
            </p>
        </form>
        <script type = "text/javascript">
          <!--
// Set submit button onsubmit property to the event handler

            document.getElementById("second").onblur = chkPasswords;
            document.getElementById("myForm").onsubmit = chkPasswords;
            // -->
        </script>
      </body>
    </html>
```

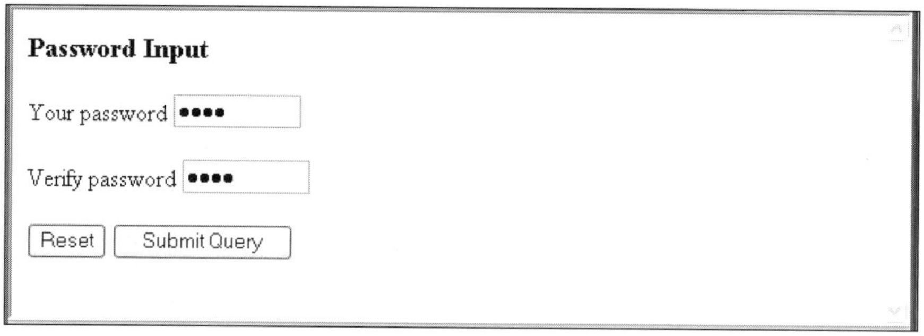

Password Input

Your password `••••`

Verify password `••••`

[Reset] [Submit Query]

FIGURE 5.5 Display of `pswd_chk.html` after it has been filled out

Figure 5.6 shows a browser display that results from pressing the Submit button on `pswd_chk.html` after different passwords have been entered.

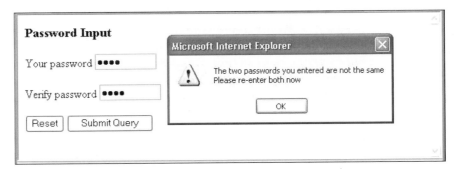

FIGURE 5.6 Display of `pswd_chk.html` after Submit has been pressed

We now consider an example that checks the validity of the form values for a name and phone number obtained from text widgets. Functions are used to check the form of each input when the values of the text boxes are changed, which is detected by the appearance of a `change` event.

In both cases, if an error is detected, an `alert` message is generated and both `focus` and `select` are called to prompt the user to fix the input. The `alert` message includes the correct format. The correct format for the name is last-name, first-name, middle-initial, where the first and last names must begin with uppercase letters and have at least one lowercase letter. Both must be followed immediately by a comma and possibly one space. The middle initial must be uppercase. It may or may not be followed by a period. There can be no characters before or after the whole name. The pattern for matching such names is as follows:

```
/^[A-Z][a-z]+, ?[A-Z][a-z]+, ?[A-Z]\.?$/
```

Note the use of the anchors, `^` and `$`, on the ends of the pattern. This prevents any leading or trailing characters. Also, notice the question marks after the spaces (following the first and last names) and after the period. Recall that the question mark qualifier means zero or one of the qualified subpattern. The period is backslashed so it matches only a period.

The correct format of the phone number is three digits and a dash, followed by three digits and a dash, followed by four digits. As with names, no characaters can precede or follow the phone number. The pattern for phone numbers is as follows:

```
/^\d{3}-\d{3}-\d{4}$/
```

The following is the complete document, `validator.html`, that displays the text boxes for a customer's name and phone number. It includes the Java-Script code to validate these inputs.

```
<?xml version = "1.0" encoding = "utf-8"?>
<!DOCTYPE html PUBLIC "-//w3c//DTD XHTML 1.1//EN"
  "http://www.w3.org/TR/xhtml11/DTD/xhtml11.dtd">
<!-- validator.html
     An example of input validation using the change and submit
     events
     -->
<html xmlns = "http://www.w3.org/1999/xhtml">
  <head>
    <title> Illustrate form input validation> </title>
    <script type = "text/javascript">
      <!--

// The event handler function for the name text box

        function chkName() {
          var myName = document.getElementById("custName");

// Test the format of the input name
//   Allow the spaces after the commas to be optional
//   Allow the period after the initial to be optional

          var pos = myName.value.search(
                  /^[A-Z][a-z]+, ?[A-Z][a-z]+, ?[A-Z]\.?$/);

          if (pos != 0) {
            alert("The name you entered (" + myName.value +
                  ") is not in the correct form. \n" +
                  "The correct form is: " +
                  "last-name, first-name, middle-initial \n" +
                  "Please go back and fix your name");
            myName.focus();
            myName.select();
            return false;
          } else
            return true;
        }

// The event handler function for the phone number text box

        function chkPhone() {
          var myPhone = document.getElementById("phone");

// Test the format of the input phone number
```

```
        var pos = myPhone.value.search(/^\d{3}-\d{3}-\d{4}$/);

        if (pos != 0) {
          alert("The phone number you entered (" + myPhone.value +
                ") is not in the correct form. \n" +
                "The correct form is: ddd-ddd-dddd \n" +
                "Please go back and fix your phone number");
          myPhone.focus();
          myPhone.select();
          return false;
        } else
          return true;
      }
      // -->
    </script>
  </head>
  <body>
    <h3> Customer Information </h3>
    <form action = "">
      <p>
        <input type = "text"  id = "custName"
               onchange = "chkName();"/>
        Name (last name, first name, middle initial)
        <br /><br />

        <input type = "text"  id = "phone" />
        Phone number (ddd-ddd-dddd)
        <br /><br />

        <input type = "reset"  id = "reset" />

        <input type = "submit"  id = "submit" />
      </p>
    </form>
    <script type = "text/javascript">
      <!--
// Set form element object properties to their
// corresponding event handler functions

        document.getElementById("custName").onchange = chkName;
        document.getElementById("phone").onchange = chkPhone;
      // -->
    </script>
  </body>
</html>
```

Figure 5.7 shows the browser screen of `validator.html` after entering a name in the correct format, followed by an invalid telephone number. The screen is shown before the user causes the phone text field to lose focus, either by pressing Enter or by clicking the left mouse button outside the phone text field.

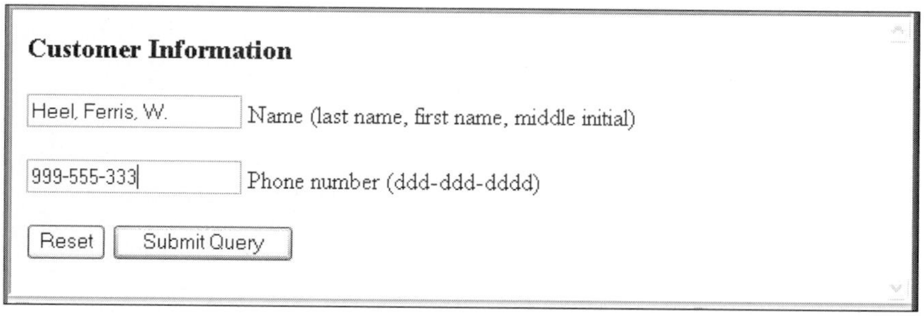

FIGURE 5.7 Display of `validator.html`, with an invalid phone number, while the phone text field has focus

Figure 5.8 shows the `alert` dialog box generated by pressing the Enter button in the phone text field of the screen of Figure 5.7.

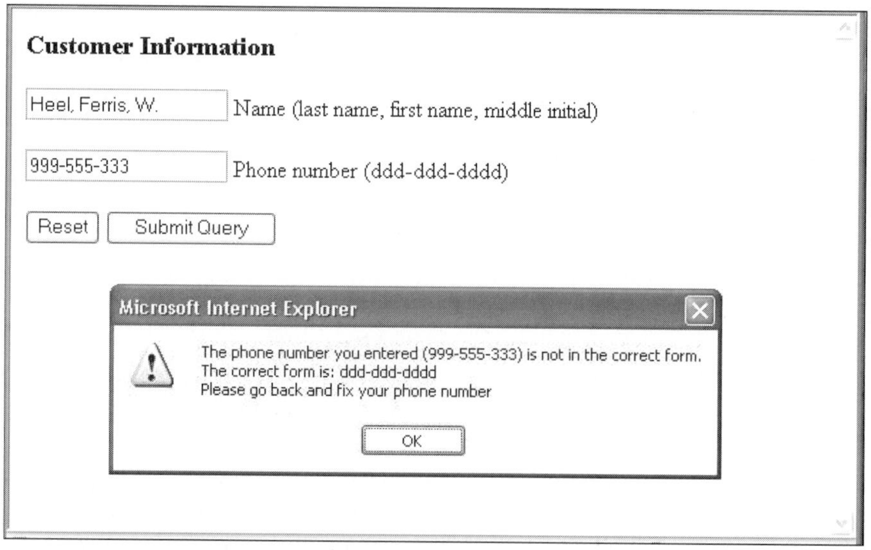

FIGURE 5.8 The message created by entering an invalid telephone number in `validator.html`

5.8

THE DOM 2 EVENT MODEL

The DOM 2 event model does not include the features of the DOM 0 event model. However, there is no chance that support for those features will be dropped from browsers anytime soon. Therefore, Web authors should not hesitate to continue to use them. On the other hand, the DOM 2 event model is more sophisticated and powerful than DOM 0. The real drawback of using the DOM 2 model is that Microsoft has yet to provide support for it in its browsers.

The DOM 2 model is a modularized interface. One of the DOM 2 modules is Events, which includes several submodules, the most commonly used of which are HTMLEvents and MouseEvents. The interfaces and events defined by these modules are as follows:

Module	Event Interface	Event Types
HTMLEvents	Event	abort, blur, change, error, focus, load, reset, resize, schroll, submit, unload
MouseEvents	MouseEvent	click, mousedown, mousemove, mouseout, mouseover, mouseup

When an event occurs and there is an event handler that is called, an object that implements the event interface associated with the event type is implicitly passed to the handler. (Section 5.8.1 explains how a handler is chosen to be called.) The properties of this object has information associated with the event.

The DOM 2 event model is relatively complex. This section covers only the basics of the model. A description of the rest of the model can be found at the W3C's Web site.

5.8.1 Event Propagation

The connection between an event and the handler that deals with it is very simple in the DOM 0 event model. When the browser senses an event has occurred, the object associated with the element that caused the event is checked for event handlers. If that object has a registered handler for the particular event that occurred, that handler is executed. The event-handler connection for the DOM 2 event model is much more complicated.

Briefly, what happens is as follows. An event object is created at a node in the document tree. For that event, that node is called the *target node*. Event creation causes a three-phase process to begin.

The first of these phases is called the *capturing phase*. The event starts at the document root node and propagates down the tree to the target node. If there are any handlers for the event registered on any node encountered in this propagation, including the document node but not the target node, these handlers are checked to determine whether they are enabled. (Section 5.5.2 explains how a handler can be enabled.) Any enabled handler for the event that is found during capturing is executed. When the event reaches the target node, the second phase takes place, in which the handlers registered for the event at the target node are executed. The second phase is similar to what happens with the DOM 0 event model. After execution of any appropriate handlers at the target node, the third phase begins. This is the *bubbling phase*, in which the event bubbles back up the document tree to the document node. On this trip back up the tree, any handler registered for the event at any node on the way is executed.

Not all events bubble. For example, the load and unload events do not bubble. On the other hand, all of the mouse events do. In general, if it makes sense to handle an event farther up the document tree than the target node, the event bubbles; otherwise, it does not.

Any handler can stop the event from further propagation, using the stopPropagation method of the event object.

Bubbling is an idea that was borrowed from exception handling. In a large and complicated document, having event handlers for every element would require a great deal of code. Much of this code would be redundant, both in the handlers and in the registering of handlers for events. Therefore, it makes sense to define a way for a single handler to deal with events created from a number of similar elements. The concept is that events can be propagated to some central place for handling rather than always being handled locally. In the DOM, the natural central place for event handling is at the document or window level, so that is the direction of bubbling.

Many events cause the browser to perform some action; for example, a mouse click on a link causes the document referenced in the link to replace the current document. In some cases, we want to prevent this action from taking place. For example, if a value in a form is found to be invalid by a Submit button event handler, we do not want the form to be submitted to the server. In the DOM 0 event model, the action is prevented by having the handler return false. The DOM 2 Events interface provides a method, preventDefault, that accomplishes the same thing.

5.8.2 Event Handler Registration

The DOM 0 event model uses two different ways of registering event handlers. First, the handler code can be assigned as a string literal to the event's associated attribute in the element. Second, the name of the handler function can be assigned to the property associated with the event. Handler registration in the DOM 2 event model is performed by the method addEventListener, which is defined in the EventTarget interface, which is implemented by all objects that descend from Document.[2]

---

2. The name of this method includes "listener" rather than "handler" because in the DOM 2 specification, handlers are called *listeners*. This is also the term used in Java for widget event handlers.

The `addEventListener` method takes three parameters, the first of which is the name of the event as a string literal. For example, `"mouseup"` and `"submit"` would be legitimate first parameters. The second parameter is the handler function. This could be specified as the function code itself or as the name of a function that is defined elsewhere. The third parameter is a Boolean value that specifies whether the handler is enabled for calling during the capturing phase. If the value `true` is specified, the handler is enabled for the capturing phase. In fact, an enabled handler can *only* be called during capturing. If the value is `false`, the handler can be called either at the target node or on any node reached during bubbling.

When a handler is called, it is passed a single parameter, the `event` object. For example, suppose we want to register the event handler `chkName` on the text element whose `id` is `custName` for the `change` event. The following call accomplishes this:

```
document.custName.addEventListener(
                 "change", chkName, false);
```

In this case, we want the handler to be called at the target node, which is `custName` in this example, so we passed `false` as the third parameter.

Sometimes it is convenient to have a temporary event handler. This can be done by registering the handler for the time when it is to be used, and then deleting that registration. The `removeEventListener` method deletes the registration of an event handler. This method takes the same parameters as `addEventListener`.

With the DOM 0 event model, when an event handler is registered to a document node, the handler becomes a method of the object that represents that node. This makes every use of `this` in the handler a reference to the target node. NS7 browsers implement event handlers for the DOM 2 model in this same way. However, this is not required by the DOM 2 model, so some other browsers may not use this approach, making the use of `this` in a handler potentially nonportable. The safe alternative is to use the `currentTarget` property of `Event`, which will always reference the object on which the handler is being executed. If the handler is called through the object of the target node, `currentTarget` is the target node. However, if the handler is called during capturing or bubbling, `currentTarget` is the object through which the handler is called, which is not the target node object. Another property of `Event`, `target`, is a reference to the target node.

The `MouseEvent` interface inherits from the `Event` interface. It adds a collection of properties related to mouse events. The most useful of these are `clientX` and `clientY`, which have the *x* and *y* coordinates of the mouse cursor, relative to the upper-left corner of the client area of the browser window. The whole browser window is taken into account, so if the user has scrolled down the document, the `clientY` value is measured from the top of the document, not the top of the current display.

5.8.3 An Example of the DOM 2 Event Model

The following example is a revision of the `validator.html` document from Section 5.7, which used the DOM 0 event model. Because the revision, `validator2.html`, uses the DOM 2 event model, this document does not work with IE6. Although they are part of JavaScript, `focus` has no effect with the Netscape 7 browser. In spite of this, we have included calls to them in this document. Curiously, these functions work with IE6, but because IE6 does not implement the DOM 2 event model, this document does not work with IE6. Notice that no call to `preventDefault` appears in this document. The only event handled here is `change`, which has no default actions, so there is nothing to prevent.

```
<?xml version = "1.0" encoding = "utf-8"?>
<!DOCTYPE html PUBLIC "-//w3c//DTD XHTML 1.1//EN"
  "http://www.w3.org/TR/xhtml11/DTD/xhtml11.dtd">


<!-- validator2.html
     An example of input validation using the change and submit
     events, using the DOM 2 event model
     Note: This document does not work with IE6
     -->
<html xmlns = "http://www.w3.org/1999/xhtml">
  <head>
    <title> Illustrate form input validation with DOM 2> </title>
    <script type = "text/javascript">
      <!--
// ******************************************************** //
// The event handler function for the name text box

      function chkName(event) {

// Get the target node of the event

        var myName = event.currentTarget;

// Test the format of the input name
//  Allow the spaces after the commas to be optional
//  Allow the period after the initial to be optional

        var pos = myName.value.search(/\w+, ?\w+, ?\w.?/);

        if (pos != 0) {
          alert("The name you entered (" + myName.value +
```

```
                       ") is not in the correct form. \n" +
                       "The correct form is: " +
                       "last-name, first-name, middle-initial \n" +
                       "Please go back and fix your name");
                myName.focus();
                myName.select();
            }
        }

// ********************************************************** //
// The event handler function for the phone number text box

        function chkPhone(event) {

// Get the target node of the event

            var myPhone = event.currentTarget;

// Test the format of the input phone number

            var pos = myPhone.value.search(/^\d{3}-\d{3}-\d{4}$/);

            if (pos != 0) {
                alert("The phone number you entered (" + myPhone.value +
                       ") is not in the correct form. \n" +
                       "The correct form is: ddd-ddd-dddd \n" +
                       "Please go back and fix your phone number");
                myPhone.focus();
                myPhone.select();
            }
        }

// ********************************************************** //
        // -->
    </script>
  </head>
  <body>
    <h3> Customer Information </h3>
    <form action = "">
      <p>
        <input type = "text"  id = "custName" />
        Name (last name, first name, middle initial)
        <br /><br />
```

continued

```
            <input type = "text"  id = "phone" />
            Phone number (ddd-ddd-dddd)
            <br /><br />

            <input type = "reset" />

            <input type = "submit"  id = "submitButton" />
        </p>
    </form>
    <script type = "text/javascript">
        <!--

// Get the DOM addresses of the elements and register
//     the event handlers

        var customerNode = document.getElementById("custName");
        var phoneNode = document.getElementById("phone");
        customerNode.addEventListener("change", chkName, false);
        phoneNode.addEventListener("change", chkPhone, false);

        // -->
    </script>
  </body>
</html>
```

Note that the two event models can be mixed in a document. If a DOM 0 feature happens to be more convenient than the corresponding DOM 2 feature, there is no reason it cannot be used. Chapter 6 includes an example of the use of the DOM 2 event model for something that cannot be done with the DOM 0 event model.

5.9

THE navigator OBJECT

The navigator object indicates which browser is being used to view the XHTML document. The browser's name is stored in the appName property of the navigator object. The version of the browser is stored in the appVersion property of the navigator object. These properties allow the script to determine which browser is being used and to use processes appropriate to that browser. The following example illustrates the use of navigator, in this case just to display the browser name and version number.

```
<?xml version = "1.0" encoding = "utf-8"?>
<!DOCTYPE html PUBLIC "-//w3c//DTD XHTML 1.1//EN"
  "http://www.w3.org/TR/xhtml11/DTD/xhtml11.dtd">


<!-- navigate.html
     An example of using the navigator object
     -->
<html xmlns = "http://www.w3.org/1999/xhtml">
  <head>
    <title> Using navigator </title>
    <script type = "text/javascript">
     <!--
// The event handler function to display the browser name
//  and its version number

     function navProperties() {
        alert("The browser is: " + navigator.appName + "\n" +
          "The version number is: " + navigator.appVersion + "\n");
     }
     // -->
    </script>
  </head>
  <body onload = "navProperties()">
    <p />
  </body>
</html>
```

Figure 5.9 shows the result of displaying `navigate.html` with NS7. Figure 5.10 shows the result of displaying `navigate.html` with IE6. Notice that the version number of IE6 is 4. Microsoft intentionally set the version number to 4 because of some compatibility issues with earlier browsers. One would hope that future versions of IE will use the correct version number. Netscape is not any better in this regard. Using NS7, it displays `version 5.0`.

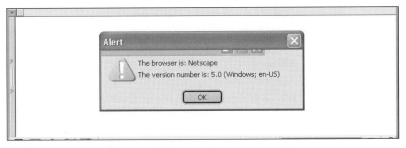

FIGURE 5.9 The `navigator` properties `appName` and `appVersion` for Netscape 7

FIGURE 5.10 The `navigator` properties `appName` and `appVersion` for Internet Explorer 6

5.10

SUMMARY

The highest levels of the execution environment of client-side JavaScript are represented with the `Window` and `Document` objects. The `Document` object includes a `forms` array property, which includes references to all forms in the document. Each element of the `forms` array has an `elements` array, which includes references to all elements in the form.

The DOM is an abstract interface whose purpose is to provide a language-independent way to access the elements of an XHTML document. Also included are the means to navigate around the structure in which the XHTML elements appear. XHTML tags are represented in JavaScript as objects; tag attributes are represented as properties.

There are three different ways to access XHTML elements in JavaScript: through the `forms` and `elements` arrays, through the names of the element and its enclosing elements, and through the `getElementById` method.

Events are simply notifications that something specific has happened that may require some special processing. Event-handling code provides that special processing. There are two distinct event models currently in use. The first is the model implemented by all browsers that support JavaScript, which we refer to as the DOM 0 model. The second is the more elaborate and powerful model defined in DOM 2.

With the DOM 0 model, there are two ways to register an event handler. First, an attribute of the tag that defines the XHTML element can be assigned the handler code. Second, the property associated with the event of the object that represents the XHTML element can be assigned the name of a function that implements the handler. The `write` method of `document` should not be used in event handlers.

With the DOM 0 model, each event has an associated tag attribute. A particular attribute may appear in several different tags. Each of these appearances is identified as a different event occurrence. The `load` and `unload` events are often used with the `<body>` tag to perform some operation when a document has been loaded or unloaded, respectively. The `click` event is used for all of the different XHTML buttons, as well as the link of an anchor tag. Form input can be conveniently checked using the `change` event. The `submit` event can also be used to check form data just before the form is submitted.

The DOM 2 event model defines three phases of event processing: capturing, target node, and bubbling. During the capturing phase, the event object travels from the document root to the target node, where the event was created. During the bubbling phase, the event travels back up the document tree to the root, triggering any handlers registered on nodes that are encountered. Event handlers can be set to allow them to be triggered during the capturing phase. Event-handler registration is done with the `addEventListener` method, which sets whether capturing-phase triggering will take place. Events can be unregistered with the `removeEventListener` method. The `currentTarget` property of `Event` has the object through which the handler was called. The `target` property has the target node object. The `mouseEvent` object has two properties, `clientX` and `clientY`, which have the coordinates of the position of the mouse cursor in the browser display window when a mouse event occurs.

The `navigator` object has information about which browser is being used, as well as its version number and other related information.

5.11 Review Questions

1. Global variables in JavaScript are properties of what object?

2. How are XHTML elements and attributes represented in the JavaScript binding to DOM?

3. What is an event?

4. What is an event handler?

5. What is the origin of the DOM 0 event model?

6. What are the two ways in which an event handler can be associated with an event generated by a specific XHTML element in the DOM 0 event model?

7. Why should `document.write` not be used in an event handler?

8. In what ways can an XHTML element acquire focus?

9. Describe the approach to addressing XHTML elements using `forms` and `elements`.

10. Describe the approach to addressing XHTML elements using `name` attributes.

11. Describe the approach to addressing XHTML elements using `getElementById`.

12. What is the disadvantage of assigning event handlers to event properties?

13. What are the advantages of assigning event handlers to event properties?

14. Why is it good to use JavaScript to check the validity of form inputs before the form data is sent to the server?

15. What three things should be done when a form input element is found to have incorrectly formatted data?

16. What exactly does the `focus` function do?

17. What exactly does the `select` function do?

18. What happens when an event handler for the `onsubmit` event returns `false`?

19. What event is used to trigger an event handler that checks the validity of input for a text button in a form?

20. What event propagation takes place in the DOM 0 event model?

21. Explain the three phases of event processing in the DOM 2 event model.

22. Give two examples of default actions of events.

23. Explain the first two parameters of the `addEventListener` method.

24. How is an event handler registered so that it will be called during the capturing phase?

25. How can an event handler be unregistered?

26. What exactly do the `clientX` and `clientY` properties store?

27. What purpose does the `navigator` object have?

5.12 Exercises

1. Modify the `radio_click.html` example to have five buttons, labeled "red," "blue," "green," "yellow," and "orange." The event handlers for these buttons must produce messages stating the chosen favorite color. The event handler must be implemented as a function, whose name must be assigned to the `onclick` attribute of the radio button elements. The chosen color must be sent to the event handler as a parameter.

2. Rewrite the document for Exercise 1 to assign the event handler to the event property of the button element. This requires the chosen color to be obtained from the `value` property of the button element rather than through the parameter.

3. Develop, test, and validate an XHTML document that has checkboxes for apple (59 cents each), orange (49 cents each), and banana (39 cents each), along with a Submit button. Each of the checkboxes should have its own `onclick` event handler. These handlers must add the cost of their fruit to a total cost. An event handler for the Submit button must produce an `alert` window with the message "Your total cost is: $xxx," where xxx is

the total cost of the chosen fruit, including 5 percent for sales tax. This handler must return `false` (to avoid actual submission of the form data).

4. Develop, test, and validate an XHTML document that is similar to that of Exercise 3. In this case, use text boxes rather than checkboxes. These text boxes take a number, which is the purchased number of the particular fruit. The rest of the document should behave exactly like that of Exercise 3.

5. Add reality checks to the text boxes of the document in Exercise 4. The checks on the text box inputs should ensure that the input values are numbers in the range of 0 to 99.

6. Range checks for element inputs can be represented as new properties of the object that represents the element. Modify the document in Exercise 5 to add a `max` property value of 99 and a `min` property value of 0. Your event handler must use the properties for the range checks on values input through the text boxes.

7. Develop, test, and validate an XHTML document that collects the following information from the user: last name, first name, middle initial, age (restricted to be greater than 17), and weight (restricted to the range of 80–300). You must have event handlers for the form elements that collect this information that check the input data for correctness. Messages in `alert` windows must be produced when errors are detected.

8. Revise the document of Exercise 1 to use the DOM 2 event model.

9. Revise the document of Exercise 3 to use the DOM 2 event model.

6

Dynamic Documents with JavaScript

Informally, a dynamic XHTML document is one that in some way can be changed while it is being displayed by a browser. The most common client-side approach to providing dynamic documents is with JavaScript. Changes to documents can occur when explicitly requested by user interactions, or at regular timed intervals.

XHTML elements can be initially positioned at any given location on the browser display. If they're positioned in a particular way, elements can be dynamically moved to new positions on the display. Elements can be made to disappear and reappear. The colors of the background and the foreground (the elements) of a document can be changed. The font, font size, and font style can be changed. Even the content of an element can be changed. Overlapping elements in a document can be positioned in a specific top-to-bottom stacking order, and their stacking order can be dynamically changed. The position of the mouse cursor on the browser display can be determined when the mouse is clicked. Elements can be made to move slowly around the display screen.

Finally, elements can be defined to allow the user to drag and drop them anywhere in the display window. This chapter discusses all of these topics.

6.1

INTRODUCTION

Dynamic XHTML is not a new markup language. It is a collection of technologies that allows dynamic changes to documents described with XHTML. Specifically, a *dynamic XHTML document* is one whose tag attributes, tag contents, or element style properties can be changed after the document has been and is still being displayed by a browser. Such changes can be made with an embedded script that accesses the elements of the document as objects in the associated Document Object Model (DOM) structure.

Support for dynamic XHTML is not uniform across the various browsers. As in Chapter 5, "JavaScript and HTML Documents," we restrict our discussion to W3C-standard approaches rather than using features defined by a particular browser vendor. All of the examples in this chapter, except the document in Section 6.11, use the DOM 0 event model and work on both Internet Explorer 6 (IE6) and Netscape 7 (NS7) browsers. The example in Section 6.11 uses the DOM 2 event model because it cannot be designed in a standard way using the DOM 0 event model. Because IE6 does not support the DOM 2 event model, this example does not work with IE6.

This chapter discusses user interactions through XHTML documents using client-side JavaScript. Chapters 10–13 of this book discuss user interactions through XHTML documents using server-side technologies.

6.2

ELEMENT POSITIONING

Before the browsers that implemented HTML 4.0 appeared, Web site authors had little control over how HTML elements were arranged in documents. In many cases, the elements found in the HTML file were simply placed in the document the way text is placed in a document with a word processor—fill a row, start a new row, fill it, and so forth. HTML tables provide a framework of columns for arranging elements, but they lack flexibility and also take a considerable amount of time to display.[1] This lack of powerful and fast element placement control ended when Cascading Style Sheets–Positioning (CSS-P) was released by the W3C in 1997.

---

1. Frames provide another way to arrange elements, but they were deprecated in XHTML 1.0 and eliminated from XHTML 1.1.

CSS-P is completely supported by IE6 and NS7. It provides the means not only to position any element anywhere in the display of a document, but also to dynamically move an element to a new position in the display, using JavaScript to change the positioning style properties of the element. These style properties, which are appropriately named `left` and `top`, dictate the distance from the left and top of some reference point to where the element is to appear. Another style property, `position`, interacts with `left` and `top` to provide a higher level of control of placement and movement of elements. The `position` property has three possible values: `absolute`, `relative`, and `static`.

6.2.1 Absolute Positioning

The `absolute` value is specified for `position` when the element is to be placed at a specific place in the document display without regard to the positions of other elements. For example, if you want a paragraph of text to appear 100 pixels from the left edge of the display window and 200 pixels from the top, you could use the following:

```
<p style = "position: absolute; left: 100px; top: 200px">
   -- text --
</p>
```

One use of absolute positioning is to superimpose special text over a paragraph of ordinary text to create an effect similar to a watermark on paper. A larger italicized font, with space between the letters in a light gray color, can be used for the special text, allowing both the ordinary text and the special text to be legible. The following XHTML document provides an example that implements this approach. In this example, a paragraph of normal text that describes apples is displayed. Superimposed on this paragraph is the somewhat subliminal message "APPLES ARE GOOD FOR YOU."

```
<?xml version = "1.0" encoding = "utf-8"?>
<!DOCTYPE html PUBLIC "-//w3c//DTD XHTML 1.1//EN"
  "http://www.w3.org/TR/xhtml11/DTD/xhtml11.dtd">

<!-- absPos.html
     Illustrates absolute positioning of elements
     -->
<html xmlns = "http://www.w3.org/1999/xhtml">
  <head>
    <title> Absolute positioning </title>
    <style type = "text/css">
```

continued

```
/* A style for a paragraph of text */

        .regtext {font-family: Times; font-size: 14pt; width: 600px}

/* A style for the text to be absolutely positioned */

        .abstext {position: absolute; top: 25px; left: 50px;
                  font-family: Times; font-size: 24pt;
                  font-style: italic; letter-spacing: 1em;
                  color: rgb(102,102,102); width: 500px}
      </style>
    </head>
    <body>
      <p class = "regtext">
        Apple is the common name for any tree of the genus Malus, of
        the family Rosaceae. Apple trees grow in any of the temperate
        areas of the world. Some apple blossoms are white, but most
        have stripes or tints of rose. Some apple blossoms are bright
        red. Apples have a firm and fleshy structure that grows from
        the blossom. The colors of apples range from green to very
        dark red. The wood of apple trees is fine-grained and hard.
        It is, therefore, good for furniture construction. Apple trees
        have been grown for many centuries. They are propagated by
        grafting because they do not reproduce themselves.
      </p>
      <p class = "abstext">
        APPLES ARE GOOD FOR YOU
      </p>
    </body>
</html>
```

Figure 6.1 shows a display of `absPos.html`.

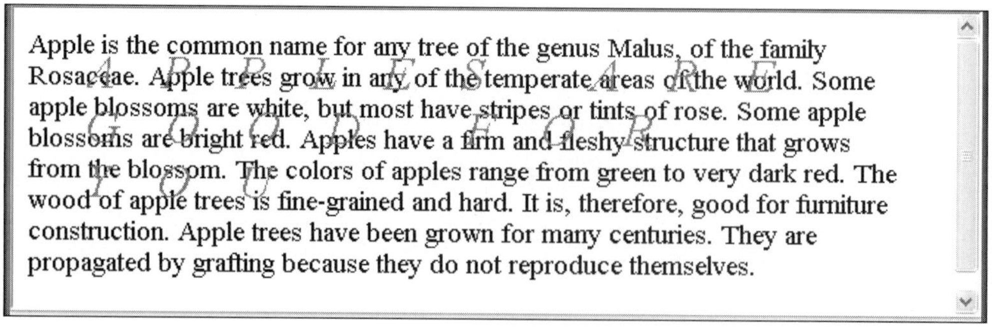

Apple is the common name for any tree of the genus Malus, of the family Rosaceae. Apple trees grow in any of the temperate areas of the world. Some apple blossoms are white, but most have stripes or tints of rose. Some apple blossoms are bright red. Apples have a firm and fleshy structure that grows from the blossom. The colors of apples range from green to very dark red. The wood of apple trees is fine-grained and hard. It is, therefore, good for furniture construction. Apple trees have been grown for many centuries. They are propagated by grafting because they do not reproduce themselves.

FIGURE 6.1 Display of `absPos.html`

Notice that a `width` property value is included in the style for both the regular and the special text. This property is used here so we can ensure that the special text is uniformly embedded in the regular text. Without it, the text would extend to the right end of the browser display window. And, of course, the width of the window could vary widely from client to client and even from minute to minute on the same client because the user can resize the browser window at any time.

When an element is absolutely positioned inside another positioned element (one that has the `position` property specified), the `top` and `left` property values are measured from the upper-left corner of the enclosing element (rather than the upper-left corner of the browser window).

To illustrate nested element placement, we modify the document `absPos.html` to place the regular text 100 pixels from the top and 100 pixels from the left. The special text is nested inside the regular text by using `<div>` and `<span>` tags. The modified document, which follows, is named `absPos2.html`.

```
<?xml version = "1.0" encoding = "utf-8"?>
<!DOCTYPE html PUBLIC "-//w3c//DTD XHTML 1.1//EN"
  "http://www.w3.org/TR/xhtml11/DTD/xhtml11.dtd">

<!-- absPos2.html
     Illustrates nested absolute positioning of elements
     -->
<html xmlns = "http://www.w3.org/1999/xhtml">
  <head>
    <title> Nested absolute positioning </title>
    <style type = "text/css">

/* A style for a paragraph of text */

    .regtext {font-family: Times; font-size: 14pt; width: 500px;
             position: absolute; top: 100px; left: 100px;}

/* A style for the text to be absolutely positioned */

    .abstext {position: absolute; top: 25px; left: 50px;
             font-family: Times; font-size: 24pt;
             font-style: italic; letter-spacing: 1em;
             color: rgb(102,102,102); width: 400px;}

    </style>
```

continued

```
    </head>
    <body>
      <div class = "regtext">
        Apple is the common name for any tree of the genus Malus, of
        the family Rosaceae. Apple trees grow in any of the temperate
        areas of the world. Some apple blossoms are white, but most
        have stripes or tints of rose. Some apple blossoms are bright
        red. Apples have a firm and fleshy structure that grows from
        the blossom. The colors of apples range from green to very
        dark red. The wood of apple trees is fine-grained and hard.
      It is, therefore, good for furniture construction. Apple trees
        have been grown for many centuries. They are propagated by
        grafting because they do not reproduce themselves.
        <span class = "abstext">
          APPLES ARE GOOD FOR YOU
        </span>
      </div>
    </body>
  </html>
```

Figure 6.2 shows a display of `absPos2.html`.

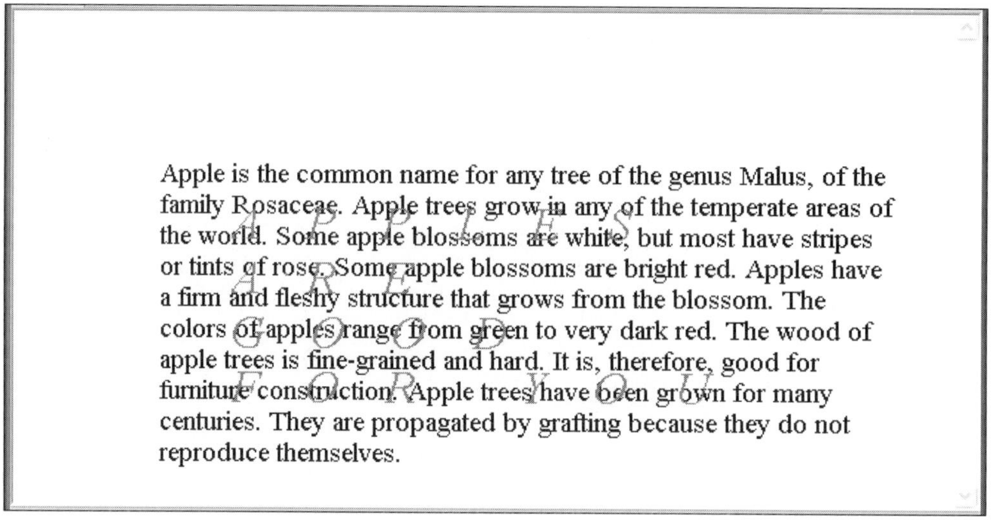

FIGURE 6.2 Display of `absPos2.html`

6.2.2 Relative Positioning

An element that has the `position` property set to `relative` but does not specify `top` and `left` property values is placed in the document as if the `position` attribute were not set at all. However, such an element can be moved later. If the `top` and `left` properties are given values, they displace the element by the specified amount from the position where it would have been placed. For example, suppose that two buttons are placed in a document, and the `position` attribute has its default value, which is `static`. They would appear next to each other in a row, assuming the current row had sufficient horizontal space for them. If `position` has been set to `relative` and the second button had its `left` property set to `50px`, the effect would be to move it 50 pixels farther to the right than it otherwise would have appeared.

In both the case of an absolutely positioned element inside another element and the case of a relatively positioned element, negative values of `top` and `left` displace the element upward and to the left, respectively.

Relative positioning can be used for a variety of special effects in element placement. For example, it can be used to create superscripts and subscripts by placing the values to be raised or lowered in `<span>` tags and displacing them from their regular positions. In the following example, a line of text is set in a normal font style in 24-point size. Embedded in the line is one word that is set in italic, 48-point, red font. Normally, the bottom of the special word would align with the bottom of the rest of the line. In this case, we want the special word to be vertically centered in the line, so its `position` property is set to `relative` and its `top` property is set to 10 pixels, which lowers it by that amount relative to the surrounding text. The XHTML document to specify this, which is named `relPos.html`, is shown here:

```
<?xml version = "1.0" encoding = "utf-8"?>
<!DOCTYPE html PUBLIC "-//w3c//DTD XHTML 1.1//EN"
  "http://www.w3.org/TR/xhtml11/DTD/xhtml11.dtd">

<!-- relPos.html
     Illustrates relative positioning of elements
     -->
<html xmlns = "http://www.w3.org/1999/xhtml">
  <head>
    <title> Relative positioning </title>
  </head>
  <body style = "font-family: Times; font-size: 24pt;">
    <p>
      Apples are <span style =
             "position: relative; top: 10px;
```

continued

```
                      font-family: Times; font-size: 48pt;
                      font-style: italic; color: red;">
          GOOD </span> for you.
      </p>
    </body>
  </html>
```

Figure 6.3 shows a display of `relPos.html`.

FIGURE 6.3 Display of `relPos.html`

6.2.3 Static Positioning

The default value for the `position` property is `static`. A statically positioned element is placed in the document as if it had the `position` value of `relative`. The difference is that a statically positioned element cannot have its `top` or `left` properties initially set or changed later. Therefore, a statically placed element cannot be displaced from its normal position and cannot be moved from that position later.

6.3

MOVING ELEMENTS

As stated previously, an XHTML element whose `position` property is set to either `absolute` or `relative` can be moved. Moving an element is simple: Changing the `top` or `left` property values causes the element to move within the display. If its `position` was set to `absolute`, the element moves to the new values of `top` and `left`; if its `position` was set to `relative`, it moves from its original position by distances given by the new values of `top` and `left`.

In the following example, an image is absolutely positioned in the display. The document includes two text boxes labeled `x coordinate` and `y coordinate`. The user can enter new values for the `left` and `top` properties of the image in these boxes. When the button labeled Move It is pressed, the values of the `left` and `top` properties of the image are changed to the given values, and the element is moved to its new position.

A JavaScript function is used to change the values of `left` and `top` in our example. Although it is not necessary, the `id` of the element to be moved is sent to the moving function, just to illustrate that the function could be used on any number of different elements. The values of the two text boxes are also sent to the function as parameters. The actual parameter values are the DOM addresses of the text boxes, with the `value` attribute attached, which provides the complete DOM addresses of the text-box values. Notice that we attach `style` to the DOM address of the image to be moved because `top` and `left` are style properties.

```
<?xml version = "1.0" encoding = "utf-8"?>
<!DOCTYPE html PUBLIC "-//w3c//DTD XHTML 1.1//EN"
  "http://www.w3.org/TR/xhtml11/DTD/xhtml11.dtd">

<!-- mover.html
     Illustrates moving an element within a document
     -->
<html xmlns = "http://www.w3.org/1999/xhtml">
  <head>
    <title> Moving elements </title>
    <script type = "text/javascript">
<!--
// **************************************************
// The event handler function to move an element

    function moveIt(movee, newTop, newLeft) {

      dom = document.getElementById(movee).style;

// Change the top and left properties to perform the move
//  Note the addition of units to the input values

      dom.top = newTop + "px";
      dom.left = newLeft + "px";
    }
// **************************************************
// -->
    </script>
  </head>
  <body>
    <form action = "">
      <p>
        x coordinate: <input type = "text"  id = "leftCoord"
                              size = "3" />
```

continued

```
                    <br />
                    y coordinate: <input type = "text"  id = "topCoord"
                                        size = "3" />
                    <br />
                    <input type = "button"  value = "Move it"
                            onclick =
                              "moveIt('nebula',
                                document.getElementById('topCoord').value,
                                document.getElementById('leftCoord').value)" />
                  </p>
                </form>
                <div id = "nebula"  style = "position: absolute;
                    top: 115px; left: 0;">
                  <img src = "../images/ngc604.jpg"
                        alt = "(Picture of a nebula)" />
                </div>
              </body>
            </html>
```

Figures 6.4 and 6.5 show the initial and new positions of an image in mover.html.

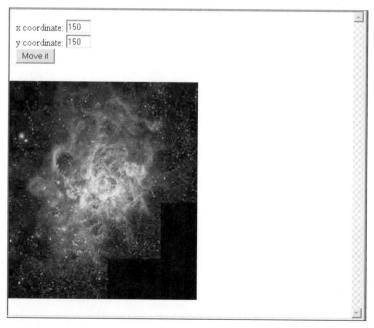

FIGURE 6.4 Display of mover.html (before pressing the Move It button)

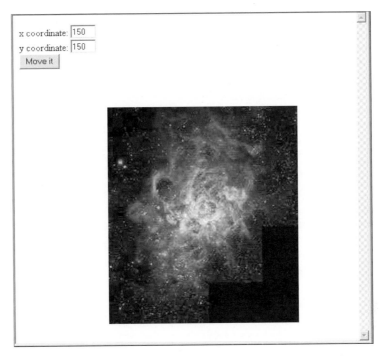

FIGURE 6.5 Display of `mover.html` (after the Move It button has been pressed)

6.4

ELEMENT VISIBILITY

Document elements can be specified to be visible or hidden with the value of their `visibility` property. The two possible values for `visibility` are, quite naturally, `visible` and `hidden`. The appearance or disappearance of an element can be controlled by the user through a button.

The following example displays an image and allows the user to toggle the image between appearing and not appearing in the document display.

```
<?xml version = "1.0" encoding = "utf-8"?>
<!DOCTYPE html PUBLIC "-//w3c//DTD XHTML 1.1//EN"
  "http://www.w3.org/TR/xhtml11/DTD/xhtml11.dtd">


<!-- showHide.html
     Illustrates visibility control of elements
     -->
```

continued

```html
<html xmlns = "http://www.w3.org/1999/xhtml">
  <head>
    <title> Visibility control </title>
    <script type = "text/javascript">
<!--
// ***********************************************************
// The event handler function to toggle the visibility
//    of the images of Saturn

    function flipImag() {
      dom = document.getElementById("saturn").style;

// Flip the visibility adjective to whatever it is not now

      if (dom.visibility == "visible")
        dom.visibility = "hidden";
      else
        dom.visibility = "visible";
    }
// ***********************************************************
// -->
    </script>
  </head>
  <body>
    <form action = "">
      <div id = "saturn"  style = "position: relative;
          visibility: visible;">
        <img src = "../images/saturn.jpg"
            alt = "(Picture of Saturn)" />
      </div>
      <p>
        <br />
        <input type = "button"  value = "Toggle Saturn"
            onclick = "flipImag()" />
      </p>
    </form>
  </body>
</html>
```

6.5

CHANGING COLORS AND FONTS

Background and foreground colors can be dynamically changed, as can the font properties of text.

6.5.1 Changing Colors

Dynamic changes to colors are relatively simple. In the following example, the user is presented two text boxes into which color specifications can be typed, one for the document background color and one for the foreground color. The colors can be specified by any of the three ways that color properties can be given anywhere else. A JavaScript function, which is called (using the `onchange` event) whenever one of the text boxes is changed, makes the change in the document's appropriate color property, `backgroundColor` or `color`. The first of the two parameters to the function specifies whether the new color is for the background or foreground; the second specifies the new color. The new color is the `value` property of the text box that was changed by the user.

In this example, the calls to the handler functions are in the XHTML text box elements. This situation allows a simple way to reference the element's DOM address. The JavaScript `this` variable is a reference to the object that represents the element in which it is referenced. A reference to such an object is its DOM address. Therefore, in a text element, the value of `this` is the DOM address of the text element. So, in our example, `this.value` is used as an actual parameter to the handler function. Because the call is in an input element, `this.value` is the DOM address of the value of the input element.

```
<?xml version = "1.0" encoding = "utf-8"?>
<!DOCTYPE html PUBLIC "-//w3c//DTD XHTML 1.1//EN"
  "http://www.w3.org/TR/xhtml11/DTD/xhtml11.dtd">

<!-- dynColors.html
     Illustrates dynamic foreground and background colors
     -->
<html xmlns = "http://www.w3.org/1999/xhtml">
  <head>
    <title> Dynamic colors </title>
    <script type = "text/javascript">
<!--
// ************************************************************
// The event handler function to dynamically set the
//  color of background or foreground
```

continued

```
      function setColor(where, newColor) {
        if (where == "background")
          document.body.style.backgroundColor = newColor;
        else
          document.body.style.color = newColor;
      }
// ***********************************************************
// -->
   </script>
 </head>
 <body>
   <p style = "font-family: Times; font-style: italic;
              font-size: 24pt" >
      This small page illustrates dynamic setting of the
      foreground and background colors for a document
   </p>
   <form action = "">
      <p>
        Background color: <input type = "text"  name = "background"
                                  size = "10"
                                     onchange = "setColor('background',
                                                 this.value)" />
          <br />
        Foreground color: <input type = "text"  name = "foreground"
                                  size = "10"
                                     onchange = "setColor('foreground',
                                                 this.value)" />
          <br />
      </p>
   </form>
 </body>
</html>
```

6.5.2 Changing Fonts

Web users are accustomed to having links in documents change color when the cursor is placed over them. Using the mouse event mouseover to trigger Java-Script event handlers, any property of a link can be changed. Thus, the font style and font size, as well as the color and background color, can be changed when the cursor is placed over a link. The link can be changed back to its original form when an event handler is triggered with the mouseout event. In the following example, the only element is a sentence with an embedded link. The foreground color for the document is the default black. The link is presented in blue. When the mouse cursor is placed over the link, its color changes to red and its font style changes to italic.

```
<?xml version = "1.0" encoding = "utf-8"?>
<!DOCTYPE html PUBLIC "-//w3c//DTD XHTML 1.1//EN"
  "http://www.w3.org/TR/xhtml11/DTD/xhtml11.dtd">

<!-- dynLink.html
     Illustrates dynamic font styles and colors for links
     -->
<html xmlns = "http://www.w3.org/1999/xhtml">
  <head>
    <title> Dynamic fonts for links </title>
    <style type = "text/css">
      .regText {font: Times; font-size: 16pt;}
    </style>
  </head>
  <body>
    <p class = "regText">
      The state of
      <a style = "color: blue;"
         onmouseover = "this.style.color = 'red';
                        this.style.font = 'italic 16pt Times';"
         onmouseout = "this.style.color = 'blue';
                        this.style.font = 'normal 16pt Times';">
         Washington
      </a>
      produces many of our nation's apples.
    </p>
  </body>
</html>
```

Figures 6.6 and 6.7 show browser displays of the dynLink.html document with the mouse cursor not over and then over the link.

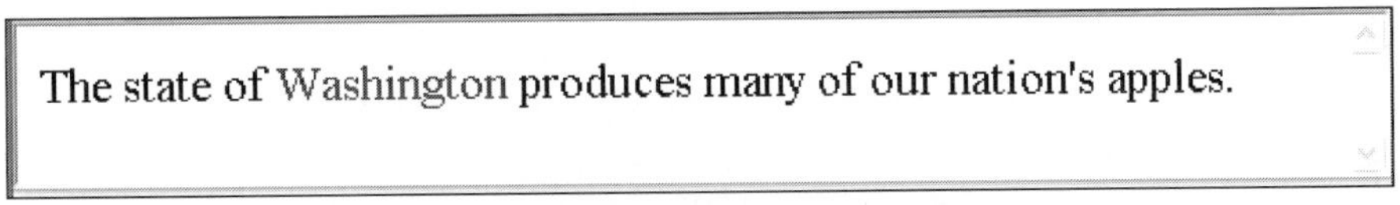

The state of Washington produces many of our nation's apples.

FIGURE 6.6 Display of dynLink.html with the cursor not over the link

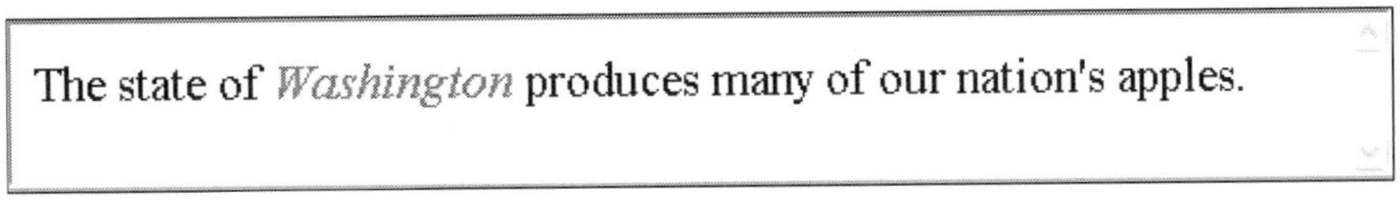

The state of *Washington* produces many of our nation's apples.

FIGURE 6.7 Display of dynLink.html with the mouse cursor over the link

6.6

DYNAMIC CONTENT

We have explored the options of dynamically changing the positions of elements, their visibility, and the colors, background colors, and styles of text fonts. This section investigates changing the content of XHTML elements. The content of an element is accessed through the `value` property of its associated JavaScript object. So, changing the content of an element is not essentially different from changing other properties of the element. The following example illustrates changing the content of a collection of text fields.

Assistance to a user filling out a form can be provided by an associated text area, often called a *help box*. The content of the help box can change, depending on the placement of the mouse cursor. When the cursor is placed over a particular input field, the help box can display advice on how the field is to be filled. When the cursor is moved away from an input field, the help-box content can be changed to simply indicate that assistance is available.

In the example, an array of messages that can be displayed in the help box is defined in JavaScript. Note that the backslash characters that terminate some of the lines of the literal array of messages specify that the string literal is continued on the next line. When the mouse cursor is placed over an input field, the `mouseover` event is used to call a function that changes the help-box content to the appropriate value (the one associated with the input field). The appropriate value is specified with a parameter sent to the handler function. The `mouseout` event is used to trigger the change of the content of the help box back to the "standard" value.

```
<?xml version = "1.0" encoding = "utf-8"?>
<!DOCTYPE html PUBLIC "-//w3c//DTD XHTML 1.1//EN"
  "http://www.w3.org/TR/xhtml11/DTD/xhtml11.dtd">

<!-- dynValue.html
     Illustrates dynamic values
     -->
<html xmlns = "http://www.w3.org/1999/xhtml">
  <head>
    <title> Dynamic values </title>
    <script type = "text/javascript">
<!--
      var helpers = ["Your name must be in the form: \n \
  first name, middle initial., last name",
```

```
      "Your email address must have the form: \
user@domain",
                  "Your user ID must have at least six characters",
                  "Your password must have at least six \
characters and it must include one digit",
                  "This box provides advice on filling out\
the form on this page. Put the mouse cursor over any \
input field to get advice"]

// **********************************************************
// The event handler function to change the value of the
//  textarea

     function messages(adviceNumber) {
        document.getElementById("adviceBox").value =
                                    helpers[adviceNumber];
}
// **********************************************************
// -->
   </script>
  </head>
  <body>
    <form action = "">
      <p style = "font-weight: bold">
        <span style = "font-style: italic">
          Customer information
        </span>
        <br /><br />
        Name: <input type = "text"  onmouseover = "messages(0)"
                    onmouseout = "messages(4)" />

        <br />
        Email: <input type = "text"  onmouseover = "messages(1)"
                    onmouseout = "messages(4)" />

        <br /> <br />
        <span style = "font-style: italic">
          To create an account, provide the following:
        </span>
        <br /> <br />
        User ID: <input type = "text"  onmouseover = "messages(2)"
                      onmouseout = "messages(4)" />

        <br />
        Password: <input type = "password"
                        onmouseover = "messages(3)"
                        onmouseout = "messages(4)" />
```

continued

```
        <br />
        <textarea id = "adviceBox"  rows = "3"  cols = "50"
                  style = "position: absolute; left: 250px;
                  top = 0px">
        </textarea>
        <br /><br />
        <input type = "submit"  value = "Submit" />
        <input type = "reset"  value = "Reset" />
      </p>
    </form>
  </body>
</html>
```

Figure 6.8 shows a browser display of the page defined by dynValue.html when the mouse cursor is over the User ID input field.

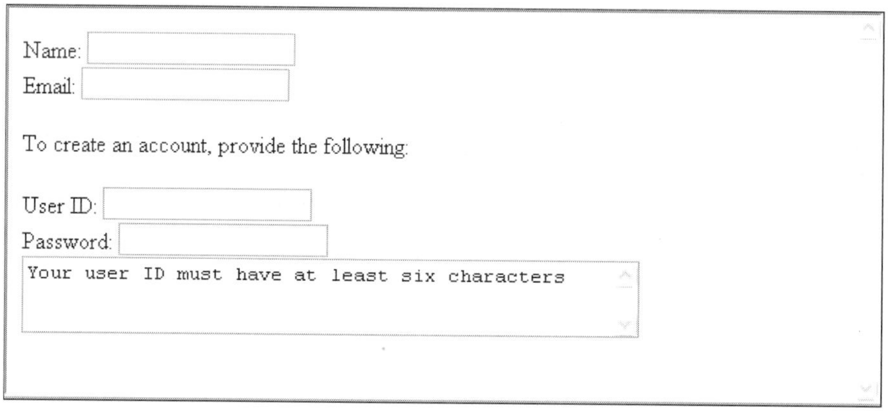

FIGURE 6.8 Display of dynValue.html

6.7

STACKING ELEMENTS

The top and left properties allow the placement of an element anywhere in the two dimensions of the display of a document. Although the display is restricted to two physical dimensions, the effect of a third dimension is possible through the simple concept of stacked elements, such as those used to stack windows in windowing systems. Although multiple elements can occupy the same space in the document, one is considered to be on top and is displayed. The top element hides the parts of the lower elements on which it is superimposed. The placement of elements in this third dimension is controlled by the z-index attribute of the element. An element whose z-index is greater than that of an element in the same space will be displayed over the other element, effectively hiding the lower element. The JavaScript style property associated with the z-index attribute is zIndex.

In the following example, three images are placed on the display so that they overlap. In the XHTML description of this, each image tag includes an onclick attribute, which is used to trigger the execution of a JavaScript handler function. The function first defines DOM addresses for the last top element and the new top element. Then the function sets the zIndex value of the two elements so that the old top element has a value of 0 and the new top element has the value 10, effectively putting it at the top. The script keeps track of which image is currently on top with the global variable top, which is changed every time a new element is moved to the top with the toTop function.

```
<?xml version = "1.0" encoding = "utf-8"?>
<!DOCTYPE html PUBLIC "-//w3c//DTD XHTML 1.1//EN"
  "http://www.w3.org/TR/xhtml11/DTD/xhtml11.dtd">


<!-- stacking.html
     Illustrates dynamic stacking of images
     -->
<html xmlns = "http://www.w3.org/1999/xhtml">
  <head>
    <title> Dynamic stacking of images </title>
    <script type = "text/javascript">
<!--
     var top = "C172";


// **********************************************************
// The event handler function to move the given element
//  to the top of the display stack

     function toTop(newTop) {

// Set the two dom addresses, one for the old top
//  element and one for the new top element

        domTop = document.getElementById(top).style;
        domNew = document.getElementById(newTop).style;
```

continued

```
// Set the zIndex properties of the two elements, and
//   reset top to the new top

        domTop.zIndex = "0";
        domNew.zIndex = "10";
        top = newTop;
      }
// ******************************************************
// -->
    </script>
    <style type = "text/css">
      .plane1 {position: absolute; top: 0; left: 0;
             z-index: 0;}
      .plane2 {position: absolute; top: 50px; left: 110px;
             z-index: 0;}
      .plane3 {position: absolute; top: 100px; left: 220px;
             z-index: 0;}
    </style>
  </head>
  <body>
    <p>
      <img class = "plane1"  id = "C172"
           src = "c172.gif"
           alt = "(Picture of a C172)"
           onclick = "toTop('C172')" />
      <img class = "plane2"  id = "cix"
           src = "cix.gif"
           alt = "(Picture of a Citation airplane)"
           onclick = "toTop('cix')" />
      <img class = "plane3"  id = "C182"
           src = "c182.gif"
           alt = "(Picture of a C182)"
           onclick = "toTop('C182')" />
    </p>
  </body>
</html>
```

Figures 6.9, 6.10, and 6.11 show the document described by stacking.html in three of its possible configurations.

FIGURE 6.9 The initial display of `stacking.html` (photographs courtesy of Cessna Aircraft Company)

FIGURE 6.10 The display of `stacking.html` after clicking on the second image (photographs courtesy of Cessna Aircraft Company)

FIGURE 6.11 The display of `stacking.html` after clicking on the bottom image (photographs courtesy of Cessna Aircraft Company)

6.8

LOCATING THE MOUSE CURSOR

Recall from Chapter 5 that every event that occurs in an XHTML document creates an event object. This object includes some information about the event. A mouse-click event is an implementation of the `MouseEvent` interface, which defines two pairs of properties that provide geometric coordinates of the position of the element in the display that created the event. One of these pairs, `clientX` and `clientY`, gives the coordinates of the element relative to the upper-left corner of the browser display window, in pixels. The other pair, `screenX` and `screenY`, also gives coordinates of the element but relative to the client computer's screen. Obviously, the former pair is usually more useful than the latter.

In the following example, `where.html`, two pairs of text elements are used to display these four properties every time the mouse button is clicked. The handler is triggered by the `onclick` attribute of the body element. An image is displayed just below the display of the coordinates but only to make the screen more interesting.

The call to the handler in this example sends `event`, which is a reference to the event just created in the element, as a parameter. This is a bit like magic because the event object is implicitly created. In the handler, the formal parameter is used to access the coordinate properties. Note that the handling of the event object is not implemented the same way in the popular browsers. The Netscape browsers send it as a parameter to event handlers, whereas Microsoft browsers make it available as a global property. The code in `where.html` works for both of these approaches by sending it in the call to the handler. It is available in the call with Microsoft browsers because it is visible there as a global variable. Of course, for a Microsoft browser, it need not be sent at all.

```
<?xml version = "1.0" encoding = "utf-8"?>
<!DOCTYPE html PUBLIC "-//w3c//DTD XHTML 1.1//EN"
  "http://www.w3.org/TR/xhtml11/DTD/xhtml11.dtd">

<!-- where.html
     Show the coordinates of the mouse cursor position
     in an image and anywhere on the screen when the mouse
     is clicked
     -->
<html xmlns = "http://www.w3.org/1999/xhtml">
  <head>
    <title> Where is the cursor? </title>
    <script type = "text/javascript">
<!--
// ******************************************************
// The event handler function to get and display the
//  coordinates of the cursor, both in an element and
//  on the screen

     function findIt(evt) {
        document.getElementById("xcoor1").value = evt.clientX;
        document.getElementById("ycoor1").value = evt.clientY;
        document.getElementById("xcoor2").value = evt.screenX;
        document.getElementById("ycoor2").value = evt.screenY;
     }
// ******************************************************
// -->
    </script>
  </head>
  <body onclick = "findIt(event)">
    <form action = "">
      <p>
        Within the client area: <br />
        x:
        <input type = "text"  id = "xcoor1"  size = "4" />
        y:
        <input type = "text"  id = "ycoor1"  size = "4" />
```

continued

```
                  <br /><br />
                  Relative to the origin of the screen coordinate system:
                  <br />
                  x:
                  <input type = "text"  id = "xcoor2"  size = "4" />
                  y:
                  <input type = "text"  id = "ycoor2"  size = "4" />
              </p>
          </form>
          <p>
            <img src = "c172.gif"  alt = "(Picture of C172)" />
          </p>
      </body>
  </html>
```

Figure 6.12 shows a browser display of where.html.

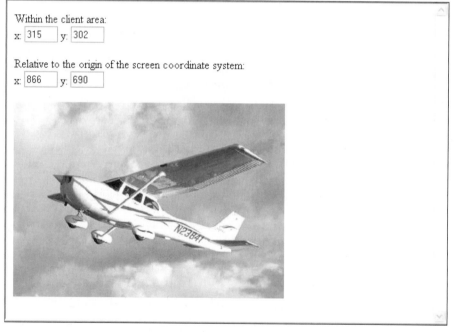

FIGURE 6.12 Display of where.html (the cursor was in the tail section of the plane)

One interesting note about the cursor-finding example is that with IE6, the mouse clicks are ignored if the mouse cursor is below the last element on the display. The NS7 browser always responds the same way regardless of where the cursor is on the display.

6.9

REACTING TO A MOUSE CLICK

The following is another example related to reacting to mouse events. In this case, the mousedown and mouseup events are used to show and hide the message "Please don't click here!" on the display under the mouse cursor whenever the mouse button is clicked, regardless of where the cursor is at the time.

```
<?xml version = "1.0" encoding = "utf-8"?>
<!DOCTYPE html PUBLIC "-//w3c//DTD XHTML 1.1//EN"
  "http://www.w3.org/TR/xhtml11/DTD/xhtml11.dtd">


<!-- anywhere.html
     Display a message when the mouse button is pressed,
     no matter where it is on the screen
     -->
<html xmlns = "http://www.w3.org/1999/xhtml">
  <head>
    <title> Sense events anywhere </title>

    <script type = "text/javascript">
<!--
// ******************************************************
// The event handler function to display the message

      function displayIt(evt) {
        var dom = document.getElementById("message");
        dom.style.left = (evt.clientX - 130) + "px";
        dom.style.top = (evt.clientY - 25) + "px";
        dom.style.visibility = "visible";
      }

// ******************************************************
// The event handler function to hide the message

      function hideIt() {
        document.getElementById("message").style.visibility =
          "hidden";
  }
// ******************************************************
// -->
    </script>
  </head>
```

continued

```
<body onmousedown = "displayIt(event);"
      onmouseup = "hideIt();">
  <p>
    <span id= "message"
          style = "color: red; visibility: hidden;
                   position: relative;
                   font-size: 20pt; font-style: italic;
                   font-weight: bold;">
        Please don't click here!
    </span>
    <br /><br /><br /><br /><br /><br /><br /><br />
    <br /><br /><br /><br /><br /><br /><br /><br />
  </p>
</body>
</html>
```

6.10

SLOW MOVEMENT OF ELEMENTS

So far, we have considered only element movements that happen instantly. These movements are controlled by changing the top and left properties of the element to be moved. The only way to move an element slowly is to move it by small amounts many times, with the moves separated by small amounts of time. JavaScript has two Window methods that are capable of this: setTimeout and setInterval.

The setTimeout method takes two parameters: a string of JavaScript code to be executed and a number of milliseconds of delay before executing the given code. For example, consider the following call:

```
setTimeout("mover()", 20);
```

This causes a 20-millisecond delay, after which the function mover is called.

The setInterval method has two forms. One form takes two parameters, exactly as does setTimeout. It executes the given code repeatedly, using the second parameter as the interval in milliseconds between executions. The second form of setInterval takes a variable number of parameters. The first parameter is the name of a function to be called, the second is the interval in milliseconds between the calls to the function, and the remaining parameters are used as actual parameters to the function being called.

The example presented here, moveText.html, moves a string of text from one position (100, 100) to a new position (300, 300). The move is accomplished by using setTimeout to call a mover function every millisecond until the final position (300, 300) is reached. The initial position of the text is set in the span element that specifies the text. The onload attribute of the body element is used to call a function, initText, to initialize the *x* and *y* coordinates to the left and top properties of the element and call the mover function.

The mover function, named moveText, takes the current coordinates of the text as parameters, moves them 1 pixel toward the final position, and then calls itself with the new coordinates using setTimeout. The recomputation of the coordinates is complicated by the fact that we want the code to work regardless of the direction of the move.

One consideration with this script is that the coordinate properties are stored as strings with units attached. For example, if the initial position of an element is (100, 100), its left and top property values both have the string value "100px". To arithmetically change the properties, we must have them as numbers. Therefore, the property values are converted to numbers in the initText function by stripping the nondigit unit parts. Then, before the left and top properties are set to the new coordinates, the units (in this case, "px") are catenated back on to the coordinates.

One other problem with our sample document is something that we have avoided so far only by luck. The problem is the use of XHTML comments to hide JavaScript and having parts of XHTML comments embedded in the JavaScript. For example, if the JavaScript statement x--; is embedded in an XHTML comment, the validator complains that the -- in the statement is an invalid comment declaration. In the JavaScript code of the following example, -- is used as a decrement operator to move the coordinates. One solution to this problem is to remove the JavaScript from the XHTML document and place it in an external file, using the src attribute of the script element to reference it. Then neither the parser nor the validator will see it. This is the approach used in our example, moveText.html, in which the JavaScript is stored in the file moveTextfuns.js.

The JavaScript script for moveText.html is as follows:

```
<?xml version = "1.0" encoding = "utf-8"?>
<!DOCTYPE html PUBLIC "-//w3c//DTD XHTML 1.1//EN"
  "http://www.w3.org/TR/xhtml11/DTD/xhtml11.dtd">

<!-- moveText.html
     Illustrates a moving text element
     Uses the JavaScript from file moveTextfuns.js
     -->
<html xmlns = "http://www.w3.org/1999/xhtml">
  <head>
    <title> Moving text </title>
    <script type = "text/javascript"
            src = "moveTextfuns.js">
    </script>
  </head>
```

continued

```html
<!-- Call the initializing function on load, giving the
        destination coordinates for the text to be moved
        -->

  <body onload = "initText()">

<!-- The text to be moved, including its initial position -->

    <p>
      <span id = 'theText' style =
                  "position: absolute; left: 100px; top: 100px;
                  font: bold 20pt 'Times Roman';
                  color: blue;"> Jump in the lake!
      </span>
    </p>
  </body>
</html>
```

```javascript
// This is moveTextfuns.js - used with moveText.html

    var dom, x, y, finalx = 300, finaly = 300;

// *************************************************** //
// A function to initialize the x and y coordinates
//  of the current position of the text to be moved,
//  and then call the mover function

    function initText() {
       dom = document.getElementById('theText').style;

    /* Get the current position of the text */

       var x = dom.left;
       var y = dom.top;

    /* Convert the string values of left and top to
       numbers by stripping off the units */

       x = x.match(/\d+/);
       y = y.match(/\d+/);

    /* Call the function that moves it */
```

```
            moveText(x, y);
       } /*** end of function initText */

// ************************************************ //
// A function to move the text from its original
//  position to (finalx, finaly)

   function moveText(x, y) {

   /* If the x coordinates are not equal, move
      x toward finalx */

      if (x != finalx)
         if (x > finalx) x--;
         else if (x < finalx) x++;

   /* If the y coordinates are not equal, move
      y toward finaly */

      if (y != finaly)
         if (y > finaly) y--;
         else if (y < finaly) y++;

   /* As long as the text is not at the destination,
      call the mover with the current position */

      if ((x != finalx) || (y != finaly)) {

   /* Put the units back on the coordinates before
      assigning them to the properties to cause the
      move */

         dom.left = x + "px";
         dom.top = y + "px";

   /* Recursive call, after a 1-millisecond delay */

         setTimeout("moveText(" + x + "," + y + ")", 1);
      }

   } /*** end of function moveText */
```

6.11

DRAGGING AND DROPPING ELEMENTS

One of the more powerful effects possible with event handling is allowing the user to drag and drop elements around the display screen. The mouseup, mousedown, and mousemove events can be used to implement this. Changing the top and left properties of an element, as we saw earlier in this chapter, causes the element to move. To illustrate drag and drop, we develop an example that creates a magnetic poetry system, showing two static lines of a poem and allowing the user to create the last two lines from a collection of movable words.

This example uses a mixture of the DOM 0 and DOM 2 event models. The DOM 0 model is used for the call to the handler for the mousedown event. The rest of the process is designed with the DOM 2 model. The mousedown event handler, grabber, takes the Event object as its parameter. It gets the element to be moved from the currentTarget property of the Event object and puts it in a global variable so it is available to the other handlers. It then determines the coordinates of the current position of the element to be moved and computes the difference between them and the coordinates of the position of the mouse cursor. These two differences, which are used by the handler for mousemove to actually move the element, are also placed in global variables. The grabber handler also registers the event handlers for mousemove and mouseup. These two handlers are named mover and dropper, respectively. The dropper handler disconnects mouse movements from the element-moving process by unregistering the handlers mover and dropper. The following is the document we have just described:

```
<?xml version = "1.0" encoding = "utf-8"?>
<!DOCTYPE html PUBLIC "-//w3c//DTD XHTML 1.1//EN"
  "http://www.w3.org/TR/xhtml11/DTD/xhtml11.dtd">

<!-- dragNDrop.html
    An example to illustrate the DOM 2 Event model
    Allows the user to drag and drop words to complete
    a short poem
    -->
<html xmlns = "http://www.w3.org/1999/xhtml">
  <head>
    <title> Drag and drop </title>
    <script type = "text/javascript">
<!--
// Define variables for the values computed by
//   the grabber event handler but needed by mover
//   event handler
```

```javascript
      var diffX, diffY, theElement;

// ******************************************************

// The event handler function for grabbing the word

   function grabber(event) {

// Set the global variable for the element to be moved

      theElement = event.currentTarget;

// Determine the position of the word to be grabbed,
//   first removing the units from left and top

      var posX = parseInt(theElement.style.left);
      var posY = parseInt(theElement.style.top);

// Compute the difference between where it is and
//   where the mouse click occurred

      diffX = event.clientX - posX;
      diffY = event.clientY - posY;

// Now register the event handlers for moving and
//   dropping the word

      document.addEventListener("mousemove", mover, true);
      document.addEventListener("mouseup", dropper, true);

// Stop propagation of the event and stop any default
//   browser action

      event.stopPropagation();
      event.preventDefault();

}  //** end of grabber

// ******************************************************

// The event handler function for moving the word

   function mover(event) {
```

continued

```
// Compute the new position, add the units, and move the word

        theElement.style.left = (event.clientX - diffX) + "px";
        theElement.style.top = (event.clientY - diffY) + "px";

// Prevent propagation of the event

        event.stopPropagation();
} //** end of mover

// ***********************************************************
// The event handler function for dropping the word

        function dropper(event) {

// Unregister the event handlers for mouseup and mousemove

        document.removeEventListener("mouseup", dropper, true);
        document.removeEventListener("mousemove", mover, true);

// Prevent propagation of the event

        event.stopPropagation();
} //** end of dropper

// ***********************************************************
// -->
    </script>
  </head>
  <body style = "font-size: 20;">
    <p>
      Roses are red <br />
      Violets are blue <br />

      <span style = "position: absolute; top: 200px; left: 0px;
                  background-color: lightgrey;"
          onmousedown = "grabber(event);"> candy </span>
      <span style = "position: absolute; top: 200px; left: 75px;
                  background-color: lightgrey;"
          onmousedown = "grabber(event);"> cats </span>
      <span style = "position: absolute; top: 200px; left: 150px;
                  background-color: lightgrey;"
          onmousedown = "grabber(event);"> cows </span>
```

```
<span style = "position: absolute; top: 200px; left: 225px;
              background-color: lightgrey;"
      onmousedown = "grabber(event);"> glue </span>
<span style = "position: absolute; top: 200px; left: 300px;
              background-color: lightgrey;"
      onmousedown = "grabber(event);"> is </span>
<span style = "position: absolute; top: 200px; left: 375px;
              background-color: lightgrey;"
      onmousedown = "grabber(event);"> is </span>
<span style = "position: absolute; top: 200px; left: 450px;
              background-color: lightgrey;"
      onmousedown = "grabber(event);"> meow </span>
<span style = "position: absolute; top: 250px; left: 0px;
              background-color: lightgrey;"
      onmousedown = "grabber(event);"> mine </span>
<span style = "position: absolute; top: 250px; left: 75px;
              background-color: lightgrey;"
      onmousedown = "grabber(event);"> moo </span>
<span style = "position: absolute; top: 250px; left: 150px;
              background-color: lightgrey;"
      onmousedown = "grabber(event);"> new </span>
<span style = "position: absolute; top: 250px; left: 225px;
              background-color: lightgrey;"
      onmousedown = "grabber(event);"> old </span>
<span style = "position: absolute; top: 250px; left: 300px;
              background-color: lightgrey;"
      onmousedown = "grabber(event);"> say </span>
<span style = "position: absolute; top: 250px; left: 375px;
              background-color: lightgrey;"
      onmousedown = "grabber(event);"> say </span>
<span style = "position: absolute; top: 250px; left: 450px;
              background-color: lightgrey;"
      onmousedown = "grabber(event);"> so </span>
<span style = "position: absolute; top: 300px; left: 0px;
              background-color: lightgrey;"
      onmousedown = "grabber(event);"> sticky </span>
<span style = "position: absolute; top: 300px; left: 75px;
              background-color: lightgrey;"
      onmousedown = "grabber(event);"> sweet </span>
<span style = "position: absolute; top: 300px; left: 150px;
              background-color: lightgrey;"
      onmousedown = "grabber(event);"> syrup </span>
<span style = "position: absolute; top: 300px; left: 225px;
              background-color: lightgrey;"
      onmousedown = "grabber(event);"> too </span>
```

continued

```
        <span style = "position: absolute; top: 300px; left: 300px;
                       background-color: lightgrey;"
              onmousedown = "grabber(event);"> yours </span>
    </p>
  </body>
</html>
```

Figure 6.13 shows a browser display of `dragNDrop.html`.

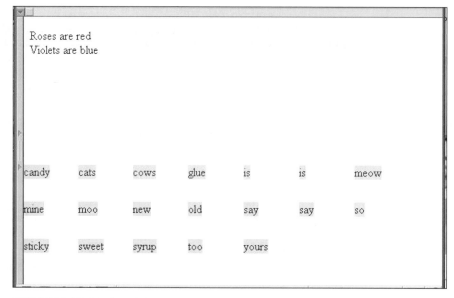

FIGURE 6.13 Display of `dragNDrop.html`

Note that the drag-and-drop process can be written with the DOM 0 event model. However, it can only be made portable by having the script detect which browser is being used and using different code for the different browsers. We have chosen to write it with the DOM 2 event model rather than deal with that untidy situation. Before long, we believe all browsers will implement the DOM 2 model.

6.12

SUMMARY

The CSS-P standard enables us to initially place XHTML elements wherever we want in a document and then move them later. Elements can be positioned at any given location in the display of a document if their `position` property is set to `absolute` or `relative`. Absolute positioning is used to place an element at a position in the display of the document relative to the upper-left corner of the display, using the `left` and `top` properties of the element. Relative positioning is used to place an element at a specified offset from the `top` and `left` coordinates of where it would have gone with the default static positioning. Relative positioning also allows an element to be moved later. Static positioning, which is the default, disallows both specific initial placement and dynamic moving of the element. An XHTML element can be made to disappear and reappear by changing its `visibility` property.

The color of the background of a document is stored in its `backgroundColor` property; the color of an element is stored in its `color` property. Both of these can be dynamically changed. The font, font size, and font style of text also can be changed.

The content of an element can be changed by changing its `value` property. An element in a document can be set to appear to be in front of other elements, and this top-to-bottom stacking order can be dynamically changed. The coordinates of the mouse cursor can be found every time a mouse button is pressed, using properties of the event object. An element can be animated, at least in a crude way, by changing its `top` and `left` properties repeatedly by small amounts. Such an operation can be controlled by the `Window` method `setTimeout`. Event handlers for the mouse events can be written to allow elements to be dragged and dropped anywhere on the display screen by the user.

6.13 Review Questions

1. Define a dynamic XHTML document.

2. If you know the `id` of an XHTML element, how can you get the DOM address of that element in JavaScript?

3. If you have a variable that has the `id` of an XHTML element, how can you get the DOM address of that element in JavaScript?

4. In what additional way can the DOM addresses of radio buttons and checkboxes be obtained?

5. What is CSS-P?

6. Describe all of the differences between the three possible values of the `position` property.

7. What are the standard values for the `visibility` property?

8. What properties control the foreground and background colors of a document?

9. What events can be used to change a font when the mouse cursor is moved over and away from an element?

10. What property has the content of an element?

11. What JavaScript variable is associated with the `z-index` property?

12. To move an element to the top of the display, do you set its `z-index` property to a large number or a small number?

13. What exactly is stored in the `clientX` and `clientY` properties after a mouse click?

14. What exactly is stored in the `screenX` and `screenY` properties after a mouse click?

15. Describe the parameters and actions of the `setTimeout` function.

6.14 Exercises

Write, test, validate, and debug (if necessary) the following documents.

1. The document must have a paragraph of at least 10 lines of text that describe you. This paragraph must be centered on the page and have space for only 20 characters per line. A light gray image of yourself must be superimposed over the center of the text as a nested element.

2. Modify the document described in Exercise 1 to add four buttons. These buttons must be labeled Northwest, Northeast, Southwest, and Southeast. When they're pressed, the buttons must move your image to the specified corner of the text. Initially, your image must appear in the northwest (upper-left) corner of the text.

3. Modify the document described in Exercise 2 to make the buttons toggle their respective copies of your image on and off so that, at any time, the document may include none, one, two, three, or four copies of your image. The initial document should have no images shown.

4. The document must have a paragraph of text that describes your home. Choose at least three different phrases (three to six words) of this paragraph and make them change font, font style, color, and font size when the mouse cursor is placed over them. Each of the different phrases must change to different fonts, font styles, colors, and font sizes.

5. The document must display an image and three buttons. The buttons should be labeled simply 1, 2, and 3. When pressed, each button should change the content of the image to that of a different image.

6. The document must contain four short paragraphs of text, stacked on top of each other, with only enough of each showing so that the mouse cursor can always be placed over some part of them. When the cursor is placed over the exposed part of any paragraph, it should rise to the top to become completely visible.

7. Modify the document of Exercise 6 so that when a paragraph is moved from the top stacking position, it returns to its original position rather than to the bottom.

8. The document must have a small image of yourself, which must appear when the mouse button is clicked at the position of the mouse cursor, regardless of the position of the cursor at the time.

9. The document must contain the statement "Save time with TIMESAVER 2.2," which continuously moves back and forth across the top of the display.

10. Modify the document of Exercise 9 to make the statement change color between red and blue every fifth step of its movement (assuming each move is 1 pixel long).

Java Applets

Applets provide another way of supporting computation in Web documents. Applets can provide interactivity and dynamic content through graphical user interface (GUI) components, as well as graphics and computation. This chapter is most accessible if the reader is already familiar with the Java programming language. Appendix A provides a brief introduction to Java for those who are already conversant in C++ and object-oriented programming. However, for those without that background, the complexity of Java and object-oriented programming is a formidable obstacle to gaining an understanding of applets in a chapter as brief as this one.

This chapter begins by providing an overview of applets and their relationship to XHTML documents. Then it describes the primary activities of applets, including initialization, starting execution, and stopping execution. Following this, attention turns to the paintComponent method, which is used to draw text and graphics both from a Java application to a display panel and from an applet to a browser screen. Next, the chapter describes the <object> tag, which connects an XHTML document to an applet, and its attributes. XHTML documents can only refer to applet files because applets cannot be directly embedded in documents, unlike scripts in languages such as JavaScript. Then the chapter covers the technique for passing parameters from an XHTML document to an applet. Following this, it describes the methods of the `Graphics` class for drawing various figures and discusses how color can be used for the output of the `paintComponent` method.

Finally, interactive applets are discussed. This requires a description of how GUI components are defined in Java and how the Java event model is used to allow those components to provide interactivity.

Java 1.1 included the Abstract Windowing Toolkit (AWT), which provided basic drawing capabilities, as well as support for GUI components and an event model to allow users to interact with programs through them. Java 1.2 introduced the Swing package, which has a different set of GUI components that are similar in appearance to those of AWT but are very different internally. This chapter covers the AWT drawing facilities and the Swing GUI components. Be aware that the discussion of AWT graphics, event handling, and Swing components is brief and covers only a small portion of what exists.

All of the Java system software can be obtained from `http://java.sun.com`.

7.1

INTRODUCTION

Applets are Java programs whose execution is controlled in a way that is quite different from that of Java application programs. The purpose of an applet is related to that of client-side JavaScript: to provide processing capability and interactivity for XHTML documents.

When the browser encounters an applet in an XHTML document, it downloads the compiled version of the applet class (the `.class` file), along with any classes that the applet uses, from the server. Then an instance of the applet class is implicitly created and executed on the browser. (A more detailed description of these processes is given in Section 7.2.) Because applets can include most of the Java language features, including widgets and event handling, they allow interactivity to be included in a document.

All applets must have some standard operations. The protocols for these common operations are gathered as method definitions in a predefined class named `JApplet`. All user-defined applets are written as subclasses of `JApplet`. Some of the methods inherited from `JApplet` are routinely overridden by user-defined applets.

The class header of an applet has the following form:

```
public class class_name extends JApplet { ... }
```

Although applets are good for graphics, they usually also display text and images. Rather than writing normal text to the screen, however, they must do this with a method that draws text into the browser display. All of the graphics and text display capabilities used in applets can also be used in Java application programs.

Learning to write simple applets requires the following: First, you must understand how applets are specified in XHTML documents and how documents and applets interact. Second, you must learn how the relevant graphics library classes are used to display text and graphical figures. Third, you must see how the methods of `JApplet` are used, often in overridden versions, to control applet execution within the operation of the browser.

The simplest way to test an applet is with the Sun Microsystems program `appletviewer`, which enables you to see what an applet does without using a browser and a server. This technique has the advantage of simplicity, but it lacks some of the reality of using a Web browser. Of course, it is not much more complicated to use a browser with local XHTML documents and applets.

When Java applets appeared, they provided the first way to include client-resident computational capability in an XHTML document. JavaScript and its close relatives, AppleScript and VBScript, provide much of what the first release of Java provided through its applets. The power and versatility of Java—and especially its classes to support graphical user interfaces—have grown considerably since its original release. Furthermore, Java now has a large collection of class libraries that provide far more descriptive power than the scripting languages.

Applets are the second technology discussed in this book that provides computational capabilities for XHTML documents. Both JavaScript scripts and Java applets are interpreted on the client by the browser, which is good for server efficiency. JavaScript is both simpler to learn and simpler to use than Java. On the other hand, Java is much more expressive than JavaScript, especially because of the extensive array of class libraries now available. Furthermore, Java is faster than JavaScript, so if anything beyond short and simple computations is required, Java has the advantage.

Another area in which there is an advantage for Java applets over JavaScript is graphics. JavaScript includes virtually no graphics capability. So, even the graphics available in Java 1.1 (an early version of Java) are far superior to anything available in JavaScript. On the other hand, JavaScript has an advantage over Java because it is directly embedded in XHTML documents, whereas applets must be downloaded from the server when needed.

By 2002, the initial excitement regarding applets had diminished significantly, and other technologies, particularly scripting languages, had taken over many of the former uses of applets. The decrease in popularity of applets was in part due to the inconsistency of support from the browser vendors. The Netscape 4 browsers included Java virtual machines (intermediate code interpreters) that supported only version 1.1 of Java. (version 1.2 of Java, which included many significant changes, was released in late 1998.) So, applets either had to be written using obsolete Java, or they would not be viewable on Netscape's browsers.[1] Up-to-date Java virtual machines were available from Sun for these browsers, but it was a sizable download, especially for those without high-speed Internet access, so many did not bother getting it. More recently,

Microsoft stopped including support for Java in their browsers, although it can be downloaded from Sun. So, for awhile, Netscape clients were required to download Java virtual machines for their browsers, and Microsoft clients now are required to download them for their browsers. Because of these problems, as well as the availability of alternative technologies, many Web sites stopped creating applets and gradually eliminated the applets they were providing.

Java has become more heavily used on the server side in the form of servlets (discussed in Chapter 11, "Servlets and Java Server Pages") than on the client side in the form of applets. However, for now at least, Java applets are still included in some legacy Web sites, and some applets are still being written. Therefore, it is worthwhile for Web professionals to be familiar with them.

7.2

THE PRIMARY APPLET ACTIVITIES

Applets must include four fundamental methods through which the browser controls their execution. All of these are inherited from `JApplet`. When an XHTML document is being interpreted and displayed by a browser and an applet is encountered, the applet class code is downloaded and instantiated. Then the browser calls the applet's `init` method, which is inherited from `JApplet` but is often overridden in the user-defined applet class. The purpose of `init`, naturally, is to allow the applet to do some initialization. For example, if the applet has user-interface components (widgets), they are normally created in `init`. Upon return from the `init` method, the browser calls the applet method `start`, which begins execution of the applet's code. The `start` method is also implicitly called when the browser user returns to a document after viewing some other document. When the browser user directs the browser to follow a link from the current page to some new page, the browser calls the applet method `stop`. When the browser is stopped by the user, it calls the applet method `destroy`, which is used to do any cleanup that might be required at the end of the applet's life.

An applet's display is actually a frame, which is a multilayered structure. We are interested in just one of those layers, the *content pane*. The content pane is where applets put their output. Note that applets do not draw anything directly in the content pane; rather, applets draw in a panel and then add the panel to the content pane. This is also true for graphics in the Java applications world. For applications, a frame is created, and the filled panel is added to that frame's content pane. For applets, the filled panel is added to the applet's content pane.

There are two distinct categories of graphics operations for applets. In one category, something is drawn using a small set of primitive drawing methods. This use of primitives, which is sometimes called *custom drawing*, is done in

---

1. Netscape 6 and 7 include up-to-date Java interpreters.

overridden versions of the paintComponent method. Custom drawing must be done outside the subclass of JApplet. Typically, a subclass of Jpanel is created and used for custom drawing. Then the applet creates an instance of the panel subclass and adds it to its content pane. The other category of graphics is the use of predefined graphics objects. Predefined graphics objects do not require the use of a paintComponent method. This means they can be placed directly in a panel that is created in the applet and then added to the applet's content pane. This is a simpler process.

7.3

THE paintComponent METHOD

As previously stated, custom painting is done with the paintComponent method. However, when paintComponent is used in an applet environment, only the browser calls it; it should never be called by user code. paintComponent takes a single parameter: an object of class Graphics, which is defined in the java.awt package. This object, which is created by the browser, provides a collection of methods for drawing text and graphics. In a sense, the Graphics object provides a graphics context for paintComponent, similar to the device context for Windows and the graphics context in X-11. The methods of Graphics must be called through the browser-generated Graphics object. The protocol of the paintComponent method is as follows:

```
public void paintComponent(Graphics grafObj) { ... }
```

Initially, we discuss creating text with paintComponent. This is done with a method named drawString, which takes three parameters: a String literal, the x coordinate of the left end of the string, and the y coordinate of the base of the string. These coordinates are given in pixels.

Before calling paintComponent, the paintComponent method of the parent class (referred to with super) is called to paint the background of the display panel.

The following is an applet that displays a welcome message. It defines a subclass of JPanel that overrides paintComponent. The overriding paintComponent method draws the message with drawstring. The applet itself (the subclass of JApplet) creates a content pane, which is a Container object, with the getContentPane method. It also instantiates the subclass of JPanel, MessagePanel, by calling its constructor in a new clause. The init method, inherited from JApplet and overriden in the example, has just one statement, which adds the panel to its content pane by sending the MessagePanel object (created by the applet) to the add method of the Container object.

```
/* Wel.java
   An applet to illustrate the display of a string
   */
import java.applet.*;
import javax.swing.*;
import java.awt.*;

// The Wel applet

public class Wel extends JApplet {

// Create a content pane and the panel

   Container messageArea = getContentPane();
   MessagePanel myMessagePanel = new MessagePanel();

// The init method, which adds the panel to the applet

   public void init() {
      messageArea.add(myMessagePanel);
   }
}

// The panel class on which the message is painted

class MessagePanel extends JPanel {
   public void paintComponent(Graphics grafObj) {
      super.paintComponent(grafObj);
      grafObj.drawString("Welcome to my home page!", 50,
                        50);
   }
}
```

The call to drawString in Wel uses default values for the font parameters to display its string parameter. These parameters can be changed. The Font class, which is defined in java.awt.Font, has three variables that specify a font name, style, and size. Objects of the Font class can be created and used to set the instance variables in the paintComponent method. The font names and styles that are available depend on the implementation. We assume here that Times Roman and Courier are available in plain, boldface, and italic styles. The font styles are specified by named constants in the Font class, PLAIN, BOLD, and ITALIC. Objects of class Font are initialized through the three parameters in its constructor that specify the font name, style, and size. For example, consider the following instantiations:

```
Font font1 = new Font ("TimesRoman", Font.PLAIN, 36);
Font font2 = new Font ("Courier", Font.ITALIC, 24);
```

The font member of a `Graphics` object is set with the method `setFont`, which takes the `Font` object as its parameter.

The following is a revision of the `Wel` applet that uses a specific font, style, and size to display the same message as the earlier version:

```java
/* Wel2.java
   An applet to illustrate the display of a string
   in a specific font, font style, and font size
   */
import java.applet.*;
import javax.swing.*;
import java.awt.*;

// The panel class on which the message will be painted

class MessagePanel extends JPanel {
    Font myFont = new Font("TimesRoman", Font.ITALIC, 24);

    public void paintComponent(Graphics grafObj) {
        super.paintComponent(grafObj);
        grafObj.setFont(myFont);
        grafObj.drawString("Welcome to my first home page!", 50,
                          50);
    }
}


// The Wel2 applet

public class Wel2 extends JApplet {

// The init method - create the content pane, instantiate
//   the message panel and add it to the content pane

    public void init() {
        Container messageArea = getContentPane();
        MessagePanel myMessagePanel = new MessagePanel();
        messageArea.add(myMessagePanel);
    }
}
```

7.4

THE <object> TAG

The <object> tag is used to reference an applet in an XHTML document. The <object> tag is similar to the <img> tag used to specify images. The purpose of both <object> and <img> is to create a space in the document display where something can be put. In the case of <object>, when used for an applet, that something is whatever the applet paints. The form of the <object> tag and the attributes it uses for applets is as follows:

```
<object codetype = "application/java"
        classid = "java:applet_class_file"
        width = "applet display width"
        height = "applet display height">
</object>
```

The applet file is the compiled .class file. The width and height specify the size in pixels of the area in which the applet will paint.

The following XHTML document defines a simple XHTML document that uses the Wel2 applet from Section 7.3.

```
<?xml version = "1.0" encoding = "utf-8"?>
<!DOCTYPE html PUBLIC "-//w3c//DTD XHTML 1.1//EN"
  "http://www.w3.org/TR/xhtml11/DTD/xhtml11.dtd">

<!-- wel2.html
     A document to test the Wel2 applet
     -->
<html xmlns = "http://www.w3.org/1999/xhtml">
  <head> <title> Wel2 </title>
  </head>
  <body>
    <p>
      <object codetype = "application/java"
              classid = "java:Wel2.class"
              width = "500"
              height = "100">
      </object>
    </p>
  </body>
</html>
```

Unfortunately, there is a portability problem with the object element, even though it is part of the HTML 4.0 standard. Although Internet Explorer 6 (IE6) recognizes the `<object>` tag, it does not recognize the `classid` attribute. Instead, it uses the `code` attribute, which was associated with the deprecated `<applet>` tag. Also, if the `code` attribute is used in an object element, the `"java:"` part of the value for the `code` attribute must be dropped. The Netscape 7 (NS7) browsers do not recognize the `code` attribute. Oddly, Sun Microsystem's `appletviewer` also requires the nonstandard attribute `code`.

Figure 7.1 shows a display of the output of `wel2.html`.

Welcome to my first home page!

FIGURE 7.1 A display of the applet `Wel2`

7.5

APPLET PARAMETERS

A user can pass parameters to Java applications through the command line to the `main` method. Because applets do not have a `main` method, this obviously will not work for them. Still, it is convenient to be able to parameterize applets, and parameters in fact can be sent to an applet from the XHTML document that calls it. This is done with the `<param>` tag, which is followed by a pair of named attributes. The first attribute is `name`, to which any name you like can be assigned. The second attribute is `value`, to which is assigned the value that you want to pass to the applet. For example, you might want to pass the size of an applet display element through a parameter, as in this example:

```
<param name = "size"
       value = "24">
```

The applet uses the `getParameter` method to get the passed parameter value. It takes as its single parameter the name of the parameter, as a `String` literal. For example, to get the `size` parameter specified previously, the following could be used:

```
String mySize = getParameter("size");
```

If `getParameter` is called but the XHTML document did not specify the requested parameter value, `null` is returned. This provides a mechanism for specifying default values for such parameters. For example, consider the following:

```
int mySize;
String pString = getParameter("size");
if (pString == null)
  mySize = 36;
...
Font myFont = new Font("TimesRoman", Font.ITALIC, mySize);
```

The parameter value returned from `getParameter` is a `String` object. If it is actually an integer value (rather than a string), it must be converted to an `int` value. This can be done with the `Integer.parseInt` method. So, the previous `if` statement must have an `else` clause to do this conversion, as in this example:

```
if (pString == null)
    mySize = 36;
else
    mySize = Integer.parseInt(pString)
```

The code to get parameters should appear in the `init` method. The following is a complete applet that does what the applet `Wel2` in Section 7.3 did, except that the size of the displayed string is a parameter that can be specified from the XHTML document.

```
/* Wel3.java
   An applet to illustrate parameters
   */
import java.applet.*;
import javax.swing.*;
import java.awt.*;

// The panel class on which the message will be painted

class MessagePanel2 extends JPanel {
    Font myFont = new Font("TimesRoman", Font.ITALIC,
                            Wel3.mySize);

    public void paintComponent(Graphics grafObj) {
        super.paintComponent(grafObj);
        grafObj.setFont(myFont);
```

```
            grafObj.drawString("Welcome to my home page!", 50, 50);
    }
}

// The Wel3 applet

public class Wel3 extends JApplet {
    static int mySize;

    public void init() {
        Container messageArea = getContentPane();
        String pString;

// Get the fontsize parameter

        pString = getParameter("size");

// If it's null, set the size to 30; otherwise, use the
//  parameter value

        if (pString == null)
            mySize = 30;
        else mySize = Integer.parseInt(pString);

// Instantiate the panel with the message and add it to
//  the content pane

        MessagePanel2 myMessagePanel = new MessagePanel2();
        messageArea.add(myMessagePanel);
    }
}
```

The XHTML document that tests Wel3 is shown here:

```
<?xml version = "1.0" encoding = "utf-8"?>
<!DOCTYPE html PUBLIC "-//w3c//DTD XHTML 1.1//EN"
  "http://www.w3.org/TR/xhtml11/DTD/xhtml11.dtd">

<!-- wel3.html
     A document to test the Wel3 applet
     -->
```

continued

```
<html xmlns = "http://www.w3.org/1999/xhtml">
  <head> <title> Wel3 </title>
  </head>
  <body>
    <p>
      <object codetype = "application/java"
              classid = "java:Wel3.class"
              width = "500"
              height = "100">
        <param name = "size"
               value = "40" />
      </object>
    </p>
  </body>
</html>
```

7.6

SIMPLE GRAPHICS

The Graphics class that the Wel2 and Wel3 applets used to put text into a document also includes methods for drawing lines, rectangles, and ovals. Although the Swing package is now used for creating GUI components, the basic graphics capabilities of Java remain in the AWT package, which is where Graphics is defined. This section describes the basic drawing methods of AWT.

7.6.1 The Coordinate System

The methods that draw lines, rectangles, ovals, and arcs require the user to specify the location of those figures. Such locations are specified in terms of the Graphics coordinate system, which has the origin at the upper-left corner. This is exactly like the JavaScript coordinate system for positioning elements.

7.6.2 Lines

The drawLine method takes four parameters that specify the locations of the two ends of the line. For example, if the following paintComponent method were called, the call to drawLine in it would draw a line from the location (20, 10) to the location (60, 80).

```
public void paintComponent(Graphics grafObj) {
  grafObj.drawLine(20, 10, 60, 80);
}
```

7.6.3 Rectangles

The `Graphics` class provides methods for drawing rectangles and rectangles with rounded corners, where either of these can be filled or not filled. Ordinary (nonrounded corners) rectangles are drawn with either of these two methods:

```
drawRect(x1, y1, width, height)
fillRect(x1, y1, width, height)
```

In both cases, the location (x1, y1) specifies the upper-left corner of the rectangle, and the other two parameters specify the lengths of the rectangle's sides in pixels.

Specifying rectangles with rounded corners requires two more parameters in the method calls: one to specify the number of horizontal pixels in the rounding and one to specify the number of vertical pixels. If these two parameters are equal, the rounding is symmetric. The names of these two methods are `drawRoundRect` and `fillRoundRect`.

The following applet, `Rectangles.java`, draws the four rectangles shown in Figure 7.2.

```java
/* Rectangles.java
   An applet to illustrate drawing rectangles
   */
import java.applet.*;
import java.awt.*;
import javax.swing.*;


// The panel class for drawing

class MyPanel extends JPanel {

    public void paintComponent(Graphics grafObj) {
        super.paintComponent(grafObj);
        grafObj.drawRect(10, 10, 80, 60);
        grafObj.fillRect(120, 10, 60, 80);
        grafObj.drawRoundRect(10, 120, 80, 60, 20, 30);
        grafObj.fillRoundRect(120, 120, 60, 80, 40, 40);
    }
}


// The Rectangles applet
```

continued

```
public class Rectangles extends JApplet {
   Container rectangleArea = getContentPane();
   MyPanel newPanel = new MyPanel();

// The init method for the applet - adds the panel to
//  the content area of the applet

   public void init() {
      rectangleArea.add(newPanel);
   }
}
```

FIGURE 7.2 A display of the output of the applet `Rectangles`

The `Graphics` class includes methods that draw so-called three-dimensional rectangles, which have shaded sides to make them appear like buttons that are either unpushed or pushed. Light shading on the left and upper sides makes a square look like an unpushed button. Dark shading on the left and upper sides makes a square look like a pushed button. The unpushed look is specified with a fifth parameter of `true`; the pushed look is specified with `false`. The name of the method for drawing these rectangles is `draw3DRect`.

7.6.4 Polygons

Polygons can be created by simply drawing a sequence of lines whose ends are connected. The points can be specified with two arrays, one consisting of the *x* coordinates and the other of the *y* coordinates. These two arrays, along with the number of points, are sent as parameters to the method `drawPolygon`. For example, an octagon could be drawn with the following applet, `Polygons`:

```
/* Polygons.java
   An applet to illustrate drawing a polygon
   */
import java.applet.*;
import java.awt.*;
import javax.swing.*;

// The panel for drawing

class PolyPanel extends JPanel {

    public void paintComponent(Graphics grafObj) {
        int xCoordinates [] = {30, 50, 64, 64, 50, 30, 16, 16, 30};
        int yCoordinates [] = {10, 10, 24, 44, 58, 58, 44, 24, 10};
        super.paintComponent(grafObj);
        grafObj.drawPolygon(xCoordinates, yCoordinates, 9);
    }
}

// The Polygons applet

public class Polygons extends JApplet {
    Container polyArea = getContentPane();
    PolyPanel newPanel = new PolyPanel();

// The init method, which adds the panel to the applet

    public void init() {
        polyArea.add(newPanel);
    }
}
```

Figure 7.3 shows a display of the octagon drawn by `Polygons`.

FIGURE 7.3 A display drawn by the applet `Polygons`

An alternative technique for specifying a polygon is to create an object of class `Polygon`, which has a constructor with the same parameters as the `drawPolygon` method. Then an alternative version of `drawPolygon`, which takes a single `Polygon` parameter, can be called, as in this example:

```
Polygon myPolygon = new Polygon(
                    xCoordinates, yCoordinates, 9);
grafObj.drawPolygon(myPolygon);
```

Polygons, like rectangles, can be filled by simply calling `fillPolygon` instead of `drawPolygon`.

7.6.5   Ovals

Drawing an oval is very similar to drawing a rectangle. In fact, the parameters to the oval-drawing methods are exactly those that could be sent to `drawRect`. The four parameters to the two oval-drawing methods, `drawOval` and `fillOval`, specify the coordinates of the upper-left corner and the width and height of the oval. A circle, of course, is just a "square" oval.

7.7

COLOR

In Java, specific colors are represented as objects of class `Color`. The `java.awt` package includes a collection of predefined `Color` objects that represent common colors, as well as methods for creating new colors and using colors in painting applets.

The Java abstract model of color uses 24 bits, with 8 bits for each of the three primary colors, red, green, and blue. The 13 predefined colors are shown in Table 7.1, along with their RGB values.

TABLE 7.1 Predefined Java Colors and Their RGB Values

Color Name	RGB Value
Color.white	255, 255, 255
Color.black	0, 0, 0
Color.gray	128, 128, 128
Color.lightGray	192, 192, 192
Color.darkGray	64, 64, 64
Color.red	255, 0, 0

TABLE 7.1 Predefined Java Colors and Their RGB Values (Continued)

Color Name	RGB Value
Color.green	0, 255, 0
Color.blue	0, 0, 255
Color.yellow	255, 255, 0
Color.magenta	255, 0, 255
Color.cyan	0, 255, 255
Color.pink	255, 175, 175
Color.orange	255, 200, 0

Any color possible with the 24-bit specification can be constructed by creating an object of type `Color`, as in the following:

```
Color myColor = new Color(x, y, z);
```

Here, x, y, and z are integer values in the range of 0 to 255, representing the red, green, and blue components of the color.

The color of the `Graphics` object can be set with the `setColor` method, as shown here:

```
grafObj.setColor(Color.magenta);
```

The background and foreground colors for a panel can be set with methods from the `Panel` class, as discussed in Section 7.8.

7.8

INTERACTIVE APPLETS

A large part of the initial interest in Java was centered on applets, and a large part of this interest came from the possibility of making XHTML documents interactive. The support for interactivity in an applet is based on the reactive GUI components (widgets) that can be put in an applet display. This section describes how GUI components can be created in an applet and how user interactions with those components can be used to trigger computations. Because you have already learned about making GUI components react to user actions with XHTML and JavaScript, this section should be relatively easy to understand.

7.8.1 Java Swing GUI Components

The Swing package, defined in `javax.swing`, includes a collection of components that are what we have called *widgets*. A label component is an object of class `JLabel`. A `JLabel` object is a static string used to label other components. For example:

```
final JLabel lab1 = new JLabel("Customer name:");
```

A button is an object of class `JButton`. The parameter to the `JButton` constructor becomes the label in the button depiction:

```
JButton myButton = new JButton("Click me");
```

A checkbox is an object of class `JCheckbox`. The constructor for checkboxes has just one parameter, the label to appear next to the checkbox:

```
JCheckbox box1 = new JCheckbox("Hamburger");
JCheckbox box2 = new JCheckbox("French Fries");
JCheckbox box3 = new JCheckbox("Milk");
```

The `JCheckbox` constructor can include a second parameter, a Boolean. If `true` is sent to the constructor, the checkbox is initially checked; otherwise, it is initially unchecked.

Radio buttons are special buttons that are placed in a button group. A button group is an object of class `ButtonGroup`, whose constructor takes no parameters. The `JRadioButton` constructor, used for creating radio buttons, takes two parameters: the label and the initial state of the radio button (`true` or `false`). After the radio buttons are created, they are put in their button group with the `add` method of the group object. Consider the following example:

```
ButtonGroup payment = new ButtonGroup();
JRadioButton box1 = new JRadioButton("Visa", true);
JRadioButton box2 = new JRadioButton("Master Charge",
                                     false);
JRadioButton box3 = new JRadioButton("Discover", false);
payment.add(box1);
payment.add(box2);
payment.add(box3);
```

A text box is an object of class `JTextField`. The simplest `JTextField` constructor takes a single parameter, the length of the box in characters. For example,

```
JTextField name = new JTextField(32);
```

The `JTextField` constructor can also take a literal string, which is displayed as its contents. The string parameter, when present, appears as the first parameter.

Recall that the `paintComponent` method cannot paint an applet directly. Rather, it is used to paint an object of a subclass of `JPanel`, which is then added to the content pane of the applet. Components must also be added to a panel, but in this case it is a simple `JPanel` object that can be created in the applet class because the `paintComponent` method is not needed. The following code creates the panel object we use in the following discussion of components:

```
JPanel myPanel = new JPanel();
```

The background color for a panel can be set with the `setBackground` method, as shown here:

```
myPanel.setBackground(Color.yellow);
```

The `setForeground` method sets the default color of everything to be drawn in the panel. For example, the following statement changes the default drawing color to blue:

```
myPanel.setForeground(Color.blue);
```

After the components have been created with constructors, they must be placed in the panel with the `add` method, as in the following:

```
myPanel.add(lab1);
```

Java defines several different objects called *layout managers* that determine how components are positioned in a panel. The default layout manager for Swing components is `BorderLayout`, which places components on the borders of the panel. This is fine for some situations. However, it is often convenient to have more control over where components are placed in a panel. For this, Java offers several alternative layout managers. One of these is `GridLayout`, which divides the panel area into rows and columns of compartments, each of which can contain a component. The parameters to the `GridLayout` constructor are the number of rows and columns, and the number of pixels between the rows and columns, respectively. The layout manager for a panel is specified with the `setLayout` method, which takes a layout manager object as its parameter. For example, consider the following code, which creates a new panel named `buttonPanel` and a `GridLayout` layout manager object for the panel:

```
JPanel buttonPanel = new JPanel();
buttonPanel.setLayout(new GridLayout(2, 3, 15, 15));
```

In this example, the panel's grid layout is specified to have two rows of three components each, with 15 pixels between the components.

The following example illustrates an applet that contains some simple GUI components. It uses a `GridLayout` manager object to put the components in a single column. Notice that the components are all placed in the panel object, which is ultimately added to the applet's content pane.

```java
/* Pizza.java
   An applet to illustrate some GUI components with a pizza
   order form
   */
import java.awt.*;
import java.applet.*;
import javax.swing.*;

public class Pizza extends JApplet {
    Container contentPane = getContentPane();

    public void init() {

// Create a panel object and set its layout manager to put
// the components in a column

        JPanel myPanel = new JPanel();
        myPanel.setLayout(new GridLayout(20, 1, 10, 10));
        myPanel.setBackground(Color.cyan);

// Create a label for the form heading and add it to the panel

        Label myLabel = new Label("Pizza Order Form");
        myPanel.add(myLabel);

// Create a text field for the customer's name and
//  address and add them to the panel

        JLabel nameLabel = new JLabel("Name:");
        JTextField myName = new JTextField(30);
        JLabel addrLabel = new JLabel("Address:");
        JTextField myAddr = new JTextField(30);
        myPanel.add(nameLabel);
        myPanel.add(myName);
        myPanel.add(addrLabel);
        myPanel.add(myAddr);

// Create radio buttons for pizza size and add them to the panel
```

```
        JLabel sizeLabel = new JLabel("Pizza Size");
        ButtonGroup sizeGroup = new ButtonGroup();
        JRadioButton s1 = new JRadioButton("small");
        JRadioButton s2 = new JRadioButton("medium");
        JRadioButton s3 = new JRadioButton("large", true);

// Put the radio buttons in the button group

        sizeGroup.add(s1);
        sizeGroup.add(s2);
        sizeGroup.add(s3);

// Put the radio buttons in the panel

        myPanel.add(sizeLabel);
        myPanel.add(s1);
        myPanel.add(s2);
        myPanel.add(s3);

// Create checkboxes for toppings and add them to the panel

        JLabel topLabel = new JLabel("Toppings");
        Checkbox top1 = new Checkbox("sausage");
        Checkbox top2 = new Checkbox("pepperoni");
        Checkbox top3 = new Checkbox("extra cheese");
        Checkbox top4 = new Checkbox("hamburger");
        Checkbox top5 = new Checkbox("olives");
        Checkbox top6 = new Checkbox("mushrooms");
        myPanel.add(topLabel);
        myPanel.add(top1);
        myPanel.add(top2);
        myPanel.add(top3);
        myPanel.add(top4);
        myPanel.add(top5);
        myPanel.add(top6);


// Now add the panel to the content pane

        contentPane.add(myPanel);

    }  // End of init()
} // End of the Pizza applet
```

Figure 7.4 shows a browser display of the applet `Pizza`.

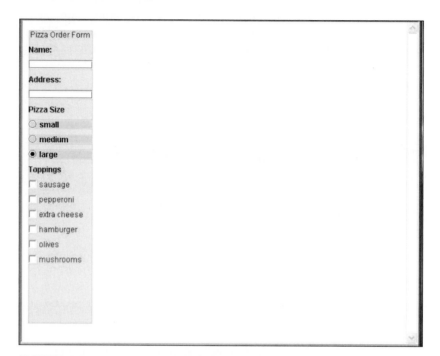

FIGURE 7.4 Results of running the `Pizza` applet

7.8.2 The Java Event Model

GUI components are not of much value unless user interactions with them trigger computations. In JavaScript, user interactions with components create events that can be caught by event handlers, which provide the computations. In Java, a similar model is used. GUI components are event generators. In Java, event handlers are called *event listeners*. Event listeners are connected to event generators through *event listener registration*. Listener registration is done with a method of the class that implements the listener interface, as described later in this section. The panel object into which the components are placed can be the event listener for those components. Only event listeners that are registered for a specific event are notified when that event occurs.

An event generator tells a listener of an event by sending a message to the listener (in other words, by calling one of the listener's methods). The listener method that receives the message implements an event handler. To make the event-handling methods conform to a standard protocol, a Java interface is used. An interface prescribes standard method protocols but does not provide implementations of those methods. This protocol could be specified by forcing the event generator to be a subclass of a class from which it would inherit the protocol. However, the `JApplet` class already has a superclass, and in Java, a class can have just one parent class. Therefore, the protocol must come from an interface. A class cannot be instantiated unless it provides definitions for all methods in the interfaces that it implements.

A class that needs to implement a listener must implement an interface for those listeners. There are many classes of events and listener interfaces. The event classes appear in two categories: semantic events and low-level events. Table 7.2 lists a few of the most commonly used classes of events.

TABLE 7.2 Event Classes

Class Name	User Actions that Create the Event Object
Semantic Event Classes	
ActionEvent	Click a button, select from a menu or list, or press the Enter button in a text field
ItemEvent	Select a checkbox or list item
TextEvent	Change the contents of a text field or text area
Low-Level Event Classes	
ComponentEvent	Resize, move, show, or hide a component
KeyEvent	Press or release a key
MouseEvent	Depress or release a mouse button, or move the cursor into or out of the component
MouseMotionEvent	Change the position of the mouse cursor over the component
FocusEvent	Get or lose focus for a component

Each semantic event listener interface prescribes one method for the handler. The low-level interfaces have several different handler methods. The handler methods for the two most commonly used semantic events are shown in Table 7.3.

TABLE 7.3 Semantic Event Listener Interfaces and Their Handler Methods

Interface	Handler Method
ActionListener	actionPerformed
ItemListener	itemStateChanged

As stated previously, the connection of a component to an event listener is made with a method of the class that implements the listener interface. Event listener registration establishes this connection. For example, because `ActionEvent` is the class name of event objects created by user actions on buttons, the `addActionListener` method is used to register a listener for buttons. The listener for button events created in a panel in an applet could be implemented in the panel. So, for a button named `button1` in a panel named `myPanel` that implements the `ActionEvent` event handler for buttons, we would register the listener with the following statement:

```
button1.addActionListener(this);
```

Each event handler method receives an event parameter that provides information about the event. Event classes have methods, such as `getState`, to access that information. For example, when called through a radio button, `getState` returns `true` or `false`, depending on whether the button was on or off, respectively.

All the event-related classes are in the `java.awt.event` package, so it must be imported to any applet class that uses events.

The following sample applet, `RadioB`, illustrates the use of events and event handling to display dynamic content in an applet. This applet constructs radio buttons that control the font style of the contents of a text field. It creates a `Font` object for each of four font styles. Each of these has a radio button to enable the user to select the style. The applet then creates a text string, whose font style will be controlled by the user through the radio buttons. The event handler `itemStateChanged` determines which radio button is pressed, after being informed by the `ItemEvent` object that a change has been made in the radio buttons. Then it sets the font style of the text string accordingly.

```
/* RadioB.java
   An applet to illustrate event handling with interactive
   radio buttons that control the font style of a text field
   */
import java.awt.*;
import java.awt.event.*;
import java.applet.*;
import javax.swing.*;

public class RadioB extends JApplet implements ItemListener {

// Make most of the variables class variables, because both init
// and the event handler must see them

    private Container contentPane = getContentPane();
    private JTextField text;
```

```
        private Font plainFont, boldFont, italicFont, boldItalicFont;
        private JRadioButton plain, bold, italic, boldItalic;
        private ButtonGroup radioButtons = new ButtonGroup();
        private JPanel myPanel = new JPanel();

// The init method is where the document is initially built

        public void init() {

// Set the background color of the panel

            myPanel.setBackground(Color.cyan);

// Create the fonts

            plainFont = new Font("Serif", Font.PLAIN, 16);
            boldFont = new Font("Serif", Font.BOLD, 16);
            italicFont = new Font("Serif", Font.ITALIC, 16);
            boldItalicFont = new Font("Serif", Font.BOLD +
                                    Font.ITALIC, 16);

// Create the test text string, set its font, and add it to the
// panel

            text = new JTextField("In what font style should I appear?",
                            30);
            myPanel.add(text);
            text.setFont(plainFont);

 // Create radio buttons for the fonts and add them to the panel

            plain = new JRadioButton("Plain", true);
            bold = new JRadioButton("Bold");
            italic = new JRadioButton("Italic");
            boldItalic = new JRadioButton("Bold Italic");
            radioButtons.add(plain);
            radioButtons.add(bold);
            radioButtons.add(italic);
            radioButtons.add(boldItalic);

// Register the event handlers to myPanel
            plain.addItemListener(this);
            bold.addItemListener(this);
```

continued

```
            italic.addItemListener(this);
            boldItalic.addItemListener(this);

// Now add the buttons to the panel

            myPanel.add(plain);
            myPanel.add(bold);
            myPanel.add(italic);
            myPanel.add(boldItalic);

// Now add the panel to the content pane for the applet

            contentPane.add(myPanel);

    }  // End of init()

// The event handler

    public void itemStateChanged (ItemEvent e) {

// Determine which button is on and set the font accordingly

if (plain.isSelected())
    text.setFont(plainFont);
else if (bold.isSelected())
    text.setFont(boldFont);
else if (italic.isSelected())
    text.setFont(italicFont);
else if (boldItalic.isSelected())
    text.setFont(boldItalicFont);

    } // End of itemStateChanged

} // End of RadioB applet
```

The RadioB applet produces the screen shown in Figure 7.5.

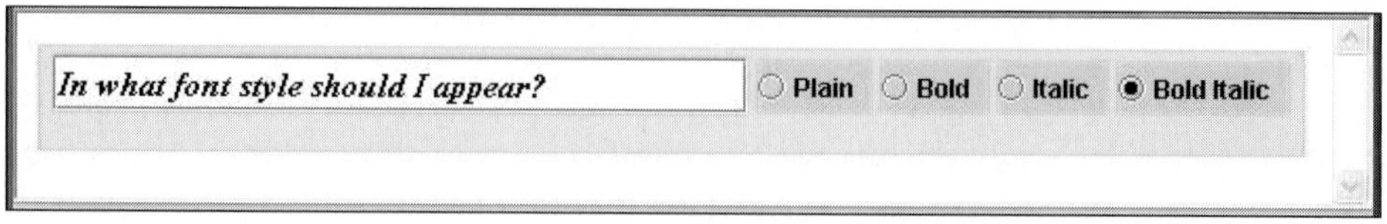

FIGURE 7.5 The output of the RadioB applet

7.9

SUMMARY

The impetus for Java's fast rise in popularity was the use of applets in constructing Web sites. An applet is a usually small collection of Java code defined in a class that is derived from `JApplet`. In objects of this class, a call is made to the `paintComponent` method, which can display a variety of things on the screen.

An XHTML tag, `<object>`, is used to inform the browser that an applet is to be downloaded from the server (or somewhere else) and run, creating something at that spot in the document. In a sense, applets are slaves to the XHTML document that calls them. The `<object>` tag also specifies the file type and the size of the area into which the applet will display and possibly some parameters to the applet.

The primary applet activities are `start`, which starts and restarts the applet; `stop`, which stops the applet's execution when the browser leaves the document that calls the applet; `destroy`, which is called when the user stops the execution of the browser; and `paintComponent`, which draws things on the screen. All of these methods are called by the browser. The `paintComponent`, `start`, and `stop` methods were described in this chapter.

Text and graphical objects are drawn by the applet with methods of the `Graphics` class. The coordinate system into which things are drawn has its origin in the upper-left corner. The `paintComponent` method takes a `Graphics` class object as a parameter. `paintComponent` calls other methods to produce the actual graphics in the applet area. The `drawString` method is used to display a character string. The `drawLine` method draws a line between two specified points. The `drawRect` and `fillRect` methods draw outlines of rectangles and filled rectangles, respectively. The `drawPolygon` and `fillPolygon` methods draw outlines of polygons and filled polygons, respectively.

Swing GUI components are implemented in Java as instantiations of their corresponding classes—for example, `JLabel` and `JButton`. The Java event model is related to that of JavaScript. Events are objects, often created by GUI components. Events are handled by methods called event listeners, which are connected to the GUI component objects. The listener object for events placed in a panel can be the panel itself. Event handlers can do virtually anything that can be done in an applet. One powerful possibility is that of dynamically changing the content of the document being displayed.

7.10 Review Questions

1. What three things happen when a browser finds a reference to an applet in an XHTML document?

2. From what class does `Applet` directly descend?

3. What are the two ways to test an applet?

4. What advantages do Java applets have over JavaScript?

5. What advantages does JavaScript have over applets?

6. What are the four fundamental methods used to control the basic operations of an applet?

7. How are the four fundamental methods for applet control called?

8. How is `paintComponent` called?

9. What parameter does `paintComponent` take and what is its origin?

10. What is the content pane of an applet?

11. Why is `paintComponent` used in a separate panel subclass?

12. Describe the parameters to `drawString`.

13. Describe the four required attributes of `<object>`.

14. Describe the attributes for `<param>`.

15. How are parameters from an XHTML document gotten into an applet that is referenced in that document?

16. Describe the parameters to `drawRect`.

17. How is the color of a `Graphics` object set?

18. How are radio buttons created in an applet?

19. What method places a GUI component into a panel?

20. Describe the parameters to a `GridLayout` constructor.

21. What is the event class for button clicks?

22. What is the event class for a checkbox selection?

23. What objects are sent notifications of GUI component events?

24. In what class is a method defined to register an event listener?

25. What event-handler method is used for button events?

7.11 Exercises

Write, test, and debug (if necessary) applets for the following specifications:

1. Modify the `We13` applet from Section 7.5 to use parameters for the font and font style, as well as the font size. Test this applet with several different sets of parameters from the XHTML document that runs it.

2. Modify the `We13` applet to place the message inside an unfilled white circle that is centered in a filled blue square. The text must be black.

3. The applet for this exercise must display the Olympic logo, which consists of five overlaid circles. Below the logo must appear the text "The United States Olympic Committee." The circles must be blue, and the text must be red. The circles part of the logo must be enclosed in an unfilled green rectangle.

4. The applet for this exercise must display four checkboxes, labeled Tacos, Chalupas, Burritos, and Nachos. Beside each checkbox there must be a text box labeled Quantity. This applet need not deal with events or event handling.

5. Modify the applet of Exercise 4 by adding event handling for the input from the user. The applet must get a number from each of the text boxes, assuming 0 if the field is not changed. It must then compute the cost of the order, assuming that tacos cost 79 cents, chalupas cost $1.19, burritos cost $1.39, and nachos cost $1.29.

6. The applet for this exercise must display two collections of six radio buttons, labeled Red, Green, Blue, Yellow, Magenta, and Cyan. The first collection must be labeled Foreground; the second must be labeled Background. These buttons must be implemented to control the foreground and background colors of the display. So that the foreground color can be seen, include a few geometric shapes and some text.

8

Introduction to XML

Some people consider the eXtensible Markup Language (XML) to be one of the most important new technologies to appear in the parade of technologies developed to support the World Wide Web. Although it has already had far-reaching effects on the storage and processing of data, its full impact will not be felt until sometime in the future. XML consists of a collection of related technologies specified by recommendations developed by the W3C. This chapter provides introductions to the most important of these.

The chapter begins with a brief discussion of the origins of XML followed by a description of some of its characteristics. The general syntactic structure of XML documents is then described. Next, the chapter details the purpose and form of document type definitions (DTDs), including the declarations of elements, attributes, and entities. A DTD provides the elements and attributes for a markup language, as well as the rules for how the elements can appear in documents. This is followed by a description of XML namespaces. Next, the chapter describes XML schemas, which provide a more elaborate way to describe the structure of XML documents than DTDs. Two different approaches to formatting XML documents, CSS and XSLT style sheets, are then discussed and illustrated with examples. Actually, XSLT style sheets are used to transform XML documents. The target of the transformations we describe is XHTML documents, which can include CSS style specifications for display. Finally, we discuss the issues associated with reading and processing XML documents. Keep in mind that this chapter describes only a tiny part of XML and its surrounding technologies.

8.1
INTRODUCTION

A meta-markup language is a language for defining markup languages. The Standard Generalized Markup Language (SGML) is a meta-markup language for documents written in virtually any language for any purpose. SGML was approved as an International Standards Organization (ISO) standard in 1986. In 1990, SGML was used as the basis for the development of HTML as the standard markup language for Web documents. The World Wide Web Consortium (W3C) began work on XML, another meta-markup language, in 1996. The first XML standard, 1.0, was published in February 1998.

Part of the motivation for the development of XML was the deficiencies of HTML. The purpose of HTML is to describe the layout of information in Web documents. To allow this, HTML defines a collection of tags and attributes. An HTML user can use only that collection of tags and attributes. One problem with HTML is that it was defined to describe the layout of information without considering its meaning. So, regardless of the kind of information you are trying to describe with HTML, all you can really describe is its general form and layout in a document. For example, suppose that a document stores a list of used cars for sale, and the color and price are included for each car. With HTML, those two pieces of information about a car could be stored as the content of paragraph elements, but there would be no way to find them in the document because paragraph tags could have been used for many different kinds of information. To describe a particular kind of information, it would be necessary to have tags indicating the meaning of the element's content. That would allow processing of specific categories of information in a document. For example, if the price of a used car is stored as the content of an element named `price`, an application could find all cars in the document that cost less than $10,000. Of course, no markup language could possibly include meaningful tags for all the different kinds of information that might be stored in documents.

Another potential problem with HTML is that it enforces few restrictions on the arrangement or order of tags in a document. For example, an opening tag can appear in the content of an element, but its corresponding closing tag can appear after the end of the element in which it is nested. An example of this is as follows:

```
<b> Now <i> is </b> the time </i>
```

Note that although this problem was evident in HTML 4, which was in use when XML was developed, it is not a problem with XHTML, for obvious reasons.

One solution to the deficiencies of HTML is for each group of users with common document needs to develop its own set of tags and attributes and then use the SGML standard to define a new markup language to meet those needs. Each application area would have its own markup language. The problem with this is that SGML is too large and complex to make this approach feasible. SGML includes a large number of capabilities that are only rarely used. A program capable of parsing SGML documents would be very large and costly to develop. In addition, SGML requires that a formal definition be provided with each new markup language. So, although having area-specific markup languages is a good idea, basing them on SGML is not.

An alternative solution to the problems of HTML is to define a simplified version of SGML and allow users to define their own markup languages based on it. XML was designed to be that simplified version of SGML. In this context, "users" means organizations of people with common data description and processing needs (rather than individual users). For example, chemists need to store chemical data in a standard way, providing a way to share data with other chemists and allowing all to use data processing tools that work on chemical data stored in the same standard format, regardless of its origin. Likewise, this is the case for many other groups with their own kinds of data to represent and process.

It is important to understand that XML was not meant to be a replacement for HTML. In fact, the two have different goals. Whereas HTML is a markup language that is meant to describe the layout of general information, as well as provide some guidance for how it should be displayed, XML is a meta-markup language that provides a framework for defining specialized markup languages. HTML itself can be defined as an XML markup language. In fact, XHTML is an XML-based version of HTML.

XML is far more than a solution to the deficiencies of HTML. It provides a simple and universal way of storing textual data of any kind. Data stored in XML documents can be electronically distributed and processed by any number of different processing applications. These applications are relatively easy to write because of the standard ways in which the data is stored. Therefore, XML is a universal data interchange language.

XML is not a markup language; it is a meta-markup language that specifies rules for creating markup languages. As a result, XML includes no tags. When designing a markup language using XML, the designer must define a collection of tags that carries the meaning of the content of the tags. As with XHTML, an XML tag and its content, together with the closing tag, are called an *element*.

Strictly speaking, a markup language designed with XML is called an *XML application*. However, a program that processes information stored in a document formatted with an XML application is also called an application. To avoid confusion, we will refer to an XML-based markup language as a *tag set*. We call documents that use an XML-based markup language *XML documents*.

XML documents can be written by hand using a simple text editor. This approach is, of course, impractical for large data collections, which are likely to be written by programs. A browser has a default presentation style for every XHTML element, which makes it possible for the browser to display any XHTML document. However, a browser cannot be expected to have default presentation styles for elements it has never seen. Therefore, the data in an XML document can be displayed by browsers or browser-like programs only if the presentation styles are provided by style sheets of some kind.

Application programs that process the data in XML documents must analyze the document before they gain access to the data. This analysis is performed by an XML processor, which has several tasks, one of which is to parse XML documents, a process that isolates the constituent parts (such as tags, attributes, and data strings) and provides them to an application. XML processors are described in Section 8.10.

Unlike most documents produced by word processing systems, XML documents have no hidden specifications. Therefore, XML documents are plain text, which is easily readable by both people and application programs (although there are no compelling reasons for people to read them).

At the time of this writing (late 2004), the vast majority of Web clients use either Internet Explorer 6 (IE6) or Netscape 7 (NS7) browsers, both of which support basic XML.

8.2
THE SYNTAX OF XML

The syntax of XML can be thought of at two distinct levels. First, there is the general low-level syntax of XML that imposes its rules on all XML documents. The other syntactic level is specified by either document type definitions (DTDs) or XML schemas. These two kinds of specifications impose structural syntactic rules on documents written with XML tag sets. DTDs and XML schemas specify the set of tags and attributes that can appear in a particular document or collection of documents, and also the orders and various arrangements in which they can appear. DTDs are described in Section 8.4. XML schemas are discussed in Section 8.6. This section describes the first level of XML syntax, that which applies to all XML documents.

An XML document can include a variety of different kinds of statements. The most common of these are the data elements of the document. XML documents may also include markup declarations, which are instructions to the XML parser, and processing instructions, which are instructions for an application program that will process the data described in the document.

All XML documents begin with an XML declaration, which has the appearance of a processing instruction but technically is not one. The XML declaration identifies the document as being XML and provides the version number of the XML standard being used. It may also specify an encoding standard. This declaration is the same as the one used in all XHTML documents in this book.

Comments in XML are the same as in HTML. They cannot contain two adjacent dashes, for obvious reasons.

XML names are used to name elements and attributes. An XML name must begin with a letter or an underscore and can include digits, hyphens, and periods. There is no length limitation for XML names. XML names are case sensitive, so Body, body, and BODY are all distinct names.

A small set of syntax rules applies to all XML documents. XHTML uses the same rules, and the XHTML markup in this book complies with them.

Every XML document defines a single root element, whose opening tag must appear on the first line of XML code. All other elements of an XML document must be nested inside the root element. The root element of every XHTML document is html. XML tags, like those of XHTML, are surrounded by pointed brackets.

Every XML element that can have content must have a closing tag. Elements that do not include content must use a tag with the following form:

<element_name />

As is the case with XHTML, XML tags can have attributes, which are specified with name/value assignments. As with XHTML, all attribute values must be enclosed by either single or double quotation marks.

An XML document that strictly adheres to these syntax rules is considered *well formed*. Consider the following simple but complete example:

```
<?xml version = "1.0" encoding = "utf-8"?>
<ad>
    <year> 1960 </year>
    <make> Cessna </make>
    <model> Centurian </model>
    <color> Yellow with white trim </color>
    <location>
       <city> Gulfport </city>
       <state> Mississippi </state>
    </location>
</ad>
```

Notice that none of the tags in this document is defined in XHTML—all are designed for the specific content of the document.

When designing an XML document, the designer is often faced with the choice between adding a new attribute to an element or defining a nested element. In some cases, there is no choice. For example, if the data in question is an image, a reference to it can only be an attribute because such a reference cannot be the content of an element. In other cases, it may not matter whether an attribute or a nested element is used. However, there are some situations in which there is a choice and one is clearly better than the other.

Sometimes nested tags are better than attributes. A document or category of documents for which you are defining tags might need to grow in structural complexity in the future. Nested tags can be added to any existing tag to describe its growing size and complexity. Nothing can be added to an attribute, however. Attributes cannot describe structure at all, so a nested element should be used if the data in question has some substructure of its own. A nested element should be used if the data is subdata of the parent element's content rather than information about the data of the parent element.

There is one situation in which an attribute should always be used: for identifying numbers or names of elements, exactly as the `id` and `name` attributes are used in XHTML. An attribute should be used if the data in question is one value from a given set of possibilities. Attributes should also be used if there is no substructure or if it is really just information about the element.

The following three versions of an element named `patient` illustrate three possible choices between tags and attributes:

```
<!-- A tag with one attribute -->
<patient name = "Maggie Dee Magpie">
   ...
</patient>

<!-- A tag with one nested tag -->
<patient>
   <name> Maggie Dee Magpie </name>
   ...
</patient>

<!-- A tag with one nested tag, which contains
     three nested tags -->
<patient>
   <name>
      <first> Maggie </first>
      <middle> Dee </middle>
      <last> Magpie </last>
   </name>
   ...
</patient>
```

In this example, the third choice is probably the best because it provides easy access to all of the parts of the data, which may be needed.

8.3

XML DOCUMENT STRUCTURE

An XML document often uses two auxiliary files: one that specifies its tag set and structural syntactic rules and one that contains a style sheet to describe how the content of the document is to be printed or displayed. The structural syntactic rules are given as either a DTD or an XML schema. Two approaches to style specification are discussed in Section 8.8 and Section 8.9.

An XML document consists of one or more entities that are logically related collections of information, ranging in size from a single character to a book chapter. One of these entities, called the *document entity*, is always physically in the file that represents the document. The document entity can be the entire document, but in many cases it includes references to the names of entities that are stored elsewhere. For example, the document entity for a technical article might contain the beginning material and ending material but have references to the article body sections, which are entities stored in separate files. Every entity except the document entity must have a name.

There are several reasons to break a document into multiple entities. It is good to define a large document as a number of smaller parts just to make it more manageable. Also, if the same data appears in more than one place in the document, defining it as an entity allows any number of references to a single copy of the data. This avoids the problem of inconsistency among the occurrences. Finally, many documents include information that cannot be represented as text, such as images. Such information units are usually stored as binary data. If a binary data unit is logically part of a document, it must be a separate entity because XML documents cannot include binary data. Such entities are called *binary entities*.

When an XML processor encounters the name of a nonbinary entity in a document, it replaces the name with the value it references. Binary entities can be handled only by applications that deal with the document, such as browsers. XML processors deal only with text.

Entity names can have any length. They must begin with a letter, a dash, or a colon. After the first character, a name can have letters, digits, periods, dashes, underscores, or colons. A reference to an entity is its name with a prepended ampersand and an appended semicolon. For example, if `apple_image` is the name of an entity, `&apple_image;` is a reference to it.

One of the common uses of entities is to allow characters that are normally used as markup delimiters to appear as themselves in a document. Because this is a common need, XML includes the entities that are predefined for XHTML, the most common of which are shown in Table 2.1 (in Chapter 2). User-defined entities can be defined only in DTDs, which are discussed in Section 8.4.

When several predefined entities must appear near each other in an XML document, their references clutter the content and make it difficult to read. In such cases, a character data section can be used. The content of a character data section is not parsed by the XML parser, so it cannot include any tags. This promise of no tags makes it possible to include special markup delimiter characters directly in the section without using their entity references. The form of a character data section is as follows:

```
<![CDATA[ content ]]>
```

For example, instead of using the line

```
The last word of the line is &gt;&gt;&gt; here
&lt;&lt;&lt;.
```

the following line could be used:

```
<![CDATA[The last word of the line is >>> here <<<]]>
```

The opening keyword of a character data section is not just CDATA; it is in effect [CDATA[. An important consequence of this is that there cannot be any spaces between the [and the C, or between the A (the last character of CDATA) and the second [.

Because the content of a character data section is not parsed by the XML parser, any entity references that are included are not expanded. For example, the content of the line

```
<![CDATA[The form of a tag is &lt;tag name&gt;]]>
```

is as follows:

```
The form of a tag is &lt;tag name&gt;
```

8.4

DOCUMENT TYPE DEFINITIONS

A document type definition (DTD) is a set of structural rules called *declarations*, which specify a set of elements that can appear in the document as well as how and where these elements may appear. Not all XML documents need a DTD. Use of a DTD is related to the use of an external style sheet for XHTML documents. External style sheets are used to impose a uniform style over a collection of documents. DTDs are used when the same tag set definition is used by a collection of documents, perhaps by a collection of users, and the collection must have a consistent and uniform structure.

The purpose of a DTD is to define a standard form for a collection of XML documents. This form is specified as the tag and attribute sets, as well as rules that define how they can appear in a document. DTDs also provide entity definitions.

All documents in the collection can be tested against the DTD to determine whether they conform to the rules it describes. Application programs that process the data in the collection of XML documents can be written to assume the particular document form. Without such structural restrictions, developing such applications would be difficult, if not impossible.

A DTD can be embedded in the XML document whose syntax rules it describes, in which case it is called an *internal DTD*. The alternative is to have the DTD stored in a separate file, in which case it is called an *external DTD*. Because external DTDs allow use with more than one XML document, they are preferable. A group of users defines a DTD for their particular kind of data and all use that DTD, which imposes structural uniformity across all of their documents.

It is common knowledge that the earlier errors in software systems are found, the less expensive it is to fix them. The situation is similar in the case of DTDs. A DTD with an incorrect or inappropriate declaration can have widespread consequences. Fixing the DTD and all copies of it is just the first step, and it is the simplest. After the correction of the DTD is completed, all documents that use the DTD must be tested against the DTD and often modified to conform to the changed DTD. Changes to associated style sheets also might be necessary.

Syntactically, a DTD is a sequence of declarations enclosed in the block of a `DOCTYPE` markup declaration. Each declaration within this block has the form of a markup declaration:

```
<!keyword ... >
```

Four possible keywords can be used in a declaration: `ELEMENT`, used to define tags; `ATTLIST`, used to define tag attributes; `ENTITY`, used to define entities; and `NOTATION`, used to define data type notations. The first three of these four kinds of declarations are described in the following sections. Because of their infrequent use, we do not discuss `NOTATION` declarations.

8.4.1 Declaring Elements

The element declarations of a DTD have a form that is related to that of the rules of context-free grammars, also known as Backus-Naur form (BNF).[1] BNF is used to define the syntax or structure of programming languages. A DTD describes the structure of a particular set of documents, so it is natural for its rules to be similar to those of BNF.

Each element declaration in a DTD specifies the structure of one category of elements. The declaration provides the name of the element whose structure is being defined, along with the specification of the structure of that element.

---

1. BNF is named after its primary designer, John Backus, and Peter Naur, who helped by providing some small modifications.

Although an XML document actually is a string of characters, it is often convenient to think of it in terms of a general tree. An element is a node in such a tree, either a leaf node or an internal node. If the element is a leaf node, its syntactic description is its character pattern. If the element is an internal node, its syntactic description is a list of its child elements, each of which can be either a leaf node or an internal node.

The form of an element declaration for elements that contain elements is as follows:

`<!ELEMENT` *element_name* (*list of names of child elements*)`>`

For example, consider the following declaration:

`<!ELEMENT memo (from, to, date, re, body)>`

This element declaration would describe the document tree structure shown in Figure 8.1.

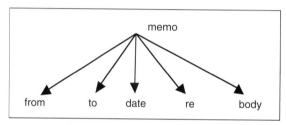

FIGURE 8.1 An example of the document tree structure for an element definition

In many cases, it is necessary to specify the number of times that a child element may appear. This can be done in a DTD declaration by adding a modifier to the child element specification. These modifiers, described in Table 8.1, are borrowed from regular expressions. Any child element specification can be followed by one of the modifiers.

TABLE 8.1 Child Element Specification Modifiers

Modifier	Meaning
+	One or more occurrences
*	Zero or more occurrences
?	Zero or one occurrence

Consider the following DTD declaration:

```
<!ELEMENT person (parent+, age, spouse?, sibling*)>
```

In this example, a `person` element is specified to have the following children elements: one or more `parent` elements, one `age` element, possibly a `spouse` element, and zero or more `sibling` elements.

The leaf nodes of a DTD specify the data types of the content of their parent nodes, which are elements. In most cases, the content of an element is type `PCDATA`, for *parsable character data*. Two other content types can be specified: `EMPTY` and `ANY`. The `EMPTY` type is used to specify that the element has no content. This is used for elements similar to the XHTML `img` element. The `ANY` type is used when the element may contain literally any content. The form of a leaf element declaration is as follows:

```
<!ELEMENT element-name (#PCDATA)>
```

8.4.2 Declaring Attributes

The attributes of an element are declared separately from the element declaration in a DTD. An attribute declaration must include the name of the element to which the attribute belongs, the attribute's name, and its type. Also, it may include a default value. The general form of an attribute declaration is as follows:

```
<!ATTLIST element_name attribute_name attribute_type [default_value]>
```

If more than one attribute is declared for a given element, the declarations can be combined, as in this example:

```
<!ATTLIST element_name
          attribute_name_1 attribute_type default_value_1
          attribute_name_2 attribute_type default_value_2
          . . .
          attribute_name_n attribute_type default_value_n
>
```

There are ten different attribute types. For this chapter, only one, `CDATA`, will be used. This type is just any string of characters.

The default value in an attribute declaration can specify either an actual value or a requirement for the value of the attribute in the XML document. Table 8.2 lists the possible default values.

TABLE 8.2 Possible Default Values for Attributes

Value	Meaning
A value	The value, which is used if none is specified in an element.
#FIXED value	The value, which every element will have and which cannot be changed.
#REQUIRED	No default value is given; every instance of the element must specify a value.
#IMPLIED	No default value is given; the value may or may not be specified in an element.

For example, suppose the DTD included these attribute specifications:

```
<!ATTLIST airplane places CDATA "4">
<!ATTLIST airplane engine_type CDATA #REQUIRED>
<!ATTLIST airplane price CDATA #IMPLIED>
<!ATTLIST airplane manufacturer CDATA #FIXED "Cessna">
```

The following XML element is valid for this DTD:

```
<airplane places = "10" engine_type = "jet"> </airplane>
```

Attributes that include #FIXED in the DTD may or may not be specified in particular element instances.

8.4.3 Declaring Entities

Entities can be defined so that they can be referenced anywhere in the content of an XML document, in which case they are called *general entities*. The predefined entities are all general entities. Entities can also be defined so that they can be referenced only in markup declarations, in which case they are called *parameter entities*.

The form of an entity declaration that appears in a DTD is shown here:

```
<!ENTITY [%] entity_name "entity_value">
```

When the optional percent sign (%) is present in an entity declaration, it specifies that the entity is a parameter entity rather than a general entity.

Consider the following example of an entity. Suppose that a document includes a large number of references to the full name of President Kennedy. You could define an entity to represent his complete name:

```
<!ENTITY jfk "John Fitzgerald Kennedy">
```

Any XML document that uses the DTD that includes this declaration can specify the complete name with just the reference &jfk;.

When an entity is longer than a few words, such as a section of a technical article, its text is defined outside the DTD. In such cases, the entity it is called an *external text entity*. The form of the declaration of an external text entity is shown here:

```
<!ENTITY entity_name SYSTEM "file_location">
```

The keyword SYSTEM specifies that the definition of the entity is in a different file, which is specified as the string following SYSTEM.

8.4.4 A Sample DTD

As an example of a DTD, consider a booklet of ads for used aircraft. In this case, the DTD describes the form of the booklet and each of its ads:

```
<?xml version = "1.0" encoding = "utf-8"?>

<!-- planes.dtd - a document type definition for
                  the planes.xml document, which specifies
                  a list of used airplanes for sale   -->

<!ELEMENT planes_for_sale (ad+)>
<!ELEMENT ad (year, make, model, color, description,
             price?, seller, location)>
<!ELEMENT year (#PCDATA)>
<!ELEMENT make (#PCDATA)>
<!ELEMENT model (#PCDATA)>
<!ELEMENT color (#PCDATA)>
<!ELEMENT description (#PCDATA)>
<!ELEMENT price (#PCDATA)>
<!ELEMENT seller (#PCDATA)>
<!ELEMENT location (city, state)>
<!ELEMENT city (#PCDATA)>
<!ELEMENT state (#PCDATA)>

<!ATTLIST seller phone CDATA #REQUIRED>
<!ATTLIST seller email CDATA #IMPLIED>

<!ENTITY c "Cessna">
<!ENTITY p "Piper">
<!ENTITY b "Beechcraft">
```

Some XML parsers check documents that have DTDs to ensure that the documents conform to the structure specified in the DTDs. These parsers are called *validating parsers*. Not all XML parsers are validating parsers. If an XML document specifies a DTD and is parsed by a validating XML parser, and the parser determines that the document conforms to the DTD, the document is called *valid*.

Handwritten XML documents often are not well formed, which means they do not follow XML's syntactic rules. These errors are detected by all XML parsers, which must report them. Because errors are common, it is important to check XML documents for well-formedness before making them available to site visitors. XML parsers are not allowed to either repair or ignore errors. Validating XML parsers detect and report all inconsistencies in documents relative to their DTDs. XML parsers are discussed in Section 8.10.

8.4.5 Internal and External DTDs

Recall that a DTD can appear inside an XML document or in an external file, as is the case with `planes.dtd`. If the DTD is included in the XML code, it must be introduced with `<!DOCTYPE` *root_name* [and terminated with]>. For example, the structure of the `planes` XML document with its DTD included is as follows:

```
<?xml version = "1.0" encoding = "utf-8"?>
    <!DOCTYPE planes [
        <!-- The DTD for planes -->
    ]>
<!-- The planes XML document -->
```

When the DTD is in its own file, the XML document includes a `DOCTYPE` declaration as its second line. This declaration has the following form:

`<!DOCTYPE` *XML_document_root_name* `SYSTEM` *"DTD_file_name"*`>`

For the `planes` example, assuming that the DTD is stored in the file named `planes.dtd`, this declaration would be as follows:

`<!DOCTYPE planes_for_sale SYSTEM "planes.dtd">`

The following is an example of an XML document that is valid for the planes DTD:

```xml
<?xml version = "1.0" encoding = "utf-8"?>

<!-- planes.xml - A document that lists ads for
                  used airplanes -->

<!DOCTYPE planes_for_sale SYSTEM "planes.dtd">
<planes_for_sale>
   <ad>
      <year> 1977 </year>
      <make> &c; </make>
      <model> Skyhawk </model>
      <color> Light blue and white </color>
      <description> New paint, nearly new interior,
            685 hours SMOH, full IFR King avionics </description>
      <price> 23,495 </price>
      <seller phone = "555-222-3333"> Skyway Aircraft </seller>
      <location>
         <city> Rapid City, </city>
         <state> South Dakota </state>
      </location>
   </ad>
   <ad>
      <year> 1965 </year>
      <make> &p; </make>
      <model> Cherokee </model>
      <color> Gold </color>
      <description> 240 hours SMOH, dual NAVCOMs, DME,
               new Cleveland brakes, great shape </description>
      <seller phone = "555-333-2222"
              email = "jseller@www.axl.com">
              John Seller </seller>
      <location>
         <city> St. Joseph, </city>
         <state> Missouri </state>
      </location>
   </ad>
</planes_for_sale>
```

8.5

NAMESPACES

It is often convenient to construct XML documents that include tag sets that are defined for and used by other documents. When a tag set is available and appropriate for a particular XML document or class of documents, it is better to use it than to invent a new collection of element types. For example, imagine that you must define an XML markup language for a furniture catalog with `<chair>`, `<sofa>`, and `<table>` tags. The catalog document must also include several different tables of specific furniture pieces, wood types, finishes, and prices. It is convenient to use XHTML table tags to define these tables rather than inventing a new vocabulary for them.

The obvious problem with using different markup vocabularies in the same document is that collisions could result between names that are defined in two or more of those tag sets. An example of this is having a `<table>` tag for a category of furniture and a `<table>` tag from XHTML for information tables. Clearly, software systems that process XML documents must be capable of unambiguously recognizing the element names in those documents. To deal with this problem, the W3C has developed a standard for XML namespaces (`http://www.w3.org/TR/REC-xml-names`).

An *XML namespace* is a collection of element names used in XML documents. The name of a namespace usually has the form of a uniform resource identifier (URI).[2] A namespace for the elements of the hierarchy rooted at a particular element is declared as the value of the attribute `xmlns`. The form of a namespace declaration for an element is shown here:

```
<element_name  xmlns[:prefix] = URI>
```

The square brackets indicate that what is within them is optional. The prefix, if included, is the name that must be attached to the names in the declared namespace. A prefix is used for two reasons. First, the URI is too long to be typed on every occurrence of every name from the namespace. Second, a URI includes characters that are illegal in XML. Note that the element for which a namespace is declared is usually the root of a document.

As an example of a namespace declaration, consider the following:

```
<birds  xmlns:bd = "http://www.audubon.org/names/species">
```

Within the `birds` element, including all of its children elements, the names from the namespace must be prefixed with `bd`, as in the following:

```
<bd:lark>
```

---

2. A URL is a URI that happens to be the Internet address of some resource.

If an element has more than one namespace declaration, these are declared as shown here:

```
<birds  xmlns:bd = "http://www.audubon.org/names/species"
        xmlns:html = "http://www.w3.org/1999/xhtml" >
```

In this example, we have added the standard XHTML namespace to the `birds` element.

One namespace declaration in an element can be used to declare a default namespace. This is done by simply leaving out the prefix in the declaration. The names from the default namespace can be used without a prefix.

Consider the following example in which two namespaces are declared. The first is declared to be the default namespace; the second defines the prefix, `cap`.

```
<states>
  xmlns = "http://www.states-info.org/states"
  xmlns:cap =
            "http://www.states-info.org/state-capitals"
  <state>
     <name> South Dakota </name>
     <population> 754844 </population>
     <capital>
        <cap:name> Pierre </cap:name>
        <cap:population> 12429 </cap:population>
     </capital>
  </state>
  <!-- More states -->
</states>
```

Each state element has name and population elements from both namespaces.

Note that attribute names are not included in namespaces. The reason they are not is that attribute names are local to elements, so a tag set may use the same attribute name in more than one element without causing ambiguity.

If an XML document uses a DTD and a prefixed name, the DTD must define an element with exactly the same prefix and name.

Because of their form, it is tempting to think that a namespace is a Web resource that lists element names. But that is never the case. The standard namespaces (for example, `http://www.w3.org/1999/xhtml`) often are valid URLs, but they are documents that describe far more than a set of element names. User-defined namespace names need not use the URI form, although that is a good way to prevent conflicts with namespace names.

8.6

XML SCHEMAS

DTDs have several disadvantages. One is that DTDs are written in a syntax unrelated to XML, so they cannot be analyzed with an XML processor. Also, it can be confusing to deal with two different syntactic forms, one to define a document and one to define its structure. Another disadvantage is that DTDs do not allow restrictions on the form of data that can be the content of a particular tag. For example, if the content of an element represents time, regardless of the form of the time data, a DTD can only specify that it is text, which could be anything. In fact, the content of an element could be an integer number, a floating-point number, or a range of numbers. All of these would be specified as text. With DTDs, there are only ten data types, none of which is numeric.

Several alternatives to DTDs have been developed, all attempts to overcome their weaknesses. XML schema, which was designed by the W3C, is one of these alternatives. We have chosen to discuss it because of its W3C support and the likelihood that it will become the primary successor to the DTD-based system. An XML schema is an XML document, so it can be parsed with an XML parser. It also provides far more control over data types than do DTDs. Data in a specific element can be required to be of any one of 44 different data types. Furthermore, the user can even define new types with constraints on existing data types. For example, a data value can be required to have exactly seven digits.

To promote the transition from DTDs to XML schemas, XML schema was designed to allow any DTD to be automatically converted to an equivalent XML schema.

8.6.1 Schema Fundamentals

Schemas can conveniently be related to the idea of a class and an object in an object-oriented programming language. A schema is similar to a class definition; an XML document that conforms to the structure defined in the schema is similar to an object of the schema's class. In fact, XML documents that conform to a specific schema are considered instances of that schema.

Schemas have two primary purposes. First, a schema specifies the structure of its instance XML documents, including which elements and attributes may appear in the instance document, as well as where and how often they may appear. Second, a schema specifies the data type of every element and attribute of its instance XML documents. This is the area in which schemas far outshine DTDs.

It has been said that XML schemas are "namespace centric." There is some truth to that depiction. In XML schemas, as in XML, namespaces are represented by names that have the form of URIs. Because they must be unique, it is customary to use URIs that start with the author's Web site address for namespaces. For example, for namespaces used in this section we use the prefix "http://cs.uccs.edu/". To this we add whatever name is connotative of the specific application.

8.6.2 Defining a Schema

Schemas themselves are written using a collection of names, or a vocabulary, from a namespace that is, in effect, a schema of schemas. The name of this namespace is http://www.w3.org/2001/XMLSchema. Some of the names in this namespace are element, schema, sequence, and string.

Every schema has schema as its root element. As already stated, the schema element specifies the namespace for the schema of schemas from which the schema's elements and attributes will be drawn. It often also specifies a prefix that will be used for the names in the schema. This namespace specification appears as follows:

```
xmlns:xsd = "http://www.w3.org/2001/XMLSchema"
```

This provides the prefix xsd for the names from the namespace for the schema of schemas.

A schema defines a namespace in the same sense as a DTD defines a tag set. The name of the namespace defined by a schema must be specified with the targetNamespace attribute of the schema element. Every top-level (not nested) element that appears in a schema places its name in the target namespace. The target namespace is specified by assigning a namespace to the target namespace attribute, as in the following:

```
targetNamespace = "http://cs.uccs.edu/planeSchema"
```

If we want the elements and attributes that are not defined directly in the schema element (they are nested inside top-level elements) to be included in the target namespace, schema's elementFormDefault must be set to qualified, as in the following:

```
elementFormDefault = "qualified"
```

The default namespace, which is the source of the unprefixed names in the schema, is given with another xmlns specification, but this time without the prefix. For example:

```
xmlns = "http://cs.uccs.edu/planeSchema"
```

An example of a complete opening tag for a schema is as follows:

```
<xsd:schema
<!-- The namespace for the schema itself (prefix is xsd) -->
```

```
      xmlns:xsd = http://www.w3.org/2001/XMLSchema
<!-- The namespace where elements defined here will be placed -->
      targetNamespace = http://cs.uccs.edu/planeSchema
<!-- The default namespace for this document (no prefix) -->
      xmlns = http://cs.uccs.edu/planeSchema
<!-- We want to put non-top-level elements in the target namespace -->
      elementFormDefault = "qualified">
```

In this example, the target namespace and the default namespace are the same.

One alternative to the preceding opening tag would be to make the XMLSchema names the default so that they need not be prefixed in the schema. Then the names in the target namespace would need to be prefixed. The following schema tag illustrates this:

```
<schema
    xmlns = "http://www.w3.org/2001/XMLSchema"
    targetNamespace = "http://cs.uccs.edu/planeSchema"
    xmlns:plane = "http://cs.uccs.edu/planeSchema"
    elementFormDefault = "qualified">
```

Notice that the name schema in this tag name need not be prefixed because its namespace is now the default. However, all of the names being created by this schema must be prefixed, both in the schema and in its instances.

8.6.3 Defining a Schema Instance

An instance of a schema must include specifications of the namespaces it uses. These are given as attribute assignments in the tag for its root element. First, an instance document normally defines its default namespace to be that defined in its schema. For example, if the root element is planes, we could have the following:

```
<planes
    xmlns = http://cs.uccs.edu/planeSchema
    ... >
```

The second attribute specification in the root element of an instance document is for the schemaLocation attribute. This attribute is used to name the standard namespace for instances, which is XMLSchema-instance. This namespace corresponds to the XMLSchema namespace used for schemas. The following attribute assignment specifies the XMLSchema-instance namespace and defines the prefix, xsi, for it:

```
xmlns:xsi = "http://www.w3.org/2001/XMLSchema-instance
```

Third, the instance document must specify the filename of the schema where the default namespace is defined. This is accomplished with the `schemaLocation` attribute, which takes two values: the namespace of the schema and the filename of the schema. This attribute is defined in the `XMLSchema-instance` namespace, so it must be named with the proper prefix. For example:

```
xsi:schemaLocation = "http://cs.uccs.edu/planeSchema
                      planes.xsd"
```

This is a peculiar attribute assignment in that it assigns two values, which are separated only by white space.

Altogether, the opening root tag of an XML instance of the `planes.xsd` schema, where the root element name in the instance is `planes`, could appear as follows:

```
<planes
    xmlns = "http://cs.uccs.edu/planeSchema"
    xmlns:xsi = "http://www.w3.org/2001/XMLSchema-instance"
    xsi:schemaLocation = "http://cs.uccs.edu/planeSchema
                          planes.xsd">
```

The purpose of both DTDs and XML schemas is to provide a technique for standardization of the tag set and structure of families of XML documents. Conformance checking of an XML document against an XML schema can be done with any one of several available validation programs. One of these, named `xsv`, is discussed in Section 8.6.7. An XML schema validation program performs two kinds of conformance checks: First, it checks to determine whether the schema is valid relative to the schema of schemas, `XMLSchema`. Second, it checks to determine whether the XML document conforms to the syntactic rules specified in the schema of which the document is an instance.

8.6.4 An Overview of Data Types

There are two categories of user-defined XML schema data types, simple and complex. A *simple data type* is one whose content is restricted to strings. A simple type cannot have attributes or include nested elements. The string restriction seems like it would make simple types a very narrow type category, but in fact it does not because a large collection of predefined data types are included in the category. Some of these are mentioned in this section. A *complex type* can have attributes and include other data types as elements.

XML schema defines 44 data types, 19 of which are primitive and 25 of which are derived. The primitive data types include `string`, `Boolean`, `float`, `time`, and `anyURI`. The predefined derived types include `byte`, `long`, `decimal`, `unsignedInt`, `postiveInteger`, and `NMTOKEN`. User-defined data types are defined by specifying restrictions on an existing type, which is then called a *base type*. Such user-defined types are derived types. Constraints in derived types are given in terms of the *facets* of the base type. For example, the `integer` primitive data type has eight possible facets: `totalDigits`, `maxInclusive`, `maxExclusive`, `minInclusive`, `minExclusive`, `pattern`, `enumeration`, and `whitespace`. Examples of user-defined data types are given in Section 8.6.5. A list of all predefined data types can be found at `http://www.w3.org/TR/xmlschema-2/#built-in-datatypes`.

Both simple and complex types can be *named* or *anonymous*. If anonymous, a type cannot be used outside the element in which it is declared.

Elements in a DTD are all global. Each has a unique name and is defined exactly once. The context of a reference to a DTD element is irrelevant. By contrast, context is essential to defining the meaning of a reference to an element in an XML schema.

Data declarations in an XML schema can be either local or global. A *local declaration* is one that appears inside an element that is a child of the `schema` element; that is, a declaration in a grandchild element of `schema` (or a more distant descendant) is a local declaration. A locally declared element is visible only in that element. This means that local elements with the same name can appear in any number of different elements with no interference among them. A *global declaration* is one that appears as a child of the `schema` element. Global elements are visible in the whole schema in which they are declared.

8.6.5   Simple Types

Elements are defined in an XML schema with the `element` tag, which is from the `XMLSchema` namespace. Recall that the prefix `xsd` is normally used for names from this namespace. An element that is named includes the `name` attribute for that purpose. The other attribute that is necessary in a simple element declaration is `type`, which is used to specify the type of content allowed in the element. For example:

```
<xsd:element name = "engine"  type = "xsd:string" />
```

An instance of the schema in which the engine element is defined could have the following element:

```
<engine> inline six cylinder fuel injected </engine>
```

An element can be given a default value using the `default` attribute. For example:

```
<xsd:element name = "engine"   type = "xsd:string"
             default = "fuel injected V-6"  />
```

Elements can have constant values, meaning that the content of the defined element in every instance document has the same value. Constant values are given with the `fixed` attribute, as in the following example:

```
<xsd:element name = "plane"   type = "xsd:string"
             fixed = "single wing"  />
```

We now turn our attention to user-defined data types, which are constrained predefined types. A simple user-defined data type is described in a `simpleType` element, using facets. Facets must be specified in the content of a `restriction` element, which gives the base type name. The facets themselves are given in elements named for the facets, using the `value` attribute to specify the value of the facet. For example, the following declares a user-defined type, `firstName`, for strings of fewer than 11 characters:

```
<xsd:simpleType name = "firstName">
    <xsd:restriction base = "xsd:string">
        <xsd:maxLength value = "10" />
    </xsd:restriction>
</xsd:simpleType>
```

The `length` facet is used to restrict the string to an exact number of characters. The `minLength` facet is used to specify a minimum length. The number of digits of a decimal number is restricted with the `precision` facet. For example:

```
<xsd:simpleType name = "phoneNumber">
    <xsd:restriction base = "xsd:decimal">
        <xsd:precision value = "7" />
    </xsd:restriction>
</xsd:simpleType>
```

8.6.6 Complex Types

Most XML documents include nested elements, so few XML schemas do not have complex types. Although there are several categories of complex element types, we restrict our discussion to those called *element-only elements*, which can have elements in their content but no text. All complex types can have attributes.

Complex types are defined with the `complexType` tag. The elements that are the content of an element-only element must be contained in an ordered group, an unordered group, a choice, or a named group. Ordered and unordered groups are discussed here.

The `sequence` element is used to contain an ordered group of elements. For example, consider the following type definition:

```
<xsd:complexType name = "sports_car">
    <xsd:sequence>
        <xsd:element name = "make"   type = "xsd:string" />
        <xsd:element name = "model"  type = "xsd:string" />
        <xsd:element name = "engine"  type = "xsd:string" />
        <xsd:element name = "year"  type = "xsd:decimal" />
```

```
        </xsd:sequence>
    </xsd:complexType>
```

A complex type whose elements are an unordered group is defined in an `all` element.

Elements and `all` and `sequence` groups can include attributes to specify the numbers of occurrences. These attributes are `minOccurs` and `maxOccurs`. The possible values of `minOccurs` are the non-negative integers, including zero. The possible values for `maxOccurs` are the non-negative integers plus the value `unbounded`, which has the obvious meaning.

Consider the following complete example of a schema:

```xml
<?xml version = "1.0" encoding = "utf-8"?>

<!-- planes.xsd
     A simple schema for planes.xml
     -->

<xsd:schema
    xmlns:xsd = "http://www.w3.org/2001/XMLSchema"
    targetNamespace = "http://cs.uccs.edu/planeSchema"
    xmlns = "http://cs.uccs.edu/planeSchema"
    elementFormDefault = "qualified">

    <xsd:element name = "planes">
        <xsd:complexType>
            <xsd:all>
                <xsd:element name = "make"
                             type = "xsd:string"
                             minOccurs = "1"
                             maxOccurs = "unbounded" />
            </xsd:all>
        </xsd:complexType>
    </xsd:element>
</xsd:schema>
```

Notice that we use the `all` element to contain the single element of the complex type, `planes`. We could have used `sequence` instead. Because there is only one contained element, it makes no difference.

An XML instance that conforms to the `planes.xsd` schema follows:

```xml
<?xml version = "1.0" encoding = "utf-8"?>

<!-- planes.xml
```

```
        A simple XML document for illustrating a schema
        The schema is in planes.xsd
        -->
<planes
  xmlns = "http://cs.uccs.edu/planeSchema"
  xmlns:xsi = "http://www.w3.org/2001/XMLSchema-instance"
  xsi:schemaLocation = "http://cs.uccs.edu/planeSchema
                        planes.xsd">
    <make> Cessna </make>
    <make> Piper </make>
    <make> Beechcraft </make>
</planes>
```

If we want the year element in the sports_car element that was defined earlier to be a derived type, we could define the derived type as another global element and refer to it in the sports_car element. For example, the year element could be defined as follows:

```
<xsd:element name = "year">
    <xsd:simpleType>
        <xsd:restriction base = "xsd:decimal">
            <xsd:minInclusive value = "1900" />
            <xsd:maxInclusive value = "2002" />
        </xsd:restriction>
    </xsd:simpleType>
</xsd:element>
```

With the year element defined globally, the sports_car element can be defined with a reference to the year with the ref attribute, as in the following:

```
<xsd:complexType name = "sports_car">
    <xsd:sequence>
        <xsd:element name = "make"  type = "xsd:string" />
        <xsd:element name = "model"  type = "xsd:string" />
        <xsd:element name = "engine"  type = "xsd:string" />
        <xsd:element ref = "year" />
    </xsd:sequence>
</xsd:complexType>
```

8.6.7 Validating Instances of Schemas

An XML schema provides a definition of a category of XML documents. However, developing a schema is of limited value unless there is some mechanical way of determining whether a given XML instance document conforms to the schema. Several XML schema validation tools are available. One of these is named xsv, an acronym for XML Schema Validator. It was developed by Henry S. Thompson and Richard Tobin at the University of Edinburgh in Scotland. If your schema and instance document are available on the Web, xsv can be used online, like the XHTML validation tool at the W3C site. This tool can also be downloaded and run on your computer. The Web site for xsv is http://www.ltg.ed.ac.uk/~ht/xsv-status.html.

The output of xsv is an XML document. When run from the command line, the output document appears on the screen with no formatting, so it is a bit difficult to read. The following is the output of xsv when run on planes.xml:

```
<?XML version='1.0' encoding = 'utf-8'?>
<xsv docElt='{http://cs.uccs.edu/planeSchema}planes'
     instanceAssessed='true'
     instanceErrors = '0'
     rootType='[Anonymous]'
     schemaErrors='0'
     schemaLocs='http://cs.uccs.edu/planeSchema -> planes.xsd'
     target='file:/c:/wbook2/xml/planes.xml'
     validation='strict'
     version='XSV 1.197/1.101 of 2001/07/07 12:10:19'
     xmlns='http://www.w3.org/2000/05/xsv' >

  <importAttempt URI='file:/c:wbook2/xml/planes.xsd'
                 namespace='http://cs.uccs.edu/planeSchema'
                 outcome='success' />
</xsv>
```

The actual output was displayed with no formatting: Each line was filled to the right end of the screen, and attribute values were broken across line boundaries in several places.

One useful thing to know about validation with xsv: If the schema is not in the correct format, the validator will report that it could not find the specified schema.

8.7

DISPLAYING RAW XML DOCUMENTS

An XML-enabled browser, or any other system that can deal with XML documents, cannot possibly know how to format the tags defined in the document (after all, someone just made them up). Therefore, if you display an XML document without a style sheet that defines presentation styles for the document's tags, you should not expect it to have formatted content. Contemporary browsers include default style sheets that are used when no style sheet is specified in the XML document. The display of such an XML document is only a somewhat

stylized listing of the XML. The Mozilla Firefox browser display of the
`planes.xml` document is shown in Figure 8.2.

This XML file does not appear to have any style information associated with it. The document tree is shown below.

```
- <!--
    planes.xml - A document that lists ads for
        used airplanes
  -->
- <!--
    <?xml-stylesheet  type = "text/css"  href = "planes.css" ?>
  -->
- <planes_for_sale>
  - <ad>
      <year> 1977 </year>
      <make> cessna </make>
      <model> Skyhawk </model>
      <color> Light blue and white </color>
    - <description>
        New paint, nearly new interior, 685 hours SMOH, full IFR King avionics
      </description>
      <seller phone="555-222-3333"> Skyway Aircraft </seller>
    - <location>
        <city> Rapid City, </city>
        <state> South Dakota </state>
      </location>
    </ad>
  - <ad>
      <year> 1965 </year>
      <make> Piper </make>
      <model> Cherokee </model>
      <color> Gold </color>
    - <description>
        240 hours SMOH, dual NAVCOMs, DME, new Cleveland brakes, great shape
      </description>
      <seller phone="555-333-2222"> John Seller </seller>
    - <location>
        <city> St. Joseph, </city>
        <state> Missouri </state>
      </location>
    </ad>
  </planes_for_sale>
```

FIGURE 8.2 A display of an XML document with the Mozilla Firefox default style sheet

Some of the elements in the display in Figure 8.2 are preceded by dashes. These elements can be elided (temporarily removed) by placing the mouse cursor over the dash and clicking the left mouse button. For example, if the mouse cursor is placed over the dash to the left of the first <ad> tag and the left mouse button is clicked, the result is as shown in Figure 8.3.

```
This XML file does not appear to have any style information associated with it. The document tree is
shown below.

- <!--
     planes.xml - A document that lists ads for
           used airplanes
  -->
- <!--
     <?xml-stylesheet  type = "text/css"  href = "planes.css" ?>
  -->
- <planes_for_sale>
  + <ad></ad>
  - <ad>
      <year> 1965 </year>
      <make> Piper </make>
      <model> Cherokee </model>
      <color> Gold </color>
    - <description>
        240 hours SMOH, dual NAVCOMs, DME, new Cleveland brakes, great shape
      </description>
      <seller phone="555-333-2222"> John Seller </seller>
    - <location>
        <city> St. Joseph, </city>
        <state> Missouri </state>
      </location>
    </ad>
</planes_for_sale>
```

FIGURE 8.3 The document of Figure 8.2 with the first ad element elided

It is unusual to display a raw XML document. This is usually done to review and check the structure and content of the document during its development.

8.8

DISPLAYING XML DOCUMENTS WITH CSS

Style sheet information can be provided to the browser for an XML document in two ways. First, a Cascading Style Sheet (CSS) file that has style information for the elements in the XML document can be developed. The other way is to use the XSLT style sheet technology, which was developed by the W3C. Although using CSS is effective, XSLT provides far more power over the appearance of the document's display. On the other hand, XSLT is not yet available on all of the most commonly used browsers. XSLT is discussed in Section 8.9.

The form of a CSS style sheet for an XML document is simple: It is just a list of element names, each followed by a brace-delimited set of the element's CSS attributes. This is the form of the rules in a CSS document style sheet. The following is a CSS style sheet for the `planes` XML document:

```
<!-- planes.css - a style sheet for the planes.xml document -->
ad { display: block; margin-top: 15px; color: blue;}
year, make, model { color: red; font-size: 16pt;}
color {display: block; margin-left: 20px; font-size: 12pt;}
description {display: block; margin-left: 20px; font-size: 12pt;}
seller { display: block; margin-left: 15px; font-size: 14pt;}
location {display: block; margin-left: 40px; }
city {font-size: 12pt;}
state {font-size: 12pt;}
```

The only style property in this style sheet that has not been discussed earlier in this book is `display`. This property is used to specify whether an element is to be displayed inline or in a separate block. These two options are specified with the values `inline` and `block`. The `inline` value is the default. When `display` is set to `block`, the content of the element is usually separated from its sibling elements by line breaks.

The connection of an XML document to a CSS style sheet is established with the processing instruction `xml-stylesheet`, which specifies the particular type of the style sheet via its `type` attribute and the name of the file that stores the style sheet via its `href` attribute. For the `planes` example, this processing instruction is as follows:

```
<?xml-stylesheet type = "text/css" href = "planes.css" ?>
```

Figure 8.4 shows the display of `planes.xml` using the `planes.css` style sheet.

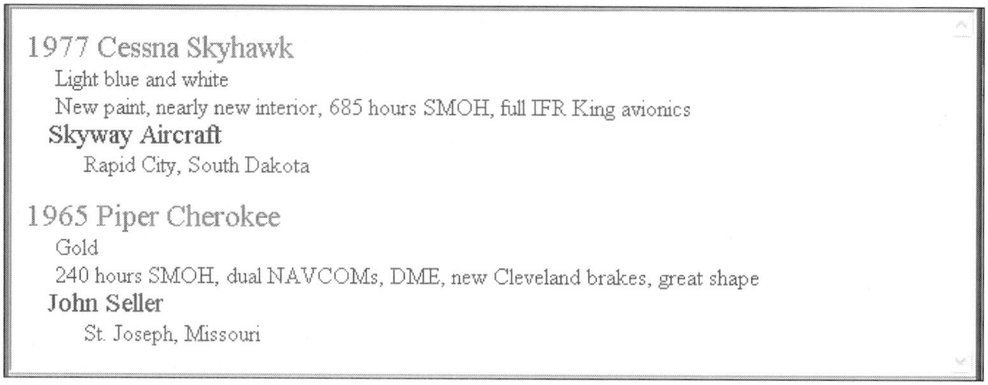

1977 Cessna Skyhawk
   Light blue and white
   New paint, nearly new interior, 685 hours SMOH, full IFR King avionics
Skyway Aircraft
   Rapid City, South Dakota

1965 Piper Cherokee
   Gold
   240 hours SMOH, dual NAVCOMs, DME, new Cleveland brakes, great shape
John Seller
   St. Joseph, Missouri

FIGURE 8.4 The result of using a CSS style sheet to format `planes.xml`

8.9

XSLT STYLE SHEETS

The eXtensible Stylesheet Language (XSL) Family is a family of recommendations for defining XML document transormations and presentation. It consists of three related standards: XSL Transformations (XSLT), XML Path Language (XPath), and XSL Formatting Objects (XSL-FO). Each of these has an importance and use of its own. Together, they provide a powerful means of formatting XML documents. Because XSL-FO is not yet implemented by any popular browser, we do not discuss it in this book.

XSLT style sheets are used to transform XML documents into different forms or formats, perhaps using different DTDs. One common use for XSLT is to transform XML documents to XHTML documents, primarily for display. In the transformation of an XML document, element content can be moved and/or modified, sorted, or converted to attribute values, among other things. XSLT style sheets are XML doucments, so they can be validated against DTDs. They can even be transformed using other XSLT style sheets. The XSLT standard is given at `http://www.w3.org/TR/xslt`. XSLT stylesheets and their uses are the primary topics of this section.

XPath is a language for expressions, which are often used to identify parts of XML documents, such as specific elements that are in specific positions in the document or elements that have particular attribute values. XSLT requires such expressions to specify tranformations. XPath is also used for XML document querying languages, such as XQL, and for building new XML document structures using XPointer. The XPath standard is given at `http://www.w3.org/TR/xpath`. This chapter uses simple XPath expressions in the discussion of XSLT but does not explore them further.

8.9.1   Overview of XSLT

XSLT is actually a functional-style programming language. Included in XSLT are functions, parameters, names to which values can be bound, selection constructs, and conditional expressions for multiple selection. The syntactic structure of XSLT is XML, so each statement is specified with an element. This makes XSLT documents appear very different from programs in a typical programming language, but not completely different from programs written in LISP-based functional languages such as COMMON LISP and Scheme.

XSLT processors take as input an XML document and an XSLT document. The XSLT document is the program to be executed; the XML document is the input data to the program. Parts of the XML document are selected, possibly modified, and merged with parts of the XSLT document to form a new document, which is sometimes called an *XSL document*. Note that the XSL document is also an XML document, which could be again the input to an XSLT processor. The output document can be stored for future use by applications, or it may be immediately displayed by an application, often a browser. Neither the XSLT document nor the input XML document is changed by the XSLT processor.

The transformation process by an XSLT processor is shown in Figure 8.5.

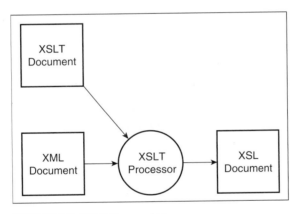

FIGURE 8.5 XSLT Processing

An XSLT document consists primarily of one or more templates, which use XPath to describe element/attribute patterns in the input XML document to be processed. Each template has associated with it a section of XSLT "code," which is "executed" when a match to the template is found in the XML document. So, each template describes a function, which is executed whenever the XSLT processor finds a match to the template's pattern.

An XSLT processor sequentially examines the input XML document, searching for parts that match one of its templates. XML documents consist of nodes, where nodes are elements, attributes, comments, text, and processing instructions. If a template matches an element, the element is not processed until the closing tag is found. When a template matches an element, the child elements of that element may or may not be processed themselves.

The XSLT model of processing XML data is called the *template-driven model*, which works well when the data consists of multiple instances of highly regular data collections, as with files of records. XSLT can also deal with irregular and recursive data, using template fragments in what is called the *data-driven model*. A single XSLT style sheet can include the mechanisms for both the template- and data-driven models. The discussion of XSLT in this chapter is restricted to the template-driven model.

To keep the complexity of our discussion manageable, we focus on tranformations that are related to presentation. The examples in this section were processed with the XSLT processor that is part of IE6.

8.9.2 XSL Transformations for Presentation

Although XSLT style sheets can be used to control page layout, including orientation, writing direction, margins, and page numbering, this chapter discusses only the simplest of formatting specifications for the smallest units of information. XSLT includes more than 50 formatting object (element) types and more than 230 properties, so it is a large and complex tag set.

In this section, we assume that the XSLT processor processes an XML document with its associated XSLT style sheet document and produces as its output document an XHTML document to display.

An XML document that is to be used as data to an XSLT style sheet must include a processing instruction to inform the XSLT processor that the style sheet is to be used. The form of this instruction is as follows:

```
<?xml-stylesheet type = "text/xsl" href =
                        "XSL_stylesheet_name" ?>
```

As a simple example of an XML document that can be used to illustrate XSLT formatting, consider the following:

```
<?xml version = "1.0" encoding = "utf-8"?>
<!-- xslplane.xml -->
<?xml-stylesheet type = "text/xsl"  href = "xslplane.xsl" ?>
<plane>
    <year> 1977 </year>
    <make> Cessna </make>
    <model> Skyhawk </model>
    <color> Light blue and white </color>
</plane>
```

Notice that this document specifies xslplane.xsl as its XSLT style sheet.

An XSLT style sheet is an XML document whose root element is the special-purpose element stylesheet. The stylesheet tag defines namespaces as its attributes and encloses the collection of elements that defines its transformations. It also identifies the document as an XSLT document. The namespace for all XSLT elements is specified with a W3C URI. If the stylesheet includes XHTML elements, the stylesheet tag also specifies the XHTML namespace. Consider the following stylesheet tag:

```
<xsl:stylesheet xmlns:xsl =
                "http://www.w3.org/1999/XSL/Format"
              xmlns = "http://www.w3.org/1999/xhtml">
```

Notice that the prefix for XSLT elements is `xsl` and the default namespace is that for XHTML.

A stylesheet document must include at least one `template` element. The template opening tag includes a `match` attribute to specify an XPath expression to select a node in the XML document. The content of a template element specifies what is to be placed in the output document. If a template element is thought of as a subprogram, the opening tag states where the subprogram is to be applied. The content of the element is the body of the subprogram, specifying what is to be done.

In most XSLT documents, a template is included to match the root node of the XML document. This can be done in two ways, one being to use the XPath expression "/", as in the following:

```
<xsl:template match = "/">
```

Notation similar to that used to specify UNIX directory addresses is used. The alternative to using "/" is to use the actual root of the document. In the example, `xslplane.xml`, the document root is `plane`. Every XSLT style sheet should include a template for the root node. If the output of the XSLT processor is an XHTML document, the template that matches the root node is used to create the XHTML header of the output document. The header code appears as the content of the template element. An example of a complete template element follows:

```
<xsl:template match = "plane">
<html><head><title> Example </title></head><body>
...
</body></html>
</xsl:template>
```

To produce complete XHTML documents as output from XSLT documents, the `output` element can be included prior to the first template. This element can include `doctype-public` and `doctype-system` attributes to specify the two parts of the `DOCTYPE` declaration, respectively. For the sake of brevity, `output` elements are not included in the XSLT examples in this chapter.

Style sheets nearly always have templates for specific nodes of the XML document, which are descendants of the root node, as in this example:

```
<xsl:template match = "year">
```

XPath expressions that begin with the slash are absolute addresses within the document. Those that do not begin with a slash are relative addresses. The value "year" in the preceding example is obviously a relative address. Relative addresses are relative to the "current" node of the XML document, which is the last node found by the XSLT processor in the XML document.

The template for the root node is implicitly applied. However, all other templates in an XSLT document must be explicitly applied to the XML document. This can be done in several ways. The apply-templates element applies appropriate templates to the descendant nodes of the current node. This element can include a select attribute to specify the descendant nodes whose templates should be applied. If no select attribute is included, the XSLT processor will apply a template to every descendant node. For those nodes for which the XSLT document has not defined a template, a default template is used. For example, both text and attributes have default templates that output them as text.

Template elements include two distinct kinds of elements: those that literally contain content and those that specify content to be copied from the associated XML document. XSLT elements that represent XHTML elements often are used to specify content. These have the appearance of their associated XHTML elements. For example, consider the following XHTML element:

```
<span style = "font-size: 14"> Merry Christmas! </span>
```

All XSLT elements that represent XHTML elements are copied by the XSLT processor to the output document being generated. Note that all XHTML elements that appear in an XSLT document must conform to the syntactic restrictions that apply to XML (and XHTML) elements.

In many cases, the content of an element of the XML document is to be copied to the output document. This is done with the value-of element, which uses a select attribute to specify the element of the XML document whose contents are to be copied. For example:

```
<xsl:value-of select = "AUTHOR" />
```

This element specifies that the content of the AUTHOR element of the XML document is to be copied to the output document. Because the value-of element cannot have content, it is terminated with a slash and a right pointed bracket.

The select attribute can specify any node of the XML document. This is an advantage of XSLT formatting over CSS, in which the order of data as stored is the only possible order of display.

The attribute value "." for the `select` attribute of `value-of` means to select all elements within the current element, just the current node if it contains no nested elements.[3]

The following is a complete XSLT style sheet for the XML document `xslplane.xml`, shown previously:

```
<?xml version = "1.0" encoding = "utf-8"?>
<!-- xslplane1.xsl
     An XSLT stylesheet for xslplane.xml using child templates
     -->
<xsl:stylesheet version = "1.0"
                xmlns:xsl = "http://www.w3.org/1999/XSL/Transform"
                xmlns = "http://www.w3.org/1999/xhtml">

<!-- The template for the whole document (the plane element) -->

  <xsl:template match = "plane">
    <html><head><title> Style sheet for xslplane.xml </title>
    </head><body>
    <h2> Airplane Description </h2>

<!-- Apply the matching templates to the elements in plane -->

    <xsl:apply-templates />
    </body></html>
  </xsl:template>

<!-- The templates to be applied (by apply-templates) to the
     elements in the plane element -->

  <xsl:template match = "year">
    <span style = "font-style: italic; color: blue;"> Year:
    </span>
    <xsl:value-of select = "." /> <br />
  </xsl:template>
  <xsl:template match = "make">
    <span style = "font-style: italic; color: blue;"> Make:
    </span>
    <xsl:value-of select = "." /> <br />
  </xsl:template>
```

continued

---

3. If `select` = "." is included in an `<xsl:apply-templates>` tag, it does nothing because `apply-templates` implicitly specifies all immediate child nodes.

```
    <xsl:template match = "model">
      <span style = "font-style: italic; color: blue;"> Model:
      </span>
      <xsl:value-of select = "." /> <br />
    </xsl:template>
    <xsl:template match = "color">
      <span style = "font-style: italic; color: blue;"> Color:
      </span>
      <xsl:value-of select = "." /> <br />
    </xsl:template>
</xsl:stylesheet>
```

Figure 8.6 shows an IE6 display of the output document created by the XSLT processor from `xslplane.xml` with `xslplane1.xsl`.

Airplane Description

Year: 1977
Make: Cessna
Model: Skyhawk
Color: Light blue and white

FIGURE 8.6 An output document from the XSLT processor

The XSLT document, `xslplane1.xsl`, is more general and complex than necessary for the simple use for which it was written. There is actually no need to include templates for all of the child nodes of `plane`, because the `select` clause of the `value-of` element finds them. The following XSLT document, `xslplane2.xsl`, produces the same output as `xslplane1.xsl`.

```
<?xml version = "1.0" encoding = "utf-8"?>
<!-- xslplane2.xsl
    An XSLT Stylesheet for xslplane.xml using implicit templates
    -->
<xsl:stylesheet version = "1.0"
              xmlns:xsl = "http://www.w3.org/1999/XSL/Transform"
              xmlns = "http://www.w3.org/1999/xhtml">

<!-- The template for the whole document (the plane element) -->

  <xsl:template match = "plane">
    <html><head><title> Style sheet for xslplane.xml </title>
    </head><body>
```

```
        <h2> Airplane Description </h2>
        <span style = "font-style: italic; color: blue;"> Year:
        </span>
        <xsl:value-of select = "year" /> <br />
        <span style = "font-style: italic; color: blue;"> Make:
        </span>
        <xsl:value-of select = "make" /> <br />
        <span style = "font-style: italic; color: blue;"> Model:
        </span>
        <xsl:value-of select = "model" /> <br />
        <span style = "font-style: italic; color: blue;"> Color:
        </span>
        <xsl:value-of select = "color" /> <br />
        </body></html>
    </xsl:template>
</xsl:stylesheet>
```

We now consider an XML document that includes a collection of data elements with the same structure. For example, a document named `airplanes.xml` could have a list of airplane descriptions. The XSLT template used for one plane can be used repeatedly with the `for-each` element, which uses a `select` attribute to specify an element in the XML data. The value of the `select` attribute is a pattern, which is a path expression that specifies an element. Any child elements of the specified element are included.

Consider the following XML document:

```
<?xml version = "1.0" encoding = "utf-8"?>
<!-- xslplanes.xml -->
<?xml-stylesheet type = "text/xsl" href = "xslplanes.xsl" ?>
<planes>
    <plane>
        <year> 1977 </year>
        <make> Cessna </make>
        <model> Skyhawk </model>
        <color> Light blue and white </color>
    </plane>
    <plane>
        <year> 1975 </year>
        <make> Piper </make>
        <model> Apache </model>
        <color> White </color>
    </plane>
```

continued

```
    <plane>
        <year> 1960 </year>
        <make> Cessna </make>
        <model> Centurian </model>
        <color> Yellow and white </color>
    </plane>
    <plane>
        <year> 1956 </year>
        <make> Piper </make>
        <model> Tripacer </model>
        <color> Blue </color>
    </plane>
</planes>
```

The following XSLT style sheet processes the previous XML data document:

```
<?xml version = "1.0" encoding = "utf-8"?>
<!-- xslplanes.xsl -->

<xsl:stylesheet version = "1.0"
                xmlns:xsl = "http://www.w3.org/1999/XSL/Transform"
                xmlns = "http://www.w3.org/1999/xhtml" >

<!-- The template for the whole document (the planes element) -->

    <xsl:template match = "planes">
        <h2> Airplane Descriptions </h2>

<!-- Apply the following to all occurrences of the plane element -->

        <xsl:for-each select = "plane">
            <span style = "font-style: italic"> Year: </span>
            <xsl:value-of select = "year" /> <br />
            <span style = "font-style: italic"> Make: </span>
            <xsl:value-of select = "make" /> <br />
            <span style = "font-style: italic"> Model: </span>
            <xsl:value-of select = "model" /> <br />
            <span style = "font-style: italic"> Color: </span>
            <xsl:value-of select = "color" /> <br /> <br />
        </xsl:for-each>

    </xsl:template>
</xsl:stylesheet>
```

Figure 8.7 shows an IE6 display of the document produced by an XSLT processor on `xslplanes.xml`, using the `xslplanes.xsl` style sheet.

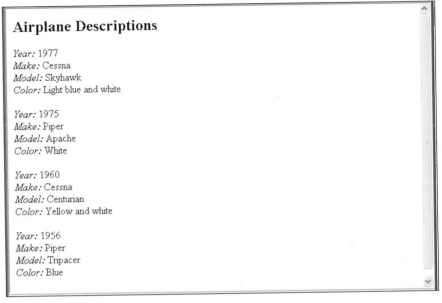

FIGURE 8.7 Using the `for-each` element for lists of elements

XSLT provides a simple way to sort the elements of the XML document before sending them or their content to the output document. This is done with the `sort` element, which can take serveral attributes. The `select` attribute specifies the node that is used for the key of the sort. The `data-type` attribute is used to specify whether the key is to be sorted as text (`"text"`) or numerically (`"number"`). By default, the sort is to ascending order. The `order` attribute can be set to `"descending"` to produce the reverse order. By inserting the following single line into the `xslplanes.xsl` document, the output will appear in ascending numeric order of the year of the airplane:

```
<xsl:sort  select = "year"  data-type = "number" />
```

8.10

XML PROCESSORS

This chapter has so far discussed the structure of XML documents, the rules for writing them, the DTD and XML schema approaches to specifying the particular tag sets and structure of collections of XML documents, and the CSS and XSLT methods of displaying the contents of XML documents. That is tantamount to telling a long story about how data can be stored and displayed, without providing any hint on how it may be processed. Although this section does not discuss processing data stored in XML documents, it does introduce approaches to making that data conveniently available to application programs that process that data.

8.10.1 The Purposes of XML Processors

Several of the purposes of XML processors have already been discussed. These are as follows: First, the processor must check the basic syntax of the document for well-formedness. Second, the processor must replace all references to entities in an XML document by their definitions. Third, DTDs and XML schemas can specify that certain values in an XML document have default values, which must be copied into the XML document during processing. Fourth, when a DTD or an XML schema is specified and the processor includes a validating parser, the structure of the XML document must be checked to ensure that its structure is legitimate.

One simple way to check the well-formedness of an XML document is with a browser that has an XML parser. Another way is to run an XML parser directly on the document. One such parser is available from the Apache XML Project Xerces-J. It can be downloaded from `http://xml.apache.org/xerces-j/index.hmtl`. This parser is written in Java and runs on any platform that has a Java virtual machine version 1.1 or later. The class from this system that checks the well-formedness of XML documents, which can be run from the command line, is named `sax.SAXCount`.[4]

Although an XML document exhibits a regular and elegant structure, that structure does not provide applications convenient access to the document's data. Because the process of the initial syntactic analysis required to expose the embedded data must be repeated for every application that processes XML documents, it was recognized early on that standard syntax analyzers for XML documents were needed. Actually, the syntax analyzers themselves need not be standard; rather, they should expose the data of XML documents in a standard application programmer interface (API). This need led to the development of two different standard APIs for XML processors. Because there are different needs and uses of XML applications, having two standards is not a negative. The two APIs parallel the two kinds of output that are produced by the syntax analyzers of compilers for programming languages. Some of these syntax analyzers produce a stream of the syntactic structures of an input program. Others produce a parse tree of the input program that shows the hierarchical structure of the program in terms of simple syntactic structures.

---

4. The term **SAX** here is borrowed from the acronym SAX, which is derived from Simple Application Programming Interface for XML.

8.10.2   The SAX Approach

The Simple API for XML (SAX) standard, which was released in May 1998, was developed by an XML users group, XML-DEV. Although not developed or supported by any standards organization, SAX has been widely accepted as a de facto standard and is now widely supported by XML processors.

The SAX approach to processing is called *event processing*. The processor scans the XML document from beginning to end. Every time a syntactic structure of the document is recognized, the processor signals an event to the application by calling an event handler for the particular structure that was found. The syntactic structures of interest naturally include opening tags, attributes, text, and closing tags. The interfaces that describe the event handlers form the SAX API.

8.10.3   The DOM Approach

The natural alternative to the SAX approach to XML document parsing is to build a hierarchical syntactic structure of the document. Given the use of DOM representations of XHTML documents to create dynamic documents in Chapter 6, "Dynamic Documents with JavaScript," this is a familiar idea. In the case of XHTML, the browser parses the document and builds the DOM tree. In the case of XML, the parser part of the XML processor builds the DOM tree. In both cases, the nodes of the tree are represented as objects that can be accessed and processed or modified by the application. When parsing is complete, the complete DOM representation of the document is in memory and can be accessed in a number of different ways, including tree traversals of various kinds as well as random accesses.

The DOM representation of an XML document has several advantages over the sequential listing provided by SAX parsers. First, it has an obvious advantage if any part of the document must be accessed more than once by the application. Second, if the application must perform any rearrangement of the document, that can most easily be done if the whole document is accessible at one time. Third, accesses to random parts of the document are possible. Finally, because the parser sees the whole document before any processing takes place, this approach avoids any processing of a document that is later found to be invalid (according to a DTD or XML schema).

In some situations, the SAX approach has advantages over the DOM method. The DOM structure is stored entirely in memory. For large documents, this requires a great deal of memory. In fact, because there is no limit on the size of an XML document, there may be some documents that cannot be parsed this way. This is not a problem with the SAX approach. Another advantage of the SAX method is speed—it is faster than the DOM approach.

The process of building the DOM structure of an XML document requires some syntactic analysis of the document, similar to that done by SAX parsers. In fact, most DOM parsers include a SAX parser as a front end.

8.11

WEB SERVICES

The movement toward Web services began in earnest when Microsoft Chairman Bill Gates introduced a concept he called BizTalk in 1999. BizTalk later was renamed .NET. The idea was to provide the technologies to allow different software in different places, written in different languages and resident on different platforms, to connect and interoperate.

The Web began as a focused Web service for information, and is still just that. Through three fundamental methods, GET, POST, and PUT, and a vast collection of public markup documents, information is provided to anyone with an Internet connection and a computer running a browser. The more general concept of a Web service is a similar technology for services. Rather than deploying documents through a Web server, services are deployed (through the same Web server). Rather than documents, access to software components is provided. Components are not downloaded, but are run on the Web server as a remote service.

Web services are of course not a completely new idea. Remote Procedure Call (RPC) is an earlier and closely related concept. RPC was invented to allow distributed components to communicate. There are two successful (widely used) RPC technologies, DCOM and CORBA. Both, however, are too complex to provide a simple and convenient way to support interoperability among the components of different systems. DCOM is proprietary, supported only by Microsoft software systems. CORBA is designed to be cross-platform, but it requires a great deal of manual integration work. DCOM uses the Object Remote Procedure Call (ORPC) protocol to interface components. CORBA uses Object Management Group's Internet Inter-ORB Protocol (IIOP). Needless to say, these two protocols are not compatible. Therefore, neither DCOM nor CORBA supports the goal of Web services—universal component interoperability.

The dream of Web services is that there will be protocols that allow all components to interoperate entirely under the control of the computers, without human intervention. That means that a when a system needs a service, it can implicitly find one on the Web and use it. Standard non-proprietary protocols and languages to support this dream have been developed, although they are not yet widely used.

There are three roles that are required to provide and use Web services: service providers, service requestors, and a service registry. A service provider must develop and deploy software that provides a service. This service must have a standard description. The W3C language designed for writing such descriptions is Web Services Definition Language (WSDL, pronounced "wizdill"), which is an XML-based format. The WSDL description is published on a Web server, similar to a Web-accessible document. It is used to describe the specific operations provided by the Web service, as well as the protocols for the messages the Web service can send and receive.

A Web services registry is created with another standard protocol, Universal Description, Discovery and Integration Service (UDDI). UDDI also provides methods of querying a Web services registry to determine what specific services are available. So, a requestor queries a registry with a WSDL query, to which the registry responds with the protocol of how the requestor may interact with the requested Web service. UDDI has two kinds of clients, service providers and clients who want to find and use Web services.

The Standard Object Access Protocol (SOAP) is an XML-based specification that defines the forms of messages and RPCs. SOAP, which uses HTTP, supports the exchange of information among distributed systems. A SOAP message, which is an XML document, includes a description of a method call called an *envelope*. The body of a SOAP message is either a request, which is an RPC, or a response, which contains values returned from the called method, or service. SOAP messages are sent with the HTTP POST method.

Chapter 14, "Introduction to ASP.NET," discusses Web services provided through ASP.NET.

8.12

SUMMARY

XML is a simplified version of SGML, which is a meta-markup language. XML provides a standard way for a group of users to define the structure of their data documents, using a subject-specific markup language.

XML documents can include elements, markup declarations, and processing instructions. Every XML document has the form of a single document tree, so there can be just one root element.

An XML document is a document entity that can include any number of references to other entities defined elsewhere. An entity can be several different things, including plain text and references to images.

A DTD is a document that describes the syntactic structure of an XML document or collection of documents that uses a particular tag set. A validating XML parser compares a document it is analyzing to its DTD, if one is specified. If no DTD is specified for an XML document, only well-formedness can be checked during parsing. A DTD has declarations for elements, attributes, entities, and notations. An element declaration specifies the name of the element and its structure. If an element represents an internal node in the document tree, its structure is a list of the children nodes. Any internal node can include a modifier that specifies the number of times that its children nodes can or must appear. A leaf node's structure is usually either empty or plain text.

A DTD attribute declaration specifies the attribute's name, the name of its associated element, the type of its values, and optionally a default value. In many cases, the type of an attribute value is simply text. The default value can be an actual value, but it may also specify something about the value. There are several predefined entities that represent the special characters that are used as markup delimiters. A character data section can be used to allow these special characters to appear as themselves, without using entities. A DTD specification could appear embedded in an XML document, but this makes it inconvenient to use for other documents.

An XML document can include the predefined element names for some other application, such as the names of the elements of XHTML. To avoid name clashes between these different sources of names, XML uses the concepts of namespaces and name prefixes, which indicate the namespace of a name in a document. Namespaces are specified in declarations as URIs. A default namespace can be declared for a document. Names from the default namespace can be used without being prefixed.

XML schemas provide an alternative to DTDs. XML schemas allow much stricter control over the structure and especially the data types of an XML document. A schema defines the structure of a class of XML documents. The documents that conform to a specific schema are considered instances of that schema. Because a schema is itself an XML document, it is the instance of a schema, XMLSchema. A schema specifies a target namespace with the targetNamespace attribute. The target namespace is also often named as the default namespace. Schemas can define simple and complex data types. Simple data types cannot contain other elements or attributes. One common category of complex types are those that can contain other elements but no text. There are many predefined types. Users are allowed to define new simple types as constrained versions of existing simple types, using facets. Users can also define new complex types. Instances of schemas can be validated with several different validation programs that are now available, among them xsv.

An XML parser includes a default style sheet, which is used when no other style sheet is specified by the document being parsed. The default style sheet simply produces a somewhat stylized listing of the XML. CSS style sheets can be used with XML documents to provide formatting information. Such a CSS style sheet has the form of an external CSS style sheet for XHTML.

XML documents can also be formatted with XSLT style sheets. XSLT style sheets specify document transformations and can include XHTML and CSS presentation information. XSLT style sheets define templates into which XML document elements are mapped. An XSLT processor creates an output document from the XML document and the XSLT style sheet. If the style sheet includes XHTML style specifications, the document will have style information embedded in its elements. XSLT style sheets actually are XML applications. An XSLT style sheet can have a template that is reused for any number of occurrences of a document branch in the associated XML document.

XML applications require that the nodes (tags, attributes, text, etc.) of the XML document be provided in some standard way by the XML parser. The two ways in which this is done are the SAX approach, which calls an event handler for each node it finds, and the DOM approach, which provides a complete tree structure of the whole document.

A Web service is a method that resides and is executed on a Web server, but which can be called from any computer on the Web. The standard technologies to support Web services are WSDL, UDDI, SOAP, and XML.

8.13 Review Questions

1. Is XML more closely related to SGML or HTML?

2. What is the main deficiency of HTML?

3. What is the goal of HTML?

4. What is the goal of XML?

5. What are the two primary tasks of a validating XML parser?

6. In what way are nested tags better than attributes?

7. What is a document entity?

8. Why should a document be broken into multiple entities?

9. What is a binary entity?

10. How does an XML parser handle binary entities?

11. What is the purpose of a DTD?

12. Why is it better to find an error in a DTD before it is used?

13. What are the four possible keywords in a DTD declaration?

14. What are the meanings of the modifiers (+, *, and ?) that can be used in element declarations?

15. Explain the three types that can be used to describe data in an element declaration.

16. What are the four possible parts of an attribute declaration in a DTD?

17. Describe the meanings of the default attribute values #REQUIRED and #IMPLIED.

18. What is the difference between general and parameter entities?

19. Why do some special characters have predefined entity references?

20. What is the purpose of a character data section?

21. How does the XML parser distinguish between a general entity and a parameter entity?

22. What does the keyword SYSTEM specify in an entity declaration?

23. What is the syntactic form of an internal DTD?

24. What is the markup vocabulary of a markup language?

25. What is an XML namespace?

26. What are the two primary advantages of XML schemas over DTDs?

27. From where do the names used in defining an XML schema come?

28. What three namespaces are normally named in an XML schema?

29. What is the form of the assignment to the `schemaLocation` attribute?

30. What are the differences between simple and complex XML schema types?

31. Define local and global declarations in an XML schema.

32. What is a facet?

33. What are the four categories of complex types in an XML schema?

34. What is the difference between the `sequence` and `all` schema elements?

35. Why would you use a CSS style sheet for an XML document?

36. How does an XSLT processor use an XSLT style sheet with an XML document?

37. What is a `template` element of an XSLT style sheet?

38. What two kinds of elements are included in XSLT style sheets?

39. What does the `value-of` XSLT element do?

40. What does the `select` attribute of the `value-of` element do?

41. What does the `for-each` element of an XSLT style sheet do?

42. What is produced by a SAX parser?

43. What is produced by a DOM parser?

44. What advantages does a SAX parser have over a DOM parser?

45. What advantages does a DOM parser have over a SAX parser?

46. Explain the ultimate goal of Web services.

47. Describe the three roles in Web services.

48. What is UDDI?

49. What is SOAP?

8.14 Exercises

Write, test, and debug (if necessary) the following documents.

1. Create a DTD for a catalog of cars, where each `car` has the child elements `make`, `model`, `year`, `color`, `engine`, `number_of_doors`, `transmission_type`, and `accessories`. The `engine` element has the child elements `number_of_cylinders` and `fuel_system` (carbureted or fuel-injected). The `accessories` element has the attributes `radio`, `air_conditioning`, `power_windows`, `power_steering`, and `power_brakes`, each of which is required and has the possible values `yes` and `no`. Entities must be declared for the names of popular car makes.

2. Create an XML document with at least three instances of the car element defined in the DTD of Exercise 1. Process this document using the DTD of Exercise 1 and produce a display of the raw XML document.

3. Create an XML schema for the XML document described in Exercises 1 and 2.

4. Create a CSS style sheet for the XML document of Exercise 2 and use it to create a display of that document.

5. Create an XSLT style sheet for one car element of the XML document of Exercise 2 and use it to create a display of that element.

6. Modify the XSLT style sheet of Exercise 5 to format all the car elements in the XML document of Exercise 2 and use it to create a display of the whole document.

7. Design an XML document to store information about patients in a hospital. Information about patients must include name (in three parts), Social Security number, age, room number, primary insurance company—including member identification number, group number, phone number, and address—secondary insurance company (in the same subparts as for the primary insurance company), known medical problems, and known drug allergies. Both attributes and nested tags must be included. Make up sample data for at least four patients.

8. Write a DTD for the document described in Exercise 7 with the following restrictions: the name, Social Security number, age, room number, and primary insurance company are required. All the other elements are optional, as are middle names.

9. Create a CSS style sheet for the XML document of Exercise 7 and use it to create a display of that document.

10. Create an XSLT style sheet for one patient element of the XML document of Exercise 7 and use it to create a display of that element.

11. Modify the XSLT style sheet of Exercise 6 to format all the patient elements in the XML document of Exercise 7 and use it to create a display of the whole document.

The Basics of Perl

Our primary interest in Perl in this book is its widespread use for Common Gateway Interface (CGI) programming. However, it is beneficial to most programmers to become familiar with Perl's capabilities. Perl is a flexible, powerful, widely used programming language—and it would be so even if CGI programming did not exist. This chapter takes you on a quick tour of Perl, introducing most of the important concepts and constructs but leaving out many of the details of the language. In spite of its brevity, however, if you are an experienced programmer, you can learn to write useful Perl programs by studying this chapter. The similarity of Perl to other common programming languages, especially C and JavaScript, makes this relatively easy, at least for those who know one of those two languages. If you want more details, there are numerous books dedicated solely to Perl.

This chapter begins with a description of Perl's scalar values and variables and their use in expressions and assignment statements. Next, it covers control expressions and the collection of control statements available in Perl. It then introduces Perl's two built-in data structures, arrays and hashes, and references. This is followed by a description of functions and how they are defined and called, including the peculiar way (for a high-level language) parameters are passed. Finally, the chapter covers Perl pattern matching and the basic operations of file input and output. Although we attempt to describe Perl in a single chapter, do not be misled into thinking that this is a small or simple language—it is neither.

9.1

ORIGINS AND USES OF PERL

Perl began as a relatively small language with the modest purpose of including and expanding on the operations of the text-processing language awk and the system administration capabilities of the UNIX shell languages, initially sh. Perl was first released in 1987 after being developed and implemented by Larry Wall. Since then it has grown considerably, borrowing features from other languages as well as inventing a few of its own.[1] Along the way, it picked up support for communications using sockets, a module construct, and a form of object-oriented programming. Its text pattern-matching capabilities are elaborate and powerful, which is one of the reasons it became the most popular language for CGI programming. Perl's pattern matching has been copied into several other languages, including JavaScript and PHP. Perl is now used for many of the small to medium-size programming projects formerly done in C.

Perl is a language whose implementation is between compiled (to machine code) and interpreted languages. Perl programs are compiled to an intermediate form, in part to check for errors but mostly to make possible impressive runtime performance even though it is interpreted. When we refer to perl, we mean the Perl language processing system, which compiles and interprets programs. The perl system includes a debugger, among other things.

Perl has been ported to every common computing platform, from the various versions of UNIX to Windows and everything in between.

9.2

SCALARS AND THEIR OPERATIONS

Perl has three categories of variables—scalars, arrays, and hashes—each identified by the first character of their names ($ for scalar variables, @ for array variables, and % for hash variables). This section discusses the important characteristics of the most commonly used kind of variables, namely, scalars. Scalar variables can store three different kinds of values: numbers, character strings, and references, which are addresses. We postpone discussing references until Section 9.7.

---

1. See http://history.perl.org/ for more on the evolution of Perl.

The numeric values stored in scalar variables are represented in double-precision floating-point form. Although there is a way to suggest (to the compiler) that integer operations be used on scalar numeric values, in most cases the operations are done in double-precision floating point. Character strings are treated as scalar units in Perl. They are not arrays of individual characters.

9.2.1 Numeric and String Literals

Numeric literals can have the forms of either integers or floating-point values. Integer literals are strings of digits. Floating-point literals can have either decimal points or exponents or both. Exponents are specified with an uppercase or lowercase e and a possibly signed integer literal. The following are legal numeric literals:

```
72   7.2   .72   72.   7E2   7e2   .7e2   7.e2   7.2E-2
```

Integer literals can be written in hexadecimal (base 16) by preceding their first digit with either 0x or 0X.

String literals can appear in two forms, depending on whether their delimiters are single quotes (') or double quotes ("). Single-quoted string literals cannot include characters specified with escape sequences, such as newline characters specified with \n.[2] If an actual single-quote character is needed in a string literal that is delimited by single quotes, the embedded single quote is preceded by a backslash, as in this example:

```
'You\'re the most freckly person I\'ve ever met'
```

If an escape sequence is embedded in a single-quoted string literal, each character in the sequence is taken literally as itself. For example, the sequence \n in the following string literal will be treated as two characters, a backslash and an n:

```
'You have freckles, \n but I don\'t'
```

If a string literal with the same characteristics as single-quoted strings is needed but you want to use a different delimiter, precede the delimiter with q, as in this example:

```
q$I don't want to go, I can't go, I won't go!$
```

---

2. An *escape sequence* is one or two special characters followed by another character. The special character or characters change the meaning of the following character for that single appearance. For example, \n means a newline character, not a backslash followed by the letter n.

If the new delimiter is a parenthesis, a brace, a bracket, or a pointed bracket, the left element of the pair must be used on the left, and the right element must be used on the right. For example,

```
q<I don't want to go, I can't go, I won't go!>
```

Double-quoted string literals differ from single-quoted string literals in two ways: First, they can include special characters specified with escape sequences; second, embedded variable names are interpolated into the string, which means that their values are substituted for their names. We discuss the first of these differences here; the other will be discussed in Section 9.2.2.

In many situations, we want to include special characters that are specified with escape sequences in string literals. For example, if we want the words on a line to be spaced by tabs, we use a double-quoted literal with embedded escape sequences for the tab character:

```
"Completion % \t Yards \t Touchdowns \t Interceptions"
```

A double quote can be embedded in a double-quoted string literal by preceding it with a backslash.

A different delimiter can be specified for string literals with the characteristics of double-quoted strings by preceding the new delimiter with qq:

```
qq@"Why, I never!", said she.@
```

The null string (one with no characters) can be denoted with either `''` or `""`.

9.2.2   Scalar Variables

The names of all scalar variables, whether predefined or programmer defined, begin with dollar signs ($). The part of a scalar variable's name that follows the dollar sign is similar to the names of variables in other programming languages. It begins with a letter, which can be followed by any number of letters, digits, or underscore characters. There is no limit to the length of a variable name, and all of its characters are significant.[3] The letters in a variable name are case sensitive, meaning that $FRIZZY, $Frizzy, $FrIzZy, and $frizzy are all distinct names. However, by convention, programmer-defined variable names do not include uppercase letters.

As mentioned earlier, double-quoted string literals that contain the names of variables have the values of those variables included in, or interpolated into, the string. Consider the following string literal:

---

3. Well, at least no practical limit. Actually, a name can have no more than 255 characters.

```
"Jack is $age years old"
```

If the value of $age is 47, this string has the following value:

```
"Jack is 47 years old"
```

To place a variable name in a double-quoted string but not have it interpolated, the variable's name is preceded by a backslash. For example:

```
"The variable with the result is \$answer"
```

In Perl, variables are not explicitly declared; the compiler declares a variable implicitly when it first encounters the variable's name in a program.

A scalar variable that has not been assigned a value by the program has the value undef. The numeric value of undef is 0; the string value of undef is the null string (" ").

Perl includes a large number of predefined, or *implicit*, variables. The names of implicit scalar variables begin with dollar signs. The rest of the name of an implicit variable is often just one more special character, such as an underscore (_), a circumflex (^), or a backslash (\). You will see many uses of these implicit variables in this chapter and the next.

The Perl software system includes extensive documentation. Specific parts of this documentation can be retrieved with the command perldoc followed by a topic. For example, a list of all Perl predefined variables can be found by typing the following:

```
perldoc perlvar
```

9.2.3 Numeric Operators

Most of Perl's numeric operators are similar to those in other common programming languages, so they should be familiar to most readers. These are the binary operators + for addition, − for subtraction, * for multiplication, / for division, ** for exponentiation, and % for modulus.[4] In addition, there are the unary operators for addition, subtraction, decrement (−−), and increment (++). The decrement and increment operators can be either prefix or postfix.

Except under unusual circumstances, numeric operations are done in double-precision floating point. So, whereas the expression 5 / 2 may evaluate to 2 in many other languages, in Perl it evaluates to 2.5.

The precedence rules of a language specify which operator is evaluated first when two operators that have different levels of precedence appear in an expression, separated only by an operand. The associativity rules of a language specify which operator is evaluated first when two operators with the same precedence

---

4. $x % $y produces the remainder of the value of $x after division by $y.

level appear in an expression, separated only by an operand. The precedence and associativity of the numeric operators are given in Table 9.1.

TABLE 9.1 Precedence and Associativity of the Numeric Operators

Operator	Associativity
++, --	Nonassociative*
unary +, −	Right
**	Right
*, /, %	Left
binary +, −	Left

The operators listed first have the highest precedence.
*An operator is nonassociative if two of them cannot appear in an expression separated only by an operand.

9.2.4 String Operators

Perl strings are not stored or treated as arrays of characters; rather, a string is a single unit. The two string operators are described in this section. The most commonly used string functions are introduced in Section 9.2.5.

String catenation is specified with the operator denoted by a period. For example, if the value of $first is "Freddie", the value of the expression

```
$first .  " Freeloader"
```

is

```
"Freddie Freeloader"
```

The repetition operator is specified with an x. It takes a string as its left operand and an expression that evaluates to a number as its right operand. The left operand is replicated the number of times equal to the value of the right operand. For example, the value of

```
"More! "  x  3
```

is

```
"More! More! More! "
```

9.2.5   String Functions

Functions and operators in Perl are closely related. In fact, in many cases they can be used interchangeably. For example, if there is a predefined unary operator named `doit` that takes one parameter, it can be treated as an operator, as in the following example:

```
doit x
```

Or it could be treated as a function, as in the following:

```
doit(x)
```

A function with no parameters can be called with empty parentheses or no parentheses at all.

Table 9.2 lists the most commonly used string functions.

TABLE 9.2 String Functions

Name	Parameter(s)	Actions
chomp	A string	Removes any terminating newline characters* from its parameter; returns the number of removed characters
length	A string	Returns the number of characters in its parameter string
lc	A string	Returns its parameter string with all uppercase letters converted to lowercase
uc	A string	Returns its parameter string with all lowercase letters converted to uppercase
hex	A string	Returns the decimal value of the hexadecimal number in its parameter string
join	A character and the strings catenated together with a list of strings	Returns a string constructed by catenating the strings of the second and subsequent strings together, with the parameter character inserted between them

*The newline character may actually be two characters, as is the case with Windows.

When an operator or function that expects a numeric operand is given a string, the string is converted to a number. If the string does not represent a number, zero is used. When an operator or function that expects a string operand is given a number, the number is converted to a string.

9.3

ASSIGNMENT STATEMENTS AND SIMPLE INPUT AND OUTPUT

Among the most fundamental constructs in most programming languages are assignment statements and the statements or functions that provide keyboard input and screen output. The next subsections introduce these as they appear in Perl.

9.3.1 Assignment Statements

Perl's assignment statements are the same as those of C and its descendents. The simple assignment operator is =, used in this example:

```
$salary = 47500;
```

Compound assignment operators are binary operators with the simple assignment operator catenated to their right side. For example, the statement

```
$sum += $value;
```

is the same as this statement:

```
$sum = $sum + $value;
```

Notice that these sample assignment statements are terminated by semicolons. All Perl statements except those at the end of blocks (see Section 9.4) must be terminated by semicolons.

Comments in Perl are specified using the pound sign (#). Any text following a # on a line is ignored by the compiler (unless the # is in a literal string).

9.3.2 Keyboard Input

All input and output in Perl is uniformly thought of as file input and output. Files have external names but are referenced in programs through internal names, called *filehandles*. There are three predefined filehandles: STDIN, which is a program's normal input stream (by default, the keyboard); STDOUT, which is a program's normal output stream (by default, the screen); and STDERR, which is a program's normal output stream for error messages (usually also associated with the screen).

The line input operator[5] is different from other operators. It is specified with a pair of pointed brackets <>, with its operand, if one is provided, embedded between the brackets. For example, to get a line from STDIN:

```
$in_data = <STDIN>;
```

The line input operator gets all characters typed on the keyboard up to and including the newline character. In many cases, the newline character is not wanted, so the following idiom is common:

```
chomp($in_data = <STDIN>);
```

9.3.3   Screen Output

Output is directed to the screen with the print function (or operator). We prefer to treat it as an operator. The operand for print is one or more string literals, separated by commas. No implicit newline character is appended to the last string operand, so if one is needed, it must be included, as in the following:

```
print "This is pretty easy \n";
```

Many screen output lines include the value of one or more program variables. Because the variable names in a double-quoted string are interpolated, this is easy. The printf function from C is also available in Perl, including format codes such as %7d and %5s.

The following trivial program illustrates some of what we have discussed so far:

```
# quadeval.pl — A simple Perl program
#   Input: Four numbers, representing the values of
#          a, b, c, and x
# Output: The value of the expression
#          axx + bx + c
# Get input
print "Please input the value of a ";
$a = <STDIN>;
print "Please input the value of b ";
$b = <STDIN>;
print "Please input the value of c ";
$c = <STDIN>;
```

continued

---

5. Note that the line input operator is also used to get input from places other than the keyboard, as we explain later. The line input operator is sometimes called the *angle operator*; it is also sometimes called the *diamond operator*.

```
print "Please input the value of x ";
$x = <STDIN>;
# Compute and display the result
$result = $a * $x * $x + $b * $x + $c;
print "The value of the expression is: $result \n";
```

Under Windows and UNIX, a Perl program can be run from the operating system command-line prompt, by typing `perl` followed by the filename where the Perl program is stored, as in the following:

```
perl quadeval.pl
```

This executes the program named `perl`, which is the Perl compiler/interpreter. It causes the program in the file `quadeval.pl` to be compiled and interpreted. If you want a compilation without the interpretation, just to check the syntactic correctness of your program, include the `-c` flag after the `perl` command. It is always a good idea to include the `-w` flag, which causes `perl` to produce warning messages for a variety of suspicious things it may find in your program. This is useful because Perl is a very forgiving language.

The line input operator can be used to get input from a file specified as a command-line argument, which can appear at the end of the `perl` command. The operator in this case is empty pointed brackets. For example, if `perl` is run with the command

```
perl —w quadeval.pl quad.dat
```

then the following statement puts the first line from the file `quad.dat` into `$input`:

```
$input = <>;
```

An alternative way to run Perl programs is discussed in Chapter 10, "Using Perl for CGI Programming."

9.4

CONTROL STATEMENTS

Perl has a powerful collection of statements for controlling the execution flow through its programs. This section introduces the control expressions and control statements of Perl.

9.4.1 Control Expressions

The expressions upon which statement control flow is based are either scalar-valued expressions, relational expressions, or compound expressions. If the value of a scalar-valued expression is a string, it is true unless it is either the empty string ("") or a zero string ("0").[6] If the value is a number, it is true unless it is zero (0).

Relational operators can have any scalar-valued expression for their operands. Perl has two sets of relational operators, one for numeric operands and one for string operands. Table 9.3 lists the relational operators.

TABLE 9.3 Relational Operators

Operation	Numeric Operands	String Operands
Is equal to	==	eq
Is not equal to	!=	ne
Is less than	<	lt
Is greater than	>	gt
Is less than or equal to	<=	le
Is greater than or equal to	>=	ge
Compare, returning −1, 0, or +1	<=>	cmp

If a string relational operator is given a numeric operand, the value of that operand is coerced (implicitly converted) to a string. Likewise, the numeric operators coerce string operands to numbers. In some cases, the value produced by a coercion may not be intuitive. For example, when the string 'George' is used as an operand of >, it is coerced to zero. Coercions do not produce error or warning messages when an operand must be coerced, even if the coercion is required only because the programmer typed the wrong operand. These coercions are obviously dangerous because they prevent the system from detecting some programmer errors, so be careful to use the relational operator that is appropriate for the operands.

The first six relational operators in Table 9.3 produce +1 if true, "" if false.

The <=> and cmp operators compare their operands and produce −1 if the left operand is less than the right operand, 0 if they are equal, and +1 if the left operand is greater than the right operand. These operators are useful with the sort operator, which is discussed in Section 9.8.4.

---

6. This can be misinterpreted. The string "0.0" may look like a false value, but because it is not precisely "0", it is true.

Perl has two sets of operators for the AND, OR, and NOT Boolean operations. These two sets have the same semantics but different precedence levels. The operators with the higher precedence level are `&&` (AND), `||` (OR), and `!` (NOT). Those with the lower precedence are `and`, `or`, and `not`. The precedence of these latter operators is lower than any other operators in Perl, so no matter what operators appear in their operands, these operators will be evaluated last.

The precedence and associativity of all operators discussed so far in this chapter are shown in Table 9.4.

TABLE 9.4 Operator Precedence and Associativity

Operator	Associativity
`++`, `--`	Nonassociative
`**`	Right
unary `+` and `-`, and	Right
`*`, `/`, `%`, `x`	Left
`+`, `-`, `.`	Left
`>`, `<`, `>=`, `<=`, `lt`, `gt`, `le`, `ge`	Nonassociative
`==`, `!=`, `<=>`, `eq`, `ne`, `cmp`	Nonassociative
`&&`	Left
`||`	Left
`=`, `+=`, `-=`, `*=`, `**=`, `/=`, `%=`, `&=`, `&&=`, `||=`, `x=`	Right
`not`	Right
`and`	Left
`or`	Left

Highest-precedence operators are listed first.

Because assignment statements have values (the value of an assignment is the value assigned to the left-side variable), they can be used as control expressions. One common use of this is for an assignment statement that uses `<STDIN>` as its right side. The line input operator returns the empty string when it gets the end-of-file (EOF) character, so this can be conveniently used to terminate loops. For example:

```
while ($next = <STDIN>) { … }
```

The keyboard EOF character is Ctrl+D for UNIX, Ctrl+Z for Windows, and CMD+. (period) for Macintosh systems.

9.4.2 Selection and Loop Statements

Control statements require some syntactic container for sequences of statements whose execution they are meant to control. Perl uses the block for this container. A block is formed by putting braces ({}) around a sequence of statements. Blocks can have local variables, as you will see in Section 9.8. A *control construct* is a control statement and the block whose execution it controls.

Perl's `if` statement is similar to that of other languages. The only thing a bit different is that both the then clause and the else clause must always be blocks. For example, the following construct is illegal:

```
if ($a > 10)
    $b = $a * 2;   # Illegal — not a block
```

To be legal, the then clause must be a block, as in this example:

```
if ($a > 10) {
    $b = $a * 2;
}
```

An `if` construct can include `elsif` (note that it is *not* spelled "elseif") clauses, which provide a way of having a more readable sequence of nested `if` constructs. For example:

```
if ($snowrate < 1) {
    print "Light snow \n";
} elsif ($snowrate < 2) {
    print "Moderate snow \n";
} else
    print "Heavy snow \n";
}
```

Perl has an `unless` statement, which is the same as its `if` statement except that the inverse of the value of the control expression is used. This is convenient if you want a selection construct with an else clause but no then clause. The following construct illustrates an `unless` statement:

```
unless ($sum > 1000) {
    print "We are not finished yet! \n";
}
```

The Perl `while` and `for` statements are similar to those of C and its descendents. The bodies of both must be blocks. The general form of the `while` statement is as follows:

```
while (control expression) {
    # loop body statement(s)
}
```

The `until` statement is similar to the `while` statement except that the inverse of the value of the control expression is used.

Perl's `for` statement is most often used for loops controlled by counters. The general form of the `for` statement is as follows:

```
for (initial expression; control expression; increment expression) {
    # loop body statement(s)
}
```

Both the initial expression and the increment expression can be multiple expressions, separated by commas. The following `for` statement illustrates its use in forming a simple counter-controlled loop:

```
$sum = 0;
for ($counter = 1; $counter <= 100; $counter++) {
    $sum += $counter;
}
```

The operators `last` and `next` provide a way to exit a loop (or any block). These are exactly like the `break` and `continue` statements of C except they can include labels, which allow more than one loop or block to be exited. Consider the following skeletal example:

```
BIGLOOP:
while (...) {
    while (...) {
        ...
        if (...) {last BIGLOOP;}
        ...
    }
    ...
}
```

In the code, the `last` operator transfers control out of both loops.

Perl has no `switch` statement.

The implicit variable $_ is frequently used in Perl programs, most often as the default parameter in a function call and as the default operand of an operator.

It is also the default target for the input operator. For example, consider the following statement:

```
<STDIN>;
```

This statement gets a line from the keyboard and assigns it to $_.
    The following example illustrates some of the uses of $_:

```
while (<STDIN>) {
    print;
    chomp;
    if ($_ eq "redhead") {
        print "I've finally found one! \n";
    }
}
```

There are three uses of $_ in this while construct: as the target of the input line operator, as the default parameter to print, and as the default operand of chomp. As you might suspect, the heavy use of $_, especially when it is only implied, is not highly regarded by some software developers who normally use other programming languages.

9.5

FUNDAMENTALS OF ARRAYS

Arrays in Perl are more flexible than those of most of the other common languages. This is a result of three fundamental differences between Perl arrays and those of other common languages such as C, C++, and Java. First, the length of a Perl array is dynamic—it can grow or shrink any time during program execution. Second, Perl arrays can have absent elements. For example, a Perl array may have only three elements, but those elements may have the subscripts 10, 100, and 352. Third, a Perl array can store different types of data. For example, an array may have some numeric elements and some string elements.

9.5.1 List Literals

A *list* is an ordered sequence of scalar values. A *list literal*, which is a parenthesized list of scalar values, is the way a list value is specified in a program. Arrays store lists, so list literals serve as array literals. Because each list element can be any kind of scalar value, a list literal can be any combination of them. An expression can also be used to describe an element of a list literal. For example:

```
(3.14149 * $radius, "circles", 17)
```

9.5.2 Arrays

We use the term *array* to denote a variable that stores lists. All array names begin with an at sign (@), which puts them in a namespace that is different from that of the scalar variable names. Arrays can be assigned list literals or other arrays. Consider the following examples:

```
@list =  ('boy', 'girl', 'dog', 'cat');
@creatures = @list;
```

When an array is assigned to another array, as in the second assignment statement above, a new array is created for the target variable (@creatures in the example). This is different from C, where array names without subscripts are treated as pointers, and an array assignment such as the preceding example would result in the target variable being set to the address of the assigned array. In Perl, array names without subscripts are never treated as pointers.

The context of an assignment statement depends on the type of the target variable—if it is a scalar, the context is scalar; if it is an array or a list, it is called list context. If an array is used in scalar context, the array's length (the number of elements that are in the array) is used. For example, the following statement assigns 4 to $len because there are four elements in @list:

```
$len = @list;
```

A list literal that contains only scalar variable names can be the target of a list assignment:

```
($first, $middle, $last) = ("George", "Bernard", "Shaw");
```

Such an assignment is called a *list assignment.*

If the target of a list assignment includes an array, all remaining values on the right side go to the array. Therefore, if an array is in the target of a list assignment, it must appear last.

All Perl array elements use integers as subscripts, and the lower-bound subscript of every array is zero. Array elements are referenced through subscripts delimited by brackets ([ ]). A subscript can be any numeric-valued expression. Because an array element is always a scalar, the scalar version of the array's name is used when a subscript is attached:

```
@list = (2, 4, 6, 8);
$second = $list[1];  # Sets $second to 4
```

Though it makes some sense, this use of a scalar name to reference an element of an array is confusing to most Perl beginners.

It is essential to remember that scalar and array variables are in distinct namespaces. When a scalar name is followed by a subscript, it is no longer in the scalar namespace—the subscript moves it to the array namespace. Therefore, there is no connection between $a and $a[5].

The length of an array is dynamic; the highest subscript to which a value has been assigned determines the current length of the array:

```
$list = ("Monday", "Tuesday", "Wednesday", "Thursday");
$list[4] = ("Friday");
```

Here, the length of @list is now 5. Note that the length of an array is determined by the highest used subscript, which may be unrelated to the number of elements in the array.

Consider the following code:

```
@list = (2, 4, 6);
$list[27] = 8;
```

Now @list has four elements, but its length is 28. It has 24 vacant positions, which do not have elements.

The last subscript of @list can be referenced as $#list. So, the length of @list is $#list + 1. The last subscript of an array can be assigned to set its length to whatever you want, as in this example:

```
$#list = 999;
```

As discussed previously, two different contexts of a variable name or expression exist: scalar and list. An expression assigned to a scalar variable is in scalar context; an expression assigned to an array or list is in list context. Some of Perl's operators force either scalar or list context on their operands. Likewise, some functions force either scalar or list context on their parameters. Scalar context can be forced with the pseudo function scalar, as shown here:

```
scalar(@list)
```

There is no way to force list context on an expression.

9.5.3 The foreach Statement

The foreach statement is used to process the elements of an array. For example, the following code will divide all of the values in @list by 2:

```
foreach $value (@list) {
    $value /= 2;
}
```

The scalar variable in a foreach becomes an alias (a new name) for each of the array's elements, one at a time. So, although the assignment statement in this `foreach` body appears to be changing the scalar variable `$value`, it is in fact changing the values of the elements of the array `@list`.

The scalar variable that appears in the `foreach` statement is local to the `foreach` construct. So, if the program has another variable with the same name, the one in the `foreach` will not interfere with the one used outside the construct.

If the array specified in a `foreach` statement has vacant spaces, `foreach` behaves as if the vacant elements existed and had the value `""`. For example, suppose an array is defined as follows:

```
$list[1] = 17;
$list[3] = 34;
```

Now consider the following loop:

```
foreach $value (@list) {
    print "Next: $value \n";
}
```

This loop produces the following:

```
Next:
Next: 17
Next:
Next: 34
```

9.5.4 Built-In Functions for Arrays and Lists

This section introduces a few of the many built-in functions that are part of Perl.

9.5.4.1 Array Functions

As with other Perl functions, these can be treated as either operators or functions—operators if the parameters are not parenthesized, functions otherwise. It is common to need to place new elements on one end or the other of an array. Perl has four functions for these purposes: `unshift` and `shift`, which deal with the left end of arrays; and `pop` and `push`, which deal with the right end of arrays.

The `shift` function removes and returns the first element of its given array parameter. For example, the following statement removes the first element of `@list` and places it in `$first`:

```
$first = shift @list;
```

The subscripts of all of the other elements in the array are reduced by 1 as a result of the shift operation. The pop function removes and returns the last element of its given array operand. In this case, there is no change in the subscripts of the array's other elements.

The unshift function takes two parameters: an array and a scalar or list. The scalar or list is appended to the beginning of the array. This results in an increase in the subscripts of all other array elements. The push function also takes an array and a scalar or a list. The scalar or list is added to the high end of the array:

```
@list = (2, 4, 6);
push @list, (8, 10);
```

The value of @list is now (2, 4, 6, 8, 10).

Either pop and unshift or push and shift can be used to implement a queue in an array, depending on the direction the queue should grow.

9.5.4.2 List Functions

List functions take lists as parameters. Because lists are immutable, these functions cannot change their list parameters. Instead, they yield new lists.

The split function is used to break strings into parts using a specified character as the basis for the split. The resulting substrings are placed in a specified array, as in this example:

```
$stoogestring = "Curly Larry Moe";
@stooges = split(" ", $stoogestring);
```

The three elements of @stooges are now "Curly", "Larry", and "Moe".

The sort function takes an array parameter and uses string comparison to sort the elements of the array into alphabetic order in the returned list. For example:

```
@new_names_list = sort @names_list;
```

Recall that if either operand of a string comparison (relational) operator is not a string, it is coerced to a string before the comparison operation takes place. It is possible to supply a comparison function to allow sort to sort all kinds of data. Do not use the sort operator to sort numbers if you do not supply a comparison function. If you do, sort will convert the numbers to strings, and you probably will not get what you expected. Section 9.8.4 discusses the use of the sort function for other orders and for nonstring array elements.

The qw function can be used on a sequence of unquoted strings to quote all of them, as in this example:

```
qw(peaches apples pears kumquats)
```

This call to qw produces the following:

```
("peaches", "apples", "pears", "kumquats")
```

Notice that spaces, not commas, separate the list elements in the call to qw.

The die list operator is similar to the print function, which also can be considered a list operator. It takes a variable number of string parameters, catenates them, sends the result to STDERR, and terminates the program. For example:

```
die "Error -- division by zero in function fun2";
```

9.5.5 An Example

The following example illustrates a simple use of an array. A file of names, whose name is specified on the command line, is read. The names are converted to all uppercase letters, and the array is sorted and displayed.

```perl
# process_names.pl - A simple program to illustrate
#                    the use of arrays
#  Input: A file, specified on the command line, of
#         lines of text, where each line is a person's
#         name
# Output: The input names, after all letters are converted
#         to uppercase, in alphabetical order

$index = 0;

# Loop to read the names and process them

while($name = <>) {

# Convert the name's letters to uppercase and put it in
#   the names array

    $names[$index++] = uc($name);
}

# Display the sorted list of names

print "\nThe sorted list of names is:\n\n\n";
foreach $name (sort @names) {
    print ("$name \n");
}
```

9.6

HASHES

Associative arrays are arrays in which each data element is paired with a key, which is used to find the data element. Because hash functions are used to find specific elements in an associative array, Perl associative arrays are called *hashes*. The two fundamental differences between arrays and hashes are as follows: First, arrays use numeric subscripts to address specific elements, whereas hashes use string values (the keys) for element addressing. Second, the elements in arrays are ordered by subscript, but the elements in hashes are not. In a sense, elements of an array are like those in a list, whereas elements of a hash are like those in a set, where order is irrelevant. The actual arrangement of the elements of a hash in memory is determined by the hash function used to insert and access them.

Names of hash variables begin with percent signs (%), which places them in their own namespace. List literals may be used to initialize hash variables. The symbols => can be used between a key and its associated data element, or value, in a list literal used to initialize a hash variable. Commas can also be used, but they do nothing to connote the fact that it is a literal hash value:

```
%kids_ages = ("John" => 35, "Genny" => 33, "Jake" => 19,
              "Darcie" => 18);
```

Arrays also can be assigned to hashes, with the sensible semantics that the odd-subscripted elements of the array become the values of the hash, and the even-subscripted elements of the array become the keys of the hash. Hashes also can be assigned to arrays.

An individual value element of a hash can be referenced by "subscripting" the hash name with a key. Braces are used to specify the subscripting operation. The name of a reference to a hash element begins, of course, with a dollar sign instead of the percent sign (because it is a scalar value):

```
$genny_age = $kids_ages{"Genny"};
```

New values are added to a hash by assigning the value of the new element to a reference to the key of the new element, as in this example:

```
$kids_ages{"Aidan"} = 2;
```

An element is removed from a hash with the `delete` operator, as shown here:

```
delete $kids_ages{"Genny"};
```

A hash can be set to empty in two ways: First, an empty list can be assigned to the hash. Second, the undef operator can be used on the hash. These two approaches are illustrated with the following statements:

```
%kids_ages = ();
undef %kids_ages;
```

The exists operator is used to determine whether an element with a specific key is in a hash. For example:

```
if (exists $kids_ages{"Freddie"}) ..
```

The keys and values of a hash can be extracted into arrays with the operators keys and values, respectively:

```
foreach $child (keys %kids_ages) {
  print "The age of $child is $kids_ages{$child} \n";

}
```

```
@ages = values %kids_ages;
print "All of the ages are: @ages \n";
```

If a hash variable is embedded in a double-quoted string literal, its keys and values are not interpolated into the string. To display all of the keys and values of a hash, first assign it to an array and then print the array.

Perl has a predefined hash named %ENV that stores operating system environment variables. Environment variables are used to store information about the system on which perl is running. The environment variables and their respective values in %ENV can be accessed by any Perl program. The keys of %ENV are the names of the environment variables; the values are, of course, their values. All of the environment variables and their values of a specific system can be displayed with the following:

```
foreach $key (sort keys %ENV) {
    print "$key = $ENV{$key} \n";
}
```

In Chapter 10, we will make use of environment variables.

9.7

REFERENCES

A *reference* is a scalar variable that references another variable or a literal. So, the value of a reference variable is an address. Although Perl's references are related to the pointers in C and C++, they are less flexible and much safer. The address of an existing variable is obtained with the backslash operator on the name of that variable:

```perl
$age = 42;
$ref_age = \$age;
@stooges = ("Curly", "Larry", "Moe");
$ref_stooges = \@stooges;
```

A reference to a list literal is created by putting the literal value in brackets, as follows:

```perl
$ref_salaries = [42500, 29800, 50000, 35250];
```

A reference to a hash literal is created by putting the literal value in braces:

```perl
$ref_ages = {
    'Curly' => 41,
    'Larry' => 38,
    'Moe' => 43,
};
```

A reference can specify two different values: its own, which is an address, or the value at that address. The process of making an appearance of a reference variable specify the latter is called *dereferencing*. All dereferencing in Perl is explicit. So, if you want the value to which a reference points rather than the address value of the reference, you must use different syntax on the reference's name. There are two ways to do this in Perl. First, an extra dollar sign can be appended to the beginning of the reference's name. For example, the value of `$$ref_age` is 42 rather than the address of `$age`.

If the reference is to an array or hash, there is a second way to specify dereferencing, which is to use the `->` operator between the variable's name and its subscript. For example, the following two assignment statements are equivalent:

```perl
$$ref_stooges[3] = "Maxine";
$ref_stooges -> [3] = "Maxine";
```

9.8

FUNCTIONS

Subprograms are central to the usefulness of any programming language. Perl's subprograms are all functions, as in its ancestor language, C. This section describes the basics of Perl functions.

9.8.1 Fundamentals

A *function definition* includes the function's header and a block of code that describes its actions. Neither parameter specifications nor a return value type are part of a Perl function definition. A *function header* is the reserved word sub and the function's name. A *function declaration* is a message to the compiler that the given name is a function that will be defined somewhere in the program. Syntactically, a function declaration is the function header without the block. Because forward calls to functions are legal, it does not matter where their definitions appear in a program. We prefer to put them at the beginning.

A function that returns a value that is to be used immediately is called in the position of an operand in an expression (or as the whole expression). A function that either does not return a value or returns a value that is not to be used can be called by a standalone statement.

A function that has been previously declared can be treated as a list operator, meaning that calls to it need not include the parentheses.

A function definition can specify the value it returns in two ways, implicitly and explicitly. The return function takes an expression as its parameter. The value of the expression is returned when the return is executed. A function can have any number of calls to return, including none. If there are no calls to return in a function or if execution arrives at the end of the function without encountering a return, its returned value is the value of the last expression evaluated in the function. For example, consider the following two function definitions:

```
sub product1 {
    return($first * $second);
}
sub product2 {
    $first * $second;
}
```

The following two calls produce the same result:

```
$p1 = product1();
$p2 = product2();
```

9.8.2 Local Variables

Variables that are implicitly declared have global scope—that is, they are visible in the entire program. It is usually best for variables used in a function that are not used outside the function to have local scope, meaning that they are visible and can be used only within the block of the function. Such variables are declared to have local scope in a function by including their names as parameters to the my function. Initial values of local variables can be part of their declaration:

```
my $count = 0;
```

If more than one variable is declared by a call to my, they must be placed in parentheses, as in this example:

```
my($count, $sum) = (0,0);
```

Notice the use of the list assignment to initialize these local variables.

If the name of a local variable conflicts with that of a global variable, the local variable is used. This is the advantage of local variables: When you make up their names, you need not be concerned that a global variable with the same name may exist in the program.

Perl includes a second kind of local variables, which are declared with the local reserved word. The scope of such variables is dynamic, which makes them much different from my variables, whose scope is static. We do not discuss this second kind of local variables here. When we say a variable is local, we mean it has local scope and is defined with my.

9.8.3 Parameters

The parameter values that appear in a call to a function are called *actual parameters*. The parameter names used in the function, which correspond to the actual parameters, are called *formal parameters*. Two common models of parameter transfers are used in the linkage between a function and its caller: pass by value and pass by reference. Pass-by-value parameters, which are usually implemented by sending values to the function, provide one-way communication to the called function. Pass-by-reference parameters, which are often implemented by passing the addresses of variables to the function, provide two-way communication between the function and its caller.

All Perl parameters are communicated through a special implicit array, @_. When a function is called, the values of the actual parameters specified in the call are placed in @_. If an actual parameter is an array, all of the array's elements are placed in @_. When a hash is used as an actual parameter, its value is flattened into an array, and its values are moved to @_. Every function has its own version of @_, so if a function calls another function, the values in the caller's @_ are not affected by the call.

If the values in @_ are manipulated directly in the called function, the parameters have pass-by-reference semantics, as in this example:

```
sub plus10 {
    $_[0] += 10;
}
plus10($a);
```

The call to plus10 results in 10 being added to $a. If you call this function with a literal—by mistake, of course—it has no effect, not even that of producing an error message.

Pass-by-value parameters are implemented by assigning the passed values in @_ to local variables. For example:

```
sub fun1 {
    my($a, $b) = @_;
    return ++$a * ++$b;
}
```

This function adds 1 to the values of each of the two actual parameters, multiplies the two resulting values, and returns the product, without affecting the values of the two actual parameters.

References to variables can be used as actual parameters, which provides pass-by-reference semantics. For example, the following function subtracts 1 from the first n elements of a given array, where the address of the array is the parameter.

```
sub sub1 {
    my $ref_list = $_[0];
    my $count;
    my $len = $#$ref_list + 1;

    for ($count = 0; $count < $len;
        $$ref_list[$count++]--){
    }
}
```

The following is an example of a call to sub1:

```
sub1(\@mylist);
```

9.8.4 The sort Function, Revisited

Recall that the sort function, as introduced in Section 9.5.4.2, takes a single array parameter and sorts that array, treating the elements as strings (coercing elements that are not strings to strings). This does not work for numbers because, when coerced to strings, 124 belongs before 2.

A more flexible and useful form of `sort` takes another parameter, which is a block of code of a particular form that provides a comparison operation for the sort process.[7] This block parameter appears as the first parameter. The comparison process must return a negative number if the first value being compared belongs before the second, zero if the two values are equal, and a number greater than zero if the two values must be interchanged. The two values to be compared are referenced in the comparison with the names `$a` and `$b`. These variables, which act as formal parameters, are used in pass-by-reference mode. Therefore, they should not be changed in the comparison code. The two relational operators, `<=>` and `cmp`, are normally used for the comparison. Recall that they return exactly what is needed by the sort process.

For example, to sort numbers in the array `@list` into ascending order, the following could be used:

```
@new_list = sort {$a <=> $b}, @list;
```

To sort the same array into descending order, the two variables `$a` and `$b` are interchanged in the comparison, as in the following:

```
@new_list = sort {$b <=> $a}, @list;
```

Likewise, to sort strings in the array `@names` into reverse alphabetic order, the following could be used:

```
@new_names = sort {$b cmp $a}, @names;
```

9.8.5 An Example

What follows is an example of a program that uses a function to compute the median of a given array of numbers. The address of the array is passed to the function and is moved to a local variable there. There is no need to pass the length of the array because the function can easily determine the array's length. The precise specification for the function is given in its initial comments.

```
# tst_median.pl - a program to test a function that
#                 computes the median of a given array

# median - a function
```

continued

---

7. Actually, the parameter also could be a function name, or a scalar variable that has either the name or a reference to a function.

```perl
# Parameters:
#      A reference to an array of numbers
# Return value:
#      The median of the array, where median is the
#      middle element of the sorted array, if the
#      length is odd; if the length is even, the median
#      is the average of the two middle elements of the
#      sorted array

sub median {
    my $ref_list = $_[0];

# Compute the length of the passed array

    my $len = $#$ref_list + 1;

# Sort the parameter array

    @list = sort {$a <=> $b} @$ref_list;

# Compute the median

    if ($len % 2 == 1) {   # length is odd
        return $list[$len / 2];
    } else {   # length is even
        return ($list[$len / 2] + $list[$len / 2 - 1]) / 2;
    }

}   # End of function median

# Begin main program
# Create two test arrays, one with odd length and one with
#   even length

@list1 = (11, 36, 5, 20, 41, 6, 8, 0, 9);
@list2 = (43, 77, 11, 29, 8, 51, 9, 18);

# Call median on both arrays and display the results

$med = median(\@list1);
print "The median of the first array is: $med \n";
$med = median(\@list2);
print "The median of the second array is: $med \n";
```

The output of this program is as follows:

```
The median of the first array is: 9
The median of the second array is: 23.5
```

9.9
PATTERN MATCHING

Regular expressions in JavaScript were discussed in Chapter 4, "The Basics of JavaScript." Because JavaScript regular expressions are based directly on those of Perl, we greatly abbreviate our discussion of them here. The pattern-matching operations of Perl are different from those of JavaScript.

9.9.1 The Basics of Patterns and Pattern Matching

Within a pattern, "normal" characters match themselves. *Normal* means that they are not metacharacters, which are characters that have special meanings in some contexts in patterns. The metacharacters are these:

```
\ | ( ) [ ] { } ^ $ * + ? .
```

Metacharacters can themselves be matched by being immediately preceded by a backslash. Before discussing the use of metacharacters in patterns, we show how normal characters are used. Because they match themselves, this is simple. As in JavaScript, patterns are normally delimited by slashes.

The period matches any character except newline. Therefore, the following pattern matches `"snowy"`, `"snowe"`, and `"snowd"`, among others:

```
/snow./
```

Character classes are used to abbreviate lists of characters that are logically ORed together in a pattern. For example, the following character class matches `'a'`, `'b'`, or `'c'`:

```
[abc]
```

If a circumflex character (^) is the first character in a character class, it inverts the specified set. For example, the following character class matches any character that is not a vowel:

```
[^aeiou]
```

Note that metacharacters are not special in a character class, so if a period is included in a character class, it need not be backslashed.

Several of the most frequently used character classes are predefined and can be specified by their names. Among these are \d, which matches any digit, and \s, which matches whitespace characters.

In many cases, it is necessary to repeat a character or character-class pattern. To repeat a pattern, a numeric quantifier, delimited by braces, is attached. For example, the following pattern matches xyyyyz:

```
/xy{4}z/
```

The following pattern matches phone numbers that have dashes separating their three parts:

```
/\d{3}-\d{3}-\d{4}/
```

There are also three symbolic quantifiers: asterisk (*), plus (+), and question mark (?). The asterisk means zero or more repetitions, the plus means one or more repetitions, and the question mark means one or none. For example, the following pattern matches strings that begin with any number of x's (including zero), followed by one or more y's, possibly followed by z:

```
/x*y+z?/
```

These quantifiers are often used with the predefined character class names, as in the following pattern, which matches a string of one or more digits followed by a decimal point and possibly more digits:

```
/\d+\.\d*/
```

Anchored patterns are often useful. A circumflex (^) anchor given at the beginning of a pattern specifies that the match must occur at the left end of the string. Similarly, a dollar sign ($) given at the end of the pattern specifies that the match must occur at the right end of the string. For example, the pattern

```
/^son/
```

matches "sonny boy" but not "Johnson". Likewise, the pattern

```
/son$/
```

matches "Johnson" but not "sonny boy".

Modifiers can be attached to patterns to change how they are used, thereby increasing their flexibility. The modifiers are specified as letters just after the right delimiter of the pattern. The i modifier makes the letters in the pattern match either uppercase or lowercase letters in the string. The x modifier allows whitespace to appear in the pattern. Because comments are considered whitespace, this provides a way to provide explanatory comments in the pattern.

In Perl, the pattern-matching operation is specified with the operator m. When slashes are used as delimiters, the m operator is not required. Therefore, just a slash-delimited regular expression is a complete pattern expression in Perl. The string against which the matching is attempted is, by default, the implicit variable $_. The result of evaluating a pattern-matching expression is either true or false. The following is a pattern match against the value in $_:

```
if (/rabbit/) {
    print
        "The word 'rabbit' appears somewhere in \$_ \n";
}
```

The pattern-matching operation does not need to be always against the string in $_. The binding operator, =~, can be used to specify any string as the one against which the pattern will be matched. For example, consider the following:

```
if ($str =~ /^rabbit/) {
    print "The value of \$str begins with 'rabbit' \n";
}
```

A restricted form of the split function was introduced in Section 9.5.4.2. In that section, the first parameter to split was a single character. However, the first parameter also can be any pattern. For example, we could have the following:

```
@words = split /[ .,]\s*/, $str;
```

This statement puts the words from $str into the @words array. The words in $str are defined to be terminated with either a space, a period, or a comma, any of which could be followed by more whitespace characters.

The following sample program illustrates a simple use of pattern matching and hashes. The program reads a file of text in which the words are separated by whitespace and some common kinds of punctuation such as commas, periods, semicolons, and so forth. The objective of the program is to produce a frequency table of the words found in the input file. A hash is an ideal way to build the word-frequency table. The keys can be the words, and the values can be the number of times they have appeared. The split operator provides a convenient way to split each line of the input file into its words. For each word, the program uses exists on the hash to determine whether the word has occurred before. If so, its count is incremented; if not, the word is entered into the hash with a count of 1.

```
# word_table.pl
#   Input: A file of text in which all words are separated by white-
#          space or punctuation, possibly followed by whitespace,
#          where the punctuation can be a comma, a semicolon, a
#          question mark an exclamation point, a period, or a colon.
#          The input file is specified on the command line
# Output: A list of all unique words in the input file,
#          in alphabetical order
#
#


# Main loop to get and process lines of input text

while (<>) {

# Split the line into words

    @line_words = split /[ .,;:!?]\s*/;

# Loop to count the words (either increment or initialize to 1)

    foreach $word (@line_words) {
        if (exists $freq{$word}) {
            $freq{$word}++;
        } else {
            $freq{$word} = 1;
        }
    }
}


# Display the words and their frequencies

print "\n Word \t\t Frequency \n\n";
foreach $word (sort keys %freq) {
    print " $word \t\t $freq{$word} \n";
}
```

Notice that the two normally special characters, . (period) and ? (question mark), are not backslashed in the pattern for split in this program. The reason is that, as mentioned previously, the normally special characters for patterns (metacharacters) are not special in character classes.

9.9.2 Remembering Matches

The part of the string that matched a part of the pattern can be saved in an implicit variable for later use. The part of the pattern whose match you want to save is placed in parentheses. The substring that matched the first parenthesized part of the pattern is saved in $1, the second in $2, and so forth. As an example, consider the following:

```
"4 July 1776" =~ /(\d+) (\w+) (\d+)/;
print "$2 $1, $3 \n";
```

This displays the following:

```
July 4, 1776
```

In some situations, it is convenient to be able to reference the parts of the string that preceded the match, the part that matched, or the part that followed the match. These three strings are available after a match through the implicit variables $`, $&, and $´, respectively.

9.9.3 Substitutions

Sometimes the substring of a string that matched a pattern must be replaced by another string. Perl's substitute operator is designed to do exactly that. The general form of the substitute operator is as follows:

s / *Pattern* / *New_String* /

Pattern is the same as the patterns used by the match operator. *New_String* is what is to replace the part of the string that matched the pattern. Consider the following example:

```
$_ = "It ain't going to rain no more, no more";
s/ain't/is not/;
```

This changes "ain't" to "is not".

The substitute operator can have two modifiers, g and i. The g modifier tells the substitute operator to find all matches in the given string and replace all of them:

```
$_ = "Rob, Robbie, and Robette were siblings";
s/Rob/Bob/g;
```

This changes the string to "Bob, Bobbie, and Bobette were siblings".

The i modifier can also be used with the substitute operator, as in this code:

```
$_ = "Is it Rose, rose, or ROSE?";
s/Rose/rose/ig;
```

This changes the string to "Is it rose, rose, or rose?".

All of the other details of Perl regular expressions can be found by typing the following:

```
perldoc perlre
```

9.9.4   The Transliterate Operator

Perl has a transliterate operator, tr, which translates a character or character class to another character or character class, respectively. For example, the following statement replaces all semicolons in $_ with colons:

```
tr/;/:/;
```

This particular operation can also be done with the substitute operator, as follows:

```
s/;/:/g;
```

The following statement transforms all uppercase letters in $_ to lowercase letters:

```
tr/A-Z/a-z/;
```

Specific characters can be deleted from a string by using a null substitution character. For example, this next statement deletes all commas and periods from the string in $_:

```
tr/\,\.//;
```

The transliterate operator can use the same binding operators that are used with the substitute operator.

9.10

FILE INPUT AND OUTPUT

Files are referenced through program variables called *filehandles*, whose names do not begin with special characters. To make them more readable, filehandles are often spelled using all uppercase letters. Filehandles are initialized with the open function, which opens a file for use and assigns the filehandle. The open function establishes the relationship between a filehandle and the file's external (operating system) name. Files can be opened for input or either of two kinds of output. The first parameter to open is the filehandle; the second specifies both the file's external name and how it will be used. The file's name is either a literal string or a string-valued expression. The file's usage is specified by appending one or two special characters to the beginning of the file's name. The most common of these are shown in Table 9.5.

TABLE 9.5 File Use Specifications

Character(s)	Meaning
<	Input (the default)
>	Output, starting at the beginning of the file
>>	Output, starting at the end of the existing data on the file
+>	Input from and output to the file

The > file use specification indicates the file is to be opened for output and writing is to begin at the file's beginning (overwriting any data currently written there). If the file does not exist, it is implicitly created. >> also indicates the files is to be opened for output, but the new data to be appended to the end of the file's current data. The +< file use specification is used when a file's data is to be read, processed, and rewritten to the same file, replacing the data that was read. As with <, if the file does not exist, it is an error.

Every file has an internal file pointer that points to the position in the file where the next read or write will take place. The > and < file use specifications initialize the file pointer to the beginning of the file. The >> file use specification initializes the file pointer to the end of the current data in the file. Because open can fail, it is often used with the die function, as in this example:

```
open(INDAT, "<temperatures") or
    die "Error — unable to open temperatures $!";
```

The predefined variable $! has the value of the system variable errno, which is useful for determining the reason open failed. Files are closed with the close function.

One line of text can be written to a file with the print function, using the file's filehandle as the first parameter, as shown here:

```
print OUTDAT "The result is: $result \n";
```

Notice that no comma appears between the filehandle and the string.

Lines of text can be read from a file using the line input operator, including the filehandle between the pointed brackets, as in this example:

```
$next_line = <INDAT>;
```

Multiple lines can be read from a file with the read function. Because of the overhead of starting a file read or write operation, large files are input most quickly by reading more than one line at a time. The general form of a call to read is as follows:

```
read(filehandle, buffer, length [, offset]);
```

The *offset* is optional, as indicated by the brackets. The *buffer* is a scalar variable into which the lines that have been read are placed. The *length* parameter is the number of bytes of input to be read. When included, the offset is the distance from the beginning of the buffer where the input is to go. When not included in the call to read, the offset is zero. The read function returns the number of bytes that it read and placed in the buffer. Newlines count in the read operation.

Suppose you have a file whose filehandle is ANIMALS and that has lines of 50 characters, not counting the newline. You could read five lines from this file with this statement:

```
$chars = read(ANIMALS, $buf, 255);
```

If $chars is less than 255 after this, there were not 255 characters left in the file.

The lines in the buffer can be separated into separate elements of an array with this statement:

```
@lines = split /\n/, $buf;
```

Some applications read a file, modify the data read from the file, and then rewrite the file with the modified data. The +> file use specification allows a file to be both read and written, but after the file has been read, its file pointer is left at the end of the data that has been read. To rewrite the file, its file pointer must be moved back to the file's beginning. This can be done with the seek function, which takes three parameters: the filehandle of the file, an offset, and a base position in the file. The possible base position values are 0, 1, or 2, specifying the beginning of the file, the current position of the file pointer in the file, or the end of the file, respectively. The offset is used to specify the number of bytes from the given base position. A positive value is an offset toward the end of the file (from the base position); a negative value is an offset in the direction of the beginning of the file. Most commonly, seek is used to rewind a file,[8] which sets the file pointer to the beginning of the file. This is specified with the following:

```
seek(filehandle, 0, 0);
```

When files are used to store data for CGI programs, they frequently need to be protected against corruption caused by multiple simultaneous writes. This is done with file locks, which are discussed and exemplified in Chapter 10.

9.11

AN EXAMPLE

The next sample program illustrates some of the features of Perl described in this chapter. The program reads employee records from a file and computes some statistics on the contents of the file. The precise specification for the program is included at its beginning as documentation.

```perl
# wages.pl - An example program to illustrate some of the
#              features of Perl
#   Input: A file of lines of employee data, where each line has
#          name:age:department code:salary
# Output: 1. The names of all employees whose names end with "son"
#         2. Percentage of employees under 40 years old
#         3. Average salary of employees under 40 years old
#         4. An alphabetical list of employees who are under 40
#            years old and who have salaries more than $40,000


# Open the data file and display a header for employees
#   whose names end in 'son'

open(EMPLOYEES, "employees.txt") || die "Can't open employees $!";
print "Names that end in 'son'\n\n";


# Loop to read and process the employee data

while (<EMPLOYEES>) {

# Increment the number of employees and chop off the newline
```

continued

---

8. Rewind is a holdover word from the days of magnetic tape. With magnetic tape, setting the file pointer to the beginning required the tape to be rewound.

```perl
    $total_employees++;
    chomp;

# Split the input line into its four parts


    ($name, $age, $dept, $salary) = split(/:/);

# If the name ends in 'son', print the name

    if ($name =~ /son$/) {
        print "$name \n";
    }

# If the employee is under 40, count him or her and add his or her
#   salary to the sum of such salaries

    if ($age < 40) {
        $under_40++;
        $salary_sum += $salary;

# If the salary was over 40,000, add the person and his or her
#   salary to the hash of such people

        if ($salary > 40000) {
            $sublist{$name} = $salary;
        }
    }
}

# If there was at least one employee, continue

if ($total_employees > 0) {

# If there was at least one under 40, continue

    if ($under_40 > 0) {

# Compute and display the % of employees under 40 and their
#   average salaries

        $percent = 100 * $under_40 / $total_employees;
        print "\nPercent of employees under 40 is: $percent \n";
        $avg = $salary_sum / $under_40;
        print "Average salary of employees under 40 is: $avg \n";
```

```
    # If there was at least one under 40 who earned a salary > 40,000,
    #  continue

            if (keys(%sublist)) {


# Sort and display the names of the employees under 40 with
#  with salaries > 40,000

                print "Sorted list of employees under 40",
                       " with salaries > \$40,000 \n";
                @sorted_names = sort (keys(%sublist));
                print "\nName \t\t Salary\n";
                foreach $name (@sorted_names) {
                    print "$name \t \$$sublist{$name} \n";
                }
            }
            else {
                print "There were no employees under 40 who earned";
                print "over $40,000 \n";
            }  #** of if (keys(%sublist))
        }
        else {
            print "There were no employees under 40 \n";
        }  #** of if ($under_40 > 0)
    }
    else {
        print "There were no employees\n";
    }  #** of if ($total_employees > 0)
```

9.12

SUMMARY

Perl began as a relatively small language that offered the capabilities of awk and sh, but it since has evolved to a full-blown programming language.

Perl's scalar values can be numbers, strings, or references. Numeric literals can be in either integer or floating-point form. Strings can be delimited by either single or double quotes. Variables that appear in double-quoted strings are interpolated into the string. The names of all scalar variables begin with dollar signs. Numeric expressions can use the usual complement of arithmetic operators.

There are only two string operators: catenation (.) and repetition (x). However, there is a large collection of functions and operators that perform the most commonly needed operations on strings. Assignment statement operators can be simple or compound, where the compound operators combine a binary operator with the assignment operator. Keyboard input is obtained with the line input operator using STDIN. Screen output is created with the print function.

Perl includes two sets of relational operators, one for numeric operands and one for string operands. If an operand of the wrong type appears on one of these, it is coerced to the proper type. Perl also includes two sets of Boolean operators, the only difference being the level of precedence of the two (&&, ||, and ! have higher precedence; and, or, and not have lower precedence). In all of the control constructs, the statements whose execution is to be controlled are specified by a block. The two selection statements are if and its complement unless. The two logically controlled loops are while and until. The for statement can also be used as a logically controlled loop but is usually used for counting loops. Perl has no case or switch statement.

An array is a variable that stores lists. A list literal is a parenthesized list of scalar expressions or values. The names of all arrays begin with at signs (@). Individual elements of arrays are referenced through subscripts, which are numeric-valued expressions delimited by brackets. Arrays, like scalars, need not be declared—that is, they are implicitly declared. The length of an array is determined by the highest subscript with which it has been assigned a value. The foreach statement provides a convenient way of processing all of the elements of an array. The shift, unshift, pop, and push operators provide simple ways of adding or removing an end element of an array.

A hash is an associative array, which is a data structure in which each element is actually a key/value pair. The values are the stored data; the keys are used to find specific data values. There are no hash literals, so list literals with alternating keys and values are used. A particular value element of a hash is referenced by the hash's name followed by the key's name, delimited by braces. Hash elements can be removed with the delete operator.

A reference variable stores the address of a variable or a literal. References to variables are created with the backslash operator appended to the beginning of the variable's name. A reference to a list literal is created by placing the list literal in brackets. A reference to a hash literal is created by placing the list of hash elements in braces. A reference can be dereferenced by appending a dollar sign to the beginning of its name. In the cases of arrays and hashes, the -> operator can also be used for dereferencing.

A function consists of the function header, which is the reserved word sub and the function's name, and a block that defines its actions. Local variables in functions are created with the my declaration. Function parameters are passed through the implicit array @_. To achieve pass-by-reference semantics, @_ can be directly manipulated in the function. To achieve pass-by-value semantics, the values in @_ are assigned to new local variables at the beginning of the function. Pass-by-reference semantics can also be achieved by passing references.

Perl has a powerful pattern matcher. Typically, the pattern is delimited by slashes and is matched against $_. The result of a pattern match is either true or false. String matches of subpatterns can be remembered in predefined variables by parenthesizing those subpatterns. The substitution operator is a powerful tool for modifying text. The transliteration operator is used to do literal translations of either characters or character classes.

Files are referenced through program variables called filehandles, which do not begin with any special characters. Files can be opened for input, output to the current end of the file, output to the beginning of the file, or input and output. These are specified with the open function, whose parameters are the filehandle and the file's external name as a string literal. Using a filehandle as the first parameter to print causes its output to go to that file. A single line from a file can be read using the line input operator with the filehandle. The read function can be used to read multiple lines from a file.

9.13 Review Questions

1. What are the three categories of Perl variables?

2. How many numeric data types does Perl have?

3. What is the purpose of the qq operator?

4. In what two ways do single-quoted string literals differ from double-quoted string literals?

5. What is the numeric value of undef?

6. Describe the operands and the actions of the x string operator.

7. Describe the parameters and actions of the chomp function.

8. Describe the parameters and actions of the join function.

9. What is a filehandle?

10. Under what conditions is a string used in a Boolean context considered to be true?

11. Why does Perl have two sets of relational operators?

12. What is the difference between Perl's two sets of Boolean operators?

13. What exactly does the expression <STDIN> do when executed?

14. In what three fundamental ways do Perl arrays differ from the arrays of other common high-level programming languages?

15. If an array's name appears in scalar context, what is its value?

16. What two predefined Perl functions can be used to implement a queue in an array?

17. What are the two fundamental ways in which hashes differ from arrays?

18. What statement adds the element (joe, 42) to the hash %guys?

19. How do you get the address of the scalar variable $fruit?

20. How do you get the address of a list literal?

21. What is a function declaration?

22. How do you create local variables in a function?

23. What are actual parameters? What are formal parameters?

24. What are the two ways a value can be returned from a function?

25. How does the `i` modifier change pattern matching?

26. Describe the two parameters for the substitute operator.

27. Describe the transliterate operator.

28. Describe the four file use specifications.

29. Under what circumstances is the `read` function used?

30. What is a file pointer?

31. What is one common use of the `seek` function?

9.14 Exercises

1. Write, test, and debug (if necessary) Perl programs for the following specifications.

   Input: Three numbers, a, b, and c, each on its own line, from the keyboard.

   Output: The value of the expression `10ab-((c-1)/17.44)`.

2. *Input:* A text file, specified on the command line, in which each line contains one number.

   Output: The second smallest number in the file, along with its position in the file, with 1 being the position of the first number.

3. *Input:* Three names, on separate lines, from the keyboard.

   Output: The input names in alphabetical order, without using arrays.

4. *Input:* A file of lines of text, specified on the command line.

   Output: Every input line that has more than 10 characters (not counting the newline) but fewer than 20 characters (not counting the newline) that contains the string `"ed"`.

5. *Input:* A list of numbers in a file specified on the command line.

   Output: Two lists of numbers, one with input numbers that are greater than zero, and one with those that are less than zero (ignore the zero-valued numbers).

   Method: You must first build two arrays with the required output numbers before you display any of them.

6. *Input:* A file that contains English words, where each word is separated from the next word on a line by one space, specified on the command line.

   Output: A table, in which the first column has the unique words from the input file and the second column has the number of times the word appeared in the file. No word can appear twice in the table.

   Method: Your program must use two arrays to store the table, one for the words and one for the frequency values.

7. *Input:* A file in which each line contains a string of the form `name+sales`, where in some cases the sales will be absent (but not the plus sign), specified on the command line.

   Output: A list of the names and sales numbers that remain after the following processing:

   a. Names with sales numbers are added to a hash when they are first found, along with their sales numbers.

   b. Names with absent sales numbers are deleted from the hash if they are already there.

   c. When a name appears that is already in the hash, the new sales number is added to the old sales number (the one already in the hash).

8. *Input:* A file specified on the command line that contains text.

   Output: The input text after the following modifications have been made:

   a. All multiple spaces are reduced to single spaces.

   b. All occurrences of `Darcy` are replaced with `Darcie`.

   c. All lines that begin with ~ are deleted.

   d. All occurrences of `1998` are replaced with `1999`.

9. *Input:* A file specified on the command line that contains a C program.

   Output: For each line of the input:

   a. The number of words (variables and reserved words) on the line.

   b. The number of numeric literals without decimal points on the line.

   c. The number of numeric literals with decimal points on the line.

   d. The number of braces and parentheses on the line.

   Write functions for the specifications in Exercises 10 to 12.

10. *Parameter:* An array of strings, passed by value.

    Return value: A list of the unique strings in the parameter array.

11. *Parameter:* An array of numbers.

    Return value: The average and median of the parameter array.

12. *Parameter:* A reference to an array of strings.

    Return value: A list of the unique strings in the parameter array.

Using Perl for CGI Programming

This chapter introduces the Common Gateway Interface (CGI) and discusses using Perl for CGI programming. It begins with an overview of CGI, explaining how CGI programs are linked to Web documents and how results are returned to clients from CGI programs. Next, the format of query strings is described. Then it discusses the CGI.pm module, which provides a simple and efficient way to write CGI programs in Perl. A CGI program to process a product order form is then presented. This is followed by another complete example, including the XHTML code to describe a survey form and the two CGI programs that are used to provide the processing required for the form. The chapter closes with an introduction to cookies and how they are created and used in Perl CGI programs.

10.1

THE COMMON GATEWAY INTERFACE

XHTML is a markup language and, as such, cannot by itself describe computations, allow interaction with the user, or provide access to a database. Yet these are things that are commonly needed in Web-based systems. Computations are required to provide support for all kinds of Web commerce. The Web also is now a common way to access databases—for example, for making reservations for transportation services. Such applications obviously require interaction with clients. One early response to these needs was to develop a technique for a browser to access the software resources of the server machine. Using this approach, a browser can run programs indirectly on the server, including database access systems for the databases that reside on the server. These server-based programs communicate back to the client through HTTP. The protocol that is used between a browser and software on the server is called the *Common Gateway Interface*.

Before further discussing CGI, it is useful to take a brief look at its alternatives. There are now several popular approaches to providing server-side computation, including support for dynamic documents. As just discussed, the first of these uses the CGI to run software on the server that is completely separate from markup documents. CGI is part of a general approach that is often called LAMP, which is an acronym for Linux, Apache, and MySQL. The 'P' part of the acronym is generic—it represents one of the server-side programming and/ or scripting languages, Perl, PHP, or Python. This chapter discusses using Perl and CGI. Chapter 12, "Introduction to PHP," discusses using PHP as an XHTML-embedded, server-side scripting language. This book does not cover Python, another scripting language. MySQL, a database management system, as used in conjunction with Perl, Java, and PHP in Web database access systems, is discussed in Chapter 14, "Database Access through the Web."

A second approach to providing server-side computation and dynamic documents is Microsoft's product, ASP. The latest incarnation of ASP is ASP.NET, an important part of the .NET computing platform. ASP.NET documents are mixtures of XHTML markup and either programming language code or references to external programs. These documents are compiled into classes in which the XHTML code is replaced by output statements that produce that XHTML code. ASP.NET documents can use any of the .NET programming languages. ASP.NET is discussed in Chapter 13, "Introduction to ASP.NET."

Yet another approach to providing server-side computation and dynamic documents is Java servlets and Java Server Pages (JSP). Servlets are Java classes with close connections to XHTML documents, which allow them to conveniently interact with Web clients. JSP is similar to ASP.NET in that programming code can be embedded in markup documents and programs can be referenced in documents to provide computational support. The primary difference between JSP and ASP.NET is that JSP restricts the developer to Java rather than a range of programming and scripting languages. JSP documents are converted to Java servlets before they are compiled. Both servlets and JSP are discussed in Chapter 11, "Servlets and Java Server Pages."

Now we can return to CGI. An HTTP request to run a CGI program is like any other HTTP request except that the requested file can be identified by the server as being a CGI program. Servers can identify CGI programs by their addresses on the server or by their filename extensions. When a server receives a request for a CGI program, it does not return the file—it executes the program in the file and returns that program's output.

A CGI program can produce results in a number of different forms. Most often, an XHTML document is returned, although the program may produce only the URL of an existing document. When a new document is generated, it consists of two parts: an HTTP header and a body. The header must be complete if the response is going directly to the client. It can be partial if the response is going to the client through the server, which completes the header. This is the usual process. The form of the body, which is specified in the header, can be XHTML, plain text, or even an image or audio file.

One common way for a browser user to interact with a Web server is through forms. A form is presented to the user, who is invited to fill in the text boxes and click the buttons of the form. The user submits the form to the server by clicking its Submit button. The contents of the form are encoded and transmitted to the server. The server must use a program to decode the transmitted form contents, perform whatever computation is necessary on the form data, and produce its output. Figure 10.1 shows the communications configuration for CGI.

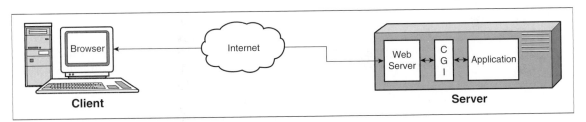

FIGURE 10.1 Communications and computation using CGI

Both CGI programs and client-side scripts, such as JavaScript, support dynamic documents. However, client-side scripts cannot access files and databases on the server.

10.2

CGI LINKAGE

This section describes how the connection between an XHTML document being displayed by a browser and a CGI program on the server is established.

CGI programs often reside in one specific directory on the server, `cgi-bin`, which is usually a subdirectory of `public_html`[1]. However, the Web server administrator can choose a different directory name and place for CGI programs. The only requirement is that the CGI programmer knows the location of CGI programs. The examples in this chapter assume that CGI programs are stored in a directory named `cgi-bin`, which is a subdirectory of the directory in which XHTML documents are stored.

A server can be configured to recognize the requested file as being a program by the extension on the file's name. For example, if the extension on the requested file's name is `.pl`, that could indicate that it is a Perl CGI program. Another extension that indicates the file is a Perl program is `.cgi`. Because CGI programs are invoked by the server, their access protection code must be set to allow this.

If a CGI program has been compiled and is in machine code, the server can invoke it directly. However, the compiled versions of Perl programs normally are not saved and are not in machine code anyway, so the `perl` system must be invoked on every Perl CGI program.[2] For UNIX-based Web servers, this can be done by adding a special line to the beginning of the program that specifies that `perl` must be run, using the remainder of the program file as input data to `perl`. This special line also must specify the location of `perl`. On UNIX systems, `perl` is often stored in `/usr/local/bin`. If so, this line is as follows:

```
#!/usr/local/bin/perl -w
```

The `#!` specifies that the program whose location follows must be executed on the rest of the file. And, of course, `/usr/local/bin/perl` is the path to the `perl` system. If `perl` resides in some other directory, that directory's name is used in place of `/usr/local/bin`. Because `!` is called "bang" in the UNIX world, the `#!` line is often called "shebang."

Windows-based Web servers do not require the shebang line in Perl CGI programs.

An XHTML document can specify a call to a CGI program using an anchor tag (`<a>`), which must include a hypertext reference attribute (`href`). In this case, a CGI program call is similar to a link to an XHTML document. The

---

1. `public_html` is the directory in which the publicly accessible XHTML document files are stored.

2. Systems are available that produce and save compiled versions of Perl programs for use on Web servers. For example, look at `http://perl.apache.org/list/mod_perl.html`.

value of `href` must be the complete URL of the CGI program's filename. Consider the following anchor tag:

```
<a href = "./cgi-bin/reply.cgi">
Click here to run the CGI program reply.cgi
</a>
```

The content of the anchor tag specifies the actual link in the XHTML. In this example, `cgi-bin`, which is a subdirectory of where the calling XHTML docment is stored, is the directory where CGI programs are stored, and `reply.cgi` is the name of the CGI program. Some educational institutions now use a system called CGI Wrap to allow students to run CGI programs in a relatively secure environment This system allows the CGI program to be in the student's directory rather than on the server system. For CGI Wrap, Perl CGI programs must use the `.cgi` extention to their filenames.

The most common application of CGI programs is form processing, so most CGI programs are not called from XHTML documents with anchor tags. Rather, they are called as a side effect of Submit button clicks, with the CGI program being specified on the action attribute of the form tag. This is exemplified in Section 10.4.2.

The following document calls a trivial Perl CGI program through its anchor tag.

```
<?xml version = "1.0" encoding = "utf-8"?>
<!DOCTYPE html PUBLIC "-//w3c//DTD XHTML 1.1//EN"
 "http://www.w3.org/TR/xhtml11/DTD/xhtml11.dtd">

<!-- reply.html
     A trivial document to call a simple Perl CGI program
     -->
<html xmlns = "http://www.w3.org/1999/xhtml">
  <head>
    <title> XHTML to call the Perl CGI program, reply.cgi
    </title>
  </head>
  <body>
    <p>
      This is our first Perl CGI example
      <br /><br />
      <a href = "./cgi-bin/reply.cgi">
      Click here to run the CGI program, reply.cgi
      </a>
    </p>
  </body>
</html>
```

We have implied that the CGI program is always on the server that sent the XHTML document to the browser. However, the `href` attribute can be assigned the URL of any CGI program on any Web server on the Internet.

The obvious next step is to describe the CGI program, `reply.cgi`, which simply returns a greeting to the browser (through the server). The connection from a CGI program to the client is through standard output. Therefore, anything the CGI program sends to standard output is sent to the server, which sends it on to the client. In a Perl CGI program, this means that the `print` function is used to communicate to the client.

As stated earlier, the HTTP response to the client can be in a variety of different forms, but it must begin with the HTTP header. The CGI program often supplies only the first line of the header; the remainder is added by the server before the response document is sent to the client. The first line of the header specifies the form of the response as a MIME content type. In this book, we consider only XHTML as the response content type, which is specified with `text/html`.

The line following the one-line header *must* always be blank. The blank line indicates the end of the HTTP header. Therefore, the first output from all Perl CGI programs that return partial headers and XHTML response bodies is generated with this statement:

```
print "Content-type: text/html \n\n";
```

Since the output of a CGI program is ultimately for the browser, it must be in the form of an HTML (or XHTML) document. Such a document is created in Perl by using `print` statements to output the XHTML text.

If the only task of a CGI program is to send one line of information, most of the program will be used to generate the required tags for the XHTML file. The following is the Perl program `reply.cgi`:

```
#!/usr/local/bin/perl -w

# reply.cgi
# This CGI program returns a greeting to the client

print "Content-type: text/html \n\n",
  "<?xml version = '1.0' encoding = 'utf-8'?> \n",
  "<!DOCTYPE html PUBLIC '-//w3c//DTD XHTML 1.1//EN'\n",
  "'http://www.w3.org/TR/xhtml11/DTD/xhtml11.dtd'>\n",
  "<html xmlns = 'http://www.w3.org/1999/xhtml'>\n",
  "<head><title> reply.cgi example </title></head>\n",
  "<body>\n",
  "<h1> Greetings from your Web server! </h1>\n",
  "</body></html>";
```

10.3

QUERY STRING FORMAT

HTTP requests made by the GET and POST methods transmit the data associated with the request to the Web server. This data is in the form of a character string called a *query string*. This section describes the format of a query string.

Query strings can be hand-written and used directly with GET and/or POST HTTP methods. However, the great majority of query strings are those that code form data and are constructed by the browser when the Submit button of the form is clicked. The following paragraphs describe query strings in terms of form data.

For each element (widget) in the form that has a value, the widget's name and that value are coded as a character string of the form *name=value* and included in the query string. A widget's value is always a character string. For example, if the value of a radio button named `payment` is `discover`, it is coded in the query string as follows:

```
payment=discover
```

If the form has more than one widget, their name/value pairs are separated by ampersands (`&`):

```
caramel=7&payment=discover
```

If there are special characters in the value of a widget, they are coded as a percent sign (`%`) followed by a two-character hexadecimal number that is the ASCII code for that character.[3] For example, the hexadecimal ASCII code for the exclamation point (`!`) is `21`, so that character is coded as `%21`. Likewise, because the hexadecimal ASCII code for a space is `20`, spaces are coded as `%20`. Suppose we had a form whose only widgets were a radio button collection named `payment` whose value was `visa` and a text widget whose name was `saying` and whose value was `"Eat your fruit!"`. The query string for this form would be as follows:

```
payment=visa&saying=Eat%20your%20fruit%21
```

Some browsers replace spaces in form data values with plus signs (`+`). For these, the previous example would be coded as follows:

```
payment=visa&saying=Eat+your+fruit%21
```

---

3. When the **GET** method is used, the query string becomes part of a URL, in which certain special characters can cause problems.

Recall from Chapter 2, "Introduction to XHTML," that the method attribute of <form> specifies one of the two techniques, get or post, used to pass the form data to the server. get is the default, so if no method attribute is given in the <form> tag, get will be used. The alternative technique is post. In both techniques, the form data is coded into a query string when the user clicks the Submit button. When the get method is used, the browser attaches the query string to the URL of the CGI program, so the data is transmitted to the server with the URL. The browser inserts a question mark at the end of the actual URL just before the first character of the query string so that the server can easily find the beginning of the query string. The server removes the query string from the URL and places it in the environment variable QUERY_STRING, where it can be accessed by the CGI program. The get method can also be used to pass parameters to the server when forms are not involved (this cannot be done with post). The main disadvantage of the get method is that some servers place a limit on the length of the URL string and truncate any characters past the limit. So, if the form has more than a few widgets, get is not a good choice.

The following is an example of a URL with a query string:

```
http://cs.ucp.edu/cgi-bin/rws/test.cgi?sender=bob&day=2
```

When the post method is used, the query string is passed through standard input to the CGI program so that the CGI program can simply read the string. The length of the query string is passed through the environment variable CONTENT_LENGTH. There is no length limitation for the query string with the post method, so it is obviously the better choice when there are more than a few widgets in the form.

The following code, as part of a CGI program that handles GET or POST requests, fetches the query string and places it is $query_string, regardless of which method was used.

```perl
$request_method = $ENV{'REQUEST_METHOD'};
if ($request_method eq "GET") {
    $query_string = $ENV{'QUERY_STRING'};
}
elsif ($request_method eq "POST") {
    read(STDIN, $query_string, $ENV{'CONTENT_LENGTH'})
}
else {
    print "Error - the request method is illegal \n";
    exit(1);
}
```

Notice that although the value of the method attribute of the form element in XHTML must be lowercase, when that value is stored in the REQUEST_METHOD environment variable, it is in uppercase.

10.4

THE CGI.pm MODULE

Much of what a CGI program must do is routine—that is, it is nearly the same for all CGI programs. Among these common tasks are creating the required tags, such as `<html>` and `</html>`, and creating form elements such as buttons and lists. Therefore, it is natural to have standard routines to do these things. CGI.pm, which was developed by Lincoln Stein, is a Perl module of functions for these common tasks.[4] The CGI.pm module is part of the standard Perl distribution. Its documentation can be obtained with the following command:

```
perldoc CGI
```

A Perl program specifies that it needs access to a particular module with the use declaration. In the case of CGI.pm, only a part of the module is usually needed. The part we need here, which is the most often used part, is named `:standard`. The following declaration provides access to this collection of resources from CGI.pm:

```
use CGI ":standard";
```

10.4.1   Common CGI.pm Functions

Many of the functions in CGI.pm produce XHTML tags. In these cases, the functions have the names of their associated XHTML tags. These functions are called *shortcuts*. Shortcut functions produce their tags by using the parameters passed to them for the attributes and content of the tag. They may also generate embedded tags. If there are no attributes and no embedded tags, the only parameter is the content of the tag. A shortcut function that takes no parameters may be called without the parentheses. For example, the following call to `br`

```
br;
```

returns

```
<br/>
```

Note that the shortcut functions do not produce any output—they simply return strings. So, to get a break in the output, use the following:

```
print br;
```

---

4. A Perl module can be thought of as a library of Perl functions.

A shortcut function may take several different kinds of parameters, including a scalar literal or variable, a reference to a hash, or a reference to an array or list. When there is just one parameter, the CGI function call has the same form as that for any other Perl function. For example, in the following call, the only parameter is the content of the tag:

```
print h1("This is the real stuff");
```

This produces the following:

```
<h1> This is the real stuff </h1>
```

CGI programs sometimes create and send forms back to the client to gather information. In the following paragraphs, we use some examples of CGI.pm functions that produce widgets. Tags can have both content and attributes. In the previous example of the h1 function, the parameter becomes the content of <h1>. Each attribute of a tag is passed in the name/value pair form that is used in a hash literal, where the name and value are separated by =>. The name of the attribute is the key in the pair, and the attribute value is its value. The attribute names are preceded by minus signs. For example, consider this call to textarea:

```
print textarea(-name => "Description",
               -rows => "2",
               -cols => "35"
);
```

This produces the following:

```
<textarea name="Description" rows=2 cols=35> </textarea>
```

Note that although we passed quoted numeric literals as actual parameters, the textarea function produced unquoted attribute values for them. We expect that this soon will be changed to conform to the XHTML standard, which requires all attribute values to be quoted.

If both attributes and content are passed to a shortcut function, the attributes are specified in a hash literal, which must be the first parameter. For example, the statement

```
print a({-href => "fruit.html"},
     Press here for fruit descriptions");
```

generates

```
<a href="fruit.html"> Press here for fruit descriptions </a>
```

One convenient characteristic of the shortcut functions is that the tags and their attributes are distributed over the parameters to the function. For example, consider this call:

```
print ol(li({-type => "square"},
        ["milk", "bread", "cheese"]));
```

Notice that a reference to the literal array, ("milk", "bread", "cheese"), is passed as a parameter to li. In this example, the li tag and its attribute are distributed over the list items. This produces the following:[5]

```
<ol>
    <li type="square" milk</li>
    <li type="square" bread</li>
    <li type="square" cheese</li>
</ol>
```

As another example, consider the following call to radio_group, in which the collection name is specified just once, and the values can be specified as a reference to an array:

```
print radio_group(-name => 'colors',
            -value => ['blue', 'green', 'yellow', 'red'],
            -default => 'blue');
```

This produces the following:

```
<input type="radio" name="colors" value="blue" checked /> blue
<input type="radio" name="colors" value="green" /> green
<input type="radio" name="colors" value="yellow" /> yellow
<input type="radio" name="colors" value="red" /> red
```

The CGI.pm functions that are not shortcuts often produce the boilerplate that is part of every XHTML document. The first thing most CGI programs must do is produce the content type line. The header function does precisely this. Specifically,

```
print header;
```

---

5. Actually, the produced XHTML is returned as a single string.

creates

```
Content-type: text/html;charset=ISO-8859-1
-- blank line --
```

Notice that CGI.pm includes the charset value ISO-8859-1 in the output of header. We do not include charset in the HTTP headers of our non-CGI.pm examples because it is the default character set. If the content type is not text/html, the alternative content type can be specified as the parameter to header.

The next required XHTML output of a CGI program is the head part of the document. This is generated by the start_html function, whose parameter specifies the title of the document. For example, the call

```
print start_html("Paul's Gardening Supplies");
```

produces

```
<?xml version="1.0" encoding="utf-8"?>
DOCTYPE html
    PUBLIC "-//W3C//DTD XHTML Basic 1.0 //EN"
    "http://www.w3.org/TR/xhtml-basic/xhtml-basic10.dtd">
<html xmlns="http://www.w3.org/1999/xhtml" lang="en-US">
<head><title> Paul's Gardening Supplies </title></head>
<body>
```

Section 10.3 describes the format of the query string. Any form-processing program must first extract the form data from the query string. This means it must be split into its name/value pairs, which then must be split to access the values. Any characters coded as hexadecimal ASCII must be decoded, and any plus signs must be replaced by spaces. The whole process of decoding the query string and setting local variables to the values in the query string can be done by calls to the CGI.pm function, param. For example, if the query string is

```
name=Bob%20Brumbel&payment=visa
```

then the following statement sets $name to "Bob Brumbel":

```
my $name = param("name")
```

So, for the whole query string, the following statement could be used:

```
my($name, $payment) = (param("name"), param("payment"));
```

This sets the local variables $name and $payment to the values of the form values for "name" and "payment" ("Bob Brumbel" and "visa", respectively).

The last XHTML code required in a document is generated with `end_html`, which produces `</body>` `</html>`.

The `CGI.pm` functions for creating XHTML tables are discussed in Section 10.5.

10.4.2   A Complete Form Example

The following XHTML code describes a form for taking sales orders for popcorn. Three text widgets are used at the top of the form to collect the buyer's name and address. These are placed in a borderless table to force the text boxes to align vertically. A second table is used to collect the actual order. Each row of this table names a product with the content of a `<td>` tag, displays the price with another `<td>` tag, and uses a text widget with `size` set to 2 to collect the quantity ordered. The payment method is input by the user through one of four radio buttons. Recall that this form also appears in Chapter 2.

```
<?xml version = "1.0" encoding = "utf-8"?>
<!DOCTYPE html PUBLIC "-//w3c//DTD XHTML 1.1//EN"
  "http://www.w3.org/TR/xhtml11/DTD/xhtml11.dtd">


<!-- popcorn.html
     This describes popcorn sales form page>
     -->
<html xmlns = "http://www.w3.org/1999/xhtml">
  <head> <title> Popcorn Sales Form </title>
  </head>
  <body>
    <h2> Welcome to Millenium Gynmastics Booster Club Popcorn
       Sales
    </h2>

<!-- The next line gives the address of the CGI program -->

    <form action = "./cgi-bin/popcorn.cgi"
         method = "post">
      <table>

<!-- Text widgets for name and address -->

       <tr>
         <td> Buyer's Name: </td>
         <td> <input type = "text" name = "name" size = "30">
         </td>
       </tr>
```

continued

```
            <tr>
              <td> Street Address: </td>
              <td> <input type = "text" name = "street" size = "30">
              </td>
            </tr>
            <tr>
              <td> City, State, Zip: </td>
              <td> <input type = "text" name = "city" size = "30">
              </td>
            </tr>
          </table>
          <br />

          <table border = "border">

<!-- First, the column headings -->

            <tr>
              <th> Product Name </th>
              <th> Price </th>
              <th> Quantity </th>
            </tr>

<!-- Now, the table data entries -->

            <tr>
              <td> Unpopped Popcorn (1 lb.) </td>
              <td> $3.00 </td>
              <td> <input type = "text" name = "unpop" size ="2">
              </td>
            </tr>
            <tr>
              <td> Caramel Popcorn (2 lb. cannister) </td>
              <td> $3.50 </td>
              <td> <input type = "text" name = "caramel" size = "2">
              </td>
            </tr>
            <tr>
              <td> Caramel Nut Popcorn (2 lb. cannister) </td>
              <td> $4.50 </td>
              <td> <input type = "text" name = "caramelnut" size = "2">
              </td>
            </tr>
```

```
      <tr>
        <td> Toffey Nut Popcorn (2 lb. cannister) </td>
        <td> $5.00 </td>
        <td> <input type = "text" name = "toffeynut" size = "2">
        </td>
      </tr>

    </table>
    <br />

<!-- The radio buttons for the payment method -->

    <h3> Payment Method: </h3>
    <p>
      <input type = "radio" name = "payment" value = "visa"
             checked = "checked" /> Visa <br />
      <input type = "radio" name = "payment" value = "mc"
        />
        Master Card <br />
      <input type = "radio" name = "payment" value = "discover"
        />
        Discover <br />
      <input type = "radio" name = "payment" value = "check" />
        Check <br />
    </p>

<!-- The submit and reset buttons -->

    <p>
      <input type = "submit" value = "Submit Order" />
      <input type = "reset" value = "Clear Order Form" />
    </p>
  </form>
  </body>
</html>
```

Figure 10.2 shows a browser display of popcorn.html. Figure 10.3 shows an example of this form after it has been filled out.

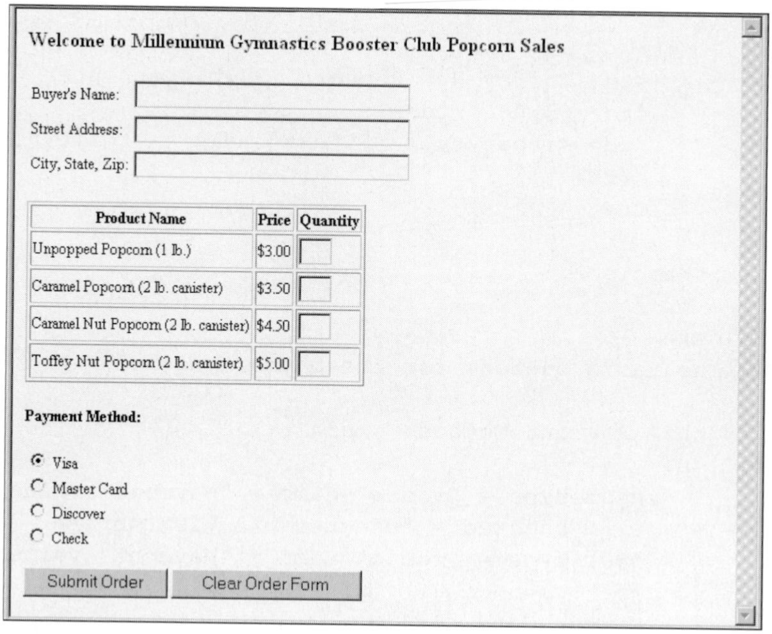

FIGURE 10.2 Display of `popcorn.html`

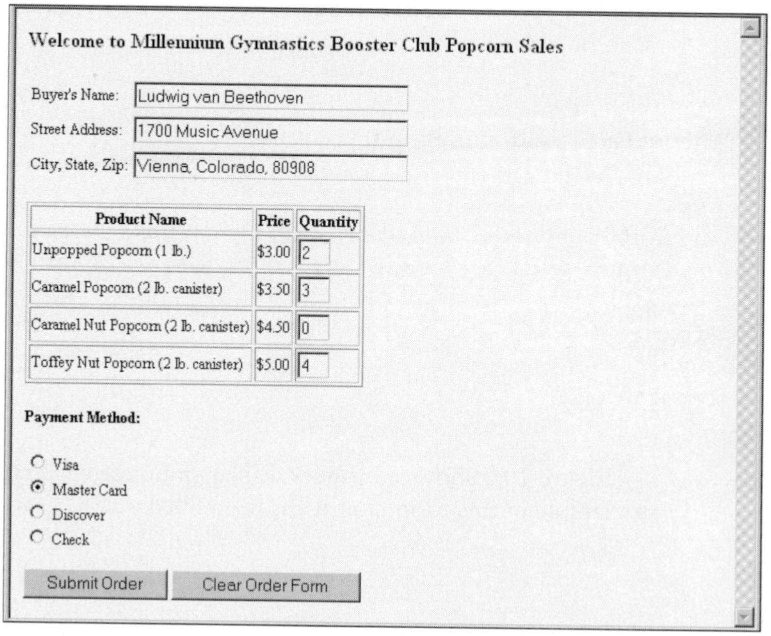

FIGURE 10.3 Display of `popcorn.html` with the form filled out

We now can consider the CGI program that will process the data from the popcorn order form. The program must compute the costs of the ordered items, determine the total sale amount, and send them back to the user as an XHTML document. The program must determine what was ordered and compute its cost. For the item orders, the program must use the values to compute the total price and total number of items in the order. Finally, this program must build the XHTML code to reply to the user who placed the order. The complete program, called `popcorn.cgi`, follows:

```perl
#!/usr/local/bin/perl

# popcorn.cgi
# A CGI program to process the popcorn sales form

use CGI ":standard";

# Initialize total price and total number of purchased items


$total_price = 0;
$total_itemi = 0;

# Produce the header part of the HTML return value

print header;
print start_html("CGI-Perl Popcorn Sales Form, using CGI.pm");

# Set local variables to the parameter values

my($name, $street, $city, $payment) =
      (param("name"), param("street"),
       param("city"), param("payment"));
my($unpop, $caramel, $caramelnut, $toffeynut) = (param("unpop"),
       param("caramel"), param("caramelnut"),
       param("toffeynut"));


# Compute the number of items ordered and the total cost

$total_price = 3.0 * $unpop + 3.5 * $caramel + 4.5 * $caramelnut +
               5.0 * $toffeynut;
$total_items = $unpop + $caramel + $caramelnut + $toffeynut;
```

continued

```
# Produce the result information for the browser and
#  finish the page

print h3("Customer:"), "\n";
print "$name<br/>\n", "$street <br/>\n", "$city <br/><br/>\n";
print "<b>Payment method:</b> $payment <br/><br/>\n";
print h3("Items ordered:"), "\n";
if ($unpop > 0) {print "Unpopped popcorn: $unpop <br/>\n";}
if ($caramel > 0) {print "Caramel popcorn: $caramel <br/>\n";}
if ($caramelnut > 0)
   {print "Caramel nut popcorn: $caramelnut <br/>\n";}
if ($toffeynut > 0)
   {print "Toffey nut popcorn: $toffeynut <br/>\n";}
print "Thank you for your order <br/><br/>\n";
print "<b>Your total bill is:</b> \$ $total_price <br/> \n";
print end_html;
```

Figure 10.4 shows the results of running popcorn.cgi on the filled-out form shown in Figure 10.3.

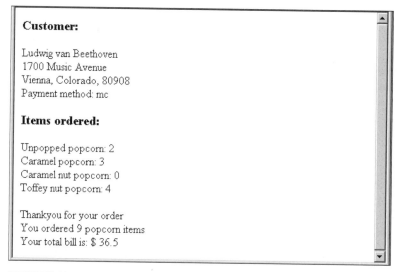

FIGURE 10.4 Output of popcorn.cgi

10.5

A SURVEY EXAMPLE

It is common for a Web document to conduct a survey of the opinions or choices of the people who visit the document. The document to gather the information is similar to the popcorn sales example. The most important difference in the CGI program that processes the inputs for a survey is that the data must be stored between visits. The obvious place to store such data is on the disk on the server. The simplest place to put this file is in the directory where CGI programs reside. We use a file in this example because of the simplicity of the data that needs to be stored. However, it many cases a database would be a better choice.

For this example, we use two CGI programs: one to process a client's response to the survey form and one to produce the latest totals from the survey.

One of the complications with this application is that more than one user may submit survey forms at the same time, which could lead to corruption of the data. For example, suppose two clients simultaneously request executions of a CGI program that reads a number from a file, increments the number, and rewrites the file. Consider the following scenario: The initial value in the file is 27. Two browsers simultaneously call the CGI program. The three steps of the CGI program (read the file, increment the value from the file, rewrite the file) can become interleaved. One possible sequence of these steps is as follows. (We name the two browser's executions of the CGI program CGI1 and CGI2.)

1. CGI1 reads the file into its variable, `counter` (value is 27).
2. CGI2 reads the file into its variable, `counter` (value is 27).
3. CGI1 increments its `counter` to 28.
4. CGI1 rewrites the file, which now has 28.
5. CGI2 increments its `counter` to 28.
6. CGI2 rewrites the file, which still has 28.

So, although the file now should have 29, it has 28.

Such multiple simultaneous accesses can be prevented by requiring the programs that access the file to lock the file before accessing it and unlock it when they are finished.[6] The Perl function `flock` can be used to both lock and unlock the file. `flock` takes two parameters: the filehandle of the file to be locked or unlocked, and the specified process (lock or unlock).

---

6. Locking the file means that all other accesses to it are temporarily blocked. Unlocking it makes it available to other accesses.

Actually, locking the file with `flock` does not block all accesses to the file; rather, it prevents any other process from acquiring the file's lock. So, it effectively blocks other processes from accessing the file only if they first attempt to lock the file. We assume for our example that no other process will attempt to use the file, so this works.

The values for the parameter to `flock` are defined in the Perl `Fcntl` module, which is made accessible with the following:

```
use Fcntl qw(:DEFAULT :flock);
```

Because closing a file implicitly unlocks it, we only need the parameter value for a write lock, which is `LOCK_EX`. The following example illustrates the process of updating a file using locking:

```
use Fcntl qw(:DEFAULT :flock);
open(TAX_DATA, "+<taxdata") or
    die "TAX_DATA could not be opened";
flock(TAX_DATA, LOCK_EX) or
    die "TAX_DATA could not be locked";
chomp($tax = <TAX_DATA>);
# update $tax
# Rewind the file so the write goes to its beginning
seek(TAX_DATA, 0, 0) or
    die "TAX_DATA could not be rewound";
print TAX_DATA $tax or
    die "TAX_DATA could not be rewritten";
close TAX_DATA or die "TAX_DATA could not be closed";
```

The survey form collects votes on what consumer electronics device the client is most likely to purchase in the next six months. The form will also collect information on the age and gender of the client. A visitor to the document can vote, see the current voting results, or both. So the document needs two links, one to the CGI program that records a vote and one that produces a table of current results. The survey document is described by the following code:

```
<?xml version = "1.0" encoding = "utf-8"?>
<!DOCTYPE html PUBLIC "-//w3c//DTD XHTML 1.1//EN"
 "http://www.w3.org/TR/xhtml11/DTD/xhtml11.dtd">

<!-- conelec.html
     A document to present the user with a consumer electronics
     purchasing survey form -->
```

```
<html xmlns = "http://www.w3.org/1999/xhtml">
  <head>
    <title> Consumer Electronics Purchasing Survey </title>
  </head>
  <body>
    <form action = "./cgi-bin/conelec1.cgi" method = "post">
      <h2> Welcome to the Consumer Electronics Purchasing Survey
      </h2>
      <p />

      <h4> Your Age Category: </h4>
      <p>
        <input type = "radio" name = "age" value = "0"
               checked = "checked" /> 10-25 <br/>
        <input type = "radio" name = "age" value = "1"/>
          26-40 <br/>
        <input type = "radio" name = "age" value = "2"/>
          41-60 <br/>
        <input type = "radio" name = "age" value = "3"/>
          Over 60 <br /> <br />
      </p>
      <h4> Your Gender: </h4>
      <p>
        <input type = "radio" name = "gender" value = "0"
               checked = "checked" /> Female <br/>
        <input type = "radio" name = "gender" value = "4"/>
          Male <br /> <br />
      </p>
      <h4> Your Next Consumer Electronics Purchase will be: </h4>
      <p>
        <input type = "radio" name = "vote" value = "0"/>
          Conventional TV <br />
        <input type = "radio" name = "vote" value = "1"/>
          HDTV <br />
        <input type = "radio" name = "vote" value = "2"/>
          VCR <br />
        <input type = "radio" name = "vote" value = "3"/>
          CD player <br />
        <input type = "radio" name = "vote" value = "4"/>
          Mini CD player/recorder <br />
        <input type = "radio" name = "vote" value = "5"/>
          DVD player <br/>
        <input type = "radio" name = "vote" value = "6"
               checked = "checked" /> Other <br /> <br/>
```

continued

```
                <input type = "submit" value = "Submit Order" />
                <input type = "reset" value = "Clear Order Form"/>
          </p>
      </form>

      <hr/>
      <p>
        To see the results of the survey so far, click
          <a href = "./cgi-bin/conelec2.cgi"> here </a>
      </p>
    </body>
</html>
```

Figure 10.5 shows the display of `conelec.html`.

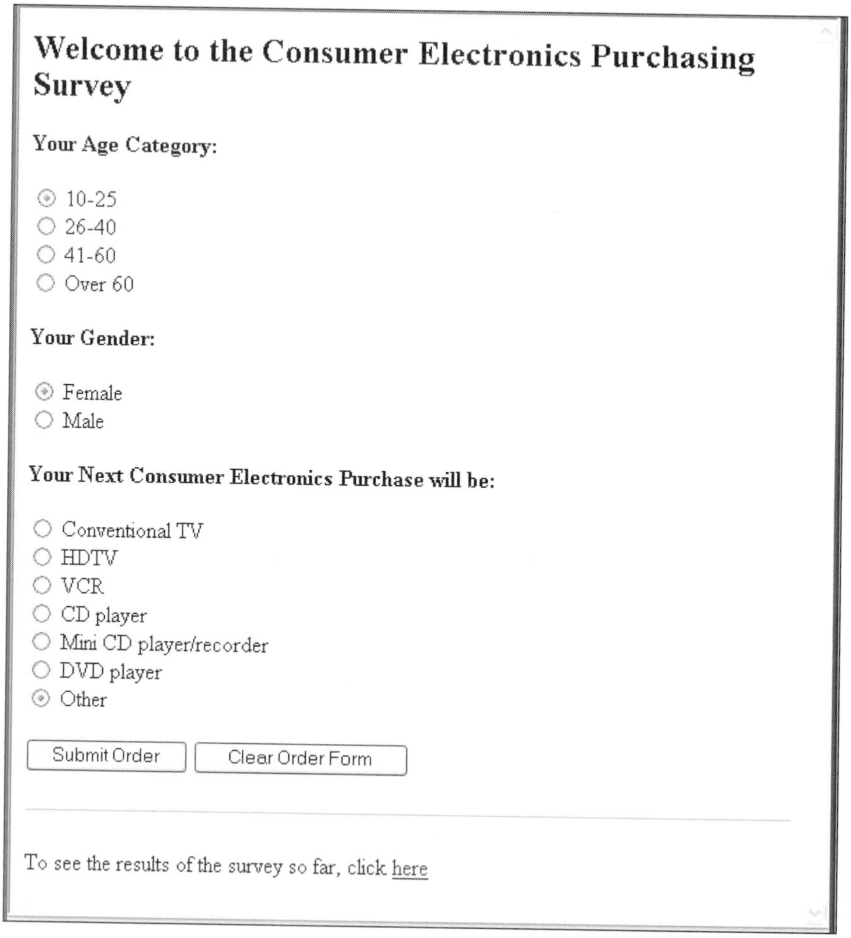

FIGURE 10.5 Display of `conelec.html`

Before we can develop either of the two CGI programs for this application, we must design the file format to be used to store the data. The simple format we will use for this file is eight strings that represent the rows of voting totals. The first four rows store the votes from female visitors; the last four are for the male visitors. Initially, the file will have eight lines, each being a string of seven zeros (one for each possible vote), separated by spaces. The file must be created and initialized to all zeros before the survey page is made public. This can be done with a text editor because it is simple text.

Note in `conelec.html` that the values 0, 1, 2, and 3 are used for the radio buttons for selecting the age group. Also, the values 0 and 4 are used for the gender selection. These values were chosen so that the index of the element of the vote data array that must be changed can be computed by adding the age group value and the gender value. For example, a male voter (gender = 4) who selects the 41–60 age group (age = 2) affects the element with the index 6.

It is always a good idea to check that file operations succeeded. In Chapter 9, "The Basics of Perl," the `die` function is used with `open` to produce an error message and terminate the program when `open` fails. In a CGI program, this is a bad idea because if a file operation fails and the program dies, the client will not know what happened. Instead, a message must be returned to the client indicating the problem. In the two CGI programs for the survey form document, a function named `error` is included to produce a message and terminate the program. Because the message must go to the client, it must be in the form of XHTML.

The CGI program that collects and records the voting data is named `conelec1.cgi`. Its tasks are as follows:

1. Get the form values.
2. Determine which row of the file must be modified.
3. Open, lock, and read the survey data file.
4. Split the affected data string into numbers and store them in an array.
5. Modify the affected array element and join the array back into a string.
6. Rewind the data file (with `seek`).
7. Rewrite and close the survey data file.

We already know how to get the widget values from the query string, and reading and writing the survey data file is relatively simple. Its lines will be read into an array of strings, one array element per row of the file. Each of the strings stores seven numbers. Because each submitted voting form changes just one element of the file, only one row must be converted from a string to an array of numbers. As previously explained, the row to be changed can be determined by adding the `age` and `gender` form data values. The `gender` form value determines which half of the file is affected. The `age` form data will determine which of the four rows of the `gender`'s half is affected. The actual change amounts to splitting the row into an array of numbers, adding 1 to one of its elements, which is determined by the particular vote, and joining the resulting array back together as a string.

The following is the CGI program to implement the processes previously described:

```perl
#!/usr/local/bin/perl

# conelec1.cgi
# This CGI program processes the consumer electronics survey form
# and updates the file that stores the survey data, survdat.dat

use CGI ":standard";
use Fcntl qw(:DEFAULT :flock);

# error - a function to produce an error message for the client
#           and exit in case of input/output errors

sub error {
    print start_html();
    print "Error - input/output error in conelec1.pl <br/>";
    print end_html();
    exit(1);
}

# Begin the main program
# Get the form values

my($age, $gender, $vote) = (param("age"), param("gender"),

# Produce the header for the reply page - do it here so error
#   messages appear on the page

print header;

# Set $index to the line index of the current vote

$index = $age + $gender;

# Open and lock the survey data file

open(SURVDAT, "+<survdat.dat") or error();
```

```
flock(SURVDAT, LOCK_EX) or error();

# Read the survey data file, unlock it, and close it

for ($count = 0; $count <= 7; $count++) {
    chomp($file_lines[$count] = <SURVDAT>);
}

# Split the line into its parts, increment the chosen device, and
#  put it back together again

@file_votes = split / /, $file_lines[$index];
$file_votes[$vote]++;
$file_lines[$index] = join(" ", @file_votes);

# Rewind the file for writing

seek(SURVDAT, 0, 0) or error();

# Write out the file data and close it (which also unlocks it)

foreach $line (@file_lines) {
    print SURVDAT "$line\n";
}

close(SURVDAT);

# Build the web page to thank the survey participant

print start_html("Thankyou");
print "Thank you for participating in our survey <br/> <br/> \n";
print end_html;
```

We now can develop the program, named `conelec2.cgi`, that produces the current status of the voting in the consumer electronics preference survey. Because there are vote totals in 56 different categories, it is best that the results be displayed in a table. Building this table in XHTML would be tedious without `CGI.pm`, and even with this module it is nontrivial.

Tables with `CGI.pm` are introduced through the following example: Suppose you want a CGI program to return a table of sales figures for the sales personnel Mary, Freddie, and Spot, including numbers for each of the five workdays of a week. The people will be the rows of the table; the days of the week will be the columns. Assume the sales figures are in three arrays,

@marysales, @freddiesales, and @spotsales, each of which has five elements. The column titles are Salesperson (for the title row), Monday,
Tuesday, Wednesday, Thursday, and Friday. The row titles for the three
arrays are Mary, Freddie, and Spot.

The table function creates an entire table, which is specified with its
parameters. If the table is to have a border, that is specified with the attribute
border. The table's caption, if there is one, is created with the caption
function:

```
caption("Sales Figures");
```

Each row of a table is created by a call to Tr. This shortcut is spelled with
an uppercase first letter because, if it were not, it would be mistaken for the Perl
transliterate operator, tr. The other parameters for Tr specify the row data of
the table. The title row is built with a call to th, and the data rows are built with
calls to td. All three functions, Tr, th, and td, take either references or arrays
as parameters. Therefore, if a literal list is to be passed, it must be constructed
with brackets. If a parameter is an array, its name must be backslashed in the
actual parameter list to specify its address.

Consider the following examples of the th shortcut function:

```
print th(['apples', 'oranges', 'grapes']);
```

produces

```
<th> apples </th>
<th> oranges </th>
<th> grapes </th>
```

and

```
@days = ('Saturday', 'Sunday');
print th(\@days);
```

produces

```
<th> Saturday </th>
<th> Sunday </th>
```

The td function is exactly like the th function.

In many cases, we want to build a table row that consists of a th element
and several td elements and treat the whole thing as a single parameter to Tr.
To treat these as a single row string, the returned values of the calls to td and th
can be catenated together. For example, the code

```
print th('9:15').td('French', '', 'French', '');
```

produces

```
<th> 9:15 </th> <td> French </td> <td> </td>
              <td> French </td> <td> </td>
```

Let us now consider a complete table specification.

```
# easy_table.pl
table({-border => "border"},
      caption("Sales Figures"),
        Tr(
          [th(["Salesperson", "Mon", "Tues", "Wed",
              "Thu", "Fri"]),
          th("Mary").td(\@maysales),
          th("Freddie").td(\@freddiesales),
          th("Spot").td(\@spotsales),
        ]
      )
    );
```

The browser display of the XHTML produced by this call to `table` is shown in Figure 10.6.

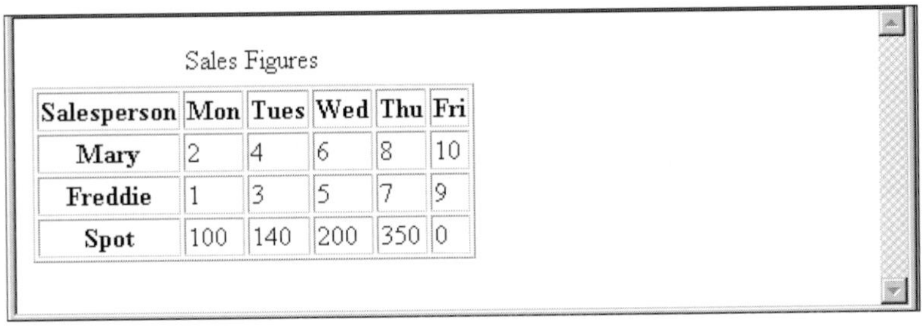

Sales Figures

Salesperson	Mon	Tues	Wed	Thu	Fri
Mary	2	4	6	8	10
Freddie	1	3	5	7	9
Spot	100	140	200	350	0

FIGURE 10.6 A table produced with `table`

Rows can have horizontal and vertical alignment attributes, specified by `align` and `valign`, respectively. These can be specified as the first parameter in the call to `Tr`.

Now we can get back to the development of the second survey-handling CGI program, `conelec2.cgi`. The basic tasks of `conelec2.cgi` are as follows:

1. Open the file and read the lines of the file into an array of strings.
2. Split the first four rows (responses from females) into arrays of votes for the four age groups.

3. Unshift row titles into the vote rows (making them the first elements).

4. Create the column titles row with th and put its address in an array.

5. Use td on each row of votes.

6. Push the addresses of the rows of votes onto the row address array.

7. Create the table using Tr on the array of row addresses.

8. Repeat steps 2 to 7 for the last four rows of data (responses from males).

Because the rows of the two result tables are nearly the same for the two tables, they are built with a subprogram, make_rows. This function takes one parameter, which is 0 for the female results table and 4 for the male results table. make_rows builds the table rows in the @rows array, which is globally accessed by the function and the calling program. The following is the CGI program to produce the vote totals tables:

```perl
#!/usr/local/bin/perl -w

# conelec2.cgi - display the survey results

# make_rows - a subprogram to make the rows of an output table

sub make_rows {
    my $index = $_[0];

# Split the input lines for females into age arrays

    @age1 = split(/ /, $vote_data[$index]);
    @age2 = split(/ /, $vote_data[$index + 1]);
    @age3 = split(/ /, $vote_data[$index + 2]);
    @age4 = split(/ /, $vote_data[$index + 3]);

# Add the row titles to the age arrays

    unshift(@age1, "10-25");
    unshift(@age2, "26-40");
    unshift(@age3, "41-60");
    unshift(@age4, "Over 60");

# Create the column titles in HTML by giving their address to the th
# function and storing the return value in the @rows array

    @rows = th(\@col_titles);
```

```
# Now create the data rows with the td function
#   and add them to the row addresses array

    push(@rows, td(\@age1), td(\@age2), td(\@age3), td(\@age4));
}   ##** end of the make_rows subprogram

# error - a function to produce an error message for the client
#            and exit in case of open errors

sub error {
    print start_html;
    print "Error - input/output error in conelec2.pl <br/>";
    print end_html;
    exit(1);
}   ##** end of the error subprogram

use CGI qw(:standard);

# Make the column titles array

@col_titles = ("Age Group", "Conventional TV", "HDTV", "VCR",
               "CD player", "MiniCD player/recorder", "DIVD player",
               "Other");
print header;

# Open and read the survey data file

open(SURVDAT, "<survdat.dat") or error();
@vote_data = <SURVDAT>;

# Create the beginning of the result Web page

print start_html("Survey Results");
print h2("Results of the Consumer Electronics Purchasing Survey");
print "<br />";

# Create the rows of the female survey results table

make_rows(0);

# Create the table for the female survey results
#   The address of the array of row addresses is passed to Tr
```

continued

```
print table({-border => "border"},
        caption(h3("Survey Data for Females")),
        Tr(\@rows)
        );

# Create the rows for the male results table

make_rows(4);

# Create the table for the male survey results
#   The address of the array of row addresses is passed to Tr

print "<br /><br />";
print table({-border => "border"},
        caption(h3("Survey Data for Males")),
        Tr(\@rows)
        );

print end_html;
```

Figure 10.7 shows the display of the table of voting results constructed by conelec2.cgi after some voting has occurred.

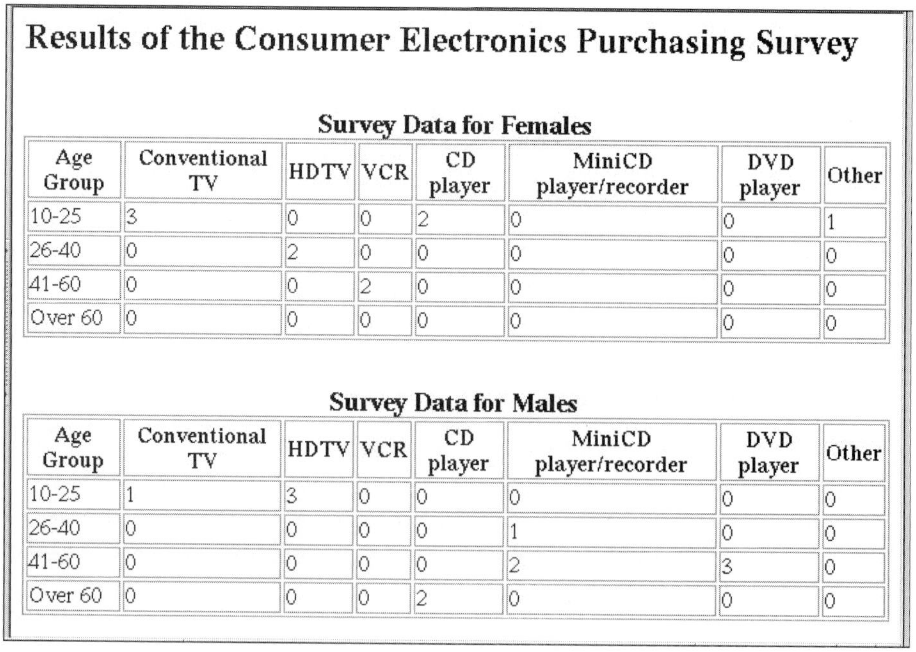

Results of the Consumer Electronics Purchasing Survey

Survey Data for Females

Age Group	Conventional TV	HDTV	VCR	CD player	MiniCD player/recorder	DVD player	Other
10-25	3	0	0	2	0	0	1
26-40	0	2	0	0	0	0	0
41-60	0	0	2	0	0	0	0
Over 60	0	0	0	0	0	0	0

Survey Data for Males

Age Group	Conventional TV	HDTV	VCR	CD player	MiniCD player/recorder	DVD player	Other
10-25	1	3	0	0	0	0	0
26-40	0	0	0	0	1	0	0
41-60	0	0	0	0	2	3	0
Over 60	0	0	0	2	0	0	0

FIGURE 10.7 Survey results page

10.6

COOKIES

A *session* is the time span during which a browser interacts with a particular server. A session begins when a browser becomes connected to a particular server. It ends when the browser ceases to be connected to that server because either it becomes connected to a different server or it is terminated. The HTTP protocol is essentially stateless—it includes no means to store information about a session that is available to a subsequent session. However, there are a number of different reasons why it is useful for the server to be capable of connecting a request made during a session to the other requests made by the same client during that session and subsequent sessions. Many Web sites now create profiles of clients by remembering which parts of the site are perused. Later sessions can use such profiles to target advertising to the client according to the client's past interests. Also, if the server recognizes a request as being from a client who has made an earlier request from the same site, it is possible to present a customized interface to that client. These situations require that information about clients be accumulated and stored.

Cookies provide a general approach to storing information about sessions on the browser system itself. The server is given this information when the browser makes subsequent requests for Web resources from the server. The identity of the browser user can be included in the information, which allows the server to present an interface to the client that is customized for that client. It also allows the server to connect requests from a particular client to previous requests, thereby connecting sequences of requests into a session.

A *cookie* is a small object of information consisting of a name and a textual value. A cookie is created by some software system on the server, such as a CGI program. Every HTTP communication between a browser and a server includes a header, which stores information about the message. A message from a browser to a server is a request; a message from a server to a browser is a response. The header part of an HTTP communication can include cookies. So, every request sent from a browser to a server, and every response from a server to a browser, can include one or more cookies.

At the time it is created, a cookie is assigned a lifetime. When the time a cookie has existed reaches its associated lifetime, the cookie is deleted from the browser's host machine. Every browser request includes all of the cookies its host machine has stored that are associated with the Web server to which the request is directed. Only the server that created a cookie can ever receive the cookie from the browser, so a particular cookie is information that is exchanged exclusively between one specific browser and one specific server. Because cookies are stored as text, the browser user can view, alter, or delete them at any time.

Because cookies allow servers to record browser activities, they are considered by some to be privacy concerns. Accordingly, browsers allow the client to change the browser setting to refuse to accept cookies from servers. This is clearly a drawback of using cookies—the clients that reject them render them useless.

The `CGI.pm` module includes support for cookies in Perl, primarily through the `cookie` function. The `cookie` function serves both to create cookies and to retrieve existing cookies from the HTTP header of a request. The form of a call to `cookie` to create a cookie is as follows:

```
cookie(-name => a_cookie_name,
       -value => a_value,
       -expires => a_time_value)
```

The `cookie` function can take three more parameters, but they are not discussed here. The cookie name can be any string. The value can be any scalar value, including references to arrays and hashes. These last two allow the creation of multiple cookies with one call. The `expires` value, which specifies the lifetime of the cookie, can be expressed in many different units. For example, `+3d` specifies three days. The other units are `s` for seconds, `m` for minutes, `h` for hours, `M` for months, `y` for years, and `now` for right now. A negative value for `expires` effectively kills the cookie.

A cookie must be placed in the HTTP header at the time the header is created. With `CGI.pm`, this means when the `header` function is called. This is done by passing the cookie as a parameter to `header`, as in the following example:

```
header(-cookie => $my_cookie);
```

When the `cookie` function is called with no parameters, it returns a hash of all of the cookies in the HTTP header of the current request. To retrieve the value of one cookie, the `cookie` function is called with the name of the cookie. For example:

```
$age = cookie('age');  # gets the value of the cookie named age
```

To display all of the cookies, both names and values, in a CGI program, we could use the following:

```
print "Cookie Name \t Cookie Value <br  />";
foreach $name (keys cookie()) {
    print "$name \t cookie($name) <br />";
}
```

Suppose we want to provide a greeting to all visitors, including a message giving the day of the week, month, and day of the month of their last visit. To do this, we could use a cookie to record the time and date of each visit. For the first visit by a client, a message could provide a first-time greeting.

For our program, we need to get the current date. The Perl `time` function returns the current time in seconds since January 1, 1970. The `localtime` function is more useful for our problem. It calls `time` and converts the number of seconds into nine values. For example, consider the following call to `localtime`:

```
($sec, $min, $hour, $mday, $mon, $year, $wday, $yday,
   $isdst) = localtime;
```

This statement sets the nine values for the current time and date, corrected for the time zone in which the Web server computer is installed. The first three scalars in the list have obvious meanings. The others have the following meanings: `$mday` is the day of the month; `$mon` is the month, coded as 0 to 11; `$year` is the number of years since 1900; `$wday` is the day of the week, coded as 0 to 6, where 0 is Sunday; `$yday` is the day of the year; and `$isdst` is a Boolean that specifies whether the given time is in daylight savings time.

The following example displays all of the nine values returned by `localtime`:

```
# time_date.pl
#   Input: None
# Output: The nine values returned by localtime
#

($sec, $min, $hour, $mday, $mon, $year, $wday, $yday,
   $isdst) = localtime;

print "\$sec = $sec\n";
print "\$min = $min\n";
print "\$hour = $hour\n";
print "\$mday = $mday\n";
print "\$mon = $mon\n";
print "\$year = $year\n";
print "\$wday = $wday\n";
print "\$yday = $yday\n";
print "\$isdst = $isdst\n";
```

The output of `time_date.pl` is:

```
$sec = 43
$min = 20
$hour = 10
$mday = 19
$mon = 2
```

```
$year = 105
$wday = 6
$yday = 77
$isdst = 0
```

For days of the week and month, we often want the names rather than numbers. This conversion is easy in Perl. The names can be put in a list, which can be subscripted by the value returned from `localtime`. For example, the following statement sets $day_of_week to the name of the current day of the week:

```
$day_of_week = (qw(Sunday Monday Tuesday Wednesday
                   Thursday Friday Saturday))[(localtime[6]];
```

The subscript 6 is that of the day of the week ($wday).

The CGI program for our problem will do the following:

1. Get the cookie named `last_time`.
2. Get the current day of the week, month, and day of the month and put them in a cookie named `last_time`.
3. Put the cookie in the header of the return document.
4. If there was no existing cookie, produce a welcome message for the first-time visitor.
5. If there was a cookie, produce a welcome message that includes the previous day of the week, month, and day of the month.

The following is the Perl program to implement these actions:

```perl
#!/usr/bin/perl
# day_cookie.pl
# - A CGI-Perl program to use a cookie to remember the
#   day of the last login from a user and display it when run

use CGI ":standard";

# Get the existing day cookie, if there was one

@last_day = cookie('last_time');

# Get the current date and make the new cookie

$day_of_week = (qw(Sunday Monday Tuesday Wednesday Thursday
                   Friday Saturday)) [(localtime)[6]];
```

```
$month = (qw(January February March April May June July
          August September October November December))
          [(localtime)[4]];
$day_of_month = (localtime)[3];
@day_stuff = ($day_of_week, $day_of_month, $month);

$day_cookie = cookie(-name => 'last_time',
                     -value => \@day_stuff,
                     -expires => '+5d');

# Produce the return document
# First, put the cookie in the new header

print header(-cookie => $day_cookie);
print start_html('This is day_cookie.pl');

# If there was no day cookie, this is the first visit

if (scalar(@last_day) == 0) {
    print "Welcome to you on your first visit to our site <br />";
}

# Otherwise, welcome the user back and give the date of the
#  last visit

else {
    ($day_of_week, $day_of_month, $month) = @last_day;
    print "Welcome back! <br /> ",
          "Your last visit was on ",
          "$day_of_week, $month $day_of_month <br />";
}

print end_html;
```

Figure 10.8 shows a browser display of a document returned by day_cookie.pl.

```
Welcome back!
You're last visit was on Friday, March 22
```

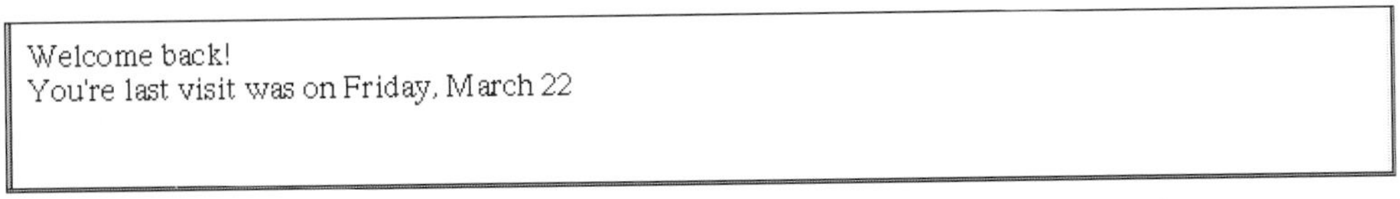

FIGURE 10.8 A document returned by day_cookie.pl

10.7

SUMMARY

CGI is the interface between an XHTML document being displayed by a browser and a program that resides on the server. An XHTML document can specify a call to a CGI program with an anchor tag that includes the Internet address of the program. CGI programs can also be called as a side effect of a Submit button being clicked. A CGI program communicates with the XHTML document that called it by sending an XHTML document back to the browser through the server. The XHTML tags in this document, as well as their content, are created by the CGI program through standard output.

XHTML forms are sections of documents that contain widgets, which are used to collect input from the user. The data specified in a form can be sent to the CGI program in either of two methods, get or post. The get method is fine for forms with relatively few widgets. It is also good for sending parameters to a CGI program when a form is not involved. The post method is more general because it has no limitation on the number of widgets included in the form. The coded data from a form is called a query string. With get, the query string is attached to the URL of the CGI program.

The values specified in a form are together called form data. When the Submit button is clicked, the query string, which is an encoded version of the form data, is created from the form data and sent to the server. Each widget that has a value is included in the query string. The format of each of these is a name/value pair, separated by an equal sign. These assignments are separated by ampersands. All special characters are coded by using a percent sign followed by the ASCII code for the character, in hexadecimal.

The CGI.pm module provides convenient aids to writing CGI programs in Perl. The shortcut functions of CGI.pm produce the tags after which they are named. Attribute values are passed to functions in CGI.pm using the form of the elements in a hash literal. The attribute names are preceded by minus signs. Parameters to functions follow the attribute values, if there are any. Tags and their attributes distribute over a list parameter. This list parameter must actually be the address of a list or array. Tables are built with table, table rows are built with Tr, table headings are built with th, and table data is created with td. Tr, th, and td allow references as parameters. The header function produces the first two lines of the return XHTML document. The start_html function produces the <head>, <title>, </title>, </head>, and <body> tags. Its parameter is used for the content of <title>. The param function takes a name as its parameter. It returns the value from the query string of that name. The end_html function produces the closing tags for <body> and <html>.

Cookies are small pieces of textual information that are exchanged between Web servers and browsers. They originate from server-based programs but are stored on browser systems. They are used to store information about a client between sessions the browser has with specific servers.

10.8 Review Questions

1. What are three categories of operations that are essential in Web documents but that cannot be done with XHTML?

2. On what system, the client or the server, do CGI programs reside when they are executed?

3. What forms are legal for the response from a CGI program?

4. What is the most common way for a client to provide information to the server?

5. What are the actions of the Submit button in a form?

6. How is the CGI program that processes the data provided by a form specified in the form?

7. Must a CGI program that processes a form reside on the server that provided the form to the client?

8. What part of the HTTP header is always provided as part of the response of a CGI program?

9. What is form data?

10. What is a query string?

11. How is a query string transmitted to the server with the `get` method?

12. How is a query string transmitted to the server with the `post` method?

13. What is the format of a query string that has multiple widget data values?

14. Why are special characters coded in query strings?

15. What is the purpose of the shortcuts in `CGI.pm`?

16. If both content and attribute values are passed to a shortcut, what is the format of these parameters?

17. Explain how tags and their attributes are distributed over the parameters to a shortcut function.

18. How are arrays passed to shortcut functions?

19. Why should a file to be read or written by a CGI program be locked against multiple simultaneous operations?

20. Where are cookies stored?

21. What is the form of the value of a cookie?

10.9 Exercises

1. Write an XHTML document that contains an anchor tag that calls a CGI program. Write the called CGI program, which returns a randomly chosen greeting from a list of five different greetings. The greetings must be stored as constant strings in the program. A random number between 0 and 4 can be computed with these lines:

```
srand;   # Sets the seed for rand
$number = int(rand 4);   # Computes a random integer 0-4
```

2. Modify the CGI program for Exercise 1 to count the number of visitors and display that number for each visitor.

3. Write an XHTML document to create a form with the following capabilities:

   a. A text widget to collect the user's name

   b. Four checkboxes, one each for the following items:

      i. Four 100-watt light bulbs for $2.39

      ii. Eight 100-watt light bulbs for $4.29

      iii. Four 100-watt long-life light bulbs for $3.95

      iv. Eight 100-watt long-life light bulbs for $7.49

   c. A collection of three radio buttons that are labeled as follows:

      i. Visa

      ii. MasterCard

      iii. Discover

4. Write a Perl CGI program that computes the total cost of the ordered light bulbs from Exercise 3, after adding 6.2 percent sales tax. The program must inform the buyer of exactly what was ordered, in a table.

5. Revise the survey sample CGI program of this chapter to make the table that displays the results of the survey have consumer electronics devices as its rows rather than its columns.

6. Revise the survey sample CGI program of this chapter to record the number of votes so far in the data file and display that count every time a vote is submitted or a survey result is requested. Also, change the output table so that its data is a percentage of the total votes for the particular age category.

7. Write an XHTML document to create a form that collects favorite popular songs, including the name of the song, the composer, and the performing artist or group. This document must call one CGI program when the form is submitted and another to request a current list of survey results.

8. Write a CGI program that collects the data from the form of Exercise 7 and writes it to a file.

9. Write a CGI program that produces the current results of the survey of Exercise 7.

10. Write an XHTML document to provide a form that collects names and telephone numbers. The phone numbers must be in the format ddd-ddd-dddd. Write a CGI program that checks the submitted telephone number to be sure it conforms to the required format and then returns a response that indicates whether the number was correct.

11. Modify the `day_cookie.pl` program to have it return the number of months, days, hours, and minutes since the last visit by the current client.

12. Write a CGI program that collects the name of every visitor (in a form text element). The program must create a cookie to save the visitor's name and include a brief personalized greeting to every repeat visitor.

11

Servlets and Java Server Pages

This chapter discusses Java server-based software, specifically servlets and Java Server Pages. First, servlets are introduced, including their general structure and common uses. The servlet methods for handling GET and POST HTTP requests are then discussed. This includes the objects used for carrying information between the client and the servlet on the server. Four complete examples are provided to illustrate servlets.

Next, the chapter describes two servlet approaches to storing information about clients: cookies, which were discussed in Chapter 10, "Using Perl for CGI Programming," and session tracking. Each of these is illustrated with a complete servlet example.

Lastly, Java Server Pages are introduced. The focus is on the JSP Standard Tag Library and the Expression Language. Java beans and scriptlets are not discussed, though they are part of Java Server Pages. Accessing values for the various kinds of form components is discussed, using implicit variables and action elements.

11.1

OVERVIEW OF SERVLETS

Simply put, a *servlet* is a server-side version of an applet. Applets are executed on a client system under the control of the browser, after being requested by the XHTML document being displayed by the browser. A servlet is a compiled Java class that is executed on the server system when requested by the XHTML document being displayed by the browser. The execution of a servlet is managed by a *servlet container*. The servlet container may run in the same process as the Web server, in a different process on the server host machine, or even on a different machine. The servlet request and response processes are supported with the HTTP protocol, so the servlet container must implement the HTTP specification. A servlet container might also define and enforce security restrictions on the execution of its servlets. Servlet containers are sometimes called *servlet engines*.

When an HTTP request is received by a Web server, the Web server examines the request. If a servlet must be called, the Web server passes the request to the servlet container. The container determines which servlet must be executed, makes sure it is loaded, and calls it. A servlet call passes two parameter objects: one with the request and one for the response. The servlet receives the input data associated with the request through the request object. This may include form data as well as the identity of the requesting client. After the servlet handles the request, its results are returned through the response object parameter in the form of an XHTML document. When finished, the servlet container returns control to the Web server.

Servlets are often used as alternatives to CGI programs. They are also used as alternatives to server extensions such as Apache modules, which users can write and add to an Apache server to extend its capabilities. Servlets have some potential advantages over CGI for providing server-based computation and server extensions. Because servlets continue to run, they are capable of saving status information, whereas CGI programs start, execute, and stop, providing no way to save such information except on the server's disk. Also, there are the general advantages that Java has over the languages typically used for CGI, such as Perl, in the areas of software reliability and maintainability.

When servlets were introduced, they were faster than CGI programs because, at that time, every execution of a CGI program required a new process to be spawned. Newer versions of Perl, such as `mod_perl`, avoid the new process creation for CGI programs, thereby eliminating the speed advantage of servlets.

11.2

SERVLET DETAILS

All servlets either implement the `Servlet` interface or extend a class that implements `Servlet`. The `Servlet` interface, which is defined in the `javax.servlet` package, declares the methods that manage servlets and their interactions with clients. The author of a servlet must provide definitions of these methods.

The `Servlet` interface declares three methods that are called by the servlet container to control servlet operation. These are `init`, which initializes a servlet and prepares it to respond to client requests; `service`, which controls how the servlet responds to client requests; and `destroy`, which takes the servlet out of service, making it unavailable for client requests. All three of these methods, which are called the *life-cycle methods*, are called by the servlet container. The `init` and `destroy` methods are called just once during the lifetime of a servlet.

The `Servlet` interface also declares two more methods: `getServletConfig`, which the servlet can use to get initialization and startup parameters for itself, and `getServletInfo`, which allows the servlet to return information about itself, such as the author and version number of the servlet.

The `GenericServlet` class is a predefined implementation of the `Servlet` interface. The `HttpServlet` class is a predefined extension to `GenericServlet`.[1] Most user-written servlets are extensions to `HttpServlet`.

In addition to the `Servlet` interface, the `javax.servlet` package contains several other interfaces required for implementing servlets. The `ServletRequest` and `ServletResponse` interfaces encapsulate the communication from the client to the servlet and from the servlet back to the client, respectively. The `ServletRequest` interface provides servlet access to `ServletInputStream`, through which input from the client flows. The `ServletResponse` interface provides servlet access to `ServletOutputStream` and also provides a method used to send information, usually in the form of an XHTML document, back to the client.

---

1. There are other extensions to `GenericServlet` (for example, to handle other protocols such as the Simple Object Access Protocol [SOAP]).

Every subclass of `HttpServlet` must override at least one of the methods of `HttpServlet`, the most common of which are shown in Table 11.1.

TABLE 11.1 Commonly Used Methods of `HttpServlet`

Method	Purpose
doGet	To handle HTTP GET requests
doPost	To handle HTTP POST requests
doPut	To handle HTTP PUT requests
doDelete	To handle HTTP DELETE requests
init	To initialize resources used by the servlet
destroy	To delete resources used by the servlet
getServletInfo	To allow the servlet to provide information about itself

The `doGet`, `doPost`, `doPut`, and `doDelete` methods are called by the server. The HTTP PUT request allows a client to send a file to be stored on the server. The HTTP DELETE request allows a client to delete a document or Web page from the server. In many cases, users are not allowed to add files to the server or delete files that are stored on the server. We focus on `doGet` and `doPost` because they are the most frequently used of the `HttpServlet` methods.

The protocol of the `doGet` method is as follows:

```
protected void doGet (HttpServletRequest request,
                      HttpServletResponse response)
    throws ServletException, java.io.IOException
```

`ServletException` is a subclass of `Exception` that serves as a wrapper for every kind of general servlet problem. `java.io.IOException` is thrown for the usual reasons. The `HttpServletRequest` object parameter, `request`, contains the client request; the `HttpServletResponse` object parameter, `response`, provides the means to communicate the response that the servlet sends back to the client.

The protocol of the `doPost` method is the same as that of `doGet`.

Servlet output to the requesting client is created by defining a `PrintWriter` object through the `HttpServletResponse` object, using the `getWriter` method. The `PrintWriter` object provides a collection of methods, such as `println`, that sends response XHTML code to the client, through the response object. The `PrintWriter` object corresponds to the standard output stream from a Perl CGI program.

Before the `PrintWriter` object is created, it is essential that the content type of the return document be set. This is done with the `setContentType` method of the `HttpServletResponse` object, as in this example:

```
response.setContentType("text/html");
```

Following this method call, the `PrintWriter` object can be created with the following:

```
PrintWriter servletOut = response.getWriter();
```

Now the `println` method of the `servletOut` object can be used to generate the XHTML markup of the document to be returned to the requesting client.

We are now ready to look at a complete servlet example. This first example servlet simply responds to a call from a form that uses the GET method. The form sends no data and requires no processing. So, the only action of the servlet is to produce an XHTML document with a message to indicate that the call was received. The call to the servlet in the form specifies the location of the servlet as the value of the `action` attribute of the form element. The servlet examples in this chapter were all run on the same machine as the browser, so the location is `localhost` (this machine), the servlet directory, and the servlet name. The following is the XHTML document that will call the servlet. Figure 11.1 shows the display created by `tstGreet.html`.

```
<?xml version = "1.0" encoding = "utf-8"?>
<!DOCTYPE html PUBLIC "-//w3c//DTD XHTML 1.1//EN"
 "http://www.w3.org/TR/xhtml11/DTD/xhtml11.dtd">

<!-- tstGreet.html
     Used to test the servlet, Greeting
     -->
<html xmlns = "http://www.w3.org/1999/xhtml">
  <head> <title> Test greeting </title>
  </head>
  <body>
    <form action = "http://localhost/servlet/Greeting"
          method = "get">
      <p>
        Press the button to enact the servlet
        <input type = "submit" value = "Enact Servlet" />
      </p>
    </form>
  </body>
</html>
```

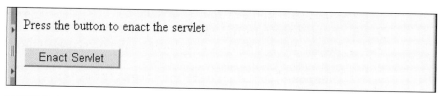

FIGURE 11.1   Display of `tstGreet.html`

The `Greeting` servlet class extends `HttpServlet` and implements the `doGet` method, which produces the XHTML response to the browser call:

```
/*  Greeting.java
    A servlet to illustrate a simple GET request
    */
import javax.servlet.*;
import javax.servlet.http.*;
import java.io.*;

public class Greeting extends HttpServlet {

    public void doGet(HttpServletRequest request,
                      HttpServletResponse response)
        throws ServletException, IOException {
        PrintWriter returnHTML;

        response.setContentType("text/html");
        returnHTML = response.getWriter();
        returnHTML.println("<html><head><title>");
        returnHTML.println("A simple GET servlet");
        returnHTML.println("</title></head><body>");
        returnHTML.println(
            "<h2> This is your servlet answering </h2>");
        returnHTML.println("</body></html>");
        returnHTML.close();
    }
}
```

Figure 11.2 shows the response from the `Greeting` servlet.

> This is your servlet answering

FIGURE 11.2   The response from the `Greeting` servlet

One popular way of running servlets is the Tomcat servlet container, which is available for free from the Apache Group at `http://www.apache.org/jakarta`. Tomcat can run as a standalone servlet container or as part of another Web server.

11.3

A SURVEY EXAMPLE

The next servlet example is more complicated and interesting than the `Greeting` servlet. Chapter 10 includes an example in which a form is used to gather responses for a survey of potential purchasers of consumer electronics products. It uses two Perl CGI programs to process the form data: one to collect responses and one to produce the current results of the survey. We now reformulate that example into a simpler form and use a single servlet both to collect the responses and produce the current results. The XHTML document for the new survey follows:

```
<?xml version = "1.0" encoding = "utf-8"?>
<!DOCTYPE html PUBLIC "-//w3c//DTD XHTML 1.1//EN"
 "http://www.w3.org/TR/xhtml11/DTD/xhtml11.dtd">


<!-- conelec2.html
    A simplified version of the consumer electronics
    survey form from chapter 10.
    This version uses a servlet for processing the form data
  -->

<html xmlns = "http://www.w3.org/1999/xhtml">
  <head>
    <title> Consumer Electronics Purchasing Survey </title>
  </head>
  <body>
    <form action = "http://localhost/servlet/Survey"
          method = "post">
```

continued

```
<h2> Welcome to the Consumer Electronics Purchasing Survey
</h2>
<p />

<h4> Your Gender: </h4>
<p>
   <input type = "radio" name = "gender" value = "female"
          checked = "checked" />
   Female <br />
   <input type = "radio" name = "gender" value = "male" />
   Male <br /> <br /> <br />
</p>
<h4> Your Next Consumer Electronics Purchase will be: </h4>
<p>
   <input type = "radio" name ="vote" value="0" />
   Conventional TV <br />
   <input type = "radio" name ="vote" value="1" />
   HDTV <br />
   <input type = "radio" name ="vote" value="2" />
   VCR <br />
   <input type = "radio" name ="vote" value="3" />
   CD player <br />
   <input type = "radio" name ="vote" value="4" />
   Mini CD player/recorder <br />
   <input type = "radio" name ="vote" value="5" />
   DVD player <br />
   <input type = "radio" name="vote" value="6"
          checked = "checked" />
   Other <br /> <br />

   <input type = "submit" value = "Submit Order" />
   <input type = "reset" value = "Clear Order Form" />
</p>
</form>
</body>
</html>
```

Figure 11.3 shows the display of `conelec2.html`.

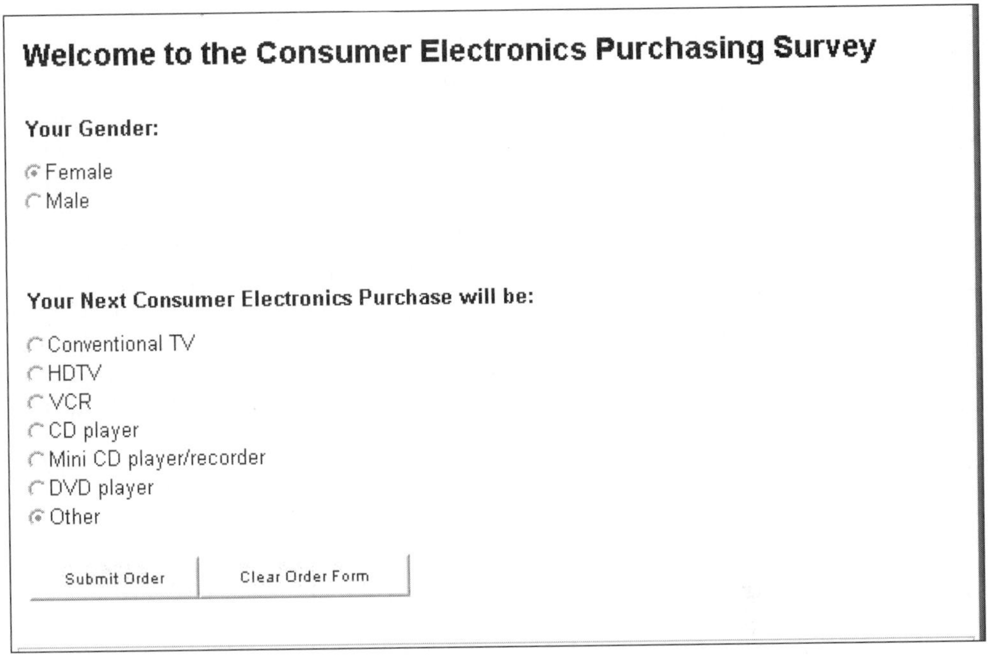

Welcome to the Consumer Electronics Purchasing Survey

Your Gender:

⊙ Female
○ Male

Your Next Consumer Electronics Purchase will be:

○ Conventional TV
○ HDTV
○ VCR
○ CD player
○ Mini CD player/recorder
○ DVD player
⊙ Other

| Submit Order | Clear Order Form |

FIGURE 11.3 Display of `conelec2.html`

Because the servlet that processes the form in this page must accumulate the results of the survey, it must create and use a file. The first time the form is submitted, the file must be created and written. For all subsequent submissions, the file is opened, read, and rewritten. The servlet will produce the current vote totals for every client that submits a form. The survey results will be just the totals for each kind of product.

The data stored in the vote totals file is an integer array of results. The approach used was to read and write the file using the `ObjectInputStream` and `ObjectOutputStream` objects, respectively. This is a simple way to write any object to a file. When used for input, the input data object is cast to an integer array. For file output, the array object is written directly to the stream.

On all calls to the servlet except the first, the servlet must read the current vote array from the file, modify it, and write it back to the file. On the first call, there is no need to read the file first because the call creates the first vote to be written to the file. The file is read through an `ObjectInputStream` object that is created by a call to the `ObjectInputStream` constructor, passing an object of class `FileInputStream`, which is itself created by passing the file's program name to the `FileInputStream` constructor. This is specified with the following statement:

```
ObjectInputStream indat = new ObjectInputStream(
        new FileInputStream(File_variable_name));
```

In this statement, indat is the program variable that references the input stream.

As was the case with the Perl CGI program in Chapter 10 that wrote to a server file, there can be concurrent accesses to the file used here. A servlet container can support multiple simultaneous executions of a servlet. To prevent corruption caused by concurrent accesses to the file, a synchronized clause can be used to enclose the file accesses. Whatever code that is in such a clause executes completely before a different execution is allowed to enter the clause.

The servlet accesses the form data with the getParameter method of the request object that was passed to the doPost method. This method takes a string parameter, which is the name of the form element. The string value of the parameter is returned. For example, if the form has an element named address, the following statement will put the value of the address form element in the variable newAddress:

```
newAddress = request.getParameter("address");
```

If the element whose name is sent to getParameter does not have a form value, getParameter returns null.

Form values that are not strings must be converted because they are all passed as strings. So, if a form value is an integer number, it is passed as a string and must be converted back to an integer value in the servlet. In Java, this is done with the parseInt method, which is defined in the wrapper class for integers, Integer. For example, to get the integer value of a parameter that is passed as the form value of an element named price, the following could be used:

```
price = Integer.parseInt(request.getParameter("price"));
```

We can now discuss the specifics of the servlet for processing the survey form data. The data file stores an array of 14 integers, seven votes for female voters and seven votes for male voters. The actions of the servlet are described in the following pseudocode algorithm:

```
If the votes data file exists
   read the votes array from the data file
else
   create the votes array
Get the gender form value
Get the form value for the new vote
   and convert it to an integer
Add the vote to the votes array
Write the votes array to the votes file
Produce the return XHTML document that shows the
   current results of the survey
```

The servlet, Survey, that implements this process is as follows:

```
// Survey.java

// This servlet processes the consumer electronics survey
//   form, updating the file that stores the survey data
//   and producing the current total votes in the survey.
//   The survey data file, survdat.dat, is stored on the Web server.

import javax.servlet.*;
import javax.servlet.http.*;
import java.io.*;
public class Survey extends HttpServlet {
    public void doPost(HttpServletRequest request,
                       HttpServletResponse response)
        throws ServletException, IOException {
        int votes[] = null;
        int index;
        int vote;
        File survdat = new File("survdat.dat");
        String gender;
        String products[] = {"Conventional TV", "HDTV", "VCR",
                             "CD Player",
                             "Mini CD player/recorder",
                             "DVD player", "Other"};

// Set the content type for the response output and get a writer

        response.setContentType( "text/html" );
        PrintWriter servletOut = response.getWriter();

// Produce the head of the output document

        servletOut.println("<html><head>");
        servletOut.println(
            "<title> Return message </title></head><body>");

// Synchronize a block for the votes file access

        synchronized(this) {

// If the file already exists, read in its data

            try {
              if (survdat.exists()) {
                ObjectInputStream indat = new ObjectInputStream(
                            new FileInputStream(survdat));
```

continued

```
                votes = (int []) indat.readObject();
                indat.close();
            }

// If the file does not exist (this is the first vote), create the
//   votes array

            else
                votes = new int[14];
        }
        catch (Exception e) {e.printStackTrace();}

// Get the gender of the survey respondee

        gender = request.getParameter("gender");

// Add the consumer electronics vote of the response to the
//   votes array

        vote = Integer.parseInt(request.getParameter("vote"));
        if (gender.equals("male")) vote += 7;
        votes[vote]++;

// Write updated votes array to disk

        ObjectOutputStream outdat = new ObjectOutputStream(
            new FileOutputStream(survdat));
        outdat.writeObject(votes);
        outdat.flush();
        outdat.close();

    }  //** end of the synchronized block

// Create the initial response information

        servletOut.println(
            "<h3>Thank you for participating in the");
        servletOut.println(" Consumer Electronics Survey</h3>");
        servletOut.println("<h4>Current Survey Results:</h4>");

// Create the total votes return information for female respondents

        servletOut.println("<h5>For Female Respondents </h5>");
        for (index = 0; index < 7; index++) {

            servletOut.print(products[index]);
```

```
                    servletOut.print(": ");
                    servletOut.println(votes[index]);
                    servletOut.println("<br />");
            }

// Create the total votes return information for male respondents

            servletOut.println("<h5>For Male Respondents </h5>");
            for (index = 7; index < 14; index++) {
                    servletOut.print(products[index - 7]);
                    servletOut.print(": ");
                    servletOut.println(votes[index]);
                    servletOut.println("<br />");
            }
            servletOut.close();
        }
    }
```

Figure 11.4 shows the results of running the survey servlet after some survey responses have been received.

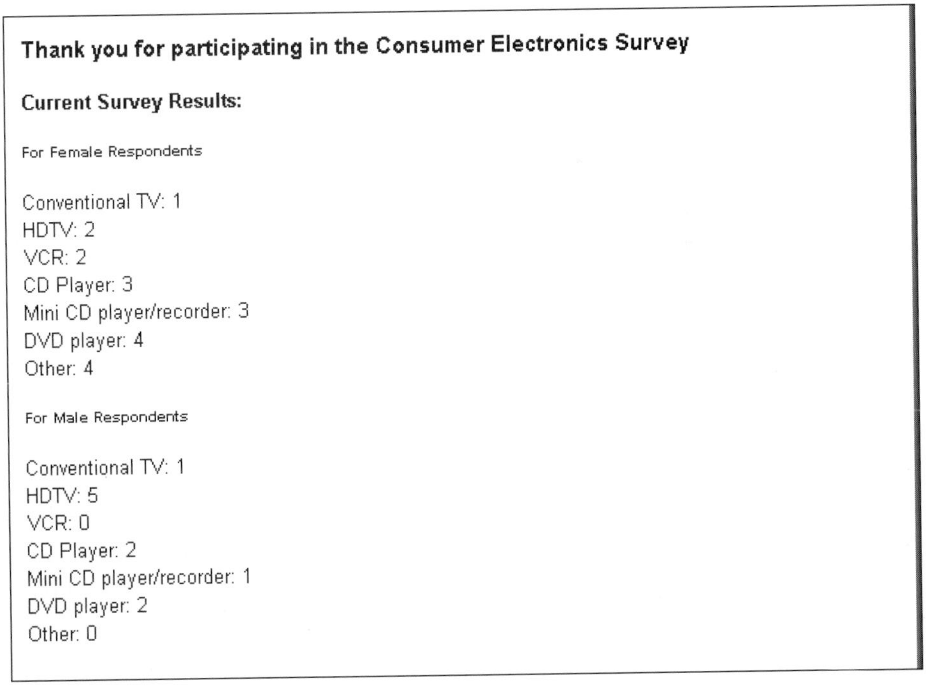

Thank you for participating in the Consumer Electronics Survey

Current Survey Results:

For Female Respondents

Conventional TV: 1
HDTV: 2
VCR: 2
CD Player: 3
Mini CD player/recorder: 3
DVD player: 4
Other: 4

For Male Respondents

Conventional TV: 1
HDTV: 5
VCR: 0
CD Player: 2
Mini CD player/recorder: 1
DVD player: 2
Other: 0

FIGURE 11.4 Results of the Survey servlet

11.4

STORING INFORMATION ON CLIENTS

Chapter 10 discussed cookies, which are used to store information about a Web client on the client's machine. The `javax.servlet` package provides the tools for creating and using cookies as well as a cookie alternative, session tracking.

11.4.1 Cookies

Recall that cookies provide a general approach to storing information about a browser user on the browser system itself. The server is given this information when the browser makes subsequent requests for Web resources from the server. The identity of the browser user can be included in the information, which allows the server to present an interface to the user that is customized for that user. It also allows the server to connect a session with a particular client to previous sessions with the same client.

On the server, a cookie associated with a servlet is an object of class `Cookie`; on a client, a cookie is just a text data value. It is good to keep these two uses of the term *cookie* distinct.

A Java cookie object has a collection of data members and methods. Among the most commonly used data members are those for storing the lifetime, or maximum age, of the cookie and for storing the cookie's name and value as strings, along with a comment, which is a string that can be used to explain the purpose of the cookie. The most commonly used `Cookie` methods are `setComment(String)`, `setMaxAge(int)`, `setValue(String)`, `getComment()`, `getMaxAge()`, `getName()`, and `getValue()`, all of whose purposes are obvious from their names.

A cookie object is created with the constructor for the `javax.servlet.http.Cookie` class. This constructor takes two parameters: the cookie name and the cookie value. For example, consider this statement:

```
Cookie newCookie = new Cookie(gender, vote);
```

By default, a cookie exists from the time it is created until the current session ends, which is when the browser that started the session is terminated. If you want the cookie to exist past the end of the current session, you must use the `setMaxAge` method of `Cookie` to give the cookie a specific lifetime. The parameter to `setMaxAge` is the number of seconds, expressed as an integer literal. Because Java integers can have values up to a maximum of about two billion, cookies can have ages that range from one second to nearly 25,000 years.

For example, the following method call gives `newCookie` a lifetime of one hour:

```
newCookie.setMaxAge(3600);
```

A cookie is attached to a response from a server with the `addCookie` method of the `HttpServletResponse` class. For example, the cookie `newCookie` can be added to the response object `myResponse` with this statement:

```
myResponse.addCookie(newCookie);
```

Note that the cookie must be added to the response before any other part of the response is created, even the content type. When cookies are used, the sequence of response creation must be as follows:

1. Add any cookies to the response with `addCookie`.
2. Set the content type of the message with `setContentType`.
3. Get a response output stream with `getWriter`.
4. Place response information in the response stream with `print` or `println`.

Once again, remember that the cookie that a browser gets and stores is not a Java object—it has no methods; it is just some data.

The browser has little to do with cookies, at least directly. Browsers accept cookies, store them on the browser system, and return them to the server that created them with each `GET` or `POST` request to that server that occurs before the session ends or the cookie's lifetime ends. All of this is done implicitly by the browser.

A cookie that is sent from the browser to the server must be explicitly received by the server. In the case of a servlet, this is done with the `getCookies` method of `HttpServletRequest`. This method returns an array of references to `Cookie` objects. The following is an example of a cookie array declaration and a subsequent call to `getCookies`:

```
Cookie theCookies [];
...
theCookies = request.getCookies();
```

Whatever cookie processing is required can be done before the cookies are attached to the response and sent back to the browser.

We'll now consider an example of a ballot form that collects client votes in an election for the esteemed position of dogcatcher. The votes submitted through this form are recorded on the server by a servlet, which handles the form. This example uses a cookie to record, on the client, whether the voter has voted before, the objective being to prevent multiple votes from the same client.

The survey form is presented with the XHTML document named `ballot.html`, which follows:

```
<?xml version = "1.0" encoding = "utf-8"?>
<!DOCTYPE html PUBLIC "-//w3c//DTD XHTML 1.1//EN"
 "http://www.w3.org/TR/xhtml11/DTD/xhtml11.dtd">


<!-- ballot.html
     Presents a ballot to the user and calls
     the VoteCounter servlet for form handling
     -->
<html xmlns = "http://www.w3.org/1999/xhtml">
  <head> <title> Ballot </title>
  </head>
  <body>
    <form action = "http://localhost/servlet/VoteCounter"
          method = "post">
      <h3> Please choose one candidate for dogcatcher </h3>
      <p>
        <input type = "radio" name = "vote" value = "Dogman" />
        Daren Dogman <br />
        <input type = "radio" name = "vote"
               value = "Taildragger" />
        Timmy Taildragger <br/>
        <input type = "radio" name = "vote" value = "Dogpile" />
        Don Dogpile <br />
      </p><p>
        <input type = "submit" value = "Submit ballot" />
      </p>
    </form>
  </body>
</html>
```

Figure 11.5 shows the display of the form described in `ballot.html`.

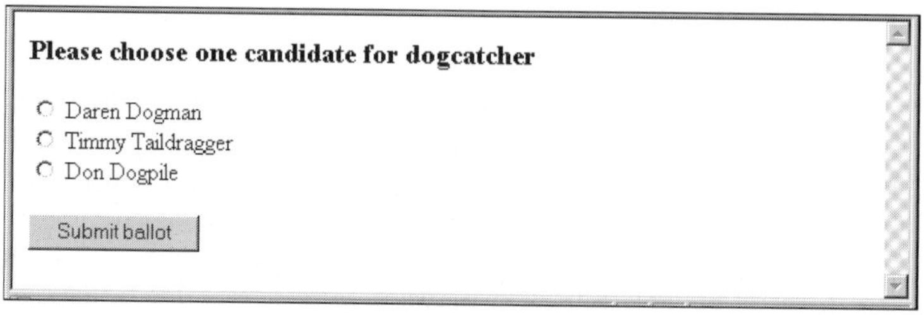

FIGURE 11.5 Display of `ballot.html`

The users of the ballot form can vote for one of three persons for dog-catcher. The form presents the three choices as radio buttons and includes a Submit button. The `action` attribute of the form specifies that it be handled by the servlet `VoteCounter`, using the `POST` method.

The vote-counting servlet has several processing responsibilities. For each ballot (request) the servlet receives, it must first determine whether a vote was actually cast. If no vote was cast, it must send an XHTML document back to the client, asking the user to mark a vote and return the ballot form. It must also ensure that a voter does not vote twice, at least for some specified period of time. To do this, a cookie is returned to each voter. Each vote submission is checked to determine whether a cookie showing that the user has already voted came along with the ballot. If the ballot contains a vote—that is, if the form has one of its radio buttons pressed—and the voter has not voted previously, the vote must be processed. Processing a vote means reading the vote totals file, updating it, and writing it back to disk storage. Finally, the servlet must produce the current vote totals for each legitimate voter, in the form of an XHTML document. The actions of the `VoteCounter` servlet are outlined in the following pseudocode algorithm:

```
If the form does not have a vote
    return a message to the client – "no vote"
else
    If the client did not vote before
        If the votes data file exists
            read in the current votes array
        else
            create the votes array
        update the votes array with the new vote
        write the votes array to disk
        make an "iVoted" cookie
        return a message to the client, including the new vote totals
    else
        return a message to the client – "Illegal vote"
```

Two utility methods are used: a predicate method to determine whether the client has voted, and a method to create the XHTML header text. The servlet code follows:

```
// VoteCounter.java
// This servlet processes the ballot form, returning a
// page asking for a new vote if no vote was made on the
// ballot. For legitimate ballots, the vote is added to
// the current totals, and those totals are presented to
// the user in a return page.
```

continued

```java
//   A cookie is returned to the voter, recording the fact
//   that a vote was received. The servlet examines all votes
//   for cookies to ensure that there is no multiple voting.
//   The voting data file, votesdat.dat, is stored on the Web
//   server.

import javax.servlet.*;
import javax.servlet.http.*;
import java.io.*;

public class VoteCounter extends HttpServlet {
    Cookie cookies[] = null;
    int index;
    PrintWriter servletOut;

    public void doPost(HttpServletRequest request,
                       HttpServletResponse response)
        throws ServletException, IOException {

        Cookie newCookie;
        int votes[] = null;
        String vote;
        File votesdat = new File("votesdat.dat");
        String candidates[] = {"Daren Dogman", "Timmy Taildragger",
                               "Don Dogpile"};

// Get cookies from the request

        cookies = request.getCookies();

// Check to see if there was a vote on the form

        vote = request.getParameter("vote");
        if (vote == null) {   // There was no vote

// Create the return page

            makeHeader(response);
            servletOut.println(
            "You submitted a ballot with no vote marked <br />");
            servletOut.println(
                "Please mark the ballot and resubmit");
        }         // end of if (vote == null)...
```

```
        else {   // There was a vote

// Check to see if this client voted before

            if (!votedBefore()) {

// No previous vote, so get the contents of the file (if the file
//  already exists)

// Syncronize block for file input/output

            synchronized(this) {

                if (votesdat.exists()) {
                    ObjectInputStream indat =
                        new ObjectInputStream(
                        new FileInputStream(votesdat));

// We need the try/catch here because readObject can throw
//   ClassNotFoundException

                    try {
                        votes = (int []) indat.readObject();
                    }
                    catch(ClassNotFoundException problem) {
                        problem.printStackTrace();
                    }
                }  //** end of if(votesdat.exists() ...

// If the file does not exist (this is the first vote), create the
//  votes array

                else
                    votes = new int[3];

// Add the new vote to the votes array

                if (vote.equals("Dogman"))
                    votes[0]++;
                else if (vote.equals("Taildragger"))
                    votes[1]++;
                else votes[2]++;
```

continued

```
// Write updated votes array to disk

                ObjectOutputStream outdat =
                    new ObjectOutputStream(
                    new FileOutputStream(votesdat));
                outdat.writeObject(votes);
                outdat.flush();
                outdat.close();
        }   //** end of synchronize block

// Attach a cookie to the response

            newCookie = new Cookie("iVoted", "true");
            newCookie.setMaxAge(5);   // Set to 5 for testing
            response.addCookie(newCookie);

// Write a response message

            makeHeader(response);
            servletOut.println("Your vote has been received");
            servletOut.println(
                "<br /> <br /> Current Voting Totals:<br />");

// Create the total votes return information

            for (index = 0; index < 3; index++) {
                servletOut.println("<br />");
                servletOut.print(candidates[index]);
                servletOut.print(": ");
                servletOut.println(votes[index]);
            }
        }  // end of if (!votedBefore() ...

        else {  // The client voted before

// Write a response message

            makeHeader(response);
            servletOut.println(
              "Your vote is illegal - you have already voted!");
            }  // end of else clause - client voted before

    }  // end of else (there was a vote)
```

```
        // Finish response document and close the stream

            servletOut.println("</body> </html>");
            servletOut.close();

    }   // end of doPost

//------------------------------------------------------------
// Method votedBefore - return true if the client voted before;
//   false otherwise

    boolean votedBefore() {
        if (cookies == null || cookies.length == 0)
            return false;
        else {

// Check the cookies to see if this user voted before

            for (index = 0; index < cookies.length; index++) {

                if (cookies[index].getName().equals("iVoted")
                    && cookies[index].getValue().equals("true"))
                    return true;

            }   // end of for (index = 0; ...

            return false;

        }   // end of if (cookies == null ...
    }   // end of votedBefore

//------------------------------------------------------------
// Method makeHeader - get the writer and produce
// the response header

    void makeHeader(HttpServletResponse response)
            throws IOException {

// Set content type for response and get a writer

            response.setContentType("text/html");
            servletOut = response.getWriter();
```

continued

```
// Write the response document head and the message

        servletOut.println("<html><head>");
        servletOut.println(
                "<title> Return message - </title></head><body>");

    }  // end of makeHeader

}  // end of VoteCounter
```

The outputs of the VoteCounter servlet for the three possibilities it handles—a nonvote ballot, a second ballot from the same client, and a ballot with a legitimate vote—are shown in Figures 11.6, 11.7, and 11.8.

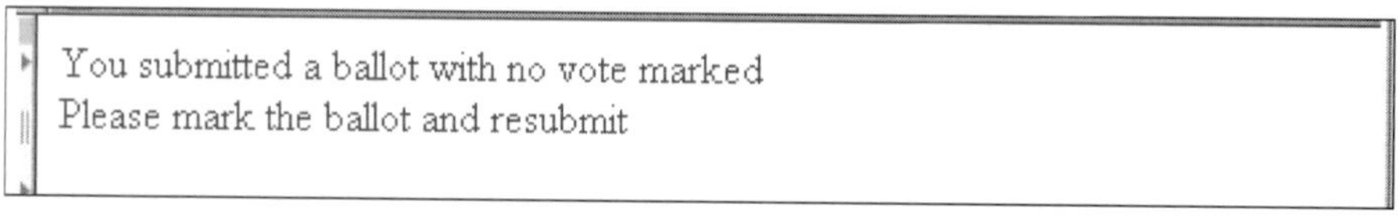

> You submitted a ballot with no vote marked
> Please mark the ballot and resubmit

FIGURE 11.6   The output of the VoteCounter servlet for a form with no vote

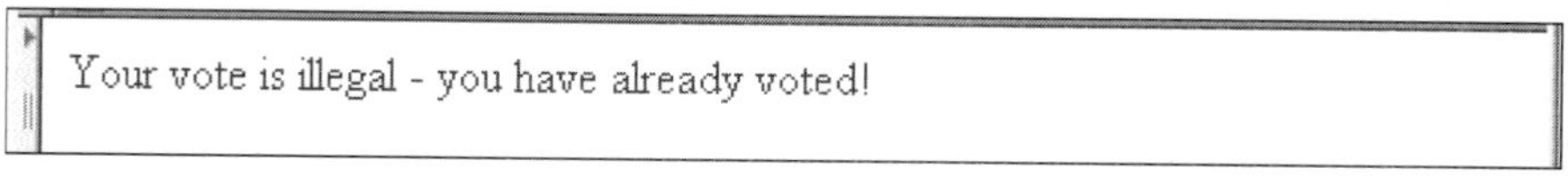

> Your vote is illegal - you have already voted!

FIGURE 11.7   The output of VoteCounter for a form with a second vote from the same client

> Your vote has been received
>
> Current Voting Totals:
>
> Daren Dogman: 3
> Timmy Taildragger: 1
> Don Dogpile: 0

FIGURE 11.8   The output of VoteCounter for a form with a legitimate vote

11.4.2   Session Tracking

In many cases, information about a session is needed only during the session. Also, the needed information about a client is nothing more than a unique identifier for the session, which is commonly used in shopping cart applications. For these cases, Java supports a simple alternative to using cookies directly for storing information about requests made by a client during a session; it is called *session tracking*. Session tracking is done using an `HttpSession` object, often called a *session object*, which can store a list of names and values. So, rather than using one or more cookies, a single session object can be used to store information about the previous requests of a client during a session. In particular, session objects often store a unique session ID for a session. One signficant way that session objects differ from cookies is that they can be stored on the server, whereas cookies are stored on the client. Session tracking can be implemented by a servlet container with cookies, in which case the session information is actually stored on the client. The most useful methods for session objects are described in the following paragraphs.

The `putValue` method takes two objects, `String` and `Object`. The `String` object represents the name of a value; the `Object` object is the value to be bound to the name. Both the name and the value are stored in the session object on which `putValue` is called. For example, if there is a session named `mySession`, we could have the following:

```
mySession.putValue("iVoted", "true");
```

The `invalidate` method takes no parameters. It invalidates or destroys the session on which it is called.

The `removeValue` method takes a `String` parameter, which it interprets as the name of a value in the session object. The action of `removeValue` is to delete the data bound to the given name.

The `getValue` method takes a `String` parameter, which it interprets as the name of a value in the session object. `getValue` returns a reference to the value bound to the given name. The value returned by `getValue` is often cast so that it can be used as a reference to a particular type. For example, consider the following statement:

```
String theValue = mySession.getValue("iVoted");
```

The `getValueNames` method takes no parameters. It returns the names of all values in the session object as an array of strings:

```
String valueNames [] = mySession.getValueNames();
```

A client request that includes a session object has that object attached to the `HttpServletRequest` object. To access such a session object, we use the `getSession` method of `HttpServletRequest`, which takes a `Boolean` object as a parameter. If the value `true` is given as a parameter and no session object is attached to the `HttpServletRequest` object, one is created and a reference to it is returned. If the value `false` is given as a parameter and there is no session object, `getSession` returns `null`.

The use of session tracking is illustrated with an alternative vote-counting servlet named `VoteCounter2`. The purpose of this servlet is the same as the earlier vote-counting servlet, which used cookies to disallow multiple votes from the same client. This example is slightly less realistic because it uses session tracking to check for multiple votes. This is unrealistic because the user can simply exit the browser, reenter the browser, which creates a new session, and vote again. In the case of the cookie voting control, the user was disallowed multiple votes for a specified period of time, regardless of how many times he or she exited and reentered the browser.[2] The following is the code for the session-tracking vote counter:

```java
// VoteCounter2.java
// This servlet processes the ballot form, returning a
//   page asking for a new vote if no vote was made on the
//   ballot. For legitimate ballots, the vote is added to
//   the current totals, and those totals are presented to
//   the user in a return page.
// This servlet uses session tracking rather than cookies.
// The voting data file, votesdat.dat, is stored on the Web server.

import javax.servlet.*;
import javax.servlet.http.*;
import java.io.*;

public class VoteCounter2 extends HttpServlet {
    PrintWriter servletOut;
    int index;
    public void doPost(HttpServletRequest request,
                       HttpServletResponse response)
        throws ServletException, IOException {
        HttpSession mySession = null;
        int votes[] = null;
        String vote;
        File votesdat = new File("votesdat.dat");
        String candidates[] = {"Daren Dogman", "Timmy Taildragger",
                        "Don Dogpile"};
```

---

2. Of course, it is easy to cheat our cookies voting system. The user either could set his or her browser to not accept cookies or could simply delete them after voting. Using a different machine for each vote would also work.

```
// Check to see if there was a vote on the form

        vote = request.getParameter("vote");
        if (vote == null) {  // There was no vote

// Create the return page

        makeHeader(response);
        servletOut.println(
            "You submitted a ballot with no vote marked");
        servletOut.println(
            "Please mark the ballot and resubmit");
    }  // end of if vote == null) ...
    else {  // There was a vote

// Check to see if this client voted before

        if (!votedBefore(mySession, request)) {

// No previous vote, so read the file (if it exists)

// Synchronize a block for the file access

            synchronized(this) {

                if (votesdat.exists()) {
                    ObjectInputStream indat =
                        new ObjectInputStream(
                        new FileInputStream(votesdat));

// We need try/catch here because readObject may throw the
//   ClassNotFoundException

                    try {
                        votes = (int []) indat.readObject();
                    }
                    catch(ClassNotFoundException problem) {
                        problem.printStackTrace();
                    }
                    indat.close();
                }  // end of if (votesdat...

// If the file does not exist (this is the first vote), create the
//   votes array
```

continued

```
                    else
                        votes = new int[3];

// Add the new vote of the response to the votes array

                    if (vote.equals("Dogman"))
                        votes[0]++;
                    else if (vote.equals("Taildragger"))
                        votes[1]++;
                    else votes[2]++;

// Write updated votes array to disk

                    ObjectOutputStream outdat =
                        new ObjectOutputStream(
                        new FileOutputStream(votesdat));
                    outdat.writeObject(votes);
                    outdat.flush();
                    outdat.close();

              }  //** end of the synchronized block

// Create a session object and set a value to indicate a vote

                    mySession = request.getSession(true);
                    mySession.putValue("iVoted", "true");

// Write a response message

                    makeHeader(response);
                    servletOut.println("Your vote has been received");
                    servletOut.println(
                        "<br/> <br/> Current Voting Totals:<br/>");

// Create the total votes return information

                    for (index = 0; index < 3; index++) {
                        servletOut.println("<br/>");
                        servletOut.print(candidates[index]);
                        servletOut.print(": ");
                        servletOut.println(votes[index]);
                    }
              }  // end of if (!votedBefore( ...
            else {  // The client voted before
```

```
      // Write a response message

                  makeHeader(response);
                  servletOut.println(
                      "Your vote is illegal - you already voted!");
              }   // end of else
          }   // end of else (there was a vote)

          servletOut.println("</body> </html>");
          servletOut.close();


      }   // end of doPost
//------------------------------------------------------------
// Method votedBefore - return true if the client voted before;
//   false otherwise

      boolean votedBefore(
              HttpSession mySession, HttpServletRequest request) {

// Get the session object, if there is one

          mySession = request.getSession(false);

// If there was no session, the vote must be okay

          if (mySession == null)
              return false;
          else {  // there was a session
              String names [] = mySession.getValueNames();
              for (index = 0; index < names.length; index++) {
                  if (names[index].equals("iVoted") &&
                    mySession.getValue(names[index]).equals("true"))
                      return true;

              }   // end of for (index = 0; ...

              return false;
          }   // end of else
      }   // end of votedBefore
```

continued

```
//-----------------------------------------------------------------
// Method makeHeader -
// get the writer and produce the response header
   void makeHeader(HttpServletResponse response)
           throws IOException {

// Set content type for response and get a writer

       response.setContentType("text/html");
       servletOut = response.getWriter();

// Write the response document head and the message

       servletOut.println("<html><head>");
       servletOut.println(
           "<title> Return message - </title></head><body>");
   } // end of makeHeader
 } // end of VoteCounter2
```

11.5

JAVA SERVER PAGES

Java Server Pages (JSP), which are built on top of servlets, provide alternative ways of constructing dynamic Web documents. It is "ways," not "way," because JSP includes several different approaches to inserting computation capability into Web documents. JSP, which was designed by Sun Microsystems, is a specification rather than a product. This means that Sun does not provide code to support JSP. Other organizations are invited to implement the specification. This encourages competition among providers, which can result in better quality software.

11.5.1 Motivations for JSP

There are several perceived problems with the servlet approach, as well as other related approaches, to providing dynamic Web documents. Among these are the problem of having the XHTML response document embedded in programming code. In the case of servlets, the entire response document is created by calls to the `writeln` method of the `PrintWriter` class. This forces all maintenance of the user interface of the document to be done on program code.

A closely related problem is that organizations often have two different kinds of personnel, with different skill sets, work on the development and maintenance of Web documents. Web designers focus on interface and presentation characteristics of Web documents. Programmers, on the other hand, design and maintain the code that processes form data and handles interactions with databases. Most personnel appear in one or the other of these two categories rather than both. Yet having XHTML code and programming code intermixed requires people from both categories to work on the same documents.

JSP takes an opposite approach to that of servlets: Instead of embedding XHTML in Java code that provides dynamic documents, code of some form is embedded in XHTML documents to provide the dynamic parts of a document. These different forms of code are what make up the different approaches used by JSP.

The basic capabilities of servlets and JSP are the same. JSP is more appropriate when the majority of the document to be returned is predefined; servlets are more commonly used when the majority of the return document is dynamically generated.

11.5.2 JSP Documents

When requested by a browser, a JSP document is processed by a software system called a JSP container. Some JSP containers compile the document when the document is loaded on the server; others compile them only when they are requested. The compilation process translates a JSP document into a servlet and then compiles the servlet. So, JSP is actually a simplified approach to writing servlets.

A JSP document consists of four different kinds of elements: directives, traditional XHTML or XML code, action elements, and scriptlets.

The XHTML or XML code in the document is used to produce the content that is fixed. This markup is called *template text*. It is the static part of the document. Everything in a JSP document that is not a JSP element is template text. Template text is not modified by JSP elements—it arrives at the browser exactly as it appears in the JSP document. The designer choice between using a servlet and a JSP document is made on the basis of the proportion of the document that is template text. The more template text there is, the better it is to use JSP. If a document is mostly dynmically generated, then a servlet is the better choice.

Action elements dynamically create content. The result of the execution of a JSP document is a combination of the template text and the output of the action elements. An action element has the form of an XHTML element: an opening tag, possibly including attributes; content, which is sometimes called the action body; and a closing tag. In fact, however, action elements represent program code that generates XHTML markup.

Action elements appear in three different categories: standard, custom, and JSP Standard Tag Library (JSTL). The standard action elements are defined by the JSP specification. These include elements for dealing with Java beans[3],

---

3. A Java bean is a reusable component. Because they are beyond the scope of this book, beans will
   not be discussed here.

including the response from a servlet or another JSP document, and dynamically generating an XML element. For example, the action element `<jsp: element>` dynamically generates an XML element, possibly with attributes and content defined by other nested actions. The `<jsp:include>` action element specifies a document file as the value of its `page` attribute. The document file is copied into the output document of the JSP document in which the `include` appears.

Custom action elements are those that are designed for a specific category of JSP documents within an organization. Because of its complexity, the development of custom action elements is not discussed in this chapter.

The JSP standard action elements are highly limited in scope and utility, so there are many commonly needed tasks that cannot be done with them. This led to a large number of different programmers defining their own custom action elements for these tasks, which was clearly a waste of effort. This situation was remedied by the development of the JSTL, which includes action elements for many commonly needed tasks. The JSTL actually consists of five libraries. The *Core* library includes elements for simple flow control, in particular selection and loop constructs, among others. The *XML Processing* library includes elements for transformations of XML documents. The *Internationalization and Formatting* library includes elements for formatting and parsing localized information. The *Relational Database Access* library includes elements for database access. The *Functions* library includes elements for Expression Language functions. (Expression Language is described below.)

Action elements specify actions that are normally described with statements from a programming language. Libraries of action elements in fact form programming languages that can be used to write dynamic actions in a markup-like form. The difference between using the action elements and using Java is twofold: First, the syntax is completely different. Second, the special tags are simpler and easier to use than their Java equivalents.

A directive is a message to the JSP container, providing information about the document and the sources of predefined action elements of the document. Directives can specify that content from other sources be included in a document. However, directives do not themselves create content.

Syntactically, directives are tags that use `<%@` and `%>` delimiters. They use attributes to communicate to the container. The most commonly used directives are `page` and `taglib`. The `page` directive can include many different attributes, but only one is required, `contentType`, which is usually set to `text/html`, as in the following:

```
<%@ page contentType = "text/html" %>
```

The `taglib` directive is used to specify a library of action elements, or tags, that are used by the document. Many JSP documents use JSTL. The URI for the JSTL is given as the value of the `uri` attribute in the `taglib` directive. Also included is the `prefix` attribute, which is assigned the abbreviation, or prefix, that the document uses for tags from the JSTL. For example, a JSP document may contain the following directive:

```
<%@ taglib prefix = "c"
   uri = "http://java.sun.com/jsp/jstl/core" %>
```

This directive specifies the URI of the JSTL Core library and sets the prefix for its elements to c. Examples of the use of Core library action elements appear in the JSP examples later in this chapter.

11.5.3 Scriptlets

Scriptlets are Java code scripts that can be embedded in JSP documents. When the JSP document is converted to a servlet, its scriptlets are simply copied into the servlet. There are four kinds of elements that can appear in a scriptlet: comments, scriptlet code, expressions, and declarations. The use of declarations can lead to threading problems, so they are rarely used. Because of this, they are not discussed here.

Scriptlet expressions are used to insert values into the response. The form of a scriptlet expression is as follows:

```
<%= expression %>
```

The expression is evaluated, and the result is converted to a `String` object, if it is not already a `String` object, and is placed in the response. Note that the expression cannot be terminated with a semicolon.

Scriptlet code is Java code that is delimited by <% and %>.

Scriptlet comments must be Java comments because scriptlets consist of Java code. This means that JSP comments (<%-- ... --%>) and XHTML comments, although both are legal in JSP documents, are not legal in scriptlets.

The following is a simple example of an XHTML document that displays a form that collects a termperature in Celsius from the client. It then calls a JSP document that uses a scriptlet to compute and display the equivalent Fahrenheit temperature.

```
<!-- tempconvert0.html
     A document that displays a form that collects a Celsius
     temperature from a client and calls a scriptlet to
     convert it to Fahrenheit
     -->

<html xmlns = "http://www.w3.org/1999/xhtml">
```

continued

```
    <head>
      <title> Get a Celsius temperature </title>
    </head>
    <body>
      <p>

<!-- Display a form to collect a Celsius temperature -->

        <form action = "tempconvert0.jsp" method = "get" >
          Celsius temperature:
          <input type = "text" name = "ctemp" />
          <input type = "submit" />
        </form>
      </p>
    </body>
</html>
```

The JSP document that is called by this document follows:

```
<!-- tempconvert0.jsp
     A document that converts a Celsius temperature received
     from tempconvert0.html to Fahrenheit
     -->

<html xmlns = "http://www.w3.org/1999/xhtml">

  <head>
    <title> Temperature converter </title>
  </head>
  <body>
    <p>
      <%

// Get the Celsius temperature from the form

        String strCtemp = request.getParameter("ctemp");
        float ftemp;

// convert the value to Fahrenheit

        ftemp = 1.8f * Integer.parseInt(strCtemp) + 32.0f;
      %>
```

```
<!-- Use an expression to display the value of the
     Fahrenheit temperature -->

     Fahrenheit temperature:

       <%= ftemp %>
   </body>
</html>
```

The XHTML and JSP documents for the temperature conversion can be combined into a single JSP document. This document has two parts: the XHTML markup to display the form to collect the Celsius temperature and the scriptlet to compute and display the Fahrenheit temperature. The document must first determine whether a request is the first or the second so that it can choose whether to display the form or compute and display the result. One way to do this is to use the `getParameter` method of the response object to get the form value and test it against the null string. If it is null, it is the first request, which requires the form must be displayed. Otherwise, the computation must be done. The following is the combined document:

```
<!-- tempconvert1.jsp
     A document that collects a Celsius temperature from a
     client and uses a scriptlet to convert it to Fahrenheit
     -->

<html xmlns = "http://www.w3.org/1999/xhtml">
  <head>
    <title> Temperature converter </title>
  </head>
  <body>
    <p>
      <%

// Get the Celsius temperature from the form

        String strCtemp = request.getParameter("ctemp");
        float ftemp;

// If this is not the first request (there was a form value),
// convert the value to Fahrenheit
```

continued

```
            if (strCtemp != null) {
              ftemp = 1.8f * Integer.parseInt(strCtemp) + 32.0f;
        %>


<!-- Use an expression to display the value of the
     Fahrenheit temperature -->

     Fahrenheit temperature:

        <%= ftemp %>

<!-- Code for the end of the then clause compound
     statement -->

        <%
          } //** end of if (strCtemp != ...
          else {
        %>

<!-- This is the first request, so display the form
     to collect the Celsius temperature -->

        <form action = "tempconvert1.jsp" method = "get" >
          Celsius temperature:
          <input type = "text" name = "ctemp" />
          <input type = "submit" />
        </form>
      </p>

<!-- Code for the end of the else clause compound
     statement -->

        <%
          } //** end of else clause
        %>
    </body>
</html>
```

In the first version of JSP, 1.1, all dynamic parts of documents were specified with scriptlets. Of course, embedding a significant amount of Java code in a JSP document defeated the goals of the JSP approach to writing servlets. Putting a large amount of Java code in an XHTML document is not better than putting a large amount of XHTML markup in a servlet. Even the simple JSP document, tempconvert1.jsp, illustrates the confusion that results from mixing Java and XHTML in a document.

Recent versions of JSP, which include the JSP Standard Tag Library (JSTL) and the JSP Expression Language, have made it unnecessary to include raw Java code in a JSP document. Furthermore, the use of scriptlets is now being discouraged. For these reasons, this chapter does not further discuss scriptlets.

The focus of the remainder of this chapter is JSP using JSTL.

11.5.4 Expression Language

The use of JSTL requires knowledge of its two primary technologies, the actual tag set of JSTL and the JSP Expression Language.

The JSP Expression Language (EL) is similar to the expressions (but only the expressions) of a scripting language such as JavaScript, at least in terms of simplicity. This similarity is most evident in the type coercion rules, which obviate most of the strict typing and explicit type conversions that are required in writing expressions in strongly typed programming languages such as Java. For example, if a string is added to a number in EL, an attempt will be made to coerce the string to a number. This makes it convenient for dealing with form data, which is always in text form but often represents data of other types. It also makes EL easier for Web designers, who are often not Java programmers. Also, EL has no control statements such as selection and loop control. These are provided by action elements from the JSTL. EL is true to its name—it is just a language for simple expressions.

Syntactically, an EL expression is always introduced with a dollar sign ($) and delimited by braces, as in the following:

```
${ expression }
```

An EL expression consists of literals, the usual arithmetic operators, implicit variables that allow access to form data, and normal variables. The literals can be numeric, either in the form of floating-point or integer values, Booleans (true or false), or strings delimited by either single or double quotes. A variable that has not been assigned a value has the value null. The only variables we will use are those created by the JSTL action elements.

EL is used to set the attribute values of action elements. Because attributes take string values, the result of the evaluation of an EL expression is always coerced to a string.

EL uses data that comes from several different sources. The most interesting of these for our discussion is the form data sent in a request form, which is made available through the implicit variable, param. The param variable stores a collection of all of the form data values. To access a particular form data value, the name of the form element is used like a property name in JavaScript, catenated on the collection name with a period. For example, if there is a form element named address, it can be accessed with the following:

```
${param.address}
```

If the form element name includes special characters, an alternative access form is used, which is to treat the element name as a subscript into the `param` array, as in the following:

```
${param['cust-address']}
```

EL defines a number of other implicit variables. Most of them are collections of values related to the request header, form values, cookies, and various scope variables. For example, the `pageContext` implicit variable is a reference to an object of class `javax.servlet.http.HttpServletRequest`, which has a long list of information about the request. Among these are `contentType`, `method`, which is the request method (GET or POST), `remoteAddr`, the IP of the client, and `contentLength`.

Although the values of EL expressions are usually implicitly placed in the result document, it is good to explicitly request such placement. This is accomplished by assigning the expression value to the value attribute of the out action element defined in the JSTL Core library. The recommended prefix for this library is `c`. To output the value of the address form element, the following could be used:

```
<c:out value = "${param.address}" />
```

The following example consists of an XHTML document with a form that solicits a temperature in Celsius from the user and a JSP document that processes the form, which in this case computes the equivalent temperature in Fahrenheit and returns an HTML document to the user with that value. The XHTML document is `tempconvert2.html`.

```
<?xml version = "1.0" encoding = "utf-8"?>
<!DOCTYPE html PUBLIC "-//w3c//DTD XHTML 1.1//EN"
 "http://www.w3.org/TR/xhtml11/DTD/xhtml11.dtd">

<!-- tempconvert2.html
     Get a temperature in Celsius and call a JSTL JSP
     document (tempconvert2.jsp) to convert it to Fahrenheit
     -->
<html xmlns = "http://www.w3.org/1999/xhtml">
  <head>
    <title> Get a Celsius temperature </title>
  </head>
  <body>
    <form action = "tempconvert2.jsp" method = "post" >
      <p>
```

```
        Celsius temperature:
        <input type = "text" name = "ctemp" /> <br />
        <input type = "submit" value = "Convert to Fahrenheit" />
      </p>
    </form>
  </body>
</html>
```

The JSP document to process the form data in `tempconvert2.html` is `tempconvert2.jsp`.

```
<!-- tempconvert2.jsp
     Convert a given temperature in Celsius to Fahrenheit.
     Called by tempconvert2.html
     -->
<%@ page contentType = "text/html" %>
<%@ taglib prefix = "c"
           uri = "http://java.sun.com/jsp/jstl/core" %>
<html xmlns = "http://www.w3.org/1999/xhtml">
  <head>
    <title> Temperature converter </title>
  </head>
  <body>
    <p>
      Given temperature in Celsius:
      <c:out value = "${param.ctemp}" />
      <br /> <br />
      Temperature in Fahrenheit:
      <c:out value = "${(1.8 * param.ctemp) + 32}" />
    </p>
  </body>
</html>
```

Note that although the JSP document, `tempconvert.jsp`, has the form of an XHTML 1.1 document, it cannot be validated as one because of the embedded JSP.

11.5.5 JSTL Control Action Elements

The Core library of JSTL includes a collection of action elements for flow control in a JSP document. The most commonly used of these are `if`, `forEach`, when, choose, and otherwise. The form of an if element that has a body, which is the most useful form, is as follows:

```
<c:if test = "boolean expression">
```

JSP elements and/or XHTML markup

```
</c:if>
```

An if element could be used to write a JSP document that served as both the requesting document and the responding document. It could determine whether the document was being processed (after being interacted with and sent to the server) by checking whether the method implicit variable had been set to "POST". For example:

```
<c:if test = "pageContext.request.method == 'POST'}">
```

JSP elements and/or XHTML markup

```
</c:if>
```

The following is a JSP document for the temperature conversion previously done with tempconvert.html and tempconvert.jsp.

```
<!-- tempconvert3.jsp
     Convert a given temperature in Celsius to Fahrenheit
     This is both the request and the response document
     -->
<%@ page contentType = "text/html" %>
<%@ taglib prefix = "c"
           uri = "http://java.sun.com/jsp/jstl/core" %>
<html xmlns = "http://www.w3.org/1999/xhtml">
  <head>
    <title> Temperature converter </title>
  </head>
  <body>

     <c:if test = "${pageContext.request.method != 'POST'}">
        <form action = "tempconvert3.jsp" method = "post" >

           Celsius temperature:
           <input type = "text" name = "ctemp" /> <br />
           <input type = "submit"
                  value = "Convert to Fahrenheit" />
```

```
        </form>
      </c:if>


      <c:if test = "${pageContext.request.method == 'POST'}">
        Given temperature in Celsius:
             <c:out value = "${param.ctemp}" />
        <br /> <br />
        Temperature in Fahrenheit:
             <c:out value = "${(1.8 * param.ctemp) + 32}" />
      </c:if>


  </body>
</html>
```

Through "view source," one can see the two versions of tempconvert3.jsp that come to the browser. These are shown in Figures 11.9 and 11.10.

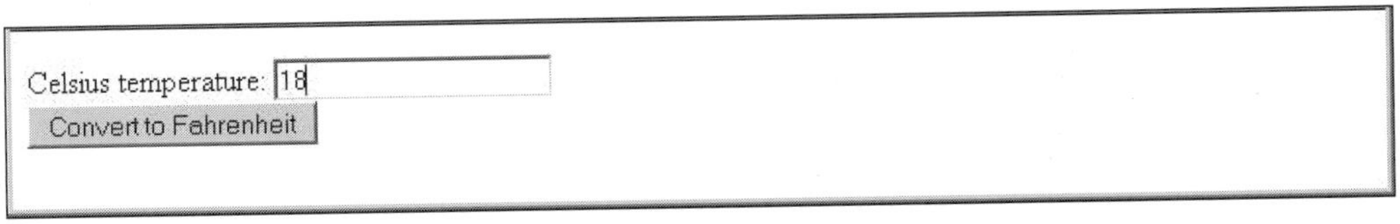

Celsius temperature: 18
Convert to Fahrenheit

FIGURE 11.9 A listing of the initial version of `tempconvert3.jsp`

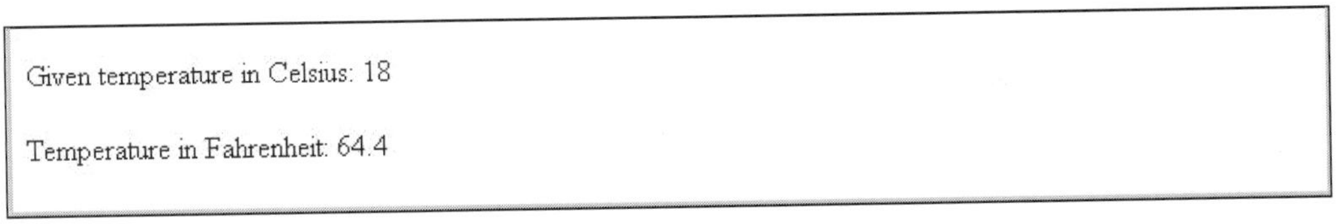

Given temperature in Celsius: 18

Temperature in Fahrenheit: 64.4

FIGURE 11.10 The listing of `tempconvert3.jsp` after submitting the original

Checkboxes and menus have multiple values. The `param` implicit variable cannot be used to determine which values are set in the document that handles forms with these components. For this, there is the `paramValues` implicit variable, which has an array of values for each form element. The `forEach` JSTL action element can be used to iterate through the elements of a `paramValues` array.

`forEach` is related to the Perl `foreach` statement—it iterates based on the elements of a collection, an iterator, an enumeration, or an array. The `items` attribute is assigned the data structure on which the iteration is based. The `var` attribute is assigned variable name to which the structure's elements are assigned. For example, consider the following checkboxes:

```
<form method = "post">
  <input type = "checkbox" name = "topping"
         value = "extracheese"
         checked = "checked" />      Extra cheese <br />
  <input type = "checkbox" name = "topping"
         value = "pepperoni" /> Pepperoni <br />
  <input type = "checkbox" name = "topping"
         value = "olives" /> Olives <br />
  <input type = "checkbox" name = "topping"
         value = "onions" /> Onions <br />
  <input type = "checkbox" name = "topping"
         value = "bacon" /> Bacon <br />
  <input type = "submit"  value = "Submit" /> <br />
</form>
```

To list the checkboxes that were checked, the following could be used:

```
Pizza Toppings:
<c:forEach items = "${paramValues.topping}"
           var = "top">
  <c:out value = "${top}"> <br />
</c:forEach>
```

The `forEach` element can also be used to control a loop body based on a counter. For this, it uses the `begin`, `end`, and `step` attributes. For example, the following could be used to simply repeat the enclosed code ten times:

```
<c:forEach begin = "1" end = "10">
  ...
c:/forEach>
```

Radio buttons must be handled differently than checkboxes. Once again, all radio buttons in a group have the same name. For this situation, JSTL has three action elements that allow the specification of a form of a switch construct. These three are `choose`, `when`, and `otherwise`. The `choose` element, which takes no attributes, encloses the whole construct. A `when` element specifies one of the selectable sequences of code. The `when` attribute, `test`, is set to an EL expression that describes the Boolean expression that controls entry into the body of the element. The `otherwise` element, which takes no attributes, specifies the code for the case when none of the Boolean expressions in the `when` elements is true. The first `when` element with a true `test` attribute is chosen, so if the `test` attributes of more than one of the `when` elements are true, only one is chosen. Consider the following example, which only displays the radio button that is currently pressed:

```
<?xml version = "1.0" encoding = "utf-8"?>
<!DOCTYPE html PUBLIC "-//w3c//DTD XHTML 1.1//EN"
 "http://www.w3.org/TR/xhtml11/DTD/xhtml11.dtd">

<!-- testradio.jsp
     Display radio buttons and use JSP to display which is
     pressed when the form is submitted
     -->

<%@ page contentType = "text/html" %>
<%@ taglib prefix = "c"
           uri = "http://java.sun.com/jsp/jstl/core" %>

<html xmlns = "http://www.w3.org/1999/xhtml">
<head> <title> Test Radio buttons </title>
</head>
<body>
  <form method = "post">
    <p>
      <input type = "radio" name = "payment"
             value = "visa" checked = "checked" />
        Visa
      <input type = "radio" name = "payment"
             value = "mc" />
        Master Charge
      <input type = "radio" name = "payment"
             value = "discover" />
        Discover
      <input type = "radio" name = "payment"
             value = "check" /> Check <br/>
      <input type = "submit" value = "Submit" />
    </p>
  </form>

<!-- If the form has been submitted, display the payment method -->

  <c:if test = "${pageContext.request.method == 'POST'}">
    You have chosen the following payment method:
    <c:choose>
```

continued

```
        <c:when test = "${param.payment == 'visa'}">
          Visa
        </c:when>
        <c:when test = "${param.payment == 'mc'}">
          Master Charge
        </c:when>
        <c:when test = "${param.payment == 'discover'}">
          Discover
        </c:when>
        <c:otherwise>
          Check
        </c:otherwise>
      </c:choose>
    </c:if>
  </body>
</html>
```

11.6

SUMMARY

A servlet is a Java program that resides on the Web server and is enacted when requests are received from Web clients. A program called a servlet container, which runs in the Web server, controls the execution of servlets. The most common uses of servlets are as server-side scripts and as alternatives to CGI programs.

The Java `Servlet` interface includes declarations of three methods: `init`, `service`, and `destroy`. The `service` method controls how the servlet responds to client requests. Most user-written servlets are extensions to the predefined abstract class `HttpServlet`, which is a predefined descendent of `GenericServlet`, which implements the `Servlet` interface. Any class that is derived from `HttpServlet` must override at least one of its methods—most often `doGet`, `doPost`, or both. The `doGet` and `doPost` methods both take two parameters: one to get the input from the client and one that makes it convenient to return results to the client. The `setContentType` method sets the MIME type for the return information. The `println` method of a `PrintWriter` object is used to actually create the return information. The `getParameter` method is used to get the form values from the inquiry string of a form submission from the client. It is called through the request object parameter.

A Web server can store information about clients on the clients themselves in two ways: by using cookies and by using session tracking. A session begins with the first client request to a Web server and ends when the client's browser is stopped. Cookies are implemented on the server as objects of the `Cookie` class, which defines a collection of methods for dealing with cookie objects. Each cookie stores a single name/value pair. The server may send a cookie to the client along with the response to the client's request. Each subsequent request made by that client to that server includes the cookies that have been sent by the server during the current session. Each cookie has a lifetime, which is assigned with the `setMaxAge` method of the `Cookie` class. Cookies are destroyed when their lifetimes end. The server attaches a cookie to its response to a client with the `addCookie` method of the response object. Cookies are obtained from a client request with the `getCookies` method of the request object.

Session tracking is an alternative to cookies for storing information on the client. In this case, the information is stored in an object of the `HTTPSession` class, often called a session object. Such an object can store an unlimited amount of information, whereas a cookie can store just one name/value pair. Session objects live only as long as the session lasts (that is, only as long as the session in which they are created). Values are inserted into a session object with the `putValue` method and are removed with the `removeValue` method. The `getValue` method takes a string as a parameter, which it uses as the name of a session object value. `getValue` returns the value associated with the given name.

JSP is a collection of several approaches to support dynamic documents on the server. It is an alternative to servlets, putting some form of code in markup, rather than the servlet approach to producing markup with Java code. JSTL provides a set of action elements that form a programming language that has the form of markup. EL is a simple expression language to be used with JSP. The `if` JSTL element provides a selection construct; the `forEach` element provides a loop construct, and `choose`, `when`, and `otherwise` provide a multiple selection construct.

Servlets should be used when there is little static content in the return document; JSP should be used when there is little dynamic content.

11.7 Review Questions

1. What potential advantages do servlets have over CGI programs?

2. What is a servlet container?

3. Describe the purpose of the life-cycle servlet methods.

4. Most user-written servlets extend what predefined class?

5. What are the purposes of the `doGet`, `doPost`, and `doPut` methods of the `HttpServlet` class?

6. Describe the two parameters to `doGet` and `doPost`.

7. What must the first markup output of a servlet to a client be?

8. What class of object is used to create XHTML output of a servlet to a client?

9. How does a servlet read form data values sent by a client to a servlet?

10. What is a session?

11. Why would a Web server need to store information on a client about the client's previous requests?

12. What is a cookie?

13. What do the methods `setMaxAge`, `setValue`, and `getComment` do?

14. How is a cookie added to a response by a servlet?

15. How does a servlet get a cookie coming from a client?

16. What is session tracking?

17. How is a name/value pair added to a session object?

18. How does a session object get the value of a name?

19. How can a servlet determine whether a session object exists for a client request?

20. Why should the use of scriplets be restricted?

21. What are the two kinds of people who develop and maintain dynamic documents?

22. What happens during the compilation process for JSP documents?

23. What is template text?

24. What are the five parts of the JSTL?

25. What is the purpose of the `taglib` directive?

26. What is the syntactic form of an EL expression?

27. What are the two ways the `param` implicit variable can be used to access form values?

28. Describe the syntax and semantics of the `forEach` element when it is used to iterate through a collection.

29. Describe the semantics of a `choose` element that includes several `when` elements.

11.8 Exercises

1. Write a servlet that uses `doGet` to return an XHTML document that provides your name, e-mail address, and mailing address, along with a brief biography of yourself. Test your servlet with a simple XHTML document.

2. Write a servlet that returns a randomly chosen greeting from a list of five different greetings. The greetings must be stored as constant strings in the program.

3. Revise the survey sample servlet, `Survey.java`, to display the results of the survey in a table, with female responses in one column and male responses in another.

4. Revise the survey sample servlet, `Survey.java`, to record the number of votes so far in the data file and then display that count every time a vote is submitted or a survey result is requested. Also, change the output table so that its data is a percentage of the total votes for the particular gender category.

5. Write the XHTML to create a form that collects favorite popular songs, including the name of the song, the composer, and the performing artist or group. This document must call a servlet when the form is submitted and another servlet to request a current list of survey results.

6. Modify the servlet for Exercise 5 to count the number of visitors and then display that number for each visitor.

7. Modify the XHTML form for the election and the servlet `VoteCounter` to allow voters to vote for one additional office. The new office is named Catcatcher. Candidates for Catcatcher are Kitty Catland, Al El Gato, Kitten Katnip, Tommie Cat, and Fred Feline. The election results must be in terms of percentage of the total vote for an office. Votes are not counted if the client did not vote for both offices.

8. Rewrite the servlets for Exercise 7 to use session tracking rather than cookies.

9. Write the XHTML to create a form with the following capabilities:

   a. A text widget to collect the user's name

   b. Four checkboxes, one each for the following items:

      i. Four 100-watt light bulbs for $2.39

      ii. Eight 100-watt light bulbs for $4.29

      iii. Four 100-watt long-life light bulbs for $3.95

      iv. Eight 100-watt long-life light bulbs for $7.49

   c. A collection of three radio buttons that are labeled as follows:

      i. Visa

      ii. MasterCard

      iii. Discover

10. Write a servlet that computes the total cost of the ordered light bulbs from Exercise 9 after adding 6.2 percent sales tax. The servlet must inform the buyer of exactly what was ordered, in a table.

11. Write the XHTML to provide a form that collects names and telephone numbers. The phone numbers must be in the format ddd-ddd-dddd. Write a servlet that checks the submitted telephone number to be sure that it conforms to the required format and then returns a response that indicates whether the number was correct.

12. Revise the survey example so that it displays the result as a horizontal bar, similar to a progress bar, ranging from 0–100.

13. Emulate the built-in session-tracking mechanism using cookies. Hint: Use one cookie for the session ID and a class variable of the servlet to store a table of session objects.

14. Write and test a JSP document that displays the form of Exercise 9 and produces the same response document as Exercise 10.

15. Write an XHTML document that displays a form that collects three numbers from the client and calls a JSP document that computes the value of multiplying the three numbers together. The JSP document must use scriptlets.

16. Write a single JSP document that does exactly what is prescribed in Exercise 15.

17. Write a single JSP document that displays a form that collects the radius of a circle. The document must include scriptlets to compute the circumference and area of the circle and display them.

12

Introduction to PHP

This chapter introduces PHP and discusses its use as a server-side scripting language. It begins with a brief look at the origins of PHP, followed by an overview of its primary characteristics and some of its general syntactic conventions. Next, the core language is introduced. Because PHP is close to both Perl and JavaScript, the discussion of its expressions and statements is brief. PHP's arrays, which are different from those of any other language, are then introduced, followed by a description of PHP's functions and their parameter-passing mechanisms. Because PHP uses the same regular expressions for pattern matching as Perl and JavaScript,[1] regular expressions are not described in this chapter. The form-handling techniques of PHP are discussed next, including a complete example. Finally, both cookies and session tracking in PHP are introduced.

---

1. Actually, PHP can use two different kinds of regular expressions, POSIX and Perl style.

Significant parts of PHP are not covered in this chapter. Among these are references and support for object-oriented programming. PHP access to databases is discussed in Chapter 14, "Database Access through the Web."

12.1

ORIGINS AND USES OF PHP

PHP was developed by Rasmus Lerdorf, a member of the Apache Group,[2] in 1994. Its initial purpose was to provide a tool to help Lerdorf track visitors to his personal Web site. In 1995, he developed a package called Personal Home Page Tools, which became the first publicly distributed version of PHP. Originally, PHP was an acronym for Personal Home Page. Later, its user community began using the recursive name PHP: Hypertext Preprocessor, which subsequently forced the original name into obscurity.

Within two years of its release, PHP was being used at a large number of Web sites. By then, it had grown beyond the abilities of a single developer, and its development was transferred to a small group of devoted volunteers. PHP is now developed, distributed, and supported as an open-source product. The PHP processor is now resident on most Web servers.

As a server-side scripting language, PHP is naturally used for form handling and database access. Database access has been a prime focus of PHP development; as a result, it has driver support for 15 different database systems. PHP supports the common electronic mail protocols POP3 and IMAP. It also supports the distributed object architectures COM and CORBA.

12.2

OVERVIEW OF PHP

PHP is a server-side, XHTML-embedded scripting language. As such, it is an alternative to CGI, Microsoft's Active Server Pages (ASP and ASP.NET), Sun's Java Server Pages (JSP), and Allaire's ColdFusion.

PHP is related to client-side JavaScript. When a browser finds JavaScript code embedded in an XHTML document it is displaying, it calls the JavaScript interpreter to execute the script. When a browser requests an XHTML document that includes PHP script, the Web server that provides the document calls the PHP processor. The server determines that a document includes PHP script by the filename extension. If it is `.php`, `.php3`, or `.phtml`, it has embedded PHP.

---

2. The Apache Group develops and distributes the Apache Web server, among other things.

The PHP processor has two modes of operation, copy mode and interpret mode. It takes a PHP document file as input and produces an XHTML document file. When the PHP processor finds XHTML code (which may include embedded client-side script) in the input file, it simply copies it to the output file. When it encounters PHP script in the input file, it interprets it and sends any output of the script to the output file. This implies that the output from a PHP script must be XHTML or embedded client-side script. This new file (the output file) is sent to the requesting browser. The client never sees the PHP script. If the user clicks on View Source while the browser is displaying the document, only the XHTML (and embedded client-side script) will be shown, for that is all that ever arrives at the client.

PHP is usually purely interpreted, as is the case with JavaScript. However, recent PHP implementations perform some precompilation, at least on complex scripts, which increases the speed of interpretation.

The syntax and semantics of PHP are closely related to the syntax and semantics of two languages already described in this book, JavaScript and Perl. This should make it relatively easy to learn, assuming the reader has learned one or both of those languages.

PHP uses dynamic typing, as does JavaScript. Variables are not type declared, and they have no intrinsic type. The type of a variable is set every time it is assigned a value, taking on the type of that value. Similar to JavaScript, PHP is far more forgiving than most common programming languages. Dynamic typing is largely responsible for this, but the dynamic nature of its strings and arrays also contributes. PHP's arrays are a merge of the arrays of common programming languages and the hashes of Perl, having the characteristics of both. There is a large collection of functions for creating and manipulating PHP's arrays.

PHP has an extensive library of functions, making it a flexible and powerful tool for server-side software development. Many of the predefined functions are used to provide interfaces to other software systems such as mail and database systems.

As is the case with JavaScript and Perl, language processors for PHP are free and easily obtainable. In addition, the PHP processor is an open-source system. It is implemented on UNIX and Windows, on which the vast majority of Web servers run. The Web site for official information on PHP is http://www.php.net.

12.3

GENERAL SYNTACTIC CHARACTERISTICS

PHP scripts either are embedded in XHTML documents or are in files that are referenced by XHTML documents. There are several ways to indicate that part of a document is a PHP script. First, the `<script>` tag can be used. However, because you will sometimes want to intermingle XHTML and PHP code on a line-to-line basis, using `<script>` can be cumbersome. Perhaps the best way is to use the opening and closing tags `<?php` and `?>`. This is the only way that works in XML and XHTML documents, and it also has the benefit of requiring little typing.

If a PHP script is stored in a different file, it can be brought into a document with the `include` construct, which takes the filename as its parameter. For example:

```
include("table2.inc");
```

This construct causes the contents of the file `table2.inc` to be copied into the document where the call appears. The included file can contain XHTML markup or client-side script, as well as PHP code, but any PHP script it includes must be the content of a `<?php` tag, even if the `include` appears in the content of a `<?php` tag. The PHP interpreter changes from interpret to copy mode when an `include` is encountered.

All variable names in PHP begin with dollar signs ($). The part of the name after the dollar sign is like the names of variables in many common programming languages: a letter or an underscore followed by any number (including zero) of letters, digits, or underscores. PHP variable names are case sensitive.

Table 12.1 lists the PHP reserved words. Although variable names in PHP are case sensitive, neither reserved words nor function names are. For example, there is no difference between `while`, `WHILE`, `While`, and `wHiLe`.

TABLE 12.1 The Reserved Words of PHP

and	else	global	require	virtual
break	elseif	if	return	xor
case	extends	include	static	while
class	false	list	switch	
continue	for	new	this	
default	foreach	not	true	
do	function	or	var	

PHP allows comments to be specified in three different ways. Single-line comments can be specified either with #, as in Perl, or with //, as in JavaScript. Multiple-line comments are delimited with /* and */, as in many other programming languages.

PHP statements are terminated with semicolons. Braces are used to form compound statements for control structures. Unless used as the body of a function definition, compound statements cannot be blocks. (They cannot define locally scoped variables.)

12.4

PRIMITIVES, OPERATIONS, AND EXPRESSIONS

PHP has four scalar types, Boolean, integer, double, and string; two compound types, array and object; and two special types, resource and NULL. In this section, only the scalar types and NULL are discussed. Arrays are discussed in Section 12.7; objects and resource types are not covered in this book.

12.4.1 Variables

Because PHP is dynamically typed, it has no type declarations. In fact, there is no way or need to ever declare the type of a variable.[3] The type of a variable is set every time it is assigned a value. An unassigned variable, sometimes called an *unbound variable*, has the value NULL, which is the only value of the NULL type. If an unbound variable is used in an expression, NULL is coerced to a value that is dictated by the context of the use. If the context specifies a number, NULL is coerced to 0; if the context specifies a string, NULL is coerced to the empty string.

A variable can be tested to determine whether it currently has a value with the IsSet function, which takes the variable's name as its parameter and returns a Boolean value. For example, IsSet($fruit) returns TRUE if $fruit currently has a non-NULL value, FALSE otherwise. A variable that has been assigned a value retains that value until either it is assigned a new value or it is set back to the unassigned state, which is done with the unset function.

If you prefer to be informed when an unbound variable is referenced, use the error_reporting function to change the error-reporting level of the PHP interpreter to 15. The following call is placed at the beginning of the script in the document file:

```
error_reporting(15);
```

The default error-reporting level is 7, which does not require the interpreter to report the use of an unbound variable.

12.4.2 Integer Type

PHP has a single integer type, named integer. This type corresponds to the long type of C and its successors, which means its size is that of the word size of the machine on which the program is run. In most cases, this is 32 bits, or a bit less (not fewer) than ten decimal digits.

---

3. Variables are sometimes declared to have nondefault scopes or lifetimes, as discussed in Section 12.8.

12.4.3   Double Type

PHP's double type corresponds to the `double` type of C and its successors. Double literals can include a decimal point, an exponent, or both. The exponent has the usual form of an `E` or an `e`, followed by a possibly signed integer literal. There need not be any digits before or after the decimal point, so both `.345` and `345.` are legal double literals.

12.4.4   String Type

Characters in PHP are single bytes. (UNICODE is not supported.) There is no character type. A single character data value is represented as a string of length 1.

String literals are defined with either single (') or double quotes (") delimiters. The difference between them is exactly as in Perl. In single-quoted string literals, escape sequences, such as \n, are not recognized as anything special, and the values of embedded variables are not substituted. (This substitution is called *interpolation*.) In double-quoted string literals, escape sequences are recognized, and embedded variables are replaced by their current values. For example, the value of

```
'The sum is: $sum'
```

is exactly as it is typed. However, assuming the current value of `$sum` is `10.2`, the value of

```
"The sum is: $sum"
```

is

```
The sum is: 10.2
```

If a double-quoted string literal includes a variable name but you do not want it interpolated, precede the first character of the name (the dollar sign) with a backslash (\). If the name of a variable that is not set to a value is embedded in a double-quoted string literal, the name is replaced by the empty string.

Double-quoted strings can include embedded newline characters that are created by the Enter key of the keyboard. Such characters are exactly like those that result from typing \n in the string.

The length of a string is limited only by the available memory on the computer.

12.4.5   Boolean Type

The only two possible values for the Boolean type are `TRUE` and `FALSE`, both of which are case insensitive. Although Boolean is a data type in the same sense as integer, expressions of other types can be used in Boolean context. If you use a non-Boolean expression in Boolean context, you obviously must know how it will be interpreted.

If an integer expression is used in Boolean context, it evaluates to FALSE if it is zero; otherwise, it is TRUE.

If a string expression is used in Boolean context, it evalutes to FALSE if it is either the empty string or the string "0"; otherwise, it is TRUE. This implies that the string "0.0" evaluates to TRUE.

Because of rounding errors, as well as the fact that the string "0.0" evaluates to TRUE, it is not a good idea to use expressions of type double in Boolean context. A value can be very close to zero, but because it is not exactly zero, it will evaluate to TRUE.

12.4.6 Arithmetic Operators and Expressions

PHP has the usual (for C-based programming languages) collection of arithmetic operators (+, -, *, /, %, ++, and --) with the usual meanings. In the cases of +, -, and *, if both operands are integers, the operation is integer and an integer result is produced. If either operand is a double, the operation is double and a double result is produced. Division is treated the same way, except that if integer division is done and the result is not an integral value, the result is returned as a double. Any operation on integers that results in integer overflow also produces a double. The operands of the modulus operator (%) are expected to be integers. If one or both are not, they are coerced to integers.

PHP has a large number of predefined functions that operate on numeric values. Some of the most useful of these are shown in Table 12.2. In this table, "number" means either integer or double.

TABLE 12.2 Some Useful Predefined Functions

Function	Parameter Type	Returns
floor	Double	Largest integer less than or equal to the parameter
ceil	Double	Smallest integer greater than or equal to the parameter
round	Double	Nearest integer
srand	Integer	Initializes a random number generator with the parameter
rand	Two numbers	A pseudorandom number greater than the first parameter and smaller than the second
abs	Number	Absolute value of the parameter
min	One or more numbers	Smallest
max	One or more numbers	Largest

The other predefined functions for number values are for doing number base conversion and computing exponents, logarithms, and trigonometric functions.

12.4.7 String Operations

The only string operator is the catenation operator, specified with a period (`.`).

String variables can be treated somewhat like arrays for access to individual characters. The position of a character in a string, relative to zero, can be specified in braces immediately after the variable's name. For example, if `$str` has the value "apple", `$str{3}` is "l".

PHP includes many functions that operate on strings. Some of the most commonly used of these are described in Table 12.3.

TABLE 12.3 Some Commonly Used String Functions

Function	Parameter Type	Returns
strlen	A string	The number of characters in the string
strcmp	Two strings	0 if the two strings are identical, a negative number if the first string belongs before the second (in the ASCII sequence), or a positive number if the second string belongs before the first
strpos	Two strings	The character position in the first string of the first character of the second string, if the second string is in the first string; `false` if it is not there
substr	A string and an integer	The substring of the string parameter, starting from the position indicated by the second parameter; if a third parameter is given (an integer), it specifies the length of the returned substring
chop	A string	The parameter with all whitespace characters removed from its end
trim	A string	The parameter with all whitespace characters removed from both ends
ltrim	A string	The parameter with all whitespace characters removed from its beginning
strtolower	A string	The parameter with all uppercase letters converted to lowercase
strtoupper	A string	The parameter with all lowercase letters converted to uppercase

Note for `strpos`: Because `false` is interpreted as zero in numeric context, this can be a problem. To avoid it, compare the returned value to zero using the `===` operator (see Section 12.6.1) to determine whether the match was at the beginning of the first string parameter (or there was no match).

12.4.8 Scalar Type Conversions

PHP, like most other programming languages, includes both implicit and explicit type conversions. Implicit type conversions are called *coercions*. In most cases, the context of an expression determines the type that is expected or required. The context can cause a coercion of the type of the value of the expression. We have already discussed some of the coercions that take place between the integer and double types and between Boolean and other scalar types. There are also frequent coercions between numeric and string types. Whenever a numeric value appears in string context, the numeric value is coerced to a string. Likewise, whenever a string value appears in numeric context, the string value is coerced to a numeric value. If the string contains a period, an e, or an E, it is converted to double; otherwise, it is converted to integer. If the string does not begin with a sign or a digit, the conversion fails and zero is used. Nonnumeric characters following the number in the string are ignored.

When a double is converted to an integer, the fractional part is dropped; rounding is not done.

Explicit type conversions can be specified in three different ways. Using the syntax of C, an expression can be cast to a different type. The cast is a type name in parentheses preceding the expression. For example, if the value of $sum is 4.777, the following produces 4:

```
(int)$sum
```

Another way to specify explicit type conversion is to use one of the functions intval, doubleval, or strval. For example, if $sum is still 4.777, the following call returns 4:

```
intval($sum)
```

The third way to specify an explicit type conversion is the settype function, which takes two parameters: a variable and a string that specifies a type name. For example, if $sum is still 4.777, the following statement converts the value of $sum to 4 and its type to integer:

```
settype($sum, "integer");
```

The type of a variable can be determined in two different ways, the first of which is the gettype function. The gettype function takes a variable as its parameter and returns a string that has the name of the type of the current value of the variable. One possible return value of gettype is "unknown". The other way to determine the type of a variable is to use one or more of the type-testing functions, each of which takes a variable name as a parameter and returns a Boolean value. These are is_int, is_integer, and is_long, which test for integer type; is_double, is_float, and is_real, which test for double type; is_bool, which tests for Boolean type; and is_string, which tests for string type.[4]

12.4.9 Assignment Operators

PHP has the same set of assignment operators as its predecessor languages, C and Perl, including the compound assignment operators such as += and /=.

12.5

OUTPUT

Any output from a PHP script becomes part of the document the PHP processor is building. Therefore, all output must be in the form of XHTML, which may include embedded client-side script.

There are three ways to create output: echo, print, and printf. The echo function can be called with or without parentheses around its parameter(s). If parentheses are included, only a single string parameter is acceptable. Otherwise, any number of parameters can appear. For example, the following statement is legal:

```
echo "Apples are red <br />", "Kumquats aren't <br />";
```

But this one is not:

```
echo("Apples are red <br />", "Kumquats aren't <br />");
```

The echo function does not return a value.

The print function is like echo, except it can never be called with more than one parameter, and it returns a value. Once again, the parentheses are optional. The returned value indicates whether the operation was completed (1 if it succeeded; 0 if it failed). The probability of failure is too small to warrant further discussion here. We will usually use print in our examples, just because it looks natural for a programming language.

Although both print and echo expect string parameters, if some other type value is given, the PHP interpreter will coerce it to a string without complaint. For example, the following statement will produce 47:

```
print(47);
```

---

4. PHP also has the is_array function to test for arrays and the is_object function to test for objects.

The `printf` function is exactly like its counterpart in C (and copied into Perl). It is used when complete control over the format of displayed data is required. A description of the syntax and semantics of `printf` can be found in any book on C.

The following simple example displays a welcome message and the current day of the week, the month, and day of the month. The date information is generated with the `date` function, whose first parameter is a string that specifies the parts of the date you want to see. In our example, `l` requests the day of the week, `F` requests the month, `j` requests the day of the week, and an `S` next to the `j` gets the correct suffix for the day (for example, `st` or `nd`). The details of `date` can be found at `http://www.php.net`. Figure 12.1 shows a display of the output of `today.php`.

```
<?xml version = "1.0" encoding = "utf-8"?>
<!DOCTYPE html PUBLIC "-//w3c//DTD XHTML 1.1 //EN"
 "http://www.w3.org/TR/xhtml11/DTD/xhtml11.dtd">

<!-- today.php - A trivial example to illustrate a php document -->
<html xmlns = "http://www.w3.org/1999/xhtml">
  <head> <title> today.php </title>
  </head>
  <body>
    <p>
      <?php
        print "<b>Welcome to my home page <br /> <br />";
        print "Today is:</b> ";
        print date("l, F jS");
        print "<br />";
      ?>
    </p>
  </body>
</html>
```

Welcome to my home page

Today is: Saturday, June 1st

FIGURE 12.1   Display of the output of `today.php`

12.6

CONTROL STATEMENTS

The control statements of PHP are not remarkable—in fact, they are very similar to those of C and its descendants. The control expression used in PHP's control statements can be any type. The interpreter evaluates the control expression and, in the cases of if and loop statements, coerces the resulting value, if necessary, to Boolean.

12.6.1 Relational Operators

PHP uses the eight relational operators of JavaScript. The usual six (>, <, >=, <=, !=, and ==) have the usual meanings. It also has ===, which produces TRUE only if both operands are the same type and have the same value, and !==, the opposite of ===. If the types of the operands of the other six relational operators are not the same, one is coerced to the type of the other. If a string is compared to a number and the string can be converted to a number (it is in fact a string version of a number, for example "42"), the string will be converted and a numeric comparison will be done. If the string cannot be converted to a number, the numeric operand will be converted to a string, and a string comparison will be done. If both operands are strings that can be converted to numbers, both will be converted and a numeric comparison will be done. This is often not always what you want. To avoid this and similar problems associated with string-to-number coercions, if either or both operands are strings that could be converted to numbers, the strcmp function should be used rather than one of the comparison operators.

12.6.2 Boolean Operators

There are six Boolean operators: and, or, xor, !, &&, and ||. The and and && operators perform the same operation, as do or and ||. The difference between these is that the precedence of and and or is higher than that of && and ||. All of PHP's binary Boolean operators are evaluated as short-circuit operators.

12.6.3 Selection Statements

PHP's if statement is like that of C. The control expression can be an expression of any type, but its value is coerced to Boolean. The controlled statement segment can be either an individual statement or a compound statement. An if statement can include any number of elseif clauses.

The switch statement has the form and semantics of that of JavaScript. The type of the control expression and the case expressions is either integer, double, or string. If necessary, the values of the case expressions are coerced to the type of the control expression for the comparisons. A default case can be included.

12.6.4 Loop Statements

The while, for, and do-while statements of PHP are exactly like those of JavaScript. PHP also has a foreach statement that is similar to the foreach in Perl. This statement will be discussed in Section 12.7.4.

The break and continue statements are similar to those of JavaScript. The break statement is used to terminate the execution of a for, foreach, while, do-while, or switch construct. The continue statement is used in loop constructs to skip the remainder of the current iteration but continue execution at the beginning of the next.

12.6.5 Alternative Compound Delimiters

The if, switch, for, and while control statements allow an alternative to the braces normally used to delimit the compound statements being controlled. The controlled compound statement's opening delimiter is the colon (:). Each of the four control statements has its own closing reserved word. These are endif, endswitch, endfor, and endwhile. For example, the following two while statements are identical in meaning:

```
while ($a < 100) {
   $a = $a * $b + 7;
   $b++;
}

while ($a < 100) :
   $a = $a * $b + 7;
   $b++;
endwhile;
```

The advantage of using the latter syntax is readability. The right brace used in the traditional form indicates that some compound statement has ended, but there is no hint as to what particular kind of construct was closed.

If this alternative syntax is used in an if statement that includes an else clause, the then clause is opened with the colon and terminated with the else reserved word. The else clause is opened with a colon and closed with endif, which closes the whole construct. For example:

```
if ($a < $b) :
   $smaller = $a;
   print("\$a is smaller <br />");
else :
   $smaller = $b;
   print("\$b is smaller <br />");
endif;
```

12.6.6   An Example

The following example is meant to illustrate the form of an XHTML/PHP document, as well as some simple mathematical functions and the intermingling of XHTML and PHP in a document. The sqrt function returns the square root of its parameter; the pow function raises its first parameter to the power of its second parameter.

Figure 12.2 displays the output of powers.php.

Powers table

Number	Square Root	Square	Cube	Quad
1	1	1	1	1
2	1.4142135623731	4	8	16
3	1.7320508075689	9	27	81
4	2	16	64	256
5	2.2360679774998	25	125	625
6	2.4494897427832	36	216	1296
7	2.6457513110646	49	343	2401
8	2.8284271247462	64	512	4096
9	3	81	729	6561
10	3.1622776601684	100	1000	10000

FIGURE 12.2   The output of powers.php

```
<?xml version = "1.0" encoding = "utf-8"?>
<!DOCTYPE html PUBLIC "-//w3c//DTD XHTML 1.1 //EN"
 "http://www.w3.org/TR/xhtml11/DTD/xhtml11.dtd">

<!-- powers.php
     An example to illustrate loops and arithmetic
     -->
<html xmlns = "http://www.w3.org/1999/xhtml">
  <head> <title> powers.php </title>
  </head>
  <body>
    <table border = "border">
      <caption> Powers table </caption>
```

```
      <tr>
        <th> Number </th>
        <th> Square Root </th>
        <th> Square </th>
        <th> Cube </th>
        <th> Quad </th>
      </tr>
      <?php
        for ($number = 1; $number <=10; $number++) {
          $root = sqrt($number);
          $square = pow($number, 2);
          $cube = pow($number, 3);
          $quad = pow($number, 4);
          print("<tr align = 'center'> <td> $number </td>");
          print("<td> $root </td> <td> $square </td>");
          print("<td> $cube </td> <td> $quad </td> </tr>");
        }
      ?>
    </table>
  </body>
</html>
```

12.7

ARRAYS

Arrays in PHP are unlike those of any other common programming language. They are best described as a combination of the arrays of a typical language and the hashes of Perl. This makes them the ultimate in flexible, built-in data structures. Array elements are like the elements of a Perl hash: Each consists of two parts, a key and a value. If the array has a logical structure that is similar to an array in another language, the keys just happen to be positive integers and are always in ascending order. If the array has a logical structure that is similar to a Perl hash, its keys are strings, and the order of its elements is determined with a hashing function. One interesting thing about PHP arrays is that they can have some elements with integer keys and some with string keys.

12.7.1 Array Creation

There are two ways to create an array in PHP. The assignment operation creates scalar variables. The same operation works for arrays—assigning a value to an element of an array that does not yet exist creates the array. For example, assuming no array named `$list` currently exists, the following statement creates one:

```
$list[0] = 17;
```

Notice that although PHP arrays are related to Perl hashes, the names of PHP arrays begin with dollar signs, like other PHP variables. If the script has a scalar variable named `$list` prior to this assignment, `$list` is now an array. If empty brackets are used in an assignment to an array, a subscript is implicitly furnished. The furnished subscript is 1 greater than the largest used so far in the array, if the array already has elements with numeric keys. If the array currently has no elements with numeric keys, the value 0 is used. For example, in the following code, the second element's subscript will be 2:

```
$list[1] = "Today is my birthday!";
$list[] = 42;
```

This example also shows that the elements of an array need not have the same type.

The second way to create an array is with the `array` construct. We call this a construct because, although the syntax of using it is the same as that of a function call, it is not a function. The parameters to `array` specify the values to be placed in a new array and sometimes also the keys. If the array is like a traditional array, only the values need to be specified. (The PHP interpreter will furnish the numeric keys.) For example:

```
$list = array(17, 24, 45, 91);
```

This assignment creates a traditional array of four elements, with the keys 0, 1, 2, and 3. If you would rather have different keys, they can be specified in the array construct, as in the following:

```
$list = array(1 => 17, 2 => 24, 3 => 42, 4 => 91);
```

An array construct with empty parentheses creates an empty array. For example, in the following statement, `$list` becomes a variable whose value is an array with no elements.

```
$list = array();
```

The following statement creates an array that is exactly like a Perl hash:

```
$ages = array("Joe" => 42, "Mary" => 41, "Bif" => 17);
```

Some built-in functions return arrays. For example, some of the functions that access databases return arrays.

PHP arrays need not be purely in the form of traditional arrays or hashes; they can be mixtures of both. For example, we could have the following:

```
$stuff = array("make" => "Cessna", "model" => "C210",
               "year" => 1960, 3 => "sold");
```

12.7.2 Accessing Array Elements

Individual array elements can be accessed by subscripting, as in other programming languages. The value in the subscript, which is enclosed in brackets, is the key of the value being referenced. The same brackets are used regardless of whether the key is a number or a string. (Recall that Perl uses braces to enclose keys in references to the elements of its hashes.) For example, the value of the element whose key is "Mary" in the $ages array can be displayed with the following statement:

```
print("Mary is $ages['Mary'] years old <br />");
```

Multiple elements of an array can be assigned to scalar variables in one statement, using the list construct. This is similar to the list assignments of Perl. For example:

```
$trees = array("oak" , "pine", "binary");
list($hardwood, $softwood, $data_structure) = $trees;
```

In this example, $hardwood, $softwood, and $data_structure are set to "oak", "pine", and "binary", repectively.

The collection of keys and the collection of values of an array can be extracted with built-in functions. The array_keys function takes an array as its parameter and returns an array of the keys of the given array. The returned array uses 0, 1, and so forth as its keys. The array_values function does for values what array_keys does for keys. For example:

```
$highs = array("Mon" => 74, "Tue" => 70, "Wed" => 67,
               "Thu" => 62, "Fri" => 65);
$days = array_keys($highs);
$temps = array_values($highs);
```

Now the value of $days is ("Mon", "Tue", "Wed", "Thu", "Fri"), and the value of $temps is (74, 70, 67, 62, 65). In both cases, the keys are (0, 1, 2, 3, 4).

12.7.3   Dealing with Arrays

A whole array can be deleted with unset, as with a scalar variable. Individual elements of an array also can be removed with unset, as in the following:

```
$list = array(2, 4, 6, 8);
unset($list[2]);
```

Now $list has three remaining elements with keys 0, 1, and 3 and elements 2, 4, and 8.

The is_array function is similar to the is_int function: It takes a variable as its parameter and returns TRUE if the variable is an array, FALSE otherwise. The count and sizeof functions, which are identical, take an array as a parameter and return the number of elements in the array. The in_array function takes two parameters—an expression and an array—and returns TRUE if the value of the expression is a value in the array; otherwise, it returns FALSE.

It is often convenient to be able to convert between strings and arrays. These conversions can be done with the implode and explode functions. The explode function explodes a string into substrings and returns them in an array. The substrings are defined by the first parameter to explode, which is a string; the second parameter is the string to be converted. For example, consider the following:

```
$str = "April in Paris, Texas is nice";
$words = explode(" ", $str);
```

Now $words contains ("April", "in", "Paris,", "Texas", "is", "nice").

The implode function does the inverse of explode. Given a separator character (or string) and an array, it catenates the elements of the array together, using the given separator string between the elements, and returns the result as a string. For example:

```
$words = array("Are", "you", "lonesome", "tonight");
$str = implode(" ", $words);
```

Now $str has "Are you lonesome tonight" (which is obviously a rhetorical question).

Internally, the elements of an array are stored in a linked list of cells, where each cell includes both the key and the value of the element. The cells themselves are stored in memory through a key hashing function so that they are randomly distributed in a reserved block of storage. Accesses to elements through string keys are implemented through the hashing function. However, the elements all have links that connect them together in the order in which they were created, which allows them to be accessed in that order if the keys are strings and in the order of their keys if the keys are numbers. Section 12.7.4 discusses the ways array elements can be accessed in order.

Figure 12.3 shows the internal logical structure of an array. Although arrays may not be implemented in this exact way, it shows how the two different access methods could be supported.

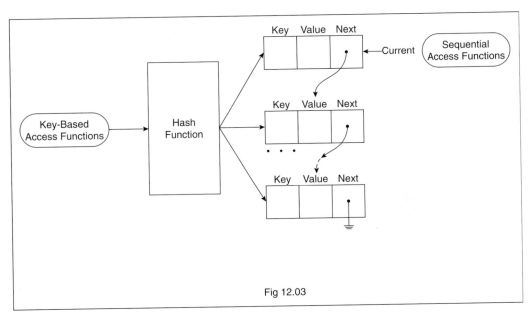

Fig 12.03

FIGURE 12.3   Logical internal structure of arrays

12.7.4   Sequential Access to Array Elements

PHP includes several different ways to access array elements in sequential order. Every array has an internal pointer, or marker, that references one element of the array. We call this the "current" pointer. This pointer is initialized to reference the first element of the array at the time the array is created. The element being referenced by the pointer can be obtained with the current function. For example, consider the following code:

```
$cities = array("Hoboken", "Chicago", "Moab", "Atlantis");
$city = current($cities);
print("The first city is $city <br />");
```

This code produces the following:

```
The first city is Hoboken
```

The "current" pointer can be moved with the next function, which both moves the pointer to the next array element and returns the value of that element. If the "current" pointer is already pointing at the last element of the array, next returns FALSE. For example, if the "current" pointer is referencing the first element of the $cities array, the following code produces a list of all of the elements of that array:

```php
$city = current($cities);
print("$city <br />");
while ($city = next($cities))
  print("$city <br />");
```

One problem with using the next function for loop control, as shown in the preceding example, occurs when the array includes an element with the value FALSE. The loop ends but not because the "current" pointer ran off the end of the array. The each function, which returns a two-element array consisting of the key and the value of the "current" element, avoids this problem. It returns FALSE only if the "current" pointer has gone past the last element of the array. The keys of the two elements of the return value from each are the strings "key" and "value". Another difference between each and next is that each returns the element being referenced by the "current" pointer and then moves that pointer. The next function first moves the "current" pointer and then returns the value being referenced by the "current" pointer. As an example of the use of each, consider the following code:

```php
$salaries = array("Mike" => 42500, "Jerry" => 51250,
                  "Fred" => 37920);
while ($employee = each($salaries)) {
  $name = $employee["key"];
  $salary = $employee["value"];
  print("The salary of $name is $salary <br />");
}
```

The output produced by this code is as follows:

```
The salary of Mike is 42500
The salary of Jerry is 51250
The salary of Fred is 37920
```

The "current" pointer can be moved backward (that is, to the element before the "current" element) with the prev function. Like the next function, the prev function returns the value of the element referenced by the "current" pointer after the pointer has been moved. The "current" pointer can be set to the first element with the reset function, which also returns the value of the first element. It can be set to the last element of the array with the end function, which also returns the value of the last element.

The `key` function, when given the name of an array, returns the key of the "current" element of the array.

The `array_push` and `array_pop` functions provide a simple way to implement a stack in an array. The `array_push` function takes as its first parameter an array. After this first parameter, there can be any number of additional parameters. The values of all subsequent parameters are placed at the end of the array. The `array_push` function returns the new number of elements in the array. The `array_pop` function takes a single parameter, the name of an array. It removes the last element from the array and returns it. The value `NULL` is returned if the array is empty.

The `foreach` statement is designed to build loops that process all of the elements of an array. This statement has two forms:

```
foreach (array as scalar_variable) loop body
foreach (array as key => value) loop body
```

In the first form, one of the array's values is set to the scalar variable for each iteration of the loop body. The "current" pointer is implicitly initialized, as with `reset`, before the first iteration. For example:

```
foreach ($list as $temp)
  print("$temp <br />");
```

This code will produce the values of all of the elements of `$list`.

The second form of `foreach` provides both the key and the value of each element of the array. For example:

```
$lows = array("Mon" => 23, "Tue" => 18, "Wed" => 27);
foreach ($lows as $day => $temp)
  print("The low temperature on $day was $temp <br />");
```

12.7.5   Sorting Arrays

The `sort` function, which takes an array as a parameter, sorts the values in the array, replacing the keys. The array can have both string and numeric values. The string values migrate to the beginning of the array in alphabetical order. The numeric values follow in ascending order. Regardless of the types of the keys in the original array, the sorted array has 0, 1, 2, and so forth as keys. This function is obviously meant for sorting traditional arrays of either strings or numbers. Although it causes no problems, it seems to be a rare situation in which one would plan on sorting arrays with both strings and numbers as values.

The `asort` function is used to sort arrays that correspond to Perl hashes. It sorts the elements of a given array by their values but keeps the original key/value associations. As with `sort`, string values all appear before the numeric values, in alphabetical order. The numeric values follow in ascending order.

The ksort function sorts its given array by keys, rather than values. The key/value associations are maintained by the process.

The rsort, arsort, and krsort functions behave like the sort, asort, and ksort functions, respectively, except they sort into the reverse orders of their counterparts.

The following example illustrates sort, asort, and ksort.

Figure 12.4 shows the output of sorting.php.

```
<?xml version = "1.0" encoding = "utf-8"?>
<!DOCTYPE html PUBLIC "-//w3c//DTD XHTML 1.1//EN"
 "http://www.w3.org/TR/xhtml11/DTD/xhtml11.dtd">


<!-- sorting.php - An example to illustrate several of the
     sorting functions -->
<html xmlns = "http://www.w3.org/1999/xhtml">
  <head> <title> Sorting </title>
  </head>
  <body>
    <?php
      $original = array("Fred" => 31, "Al" => 27,
                        "Gandalf" => "wizzard",
                        "Betty" => 42, "Frodo" => "hobbit");
    ?>
    <h4> Original Array </h4>
    <?php
      foreach ($original as $key => $value)
        print("[$key] => $value <br />");

      $new = $original;
      sort($new);
    ?>
    <h4> Array sorted with sort </h4>
    <?php
      foreach ($new as $key => $value)
        print("[$key] = $value <br />");

      $new = $original;
      asort($new);
    ?>
    <h4> Array sorted with asort </h4>
    <?php
      foreach ($new as $key => $value)
        print("[$key] = $value <br />");
```

```
      $new = $original;
      ksort($new);
   ?>
   <h4> Array sorted with ksort </h4>
   <?php
      foreach ($new as $key => $value)
        print("[$key] = $value <br />");
   ?>
  </body>
</html>
```

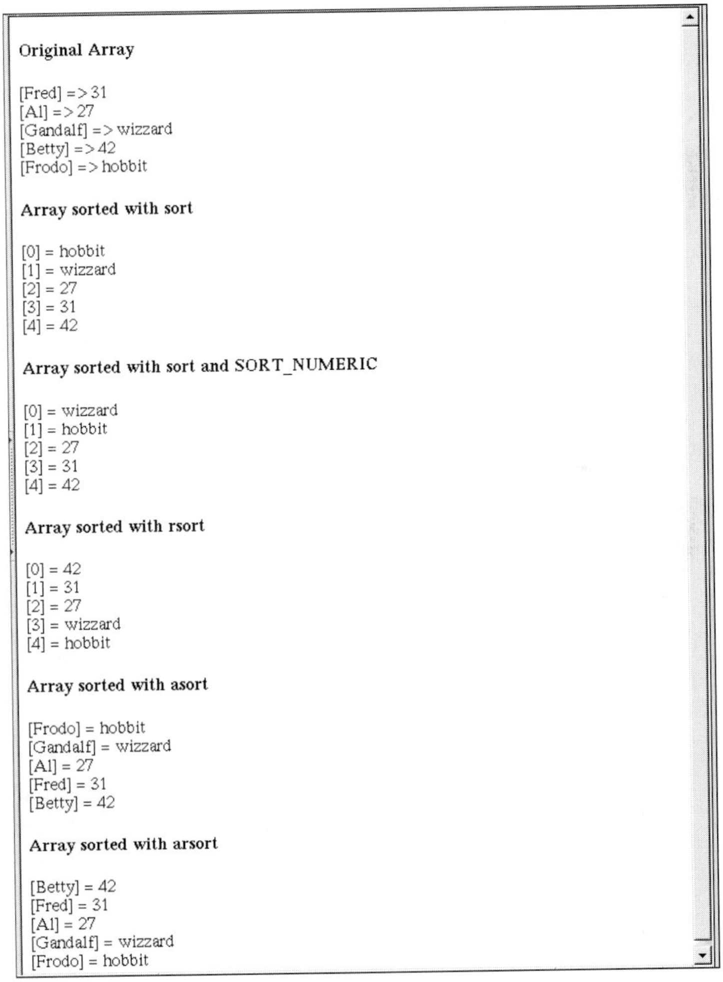

Original Array

[Fred] => 31
[Al] => 27
[Gandalf] => wizzard
[Betty] => 42
[Frodo] => hobbit

Array sorted with sort

[0] = hobbit
[1] = wizzard
[2] = 27
[3] = 31
[4] = 42

Array sorted with sort and SORT_NUMERIC

[0] = wizzard
[1] = hobbit
[2] = 27
[3] = 31
[4] = 42

Array sorted with rsort

[0] = 42
[1] = 31
[2] = 27
[3] = wizzard
[4] = hobbit

Array sorted with asort

[Frodo] = hobbit
[Gandalf] = wizzard
[Al] = 27
[Fred] = 31
[Betty] = 42

Array sorted with arsort

[Betty] = 42
[Fred] = 31
[Al] = 27
[Gandalf] = wizzard
[Frodo] = hobbit

FIGURE 12.4   The output of `sorting.php`

We have now discussed just a few of the most useful built-in functions for arrays. PHP has 57 such functions, so most remain unmentioned.

12.8

FUNCTIONS

PHP supports user-defined functions that are typical for C-based programming languages.

12.8.1 General Characteristics of Functions

The general form of a PHP function definition is as follows:

```
function name([parameters]) {
   ...
}
```

The square brackets around the parameters mean that they are optional. Because a function's definition need not appear in a document before the function is called, the placement of function definitions in a document is, strictly speaking, irrelevant. If a second definition of a function appears in a script, it is reported as an error because function overloading is not allowed and functions cannot be redefined. Function definitions can be nested, as they can in JavaScript. However, because we do not believe the benefit of nested functions is worth the additional complexity they bring to scripts that use them, they are not discussed in this chapter.

Remember that function names are not case sensitive. So, you cannot have a function named sum and another named Sum. The PHP interpreter will see them as the same function and issue an error message stating that you have two definitions for the same function.

The return statement is used in a function to specify the value to be returned to the caller. Function execution ends when a return statement is encountered or the last statement in the function has been executed. In either case, control returns to the caller. If no return statement was executed, no value is returned.

If one or more related functions are used by more than one document, it is convenient to store their definitions in a separate file and copy that file into those documents when they are requested by a client (browser). This is done using the include function, which was described in Section 12.3.

12.8.2 Parameters

As always, we call the parameters in the call to a function *actual parameters*. We call the parameters that are listed in the function definition *formal parameters*.

An actual parameter can be any expression. A formal parameter must be a variable name.

The number of actual parameters in a call to a function need not match the number of formal parameters defined in that function. If there are too few actual parameters in a call, the corresponding formal parameters will be unbound variables. If there are too many actual parameters, the excess parameters will be ignored. The absence of a requirement for matching numbers of parameters allows the language to support functions with a variable number of parameters.

The default parameter-passing mechanism of PHP is pass by value. This means that, in effect, the values of actual parameters are copied into the memory locations associated with the corresponding formal parameters in the called function. The values of the formal parameters are never copied back to the caller, so passing by value implements one-way communication to the function. This is the most commonly needed mechanism for parameter passing. However, sometimes parameters that provide two-way communication between the caller and the function are needed—for example, so a function can return more than one value. One common way to provide two-way communication is to pass the address of the actual parameter, rather than its value, to the function. Then, when the formal parameter is changed (in the function), it also changes the corresponding actual parameter. Such parameters are said to be passed by reference.

Pass-by-reference parameters can be specified in PHP in two ways. One way is to add an ampersand (&) to the beginning of the name of the formal parameter that you want to be passed by reference. Of course, passing by reference only makes sense if the actual parameter is a variable. The other way is to add an ampersand to the actual parameter in the function call. These two techniques have identical semantics. Consider the following example:

```
function add_one($first, $second, &$third) {
   $first++;
   $second++;
   $third++;
}

$a = 3;
$b = 3;
$c = 3;
add_one($a, &$b, $c);
print("\$a, \$b, and \$c are now: $a, $b, $c <br />");
```

The output of this script is as follows:

```
$a, $b, and $c are now: 3, 4, and 4
```

12.8.3 The Scope of Variables

The default scope of a variable defined in a function is local. If a variable defined in a function has the same name as a variable used outside the function, there is no interference between the two. A local variable is visible only in the function in which it is used. For example, consider the following example:

```php
function summer ($list) {
   $sum = 0;
   foreach ($list as $value)
     $sum += $value;
   return $sum;
}

$sum = 10;
$nums = array(2, 4, 6, 8);
$ans = summer($nums);
print
    ("The sum of the values in \$nums is: $ans <br />");
print("The value of \$sum is still: $sum <br />");
```

The output of this code is as follows:

```
The sum of the values in $nums is: 20
The value of $sum is still 10
```

This output shows that the value of $sum in the calling code is not affected by the use of the local variable $sum in the function. The purpose of the design of local variables is simple: A function should behave the same way regardless of the context of its use. Furthermore, when naming a variable while designing a function, the author should not need to worry about conflicts with the names of variables used outside the function.

In some cases, it is convenient for the code in a function to be able to access a variable that is defined outside the function. For this situation, PHP includes the global declaration. When a variable is listed in a global declaration in a function, that variable is expected to be defined outside the function. So, such a variable has the same meaning inside the function as outside. For example, consider the following code:

```php
$big_sum = 0;
...
/* Function summer
   Parameter: An array of integers
   Returns: The sum of the elements of the parameter
            array
```

```
        Side effect: Add the computed sum to the global,
                    $big_sum
*/
function summer ($list) {
  global $big_sum;    //** Get access to $big_sum
  $sum = 0;
  foreach ($list as $value)
    $sum += $value;
  $big_sum += $sum;
  return $sum;
}   //** end of summer


...
$ans1 = summer($list1);
$ans2 = summer($list2);
...
print
    ("The sum of all array elements is: $big_sum <br />");
```

If the global declaration were not included in the function, the script would have two variables named $big_sum, the global one and the one that is local to the function. Without the declaration, this script cannot do what it meant to do.

12.8.4   The Lifetime of Variables

In some situations, a function must be history sensitive; that is, what it does depends on what it has done before. The default lifetime of local variables in a PHP function is from the time the variable is first used (that is, when storage for it is allocated) until the function's execution terminates. To support history sensitivity, a function must have static local variables. The lifetime of a static variable in a function begins when the variable is first used in the first execution of the function. Its lifetime ends when the script execution ends. In the case of PHP, this is when the browser leaves the document in which the PHP script is embedded.

In PHP, a local variable in a function can be specified to be static by declaring it with the static reserved word. Such a declaration can include an initial value, which is only assigned the first time the declaration is reached. For example, consider the following function:

```
function do_it ($param) {
  static $count = 0;
  count++;
  print
     ("do_it has now been called $count times <br />");
  ...
}
```

This function displays the number of times it has been called, even if it is called from several different places. The fact that its local variable, $count, is static allows this to be done.

12.9

PATTERN MATCHING

PHP includes two different kinds of string pattern matching using regular expressions: one that is based on POSIX regular expressions and one that is based on Perl regular expressions. The POSIX regular expressions are compiled into PHP, but the Perl-Compatible Regular Expression (PCRE) library must be compiled before Perl regular expressions can be used. A detailed discussion of PHP pattern matching is beyond the scope of this chapter. Furthermore, Perl-style regular expressions are described in Chapter 4, "The Basics of JavaScript." Therefore, we provide only a brief description of a single PHP function for pattern matching in this section.

The preg_match[5] function takes two or three parameters, the first of which is the Perl-style regular expression as a string. The second parameter is the string to be searched. If the third parameter is included, it is the name of an array in which the pattern matches are to be stored. For example:

```
if (preg_match("/^PHP/", $str))
  print("\$str begins with PHP <br />");
else
  print("\$str does not begin with PHP <br />");
```

The preg_split function operates on strings but returns an array and uses patterns, so it is discussed here rather than with the other string functions in Section 12.4.7. preg_split takes two parameters, the first of which is a Perl-style pattern as a string. The second parameter is the string to be split.[6] For example, consider the following sample code:

```
$fruit_string = "apple : orange : banana";
$fruits = preg_split("/ : /", $fruit_string);
```

The array $fruits now has ("apple", "orange", "banana").

The following example illustrates the use of preg_split on text to parse out the words and produce a frequency-of-occurrence table.

---

5. The first part of the name, preg, is an acronym for *Perl regular*, which indicates the style of regular expression used.

6. The PHP preg_split function is exactly like the Perl split function.

```
<?xml version = "1.0" encoding = "utf-8"?>
<!DOCTYPE html PUBLIC "-//w3c//DTD XHTML 1.1 //EN"
 "http://www.w3.org/TR/xhtml11/DTD/xhtml11.dtd">

<!--    word_table.php
        Uses a function to split a given string of text into
        its constituent words. It also determines the frequency of
        occurrence of each word. The words are separated by
        whitespace or punctuation, possibly followed by whitespace.
        The punctuation can be a period, a comma, a semicolon, a
        colon, an exclamation point, or a question mark.
        The main driver program calls the function and displays
        the results.
        -->
<html xmlns = "http://www.w3.org/1999/xhtml">
<head> <title> word_table.php </title>
</head>
<body>
<?php

// Function splitter
//  Parameter: a string of text containing words and punctuation
//  Returns: an array in which the unique words of the string are
//           the keys and their frequencies are the values.

function splitter($str) {

// Create the empty word frequency array

  $freq = array();

// Split the parameter string into words

  $words = preg_split("/[ .,;:!?]\s*/", $str);

// Loop to count the words (either increment or initialize to 1)

    foreach ($words as $word) {
      $keys = array_keys($freq);
      if(in_array($word, $keys))
        $freq[$word]++;
      else
        $freq[$word] = 1;
    }
```

continued

```
      return $freq;
} #** End of splitter

// Main test driver

  $str = "apples are good for you, or don't you like apples?
          or maybe you like oranges better than apples";

// Call splitter

  $tbl = splitter($str);

// Display the words and their frequencies

  print "<br /> Word Frequency <br /><br />";
  $sorted_keys = array_keys($tbl);
  sort($sorted_keys);
  foreach ($sorted_keys as $word)
    print "$word $tbl[$word] <br />";
?>
</body>
</html>
```

The output of this script is as follows:

```
Word Frequency

apples 3
are 1
better 1
don't 1
for 1
good 1
like 2
maybe 1
or 2
oranges 1
than 1
you 3
```

12.10

FORM HANDLING

We discussed form handling using CGI with Perl in Chapter 10, "The Basics of Perl." Form handling using Java servlets was covered in Chapter 11, "Servlets and Java Server Pages." As you will soon see, form handling with PHP is simpler than either of those two approaches.

It may seem strange, but when PHP is used for form handling, the PHP script is embedded in an XHTML document, like other uses of PHP. Although it is possible to have a PHP script handle form data in the same XHTML document that defines the form, it is perhaps clearer to use two separate documents. For this latter case, the document that defines the form specifies the document that handles the form data in the action attribute of its <form> tag.

PHP can be configured so that form data values are directly available as implicit variables whose names match the names of the corresponding form elements. However, this is not allowed in many Web servers (through the configuration of PHP) because it entails a security risk. The recommended approach is to use the implicit arrays for form values, $_POST and $_GET. These arrays have keys that match the form element names and values that were input by the client. For example, if a form has a text box named phone and the form method is POST, the value of that element is available in the PHP script as follows:

```
$_POST["phone"]
```

The following is an XHTML document that presents a form for popcorn sales that is nearly identical to the one that appears in Chapter 10.

```
<?xml version = "1.0" encoding = "utf-8"?>
<!DOCTYPE html PUBLIC "-//w3c//DTD XHTML 1.1//EN"
 "http://www.w3.org/TR/xhtml11/DTD/xhtml11.dtd">


<!-- popcorn3.html - This describes the popcorn sales form -->
<html xmlns = "http:///www.w3.org/1999/xhtml">
  <head>
    <title> Popcorn Sales - for PHP handling </title>
  </head>
<body>

    <form action = "http://cs.uccs.edu/~rws/popcorn3.php"
          method = "post">
      <h2> Welcome to Millennium Gymnastics Booster Club Popcorn
          Sales </h2>
```

continued

```
        <table>

<!-- Text widgets for the customer's name and address -->

          <tr>
            <td> Buyer's Name: </td>
            <td> <input type = "text" name = "name"
                        size = "30" /></td>
          </tr>
          <tr>
            <td> Street Address: </td>
            <td> <input type = "text" name = "street"
                        size = "30" /></td>
          </tr>
          <tr>
            <td> City, State, Zip: </td>
            <td> <input type = "text" name = "city"
                        size = "30" /></td>
          </tr>
        </table>
        <p />
        <table border = "border">

<!-- First, the column headings -->

          <tr>
            <th> Product </th>
            <th> Price </th>
            <th> Quantity </th>
          </tr>

<!-- Now, the table data entries -->

          <tr>
            <td> Unpopped Popcorn (1 lb.) </td>
            <td> $3.00 </td>
            <td align = "center">
              <input type = "text" name = "unpop"
                     size = "3" /></td>
          </tr>
          <tr>
            <td> Caramel Popcorn (2 lb. canister) </td>
            <td> $3.50 </td>
```

```
              <td align = "center">
                <input type = "text" name = "caramel"
                        size = "3" /> </td>
           </tr>
           <tr>
             <td> Caramel Nut Popcorn (2 lb. canister) </td>
             <td> $4.50 </td>
             <td align = "center">
                <input type = "text" name = "caramelnut"
                        size = "3" /> </td>
           </tr>
           <tr>
             <td> Toffey Nut Popcorn (2 lb. canister) </td>
             <td> $5.00 </td>
             <td align = "center">
                <input type = "text" name = "toffeynut"
                        size = "3" /> </td>
           </tr>
         </table>
         <p />

<!-- The radio buttons for the payment method -->

         <h3> Payment Method </h3>
         <p>
           <input type = "radio" name = "payment" value = "visa"
                   checked = "checked" />
             Visa <br />
           <input type = "radio" name = "payment" value = "mc" />
             Master Card <br />
           <input type = "radio" name = "payment"
                   value = "discover" />
             Discover <br />
           <input type = "radio" name = "payment" value = "check" />
             Check <br /> <br />

<!-- The submit and reset buttons -->

           <input type = "submit" value = "Submit Order" />
           <input type = "reset" value = "Clear Order Form" />
         </p>
       </form>
     </body>
   </html>
```

Figure 12.5 shows the display of `popcorn3.html`.

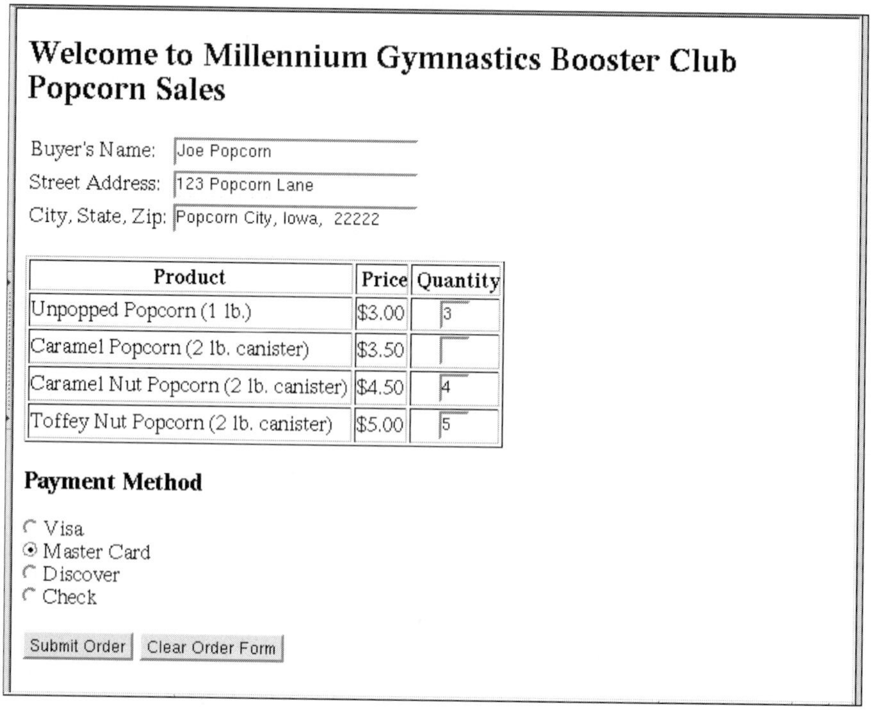

FIGURE 12.5   The display of `popcorn3.html`

The PHP script that handles the data from the form described in `popcorn3.html` follows. It uses the form data to compute the cost of each product, the total cost of the order, and the total number of ordered items. The product name, unit price, number ordered, and total cost for each product are presented to the client in a table. The table is defined with interwoven XHTML markup and PHP script. The table structure is described with XHTML, but the contents of some of the data cells are defined with PHP.

```
<?xml version = "1.0" encoding = "utf-8"?>
<!DOCTYPE html PUBLIC "-//w3c//DTD XHTML 1.1 //EN"
 "http://www.w3.org/TR/xhtml11/DTD/xhtml11.dtd">

<!-- popcorn3.php - Processes the form described in
     popcorn3.html
     -->
```

```
<html xmlns = "http://www.w3.org/1999/xhtml">
  <head>
    <title> Process the popcorn3.html form </title>
  </head>
  <body>
    <?php

// Get form data values

      $unpop = $_POST["unpop"];
      $caramel = $_POST["caramel"];
      $caramelnut = $_POST["caramelnut"];
      $toffeynut = $_POST["toffeynut"];
      $name = $_POST["name"];
      $street = $_POST["street"];
      $city = $_POST["city"];
      $payment = $_POST["payment"];

// If any of the quantities are blank, set them to zero

      if ($unpop == "") $unpop = 0;
      if ($caramel == "") $caramel = 0;
      if ($caramelnut == "") $caramelnut = 0;
      if ($toffeynut == "") $toffeynut = 0;

// Compute the item costs and total cost

      $unpop_cost = 3.0 * $unpop;
      $caramel_cost = 3.5 * $caramel;
      $caramelnut_cost = 4.5 * $caramelnut;
      $toffeynut_cost = 5.0 * $toffeynut;
      $total_price = $unpop_cost + $caramel_cost +
                     $caramelnut_cost + $toffeynut_cost;
      $total_items = $unpop + $caramel + $caramelnut + $toffeynut;

// Return the results to the browser in a table

    ?>
    <h4> Customer: </h4>
    <?php
      print ("$name <br /> $street <br /> $city <br />");
    ?>
    <p /> <p />
```

continued

```
      <table border = "border">
        <caption> Order Information </caption>
        <tr>
          <th> Product </th>
          <th> Unit Price </th>
          <th> Quantity Ordered </th>
          <th> Item Cost </th>
        </tr>
        <tr align = "center">
          <td> Unpopped Popcorn </td>
          <td> $3.00 </td>
          <td> <?php print ("$unpop"); ?> </td>
          <td> <?php printf ("$ %4.2f", $unpop_cost); ?>
          </td>
        </tr>
        <tr align = "center">
          <td> Caramel Popcorn </td>
          <td> $3.50 </td>
          <td> <?php print ("$caramel"); ?> </td>
          <td> <?php printf ("$ %4.2f", $caramel_cost); ?>
          </td>
          </tr>
        <tr align = "center">
          <td> Caramel Nut Popcorn </td>
          <td> $4.50 </td>
          <td> <?php print ("$caramelnut"); ?> </td>
          <td> <?php printf ("$ %4.2f", $caramelnut_cost); ?>
          </td>
        </tr>
        <tr align = "center">
          <td> Toffey Nut Popcorn </td>
          <td> $5.00 </td>
          <td> <?php print ("$toffeynut"); ?> </td>
          <td> <?php printf ("$ %4.2f", $toffeynut_cost); ?>
          </td>
        </tr>
      </table>
      <p /> <p />

      <?php
        print ("You ordered $total_items popcorn items <br />");
        printf ("Your total bill is: $ %5.2f <br />", $total_price);
        print ("Your chosen method of payment is: $payment <br />");
      ?>
    </body>
</html>
```

Notice that the `printf` function is used to implement the numbers that represent money, so exactly two digits appear to the right of the decimal points. Figure 12.6 displays the results of `popcorn3.php`.

Customer:

Joe Popcorn
123 Popcorn Lane
Popcorn City, Iowa, 22222

Order Information

Product	Unit Price	Quantity Ordered	Item Cost
Unpopped Popcorn	$3.00	3	$ 9.00
Caramel Popcorn	$3.50	0	$ 0.00
Caramel Nut Popcorn	$4.50	4	$ 18.00
Toffey Nut Popcorn	$5.00	5	$ 25.00

You ordered 12 popcorn items
Your total bill is: $ 52.00
Your chosen method of payment is: mc

FIGURE 12.6 The output of `popcorn3.php`

12.11

FILES

Because PHP is a server-side technology, it is able to create, read, and write files on the server system. In fact, PHP can deal with files residing on any server system on the Internet, using both HTTP and FTP protocols. We restrict our discussion to dealing with files on the server itself. Furthermore, we will cover only the simple processes of opening, reading, and writing text files. All file operations in PHP are implemented as functions.

12.11.1 Opening and Closing Files

The first step to using a file is to open it, a process that prepares the file for use and associates a program variable with the file for future reference. This program variable is called the *file variable*. The `fopen` function performs these operations. It takes two parameters: the filename, including the path to it if it is in a different directory, and a use indicator, which specifies the operation or operations you need to perform on the file. Both parameters are given as strings. The `fopen` function returns the reference to the file for the file variable. Every open file has an internal pointer that is used to indicate where the next file operation should take place within the file. We call this pointer the *file pointer*. Table 12.4 describes the possible values of the use indicator.

TABLE 12.4 File Use Indicators

Use Indicator	Description
"r"	Read only. The file pointer is initialized to the beginning of the file.
"r+"	Read and write an existing file. The file pointer is initialized to the beginning of the file; if a read operation precedes a write operation, the new data is written just after where the read operation left the file pointer.
"w"	Write only. Initializes the file pointer to the beginning of the file; creates the file if it does not exist.
"w+"	Read and write. Initializes the file pointer to the beginning of the file; creates the file if it does not exist. Always initializes the file pointer to the beginning of the file before the first write, destroying any existing data.
"a"	Write only. If the file exists, initializes the file pointer to the end of the file; if the file does not exist, creates it and initializes the file pointer to its beginning.
"a+"	Read and write a file, creating the file if necessary; new data is written to the end of the existing data.

It is possible for the fopen function to fail—for example, if an attempt is made to open a file for reading but no such file exists. It would also fail if the file access permissions did not allow the requested use of the file. The fopen function returns FALSE if it fails. PHP has a die function that is very similar to that of Perl. It simply produces a message and stops the interpretation process. The use of die with the call to fopen is exactly like that used for Perl file operations. For example, the following statement opens a file named testdata.dat for reading only:

```
$file_var = fopen("testdata.dat", "r") or
            die ("Error — testdata.dat cannot be opened");
```

The problem of fopen failing because the specified file does not exist can be avoided by determining whether the file exists with file_exists before calling fopen. The file_exists function takes a single parameter, the file's name. It returns TRUE if the file exists, FALSE otherwise.

A file is closed with the `fclose` function, which takes a file variable as its only parameter.

12.11.2 Reading from a File

The most common way to read a file in PHP is to move its contents into a scalar variable as a string. Then the impressive collection of PHP string manipulation functions can be used to process the file as a string. The `fread` function reads part or all of a file and returns a string of what was read. This function takes two parameters: a file variable and the number of bytes to be read. The reading operation stops when either the end-of-file marker is read or the specified number of bytes has been read.

Large collections of data are often stored in database systems, so only smaller data sets are stored in files. Therefore, files are often read in their entirety with a single call to `fread`. If the whole file is to be read at once, the file's length is given as the second parameter to `fread`. The best way to get the correct file length is with the `filesize` function, so a call to `filesize` is often used as the second parameter to `fread`. The `filesize` function takes a single parameter, the name of the file (not the file variable). For example, to read the entire contents of the file `testdata.dat` as a string into the variable `$file_string`, the following statement could be used:

```
$file_string = fread($file_var,
                filesize("testdata.dat"));
```

One alternative to `fread` is `file`, which takes a filename as its parameter and returns an array of all of the lines of the file. (A line is a string of non-newline characters, followed by a newline.) One advantage of `file` is that the file open and close operations are not necessary. For example, the following statement places the lines of `testdata.dat` into an array named `@file_lines`:

```
$file_lines = file("testdata.dat");
```

A single line of a file can be read with `fgets`, which takes two parameters: the file variable and a limit on the length of the line to be read. Consider the following statement:

```
$line = fgets($file_var, 100);
```

This statement reads characters from `testdata.dat` until it finds a newline character, encounters the end-of-file marker, or has read 99 characters. Note that the maximum number of characters `fgets` reads is one fewer than the limit given as its second parameter.

A single character can be read from a file with `fgetc`, whose only parameter is the file variable. When reading a file by lines or by characters, the read operation must be controlled by the detection of the end of the file. This can be done with the feof function, which takes a file variable as its only parameter. It returns a Boolean value: TRUE if the last read character of the file was the end-of-file character, FALSE otherwise.

12.11.3 Writing to a File

PHP has a single function to write to a file, fwrite.[7] It takes two parameters: a file variable and the string to be written to the file. It is possible to include a third parameter, which would be used to specify the number of bytes to be written. This parameter is rarely needed. The fwrite function returns the number of bytes written. The following is an example of a call to fwrite:

```
$bytes_written = fwrite($file_var, $out_data);
```

This statement writes the string value in $out_data to the file referenced with $file_var and places the number of bytes written in $bytes_written. Of course, this will work only if the file has been opened for writing.

12.11.4 Locking Files

If it is possible for more than one script to access a file at the same time, the potential interference of those accesses can be prevented with a file lock. The lock prevents any other access to the file while the lock is set. Scripts that use such files lock them before accessing them and unlock them when the access is completed. File locking is done in PHP with the flock function, which should sound familiar to UNIX and Perl programmers. The flock function takes two parameters: the file variable of the file and an integer that specifies the particular operation. A value of 1 specifies that the file can be read by others while the lock is set, a value of 2 allows no other access, and a value of 3 unlocks the file.

12.12

COOKIES

Cookies have been discussed in conjunction with both Perl (Chapter 10) and Java servlets (Chapter 11). This, along with the simplicity of cookies in PHP, allows our discussion here to be brief.

A cookie is set in PHP with the setcookie function. This function takes one or more parameters. The first parameter, which is mandatory, is the cookie's name given as a string. The second, if present, is the new value for the cookie, also a string. If the value is absent, setcookie undefines the cookie. The third parameter, when present, is the expiration time in seconds for the cookie, given

---

7. fread has an alias, fputs.

as an integer. The default value for the expiration time is zero, which specifies that the cookie is destroyed at the end of the current session. When specified, the expiration time is often given as the number of seconds in the UNIX epoch, which began on January 1, 1970. The `time` function returns the current time in seconds. So, the cookie expiration time is given as the value returned from `time` plus some number. For example, consider the following call to `setcookie`:

```
setcookie("voted", "true", time() + 86400);
```

This call creates a cookie named `"voted"` whose value is `"true"` and whose lifetime is one day (86,400 is the number of seconds in a day).

The `setcookie` function has three more optional parameters, the details of which can found in the PHP manual.

The most important thing to remember about creating a cookie or setting a cookie to a new value is that it must be done before any other XHTML is created by the PHP document. Recall that cookies are stored in the HTTP header of the document returned to the requesting browser. The HTTP header is sent before the body of the document is sent. The server sends the header when it receives the first of the body of the document. So, if any part of the body is created, the header is sent, and it is too late to add a cookie to the header. If you create a cookie or change the value of a cookie after even a single character of document body has been generated, the cookie operation will not be successful. (The cookie or the cookie's new value will not be sent to the browser.)

The other cookie operation is getting the cookies and their values from subsequent browser requests. In PHP, cookie values are treated much like form values. All cookies that arrive with a request are placed in the implicit `$_COOKIES` array, which has the cookie names as keys and the cookie values as values. A PHP script can test whether a cookie came with a request by using the `IsSet` predicate function on the associated variable.

As is the case with using cookies with other technologies, remember that cookies cannot be depended upon because some users set their browsers to reject all cookies. Furthermore, most browsers have a limit on the number of cookies that will be accepted from a particular server site.

12.13

SESSION TRACKING

Session tracking, which is an alternative to cookies, is supported by PHP. The idea of session tracking was discussed in Chapter 11.

In PHP, a session ID is an internal value that identifies a session. Session IDs need not be known or handled in any way by PHP scripts. PHP is made aware that a script is interested in session tracking by calling the `session_start` function, which takes no parameters. The first call to `session_start` in a session causes a session ID to be created and recorded.

On subsequent calls to session_start in the same session, the function retrieves the $_SESSION array, which stores any session variables and their values that were registered in previously executed scripts in this session.

Session key/value pairs are created or changed by assignments to the $_SESSION array. They can be destroyed with the unset operator. Consider the following example:

```
session_start();
if (!IsSet($_SESSION["page_number"]))
   $_SESSION["page_number"] = 1;
$page_num = $_SESSION["page_number"];
print("You have now visited $page_num page(s) <br />");
$_SESSION["page_number"]++;
```

If this is not the first document visited that calls session_start and sets the page_number session variable, this script will produce the specified line with the last set value of $_SESSION["page_number"]. If no document that was previously visited in this session set page_number, this script sets page_number to 1, produces the following line, and increments page_number:

```
You have now visited 1 page(s)
```

12.14

SUMMARY

PHP is a server-side, XHTML-embedded scripting language. The language is similar to both Perl and JavaScript. The PHP processor takes as input a file of XHTML/PHP, copies the XHTML to an output file, and interprets the PHP script in the input file. The output of any PHP script is written into the output file. PHP scripts are either directly embedded in XHTML files or are referenced in the XHTML files and subsequently copied into them.

PHP has four scalar types: integer, Boolean, double, and string. These are closely related to their counterparts in Perl. PHP variable names all begin with dollar signs. The language is dynamically typed. Arithmetic and Boolean expressions in PHP are very similar to those in other common languages. PHP includes a large number of functions for arithmetic and string operations. The current type of a variable is maintained internally and can be determined by a script through several different built-in functions. The echo, print, and printf functions are used to produce output, which becomes part of the PHP processor output file. The control statements of PHP are similar to those of other common programming languages.

PHP's arrays are a combination of the traditional arrays of C and its descendent languages and Perl's hashes. Arrays can be created by assigning values to their elements. This is often done with the array construct, which allows the specification of values and optionally the keys for one or more elements of an array. PHP has predefined functions for many array operations. Among these are `explode` and `implode` for converting between strings and arrays; `current`, `next`, and `prev` for fetching elements in sequential order; `each` for obtaining both the keys and values of the elements of an array in sequential order; and `array_keys` and `array_values`, which return an array of the keys and values of the array, respectively. There are also functions for stack operations on arrays. The `foreach` statement, similar to that of Perl, provides sequential access to the elements of an array. Finally, PHP has a collection of functions for sorting the elements of arrays in various ways.

User-defined functions in PHP are similar to those of other languages, except for parameter passing. Because PHP does not have pointers, pass-by-reference parameters must be specified in either the function call or the function definition. Variables used only in a function are local to that function. Access to variables used outside a function is specified with a `global` declaration. Static variables can be declared with a `static` declaration.

PHP's pattern matching can use either POSIX-style or Perl-style regular expressions. Form data is placed in user-accessible variables implicitly by the PHP system. This makes form handling very convenient.

Files are opened and prepared for reading, writing, or both with the `fopen` function, which returns a file variable. Every file has a file pointer, which maintains a position in the file where the next read or write will take place. Files can be read with `fread`, which reads as many bytes as specified in the call, up to the whole file, into a string. The lines of a file can be read into an array of strings with `file`. A single character of a file can be read with `fgetc`. The `fwrite` function is used to write to a file. Interference among simultaneous file accesses can be avoided by locking a file with `flock`.

Cookies are created and set to values with the `setcookie` function, which has parameters for the cookie name, its value, and a lifetime in seconds. Cookies created or set in a previous script are available to a current script directly through the `$_COOKIES` array. A script can test whether a cookie exists and is set to a value with `IsSet`. Session tracking is relatively simple in PHP. The `session_start` function creates a session ID. Session variables are stored in the `$_SESSION` array.

12.15 Review Questions

1. How does a Web server determine whether a requested document includes PHP code?

2. What are the two modes of the PHP processor?

3. What are the syntax and semantics of the `include` construct?

4. Which parts of PHP are case sensitive and which are not?

5. What are the four scalar types of PHP?

6. How can a variable be tested to determine whether it is bound?

7. How can you specify to the PHP processor that you want uses of unbound variables to be reported?

8. How many bytes are used to store a character in PHP?

9. What are the differences between single- and double-quoted literal strings?

10. If an integer expression appears in Boolean context, how is its Boolean value determined?

11. What happens when an integer arithmetic operation results in a value that cannot be represented as an integer?

12. If a variable stores a string, how can the character at a specific position in that string be referenced?

13. What does the chop function do?

14. What is a coercion?

15. What are the three ways the value of a variable can be explicitly converted to a specific type?

16. How can the type of a variable be determined?

17. If a string is compared with a number, what happens?

18. What is the advantage of using the unique closing reserved words such as endwhile?

19. In what two ways can arrays in PHP be created?

20. What keys are used when an array is created but no keys are specified?

21. Must all of the values of an array be of the same type?

22. Must all of the keys of an array be of the same type?

23. What exactly do the array_keys and array_values functions do?

24. What exactly does the in_array function do?

25. Explain the actions of the implode and explode functions.

26. Describe the actions of the next, reset, and prev functions.

27. What are the syntax and semantics of the two forms of the foreach statement?

28. Describe the result of using the sort function on an array that has both string and numeric values.

29. What is the difference betweeen the sort and asort functions?

30. What happens if a script defines the same function more than once?

31. Are function names case sensitive?

32. What value is returned by a function if its execution does not end by executing a `return` statement?

33. What are the two ways you can specify that a parameter is to be passed by reference?

34. How can a variable used outside a function be accessed by the function?

35. How can you define a variable in a function so that its lifetime extends beyond the time the function is in its first execution?

36. How can the value of a form element be accessed by a PHP script?

37. What is a file variable?

38. What is a file pointer?

39. What does an `fopen` function return if it fails?

40. Explain the parameters and actions of the `fread` function.

41. What is returned by the `fwrite` function?

42. How can a cookie be created in a PHP script?

43. How can a script determine whether a particular cookie exists?

44. How can a variable be saved in a session?

12.16 Exercises

Write, test, and debug (if necessary) PHP scripts for the following specifications. For Exercises 1 to 4, write functions and the code to test them.

1. *Parameter:* An array of strings.

   Return value: A list of the unique strings in the parameter array.

2. *Parameter:* An array of numbers.

   Return value: The average and median of the parameter array.

3. *Parameter:* An array of strings.

   Return value: A list of the three strings that occur most frequently in the parameter array.

4. *Parameters:* An array of numbers (pass-by-value) and two arrays (pass-by-reference).

   Return value: None.

   Result: The first pass-by-reference parameter must have the values of the given array that are greater than zero; the second must have the values that are less than zero.

5. *Parameter:* A string of numbers separated by spaces.

   Return value: The first four-digit number in the string.

6. *Parameter:* A file variable of a file of text, where the words are separated by spaces or colons.

   Return value: The word that appears most often in the file.

7. *Parameter:* A string containing words that are delimited on the left with spaces and on the right with commas, periods, or question marks.

   Return value: The three most common words in the string that have more than three letters.

8. Modify the sample script in Section 12.9, `word_table.php`, to place the output table in an XHTML table.

9. Write an XHTML document to that includes an anchor tag that calls a PHP document. Also write the called PHP document, which returns a randomly chosen greeting from a list of five different greetings. The greetings must be stored as constant strings in the script. A random number between 0 and 4 can be computed with these lines:

```
# Set the seed for mtrand with the number of microseconds
#   since the last full second of the clock
mt_srand((double)microtime() * 1000000);
$number = mtrand(0, 4);   # Computes a random integer 0-4
```

10. Write the XHTML code to create a form with the following capabilities:

    a. A text widget to collect the user's name

    b. Four checkboxes, one each for the following items:

       i. Four 100-watt light bulbs for $2.39

       ii. Eight 100-watt light bulbs for $4.29

       iii. Four 100-watt long-life light bulbs for $3.95

       iv. Eight 100-watt long-life light bulbs for $7.49

    c. A collection of three radio buttons that are labeled as follows:

       i. Visa

       ii. MasterCard

       iii. Discover

11. Write a PHP script that computes the total cost of the ordered light bulbs from Exercise 10 after adding 6.2 percent sales tax. The program must inform the buyer of exactly what was ordered, in a table.

12. Write the XHTML code to create a form that collects favorite popular songs, including the name of the song, the composer, and the performing artist or group. This document must call one PHP script when the form is submitted and another to request a current list of survey results.

13. Write the PHP script that collects the data from the form of Exercise 12 and writes it to a file.

14. Write the PHP script that produces the current results of the survey of Exercise 12.

15. Write the XHTML code to provide a form that collects names and telephone numbers. The phone numbers must be in the format ddd-ddd-dddd. Write a PHP script that checks the submitted telephone number to be sure that it conforms to the required format and then returns a response that indicates whether the number was correct.

16. Modify the PHP script for Exercise 9 to count the number of visitors and display that number for each visitor. *Hint:* Use a file to store the current count.

Introduction to ASP.NET

13.1

OVERVIEW OF THE .NET FRAMEWORK

.NET is an umbrella term for a collection of technologies that was announced by Microsoft in early 2000. In January 2002, the software to support .NET was released. It has already made significant progress in being adopted by the Web software industry. It will undoubtedly be a major factor in this industry in the near- and medium-term future.

13.1.1 Background

.NET was developed in recognition that the future of a significant part of the computing business lies in Web-based software services, in which components of a software system may reside on different computers in different places on the Internet. Prior to .NET, Microsoft's technology for distributed component-based systems was named COM.

A *component* is an encapsulation of software that can stand by itself and be used by other components, without those components knowing how the functionality of the component was implemented. Components can also be created with technologies other than COM. JavaBeans is a technology developed by Sun Microsystems to support distributed component-based computing using Java. The primary difference between JavaBeans and COM components is that COM components can be written in a variety of different programming languages—they are language neutral.

The .NET Framework is exactly that—a framework for the development and deployment of .NET software. In .NET, the central concept is that a software system or service consists of a collection of components that can be written in different languages and reside on different computers in different locations. Also, because of the diversity of employed languages, the collection of tools for development and deployment must be language neutral. These ideas permeate all of the parts of the .NET Framework.

13.1.2 The Common Language Runtime

The base technology for .NET is the Common Language Runtime (CLR), which provides language-neutral services for the processing and execution of .NET software. Among the most important services of the CLR are garbage collection, type checking, debugging, and exception handling. These services are used for all of the .NET languages.

For every .NET language, the CLR has a compiler to translate source programs to a common intermediate language, which was originally named Microsoft Intermediate Language (MSIL) but now is usually called Intermediate Language (IL). After compilation, all IL programs have the same form, regardless of the original source language. Before execution, IL programs are incrementally compiled to machine code for the host machine by a Just-In-Time (JIT) compiler, which is part of the CLR. A JIT compiler translates a method to machine code only when the method is called. Once compiled, the machine code version of the method is kept for the duration of execution of the program so that subsequent calls do not require recompilation. Because most executions of a program do not cause all of the program's methods to be called, this is an efficient approach to compilation. In .NET, it is also possible to compile a whole program into machine code before execution begins. JIT compilers are commonly used for Java program execution. One major difference between Java's approach to program execution and that of the .NET languages is that IL programs are never interpreted, as bytecode (the Java intermediate language) programs sometimes are. In fact, the .NET Framework does not include an IL interpreter, which would be similar to the Java Virtual Machine.

13.1.3 .NET Languages

Initially, .NET included five languages: Visual Basic .NET (VB .NET), Managed C++ .NET, JScript .NET, J# .NET, and a new language, C#. VB .NET is based on VB 6.0, a language widely used for Web programming and other software development that includes graphical user interfaces (GUIs). VB .NET differs from VB in many ways, most importantly in that it is a full-fledged object-oriented language, whereas VB is not. Managed C++ .NET is a garbage-collected version of C++. JScript .NET is based on JavaScript but also provides full support for object-oriented programming. J# .NET is Microsoft's version of Java. C# is briefly described in Section 13.2. There are now 20 languages available that run under .NET, among which are COBOL, Eiffel, Fortran, Perl, and Python. Work is underway to add more languages to the list.

The multilanguage aspect of .NET sets it apart from other such systems. The advantage of supporting a variety of programming languages is that there is an easy migration path from software in many different languages to .NET. Organizations that make heavy use of any of the .NET languages can easily transition to .NET. Programmers who are experienced and skilled in almost any common language can quickly become productive in a .NET environment. Although it makes reuse much more feasible, having a system composed of components written in different languages is not all good. One important disadvantage is that it complicates maintenance.

13.1.4   The Common Language Infrastructure

To make it possible to use the CLR for multiple languages, those languages must adhere to a set of common characteristics. These are specified by the Common Language Infrastructure (CLI), which consists of two specifications, the Common Type System (CTS) and the Common Language Specification (CLS).

The CTS defines a set of types that are supported by .NET languages. It also provides a mapping from every type in each language to its corresponding common type. For example, the CTS defines a type named `Int32`, which is a 32-bit signed integer type. The C# type `int` corresponds to `Int32`. The concept of common base types is analogous to what is done with CORBA (`http://www.corba.org`), which defines a similar set of types and gives a mapping from various languages to these common types. In CTS, types occur in two natural categories, value types and reference types. Value types directly reference values in memory cells; that is, the value of a value type object is a value. A reference type is a reference to or address of a memory cell that has a value. So, the value of a reference type is not a value; it is an address.

Having common types among languages is, of course, necessary if components in those languages are expected to interoperate correctly. All types of all .NET languages derive from a single type, `System.object`.

The CLS defines the language features that must be supported by all .NET languages. .NET languages can, however, include features beyond what is specified in CLS. Of course, use of such features in a program will jeopardize the possibility of interoperation of that program with programs in languages that do not support those features. Some examples of CLS restrictions are as follows:

1. No operator overloading.
2. No pointers.
3. Identifiers are not case sensitive.

Interestingly, the new .NET language, C#, includes all three of these. However, they should not be used in C# programs that will interoperate with components written in other .NET languages that do not include them. For example, VB .NET identifiers are not case sensitive. If a C# component must interoperate with a VB .NET component, the C# component must not use two different identifiers in the interface to the VB .NET component whose only difference is case (for example, Sum and sum). To design a language that can be a .NET language, the designer must ensure that all of the CLI features are supported.

The .NET Framework includes a large collection of class libraries called the Framework Class Libraries (FCL). The initial release of FCL included more than 4,000 classes that support a wide array of application areas. For example, there are APIs for networking, reflection, Web forms, database access, and file system access. Also included are APIs for access to Windows features such as the registry, as well as other Win32 functions. These functions are called through FCL classes and are executed in the CLR.

Perhaps the most important result of having the CLI and the CLR is that components written in any of the .NET languages can use any class in the FCL. More striking, perhaps, is the result that a component in any .NET language can use classes defined in any other component written in any other .NET language. This enables calling the methods of a class written in any other .NET language. It also allows subclassing classes written in any other .NET language. For example, a C# program can subclass a class written in VB .NET. It could also call the methods of a class written in managed C++.

13.2

INTRODUCTION TO C#

This section provides a brief introduction to C#. C# is used for the examples of this chapter, but little of the language is used that will not be familiar to Java programmers.

13.2.1 Origins

C# is a new object-oriented language, designed to fit the needs of .NET programming. Like most other "new" programming languages, most of C# is not in fact new but borrowed from existing languages. C# can be thought of as the most recent iteration of the sequence of C-based languages. C++ was derived from C (and SIMULA 67), and Java was derived, at least partially, from C++. C# is derived from both C++ and Java, having been based on Java but including a number of features that are part of C++ but not Java. From Java, C# gets single inheritance, interfaces, garbage collection, the absence of global types or variables, and its level of assignment coercion. From C++, C# gets pointers, operator overloading, a preprocessor, structs, and enumerations (although its structs and enumerations differ significantly from those of C++). From Delphi and VB, C# inherits properties. Finally, from J++ (Microsoft's version of Java), C# gets delegates. Among the C# features that are new are indexes, attributes, and events. Overall, C# is less complex than C++ without giving up much of the expressivity of C++, which is also the case with Java. Although C# is more complex than Java, it is also more powerful.

13.2.2 Primitive Types and Expressions

As is the case with Java, C# has two categories of data: primitives and objects. C# includes a long list of primitive types, ranging from `byte`, which is an unsigned one-byte integer, and `char`, which is a two-byte Unicode character, to `int`, `float`, `double`, and `decimal`, which is a 16-byte decimal type that can store up to 28 decimal digits.

C# supports pointers, as in C++, though they are rarely used. They were included in the language to allow interoperability with C and C++ modules that use pointers. Any method that uses a pointer must be marked with the reserved word `unsafe` in its header.

Symbolic constants are defined by preceding the type name in a declaration with the `const` reserved word. Every symbolic constant declaration must include an initial value. For example:

```
const float pi = 3.14159265;
```

C# has the same collection of arithmetic operators as Java, so its expressions are also like those of Java.

C# has one nonprimitive value type, enumerations, which is discussed in Section 13.2.3.

13.2.3 Data Structures

The .NET FCL defines an extensive variety of collection classes, including `Array`, `ArrayList` (dynamic length arrays), `Queue`, and `Stack`. Although `Array` is a class, the syntax of array references is exactly like that of C. Because it is a class, array access is through reference variables. The following is an example of a declaration of a reference to an `int` array:

```
int[] myIntArray;
```

The variable `myIntArray` can reference any single-dimentioned array of `int` elements. An array object is created with the `new` operator, as in the following statement:

```
myIntArray = new int[100];
```

`myIntArray` now references an array of 100 integers on the heap.

The `Array` class provides a large collection of methods and properties. Among the methods are `BinarySearch`, `Copy`, and `Sort`. The most frequently used property is `Length`.

C# includes an enumeration type, which is a value type. In an enumeration type, the type's designer lists all of the possible values of the type in its declaration. Internally, enumeration values are stored as integers. In C and C++, enumeration type variables can be treated like integers, meaning they can be operated on with arithmetic operators, which for many enumeration types is nonsense. Also, it is possible to assign an integer value to an enumeration type that is not one used in the internal representation of the enumeration type. Syntactically, enumerations look like those of C++ but are actually much safer. The increased security results from the fact that enumeration types are never coerced to other types, and other types are never coerced to enumeration types. This prevents enumeration variables from having values that are not defined for the enumeration type. It also prevents arithmetic operators from being used on enumeration values. The following is an example of the definition of an enumeration type in C#:

```
enum Colors {blue, green, yellow, red, orange, purple};
```

13.2.4 Control Statements

The control statements of C# are nearly identical to those of Java (as well as the other C-based languages). Two differences are the `foreach` and `switch` statements. The `foreach` statement is a data-structure-controlled iterator. It can be used on arrays and other collections. The syntax of `foreach` is as follows:

```
foreach (type identifier in collection) { ... }
```

For example:

```
foreach (int myInt in myIntArray) { ... }
```

The `switch` statement of C# is similar to that of Java but with one important restriction. The `switch` statements of C, C++, and Java all suffer the same problem: Although, in the vast majority of cases, control should exit the construct after a selected segment has executed, the default is that control flows to the next segment after the selected segment has executed. Therefore, most segments in `switch` constructs must include a `break` statement. Leaving out the `break` is a common error in `switch` constructs. To avoid these errors, the C# `switch` has the requirement that every selectable segment in a `switch` construct must end with an unconditional branch instruction, either a `break` or a `goto`. To force control to continue to the next segment, a `goto` is used. For example, consider the following `switch` construct:

```
switch (value) {
    case -1:
        Negatives++;
        break;
    case 0:
        Zeros++;
        goto case 1;
    case 1:
        Positives++;
    default:
        Console.WriteLine("Error in switch \n");
}
```

13.2.5 Classes, Methods, and Structures

C# is a pure object-oriented programming language in the same sense as Java. There are no subprograms except methods, which can only be defined in classes (and structs) and can only be called through objects or classes. Most of the syntax and semantics of C# classes and methods are the same as those of Java. In the following paragraphs, the most important differences are discussed.

Parameters to methods can be passed by value, passed by reference, or passed by result. These three implement in mode, which is the default mode (one-way communication to the method), inout mode (two-way communication between the caller and the called method), and out mode (one-way communication from the called method to the calling method) parameter semantics, respectively. Reference variables implicitly have pass-by-reference semantics. Pass by reference is specified for value types by preceding the formal parameter with the `ref` reserved word. Pass by result is specified for value types by preceding the formal parameter with the `out` reserved word.

In some object-oriented languages, such as Java, it is relatively easy to write methods that accidentally override inherited methods.[1] This happens because

---

1. This would only happen if the author of the inherited method wants to allow it to be overriden somewhere among the class descendents. If the method should never be overriden, it is marked `final`, which prevents all descendent classes from overriding it.

the author of the new method either forgets or is unaware that a method with the same name already exists in the class ancestry. To avoid this error, C# requires any method that is allowed to be overriden to be marked `virtual`. Furthermore, any method that is meant to override an inherited method must be marked `override`. If a method is defined that has the same protocol as an inherited method but is not meant to override it, it must be marked `new`. Such a method hides the inherited version.

A C# method can take a variable number of parameters as long as all are of the same type. The method defines just one parameter, an array with the `params` qualifier. For example:

```
void SumInts(params int [] intValues) { ... }
```

This method can be called with an array or a list of integer expressions. For example:

```
int [] myIntArray = new int[6] {2, 4, 6, 8, 10, 12};
sum1 = SumInts(myIntArray);
sum2 = SumInts(10, i, 17, k);
```

A struct in C++ is very similar to a class. In C#, however, a struct is quite different from the classes of the language. A C# struct is a lightweight class that does not support inheritance or subclassing. However, C# structs can implement interfaces and have constructors. They are value types, which means they are allocated on the runtime stack. The syntactic form of a struct declaration is identical to that of a class, except the reserved word `struct` is used in place of `class`. All C# primitive types are implemented as structs.

13.2.6 Properties

One problem in object-oriented programming languages is the conflict between the theoretical goal of having all data in classes be hidden from code outside the class (by defining it to be private) and the occasional need for other classes to access or modify such data. In many languages, the solution is to define accessor methods that provide indirect access to private data fields. C# borrows the Delphi and VB solution, properties. A *property* is a special data field of a class that can provide get and set accessors. Neither of these needs to be explicitly called—they are implicitly called when code accesses or modifies the property's data. Consider the following example of a property named `DegreeDays`, which defines a private data field, `degreeDays`, and provides indirect access to it:

```
public class Weather {
  public int DegreeDays {
    get {
      return degreeDays;
    }
```

```
    set {
      degreeDays = value;
    }
  private int degreeDays;
  }  //** end of property DegreeDays
  ...
}  //** end of class Weather
...
Weather w = new Weather();
...
w.degreeDays += degreeDaysToday;
```

In the last assignment statement of this code, the data field of the DegreeDays property, degreeDays, is accessed implicitly through the get method. It is also modified, implicitly through the set method, in the same statement. In effect, the property allows access to a private date field. Note the use of the implicit variable value in the set method, which references the value of the property's data. One advantage of a property over simply making the field public is that read-only access can be provided (by defining a get method but not a set method). Furthermore, the set method can be defined to restrict the range of values that can be assigned to the data field.

13.2.7   Delegates

Delegates are object-oriented method pointers. They are reference types for methods of specific protocols. Delegates are created with declarations such as the following:

```
public delegate void AHandler(
                object o, System.EventArgs e);
```

The AHandler delegate can reference any method that returns void and takes parameters of object and System.EventArgs types. (This is the protocol for event handlers in C#.) This delegate encapsulates all such methods that are subscribed to it. The delegate maintains a list of the methods that have been subscribed to it. Subscribing a method to a delegate is similar to the process of registering an object to be an event listener for a particular event in Java. The subscribed methods can be called through the delegate. In Section 13.4.4, delegates will be used for event handling of form widget events. The subscription process will be described there.

13.2.8   Program Structure

In contemporary object-oriented programming languages, programs have access to large, comprehensive, and complex class libraries that provide services and commonly needed types. For .NET, this is the FCL. The most commonly used part of the .NET FCL is System. This class defines a namespace for its constituents, also named System. The System namespace provides classes for input and output, string manipulation, threading, and collections, among others. One of the input and output classes of System, Console, supports console applications, which are those that are not interactive. Console applications are run from a command prompt rather than through a graphical user interface. The Console class has methods ReadLine and WriteLine to read strings from the keyboard and write strings to the screen, respectively.

The using statement is used to abbreviate the names of classes in a namespace. For example,

```
using System;
```

allows the program to access the classes defined in System without using the prefix System on the names of those classes. For example, if using System is not included in a program, WriteLine must be called with System. Console.WriteLine. However, if using System is included, then WriteLine can be called with Console.WriteLine.

The main method of every C# program is named Main (not main). Main need not have a parameter, and it can return either int or void.

An example of a minimal but complete program follows:

```
using System;
public class myTester {
  public static void Main() {
    Console.WriteLine("Howdy!");
  }
}
```

13.2.9   File Storage for Programs

Any number of public classes and/or interfaces can be stored in one file.[2] Every class in a file can define a Main method. If the file has more than one Main method, the compiler must be told which one should be called first. This is done on the compile comand-line command, csc. For example, if the particular Main method that is to begin execution in the file myClassFile.cs is in the class myMainClass, the file must be compiled with the following:

```
csc myClassFile.cs  /main:myMainClass
```

---

2. This differs from Java, in which a file can contain only one public class.

Unlike Java, C# class names and the files where the classes are stored need not be related. Names of files for class definitions should use the `.cs` extension, but that is not required.

13.3

INTRODUCTION TO ASP.NET

ASP.NET is a large and complex topic. This section provides a brief introduction to the fundamentals of ASP.NET.

13.3.1   The Basics

ASP.NET (ASP is an acronym for Active Server Pages) is a Microsoft technology for building dynamic Web documents. Dynamic ASP.NET documents are supported by programming code executed on the Web server. Although ASP.NET documents can also include client-side scripts, we focus on the server side. ASP.NET is based on its predecessor, ASP, which allowed embedded scripts written in either JScript (Microsoft's JavaScript) or VBScript, a scripting dialect of VB. Both of these languages are purely interpreted, making their execution much slower than that of code written in compiled languages. In ASP, the embedded scripts were interpreted on the server. There are a few problems with this approach to providing server-side dynamic documents. First, documents that include both scripting code and XHTML are complex, especially if they are large. Mixing markup and programming code, which mixes presentation and business logic, creates a confusing document. Furthermore, Web markup designers and programmers must deal with the same document. Second, purely interpreting scripts before delivering documents is inefficient. Third, there is the problem of reliability of code written in scripting languages, in part because they use either dynamic typing or relaxed typing rules. Also, in some scripting languages array index ranges are not checked.

As we saw in Chapter 11, "Servlets and Java Server Pages," JSP offers one solution to these problems: Use Java to describe the computation associated with user interactions with Web documents. The Java language is much more reliable than the scripting languages, largely because of the strict type checking and array index range checking. Furthermore, compiled Java code is faster than interpreted scripting code. Finally, although Java can be directly embedded in XHTML documents with JSP, it is entirely separate when JavaBeans are used.

ASP.NET provides an alternative to JSP, with two major differences: First, ASP.NET allows the server-side programming code to be written in any of the .NET languages. Second, in ASP.NET all programming code is compiled.

Programming code that is part of a Web application but resides outside the ASP.NET document (the XHTML document file) is placed in a file called the *code-behind* file. This is a good approach to adding code to a document to produce a dynamic document because it clearly separates the static XHTML from the code. This separation cleanly reflects the difference between the kinds of people who design these two kinds of artifacts. It also simplifies both the ASP.NET document and the code file.

Every ASP.NET document is compiled into a class, which resides in an assembly. An assembly is the unit in which compiled classes are stored in .NET. Compiling a markup document, which may or may not include embedded programming code, into a class is an abrupt departure from other approaches to developing Web resources. From a programmer's point of view, developing dynamic Web documents (and the supporting code) in ASP.NET is similar to developing non-Web applications. Both involve defining classes based on library classes, implementing interfaces from a library, and calling methods defined in library classes. An application class uses and interacts with existing classes. In ASP.NET, this is exactly the same for Web applications. Web documents are designed by designing classes.

The class to which an ASP.NET document is compiled is a descendent of `System.Web.UI.Page`, from which it inherits a collection of members. Among the most commonly used of these are the `Request` and `Response` objects, the `HTMLControls` and `WebControls` classes, and the `IsPostBack` property. The `Write` method of the `Response` object is used to create output from an ASP.NET document. The two controls classes define the large collection of server-side widgets that are available to ASP.NET documents. Sample documents that use the controls classes appear in Section 13.4. The `IsPostBack` property is used to determine whether the current request is a result of a user interaction with a form (as opposed to an initial request for a document). Its use is illustrated in a sample document in Section 13.4.2.

ASP.NET documents that do not use code-behind files are compiled into direct subclasses of `Page`. Code-behind files also are compiled into subclasses of `System.Web.UI.Page`. We call the class that results from compiling the ASP.NET document the *document class*. Note that a document class is pure C# source code rather than an intermediate code version.[3] Document classes that use a code-behind file are subclasses of the code-behind class. The code-behind class is an intermediate class between the document class and `System.Web.UI.Page`. So, programming code in an ASP.NET document inherits from both `Page` and the class of the code-behind file. Inheritance diagrams for ASP.NET documents with and without code-behind files are shown in Figure 13.1.

---

3. This is technically a misuse of the term "compile," although ASP.NET documents are translated from their original form to C# programs.

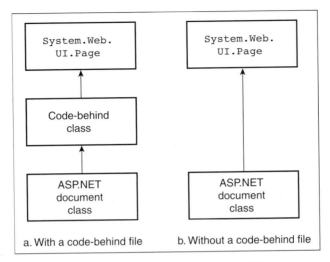

FIGURE 13.1 Inheritance Diagrams for ASP.NET documents with and without code-behind files

13.3.2 ASP.NET Documents

ASP.NET documents can include a number of different elements. First, they can contain XHTML markup, including standard XHTML comments. This markup can include static XHTML, XHTML elements made dynamic by client-side scripts, and XHTML elements made dynamic by server-side code. Second, an ASP.NET document can include one or more directives, the most common of which is @Page, which can have any of a large number of different attributes. Third, documents can have *render blocks*, which use the <% opening tag and %> closing tag and have programming code as content. This code, which cannot include subprogram definitions, is placed in a function of the class of the document when the document is translated to a class. This function's body typically consists of method calls and output statements to create the static XHTML of the document. The function is executed when the document class is executed (which produces the XHTML document that is returned to the requesting browser). Fourth, documents can include programming code as the content of script elements that include the attribute runat set to "server". Such code is called a *declaration block* because it is not implicitly executed. Subprograms, including event handlers, are defined in declaration blocks. The code in declaration blocks is inserted directly into the class created for the document. Finally, documents can include server-side comments, which appear in elements that use the opening tag <%-- and the closing tag --%>.

Directives appear in the same tag form as render blocks. Their names begin with at signs (@), although in a document the at sign is not usually attached to the name. For example, the general form of a directive is as follows:

```
<%@ directive-name attributes %>
```

The only directive required in every ASP.NET document that includes embedded programming code is @Page. For these documents, the @Page directive must minimally include a Language attribute, which is assigned the name of the .NET language that is used for embedded programming code in the document. This, of course, is necessary to inform the CLR which compiler is to be used to compile the document.

At this point, an example is in order. The following simple ASP.NET document uses C# code in a render block to call a subprogram, defined in a declaration block, to create an array of ten random numbers. The render block code then displays the array.

```
<!-- ex1.aspx
     A simple example of an ASP.NET document
     It uses a function to fill an array with pseudorandom numbers,
     which are then displayed
     -->
<%@ Page language="c#" %>

<html>
  <head> <title> Ex1 </title>

    <script runat = "server">

// Build a pseudorandom number method

     Random randomGen = new Random();
     string msg;
     private int [] myArray = new int[10];

// A method to fill the array with pseudorandom numbers

     public void fillArray() {
        for (int index = 0; index < 10; index++)

// Generate a pseudorandom number in the range of 0 to 100

          myArray[index] = randomGen.Next(0, 100);
     }
    </script>
  </head>
  <body>

<!-- Code to call the fillArray method and display the array
```

```
<% fillArray();
   Response.Write(
     "<br /> <b>The array's contents are: </b><br /><br />");
   for (int index = 0; index < 10; index++) {
     msg = string.Format("The element at {0} is: {1} <br />",
                            index, myArray[index]);
     Response.Write(msg);
   }

%>
</body>
</html>
```

`Response.Write` writes its string parameter to the response buffer, which will go back to the client. This example uses the `Format` method of `string` to create the output strings in the loop, which must be formatted with the values from two variables.

13.3.3   Code-Behind Files

As stated in Section 13.3.1, it is better to keep programming code separate from documents, which also separates program logic from presentation. This is done in ASP.NET by storing programming code in code-behind files.

To illustrate the difference between declaration blocks and code-behind files, `ex1.aspx` is rewritten as `ex2.aspx` and the code-behind file `ex2.aspx.cs`, which are shown below. Notice that the `@Page` directive in this ASP.NET document includes two new attributes. The `Inherits` attribute specifies that this document inherits from its code-behind file's class. The name used for this attribute is the same as the base name of this file. Also included is the `Src` attribute, which gives the full name of the code-behind file. When the `Src` attribute is included, the code-behind file is implicitly compiled the first time its associated ASP.NET document is requested. If the code-behind file is updated, the next request for the associated ASP.NET file implicitly causes its recompilation.

If the `Src` attribute is absent, the code-behind file must be explicitly compiled and placed in the `bin` subdirectory of the directory in which the ASP.NET document is stored, before the associated ASP.NET document is requested. This approach has the advantage of allowing the detection and repair of syntax errors in the code-behind file before deployment.

The easiest way to create .NET software is Microsoft's Visual Studio .NET, although we do not discuss its use in this book. All of the examples in this chapter were developed using a simple text editor. This makes the examples cleaner and simpler to discuss and understand.

```
<!-- ex2.aspx
     A simple example of an ASP.NET document with a code-behind file
     It has the same functionality as ex1.aspx
     -->
<%@ Page language="C#" Inherits = "ex2" Src = "ex2.aspx.cs" %>

<html>
  <head> <title> Ex2 </title>
  </head>
  <body>

<!-- Code to call the fillArray method and display the array

    <% string msg;
       fillArray();
       Response.Write(
         "<br /> <b>The array's contents are: </b><br /><br />");
       for (int index = 0; index < 10; index++) {
         msg = string.Format("The element at {0} is: {1} <br />",
                             index, myArray[index]);
         Response.Write(msg);
       }
    %>
  </body>
</html>
```

```
// ex2.aspx.cs
//    The code behind file for ex2.aspx
//    Includes a function to build an array of ten pseudorandom
//    numbers

using System;
using System.Web;
using System.Web.UI;

public class ex2 : Page {

// Build a pseudorandom number method

  Random randomGen = new Random();
  protected int [] myArray = new int[10];
```

```
// A method to fill the array with pseudorandom numbers

  public void fillArray() {
    for (int index = 0; index < 10; index++)

// Generate a pseudorandom number in the range of 0 to 100

      myArray[index] = randomGen.Next(0, 100);
  }
}
```

13.4

ASP.NET CONTROLS

Widgets, or form elements in ASP.NET documents, are called *controls*. Code associated with these controls is executed on the server, so they are called *server controls*. A server control is an event handler. The server control associated with a widget handles events that originate at that widget. Unlike a JavaScript or applet event handler, server controls execute on the server. There are two categories of ASP.NET server controls, HTML controls and Web controls.

13.4.1 HTML Controls

The ASP.NET namespace `System.Web.UI.HTMLControls`, which is implicitly available to all ASP.NET documents, includes the HTML controls. HTML controls are closely related to XHTML form elements. However, HTML controls were designed to allow interactions with server-side programming code. These interactions include the possibility of server-side programming code that can dynamically change the appearance and functionality of HTML controls because the attributes that control these are exposed by the objects that represent the controls in the document class. Furthermore, many HTML controls can raise one of two events when they are manipulated by the client. These two events are `ServerClick`, which corresponds to the JavaScript click event, and `ServerChange`, which corresponds to the JavaScript change event. The most commonly used HTML control types, their corresponding XHTML elements, and the events they raise are shown in Table 13.1.

Notice that some of the HTML control types are not form elements. Users cannot interact with them. They have types to provide program access to their attributes to allow them to be changed dynamically.

TABLE 13.1 HTML control types, corresponding XHTML elements, and their events

Control Type	XHTML Element	Event
HtmlHidden	`<input type = "hidden">`	ServerChange
HmtlInputButton	`<input type = "button">`	ServerClick
	`<input type = "submit">`	ServerClick
	`<input type = "reset">`	ServerClick
HtmlInputCheckBox	`<input type = "checkbox">`	ServerChange
HtmlInputRadioButton	`<input type = "radio">`	ServerChange
HtmlInputText	`<input type = "text">`	ServerChange
	`<input type = "password">`	ServerChange
HtmlAnchor	`<a>`	ServerClick
HtmlButton	`<button>`	ServerClick
HtmlSelect	`<select>`	ServerChange
HtmlTextArea	`<textarea>`	ServerChange
HtmlForm	`<form>`	None
HtmlTable	`<table>`	None
HtmlTableCell	`<td> and <th>`	None
HtmlTableRow	`<tr>`	None
HtmlGenericControl	Nonform elements	None

Server-side controls that appear in ASP.NET documents compile into fields or members of the document class. The id of the control becomes the name of the field in the document class. Therefore, all server-side controls must have id attributes. Also, a control is specified to be a server-side control by including the runat attribute set to "server". Without this, the control is just a static XHTML widget. For example, suppose the document includes the following:

```
<form runat = "server">
  <input type = "text"  id = "address"
         runat = "server" />
  ...
</form>
```

For this form, the document class would have the following field:

```
protected HtmlInputText address;
```

Notice that the `<form>` tag in the preceding example does not include an `action` attribute. This is the case in all ASP.NET documents. The reason is that all programming actions that result from user interactions with controls are defined in the ASP.NET document itself or in its code-behind file.

The HTML control class is derived from the generic `HtmlControl` class, from which the methods and properties that are used for all HTML controls are inherited. For example, the `Attributes` collection has a name/value pair for each attribute of the element. Methods and properties that are specific for an element are defined in the element's class. For example, the `HtmlAnchor` class includes the `Href` property.

The difference between HTML controls and ordinary static XHTML widgets is that the HTML controls are converted to objects in the document class. This means the controls and their attributes, which includes their styles, are available to and can be modified by the code of the document. As previously stated, an XHTML widget is converted to an HTML control simply by adding the `runat` attribute set to `"server"`. For example, consider the following XHTML text box:

```
<input type = "text"  id = "address" />
```

The following is the same text box, but as an HTML control:

```
<input type = "text"  id = "address"  runat = "server" />
```

13.4.2   Life Cycle of a Simple ASP.NET Document

An ASP.NET document that includes a form serves both to describe the initial content of an XHTML document for browser display and to provide the event handling to process user interactions with the form in the document. So, for all ASP.NET documents that include forms, there are two kinds of requests. First, there is an initial request, which results in the requested document and its form being displayed for the client. Second, there is a request made after the form has been changed by the client. This kind of request is called a *postback* because the form values are posted back to the document on the server. To clarify the sequence of events that takes place for an ASP.NET document that includes a form, consider the following simple document example:

```
<!-- ex3.aspx
     A simple example of an ASP.NET document with HTML controls.
     It uses textboxes to get the name and age of the client,
     which are then displayed.
     -->
<%@ Page language="c#" %>
```

continued

```
<html>
  <head> <title> Ex3 </title>
  </head>
  <body>
    <form runat = "server">
      <p>
        Your name:
        <input type = "text" id = "name" runat = "server" />
        <br />
        Your age:
        <input type = "text" id = "age" runat = "server" />
        <br />
        <input type = "submit" value = "Submit" />
      <br />
      <% if (IsPostBack) { %>
        Hello <%= name.Value %> <br />
        You are <%= age.Value %> years old <br />
        <% } %>
      </p>
    </form>
  </body>
</html>
```

Notice that both the form and the controls in the form must include the runat attribute set to "server".

ASP.NET implicity stores the control state of a document class instance before the server returns the output of the instance to the client. This information is stored in a hidden widget of the instance named ViewState. When the document is posted back to the server, the ViewState data is used to implicitly initialize the new instance. Of course, ViewState will not have element values on the first postback. After initialization using ViewState, the client input from the form is used for a second initialization of the instance. Therefore, any widget whose value is not input by the client retains its previous value. ViewState provides implicit form state preservation between requests.

The following is a list of the things that happen if this document is requested, is delivered to the browser, has its text boxes filled in by the user, is posted back to the server, and finally is returned to the browser. Note that a number of events are raised during this processing, although none is described in the following.

1. The client requests ex3.aspx, the original ASP.NET document.
2. A document class is created by compiling the requested document. Then the constructor of that class is invoked.

3. The control state of the instance is initialized with the `ViewState` data (On the initial request, there is no `ViewState` data.)

4. The form data of the request is used to set the control state of the document class instance. (On the initial request, there is no form data.)

5. The current state of the instance is recorded in the `ViewState` hidden field.

6. The instance is executed and the results returned to the client.

7. The class and its instance are deleted on the server.

8. The client interacts with the form of the document.

9. The client causes a postback to the server.

10. A document class is created by compiling the requested document. Then the constructor of that class is invoked.

11. The control state of the instance is initialized with the `ViewState` data.

12. The form data of the request is used to set the control state of the document class instance.

13. The current state of the class is recorded in `ViewState`.

14. The instance is executed and the results returned to the client; the class and its instance are deleted on the server.

The document created by the document class that was compiled from the `ex3.aspx` document, after it has had its form filled by the client, is as follows:

```
<!-- ex3.aspx
     A simple example of an ASP.NET document with HTML controls.
     It uses textboxes to get the name and age of the client,
     which are then displayed.
     -->

<html>
  <head> <title> Ex3 </title>
  </head>
  <body>
    <form name="_ct10" method="post" action="ex3.aspx id="_ct10">
<input type="hidden" name="_VIEWSTATE"
value="dDwxMTYxOTE0NDI7Oz4rK1loC8s5yMYUcQVQuGFG7BGQzg==" />

    <p>
      Your name:
      <input type = "text" id = "name" runat = "server" />
      <br />
```

continued

```
      Your age:
      <input type = "text" id = "age" runat = "server" />
      <br />
      <input type = "submit" value = "Submit" />
  <br />

      Hello mike <br />
      You are 47 years old <br />

    </p>
  </form>
</body>
</html>
```

This document differs from the original version of `ex3.aspx` in three areas. First, it includes the `ViewState` hidden control, which has a coded version of the form data. Second, the form has an internal name and ID (`_ct10`). Third, the render block to produce the return XHTML has been replaced by its output.

A postback can be initiated by a user in more than one way. Of course, a postback occurs if the user clicks the Submit button of a form. It also happens when any button is clicked. You have the option of having a postback happen when a checkbox is clicked or a select item is selected. This is controlled by the `AutoPostBack` property of the control. If `AutoPostBack` is set to `"true"`, then a change in the control's value causes a postback.

13.4.3   Page-Level Events

There are two levels of events that can be raised while an ASP.NET document is being processed. There are the control events, `ServerClick` and `ServerChange`, raised by the HTML controls and discussed in Section 13.4.4. And there are the four page-level events. These events actually are created by the `Page` class. These are `Init`, which is raised immediately after a document class is instantiated; `Load`, which is raised just after the instance has its state set from form data and `ViewState`; `PreRender`, which is raised just before the instance is executed to construct the client response document; and `Unload`, which is raised just before the instance is discarded.

There are two ways to design and register handlers for the page-level events. The first is to write the handlers using predefined names that are implicitly registered when the document class is created. This implicit handler registration is called *auto event wireup*. It is controlled by the `@Page` directive attribute, `AutoEventWireup`, which has the default value of `true`. If set to `false`, the implicit registration is not done, and registration must be done manually. The names of the handlers that are implicitly registered are `Page_Load`, `Page_Unload`, `Page_PreRender`, and `Page_Init`. All return void and take a parameter of type `System.EventArgs`. The protocols of these are as follows:

```
public void Page_Unload(System.EventArgs e) { ... }
public void Page_Load(System.EventArgs e) { ... }
public void Page_PreRender(System.EventArgs e)
                                            { ... }
public void Page_Init(System.EventArgs e) { ... }
```

`Page_Init` is used in an example in Section 13.4.4.

The second way to design and register event handlers for page-level events is to override the virtual handler methods defined in the `Page` class. Such handlers must be manually registered in the document. This approach is not further discussed here.

13.4.4 Control Events

There are two ways to create and register event handlers for HTML controls. The first of these is similar to the way JavaScript client-side event handlers are registered through XHTML attributes. The attributes are named `OnServerClick` and `OnServerChange`, which correspond to the two control events for HTML controls. The handlers for HTML controls all use the following protocol: They return `void` and take two parameters, the first of type `object` and the second of type `System.EventArgs`. This is the protocol for the `EventHandler` delegate, which provides the standard event handling approach for CLR. For example, consider the following event handler for a text box control, along with the control:

```
protected void TextboxHandler(object src,
                              System.EventArgs e) {
  ...
}
...
<input type = "text"  id = "Name"
       OnServerChange = "TextBoxHandler"
       runat = "server" />
```

The second way to write and register event handlers is to use the standard CLR approach, which uses delegates for handler registration. The events are of the generic `EventHandler` delegate type. There are three steps to creating and registering event handlers: First, the event handler is written as a function with the return type and parameter types of `EventHandler`. Second, a new instance of the delegate type is created using new, passing the name of the event handling function to the constructor. Third, the delegate instance must be subscribed to the event property of the control by adding it to any delegates already subscribed there. The second and third parts of this process are usually combined into one statement and placed in a `Page_Init` handler so that they are accomplished before the document class instance is executed. In the following example, the same text box and handler as previously shown are repeated, this time using delegates.

```
// The event handler

protected void TextboxHandler(object src,
                              System.EventArgs e) {
   ...
}


// Use a Page_Init handler to create and subscribe the
// handler

protected void Page_Init(object src, EventArgs e) {
  Name.ServerChange +=
                new EventHandler(TextboxHandler);
}
...


<!-- The text box -->

<input type = "text"  id = "Name"  runat = "server" />
```

We can now revise the life cycle of an ASP.NET document request to include event creation for both page-level and control events. This time we list only a single request cycle (rather than including a postback cycle).

1. The client requests `ex3.aspx`, the original ASP.NET document.
2. A document class is created by compiling the requested document. Then the constructor of that class is invoked.
3. The `Page` event `Init` is raised.
4. The control state of the instance is initialized with the `ViewState` data. (On the initial request, there is no `ViewState` data.)
5. The form data of the request is used to set the control state of the document class instance. (On the initial request, there is no form data.)
6. The `Page` event `Load` is raised.
7. Server-side control events are raised.
8. The `Page` event `PreRender` is raised.
9. The current control state of the instance is recorded in the `ViewState` hidden field.
10. The instance is executed and the results returned to the client.
11. The `Page` event `Unload` is raised.
12. The class and its instance are deleted on the server.

13.4.5 Web Controls

Web controls are based on the controls of VB. The `System.Web.UI.WebControls` namespace includes the Web controls. This is a larger and richer collection of controls than the HTML controls. In addition to controls that correspond to the ordinary XHTML widgets, there many more. For example, there are controls for checkbox lists, radio button lists, drop-down lists, and list boxes. In addition, there are the special controls for form data validation and data binding.

The complete one-to-one correspondence between HTML controls and the XHTML widgets is absent with the Web controls. The most commonly used Web control types are shown in Table 13.2.

TABLE 13.2 Commonly used Web controls and related XHTML elements

Web Control Type	XHTML Element
AdRotator	None

Button	`<input type = "button" />`
	`<input type = "submit" />`
	`<input type = "reset" />`

Calender	None
Checkbox	`<input type = "checkbox" />`
CheckBoxList	None
DropDownList	`<select>`
Label	None
RadioButton	`<input type = "radio" />`
RadioButtonList	None
Table	`<table>`
TableCell	`<th>, <td>`
TableRow	`<tr>`
TextBox	`<input type = "text" />`

Some additional Web control types are described in the following paragraphs. All of the Web controls are in the `asp` namespace, so the tag names are all qualified with `asp:`. For example, a text box control is specified with the following:

```
<asp:textbox id = "phone"  runat = "server" />
```

In addition to having a more consistent programing interface than the HTML controls, the Web controls collection provides controls that do not correspond to XHTML widgets and are rendered as combinations of widgets. Among these are `Xml`, `Panel`, `AdRotator`, and the list controls. The `Xml` control provides the ability to include XSL transformations on XML input as part of the output XHTML document. The `Panel` control provides a container for other controls, for those situations where you want to control the position or visibility of the contained controls as a unit. The `AdRotator` provides a way to implicitly produce different content on different requests.

The `ListControl` class has four subclass controls. Two of these are familiar, `DropDownList` and `ListBox`, both of which are converted to XHTML select elements. The `ListBox` control can display one or more of its items. The number of display items defaults to 4 but can be set to any number. A vertical scrollbar is implicitly included if the control has more items than the number it can display. More than one item in a `ListBox` can be selected. The `DropDownList` control remains hidden until the user clicks its button. The browser chooses the number of items displayed when the drop-down button is clicked. `DropDownList` controls do not allow multiselection mode.

The two other `ListControl` subclass controls are `CheckBoxList` and `RadioButtonList`. Both of these are normally translated to table XHTML elements. In both cases, the purpose is to allow programming code access to the list items in the lists. This supports the possibility of adding and/or deleting list items dynamically as the result of user interaction. It also makes it possible for list items to be fetched from a database or other external source.

13.4.6 Creating Control Elements with Code

Server-side controls can be specified for an ASP.NET document in two distinct ways: using markup or using programing code. For example, a button can be created with the following markup:

```
<asp:button id = "helpButton"  Text = "help"
            OnClick = "OnClickHandler"
            runat = "server" />
```

The same button could be created with C# code, as in the following:

```
protected Button helpButton = new Button();
helpButton.Text = "help";
helpButton.id = "helpButton";
helpButton.OnClick = "OnClickHandler";
helpButton.runat = "server";
```

There are two problems with creating controls with program code: First, clearly it requires more typing. Second, the placement of the control on the document display is problemmatic. It has to be added to something in the document. To control the placement, a placeholder element is specified in the markup. Then the control can be added using the ID of the placeholder. This gives the exact position within the document for the control. For example, the placeholder could be specified with the following:

```
<asp:placeholder id = "buttonPlace"  runat = "server" />
```

The following statement places the button at the position where the placeholder element appeared:

```
buttonPlace.Controls.Add(helpButton);
```

More than one control can be put in a placeholder. They are maintained in a property of the placeholder element, `Controls`. So, the `Controls` property is a collection of controls elements. The order in which controls are added to the placeholder's `Controls` property determines the order in which the controls will appear in the display.

Although it is easier to create elements with markup, modifying elements is a good use of program code. For example, the list items of a select element could be added with program code, after the select element had been specified in markup. This would be especially useful if the list items came from some other data source. Program code is also useful for modifying the attributes of markup-created element.

13.4.7 Response Output for Controls

The first two sample ASP.NET documents of this chapter used the `Response.Write` method to place text in the response buffer. This is not a viable approach when there are controls in the document because the output from `Response.Write` goes to the beginning of the buffer rather than the position among the controls of the call to `Response.Write` (assuming the code is embedded in the ASP.NET document). As a more effective alternative, the text can be placed in a label control, which produces the text at the position of the label control in the response buffer. The text is assigned to the `Text` property of the label control. For example, suppose the document includes the following (at the position where the output text should be):

```
<asp:label id = "output"  runat = "server" />
```

The following places the given text at that position of the label in the response buffer:

```
<% string msg = string.Format(
              "The result is {0} <br />", result);
   output.Text = msg; %>
```

Of course, the program code could also appear in a code-behind file. In this example, the `string.Format` method is used to create a formatted string that consists of literal text and the value of a variable, which has been converted to text by `Format`.

13.4.8 An Example

The following example creates a textbox, a drop-down list, and a button in an ASP.NET document. It uses code in a code-behind file to fill in the list items of the drop-down list. The document also includes a label control to provide a place for the return message from the code-behind file. The code-behind file also includes a handler for the button, which confirms to the user the selected item.

The list items are added to the select element with the `Add` method of the `Items` property of the select. Each new item is created with a call to the list item constructor, `ListItem`, passing the value of the new item. For example, to add a list item with the value "red" to the select control with the ID `mySelect`, the following could be used:

```
mySelect.Items.Add(new ListItem("red"));
```

The button handler in the example will return a message to the client, giving both his or her name as well as the chosen select item, which in this case is a color. The client name is retrieved from the `name` textbox of the document, using the `Text` property of the textbox. The chosen color is retrieved from the form with the `SelectedItem` property of the drop-down list.

The ASP.NET document and its code-behind file follow:

```
<!-- ex4.aspx
     An example of an ASP.NET document that creates a textbox,
     a drop-down list, a submit button, and a label.
   A code-behind file is used to populate the drop-down list and
     handle the button clicks. The label is used for the return
     message
     -->
<%@ Page language="c#" Inherits = "ex4" Src = "ex4.aspx.cs" %>

<html>
  <head> <title> Ex4 </title>
  </head>
  <body>
    <form runat = "server">
      Name: <asp:TextBox runat = "server" id = "name" />
```

```
      <br /><br />
      Favorite Color:<asp:DropDownList runat = "server"
                                        id = "color" />
      <br /><br />
      <asp:button  runat = "server" id = "submit"
                   text = "Submit" OnClick = "OnClickHandler" />
      <br /><br />
      <asp:label id = "message" runat = "server" />
    </form>
  </body>
</html>
```

```
// ex4.aspx.cs
//    The code behind file for ex4.aspx.
//    In an OnLoad handler, it populates the drop-down
//    list created in the associated ASP.NET document.
//    It also includes a handler for the button, which
//    produces a message to the client, including the
//    client's name and the chosen item from the drop
//    down list

using System;
using System.Web;
using System.Web.UI;
using System.Web.UI.WebControls;

public class ex4 : System.Web.UI.Page {
   protected DropDownList color;
   protected TextBox name;
   protected Button submit;
   protected Label message;


// OnLoad handler to populate the dropdownlist


   override protected void OnLoad(EventArgs e) {
     if (!IsPostBack) {
       color.Items.Add(new ListItem("blue"));
       color.Items.Add(new ListItem("red"));
```

continued

```
        color.Items.Add(new ListItem("green"));
        color.Items.Add(new ListItem("yellow"));
    }
  }

// Handler for the button

  protected void OnClickHandler(object src, EventArgs e) {
    string newMsg = string.Format(
        "Hi {0}, your favorite color is {1}",
        name.Text, color.SelectedItem);
    message.Text = newMsg;
  }
}
```

13.4.9   Validation Controls

In Chapter 5, "JavaScript and HTML Documents," client-side form data validation with JavaScript was discussed. Although there are strong reasons for
doing form data validation on the client, there are also reasons to do it again on
the server. First among these is that client-side validation can be subverted by a
devious client. In some cases, form data goes directly into a database, which
could be corrupted by bad data. So, it is worthwhile to do form data validation
on both the client and the server side. In the following paragraphs, we introduce
the ASP.NET Web controls designed to make server-side form data validation
relatively easy.

There are six validation controls defined in the Web controls collection.
The four most commonly used of these controls, along with their properties
and values, are shown in Table 13.3.

The two validation controls that are not shown in Table 13.3 are one for
custom validation, which is done in functions, and one to produce a summary of
all of the error messages produced during server-side validation.

Validation controls are placed immediately after the controls whose values
they are to validate. This placement is necessary so the error messages produced
by the validation controls appear next to the controls being validated. The
actual error message is specified in the `ErrorMessage` attribute of the validation control. The validation control is connected to the control it is to validate
with the `ControlToValidate` attribute, which is set to the ID of the control.
The `Display` attribute is used to specify how the error message will be displayed. The value `"Static"` means that space is reserved on the displayed document for the message. The value `"Dynamic"` means space for the message is
not reserved. The value `"None"` means no error message will be displayed,
although the error is still recorded in a log. Validation controls must also
include the `runat` attribute set, of course, to `"server"`.

TABLE 13.3 Validation Controls and their properties

Control	Properties	Values
RequiredFieldValidator	None	None
CompareValidator	Operator	Equal, NotEqual, GreaterThan, GreaterThanEqual, LessThan, LessThanEqual, DataTypeCheck
	Type	String, Currency, Date, Double, Integer
	ValueToCompare	Constant
	ControlToCompare	Another control
RangeValidator	MaximumValue	Constant
	MinimumValue	Constant
	Type	String, Currency, Date, Double, Integer
RegularExpressionValidator	ValidationExpression	Regular expression

The following example, `ex5.aspx`, illustrates some of the validation controls.

```
<!-- ex5.aspx
     An example of an ASP.NET document to illustrate server-side
     validation Web controls.
     It uses Web control textboxes to get the name, phone number,
     and age of the client. These three are validated on the
     server
     1. The name must be present
     2. The phone number must be in the form ddd-ddd-dddd
     3. The range of the age must be 10 to 110
     -->
<%@ Page language="c#" %>

<html>
  <head> <title> Ex5 </title>
  </head>
```

continued

```
<body>
  <form runat = "server">
    <p>
      Your name:
      <asp:TextBox  id = "name" runat = "server" />
      <asp:RequiredFieldValidator
        ControlToValidate = "name"
        Display = "Static"
        runat = "server"
        ErrorMessage = "Please enter your name">
      </asp:RequiredFieldValidator>
      <br />

      Your phone number:
      <asp:TextBox  id = "phone" runat = "server" />
      <asp:RegularExpressionValidator
        ControlToValidate = "phone"
        Display = "Static"
        runat = "server"
        ErrorMessage = "Phone number form must be ddd-ddd-dddd"
        ValidationExpression = "\d{3}-\d{3}-\d{4}">
      </asp:RegularExpressionValidator>
      <br />

      Your age:
      <asp:TextBox  id = "age" runat = "server" />
      <asp:RangeValidator
        ControlToValidate = "age"
        Display = "Static"
        runat = "server"
        MaximumValue = "110"
        MinimumValue = "10"
        Type = "Integer"
        ErrorMessage = "Age must be in the range of 10 to 110">
      </asp:RangeValidator>
      <br />

      <input type = "submit" value = "Submit" />
    </p>
  </form>
</body>
</html>
```

The name text box is validated to ensure that a name is given. The phone number text box is validated to ensure that it matches the given regular expression. (Regular expressions are described in Chapter 9, "The Basis of Perl.") The age text box is validated to ensure that the given age is at least 10 but not greater than 110.

Figure 13.2 shows the display of the `ex4.aspx` document after some of the fields have been filled incorrectly, which results in the appearance of error messages to the right of the text boxes.

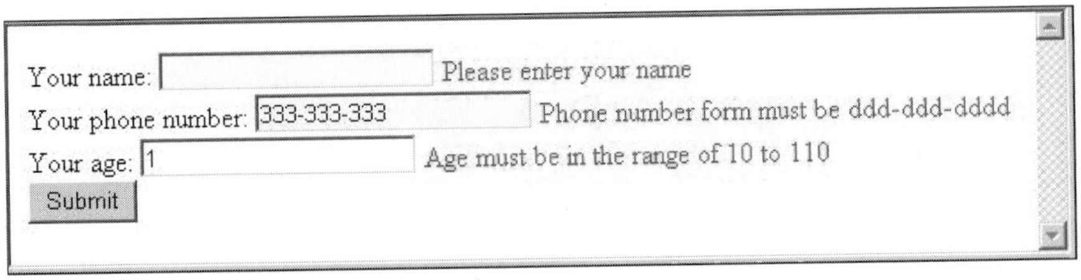

Figure 13.2 Display of `ex4.aspx` after some text boxes have been filled

13.5

WEB SERVICES

Web services, which were introduced in Chapter 8, "Introduction to XML," use technologies that have only recently been developed. In brief, a Web service is a collection of one or more related methods that can be called by remote systems using standard protocols on the Web. Microsoft is one of the companies that provides Web services. The most widely used Microsoft Web service is Passport, which identifies and authenticates users, among other things.

The .NET Framework provides several kinds of support for the construction and advertisement of Web services. The most powerful support tool is Visual Studio .NET, which is not discussed in this book. However, even without Visual Studio .NET, it is relatively easy to create and advertise Web services with the .NET Framework.

13.5.1 Constructing Web Services

In .NET, a Web service is simply a special kind of class, which can be written in any .NET programming language. The Web service class can be stored in a file with the extension `.asmx` (just like any ASP.NET Web application). In most cases, however, the `.asmx` file stores only a directive—the code is in a code-behind file with a further extension in its name. If the code is written in C#, the extension on the code-behind file would be `.asmx.cs`. The structure of the directive in the `.asmx` file is illustrated in the following example:

```
<%@ WebService Language = "C#"
               Codebehind = "Service1.asmx.cs"
               Class = "MyWebService1.Service1" %>
```

This example directive, which is in the file named `Service1.asmx`, indicates the Web service is a class written in C#, whose code-behind file is named `Service1.asmx.cs`. The class itself is named `Service1` and is in the `MyWebService1` namespace.

Following is a simple Web service class, `Service1.asmx.cs`, which defines a service method `Sum3` that takes three integers as parameters and returns the sum of the three given numbers.

```
using System;
using System.Web.Services;

namespace MyWebService1 {
[WebService(Namespace =
        "http://www.sebesta.com/webservices/")]

  public class Service1 :
          System.Web.Services.WebService {
    [WebMethod]
    public int Sum3(int first, int second, int third) {
      int sum;
      sum = first + second + third;
      return sum;
    }
  }
}
```

This code-behind file imports `System.Web.Services` and inherits from the `WebService` class, which is defined in `System.Web.Services`. The `WebService` class provides various kinds of support for Web services, including the `WebMethodAttribute` class and the `Context` object, which contains information about the HTTP request that invokes the Web service.

The line that begins `"[WebService"` is used to define a namespace for Web services on this server. If it is not included, a default generic namespace is used, which could cause conflicts with other Web services. The one method of `Service1` is marked `[WebMethod]` to specify that it is to be made available as a Web service. `WebMethod` is an attribute of the `WebMethodAttribute` class.[4] A Web service class can include methods that are not Web services—they are those that are not marked with `[WebMethod]`.

An `.asmx` file that defines a Web service can be viewed with an IE browser, which illustrates some of what the .NET system creates when a Web service class file is built. The display of the example Web service is shown in Figure 13.3.

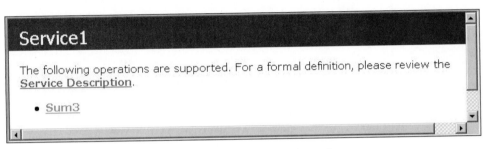

Figure 13.3 An IE browser display of the `Service1` Web service

Figure 13.3 shows that the display includes a link (`Service Description`) to a Web Service Description Language (WSDL) description of the Web service, which has the required formats for requests and responses to the methods of the Web service. Recall that WSDL is an XML-based markup language for defining the protocols of Web services. The formats given in the service description are provided for the Simple Object Access Protocol (SOAP), HTTP GET, and HTTP POST protocols. SOAP is also an XML-based markup language. The first part of the service description for our example is shown in Figure 13.4.

---

4. An attribute is used to indicate something special about a declaration.

```
<?xml version="1.0" encoding="utf-8" ?>
- <definitions
    xmlns:http="http://schemas.xmlsoap.org/wsdl/http/"
    xmlns:soap="http://schemas.xmlsoap.org/wsdl/soap/"
    xmlns:s="http://www.w3.org/2001/XMLSchema"
    xmlns:s0="http://www.sebesta.com/webservices/"
    xmlns:soapenc="http://schemas.xmlsoap.org/soap/encoding/"
    xmlns:tm="http://microsoft.com/wsdl/mime/textMatching/"
    xmlns:mime="http://schemas.xmlsoap.org/wsdl/mime/"
    targetNamespace="http://www.sebesta.com/webservices/"
    xmlns="http://schemas.xmlsoap.org/wsdl/">
- <types>
    - <s:schema elementFormDefault="qualified"
        targetNamespace="http://www.sebesta.com/webservices/">
      - <s:element name="Sum3">
        - <s:complexType>
          - <s:sequence>
              <s:element minOccurs="1" maxOccurs="1"
                name="first" type="s:int" />
              <s:element minOccurs="1" maxOccurs="1"
                name="second" type="s:int" />
              <s:element minOccurs="1" maxOccurs="1"
                name="third" type="s:int" />
            </s:sequence>
          </s:complexType>
        </s:element>
      - <s:element name="Sum3Response">
        - <s:complexType>
          - <s:sequence>
              <s:element minOccurs="1" maxOccurs="1"
                name="Sum3Result" type="s:int" />
            </s:sequence>
          </s:complexType>
        </s:element>
        <s:element name="int" type="s:int" />
      </s:schema>
  </types>
```

Figure 13.4 The first part of a service description

Also displayed in Figure 13.3 are the names of the Web service methods. Our example has just one method, Sum3. Each method name is a link to a test document for the method. Parameters can be given to the tester, which runs the method and displays the results when the Invoke button is clicked. Figure 13.5 shows the tester for the Sum3 method, including test values.

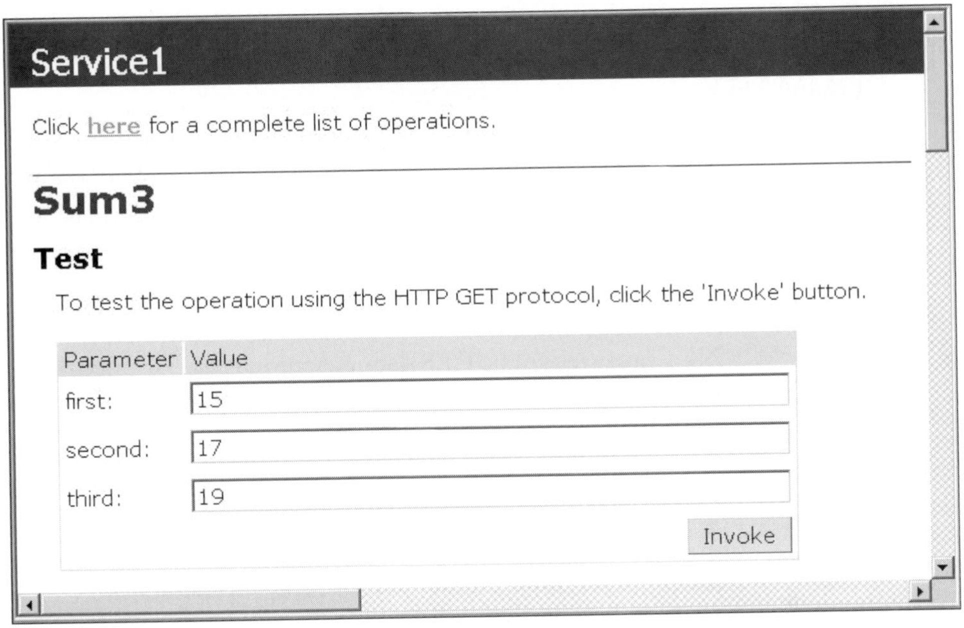

Figure 13.5 The test display for the Sum3 service method

Clicking the Invoke button of the Sum3 tester produces the screen display shown in Figure 13.6.

Figure 13.6 The result of invoking the Sum3 tester

13.5.2 Advertising Web Services

If a client has the URL of a Web service, he or she can easily use it. However, the more general situation is that a potential client does not know the URL of a possibly useful Web service. There are two approaches used with .NET to make Web services available to clients: with a Web services discovery document and with a Web services directory written with the Universal Description, Discovery, and Integration (UDDI) language. In both cases, a directory of all Web services provided by a Web site is made available to potential clients through a single URL on the site.

13.6

SUMMARY

.NET is a collection of technologies that supports the development and deployment of distributed component-based software systems written in variety of languages. The .NET Framework is a generic support structure for the .NET family of languages. The CLR is a runtime system, including JIT compilers that support the execution of .NET software. There are now 20 .NET languages, with more on the way. The CTS defines a set of types that must be supported by .NET languages. The CLS defines a minimal set of language features that must be supported by .NET languages. Software in any .NET language can interact in a variety of ways with software written in any of the other .NET languages.

The primary .NET language, C#, was designed specifically for the .NET system. C# is based on Java but includes some features of other languages, notably C++, VB, and Delphi, as well as some new language features. Among its features are a type-safe enumeration type, an improved `switch` construct, a `foreach` statement, some new controls on method inheritance, a value type struct, and properties.

ASP.NET is an approach to server-side support of dynamic documents. It is similar to JSP but is language neutral. Programming code can reside in an ASP.NET document or in a separate file called a code-behind file. In either case, the code is compiled before it is executed. Every ASP.NET document is compiled into a class before it is used, regardless of whether it contains programming code. All such classes are subclasses of the predefined class, `Page`, unless they have code-behind files, in which case the code-behind file inherits from `Page` and the class for the ASP.NET document inherits from the code-behind file.

ASP.NET documents consist of XHTML, programming code (either in script elements or render blocks), directives, server-side comments, and server-side controls. Server-side controls include the `runat` attribute set to `"server"`. The only required directive is `@Page`, which must include the `Language` attribute, which specifies the language used for the programming code, either embedded or in a code-behind file. A code-behind file can be either precompiled or dynamically compiled only after it has been changed and the associated ASP.NET document has been requested. Just as JavaBeans are the best way to use Java in a dynamic document, code-behind files are the best way to use a .NET language to support dynamic documents.

There are two categories of ASP.NET controls, HTML controls and Web controls. HTML controls closely parallel the widgets of XHTML. These controls result in objects in the compiled `Page`-derived class, whereas the static XHTML code of a document is simply emitted by the execution of the `Page`-derived class. An HTML control can create one of the two events, `ServerClick` or `ServerChange`, which can be handled by server-side code. The `id` attribute value of an HTML control becomes the associated variable's name in the compiled version of the document.

The state of an ASP.NET document is implicitly maintained between requests with the ViewState hidden field.

There are four page-level events defined in the Page class: Init, Load, Unload, and PreRender. These events can be handled in server-side code. The handlers can be implicitly registered by naming them with predefined names and using the proper protocol. Alternatively, they can be subscribed to the event handler delegate, EventHandler.

Control event handlers can be registered in two ways, either by referencing them on an attribute on the control or by using the EventHandler approach that can be used for page-level event handlers.

The Web controls collection is richer than the HTML controls collection, and they make programming interactions easier.

The .NET Framework provides significant assistance in building Web services.

13.7 Review Questions

1. What is a component?

2. What is the difference between a JavaBean and a .NET component?

3. When does a JIT compiler perform its translation of a method?

4. What is the primary benefit of the multilanguage aspect of .NET?

5. What part of the .NET system controls the execution of programs?

6. Explain how a JIT compiler works.

7. Describe briefly the two parts of the CLI.

8. On what languages is C# based?

9. Explain two reasons why C# enumeration types are safer than those of C++.

10. Explain how the switch statement of C# is safer than that of Java.

11. What parameter-passing methods are available in C# that are not available in Java?

12. What characteristic is specified by attaching virtual to a C# method?

13. What does is mean when a C# method includes the new modifier?

14. Where are C# struct objects allocated?

15. Explain properties and why they are useful.

16. What is a delegate, and what is one common use for delegates?

17. What is console input and output?

18. What are the two kinds of disadvantages of scripting languages when used for supporting dynamic documents?

19. What exactly is a code-behind file?

20. From what class does an ASP.NET document class that does not use a code-behind file inherit?

21. From what class does an ASP.NET document class that does use a code-behind file inherit?

22. What kind of code is placed in a render block?

23. What kind of code is placed in a script element?

24. Describe what is specified by the @Page attribute Src.

25. What are the two categories of ASP.NET server controls?

26. What are the two events that can be raised by the HTML controls?

27. Do all of the HTML controls raise events?

28. What is the syntactic difference between an XHTML widget and its corresponding HTML control?

29. Why do ASP.NET server-side forms not require an action attribute?

30. What is a postback?

31. What is the purpose of the hidden control ViewState?

32. How can an HTML checkbox control be forced to cause a postback when it is checked?

33. What are the four page-level events?

34. Explain auto event wireup.

35. Explain briefly the two ways to create and register event handlers for HTML controls.

36. What is the purpose of the Xml control?

37. Why should form data validation be done on the server as well as the client?

38. What is the difference between an HTML control that includes the runat attribute set to "server" and one that does not?

13.8 Exercises

1. Modify the ASP.NET document `ex1.aspx` to get a number between 10 and 100 from the keyboard. The code must verify that the number is in the correct range and then fill the array, which must be defined to have 100 elements, with random numbers and display the values.

2. Modify the ASP.NET document `ex2.aspx` and its accompanying code-behind file, `ex2.aspx.cs`, to the specification of Exercise 1.

3. Modify the ASP.NET document `ex3.aspx` to also use radio buttons to get the marital status of the user (single, married, divorced, widowed) and display the result.

4. Modify the ASP.NET document `ex4.aspx` and its accompanying code-behind file, `ex4.aspx.cs`, to add the following: a textbox for the user's address and a drop-down list for favorite category of music (rock, rap, country, classical, jazz), which must be populated in the code-behind file. The values of the new controls must be output when a postback is done.

5. Modify the ASP.NET document `ex5.aspx` to add the following: a textbox for address, which the document must validate to ensure it begins with a number, which is followed by a space and a text string that includes only letters; and a textbox to collect a social security number, which must be validated to ensure it is in the form ddd-dd-dddd, with no other characters in the textbox.

Database Access through the Web

This chapter begins with brief introductions to relational databases and the Structured Query Language. Then it discusses several different architectures for database access. Next, the primary commands of the MySQL relational database system are introduced. This is followed by three sections, each of which describes a different approach to accessing databases through the Web using MySQL. First, Perl's DBI/DBD architecture is introduced and used to write a CGI program that uses MySQL to access a database. Next, the chapter discusses the use of server-side scripting for building systems for Web access to a database, using PHP as the sample language. Finally, Java's JDBC, which provides database access from Java programs, is discussed. Both Java applications and servlets are considered. In all three approaches, a complete example is provided.

14.1

RELATIONAL DATABASES

A database is a collection of data organized to allow relatively easy access for retrievals, additions, modifications, and deletions. A number of different approaches to structuring data have been developed and used for databases. The most widely used of these are called *relational database systems*. The original design for relational databases, developed by E. F. Codd in the late 1960s, was based on Codd's mathematical theory of data. A significant number of books have been written to describe the structure and use of relational databases, so it clearly is a large and complex topic. Because just one section of one chapter of this book is devoted to it, that section can provide only a quick overview. However, that is all that is necessary for our discussion of database access through the Web.

A relational database is a collection of tables of data. Each table can have any number of rows and columns of data, and the data itself can have a variety of different forms. The columns of a table are named. Each row usually contains a value for each column. The rows of a table are often referred to as *entities*. The collection of values in a row represents the *attributes* of the entity. Most tables have one column for special data values that uniquely identify the rows of the table. The values in this special column are called the *primary keys* of the table. Mathematically, the entities of a table are elements of a set, so they must be unique. Both data values and primary key values in a table are sometimes called *fields*.

One way to introduce the basic ideas of a relational database is to develop a simple example. Suppose we need a database that stores information about used Corvette automobiles for sale. We could just make a table named `Corvettes` with a column for the primary key of an entity, which could simply be a sequence of numbers. The table could have a column for the body style of the car, one for the year of manufacture, and one for the state where the car is for sale. It would also be useful to include information about the optional equipment of the cars. If six different kinds of equipment were interesting, that would require six more columns in the table.

The six columns of the `Corvettes` table for equipment are wasteful of memory. A better design is to use a second table—say, `Equipment`—to store the various kinds of equipment in which we are interested, such as CD players and automatic transmissions. This table could have just two columns: a primary key and the specific equipment. It would need just six rows.

To make this work, we need a way to relate cars to equipment. This need can be met with a cross-reference table, which has just two columns: one with primary keys from the `Corvettes` table and one with primary keys of the `Equipment` table. We could name this table `Corvettes_Equipment`. Each car in the `Corvettes` table could have several rows in `Equipment`, one for each specific option with which the car is equipped. This table does not need, and therefore does not have, a primary key column.

Another way to store the data in less memory is to not store state names in the main table. Instead, we could move the state names to a new table—say, `States`—and have references to it in the `Corvettes` table. A primary key to the `States` table, which could be just an integer, would require far less space than a typical state name. A logical data model of the database could be as shown in Figure 14.1.

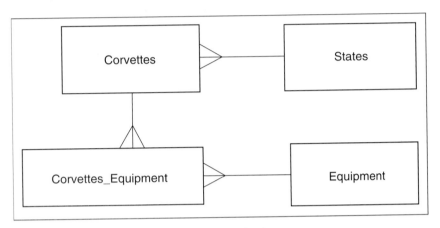

FIGURE 14.1 The logical data model for a database

The lines between the tables indicate the relationships between the connected tables. For example, the relationship between `Corvettes` and `States` is many to one: There may be many cars for sale in one state, but each car is in just one state. All of the relationships in our model are either one-to-many or many-to-one, depending on your point of view. Note that if we had not used the cross-reference table for this database, the relationship between `Corvettes` and `Equipment` would have been many-to-many.

The implementation of the database is illustrated with short examples of the required tables in Figures 14.2 to 14.5. This database will be used in the remainder of the chapter.

Equip_id	Equip
1	Automatic
2	4-speed
3	5-speed
4	6-speed
5	CD
6	Leather

FIGURE 14.2 The `Equipment` table

Vette_id	Body_style	Miles	Year	State
1	coupe	18.0	1997	4
2	hatchback	58.0	1996	7
3	convertible	13.5	2001	1
4	hatchback	19.0	1995	2
5	hatchback	25.0	1991	5
6	hardtop	15.0	2000	2
7	coupe	55.0	1979	10
8	convertible	17.0	1999	5
9	hardtop	17.0	2000	5
10	hatchback	50.0	1995	7

FIGURE 14.3 The Corvettes table

State_id	State
1	Alabama
2	Alaska
3	Arizona
4	Arkansas
5	California
6	Colorado
7	Connecticut
8	Delaware
9	Florida
10	Georgia

FIGURE 14.4 The States table

Vette_id	Equip
1	1
1	5
1	6
2	1
2	5
2	6
3	1
3	6
4	2
4	6
5	1
5	6
6	2
7	4
7	6
8	4
8	5
8	6
9	4
9	5
9	6
10	1
10	5

FIGURE 14.5 The `Corvettes_Equipment` cross-reference table

14.2

AN INTRODUCTION TO THE STRUCTURED QUERY LANGUAGE

The Structured Query Language (SQL) is a standard language for specifying accesses and modifications to relational databases. SQL was originally standardized by the American National Standards Institute (ANSI) and the International Standards Organization (ISO) in 1986. SQL was significantly expanded and modified in its early years, the result of which was standardized in 1992. This version is often called SQL-2.[1] SQL can be pronounced as either "S-Q-L" or "sequel."

SQL is supported by the databases provided by all major database vendors and is a standard that has truly become *the* standard. It is used to create, query, and modify relational databases, regardless of the particular database vendor.

SQL is quite different from programming languages; it is actually more like a structured form of English. It was designed to be easily understood and useful for any vendor's database. This section describes some of the basic SQL commands.

The SQL reserved words are not case sensitive, which means that `SELECT`, `select`, and `Select` are equivalent. However, the names of tables and table columns may or may not be case sensitive, depending on the particular database. The whitespace separating reserved words and clauses is ignored, so commands can be spread across several lines if that is convenient. Single quotes (`'`) are used to delimit character strings.

14.2.1 The `CREATE TABLE` SQL Command

A table in a database can be created with the `CREATE` command, whose general form is as follows:

```
CREATE TABLE table_name (
    column_name_1      data_type constraints,
    column_name_2      data_type constraints,
    ...
    column_name_n      data_type constraints)
```

A large number of different data types exist for table data, including `INTEGER`, `REAL`, and `CHAR`(*length*).[2] There are also several different constraints, which can be somewhat different among various database vendors. Constraints are restrictions on the values that can appear in a column of a table. One common constraint is `NOT NULL`, which means that every row in the table

---

1. The current version of the SQL standard is SQL-3. It has not yet become widely used.
2. More SQL data types and their corresponding Java data types are shown in Table 14.1 in Section 14.7.

must have a value in a column that has this constraint. Another common one is `PRIMARY KEY`, which means the column that has this constraint has a unique value for each row in the table. For example, you could have this:

```
CREATE TABLE States(
    State_id INTEGER PRIMARY KEY NOT NULL,
    State CHAR(20));
```

In some situations, table columns are referenced by position number rather than by names. The columns of a table are numbered starting with 1; that is, the first column is column 1.

14.2.2 The INSERT SQL Command

The `INSERT` command is used to add a row of data to a table. Its general form is as follows:

```
INSERT INTO table_name(column_name_1, column_name_2, ...,
    column_name_n)
VALUES (value_1, value_2, ..., value_n)
```

The correspondence between the column names and the values is positional: The first value goes into the column that is named first, and so forth. If `INSERT` is used on a table that has a column with the constraint `NOT NULL` and that column is not named in the `INSERT`, an error will be detected and reported. As an example of an `INSERT` command, consider the following:

```
INSERT INTO Corvettes(Vette_id, Body_style, Miles, Year,
                        State)
VALUES (37, 'convertible', 25.5, 1986, 17);
```

14.2.3 The SELECT SQL Command

`SELECT` clauses are used to specify queries of a database, which is how particular information is requested. The `SELECT` command has three clauses: `SELECT`, `FROM`, and `WHERE`. The general form is as follows:

```
SELECT column names   FROM table names   [WHERE condition]
```

The brackets here indicate that the `WHERE` clause is optional.[3] The `SELECT` clause specifies the columns, or attributes, of a table. The `FROM` clause specifies

---

3. Actually, although the **WHERE** clause is often used, several other clauses can also appear in a **SELECT** command.

the table or tables to be searched.[4] For example, the following query produces a list of all the values from the `Body_style` column of the `Corvettes` table:

```
SELECT Body_style FROM Corvettes;
```

The `WHERE` clause is used to specify constraints on the rows of the specified tables that are of interest. The following query produces a list of all the values from the `Body_style` column of the `Corvettes` table that have a `Year` column value greater than 1994:

```
SELECT Body_style FROM Corvettes WHERE Year > 1994;
```

An asterisk (*) as the `SELECT` clause value means to select all the columns of the specified table that meet the condition specified in the `WHERE` clause.

14.2.4 The UPDATE SQL Command

The `UPDATE` command is used to change one or more of the values of a row of a table. Its general form is shown here:

```
UPDATE  table_name
SET  column_name_1 = value_1,
     column_name_2 = value_2,
        ...,
     column_name_n = value_n
WHERE  column_name = value
```

The `WHERE` clause in an `UPDATE` command specifies the primary key of the row to be updated. For example, to correct an error, you could change the year of the row with `Vette_id = 17` in the `Corvettes` table to 1996 with this command:

```
UPDATE Corvettes
SET Year = 1996
WHERE Vette_id = 17;
```

14.2.5 The DELETE SQL Command

One or more rows of a table can be deleted with the `DELETE` command, whose general form is as follows:

```
DELETE FROM  table_name
WHERE  column_name = value
```

---

4. A `SELECT` command that specifies more than one table produces a join of the tables. Join operations are discussed in Section 14.2.7.

The WHERE clause specifies the primary key of the row to be deleted. For example, if the car with the Vette_id value 27 is sold and should no longer be in the database, you could remove it from the Corvettes table with this command:

```
DELETE FROM Corvettes
WHERE Vette_id = 27;
```

The WHERE clause of a DELETE command can specify more than one row of the table, in which case all rows that satisfy the WHERE clause are deleted.

14.2.6   The DROP SQL Command

The DROP command can be used to delete either whole databases or complete tables. The general form is as follows:

```
DROP (TABLE | DATABASE) [IF EXISTS] name
```

In this line, the parentheses and brackets are metasymbols. DROP is used with either TABLE or DATABASE. The IF EXISTS clause is included if you want to avoid errors if the named table or database may not exist. For example:

```
DROP TABLE IF EXISTS States;
```

14.2.7   Joins

Suppose you want to produce a list of all Corvettes in the database that have CD players. To do this, you need information from two tables, Corvettes and Equipment. The connection between these two tables is through the cross-reference table Corvettes_Equipment. The SELECT command allows the temporary construction of a kind of virtual table that includes information from the Corvettes and Equipment tables, using the Corvettes_Equipment table as the basis for producing the desired result. Such a virtual table is built with a *join* of the two tables. A join is specified with a SELECT command that has two tables named in the FROM clause and uses a compound WHERE clause. The WHERE clause for our example must have three conditions. First, the Vette_id column from the Corvettes table must match the Vette_id column from the Corvettes_Equipment table. This restricts the rows of the Corvettes_Equipment table to those associated with the row of interest in the Corvettes table. Second, the Equip column from the Corvettes_Equipment table must match the Equip_id column of the Equipment table. This restricts the rows of the Equipment table to those associated with the row of interest of the Corvettes_Equipment table. Finally, the Equip column from the

Equipment table must be CD. The complete SELECT command to extract the cars with CD players is shown here:

```
SELECT Corvettes.Vette_id, Corvettes.Body_style,
       Corvettes.Miles, Corvettes.Year, Corvettes.State,
       Equipment.Equip
FROM Corvettes, Equipment
WHERE Corvettes.Vette_id = Corvettes_Equipment.Vette_id
   AND Corvettes_Equipment.Equip = Equipment.Equip_id
   AND Equipment.Equip = 'CD';
```

This query produces the following result:

VETTE_ID	BODY_STYLE	MILES	YEAR	STATE	EQUIPMENT
1	coupe	18.0	1997	4	CD
2	hatchback	58.0	1996	7	CD
8	convertible	17.0	1999	5	CD
9	hardtop	17.0	2000	5	CD
10	hatchback	50.0	1995	7	CD

Notice that all references to columns in this query are prefixed with the table names. This is necessary only when the column names are not unique to one table, as is the case for the Vette_id column, which appears in both the Corvettes and the Corvettes_Equipment tables. However, even if the column names are unique, including the table names makes the query more readable.

As another example of a join, notice that the State column of the Corvettes table does not store state names. Instead, it stores row references to the States table, which stores state names. Any user who submits a query on the Corvettes table would likely prefer that the state's names be returned rather than the reference to the States table. This can be easily accommodated in SQL. For example, suppose you want to get a list of the Corvettes for sale in California. This could be obtained with the following command:

```
SELECT Vette_id, Body_style, Year, States.State
FROM Corvettes, States
WHERE Corvettes.State = States.State_id AND
      States.State = 'California';
```

This query produces the following result:

VETTE_ID	BODY_STYLE	MILES	YEAR	STATE
5	hatchback	25.0	1991	California
8	convertible	17.0	1999	California
9	hardtop	17.0	2000	California

We have now introduced enough SQL to make the topics in the remainder of this chapter understandable.

14.3

ARCHITECTURES FOR DATABASE ACCESS

A database can be made available to its users in several ways. The most common of these are briefly introduced in the following subsections.

14.3.1 Client/Server Architectures

The basic client/server architecture of the Web was discussed earlier in this book. In any client/server configuration, part of the work is done by the client, and part is done by the server. A client/server database access architecture is very similar. The clients provide a way for users to input requests to a database that is resident on a computer that runs a database server. Results of requests to the server are returned to the client, which may use them in subsequent computations or simply display them for the user. A database server implements a data manipulation language that presents an interface to clients. This language can directly access and update the database. In its simplest form, a client/server database configuration has only two components, the client and the server. Such systems are called *two-tier* systems.

In some cases, two-tier systems are adequate. For example, in simple uses of the Web, the server provides HTML documents, and the client displays them. There is little computation to be divided between the two. However, some other applications require a great deal more complexity than the Web. In recent years, large database servers have been replaced by multiple smaller servers, thus lessening the capabilities of the individual servers to deal with increasing application complexity. At the same time, client systems have grown in power and sophistication. It would seem natural for the computational load in client/server systems to gravitate toward the clients. Unfortunately, there are other problems with this solution—specifically, if any part of the application is moved to the clients, there is the problem of keeping the clients current with changes in the applications that use the database. This is clearly a serious problem if there are a large number of clients.

The most common solution to the problems of two-tier systems is to add a third component, thereby hatching a three-tier architecture. The first tier has the Web browser, which provides the user interface. The middle tier of such a system usually has the Web server and the applications that require database access. The third tier in the system has the database server and the database itself. The architecture of a three-tier Web-based database access system has the form shown in Figure 14.6.

FIGURE 14.6 Three-tier architecture of a Web site supported by databases

14.3.2   Database Access with Embedded SQL

Most database vendors have developed techniques for embedding SQL process-ing capability into at least one common programming language. The C lan-guage is often chosen as a host. The host language is extended with additional reserved words and syntax to allow SQL statements to appear in its programs. For example, in C, there might be a construct such as this:

```
EXEC SQL
    -- some SQL statement;
```

This embedded code is translated to C statements by a preprocessor before the host program is compiled. The preprocessor for the extensions is provided by the database vendor.

Many database applications have been developed in languages that have been enhanced in this way. This approach has several advantages, one of which is that you have the computational capability supported by the host language and the database access power provided by SQL in one relatively simple package. The most important disadvantage of embedding SQL in a host language is that applications developed this way are not necessarily portable among database sys-tems because different vendors can design different extensions for the host lan-guage. As we will see in Section 14.3.6, this is not a problem if the extensions are defined by the language's designers rather than by database vendors.

14.3.3   The Microsoft Access Architecture

Microsoft Access is a tool for implementing database applications that can access virtually any common database. It provides access to different database systems in two different ways: through its Jet database engine or through the Open Database Connectivity (ODBC) standard. ODBC specifies an application programming interface (API) for a set of objects and methods that serves as an interface to different databases. Each database must have a driver, which is an implementation of these objects and methods. Vendors for most common data-bases provide ODBC drivers. By using ODBC, an application can include SQL statements (through the ODBC API) that work with any database for which a driver has been installed. A system called the *ODBC driver manager*, which runs on the client computer, chooses the proper driver for a request on a specific database.

14.3.4 The Perl DBI/DBD Architecture

Perl programs use a two-stage system to access databases. First, the database interface (DBI) module provides a collection of methods and attributes that allows generic SQL access to databases. The second stage is the direct database interface, called a database driver (DBD), which is specific to the particular SQL database being used. There are DBDs for most common relational databases. Programmers use the Perl DBI to write applications, which are nearly independent of the particular database to be used. The Perl DBI module is discussed in Section 14.5.

Perl CGI programs provide Web access to databases, using the DBI and the DBDs.

14.3.5 PHP and Database Access

PHP includes support for a wide variety of database systems. For each supported database system, there is an associated API. These APIs provide the interface to the specific systems. For example, the MySQL API includes functions to connect to a database and apply SQL commands against the database. Web access to a database using PHP is a natural architecture because PHP scripts are called through HTML documents from browsers. Using PHP and MySQL for database access is discussed in Section 14.6.

14.3.6 The Java JDBC Architecture

The Java JDBC architecture is a Java API for database access.[5] JDBC is very similar to ODBC, at least in terms of purpose. Both have the X/OPEN SQL Call Level Interface (SQL CLI) in their heritages.

JDBC provides a standard set of interfaces between applications that use databases and the low-level access software that actually manipulates the databases, which is supplied by the database vendor and is dependent on the particular brand of database being used. JDBC allows applications to be independent of the database system being used, as long as a JDBC driver is installed on the platform on which the application is run.

The advantages of JDBC are basically those of Java: The language is expressive and relatively safe, and programs are highly portable among platforms. The disadvantage of JDBC is that Java/JDBC programs are more complex than programs that accomplish the same things but are written in Perl or PHP.

---

5. JDBC sounds like an acronym for Java Database Connectivity, but Sun Microsystems has been known to deny this. In fact, Sun has registered JDBC as a trademark but has not done the same for Java Database Connectivity.

JDBC is described in Section 14.7.

Figure 14.7 shows the most common database access architecture. Microsoft's Access architecture uses ODBC for its database API. For Perl, the API is DBI. PHP uses collections of functions as APIs for different databases. Java has JDBC as its database API.

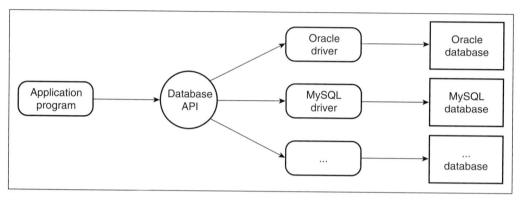

FIGURE 14.7 Common Database Access Architecture

14.4

THE MYSQL DATABASE SYSTEM

MySQL is a free, highly efficient, widely used database system that implements SQL. MySQL software and documentation can be downloaded from `http://www.mysql.org`. Some Linux system distributions, such as the one from Red Hat, include MySQL. This section describes a small part of MySQL. As with other software systems illustrated in this book, we do not discuss how to install or manage MySQL. These are usually system administration tasks. We only cover the use of MySQL, not its administration.

The first step to using MySQL is logging in to the MySQL system, which is done with the following command (at the command line of the operating system):

```
mysql [-h host] [-u username] [database_name] [-p]
```

The parts of this command that are in square brackets are optional. The *host* is the name of the server running MySQL; if absent, MySQL assumes it is the user's machine. If *username* is absent, it assumes that the name you used to log on to the machine is the correct username. If *database_name* is given, that database is selected as the focus of MySQL, making it the object of subsequent commands. If –p is included, it means a password is required, for which MySQL will ask.

Once you have successfully logged in to MySQL, it is ready to receive commands. Although it is called "logging on," what you are actually doing is starting execution of the MySQL system.

If the database to be accessed already exists but its name was not included when logging in to MySQL, the use command can be used to focus on the database of interest. For example, if we want to access a database named cars, we could use the following:

```
use cars;
```

This is sometimes called making a specific database the "current" database for the MySQL server. The MySQL response to this command is as follows:

```
Database changed
```

This seems odd because no change has been made to a database. Note the semicolon at the end of the use command—it is essential. All MySQL commands must be terminated with semicolons. If a command is given without a semicolon, MySQL will wait indefinitely for one. Until a semicolon is found, MySQL behaves as if the remainder of the command will follow.

If a database is not specified when logging in to MySQL and a database command is given before use is used to focus on a database, the following error message will be issued:

```
ERROR 1046: No Database Selected
```

If a new database is to be created, the database itself must be created first and then the tables that will make up the database. A new database is created with the SQL CREATE DATABASE command. For example:

```
CREATE DATABASE cars;
```

This command also elicits an odd response from MySQL:

```
Query ok, 1 row affected (0.05 sec)
```

The time given varies with the speed of and load on the host machine.

The tables of a database are created with the CREATE TABLE command, whose syntax is that of SQL. For example:

```
CREATE TABLE Equipment
    (Equip_id  INT  UNSIGNED  NOT NULL  AUTO_INCREMENT
             PRIMARY KEY,
     Equip  CHAR(10)
    );
```

The INT and UNSIGNED parts of the Equip_id column indicate the data type. The AUTO_INCREMENT is a MySQL convenience. It specifies that the values of this column need not be given when populating the table. The values 1, 2, 3, and so forth will be implicitly assigned. The value NULL is given in place of a value for a column so specified when populating the table with INSERT. A large number of different data types are possible for field values. The most common of these are CHAR (*length*), INT, and FLOAT (*total*, *fractional*), where *total* specifies the total number of characters, including both digits and the decimal point, and *fractional* gives the number of digits to the right of the decimal point.

The SHOW command can be used to display the tables of the database, as in the following:

```
SHOW TABLES;
```

If our sample database, cars, is the database of current focus, this produces the following:

```
--------------
show
--------------

+--------------------+
|                    |
| Tables_in_cars     |
|                    |
+--------------------+
| Corvettes          |
| Corvettes_Equipment|
| Equipment          |
| States             |
+--------------------+
```

The DESCRIBE command can be used to display the description of the structure of a table. For example,

```
DESCRIBE Corvettes;
```

produces the following:

Field	Type	Null	Key	Default	Extra
Vette_id	int(10) unsigned		PRI	NULL	auto_increment

```
|Body_style |char(12)          |       |     |        |            |          |
+-----------+------------------+-------+-----+--------+------------+----------+
|Miles      |float(4,1)        |       |     |0.0     |            |          |
+-----------+------------------+-------+-----+--------+------------+----------+
|Year       |int(10) unsigned  |       |     |0       |            |          |
+-----------+------------------+-------+-----+--------+------------+----------+
|State      |int(10) unsigned  |       |     |0       |            |          |
+-----------+------------------+-------+-----+--------+------------+----------+
```

The other MySQL commands that are needed here—INSERT, SELECT, DROP, UPDATE, and DELETE—are all implementations of their corresponding SQL commands. Therefore, their descriptions need not be repeated in this section.

14.5

DATABASE ACCESS WITH PERL AND MYSQL

Access to a database from a Perl program is a two-stage process. A standard Perl object-oriented module, DBI (for *data*base *i*nterface), provides an API for database access. An application program uses the methods and attributes of DBI to specify database accesses. The second stage of database access from Perl is a database driver (DBD) module. Each different database system requires its own driver, which is the interface to the actual database. So, a Perl program uses DBI to access a specific DBD, which accesses the physical database. This approach allows a Perl database application program to be relatively independent of the particular database it will access.

14.5.1 The DBI Module

The DBI module provides a large number of different methods and attributes, only a few of which are discussed in this section. A more complete description of DBI can be obtained by typing `perldoc DBI` at the operating system command.

The user interface design of DBI is related to that for files in Perl. Database operations are referenced through a database handle, which is defined by an operation that opens the database for access. DBI is used as an object-oriented module, so its methods and attributes are referenced through a reference variable. The first step in database access is to open the database and set a database handle variable to reference the object that represents the database in the application program. Before any DBI operations can be done, the DBI module must be made available with a `use` statement:

```
use DBI;
```

This statement creates a `DBI` object, which can be referenced through the variable `DBI`.

A database is opened with the `DBI` class method `connect`, which takes three parameters, although the last two are optional. Its protocol is as follows:

```
$dbh = DBI->connect("DBI:driver_name:database_name"
                    [, username][, password]);
```

The first parameter specifies the DBI module name, the database driver name, and the name of the database to which the connection is to be made. The driver name for MySQL is `mysql`. If the username is not specified, the login name is used; if the database does not require a password, one need not be included. For example, we could have the following:

```
$dbh = DBI->connect("DBI:mysql:cars");
```

This creates a database handle, `$dbh`, for the `cars` database. It assumes the username of the user who logged in is to be used for database access. Finally, it assumes the database does not need a password.

Because the connect operation can fail (for example, if the specified database does not exist), the call to `connect` is usually called in conjunction with a `die` operator. When `connect` fails, it returns an object that evaluates to `false`. In this case, `connect` also produces an error message that is returned from the `errstr` method of the handle it returns. Therefore, the following is a typical call to `connect`:

```
$dbh = DBI->connect("DBI:mysql:cars") or
   die "Error — unable to open cars: $dbh->errstr\n";
```

In the `die` expression, `$dbh->errstr` refers to an error message.

The database handle is actually an object that encapsulates the DBD for the specific database to be accessed. A Perl program can have connections to any number of different databases, each of which could be from a different vendor. Once the database is open and the connection to it has been made, it can be accessed. Although the handle method `do` can be used to request the execution of a SQL command, it is sometimes more convenient to first create a compiled version of a SQL command with the method `prepare`, which returns an object reference to the command. This object is called a *statement handle*. Once the statement handle has been created, it can be executed with the statement method `execute`. For example, the second query from Section 14.2.7 could be compiled with the following:

```
$sth = $dbh->prepare("SELECT Vette_id, Body_style, Year,
                             States.State
                      FROM Corvettes, States
                      WHERE Corvettes.State = States.State_id
                             AND
                             States.State = 'California'");
```

Because `execute` can fail, the call to it is usually combined with a call to `die`. For example:

```
$sth->execute() or
        die "Error — unable to execute query: $dbh->errstr\n";
```

The `$sth` statement handle object now has the results of the executed query.

In general, to properly display the results of database queries, the names of the result columns are needed. The statement handle object has an attribute, `NAME`, which is a reference to an array that has the names of the columns in the result. The attributes are stored in a hash, so `NAME` is used as a hash subscript to get the array of column names, as in the following:

```
$col_names = $sth->{NAME};
```

The rows of the returned value can be gotten with the `fetchrow_array` method of the statement handle object. This method returns a reference to an array with the next row of the result. If there are no more rows in the result, `fetchrow_array` returns `false`.

When the program is finished with a particular statement handle, it should call the `finish` method on the object. At the end of the program, the `disconnect` method of the database handle should be called.

14.5.2   An Example

Putting database field data into an HTML document creates a potential problem. A field retrieved from the database may contain characters that are special in HTML, namely >, <, ", or &. These can be converted to their corresponding HTML entities with the `CGI.pm` function `escapeHTML`, which is used in the following example.

The following is a complete CGI Perl program, `access_cars.pl`, which takes a query from a text-area widget of a form in an HTML document. The program connects to the `cars` database, performs the query, and displays the results in a table.

```perl
#!/usr/bin/perl -w
# access_cars.pl
# A CGI program to illustrate using MySQL from Perl

# Get access to DBI and CGI

use DBI;
use CGI ":standard";

print header();
print start_html("CGI-Perl MySQL database access");

# Create the connection to the database, cars

my $dbh = DBI->connect("DBI:mysql:cars", "root", "");

if (!$dbh) {
    print "Error connecting to database; $dbh->errstr\n";
}

# Get the query and display it

my $query = param("query");
print "<p> <b> The query is: </b>", $query, "</p>";

# Build a statement object for a SELECT SQL command

my $sth = $dbh->prepare($query);

# Execute the statement

$sth->execute or
    die "Error - unable to execute query: $dbh->errstr\n";

# Get a reference to the column names in the returned value and
#  display the column names as the first table row

print "<table> <caption> <h2> Query Results </h2> </caption>",
      "<tr align = 'center'>";
my $col_names = $sth->{NAME};
foreach $field_name (@$col_names) {
    print "<th> $field_name </th>";
}
```

```
print "</tr>";

# Get the rows of the result and display them in the table

while (@result_rows = $sth->fetchrow_array) {
    print "<tr align = 'center'>";

    while ($#result_rows >= 0) {
        $field = shift @result_rows;

# Replace the HTML special characters with their entities

        $field = escapeHTML($field);
        print "<td> $field </td>";
    }

    print "</tr>";
}

print "</table>";
$sth->finish;
$dbh->disconnect;
print end_html();
```

Figure 14.8 shows a browser display of the output of `access_cars.pl`.

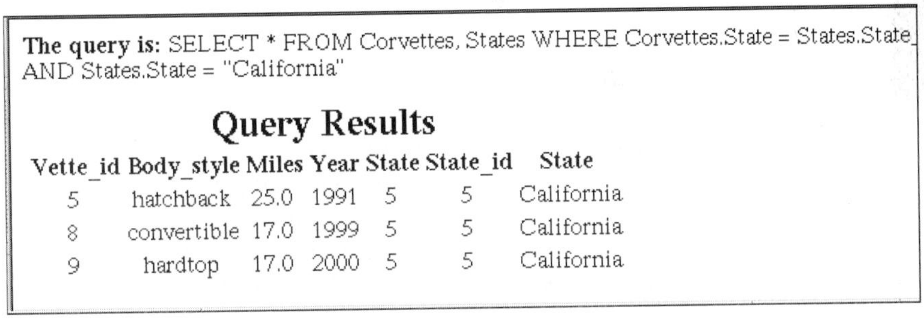

The query is: SELECT * FROM Corvettes, States WHERE Corvettes.State = States.State AND States.State = "California"

Query Results

Vette_id	Body_style	Miles	Year	State	State_id	State
5	hatchback	25.0	1991	5	5	California
8	convertible	17.0	1999	5	5	California
9	hardtop	17.0	2000	5	5	California

FIGURE 14.8   Display of the output of `access_cars.pl`

There is, of course, much more to DBI than we have given here. However, there is sufficient information to get the reader started learning it, which was our goal.

14.6

DATABASE ACCESS WITH PHP AND MYSQL

PHP access to a database is often done with two HTML documents: one to collect a user request for a database access and one to host the PHP code to process the request and generate the return HTML document. The user request collector is a simple HTML document. Therefore, this section is primarily about the database connection and processing.

14.6.1 Potential Problems with Special Characters

In Section 14.5.2, we explained the potential problem with characters in a database that are special in HTML (>, <, ", and &). PHP includes a function, `htmlspecialchars`, that replaces all occurrences of these four special characters in its parameter with their corresponding entities. For example, consider the following code:

```
$str = "Apples & grapes <raisins, too>";
$str = htmlspecialchars($str);
```

After the interpretation of this code, the value of `$str` has the following value:

```
"Apples &amp; grapes &lt;raisins, too&gt;"
```

This string is now ready to be made the content of an HTML tag without causing any browser confusion.

Another problem with special characters can occur with PHP scripts that get values through GET, POST, or from a cookie. Strings from these sources could include single quotes, double quotes, backslashes, and NULL characters, all of which could possibly cause problems if they are used in other strings in a script. To avoid these problems, the PHP system has an implicit backslashing function named `magic_quotes_gpc`, which can be turned on or off in the PHP.ini file. When this function is enabled, which is the default, all values received in a script from $_POST, $_GET, and $_COOKIE have backslashes implicitly inserted in front of all single quotes, double quotes, backslashes, and NULL characters. This avoids any problems that could be caused by those characters. For example, if the string O'Reilly is fetched from $_POST, it would be converted by `magic_quotes_gpc` to O\'Reilly. Unfortunately, this causes other problems. If the script compares the name to a nonslashed version, the comparison will fail. Furthermore, even displaying the name will show the backslash.

This problem is relevant here because we want to have a PHP script get SQL commands from a text box in an XHTML document. For example, suppose `magic_quotes_gpc` is on and the value for a query obtained from a text box on a form is as follows:

```
SELECT * FROM Corvettes WHERE Body_style = 'coupe'
```

If the name of the text box is `query`, its value is put in `$query` with the following statement:

```
$query = $_POST['query'];
```

The value of `$query` is converted to the following by `magic_quotes_gpc`:

```
SELECT * FROM Corvettes WHERE Body_style = \'coupe\'
```

Unfortunately, this string is not a legal SQL command (because of the backslashes). If it is sent to MySQL as a command, MySQL will reject it and report an error. Therefore, if complete SQL commands are to be collected from a form, as is done with the Perl/CGI program `access_cars.pl`, `magic_quotes_gpc` must be disabled in `PHP.ini` to avoid the extra backslashes. The alternative to changing the value of `magic_quotes_gpc` is to remove the extra slashes in the PHP script with the predefined function `stripslashes`, as in the following:

```
$query = stripslashes($query);
```

14.6.2 Connecting to MySQL and Selecting a Database

The PHP function `mysql_connect` connects a script to a MySQL server. This function takes three parameters, all of which are optional. The first is the host that is running MySQL; the default is localhost (the machine on which the script is running). The second parameter is the username for MySQL; the default is the username in which the PHP process runs. The third parameter is the password for the database; the default is blank (works if the database does not require a password). For example, if the default parameters were acceptable, we could use the following:

```
$db = mysql_connect();
```

Of course, the connect operation could fail, in which case the value returned would be `false` (rather than a reference to the database). Therefore, the call to `mysql_connect` usually is used in conjunction with `die`.

The connection to a database is terminated with the `mysql_close` function. This function is not necessary when using MySQL through a PHP script because the connection will be closed implicitly when the script terminates.

When running MySQL from the command line, a database must be selected as the current, or focused, database. This is also necessary when using MySQL through PHP; it is accomplished with the `mysql_select_db` function, as in the following:

```
mysql_select_db("cars");
```

14.6.3 Requesting MySQL Operations

MySQL operations are requested through the `mysql_query` function. Typically, the operation, in the form of a string literal, is assigned to a variable. Then `mysql_query` is called with the variable as its parameter. For example:

```
$query = "SELECT * from Corvettes";
$result = mysql_query($query);
```

The return value from `mysql_query` is used to identify, internally, the data that resulted from the operation. In most cases, the first thing to do with the result is determine the number of rows. This is obtained with the `mysql_num_rows` function, which is given the result value returned by `mysql_query`, as in the following:

```
$num_rows = mysql_num_rows($result);
```

The number of fields in a result row can be determined with `mysql_num_fields`, as in the following statement:

```
$num_fields = mysql_num_fields($result);
```

The rows of the result can be retrieved into several different forms. We will use `mysql_fetch_array`, which returns an array of the next row. Then the field values can be obtained by subscripting the return array with the column names. For example, if the result of a query had columns for `State_id` and `State`, we could display the results with the following code:

```
$num_rows = mysql_num_rows($result);

for ($row_num = 1; $row_num <= $num_rows; $row_num++) {
    $row = mysql_fetch_array($result);
    print "<p> Result row number" . $row_num .
        ". State_id: ";
    print htmlspecialchars($row["State_id"]);
    print " State: ";
    print htmlspecialchars($row["State"]);
    print "</p>";
}
```

The situation in which the column names are not known is considered in Section 14.6.4, which includes a complete example of accessing a database through PHP and MySQL.

14.6.4   A PHP/MySQL Example

One simple example of Web access to a database is to use an HTML form to collect a query from a user, apply the query to the database, and return a document that shows the results of the query. The form that allows users to input queries is simple. The PHP script to connect to the database and perform the query is also relatively simple—we have done all of this in Section 14.6.3. All that remains is to get the results into a form that is easy to present to the user. The example of displaying query results in Section 14.6.3 was easy because the names of the columns of the result were known and the results were not put in a table.

The rows of the result of a query are PHP arrays, which are also arrays. Such an array has double sets of elements, one with numeric keys and one with string keys. For example, if a query gets a row with the field values (1, Alabama), the row actually stores four hash elements, two with numeric keys and two with string keys. For the States table of the cars database, the result row would actually have the following:

```
((0, 1), (State_id, 1), (1, Alabama), (State, Alabama))
```

If a row is indexed with numbers, the element values are returned. For example, if a row of the result of a query is in $row, then $row[0] is the value of the first field in the row, $row[1] is the value of the second field, and so forth. The rows could be indexed with strings, in which case $row["State"] would have the value Alabama. As a result of this double storage of result fields, the result rows have twice as many elements as there are fields in the result. If only the values are needed, they can be fetched from the value part of every other hash element, beginning with the second (the element with subscript 1). The following will display all of the field values in the result row in $row:

```
$values = array_values($row);
for ($index = 0; $index < $num_fields; $index++)
    print "$values[2 * $index + 1] <br />";
```

When the results are being returned as HTML content, it is always a good idea to use htmlspecialchars on the field values.

Getting the column labels from the results of a MySQL query can be confusing. From the example of the actual contents of a result array previously shown, the column labels are the keys of the odd-numbered elements of the array (State_id and State). The keys can be displayed in the same way the values were displayed previously.

```
$keys = array_keys($row);
for ($index = 0; $index < $num_fields; $index++)
  print "$keys[2 * $index + 1] <br />";
```

The following is the HTML document `carsdata.html` to collect queries on the `cars` database from the user.

```html
<!-- carsdata.html
     Uses a form to collect a query against the cars
     database.
     Calls the PHP script, access_cars.php to perform
     the given query and display the results
     -->
<html>
  <head><title> Access to the cars database </title>
  </head>
  <body>
    <p>
      Please enter your query:
      <br />
      <form action  = "access_cars.php" method = "post">
        <textarea  rows = "2"  cols = "80" name = "query" >
        </textarea>
        <br /><br />
        <input type = "reset"  value = "Reset" />
        <input type = "submit"  value = "Submit request" />
      </form>
    </p>
  </body>
</html>
```

The following HTML document, `access_cars.php`, processes a query and returns the results in a table.

```html
<!-- access_cars.php
     A PHP script to access the cars database
     through MySQL
     -->
<html>
<head>
<title> Access the cars database with MySQL </title>
</head>
```

```php
<body>
<?php

// Connect to MySQL

$db = mysql_connect("localhost", "rws", "");
if (!$db) {
    print "Error - Could not connect to MySQL";
    exit;
}

// Select the cars database

$er = mysql_select_db("cars");
if (!$er) {
    print "Error - Could not select the cars database";
    exit;
}

// Get the query and clean it up (delete leading and trailing
// whitespace and remove backslashes from magic_quotes_gpc)

$query = $_POST['query'];
trim($query);
$query = stripslashes($query);

// Display the query, after fixing html characters

$query_html = htmlspecialchars($query);
print "<p> <b> The query is: </b> " . $query_html . "</p>";

// Execute the query

$result = mysql_query($query);
if (!$result) {
    print "Error - the query could not be executed";
    $error = mysql_error();
    print "<p>" . $error . "</p>";
    exit;
}

 // Display the results in a table
```

continued

```php
print "<table><caption> <h2> Query Results </h2> </caption>";
print "<tr align = 'center'>";

// Get the number of rows in the result, as well as the first row
//   and the number of fields in the rows

$num_rows = mysql_num_rows($result);
$row = mysql_fetch_array($result);
$num_fields = mysql_num_fields($result);

// Produce the column labels

$keys = array_keys($row);
for ($index = 0; $index < $num_fields; $index++)
    print "<th>" . $keys[2 * $index + 1] . "</th>";

print "</tr>";

// Output the values of the fields in the rows

for ($row_num = 0; $row_num < $num_rows; $row_num++) {
    print "<tr align = 'center'>";
    $values = array_values($row);
    for ($index = 0; $index < $num_fields; $index++) {
        $value = htmlspecialchars($values[2 * $index + 1]);
        print "<th>" . $value . "</th> ";
    }

    print "</tr>";
    $row = mysql_fetch_array($result);
}
print "</table>";
?>
</body>
</html>
```

Figure 14.9 shows a browser display of the results of access_cars.php on the given query.

```
The query is: SELECT Vette_id, Body_style, Year, Miles, States.State FROM Corvettes,
States WHERE Corvettes.State = States.State_id AND States.State = 'Connecticut'
```

Query Results

Vette_id	Body_style	Year	Miles	State
2	hatchback	1996	58.0	Connecticut
10	hatchback	1995	50.0	Connecticut

FIGURE 14.9   Display of the return document from `access_cars.php`

The two documents, `carsdata.html` and `access_cars.php`, which together collect a query from a user, apply it to the database, and return the results, can be combined. After inserting the XHTML markup from `carsdata.html` into `access_cars.php`, several modifications and additions must be made to the resulting document. First, the `action` attribute of the form must be changed to be self referential. One simple way to do this is to change the value to the name of the combined file. Next, there is the issue of how to get the PHP processor to produce the query collection markup the first time the document is requested and interpret the query processing code on the next request. The commonly used approach to this is to create a hidden input element that sets its value when the document is first displayed. The PHP code in the document checks the value of the hidden element to determine whether the action is to display a textarea to collect a query or to apply the query to the database and display the result. The hidden element is defined with markup as shown here:

```
<input type = "hidden"  name = "stage"  value = "1" />
```

The PHP code to test the value of the hidden element has the following form:

```
$stage = $_POST["stage"];
if (!IsSet($stage)) { ... }
```

The then clause of this selector would contain the display of the form to collect the query. The else clause would contain the query processing and result display code. The combination of `carsdata.html` and `access_cars.php`, named `access_cars2.php`, follows.

```
<!-- access_cars2.php
     A PHP script to both get a query from the user and
     access the cars database through MySQL to get and
     display the result of the query.
     -->
<html>
  <head>
    <title> Access the cars database with MySQL </title>
  </head>
  <body>
<?php
$stage = $_POST["stage"];
if (!IsSet($stage)) {
?>
    <p>
      Please enter your query:
      <br />
      <form  method = "POST"  action = "access_cars2.php" >
        <textarea  rows = "2"  cols = "80"  name = "query">
        </textarea>
        <br /><br />
        <input type = "hidden"  name = "stage"  value = "1" />
        <input type = "submit"  value = "Submit request" />
      </form>
    </p>
<?php
} else {  // $stage was set, so process the query

// Connect to MySQL

  $db = mysql_connect("localhost", "rws", "");
  if (!$db) {
    print "Error - Could not connect to MySQL";
    exit;
  }

// Select the cars database

  $er = mysql_select_db("cars");
  if (!$er) {
    print "Error - Could not select the cars database";
    exit;
  }
```

```
// Clean up the given query (delete leading and trailing
whitespace)

  $query = $_POST['query'];
  trim($query);

// Fix the query for browser display and display it

  $query_html = htmlspecialchars($query);
  print "<p> <b> The query is: </b> " . $query_html . "</p>";

// Execute the query

  $result = mysql_query($query);
  if (!$result) {
    print "Error - the query could not be executed";
    $error = mysql_error();
    print "<p>" . $error . "</p>";
    exit;
  }

// Display the results in a table

  print "<table><caption> <h2> Query Results </h2> </caption>";
  print "<tr align = 'center'>";

// Get the number of rows in the result, as well as the first row
//   and the number of fields in the rows

  $num_rows = mysql_num_rows($result);
  $row = mysql_fetch_array($result);
  $num_fields = mysql_num_fields($result);

// Produce the column labels

  $keys = array_keys($row);
  for ($index = 0; $index < $num_fields; $index++)
    print "<th>" . $keys[2 * $index + 1] . "</th>";

  print "</tr>";

// Output the values of the fields in the rows
```

continued

```
    for ($row_num = 0; $row_num < $num_rows; $row_num++) {
      print "<tr align = 'center'>";
      $values = array_values($row);
      for ($index = 0; $index < $num_fields; $index++){
        $value = htmlspecialchars($values[2 * $index + 1]);
        print "<th>" . $value . "</th> ";
      }

      print "</tr>";
      $row = mysql_fetch_array($result);
    }
    print "</table>";
  }
  ?>
</body>
</html>
```

14.7

DATABASE ACCESS WITH JDBC AND MYSQL

This section describes JDBC and its use with MySQL to create, modify, and query relational databases. Subsections 14.7.1 to 14.7.4 describe the use of JDBC with MySQL in a non-Web environment. Subsection 14.7.5 discusses using servlets and the Web with JDBC and MySQL.

14.7.1 Approaches to Using JDBC Outside the Web

JDBC is a Java API for database access. A Java program can use JDBC to connect to a database and send SQL commands to the database as the parameter of a JDBC method.

The Java interfaces that define JDBC are included in the `java.sql` package, which is part of the standard Java distribution. So, if you have a relatively recent version of Java, you have the `java.sql` package and JDBC. JDBC runs in a client/server configuration in which the classes that implement the JDBC interfaces serve as the client.

The simplest configuration in which JDBC can be used is through a JDBC driver designed for the target database. If such a driver exists—and they do now for all widely used databases—a two-tier configuration for using the database through JDBC is straightforward. The application talks to the JDBC driver, which in turn talks to the database server (see Figure 14.10). One minor disadvantage of this configuration is that every database requires its own JDBC driver, and every driver that will be used by a client must be installed on that client's machine.

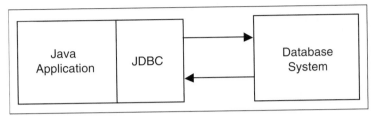

FIGURE 14.10   Using JDBC directly

The second way to use JDBC is through a third-tier computer that runs the JDBC drivers for the databases being accessed. The software that runs on the third-tier computer is often called *middleware*. In this case, the client must run a middleware client system that communicates with the middleware server, which in turn communicates with the database through the database server (see Figure 14.11). One advantage of this approach is that the package that implements the middleware client system provides support for all databases. Some database vendors add nonstandard extensions to the JDBC interfaces that they implement as their JDBC drivers. By using the middleware computer, the extensions can be used without affecting the database independence of the application. Another advantage is that the client computer never needs to connect directly to the database server computer. This allows applets, which are not allowed to connect to any computer except the one that served the applet to the client, to be used for JDBC database access. The middleware computer can serve the applet to the client.

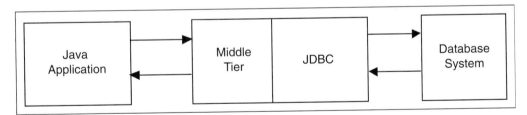

FIGURE 14.11   Using JDBC through a midtier computer

14.7.2   JDBC and MySQL

This section describes the mechanisms for using JDBC to perform simple SQL operations on an existing database. The first step in developing a JDBC application is to establish a connection between the application and the database interface, or driver. The `java.sql` package includes all the classes and interfaces that support JDBC. The `DriverManager` class provides the method `getConnection`, which makes the connection to the database. This class must select the correct driver for the database from those that have been registered.

The general form of a reference to a database for the connection operation is shown here:

jdbc:*subprotocol_name*:*more_info*

The *subprotocol_name* part is used to specify the driver for the database. For a MySQL database, the *subprotocol_name* is `mysql`. The *more_info* part is dependent on the subprotocol being used. If the database is local, it may be just the name of the database. If the database is somewhere else on the Internet, it may be the URL of the database. In the case of a database being on the same machine as the client, the *more_info* part includes `localhost` and the name of the database followed by a username and a password for the database. The username and password are attached to the database address in the same way HTML `GET` parameters are attached to a URL. For the sample MySQL database `cars`, assuming root is the user and there is no password, the reference is as follows:

jdbc:mysql://localhost/cars?user=root

A database driver may be registered in two ways, one fairly general and the other very specific. The general approach is to have the system property `jdbc.drivers` maintain a list of drivers. An application can add a new driver to this property by assigning the driver's class address to the property. For example, consider this statement:

jdbc.drivers = org.gjt.mm.mysql.Driver;

Here, `org.gjt.mm.mysql.Driver` is the name of the MySQL JDBC driver class that is used in the examples in this section. (The driver can be downloaded from `http://www.mysql.org`.) The only other requirement to make the driver usable is that it be loadable by the application, which means that it must be stored in a place where the application can access it. The driver manager is responsible for choosing the correct driver from those that are registered.

The less general way of registering a driver is to do it manually with the `forName` method of the `Class` class, giving the name of the driver class as a parameter:

Class.forName("org.gjt.mm.mysql.Driver").newInstance();

This approach is adequate if the application will be used exclusively for databases from one specific vendor.

The connection to a database from an application is made by creating a `Connection` object with the `getConnection` method of the `DriverManager` class. For the sample database `cars` and the MySQL database system, the `Connection` object can be created with the following statement:

```
myCon = DriverManager.getConnection(
                "jdbc:mysql://localhost/cars?user=root");
```

The `Connection` object is used to specify all database operations from the JDBC application.

After the appropriate database driver is registered and the connection is established to the database, a JDBC application can access the database using SQL commands. The first step in using SQL from a Java program is to create a `Statement` object through which one of the `Statement` methods can be used to actually issue the command. The `Statement` object is created with the `createStatement` method of the `Connection` class. If `myCon` is the `Connection` object, the following can be used:

```
Statement myStmt = myCon.createStatement();
```

SQL commands are created as `String` objects, as in this example:

```
final String sql_com =
 "UPDATE Corvettes SET Year = 1991 WHERE Vette_id = 7";
```

From the JDBC point of view, there are two categories of SQL commands: the action commands, which include `INSERT`, `UPDATE`, `DELETE`, `CREATE TABLE`, and `DROP TABLE`; and the query command, `SELECT`. The action commands are executed through the `executeUpdate` method of the `Statement` object. For example, the previous SQL command `sql_com` can be executed with this statement:

```
myStmt.executeUpdate(sql_com);
```

The `executeUpdate` method returns the number of rows that were affected by the command that it sent to the database.

A `SELECT` SQL command can be executed by sending it as the actual parameter to the `executeQuery` method of the `Statement` object. Executing a `SELECT` command differs from executing an action command in that the `SELECT` command is expected to return a part of the data found in the database. So, a call to `executeQuery` must be assigned to a program variable. The class of this variable must be `ResultSet`, which is structured to store such results and which has methods to provide access to the data of the result. Consider this example:

```
ResultSet result;
final String sql_com =
     "SELECT * FROM Corvettes WHERE Year <= 1990"
result = myStmt.executeQuery(sql_com);
```

Objects of the ResultSet class are similar to objects of classes that implement the related interface Enumeration. In both cases, the elements of the object are accessed through an iterator method. In the case of Enumeration, the iterator method is called nextElement; in the case of ResultSet, it is called next. The next method is a predicate—it returns a Boolean value, depending on whether there is another element in the ResultSet object. Its action is to make the next element of the ResultSet object the current one—that is, the one that can be accessed through one of the access methods provided by ResultSet. Initially, there is no current element of a ResultSet object. Therefore, next must be called to make the first element current. The elements of a ResultSet object are typically accessed in a loop such as this one:

```
while(result.next()) {
    // access and process the current element
}
```

Here, result is the object returned by executeQuery.

The actual structure of a ResultSet object is not visible to the application, so it is irrelevant. The information in a ResultSet object is extracted through a collection of access methods. Each element of a ResultSet object represents the information in a row of the result of the query operation. Field values in the rows can be extracted by the access methods, whose names are in this general form:

get*Type_name*

Here, the *Type_name* part is one of the Java data types, either a primitive type such as int or float or a class such as String.

There are actually two of each of the named access methods: one that takes an int parameter, which specifies the column number, starting at 1; and one that takes a String parameter, which specifies the column name. For example, suppose the first row of the ResultSet object for the SELECT specified previously happened to be this:

```
3, "convertible", 13.5, 2001, 1
```

Assuming that the variable style is defined to be a String object, the value of the Body_style column "convertible" could be obtained with either of the following two method calls:

```
style = result.getString("Body_style");
```

```
style = result.getString(2);
```

The SQL data types do not perfectly match the Java data types. Some of the most commonly used SQL data types and their Java counterparts are shown in Table 14.1.

TABLE 14.1 Common SQL Data Types and Their Java Counterparts

SQL Data Type	Java Data Type
`INTEGER` or `INT`	`int`
`SMALLINT`	`short`
`FLOAT(`n`)`	`double`
`REAL`	`float`
`DOUBLE`	`double`
`CHARACTER(`n`)` or `CHAR(`n`)`	`String`
`VARCHAR(`n`)`	`String`
`BOOLEAN`	`boolean`

The get*Type_name* methods attempt to convert SQL data types to equivalent Java data types. For example, if `getString` is used to fetch an `INTEGER` value, the number will be converted to a `String` object.

14.7.3   A Complete JDBC/MySQL Example

This section provides a complete Java/JDBC application that executes a single `SELECT` SQL command on the `cars` database and displays the results. This application is structured as four methods. The `main` method creates an object of the class type and defines a constructor that calls the three other methods of the class, `connector`, `select`, and `closer`. The `connector` method registers the MySQL driver, makes the connection to the `cars` database, and creates the statement object for the query. The `select` method defines the query, performs it against the database, and produces a display of the results. The `closer` method only closes the connection to the database.

```
// Query.java
//   This Java/JDBC example connects to the cars database, uses
//   a query to select all rows of the Corvettes table in which
//   the Year column is less than 1992, and displays the results
```

continued

```java
import java.sql.*;

public class Query {

    // Create connection and statement objects

    private Connection  myCon;
    private Statement    myStmt;

    // The main method - creates an instance of Query

    public static void main(String[] args) {

        // Create the Query object

        Query que = new Query();
    }

        // The Query constructor

    public Query() {
        try {
            connecter();
            select();
            closer();
        }
        catch (SQLException sqlEx) {
            System.err.println(sqlEx);
        }
    }

    // connecter method
    //     Register the database driver and create the database
    //     connection and query statement objects

    void connecter() throws SQLException {
        try {

            // Register the MySQL database driver

            Class.forName("org.gjt.mm.mysql.Driver").newInstance();

            // Create the connection object
```

```
        myCon = DriverManager.getConnection (
                    "jdbc:mysql://localhost/cars?user=root);

        // Create the statement object for the query

        myStmt = myCon.createStatement();

    } //* end of try clause

    catch (SQLException sqlEx) {
        throw sqlEx;
    }
    catch (Exception e) {
        System.err.println(e);
    }
} //* end of the connecter method


// select method - create the SQL command string,
// execute it, and display the results

void select() throws SQLException {

    // Create the SELECT command as a String

    final String select_sql =
                "SELECT * FROM Corvettes WHERE Year > 1992";

    // Perform the query

    ResultSet result = myStmt.executeQuery(select_sql);

    // Display output headings

    System.out.println(
        "\n\n\t\t1993-2001 Corvettes For Sale\n");
    System.out.println(
        "Vette_id\tBody_style \tMiles \tYear \tState");
    System.out.println();

    // Display the rows of the result
```

continued

```
    while(result.next()) {
        int id = result.getInt("Vette_id");
        String body = result.getString("Body_style");
        float miles = result.getFloat("Miles");
        int year = result.getInt("Year");
        int state = result.getInt("State");
        System.out.println(id + "\t\t" + body + "\t" + miles +
                            "\t" + year + "\t" + state);
    }

}

// closer method - close the database connection

void closer() throws SQLException {
    myCon.close();
}
}
```

The results of running this program are as follows:

	1993-2001 Corvettes For Sale			
Vette_id	Body_style	Miles	Year	State
1	coupe	18.0	1997	4
2	hatchback	58.0	1996	7
3	convertible	13.5	2001	1
6	hardtop	15.0	2000	2
8	convertible	17.0	1999	5
9	hardtop	17.0	2000	5
10	hatchback	50.0	1995	7

14.7.4 Metadata

If the same person both designs and uses a database, the approaches used in Sections 14.7.2 and 14.7.3 to display database tables and the results of queries are adequate. However, if you are writing an application that must work with any database—that is, the exact structure of the database is not known—you must be able to get table names and column names from the database. Also, the types of the data in the result rows must be known. Information that describes the database itself or some part of the database is called *metadata*. There are two kinds of metadata: metadata that describes the database and metadata that describes a ResultSet object that is returned by the execution of a query.

A method of the `Connection` object, `getMetaData`, creates an object of `DatabaseMetaData` type, which can be used to get information about a database. For example:

```
DatabaseMetaData dbmd = myCon.getMetaData();
```

To deal with the many different configurations of databases, many different methods are defined in the `DatabaseMetaData` class. Fortunately, most of these are infrequently used, and we can illustrate the use of metadata through just one that is commonly used, `getTables`. Although `getTables` returns a variety of information, here we are interested only in table names.

The `getTables` method takes four parameters, only the last of which interests us. The last actual parameter to `getTables` specifies an array of `String` objects with just one element, which is set to the value `"TABLE"`. The other three actual parameters can be `null`. The `getTables` method returns a `ResultSet` object that has information about the tables of the database, the third row of which has the table names. Assuming that the `Connection` object for a database is `myCon`, the code to produce a list of the names of the tables in the database is as follows:

```
String tbl[] = {"TABLE"};
DatabaseMetaData dbmd = myCon.getMetaData();
result = dbmd.getTables(null, null, null, tbl);
System.out.println("The tables in the database are: \n\n");
while (result.next()) {
    System.out.println(result.getString(3));
}
```

Adding this code to the program `Query.java` produces the following output:

```
The tables in this database are:
CORVETTES
CORVETTES_EQUIPMENT
EQUIPMENT
STATES
```

Fetching metadata about the result of a query on a database is more complicated than getting the table names. The metadata for a query result has a different structure than that for the general database information. For the query result, the metadata is stored in an object of the `ResultSetMetaData` class. An object of this class is returned from the `ResultSet` object when the `getMetaData` method is called, as in this example:

```
ResultSetMetaData resultMd = result.getMetaData();
```

Using the `resultMd` object, the number of columns and their names, types, and sizes can be determined through the methods of `ResultSetMetaData`. The number of columns is returned by `getColumnCount`. The name of the *i*th column is returned by `getColumnLabel(i)`.

Using these objects and methods, the code in `Query.java` can be rewritten to create a display of the column names of the result produced by the query. The code to do this is given here:

```
// Create an object for the metadata

ResultSetMetaData resultMd = result.getMetaData();

// Loop to fetch and display the column names

for (int i = 1; i <= resultMd.getColumnCount(); i++) {
    String columnName = resultMd.getColumnLabel(i);
    System.out.print(columnName + "\t");
}

System.out.println("\n");
```

The display produced by this code is as follows:

```
Vette_id      Body_style      Miles    Year    State
```

This is exactly what we had hard-wired into the original version of `Query.java`.

The problem of not knowing the types of the data in the result rows has a simple solution: The data can be converted to strings with `getString`, a method of the result object. This is illustrated in Section 14.7.5.

14.7.5   JDBC and Servlets

Using JDBC in a servlet is not very different from using it in a Java application. For example, suppose we have an HTML document that collects a database query in a text box, similar to `carsdata.html`, which is used in Section 14.6.4 as the user interface to the PHP/MySQL example. In this case, the document calls a servlet to perform the query. The servlet could use its `init` method to establish the database connection and create the `Statement` object for the query method, `executeQuery`. These operations could be specified in the `doPost` method, but that would require reconnection to the database with every query. In the `init` method, they only happen once.

The `doPost` method could perform the query operations and build the return document of the results of the query.

The situation here is different from that of the application `Query.java` in that the query is not fixed. Thus, the approaches described in Section 14.7.4

must be used to produce column labels and the data of the resulting rows. Furthermore, because the number of columns in the result is not known, the query results should be placed in an HTML table so that the output will have a presentable appearance.

The following is a servlet that accepts queries from its HTML document. It performs the queries against the `cars` database and returns an HTML document of the results.

```java
// JDBCServlet.java
//  This servlet receives an SQL query from its HTML document,
//    connects to the cars database, performs the query on the
//    database, and returns an HTML table of the results of the
//    query


import javax.servlet.*;
import javax.servlet.http.*;
import java.io.*;
import java.util.*;
import java.sql.*;

public class JDBCServlet extends HttpServlet {
   private Connection myCon;
   private Statement myStmt;

   // The init method - instantiate the db driver, connect to the
   //  db, and create a statement for an SQL command

   public void init() {

     // Instantiate the driver for MySQL

     try {
       Class.forName("org.gjt.mm.mysql.Driver").newInstance();
     }
     catch (Exception e) {
       e.printStackTrace();
     }

     // Create the connection to the cars db

     try {
```

continued

```
        myCon = DriverManager.getConnection (
              "jdbc:mysql://localhost/cars?user=root");
    }
    catch (SQLException e) {
      e.printStackTrace();
    }

    // Create the statement for SQL queries

    try {
      myStmt = myCon.createStatement();
    }
    catch (Exception e) {
      e.printStackTrace();
    }
}  //** end of the init method

// The doPost method - get the query, perform it, and produce
//   an HTML table of the results

public void doPost(HttpServletRequest request,

              throws ServletException, IOException {
  ResultSet result;
  String query, colName, dat;
  int numCols, index;
  ResultSetMetaData resultMd;

  // Get the SQL request command

  query = request.getParameter("Query");

  // Set the MIME type and get a writer

  response.setContentType("text/html");
  PrintWriter out = response.getWriter();

  // Create the initial html and display the request

  out.println("<html>");
  out.println("<head><title>JDBCServlet</title></head>");
  out.println("<body>");
  out.print("<p><b>The query is: </b>" + query + "</p>");
```

```
// Perform the query

try {
  result = myStmt.executeQuery(query);

// Get the result's metadata and the number of result rows

  resultMd = result.getMetaData();
  numCols = resultMd.getColumnCount();

  // Produce the table header and caption

  out.println("<table border>");
  out.println("<caption> <b> Query Results </b> </caption>");
  out.println("<tr>");

  // Loop to produce the column headings

  for (index = 1; index <= numCols; index++) {
    colName = resultMd.getColumnLabel(index);
    out.print("<th>" + colName + "</th>");
  }

out.println("</tr>");

// Loop to produce the rows of the result

while (result.next()) {
  out.println("<tr>");

  // Loop to produce the data of a row of the result

  for (index = 1; index <= numCols; index++) {
    dat = result.getString(index);
    out.println("<td>" + dat + "</td>");
  }  //** end of for (index = 0; ...

  out.println("</tr>");
}  //** end of while (result.next()) ...

out.println("</table>");

}  //** end of try
```

continued

```
    catch (Exception e) {
      e.printStackTrace();
    }  //** end of catch

    out.println("</body></html>");
  }  //** end of doPost method
}  //** end of class JDBCServlet
```

Figure 14.12 shows a browser display of the output of `JDBCServlet` on a given query.

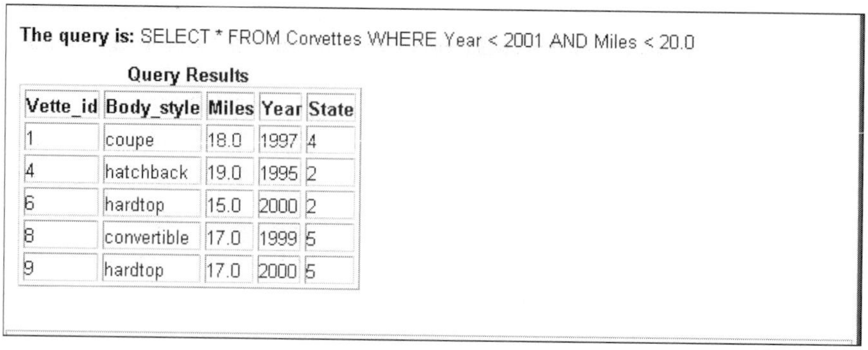

The query is: SELECT * FROM Corvettes WHERE Year < 2001 AND Miles < 20.0

Query Results

Vette_id	Body_style	Miles	Year	State
1	coupe	18.0	1997	4
4	hatchback	19.0	1995	2
6	hardtop	15.0	2000	2
8	convertible	17.0	1999	5
9	hardtop	17.0	2000	5

FIGURE 14.12   Display of the results of `JDBCServlet`

14.8

SUMMARY

A relational database consists of a collection of related tables of data. Most tables include a column of primary keys, which uniquely identify the rows. A cross-reference table contains no data; instead, it contains the primary keys of two data tables, providing a many-to-many relationship between the data in the two tables.

SQL is a standard language for specifying accesses and modifications to relational databases. All commonly used relational database systems support SQL. The most frequently used SQL commands are CREATE, SELECT, INSERT, UPDATE, and DELETE.

The CREATE command specifies a table name and a list of column names and their associated constraints. The SELECT command specifies one or more columns of one or more tables, along with a Boolean expression that provides a constraint on the data in the specified columns. SELECT is a complex and powerful tool. The INSERT command specifies a table name, a list of column names, and a list of values that correspond to the column names. The `UPDATE` command specifies a table name and a list of column name/value pairs, along with a specific primary key value. The `DELETE` command specifies a table name and the primary key of a specific column.

A join operation, which can be specified by a `SELECT` command, creates a new table by joining part of the data of one table with part of the data of another table. The objective of a join is to make information available to the user that is not stored in a single table.

A two-tier client/server architecture is common. In it, a client machine communicates directly with a server machine. The Web is an example of a two-tier client/server configuration. A third tier is used in a client/server architecture when it is better for one or both of the client or the server to communicate only indirectly with the other.

One approach to building database applications is to extend a general-purpose programming language so that it can specify SQL commands and interact with a database through them. The disadvantage of this is that such applications are not likely to be portable among the databases of different vendors. Microsoft's Access system provides a way to access the databases of most common vendors through an interface called ODBC. Because ODBC has been implemented by most vendors for their databases, this approach provides a way to develop portable applications.

MySQL is a relational database server that implements SQL. There are drivers for MySQL for most common database APIs, including Perl DBI, PHP, and JDBC.

Perl's DBI module provides an object through which Perl programs can connect to databases and use SQL to perform operations. SQL commands are often precompiled with the `prepare` method. Such commands are executed with the `execute` method. Column names for query results are obtained through the `NAME` attribute of the `DBI` object.

PHP has implemented APIs for most common database systems. The MySQL API for PHP includes functions for connecting to a database (`mysql_connect`), executing SQL commands (`mysql_query`), and retrieving rows from query results (for example, `mysql_fetch_array`). Getting the column names for query results is a bit confusing but not difficult.

The goal of JDBC is related to that of ODBC, except that it is part of one general-purpose programming language, Java. There are drivers for JDBC for all common database systems. A JDBC application must create a connection to a database for which there is a JDBC driver available. Then it creates a `Statement` object into which can be stored a SQL command as a string. The command can be executed by passing it as a parameter to a method through the `Statement` object. The return value from the execution of a `SELECT` command is an object of `ResultSet` type, which stores the rows that were extracted from the database. Actual data values are obtained from the returned object through a collection of methods called through the object.

Metadata is data about the database rather than data stored in the database. It is common to need information about the result object returned from the execution of a SELECT command. This information is obtained by a method called through the result object. Specific information is obtained by methods called through the metadata object.

14.9 Review Questions

1. What is the purpose of the primary keys of a table in a relational database?

2. What is the purpose of a cross-reference table?

3. How are string literals delimited in SQL?

4. What does the NOT NULL constraint specify in a column of a CREATE TABLE SQL command?

5. What does an asterisk specify when it appears as the value of a SELECT clause?

6. What is specified by the WHERE clause of a SELECT command?

7. How are the column names associated with the values in an INSERT command?

8. What is the purpose of an UPDATE command?

9. What exactly is a table join, and how is one specified in SQL?

10. What is the purpose of a third tier in a client/server configuration for Web access to a database?

11. Why are two-tier client/server configurations sometimes inadequate?

12. Explain how SQL database access can be provided by extending a programming language.

13. What is the disadvantage of embedding SQL in a programming language?

14. What is ODBC, and why is it useful?

15. What does the Perl DBI module provide?

16. What is the relationship between ODBC and JDBC?

17. What is MySQL?

18. What does the MySQL constraint auto_increment do?

19. What is the form of the first parameter to the Perl DBI method connect?

20. What does the Perl DBI prepare method do?

21. What is a Perl DBI statement handle?

22. What is the problem with quotes in a SQL command obtained from a form element in an HTML document?

23. What is the purpose of the PHP `mysql_select_db` function?

24. How can a PHP program determine the number of rows in a query result?

25. What does the PHP function `mysql_fetch_array` do?

26. Explain the exact form of the value returned by `mysql_fetch_array`.

27. Explain the two ways of using JDBC.

28. What advantage does a third-tier computer provide when using JDBC?

29. What method of what class is used to connect to a database when using JDBC?

30. Explain the two ways to register a JDBC driver.

31. What purpose does a `Statement` object serve when using SQL through JDBC?

32. What method of what class is used to execute a SQL action command?

33. What method of what class is used to execute a `SELECT` command?

34. What class of object is returned from the `executeQuery` method?

35. How can a program iterate through the object returned by `executeQuery`?

36. What is the form of the methods used to extract values from the object returned by `executeQuery`?

37. What is metadata?

38. How is the collection of metadata extracted from a database?

39. What are the two ways column labels can be obtained from an object of metadata?

14.10 Exercises

1. Use MySQL to create a database of information about used trucks for sale, similar to the `cars` database used in this chapter. Make up equipment that characterizes trucks. Get the raw data from the ad section of your local newspaper. Instead of the states in the `cars` database, divide your town into four sections and use them.

2. Modify and test the program `access_cars.pl` to handle `UPDATE` and `INSERT` SQL commands.

3. Modify and test the program `access_cars.php` to handle `UPDATE` and `INSERT` SQL commands.

4. Modify and test the program `Query.java` to use metadata to produce the column names.

5. Modify and test the program `Query.java` to handle UPDATE and INSERT SQL commands.

Introduction to Java

This appendix provides a quick introduction to Java for programmers who are familiar with C++ and object-oriented programming. It covers only a small part of Java, focusing on the features needed to understand Java programs similar to those discussed in this book. In some cases—for example, concurrency—the discussion of a topic can be found in the chapter of the book in which it is used, rather than in this appendix.

This appendix begins with a broad overview of the features and capabilities of Java. The data types and data structures of Java are then discussed, as well as the control statements. Next, it introduces the class definitions of Java, including some of the details of data and method definitions. Java interfaces, which provide a limited kind of multiple inheritance, are then discussed. This is followed by a description of Java exception handling.

A.1

OVERVIEW OF JAVA

Java is based on C++, so it is closely related to that language. However, some parts of C++ were left out of the design of Java in an attempt to make it smaller and simpler. Other C++ features were redesigned in Java. Java also includes some constructs that are not part of C++. In comparison with C++, Java can be characterized by the following categories of differences: exclusive support for object-oriented programming, no user-defined overloading, implicit deallocation of heap objects, use of interfaces, lack of pointers, and far fewer type coercions.

C++ was designed originally as an extension to C to provide support for object-oriented programming. Because virtually nothing was left out of C, C++ supports procedure-oriented programming as well as object-oriented programming. Java does not support procedure-oriented programming. In practical terms, this means that subprograms in Java can only appear as methods defined in class definitions. The same is true for data definitions. Therefore, all data and functionality are associated with classes, and therefore with objects.

C++ allows users to define new operations that are specified by existing operator symbols. For example, if a user defines a class to support complex numbers, he or she can overload the definitions of + and – so that they can be used as binary operators for complex objects. For the sake of simplicity, Java does not allow user-defined operator overloading.

In C++, user programs can both allocate and deallocate storage from the heap. This leads to a number of different programming problems, including the possibility of dangling pointers. A dangling pointer is one that is pointing to a memory cell that has been explicitly deallocated from its previous use and possibly reallocated to a new use. Some of these problems are avoided by making heap storage deallocation a system responsibility rather than a user one. In Java, all heap storage deallocation is implicit and a technique named *garbage collection* is used to reclaim heap storage that has been implicitly deallocated.

In C++, a user program can define a class to extend two or more different classes, thereby making use of multiple inheritance. Although multiple inheritance is sometimes convenient, it has some disadvantages, among them the possibility of designing programs whose complexity makes them difficult to understand. For this reason, Java does not support multiple inheritance. In its place, Java has interfaces, which provide some of the functionality of multiple inheritance. Interfaces are discussed in Section A.4.

Pointers are notoriously risky, especially when pointer arithmetic is allowed. Java does not include pointers. Instead, Java provides references, which are also supported by C++, though in a somewhat different way. Reference variables in Java are used to reference objects, rather than memory cells, so they cannot be used as the operands of arithmetic operators. This, in conjunction with the lack of a deallocation operator for heap objects, makes references far safer than the pointers of C++.

In C++, as in many other programming languages, it is legal to assign a value of any numeric type to a variable of any other numeric type. This requires the compiler to build type conversion code, called *coercions*, into the program. Half of these conversions are narrowing conversions, in which it may not be possible to convert the value into even an approximation in the new type. For example, in C++ it is legal to assign a `float` value to an `int` variable, although this is a narrowing conversion. For example, `float` values such as `1.23E15` cannot be converted to anything close to that value as an `int` value. Java does not allow narrowing coercions in assignment statements. It is syntactically illegal to write such an assignment statement. This results in an increase in the overall safety of programs written in Java over those written in C++.

The control statements of Java are almost exactly like those in C++. One difference is that control expressions in control statements in Java must have Boolean values, whereas in C++ the control expression can be either Boolean or a numeric type. For example, in Java, the following statement is illegal:

```
if (2 * count) ...
```

Output to the screen from a Java application is through the object `System.out`, which represents the console window associated with the application. This object has two methods, `print` and `println`, which do something similar to what you would expect given their names. Both take a string parameter, but also permit variables as parameters. The values of non-`String` variables that appear in the parameter to `System.out.print` or `System.out.println` are implicitly converted to strings. The `print` method produces a string of output to the screen without attaching a newline character to the end. The `println` method does what `print` does, except that it attaches a newline character to the end. The string parameter to `print` and `println` is often specified as a catenation of several strings, using the + catenation operator. The following method calls illustrate the use of `print` and `println`.

```
System.out.println("Apples are good for you");
System.out.println("You should eat " + numApples +
                    " apples each week");
System.out.print("Grapes ");
System.out.println("are good, too");
```

If `numApples` is 7, these statements produce the following display:

```
Apples are good for you
You should eat 7 apples each week
Grapes are good, too
```

Naming conventions used in Java are as follows:

1. Class and interface names begin with uppercase letters.
2. Variable and method names begin with lowercase letters.
3. Package names are all lowercase letters.
4. Constant names are all uppercase letters, with underscores used as separators.
5. Except for package and constant names, when a name consists of more than one word, the first letters of all embedded words are capitalized.
6. Except for constant names, all but the first letters of embedded words are lowercase.

Java does not have an address-of operator (& in C++), a dereference operator (unary * in C++), or an operator to return the size of a type or object (sizeof in C++).

A.2

DATA TYPES AND STRUCTURES

In both C++ and Java, there are two kinds of data values: primitives and objects. This is a compromise design, for it provides efficiency in arithmetic operations on primitive values at the expense of complicating the object model of the language. Arithmetic operations can be done very quickly on primitive values, but are more costly when the operands are objects.

C++ has three different kinds of variables for objects: those whose value is a stack-allocated object, pointers that reference heap-allocated objects, and references that reference heap-allocated objects. In Java, there is only one way to reference an object, namely, through a reference variable. This simplicity is possible because all objects are allocated from the heap and there are no pointer variables in Java.

The Java primitive types are int, float, double, char, and boolean. Operations on primitive values are similar to those in other programming languages. Each of the primitive types has a corresponding *wrapper class*, which is used when it is convenient to treat a primitive value as an object.[1] The Java wrapper classes are named with the name of the associated primitive type, except that the first letter is capitalized. For example, the wrapper class for

---

1. These classes are called wrapper classes because they in effect wrap a primitive value so it looks like an object.

double is Double. An object of a wrapper class is created with the new operator and the class's constructor, as in the following:

```
Integer wrapsum = new Integer(sum);
```

One of the purposes of wrapper classes is to provide methods that operate on primitive values. For example, a float value can be converted to a string by creating an object for it and using the toString method on that object. To convert the float value speed to a String object, the following could be used:

```
float speedObj = new Float(speed);
String speedStr = speedObj.toString();
```

As stated previously, all objects are referenced through reference variables. Reference variables are defined the same way as primitive variables. For example,

```
int sum;
String str1;
```

In this example, sum is a primitive variable of type int, and str1 is a reference variable that can reference a String object, initially set to null.

Although an array of characters can be created and used in Java, it is more convenient to use the String and StringBuffer classes for character strings. String objects are immutable strings of characters. They can be created in two ways: either with the new operator or implicitly, as illustrated with the following declarations:

```
String greet1 = new String("Guten Morgan");
String greet2 = "Guten Morgan";
```

These two strings are equivalent. All Java String and StringBuffer objects use 2 bytes per character because they use the Unicode character codings, which are 16 bits wide.

String catenation, which is specified with the plus operator (+), can be used on String objects, as in the following:

```
greet3 = greet3 + " New Year";
```

There are a number of methods that can be called through String objects to perform more or less standard string operations—for example, charAt, substring, concat, and indexOf. The equals method of String must be used to compare two strings for equality. Because strings are objects, the == operator is of no use between strings.

If a string must be manipulated, it cannot be a `String` object (because `String` objects cannot be changed). For this situation, a `StringBuffer` object can be used. `StringBuffer` objects are created with `new`, as in the following example:

```
StringBuffer greet3 = new StringBuffer("Happy");
```

The `StringBuffer` class has a collection of methods to manipulate its objects. Among them are `append`, which appends a given value to the end of the object; `delete`, which deletes one or more characters from the object; and `insert`, which inserts a value into its string object. In the cases of `append` and `insert`, if the given parameter is not a string, it is implicitly converted to a string.

In Java, arrays are objects of a class that has some special functionality. Array objects, like all other objects, are always referenced through reference variables and are always allocated on the heap. Array objects can be created with statements having the following form:

```
element_type array_name[ ] = new element_type[length];
```

For example,

```
int[] list1 = new int[100];
float[] list2 = new float[10];
```

If an array reference variable has been previously created, as with

```
int[] list3;
```

an object can be created with

```
list3 = new int[200];
```

As with other related languages, the subscript ranges of Java arrays always begin with zero. In a departure from C++, all references to array elements are checked to be sure the subscript values are within the defined subscript ranges of the array. Therefore, it is not possible to reference or assign an array element that does not exist. When a subscript that is out of range is detected, the exception `ArrayIndexOutOfBoundsException` is thrown. Java exception handling is discussed in Section A.5.

Java does not have the `struct` and `union` data structures that are part of C++. It also does not have the `unsigned` types or the `typedef` declaration.

A.3

CLASSES, OBJECTS, AND METHODS

There are several important differences between C++ class definitions and those of Java. All Java classes have a parent class, whereas in C++ a class need not have a parent. The parent of a class is specified in the class definition with the `extends` reserved word. The general form of a class definition is

```
[modifiers] class class_name [extends parent_class] { ... }
```

The square brackets here indicate that what they delimit is optional. Three different modifiers can appear at the beginning of a class definition: `public`, `abstract`, and `final`. The `public` modifier makes the class visible to classes that are not in the same package (packages are described later in this section). The `abstract` modifier specifies that the class cannot be instantiated. An abstract class is designed to be a class model that can be extended by nonabstract classes. The `final` modifier specifies that the class cannot be extended.

The root class of all Java classes is `Object`. A class definition that does not specify a parent is made a subclass of `Object`.

In C++, the visibility of variables and member functions (methods) defined in classes is specified by placing their declarations in `public`, `private`, or `protected` clauses. In Java, these same reserved words are used, but on individual declarations rather than on clauses. The meanings of these access modifiers are the same as in C++.

In addition to the access modifiers, a variable declaration can include the `final` modifier, which specifies that the variable is actually a constant, in which case it must be initialized. Java does not use C++'s `const` reserved word to specify constants.

In Java, all methods are defined in a class. Java class methods are specified by including the `static` modifier in their definitions. Any method without `static` is an instance method. Methods can also have several other modifiers. Among these are `abstract` and `final`. The `abstract` modifier specifies that the method is not defined in the class. The `final` modifier specifies that the method cannot be overridden.

Whereas C++ depends on classes as its only encapsulation construct, Java includes a second one at a level above classes, the *package*. Packages can contain more than one class definition, and the classes in a package are similar to the friend classes of C++. The entities defined in a class that either are public or protected or have no access specifier are visible to all other classes in the package. This is an expansion of the definition of protected as used in C++, in which protected members are visible only in the class in which they are defined and in subclasses of that class. Entities without access modifiers are said to have *package scope*, because they are visible throughout the package. Java therefore has less need for explicit friend declarations and in fact does not include either the

friend functions or friend classes of C++. Packages, which often contain libraries, can be defined in hierarchies. The standard class libraries of Java are defined
in a hierarchy of packages.

A file whose class definitions are to be put in a named package includes a
package declaration, as in the following example:

```
package cars;
```

The external visibility of entities in a class is controlled by the accessibility
modifiers on the entities. Entities from other classes that are visible can be referenced through their complete name, which begins with the name of the package in which the class is defined and includes the name of the class in which the
entity is defined. For example, if we have a package named weatherpkg, which
includes a class named WeatherData, which defines a public variable named
avgTemp, avgTemp can be referenced in any other class where it is visible with
the following:

```
weatherpkg.WeatherData.avgTemp
```

An import statement provides a way to abbreviate such imported names.
For example, suppose we include the following statement in our program:

```
import weatherpkg.WeatherData;
```

Now the variable avgTemp can be accessed directly (with just its name). The
import statement can include an asterisk instead of a class name, in which case
all classes in the package are imported. For example:

```
import weatherpkg.*;
```

A Java application program is a compiled class that includes a method
named main. The main method of a Java application is where the Java interpreter begins. The following illustrates the simplest kind of Java application
program:

```
public class Trivial {
  public static void main (String[] args) {
    System.out.println("A maximally trivial Java
                        application");
  }
}
```

The modifiers on the main method are always the same. It must have public accessibility, and it cannot be extended. The void modifier indicates that
main does not return a value. The only parameter to main is an array of strings
that contains any command-line parameters from the user. In many cases,

command-line parameters are not used. When they are used, the interpreter passes them to main as strings.

In C++, methods can be defined in a somewhat indirect way: The protocol is given in the class definition, but the definition of the method appears elsewhere. In Java, however, method definitions must appear in their associated classes.

As with C++, Java constructors have the same names as the classes in which they appear. C++ uses destructor methods to deallocate heap storage for instance data members, among other things. Because Java uses implicit heap deallocation, it does not have destructors.

In some object-oriented programming languages, including C++, method calls can be bound to methods either statically (at compile time) or dynamically (during run time). In C++, the default binding of method calls to methods is static. Only methods defined to be virtual are dynamically bound. In Java, the default is dynamic.

Objects of user-defined classes are created with new. As with array objects, a reference variable is required to access an object, but both the reference variable and the object can be created in the same statement. For example:

```
MyClass myObject1;
myObject1 = new MyClass();
MyClass myObject2 = new MyClass();
```

The two reference variables, myObject1 and myObject2, refer to new objects of class MyClass.

As is the case with C++, Java classes can have instance or class variables or both. There is a single version of a class variable per class; there is an instance variable for every instance of the class in which it is defined. Both instance and class variables that are not explicitly initialized in their declarations are implicitly initialized. Numeric variables are implicitly initialized to zero, Boolean variables are initialized to false, and reference variables are initialized to null.

Inside the methods of a class, instance variables are referenced directly. In other classes, instance variables are referenced through the reference variables that point at their associated objects. For example:

```
class MyClass extends Object {
    public int sum;
    ...
}
MyClass myObject = new MyClass();
```

In other classes that either import MyClass or are defined in the same package, the instance variable sum can be referenced with

```
myObject.sum
```

Similar to class methods, class variables are specified by preceding their declarations with the `static` reserved word.

The following is an example of a class definition that illustrates some of the aspects of Java we have discussed. It implements a stack in an array:

```java
import java.io.*;
class Stack_class {
  private int [] stack_ref;
  private int max_len,
              top_index;
  public Stack_class() {  // A constructor
    stack_ref = new int [100];
    max_len = 99;
    top_index = -1;
  }
  public void push(int number) {
    if (top_index == max_len)
      System.out.println("Error in push--stack is full");
    else stack_ref[++top_index] = number;
  }
  public void pop() {
    if (top_index == -1)
      System.out.println("Error in pop--stack is empty");
    else --top_index;
  }
  public int top() {return (stack_ref[top_index]);}
  public boolean empty() {return (top_index == -1);}
}
```

An example class that uses `Stack_class` follows:

```java
public class Tst_Stack {
  public static void main(String[] args) {
    Stack_class myStack = new Stack_class();
    myStack.push(42);
    myStack.push(29);
    System.out.println("29 is: " + myStack.top());
    myStack.pop();
    System.out.println("42 is: " + myStack.top());
    myStack.pop();
    myStack.pop();  // Produces an error message
  }
}
```

We must note here that a stack is a silly example for Java because the Java library includes a class definition for stacks.

A.4

INTERFACES

Java directly supports only single inheritance. However, it includes a construct similar to a virtual class, called an *interface*, that provides something closely related to multiple inheritance. An interface definition is similar to a class definition except that it can contain only named constants and method declarations (not definitions). So, an interface is no more than what its name indicates, just the specification of a class. (Recall that a C++ abstract class can have instance variables, and all but one of the methods can be completely defined.) The typical use of an interface is to define a class that inherits both some of the methods and variables from its parent class and implements an interface as well.

Applets are programs that are interpreted by a Web browser after being downloaded from a Web server. Calls to applets are embedded in the HTML code that describes an HTML document. These applets all need certain capabilities, which they can inherit from the predefined class `Applet`. When an applet is used to implement animation, it is often defined to run in its own thread of control. This concurrency is supported by a predefined class named `Thread`. However, an applet class being designed to use concurrency cannot inherit from both `Applet` and `Thread`. Java therefore includes a predefined interface named `Runnable` that supplies the interface (but not the implementation) to some of the methods of `Thread`. The syntax of the header of such an applet is exemplified by the following:

```
public class Clock extends Applet implements Runnable
```

Although this code appears to provide multiple inheritance, in this case it requires a further complication. For an object of the `Clock` class to run concurrently, a `Thread` object must be created and connected to the `Clock` object. The messages that control the concurrent execution of the `Clock` object must be sent to the corresponding `Thread` object. This is surely an inelegant and potentially confusing necessity. Concurrency and Java threads are discussed in Chapter 7, "Java Applets."

A.5

EXCEPTION HANDLING

Java's exception handling is based on that of C++, but is designed to be more faithful to the object-oriented language paradigm.

A.5.1 Classes of Exceptions

All Java exceptions are objects of classes that are descendants of the `Throwable` class. The Java system includes two system-defined exception classes that are subclasses of `Throwable`: `Error` and `Exception`. The `Error` class and its descendants are related to errors that are thrown by the Java interpreter, such as running out of heap memory. These exceptions are never thrown by user programs, and they should never be handled there. The two system-defined direct descendants of `Exception` are `RuntimeException` and `IOException`. As its name indicates, `IOException` is thrown when an error has occurred in an input or output operation, all of which are defined as methods in the various classes defined in the package `java.io`.

System-defined classes that are descendants of `RuntimeException` exist. In most cases, `RuntimeException` is thrown when a user program causes an error. For example, `ArrayIndexOutOfBoundsException`, which is defined in `java.util`, is a commonly thrown exception that descends from `RuntimeException`. Another commonly thrown exception that descends from `RuntimeException` is `NullPointerException`.

User programs can define their own exception classes. The convention in Java is that user-defined exceptions are subclasses of `Exception`.

A.5.2 Exception Handlers

The exception handlers of Java have a form similar to those of C++, except that the parameter of every `catch` must be present and its class must be a descendant of the predefined class `Throwable`.

The syntax of the `try` construct in Java is exactly like that of C++.

A.5.3 Binding Exceptions to Handlers

Throwing an exception is quite simple. An instance of the exception class is given as the operand of the `throw` statement. For example, suppose we define an exception named `MyException` as follows:

```java
class MyException extends Exception {
  public MyException() {}
  public MyException(String message) {
    super (message);
  }
}
```

The first constructor in this class does nothing. The second sends its parameter to the parent class (specified with `super`) constructor. This exception can be thrown with

```java
throw new MyException();
```

The creation of the instance of the exception for the throw could be done separately from the throw statement, as in the following:

```
MyException myExceptionObject = new MyException();
...
throw myExceptionObject;
```

Using the constructor with the parameter, our new exception could be thrown with

```
throw new MyException
    ("a message to specify the location of the error");
```

The binding of exceptions to handlers in Java is less complex than in C++. If an exception is thrown in the compound statement of a try construct, it is bound to the first handler (catch function) immediately following the try clause whose parameter is the same class as the thrown object or is an ancestor of it. If a matching handler is found, the throw is bound to it and is executed.

Exceptions can be handled and then rethrown by including a throw statement without an operand at the end of the handler. The newly thrown exception will not be handled in the same try where it was originally thrown, so looping is not a concern. This rethrowing is usually done when some local action is useful but further handling by an enclosing try clause or a caller is necessary. A throw statement in a handler could also throw some exception other than the one that transferred control to this handler; one particular exception could cause another to be thrown.

A.5.4   Exception Propagation

When a handler is found in the sequence of handlers in a try construct, that handler is executed and program execution continues with the statement following the try construct. If none is found, the handlers of enclosing try constructs are searched, innermost first. If no handler is found in this process, the exception is propagated to the caller of the method. If the method call was in a try clause, the search for a handler continues in the attached collection of handlers in the clause. Propagation continues until the original caller is found, which in the case of an application program is main. If no matching handler is found anywhere, the program is terminated. In many cases, exception handlers include a return statement to terminate the method in which the exception occurred.

To ensure that exceptions that can be thrown in a try clause are always handled in a method, a special handler can be written that matches all exceptions that are derived from Exception, simply by defining the handler with an Exception type parameter, as in the following:

```
catch (Exception genericObject) {
...
}
```

Because a class name always matches itself or any ancestor class, any class derived from `Exception` matches `Exception`. Of course, such an exception handler should always be placed at the end of the list of handlers, because it will block the use of any handler that follows it in the `try` construct in which it appears. The search for a matching handler is sequential, and the search ends when a match is found.

The object parameter to an exception handler is not entirely useless, as it may have appeared to be so far in this discussion. During program execution, the Java run-time system stores the class name of every object in the program. The method `getClass` can be used to get an object that stores the class name, which itself can be gotten with the `getName` method. So, we can retrieve the name of the class of the actual parameter from the `throw` statement that caused the handler's execution. For the handler above, this is done with

```
genericObject.getClass().getName()
```

The message associated with the parameter object, which is created by the constructor, can be obtained with

```
genericObject.getMessage()
```

A.5.5   The `throws` Clause

The `throws` clause of Java has an appearance and placement (in a program) similar to that of the `throw` specification of C++. However, the semantics of `throws` is completely different from that of the C++ `throw` clause.

The appearance of an exception class name in the `throws` clause of a Java method specifies that that exception class or any of its descendant exception classes can be thrown by the method. For example, when a method specifies that it can throw `IOException`, it means it can throw an `IOException` object or an object of any of its descendant classes, such as `EOFException`.

Exceptions of class `Error` and `RuntimeException` and their descendants are called *unchecked exceptions*. All other exceptions are called *checked exceptions*. Unchecked exceptions are never a concern of the compiler. However, the compiler ensures that all checked exceptions a method can throw are either listed in its `throws` clause or are handled in the method. The reason that exceptions of the classes `Error` and `RuntimeException` and their descendants are unchecked is that any method could throw them.

A method cannot declare more exceptions in its `throws` clause than the method it overrides, though it may declare fewer. So, if a method has no `throws` clause, neither can any method that overrides it. A method can throw any exception listed in its `throws` clause, along with any of the exceptions' descendant classes. A method that does not directly throw a particular exception but calls another method that could throw that exception must list the exception in its `throws` clause. This is the reason the `buildDist` method (in the example in

Section A.5.6), which uses the readLine method, must specify IOException in the throws clause of its header.

A method that calls a method that lists a particular checked exception in its throws clause has three alternatives for dealing with that exception. First, it can catch the exception and handle it. Second, it can catch the exception and throw an exception that is listed in its own throws clause. Third, it could declare the exception in its own throws clause and not handle it, which effectively propagates the exception to an enclosing try clause, if there is one, or to the method's caller if there is no enclosing try clause.

Java has no default exception handlers, and it is not possible to disable exceptions.

A.5.6   An Example

The following example program illustrates two simple uses of exception handlers. The program computes and prints a distribution of input grades by using an array of counters. There are ten categories of grades (0–9, 10–19, . . . , 90–100). The grades themselves are used to compute indexes into an array of counters, one for each grade category. Invalid input grades are detected by trapping indexing errors in the counter array. A grade of 100 is special in the computation of the grade distribution, because the categories all have ten possible grade values, except the highest, which has eleven (90, 91, . . . , 100). (The fact that there are more possible A grades than Bs or Cs is conclusive evidence of the generosity of teachers.) The grade of 100 is also handled in the same exception handler that is used for invalid input data. Following is a Java class that implements this algorithm.

```java
import java.io.*;
// The exception definition to deal with the end of data
class NegativeInputException extends Exception {
  public NegativeInputException() {
    System.out.println("End of input data reached");
  }   //** end of constructor
}   //** end of NegativeInputException class
class GradeDist {
  int newGrade,
      index,
      limit_1,
      limit_2;
  int [] freq = {0, 0, 0, 0, 0, 0, 0, 0, 0, 0};
  void buildDist() throws IOException {
//   Input: A list of integer values that represent
//          grades, followed by a negative number
```

continued

```
// Output: A distribution of grades, as a percentage for
//          each of the categories 0-9, 10-19, ...,
//          10-100.
  DataInputStream in = new DataInputStream(System.in);
  try {
    while (true) {
      System.out.println("Please input a grade");
      newGrade = Integer.parseInt(in.readLine());
      if (newGrade < 0)
        throw new NegativeInputException();
      index = newGrade / 10;
      try {
        freq[index]++;
      } //** end of inner try clause
      catch(ArrayIndexOutOfBoundsException) {
        if (newGrade == 100)
          freq [9]++;
        else
          System.out.println("Error - new grade: " +
                             newGrade + " is out of range");
      } //** end of catch (ArrayIndex...
    } //** end of while (true) ...
  } //** end of outer try clause
  catch(NegativeInputException) {
    System.out.println ("\nLimits     Frequency\n");
    for (index = 0; index < 10; index++) {
      limit_1 = 10 * index;
      limit_2 = limit_1 + 9;
      if (index ==9)
        limit_2 = 100;
      System.out.println("" + limit_1 + " - " +
        limit_2 + "        " + freq [index]);
    } //** end of for (index = 0; ...
  } //** end of catch (NegativeInputException ...
} //** end of method buildDist
```

The exception for a negative input, NegativeInputException, is defined in the program. Its constructor displays a message when an object of the class is created. Its handler produces the output of the method. The ArrayIndexOutOfBoundsException is predefined and is thrown by the interpreter. In both of these cases, the handler does not include an object name in its parameter. In neither case would a name serve any purpose. Note that all handlers get objects as parameters, but they are often not useful.

A.6

SUMMARY

Although Java is based on C++, it differs from that language in a variety of ways. The primary differences are Java's exclusive support for object-oriented programming, its lack of user-defined overloaded operators, its implicit deallocation and reclamation of heap objects, its interfaces, its lack of pointers, and its lower number of type coercions in assignment statements. Most of these differences were motivated by the perceived safety risks of C++.

Like C++, Java has primitive types and objects. Character strings can be stored as either String or StringBuffer objects, where String objects cannot be changed but StringBuffer objects can. Arrays are objects with special behavior. Array indices are always checked for range in Java.

Every Java class has a single parent class. Java does not have the public and private class derivations of C++. Java class derivation is always the same. Java has an additional encapsulation mechanism (besides the class)—the package. Entities defined in classes that do not specify a visibility have package scope, which makes them visible to all other classes in the package. Only one class in a package can be public. Rather than having public, private, and protected clauses in class definitions, the individual entities in Java classes can be defined to be public, private, or protected. All methods defined for a class are defined in the class. All binding of method calls to methods in Java is dynamic, unless the method is defined to be final, in which case it cannot be overridden and dynamic binding serves no purpose.

Class variables and class methods are specified to be static. In the absence of the static reserved word, variables are instance variables and methods are instance methods.

An interface defines the protocol of a class, but contains no variable definitions or method definitions. Interfaces are used to provide some of the benefits of multiple inheritance without all of the complexity of multiple inheritance. A class that implements an interface provides definitions for the methods of the interface.

Exception handling in Java is similar to that of C++, except that only objects of classes that descend from the predefined class Throwable can be exception objects. Propagation of exceptions is simpler in Java than it is in C++. The throws clause of Java is related to the throw clause of C++, but not closely. In Java, an exception class that appears in a throws clause means that the method in which throws appears can throw exceptions of that class or any of its descendants. A method cannot declare more exceptions in its throws clause than the method it overrides. A method that calls a method that can throw a particular exception must either catch and handle the exception, catch the exception and throw an exception that is declared in its throws clause, or declare the exception in its throws clause.

Index